James Latham, 'Tottenham in his boots', 1735,
National Gallery of Ireland, Dublin

BLUE GUIDE

IRELAND

Ian Robertson

A & C Black
London   MULTNOMAH COUNTY LIBRARY

W W Norton
New York

Fifth edition 1987

Published by A & C Black (Publishers) Limited
35 Bedford Row, London, WC1R 4JH

© Copyright A & C Black (Publishers) Limited 1987

Published in the United States of America by
W W Norton & Company, Incorporated
500 Fifth Avenue, New York, NY 10110

Published simultaneously in Canada by
Penguin Books Canada Limited
2801 John Street, Markham, Ontario L3R 1B4

British Library Cataloguing in Publication Data

Ireland.—5th ed.—(Blue guide)
  1. Ireland—Description and travel—
  1981– —Guide-books
  I. Robertson, Ian, 1928–   II. Series
  914.15′04824   DA980

  ISBN 0–7136–2843–X

ISBN 0–393–30367–5   USA

Printed and bound in Great Britain by
William Clowes Limited, Beccles and London

PREFACE

This fifth edition of *Blue Guide Ireland* has again been revised substantially, updated, and entirely reset. It is also the first to include a selection of illustrations. The island is again described from the view of the traveller by road, for roads remain the main channel of communication throughout Ireland, as it was when they were surveyed in the 1770s by George Taylor and Andrew Skinner, and before, although of course much has been done since to improve many of them, and more so during recent years: indeed there are few remaining areas of Europe where there can be found such a combination of good roads, uncluttered by heavy traffic for the most part, and running through delightful country, still comparatively unspoilt.

Maurice Craig (author of a valuable contribution to this Guide) has written in his 'The Architecture of Ireland' that 'Nothing of any antiquity in Ireland is made of anything but stone, and nearly all the stone is grey. The somewhat melancholy but undeniably appealing beauty of large tracts of the West, is matched only by the ingenuity of garage-proprietors and hoteliers in enlivening the foreground with Xirrelevant banalities. Yet in time the eye can train itself to disregard what is actually to be seen, and to dwell only on what is worth seeing. That is the intention of this book'. It is also the intention of this Guide. Ireland has numerous picturesque ruins—of castles, churches and monasteries—the reasons for which will be further discussed in the Historical Introduction. As Desmond Guinness has pointedly remarked in his study of Irish houses and castles: 'As in France, where the word *château* so conveniently means both house and castle, so in Ireland *castle* can have the double meaning—"above at the castle" might turn out to refer to some sober, classical house'. Many visitors may also be surprised to find so many churches being denominated cathedrals!

The latter part of the Introduction to the History of Ireland has been written by Professor **John A. Murphy** of the University College at Cork, who has succinctly described recent events. The Editor must express his obligation to Professor Murphy for having brought to his attention several infelicities in the earlier sections of this Introduction, together with a number of errors of fact and interpretation.

Jane Fenlon has contributed the Introduction to Irish Art, commissioned for this edition.

In this Guide the use of the name *Ireland*, unless otherwise specified, refers to the island as a geographical unity. The provinces of Leinster, Munster, Connacht, and the counties of Donegal, Cavan, and Monaghan of Ulster have since 1948 been described as the *Republic of Ireland* (previously, from December 1921, the Irish Free State; the name *Éire* being restricted to texts in the Irish language). The other *Six Counties* of Ulster, still remaining part of the United Kingdom, are denominated thus or *Northern Ireland* rather than, misleadingly, Ulster. It would be equally misleading to pretend that the recurrent 'troubles' in Northern Ireland have not had an adverse effect on the number of visitors in recent decades, but it should be emphasised that the unprejudiced and prudent traveller will very soon realise that almost all its undisturbed and beautiful countryside and coastline is entirely safe and may be explored without any apprehension. Some material damage—mainly in a few towns—will be seen: some from bombing; but much more from discreditable demolitions by developers; nevertheless, a surprising number of the better individual buildings have survived, and many have been restored. A large number have been listed for protection recently, and an increasing amount of renovation and preservation is taking place throughout the island.

Ireland is tourist conscious, for it relies to a large extent on this form of invisible export. Tourist offices are usually competently staffed, and there is more professionalism in the sensitive field of providing guidance and offering hospitality. Hotels, their standards supervised by the Tourist Board of Ireland (Bord Fáilte) and the Northern Ireland Tourist Board respectively, are found throughout Ireland, and are no longer listed in this guide, for national, regional, and municipal tourist offices can provide up-to-date information of this nature, together with details of the latest prices and facilities; likewise with restaurants. Unfortunately the prices of many have substantially increased within recent years. Times of admission to monuments and museums are also no longer included: to do so would inevitably misinform the traveller in a high proportion of cases, while tourist offices have current information.

Most of the revisions—the amount of alteration varying from very minor correction to the addition of considerable new matter—have been made from personal observation on the spot, but as it is virtually impossible to visit in person every locality, every ruined church and monastery, etc. when revising so comprehensive a guide, certain omissions will have inevitably occurred. The readers' co-operation is therefore solicited. Any constructive suggestions for the improvement of future editions will be welcomed and acknowledged by the Editor, who alone is responsible for all inexactitudes, shortcomings, inconsistencies, and solecisms. He would also welcome the recommendation that a building be deleted, for example, which perhaps did not merit inclusion. While the use of asterisks may be considered subjective and inconsistent they do help the hurried traveller to pick out those things which the general consensus of opinion (modified occasionally by the Editor's personal xprejudice, admittedly) considers he should not miss. Selection remains the touchstone by which guidebooks are judged, and it is hoped that this edition will provide a balanced account of most aspects of Ireland without intentionally neglecting any which might appeal to the traveller, and without being too exhaustive as to leave him no opportunity of discovering additional pleasures for himself.

In addition to those providing facilities and material assistance, or offering information and advice, who were listed at this point in the previous edition, the following must be mentioned: *Tim Magennis*, and *Paddy Tutty* of that excellent organisation **Bord Fáilte** in Dublin, and *Anthony Donegan* and *Mark Rowlette* at their London office; and to *Rosemary Evans* in particular at the **Northern Ireland Tourist Board**, together with managers and staff of tourist offices in Omagh, Galway, Nenagh, Dundalk, and Limerick.

Thanks must be also recorded for the help provided by *Daniel C. Lynch*, Office of Public Works, Dublin; *Vivien Igoe*, Kilmainham Hospital; *Homan Potterton*, and *Wanda Ryan*, National Gallery of Ireland; *Valerie Bond*, An Taisce; *Michael Ryan*, National Museum, Dublin; *Brian Kennedy*, Ulster Museum, Belfast; *Michael O'Shea* and *Anne Reynolds*, Russborough; *Michael Baylor*, Department of Foreign Affairs, Dublin; the Vicar of St. Peter's, Drogheda; *Muriel McCarthy*, Marsh's Library, Dublin; *Dr J. A. Claffey*, Tuam, and *Elizabeth Cavanagh*, Ulster Architectural Heritage Society. While it may be invidious to mention them, the Editor must acknowledge the exceptional hospitality of *Joan O'Hara* (Coopershill, Riverstown); *Anne* and *Patrick Foyle* (Rosleague Manor, Letterfrack); *John* and *Lucy Madden* (Hilton Park, Scotshouse, Clones); and *Mrs B. Young* (Lorum Old Rectory, Muine Bheag).

For permission to reproduce illustrations the publishers would like to thank: Bord Fáilte (Irish Tourist Board), the Northern Ireland Tourist Board, the National Gallery of Ireland, Ulster Museum, the National Museum of Ireland, the Chester Beatty Library and Gallery of Oriental Art, the Commissioners of Public Works in Ireland, the Meteorological Service.

A NOTE ON BLUE GUIDES

Prior to the outbreak of the First World War, the editors of the English editions of the German Baedeker Guides, marketed from 1908 by T. Fisher Unwin, were Finlay and James Muirhead. During 1915, with influential backing, the editors acquired the copyright of the majority of the famous 'Red' Hand-Books formerly published by John Murray, the standby of English travellers for the previous three-quarters of a century. (The 8th and last edition of their *Hand-Book for Travellers in Ireland*, published in 1921, had in fact been distributed by Edward Stanford.) Muirhead had also bought the copyright of a series published by Macmillan, who were to market the new series, the first of which was announced for publication by Muirhead Guide-Books Limited by early 1916. In the following year an agreement for mutual co-operation with Hachette et Cie of Paris was entered into: the French house, which had previously published the blue cloth-bound Guides Joanne—named after their first editor, Adolphe Joanne (1813–81), were to handle a translation of a guide to London, which was in fact the first 'Guide Bleu'; this, and other guides originating with Muirhead, were entitled **The Blue Guides** (further distinguishing them from the red Baedekers and Murrays). In 1927 a new agreement was made, which lapsed after six years.

Meanwhile, in 1931, the Blue Guides had been bought by Benn Brothers, and in 1934 L. Russell Muirhead (1896–1976), Finlay Muirhead's son, became editor. The first *Blue Guide to Ireland* was published in 1932, still relying heavily on Murray, with radically revised editions appearing in 1949, 1962, and 1979. In 1963 Muirhead was succeeded by *Stuart Rossiter* (1923–82), who had been his assistant since 1954, under whom the present editor undertook the revision of his first Blue Guide in 1971. Paul Langridge was House Editor in the decade 1975–85, after which he was succeeded by Tom Neville. The series has continued to grow spectacularly, with over 30 titles currently in print.

In April 1984, a year after Benn Brothers had itself been taken over by Extel, their guide-book publishing side, Ernest Benn Ltd, was bought by A. & C. Black, who had themselves a long history of guide-book publishing, beginning in 1826 with 'Black's Economical Tourist of Scotland', and including several written by Charles Bertram Black, eldest son of the firm's founder. The hey-day of Black's guide-book publishing was perhaps in the 1890s, when more than 55 titles were in print. In 1984 A. & C. Black also acquired the well-known series of *Red Guides*, previously published by Ward Lock.

In *Blue Guide Literary Britain and Ireland* (1985) several pages are devoted to 'James Joyce in Dublin', at the same time quoting Joyce's observation that 'if you wished to enjoy *Ulysses*, you should not make enjoyment more difficult by going to look at a changed Dublin'. Still, many people do search for such citations; and there are of course a number of references to Joyce in *Blue Guide Ireland* (apart from recording numerous other literary associations). A few lines from the concluding chapter of 'Gulliver's Travels' might perhaps be pertinent here: 'I know very well, how little Reputation is to be got by Writings which require neither Genius nor Learning, nor indeed any other Talent, except a good Memory, or an exact *Journal*. I know likewise, that Writers of Travels, like *Dictionary*-Makers, are sunk into Oblivion by the Weight and Bulk of those who come last, and therefore lie uppermost. And it is highly probable, that such Travellers who shall hereafter visit the Countries described in this Work of mine, may by detecting my Errors, (if there be any) and adding many new Discoveries of their own, jostle me out of Vogue, and stand in my Place; making the World forget that I ever was an Author. This indeed would be too great a Mortification if I wrote for Fame: But as my sole Intention was the PUBLIC GOOD, I cannot be altogether disappointed'.

CONTENTS

MAPS

PLANS

EXPLANATIONS

Type. The main routes are described in large type. Smaller type is used for sub-routes, excursions, or detours, and for historical and preliminary paragraphs, and (generally speaking) for descriptions of greater detail or minor importance.

Asterisks indicate points of special interest or excellence.

Total and intermediate **Distances**, measured in kilometres (km) are given at the commencement of each route, together with the total distance in miles; and the total length is also given in kilometres at the beginning of each sub-route described. While Northern Ireland has not yet become metric as far as distances are concerned, the rest of the island is becoming so progressively. Therefore on routes entirely in the North distances are still indicated in miles, and also in those sections extending into the North. Road distances along the routes themselves record the approx. distance between the towns and villages, etc. described, but it should be noted that with the realignment of many roads and the building of by-passes it is almost certain that these distances will vary slightly from those measured by motorists on their milometers.

Heights etc. The measurements of buildings have been expressed in metres (m), as have the altitudes of hills, cliffs, and mountains.

Populations, given in round figures, for both the Republic and Northern Ireland, accord with the census of 1978. They are not given for places with less than 500 inhabitants.

Place-names. While every attempt has been made to achieve consistency with the spelling of surnames, place-names and other 'Barbarous Denominations'—to use Swift's description—this has on occasions been impossible, particularly with the Gaelic, which may be printed in a variant form on the Ordnance Survey Maps; these however are in the process of revision and codification. In cases when two forms are in common usage, such as Dún Laoghaire and Dunleary, both names appear in the index.

Abbreviations. In addition to the generally accepted and self-explanatory abbreviations, the following occur in the Guide:

C = Century
C. of I. = Church of Ireland (Protestant)
km = kilometres
m = metres
NT = National Trust
Pl. = Plan
R = Room
R.C. = Roman Catholic
Rte = Route

INTRODUCTION TO IRISH HISTORY

The earlier period is also covered in part in the section on Irish Antiquities.

It is probable that the earliest settlers, largely hunters, reached the north of Ireland across the narrow strait from Britain in c 6000 BC, although there is increasing evidence of mesolithic settlement in the midlands and south. With the arrival of new groups of people, hunting-gathering gave way to farming during the neolithic period (c 3000 BC). The impressive civilisation of the era is known to us through excavations around *Lough Gur*, among other sites. The most imposing monuments of neolithic culture, predating the Egyptian pyramids, are in the Boyne valley, notably the great passage-grave at *Newgrange* (2800–2400 BC). In about 2000 BC metal-workers and potters ushered in a new stage of development, and numerous artefacts of this early Bronze Age have been recovered, while by c 1200 BC more sophisticated manufactures and a greater variety of objects were being produced. These prehistoric people probably lived in daub and wattle huts in small settlements with their cattle protected by a stockade; some habitations took the form of lake-dwellings or *crannógs*, built on artificial islands in the numerous loughs.

By 600 BC iron-using tribes from central Europe, speaking a Celtic language, were settling in Ireland, and soon dominated the indigenous inhabitants. They were followed in the 2C BC by a second wave, and at this stage there is evidence of the *La Tène* culture. By 150 BC the **Celts** were thoroughly established. Finds from this period, among them golden torques and ornamented scabbards, etc., are concentrated in Connacht and Ulster. Their 'capital' was probably near present-day Armagh, at *Emania* or *Emain Macha* (the Isamnion of Ptolemy's map), which, legend says, was destroyed by tribes from Connacht in the mid 5C.

The *Romans* never considered Ireland (or *Hibernia*) worthy of invasion, and therefore their civilising and disciplining influences never had any affect there. During the earlier centuries of the Christian era the island—now dominated by one language and culture—comprised some 150 or so *tuatha* or 'kingdoms', each tuath being controlled by a minor king (*rí tuaithe*) subject to a more powerful but still petty king (*ruiri*), who in turn put himself under the protection of one of five provincial kings (*rí ruirech* or *rí cóicid*). It was still a simple agrarian economy; the unit of currency was the cow (a female slave was reckoned to equal six young heifers); and *Brehon law* specified the relationship of each person in the *fine* (or extended family group), the complex stratification of Irish society, and varying forms of patronage, etc.

Tribes fought for survival and supremacy. Certain provincial kings or chieftains claimed to be *Ard Rí* or 'High Kings' at *Tara*, although they were not generally recognised as such. Among them were the descendants of the legendary Niall of the Nine Hostages, who is said to have reigned in the early 5C.

Scholars from Gaul, among them *St. Declan of Ardmore*, sought refuge in Ireland during the barbarian invasions, and Christians were already sufficiently numerous by 431 to justify the appointment of a bishop by Rome. Although there is some doubt as to when in the 5C **St. Patrick** landed in Ireland on his missionary enterprise, we know something of his background from his own 'Confessio'. A native of Roman Britain, he had already spent six years of his youth herding cattle on

Slemish Mountain (Antrim), having been enslaved by Irish raiders, but he had escaped to Gaul in a ship carrying wolfhounds. Intent on converting these pagan Gaels, he later returned, perhaps landing near Saul (close to Downpatrick), and most of his activity seems to have taken place in the northern half of the island, his successors likewise evangelising the same area. St. Patrick fixed his seat at Armagh, and introduced the episcopal system of ecclesiastical government. Monasteries were soon to become centres of monkish learning, and eventually the more important churches were controlled by the monastic hierarchy. Among the more influential were those of *Kildare* (*St. Brigid*), *Clonfert* (*St. Brendan* 'the Navigator'), and *Clonmacnoise* (*St. Kieran*), while *St. Columcille* (Columba) crossed to Scotland in 563 to found a monastery on Iona; more remote sites, such as *Skellig Michael*, were chosen by the more austere communities. There were, unusually, no Christian martyrs, although some resistance was encountered from the pagan druids, the natives for the most part accepting the new teaching, although pre-Christian beliefs and practices lived on.

By the 6C Irish missionaries were already crossing to the European mainland. In c 600 *St. Columbanus* (or Colmán) set out for Luxeuil in France; *St. Gall* was the founder of a monastery in Switzerland; *Virgilius* (or Fergil) became bishop of Salzburg; *St. Kilian* was known as the Apostle of Franconia; *St. Fursa* founded Péronne. By the early 9C this wave of missionaries to the Continent had been replaced by more scholarly monks, among them *Clement Scotus*, the grammarian; *Dicuil*, the geographer; *Sedulius*, the biblical commentator; and most influential, *John Scotus* (Erigena, or Eriugena; fl. 850)—not to be confused with the 13C 'Doctor Subtilis' Joannes Scotus (or Duns Scotus).

Many of these monks were skilled smiths or scribes, as can be seen in numerous relics of ecclesiastical metalwork such as the Ardagh Chalice, and illuminated gospels of the seventh and succeeding centuries, among them the *Book of Durrow* and the *Book of Kells*. These would have been placed in leather satchels—a practice Lord Curzon observed in Greek and Coptic monasteries a millennium later—and hung up beyond the reach of rats. Stone oratories and chapels, such as those at *Glendalough*, *Killaloe*, and *Kells*, and that of *Gallarus* on the Dingle peninsula, were constructed. At a later date tall Round Towers were raised with the triple purpose of belltower to summon the lay brothers in from the fields, a look-out post, and as a sanctuary when danger was imminent.

The first of several **Viking** raids on Ireland took place in 795. Their long shallow-draught clinker-built vessels would appear over the horizon, and land an armed crew of warriors in search of loot, as is evident by the contents of museums on the west coast of Norway. No place was safe. Any sandy strand or iron-bound fjord would be suitable for such landings; and even Skellig Michael was pillaged. Their sporadic incursions gathered impetus, and larger fleets arrived—as many as 60 sail were seen riding at anchor off the mouth of the Boyne in 837, and Clonmacnoise was plundered by ships brought up the Shannon. By 841 their first fortified settlements had been established, at *Annagassan* on the Louth coast, and near the mouth of the Liffey.

These raids were frequently resisted, and in 845 *Máel Sechnaill*, king of Meath, himself killed *Thorgestr* (or Turgesius), one of the Viking chieftains. But during the next 150 years anarchy prevailed in Ireland among the numerous smaller tuatha; little was done to stop the Vikings making further settlements along the coast at Cork and Limerick, and—as confirmed by the names—Wicklow, Wexford, and

Waterford. They carried on a brisk trade, and intermarried. The site of their burial-mound (or *Haugen*) in Dublin later became known as Hoggen Green (now College Green). In 967 the Irish under *Mathgamain* sacked Limerick. *Brian Boru*, his brother, the chief of Munster, one of a line of chieftains engaged in the general struggle for power, became High King in 1002, with his base at *Cashel*. He later confirmed the archbishop of Armagh as primate, and the Book of Armagh, in recording his formal visit to that ecclesiastical capital, is inscribed 'Brian Imperator Scotorum' (Emperor of the Irish).

Meanwhile the Irish had adapted both the ornaments of the Scandinavians, and their arms and armour. In 1014 Brian Boru attacked the Vikings at *Clontarf*, near Dublin. Here, although both Brian and his eldest son were killed, their enemies were badly beaten. But, with no successor strong enough to consolidate their ascendancy, the Irish again relapsed into comparative political anarchy. Between 1070 and 1130 Dublin was controlled in turn by kings of Leinster, Munster, and Connacht. Among them were the chieftains of seven or eight loosely formed rival provinces, a situation which did little to provide stability, each High King reigning *co fresabra* ('with opposition').

In the 1150s the struggle for power lay between the *King of Ailech* in the North and *Rory O'Connor* of Connacht, the former supported by *Dermot MacMurrough*, while *O'Rourke of Breffni* was allied to O'Connor. In 1152 Dermot raided Breffni and abducted O'Rourke's wife *Dervorgilla* (with her connivance, it is said). She returned (or was returned) the following year and retired to the nunnery of *Mellifont* (the first Cistercian house in Ireland, consecrated in 1157), where she died in 1193. Meanwhile, the balance of power being momentarily in his favour, O'Rourke, determined to get his own back, had attacked *Ferns*, and forced Dermot to flee (August 1166).

Reaching Bristol, Dermot crossed to France to seek the aid of Henry II, who, readily accepting Dermot's offer of fealty, granted him permission to recruit allies among his subjects. Thus encouraged, Dermot returned to Bristol and entered Wales, there approaching *Richard Fitz-Gilbert de Clare*, 2nd earl of Pembroke and Striguil, better known as '**Strongbow**'. Dermot promised his daughter Eva in marriage, and the succession to the kingdom of Leinster, if Pembroke took up his cause.

A number of ANGLO-NORMAN (and Norman-Welsh) knights, including the *Geraldines*, agreed to cross to Ireland when they were properly organised, but Dermot impatiently returned alone, only to be attacked once more by O'Rourke and O'Connor. He ostensibly submitted, even paying gold to the former in compensation for his earlier transgressions.

In early May 1169 an expeditionary force from Wales landed at *Bannow Bay* and, joining Dermot, marched on Wexford, where the Vikings capitulated. This vanguard was followed by a substantial contingent which disembarked at *Baginbun*, commanded by *Raymond Fitzgerald 'le Gros'*, and shortly Strongbow himself arrived with the main army near Waterford. Here Strongbow, joining forces with 'Le Gros', assaulted the town, and some days later his marriage with Eva was celebrated. Dermot then led the army towards Dublin, still largely in control of the Norsemen, allied to Rory O'Connor and O'Rourke. It soon fell to the invaders, although some months later they had to sustain a determined counter-attack, in which *Hasculf*, the chief of the Norsemen, was captured and beheaded. Although the combined forces of the Irish kings also endeavoured to starve their enemies out, they were themselves surprised and scattered. Dermot died in 1171, and Strongbow took control of the Kingdom of Leinster.

Henry II, on hearing of these successes, was worried that Strongbow might set up an independent kingdom in Ireland. Armed with the Bull *Laudabiliter* from the English Pope Adrian IV (obtained in advance for such contingencies) authorising him to reform the wayward Irish Church, the king landed with a fully-equipped army at Waterford in October 1171. *Lawrence O'Toole*, archbishop of Dublin, and other bishops assembled at Cashel, did homage, and the secular powers did likewise at Dublin. Leinster was granted to Strongbow (as Henry's viceroy); Meath, as a counterbalance, to *Hugh de Lacy*; Ulster to *John de Courcy*; while the king reserved for himself, in the name of the citizens of Bristol, the town of Dublin and a coastal strip. By the *Treaty of Windsor* (1175) Rory O'Connor's sovereignty over Connacht was confirmed, and the Church submitted to Rome at the *Synod of Lismore*. Having, in his estimation, put his Irish house in order, Henry returned to England, well satisfied with having made such a large addition to his empire at so little cost.

But the Normans still had to control these territories. Strongbow suffered setbacks at Limerick, when faced with the armies of *O'Brien, king of Thomond*, and only won the city with the help of Raymond le Gros. Strongbow died in 1176, and was buried in the cathedral of Christ Church, Dublin. He was succeeded by *William de Burgo* as viceroy. De Courcy invaded Ulster, took Downpatrick, and broke the power of *MacDunlevy* in battle (June 1177). At *Carrickfergus* he built a castle, the first of many stone fortresses erected to consolidate these conquests. Too often it was merely the hinterland of these strong points—frequently only a motte and bailey within a wooden palisade—that the Normans controlled, and it has been stated that the weakness of the Norman 'conquest' of Ireland was that it was too haphazard, and not undertaken in a more systematic fashion.

Other areas which had been left in Gaelic Irish hands were encroached upon by the land-hungry Normans, among them Munster. Family alliances were made; and intermarriage with Irish princesses took place, but too often the native tribes were forced into the remoter hills, although occasionally there were successful retaliatory campaigns, as in 1261, when the *MacCarthys* attacked the Geraldines (Fitzgeralds) at *Callan*, near Kenmare. In 1235 Connacht had been invaded by the de Burghs and their allies, but here, as often elsewhere, there were never enough Normans in the area to consolidate and feudalise it entirely.

Between 1224 and c 1280 the Dominicans, followed by the Franciscans, Carmelites, and Augustinians, entered Ireland, and, generally welcome, began to construct friaries. At the same time the administrative machine was established and the jury system introduced; sheriffs were appointed; an Irish coinage was struck. In 1297 the first parliament assembled in Dublin. Meanwhile new towns were founded; fairs, markets, and trade guilds instituted; and the conquerors, often living in isolation, became increasingly dependent on the native Irish for both cultivators and soldiers. They soon found themselves becoming 'Irish' chiefs, adopting the language, manners, and customs of the people among whom they had chosen to settle. The old *Brehon law* often continued in force beyond the *Pale*, the district round Dublin which was subject to English law, an area the extent of which fluctuated, being largely dependent on external pressures from the unassimilated Irish (see map on p 92). But as often as not the Irish were squabbling among themselves, although occasionally authority was conceded, as it was in 1258, when the nobility of Thomond and Connacht agreed to be led by *Brian O'Neill*.

The most successful attempt at revolution or reconquest took place in 1315, when **Edward Bruce** (brother of King Robert of Scotland, who had defeated the English at Bannockburn the previous year) was invited to Ireland with his mercenary troops—known as 'gallowglasses'—to set up a united Celtic Kingdom. Landing in Antrim, he joined up with the O'Neills, and was crowned 'King' of Ireland in 1316. He was subsequently killed at the *Battle of Faughart*, near Dundalk (October 1318), when his army was broken up by *Sir John de Bermingham.*

Thirty years later Ireland was ravaged by the Black Death, which depopulated the country by perhaps as much as one-third. In 1366 a parliament assembled at Kilkenny, and its *'statutes'* attempted unsuccessfully to bring back some order to the land in which too many of the settlers had 'gone native', and left Edward III with too few reliable and unassimilated Anglo-Normans to govern on his behalf. By this time Hibernisation of even such Norman families as the conquering De Burghs had made them virtually undistinguishable from the Irish of Connacht.

In 1394 *Richard II* (the first English king to visit Ireland since John, in 1210) landed at Waterford with a large army, intent on bringing to heel the irascible king of Leinster, *Art MacMurrough Kavanagh*. He also received homage from *Niall More O'Neill*, who controlled Ulster. But these submissions were only temporary, and even a second visitation in 1399 was unsuccessful in achieving a settlement. In consequence of his untimely absence in Ireland, Richard lost his English throne to Henry Bolingbroke and the Lancastrian dynasty.

During the 15C the rival feuding houses of the *Fitzgeralds, Earls of Kildare* and of *Desmond*, and the *Butlers, Earls of Ormonde* (with their headquarters at Kilkenny), divided and ruled the country, each in their spheres of influence, and, frequently in conflict with each other—as at the *Battle of Pilltown* (1462)—maintained a precarious peace. Within six years of this battle, *Thomas, 7th Earl of Desmond,* accused of treason by *John Tiptoft, Earl of Worcester*, who was sent to replace him, was beheaded, a summary measure which caused stunned reaction among the Irish. From 1478 *Gerald Fitzgerald, 8th Earl of Kildare,* was Lord Deputy. When in 1495 he was arraigned by *Henry VII* for burning down the cathedral of Cashel, the candour of his reply, 'that he did so because he thought the archbishop was inside', reputedly so delighted the king that he was forthwith reappointed in his office, which he still held at the accession of Henry VIII. Among the more serious rebellions he had to put down was that of *Ulicke Burke* of Clanricarde, whom he vanquished at *Knockdoe*, near Galway, in 1504.

In 1494, *Sir Edward Poynings*, sent over by Henry VII, convoked a parliament at Drogheda, which ended in the enactment of *Poynings' Law*. This allowed Irish parliaments to meet only with the consent of the English king if he approved of the measures they proposed. Poynings' Law was to limit the independence of the Irish parliament for almost 300 years.

It was not only the cathedral of Cashel which was in ruins. In general the Church had sunk into a deplorable state of neglect, although some friars kept the faith sufficiently alive to resist the reforms and innovations of *Henry VIII* after his break with Rome. Monasteries within the Pale were dissolved after 1539. Within three years the first Jesuits had infiltrated into the island.

Meanwhile the Butlers attempted (through Wolsey) to discredit the great Kildare's son *Garret Oge* in the eyes of Henry VIII, and *Sir*

William Skeffington was appointed as Deputy. While Garret Oge was in London (1534), his son, known as *'Silken' Thomas*—so called because his followers wore a silk fringe on their helmets—was tricked into rebellion. Kildare's castle at Maynooth was stormed, and young Thomas (now 10th earl), together with five uncles, was executed in London in 1537. The rule of the Fitzgeralds had ended.

No longer would any Irishman hold the office of viceroy; in future the English king—Henry was formally declared 'king of Ireland' by the Irish parliament in 1541—would control the country by a combination of firmness and diplomacy. In return for submission to him, he regranted to Irish chiefs their property and title under English law. The Fitzgeralds of Desmond, the Roches, Barrys, Powers, MacCarthys, O'Briens, and O'Sullivans in Munster; the Butlers, Dillons, Tyrrels, Kavanaghs, O'Byrnes, O'Mores, and O'Connors of Leinster; the Burkes, O'Connors, and O'Kellys in Connacht; and in Ulster the Savages, O'Neills, O'Donnells, Maguires, MacMahon, and the O'Reillys … and many more, some forty lords in all, had ostensibly submitted by 1547, the year of Henry's death, none of them wishing to suffer the same fate as Silken Thomas.

Earldoms had been conferred on O'Brien, Burke, O'Neill, and O'Donnell, but this was not sufficient surety that they would remain faithful subjects. As a matter of policy to redress somewhat the balance of reliability, it was decided to 'plant' Ireland with colonies of Englishmen. During *Mary I*'s reign the counties of Leix and Offaly were colonised.

Elizabeth I had a more personal interest in Ireland, for her mother had been reared at Carrick-on-Suir by her cousins, the Butlers, and through them she was connected by blood with the O'Briens and O'Reillys. Some of the O'Briens became Protestants, and their sheriffs dutifully hanged many shipwrecked Spaniards washed up on the coast of Clare after the Armada had been dispersed by storms (1588). But this was only one of many clans. The seeds of dissension among others had already been sown by Henry VIII's grants of titles to the Irish nobility, for while by English law titles and lands descended through the eldest son, under Irish law the most fitted for the position was chosen (often on a hilltop site sanctified by the usage of centuries). So each clan was before long split up into rival groups, for example, the *Queen*'s O'Reilly, and the *O'Reilly*'s O'Reilly. This internal feuding facilitated annexation and conquest. But, although the country was gradually brought into submission to the Crown and the independence of the native and Gaelicised princes destroyed, the reformed Protestant faith never won popular acceptance and the great bulk of the population remained true to ancestral Catholicism. Nevertheless, by the end of Elizabeth's reign some 400 monasteries had been virtually suppressed, although certain friaries, of which there were some 240 altogether, survived longer.

By 1585 the queen controlled much of the provinces of Leinster, Connacht, and Munster, the rebellion of the last (1579) having been crushed with some severity. More plantations took place, the rebellious landowners being dispossessed. Some of the Earl of Desmond's territory, for example, was granted to *Sir Walter Raleigh*, who in turn sold it to *Richard Boyle*, later *earl of Cork*, who colonised it. *Edmund Spenser*, somewhat of a political reactionary, was also well rewarded for his services in Ireland, where he spent most of the last two decades of his life.

But Ulster could only be tamed by war with *Hugh O'Neill, 2nd Earl of Tyrone*, who, although winning the *Battle of Yellow Ford* (near

Armagh) against *Sir Henry Bagenal* in 1598, was less successful when involved in offensive operations outside Ulster. His collaboration with a Spanish expeditionary force at *Kinsale* in late 1601 ended in a rout. Long before that fateful event, the country had been laid waste by *Sir George Carew* in Munster, and by *Lord Mountjoy*, the Lord Deputy, in Ulster. O'Neill submitted at Mellifont in 1603, and retained his property and title. But, after four years of various pressures, he set sail with *Rory O'Donnell*, 1st Earl of Tyrconnel, embarking at Rathmullen (September 1607) for exile on the Continent. With them sailed the flower of many Ulster families, an irreversible decision known as the '**Flight of the Earls**'. Their estates, consisting of c 750,000 acres (300,000 hectares) including those of their sub-tenants, were duly confiscated.

King James resolved to bring in his own countrymen, who, as he expressed it, would be able to skip about the bogs as well as the Irish. The land was divided into lots and granted to the enterprising Protestant gentry of the Scottish lowlands (apart from some English), who settled there with their families and dependents, mainly in the present counties of Donegal, Derry, Tyrone, Fermanagh, Armagh, and Cavan. A few of the old proprietors also received land, but the remainder were ordered to quit the province. The repercussions of these high-handed confiscations are still with us.

The policies of *Sir Thomas Wentworth*, Earl of Strafford, Lord Deputy in 1633–40, did much to provoke discontent and widespread antagonism, and the general desperation of the native Irish chiefs precipitated the Rebellion of 1641, an opportunity awaited by many old families, driven abroad or into the hills, who now attempted to recover their patrimony by the sword. A polarisation of forces took place rapidly, although there was some confusion of sympathies. A projected attack on Dublin Castle was forestalled, but local risings went according to plan. *Sir Phelim O'Neill*, protesting loyalty to the Crown, led the Ulster Irish, and laid siege to Drogheda until pressed back by government reinforcements.

The rebels met in October 1642 in the *Confederation of Kilkenny*. It was an alliance of Irish Catholics, both native Irish and old English descendants of pre-Protestant colonists, in defence of their religion, property, and political rights. A number of exiles returned to support the Confederate cause, among them *Thomas Preston* and *Owen Roe O'Neill*, while the Papal Nuncio, *Rinuccini*, later arrived with arms and men. The king, *Charles I*, negotiated with the Confederates, openly through *Ormonde*, the viceroy, who held Dublin, but also behind his back. O'Neill routed *General Monro's* forces at *Benburb* (1646), while *Murrough O'Brien* ('of the Burnings'), *Earl of Inchiquin*, held Munster for Parliament and defeated the Confederates at *Knocknanuss*, near Mallow.

There had been exaggerated reports in England of the brutality with which the Ulster planters had been treated by the embittered dispossessed Catholics. It was therefore in a spirit of revenge that **Oliver Cromwell** landed at Dublin with his army in 1649. With the death of Owen Roe O'Neill, there was virtually no general to oppose Cromwell, who relentlessly laid waste the country. *Drogheda* was stormed, and its garrison and gentry massacred, any survivors being sold as slaves in the West Indies. He likewise stormed Wexford and moved on Munster, but was temporarily halted at Clonmel, until, their ammunition exhausted, the town's defenders, led by Hugh O'Neill, slipped away to Limerick, which later fell to *Henry Ireton*. Cork declared for Parliament.

Ireland was in 'the Protector's' hands. He now proceeded with a ruthless proscription of the Catholic propertied classes: the labouring landless poor were undisturbed. Those who had opposed him lost their estates entirely and all property rights. Those who could not show their loyalty and 'constant good affection' to the English Commonwealth, were ordered to transplant themselves west of the Shannon by 1 May 1654, or to Connacht (including Clare), where they were supposed to receive some compensatory land. Confiscated estates in the rest of Ireland were parcelled out to the holders (known as '*Adventurers*') of the script issued to the government creditors in England who had helped to finance the campaign, and in settlement of officers' arrears of pay.

Most of the land in Leinster and Munster (excluding Clare) was thus redistributed. Louth and Cork were largely assigned to officers, while private soldiers who did not themselves sell out, were settled in the Golden Vale of Tipperary. Although a few properties of the old landowners of the Pale were later restored to them, the transference of land from Catholic ownership to Protestant was virtually as complete and as permanent a transformation as had occurred in Ulster under James I, a difference being that the Ulster plantation was a multi-class colony, while the new colonists were a gentry on the ascendant.

With the restoration of *Charles II* in 1660, some 500 or 600 Catholics were able under 'acts of settlement' to recover a small proportion of their original estates. The population of Ireland had grown to some 2 million inhabitants, three-quarters of them Catholic, with a small nucleus of Catholic nobility and landed gentry. They got little satisfaction when Charles was succeeded by his Catholic brother *James II*, at least not until *Lord Clarendon* was succeeded as Lord Deputy in February 1687 by *Richard Talbot, Earl* (later *Duke*) *of Tyrconnel*, who indiscreetly replaced Protestants by Catholics in the army and in key posts of the administration. In 1688 the king was deposed.

Having fled to France, James sailed to Kinsale in March 1689 with a body of troops provided by Louis XIV, and set up his government in Dublin. But he antagonised the Catholics who wanted a reversal of the land settlement and who reiterated their demand for parliamentary independence. The only armed resistance to James was from the colonists of Derry, and Enniskillen. The **Siege of Derry**, its defence organised by *Major Baker* and the *Rev. George Walker*, lasted 105 days, until the 'Mountjoy' broke the boom across the Foyle and relieved the famished city.

The following June (1690) **William of Orange** landed at Carrickfergus, and marched with the *Duke of Schomberg* and a force of 36,000 towards the river *Boyne*, where James's slightly smaller army was defeated and fell back towards the Shannon. William followed them, and soon engaged with the equally 'heroic' defenders of *Limerick*, but his approaching siege-train was brilliantly intercepted and destroyed by *Patrick Sarsfield*. The war dragged on. In June 1691 *Gen. Ginkel* won a resounding victory at *Aughrim*, and in October the *Treaty of Limerick* brought the struggle to an end. Catholics were offered (ambiguously) the same rights of worship as they had enjoyed in the reign of Charles II, but there was confiscation of the property of those who had left for France, and of some other Jacobites. The draft of the treaty was in the event dishonoured, but through no fault of the king. Some 14,000 troops, known in Irish history as the 'Wild Geese', chose to seek service in Continental armies. The new Irish parliament, now entirely dominated by Protestants, and still subordinate to Westminster, set about entrenching their position by passing a number of

Penal Laws.

These forbade Catholics to buy land, or take leases for more than 31 years, although it occasionally happened that Protestants held land on trust for their Catholic neighbours. They could not hold commissions or enter the liberal professions, or even own a horse worth £5; they were forbidden to teach, and the orphaned child of Catholic parents was educated as a Protestant. Protestant dissenters also suffered disqualifications under the *Test Act* of 1704. But priests continued, even if illegally, to offer mass at 'scathláns' (or open-air altars), and by the beginning of the second quarter of the century chapels were being opened in the side streets. Not many decades later, the pragmatic and generous Anglican *Frederick Hervey, Earl of Bristol* and *Bishop of Derry*, allowed his Mussenden Temple to be used for the celebration of mass once a week by the local Catholic priest, and both the priest and his horse were provided for in his will!

A number of landlords preferred to apostasise, and became members of the established Church, but the poverty-stricken peasantry kept their faith and continued to pullulate in their cabins in conditions which aroused Jonathan Swift, dean of St. Patrick's Cathedral, Dublin, and others, to attack the complacent society which tolerated them. Few people in England had much idea of these terrible conditions, as confirmed by Swift in 'The Drapier's Letters' (1724), writing: 'As to Ireland, they know little more than they do of Mexico; further than it is a Country subject to the King of England, full of Boggs, inhabited by wild Irish Papists; who are kept in Awe by mercenary troops sent from thence: And their general Opinion is, that it were better for England if this whole Island were sunk into the Sea: For, they have a tradition, that every Forty years there must be a Rebellion In Ireland' (sic).

In 1741 there was a serious famine, and in 1761 Munster was visited by agrarian disturbances instigated by the so-called *Whiteboys* (named after the white smocks they wore), and other secret societies proliferated.

The urban population, in comparison, prospered. In 1731 the *Royal Dublin Society* was founded by *Thomas Prior* with the aid of *Dr Samuel Madden*, for the encouragement of agriculture, forestry, and the arts and crafts. Numerous Catholics presented loyal addresses when Britain was confronted with a Catholic coalition during the *Seven Years' War*. Many dispossessed Catholics engaged in trade, and their increasing wealth enabled them to press for admission to the army, the law, and the political franchise. By 1778 the first Catholic relief act was introduced by *Luke Gardiner*, allowing them to take longer leases, while **Henry Grattan** and other sympathetic Protestant leaders attempted the removal of their other disabilities.

Dublin, new districts of which were being built in the Georgian taste, had by now grown to be the centre of a society in the ascendant, even if many landowners lived in cultivated (or vicious) idleness away from their estates, which, with the increasing value of land, they were now able to sub-let at considerable profit. In the 1790s some hundred peers of various degrees lived in the capital.

But there were dark sides to Dublin society: between 1784 and 1796, out of 25,352 children entered in the books of the Foundling Hospital, 17,253 died, either in that institution or after being put out to nurse in the country.

The outbreak of the *American War of Independence* (1775), with which so many Irishmen, as fellow 'colonists', openly sympathised (even if they volunteered to defend their own island against possible attack, as it had been so denuded of regular English troops) did much to bring about a relaxation of the political control of Ireland from Westminster. The *Act of Renunciation* of 1783 conceded the independence of the Irish parliament though this was still largely run by Protestants intolerant of pressure to reform themselves, and in spite of the 'patriot' group led by Grattan, *Henry Flood*, and *James Caulfeild, Earl of Charlemont*. The archbishoprics, offices of considerable political importance, and the chief offices of state, were still restricted to men of English birth. *James Napper Tandy's* attempt to set up a counter-assembly was a failure.

Yet national awareness and unity manifested itself in a number of notable material forms: the *Bank of Ireland* was founded; the *Four Courts* were built; and canals were driven across the island from Dublin to the Shannon to improve communications: the *Grand Canal* was completed in 1804; the *Royal Canal* in 1817.

But further agrarian discontent, the spread of French Revolutionary ideas, and natural impatience engendered by the frustration of Catholic hopes, led to the formation in Belfast of **Theobald Wolfe Tone**'s *Society of United Irishmen* (October–November 1791). Another association, the *Orange Order*, was formed in September 1795 in Ulster after rural rioting between Catholics and Protestants in competition for land. Protestants proclaimed their right to it as descendants of the original planters; what right had the descendants of the original owners? In co-operation with Napper Tandy, the Dublin Branch of Wolfe Tone's society (suppressed May 1794) continued to agitate for reform and emancipation, but the Irish parliament sensed treasonable activity.

In this they were right, for, in desperation, the United Irishmen turned to violence and Tone, seeking aid from France, returned with an invading fleet bound for *Bantry Bay* (December 1796), However, it was dispersed by adverse weather. *Lord Edward Fitzgerald*, another United Irishman and revolutionary, was mortally wounded when evading capture in Dublin (May 1978), and rebellion was widespread in Wexford and Waterford, until converging columns under *General Lake* crushed the rising at *Vinegar Hill* (June 1798). Survivors were ruthlessly hunted down. In August, *Géneral Humbert*, with a French expeditionary force, landed at *Killala*, but surrendered to *Cornwallis*, the viceroy, at *Ballinamuck* on 23 September. In October Tone was taken prisoner when a small French fleet was captured in *Lough Swilly*. The following month he anticipated execution by taking his own life.

The danger of invasion of Ireland—of having England's back-door opened to enemies—led *William Pitt* to put in hand his long-projected suppression of the Irish parliament by a **Union** (which was to come into effect from 1 January 1801). Renewed promises of emancipation induced Catholic leaders to acquiesce. Pitt's proposal, supported by *John Fitzgibbon, Earl of Clare* and Lord Chancellor ('Black Jack'), was presented to the Irish parliament in 1799. Not unnaturally it was opposed by the great landowners who represented the counties, and also by the country at large. Placemen voted in obedience to the government, and many of the borough members were brought over by bare-faced bribery. The proposal was again presented to the Commons in 1800. The compulsive oratory of Grattan and the popular detestation of the measure were powerless: the Irish parliament was extinguished. The Union ruined Dublin and the Irish aristocracy, because with the political centre shifting to London, many landowners followed it, taking with them their rents, and became long-term absentee landlords; others retired in disgust to their provincial estates, some to vegetate, others to 'improve' them. What were formerly impressive Georgian mansions became abandoned and derelict over the years and later they were divided up into tenements.

With the renewal of the *French War* in 1803, in which large numbers of Irishmen formed part of the British army and navy, there was a renewal of agitation, but *Robert Emmet's* rising, precipitated by an explosion of a store of arms, was abortive, and he was executed. In spite of Pitt's promises, *George III* arbitrarily refused assent to Catholic emancipation.

It was not until 1823 that Catholics found their champion in **Daniel O'Connell**, a young and eloquent lawyer, who, with *Richard Lalor Sheil*, set out to broaden the base of the *Catholic Association*, seeking to represent the interests of the tenant farmers. In 1828 he presented himself for election, representing Clare, to the British Parliament (where he, as a Catholic, could not sit) and was elected by 2057 votes against 982. So dangerous did the general agitation become that both the *Duke of Wellington*, the Dublin-born Prime Minister, and *Sir Robert Peel*, the Home Secretary, yielded.

The **Emancipation Act** of 1829 removed the oath administered on entering Parliament, to which no Catholic could commit himself, and O'Connell was able to take his seat. The repeal of the 'Union' and the restoration of Grattan's 'Irish Parliament' were his next objects, and he set about the organisation of mass meetings throughout the country. But O'Connell's failing health, the secession of the '**Young Ireland' Party**, who, with *John Mitchel* and *William Smith O'Brien*, advocated force, and the Famine, caused the essential impetus of the Repeal movement to be lost before his death in 1847. O'Connell's last public act was to preside at a meeting in Dublin which entreated the government to prohibit the export of corn or the use of grain for distilling, and to allow the navy to be used for transport, but he was largely ignored.

For in 1845—and by no means for the first time during the century—and to a calamitous extent in 1846, blight had infected the potatoes. The majority of the population subsisted on potatoes, and they were starving. Although relief was attempted and large sums were subscribed by private charity in Ireland and England, communications were bad, and food could not be properly distributed. It has been estimated that during the **Famine** years (1845–51) 800,000 died of starvation, typhus, and relapsing fever. Even greater numbers sought safety in emigration, but with many suffering from dysentery and scurvy, an unknown number did not survive the terrible journey in the overcrowded hulks frequently used in their long-distance transportation, and known as 'Coffin Ships'.

Although by far the highest proportion of emigrants sailed to North America, and considerable numbers also went to Australia, thousands made the shorter crossing to England, Wales, or Scotland, many choosing to remain in the vicinity of such ports of emigration as Liverpool. The Census of 1841 stated that there were approximately 49,000 Irish-born in Great Britain. By 1851 this had risen to 734,000 (or 3 per cent of the population of England and Wales, and almost 7 per cent of that of Scotland, where in 1848 over 60 per cent of the Glasgow Poor Law funds were spent on Irish immigrants). Often, through no fault of their own, they were illiterate, and continued to remain unskilled factory workers, or manual labourers, employed as navvies in railway construction, and—as a French observer acidly remarked—in general 'men without any definite trade, ready for anything, and good for nothing'.

Roughly two-thirds of the entire pre-Famine population of c 8 million were dependent upon agriculture for their existence. Half a million of the holdings were under 5 acres (2 hectares) in extent. Repeal of the Corn Laws turned land from tillage to pasture. More vacant land lapsed into pasture. Then commenced the 'Clearances' (or evictions) and the demolition of noisome cabins. Some of those who survived 'the Great Hunger' were able to accumulate enough money and energy to organise the struggle for tenant rights, for the land could no longer support two interests, the landlord's and the tenant's, and the majority of occupiers were tenants at will. The blow had likewise fallen on the landowners, and a third of their number, receiving no rent and unable to pay mortgage interests, were sold up in the *Encumbered Estates Court*. Many, but by no means all, of the old landlords were indulgent, but the new men who bought up the land, more often grasping, brought discredit to the class, and there was much resentment and hostility between landlord and tenant. The cottier and labourer classes were the principal victims of the Famine so that tenant farmers were by far the most numerous—and increasingly strong and self-confident— group in post-Famine society.

Meanwhile, in 1849, the year of *Queen Victoria's* first visit to Ireland, the workhouses of Ireland maintained the astonishing number of 932,000 of the total population of some 6½ million remaining after the Famine. The population continued to fall each year as emigration persisted. The census of 1861 gives some indication of what living conditions were like at that time. 1,079,062 *families* (not counting their livestock) lived in 579,042 cabins, of which 89,374 had only *one* room, while another 553,496 families occupied a further 489,000 dwellings of two or more rooms. Urban conditions were no better: 40,000 lived in the parish of St. Nicholas (Dublin), with a density of 195 persons per acre!

Conditions in parts of the northern province of Ulster were different from the rest of the island, for it was the 'Ulster Custom' that tenant farmers should enjoy a greater degree of security for their holdings, could sell their interest, and claim compensation for improvements; and secondly, with the rapid industrial expansion of Belfast, there was, to a certain extent, increasing prosperity. Many workers preferred *some* income and a brick-built urban terrace, and the chance of *some* education for their children, to a pittance in a rural cabin and the virtual illiteracy of a 'hedge' school. The connections with industrial England were stronger; the continuance of the Union seemed sensible to the hard-working thrifty Presbyterian. The pursuit of denominational interests by the different churches was often a cause of frustration to educationalists.

Too many Irish politicians seemed more interested in advancing their careers than in co-operating with those endeavouring to improve the lot of the tenant farmer, and in the elections of 1852 only about 40 of the 103 members representing Ireland supported the **Tenant Right League**, which two years earlier had been formed by *Charles Gavan Duffy*. Gavan Duffy (who eventually emigrated to Australia, in 1855, where he became Prime Minister of Victoria) had also founded, with *John Blake Dillon* and *Thomas Davis*, the most influential journal of the day, '*The Nation*'. First published in 1842, it often contained provocative articles on the land question by *James Finton Lalor*. Altruistically, Gavan Duffy and his Young Ireland comrades sensed an opportunity for all classes and creeds to work together for the common good after the ravages of the Famine, but their desperate amateur attempt in that revolutionary year of 1848 to win self-government by armed insurrection ended in disaster.

During the next decade, nursing perfectly reasonable grievances, their successors laid the foundations of the **Irish Republican Brotherhood** (I.R.B.), otherwise known as the *Fenian movement* (1858). Among the better-known leaders were *Charles Kickham, John O'Leary*, and *Jeremiah O'Donovan Rossa*, and their membership was largely drawn from the ranks of artisans, clerks, labourers, and small farmers. The movement incurred the disapproval of the Catholic hierarchy, who were convinced that here were the seeds of revolution and irreligion. Although having strong support from the Irish in America, a Fenian rebellion in 1867 proved abortive. A number of their leaders were imprisoned for their activities, but not before they had forcefully drawn the seriousness of the Irish Question to the attention of **Gladstone**, who, in his first administration, disestablished and disendowed the Anglican Church in Ireland (1869), while in the following year he attempted to pass legislation to protect the tenantry.

Even in 1861 the Church of Ireland could claim only just over 10 per cent of the community; in Ulster the Presbyterians were c 26 per cent of the total; while between 1850 and 1900 the number of ecclesiastics (priests, monks, and nuns) for the Catholic population—c 5 million in 1850—had grown from 5000 to over 14,000, although the Catholic population had by then dwindled to c 3,350,000.

Meanwhile *Isaac Butt* had founded the **Home Rule League**, and in the election of 1874 Butt's party won over half the Irish seats, but it required a more powerful and obstructive politician than Butt to convince Westminster that the Irish were in earnest about independence, and such a one was found in **Charles Stewart Parnell**, who, supported by a number of the Fenians, succeeded Butt as leader of the party in 1877.

In December 1877, after a persistent amnesty agitation, *Michael Davitt* was released from prison, where he had been incarcerated for seven years for his previous Fenian activities. Davitt and others successfully organised agrarian demonstrations in Mayo, and in 1879 the *Land League*, now backed by the clergy, was organised, and for the next three years widespread agitation, known as the 'Land War', continued, which inevitably led to occasional outbreaks of violence. *Charles Boycott* (a land-agent for Lord Erne in Mayo), in endeavouring to defy the Land League, was duly ostracised, and the episode gave a new word to the English language.

Meanwhile Gladstone pushed through a new Land Act, allowing tenants Fixity of Tenure, Fair Rent, and Free Sale of their interest, but this was not considered drastic enough by Parnell and Davitt, who were forthwith imprisoned for their pains, as was John Dillon and other members of the Land League. By the so-called 'Kilmainham Treaty' they were released, but within days both *Lord Frederick Cavendish*, the new Chief Secretary, and his under-secretary, were assassinated in Phoenix Park by members of a new 'terrorist' organisation known as '*The Invincibles*'. Yet, in spite of this setback to a mutual understanding, sympathy had been aroused, and a large body of English opinion had become more liberal towards Irish affairs. In 1885 a Tory government passed the *Ashbourne Land Act*, which was the first to introduce a system of state-aided purchase of land by tenant farmers. Rural landlords began to sell out. Parnell kept up the pressure for Home Rule, but Gladstone's bill was defeated by the House of Commons (June 1886). Seven years later, after the death of Parnell, whose place as leader of the Irish party had been taken by *John Redmond*, another Home Rule bill was defeated by the Lords.

A facet of growing nationalism in other than the merely political field was seen in the establishment of the **Gaelic League**, founded by *Douglas Hyde* and *Eoin MacNeill* in 1893. But the Gaelic League, while not ostensibly a political-nationalist movement, in endeavouring to revive interest in the Irish language, although over-reacting to anything 'English' and weltering in legendary heroics, did much to invigorate many aspects of Irish life, particularly in the cultural and educational fields; while Irish games such as 'hurling', promoted by the *Gaelic Athletic Association* (founded 1884), were invested with special significance, and came to have a mass appeal.

The literary revival, setting out to prove that there was an Irish literature apart from the Anglo-Irish tradition, was led largely by *William Butler Yeats*, who, with *Lady Gregory* and *John Millington Synge*, founded the *Abbey Theatre*. Among the famous Irish writers of the era, not all of whom subscribed to this insular movement, were *George Bernard Shaw*, *Oscar Wilde*, *'A.E.' Russell*, *James Stephens*, and *George Moore*, in whose wake followed *James Joyce*, *Seán O'Casey*, and many other distinguished names.

Meanwhile the *Congested Districts Board* (established in 1891) grappled with the complex problems of overpopulation and underproduction, particularly in Connacht, while *Sir Horace Plunkett* reorganised the creameries (or dairies) of Ireland on co-operative lines. In 1903 a *Land Purchase Act* was carried through Parliament by *George Wyndham* (great-grandson of Lord Edward Fitzgerald), by which the landlords over the greater part of the country were bought out, and a nation of occupying owners of the fee-simple of their farms created. It was the uprooting of the Cromwellian Settlement. Not infrequently the purchasing tenant of 1903 bore the same name as the proprietor whose estate had been confiscated 250 years earlier. Unfortunately by now numerous country houses (or 'castles') had already become derelict. Within twenty years too many more were to be gutted as old scores were settled, too often as indiscriminately as the Protector had indiscriminately proscribed their original owners. In 1908 *Augustine Birrell*, chief secretary during 1907–16, established the National University.

Meanwhile, in politics new forces were emerging, foremost among them being *Sinn Féin*, which gathered impetus after the publication of **Arthur Griffith**'s 'United Irishmen' (March 1899), the first issue of 'Sinn Féin' itself appearing in May 1906. His thesis and proposal asserted that as the Act of Union of 1800 was illegal anyhow, the Irish MPs (who had been illegally sitting at Westminster for a century) should withdraw from the Imperial Parliament, sit in Dublin—where as representatives of Irish constituencies, they belonged—and set up all necessary administrative machinery themselves. Shortly, the quiescent IRB smouldered into action with the publication of *'Irish Freedom'* (1910), which appealed also to a number of young nationalist intellectuals who were increasingly concerned with the appalling squalor of urban conditions of the time: in Dublin alone, 21,000 families lived in single-room tenements.

In 1909 the *Irish Transport and General Workers' Union* had been set up by *James Connolly*, with *James* ('Jim') *Larkin*. In August 1913 the union and its employers, led by *William Martin Murphy*, were at loggerheads, and within weeks 24,000 men were locked out. They formed a *Citizen Army* to protect themselves from the officious police. The strike lasted for over eight months. Militancy had been aroused.

Redmond had also been active on the parliamentary front, and in 1912 yet another *Home Rule* bill was passed by the Commons, only—

yet again—to be defeated by the Lords (January 1913), who by now, however, could only delay, not veto, legislation. The Act was given the royal assent in September 1914, but with the proviso, understandable in the circumstances, suspending it until after the German War, which, it was assumed, would soon be over.

But in Ulster attitudes had not changed; they preferred to stand by the Act of Union which had been foisted on the country in 1800. Under the leadership of the intransigent **Edward Carson**, backed by some Conservatives, over 200,000 *Ulster Volunteers* were raised (January 1913), entirely illegally, ostensibly to defend their 'rights' to remain united with Great Britain, and largely subscribed to by the Orangemen. The *'Curragh Incident'* (March 1914), in which Irish-based British officers intimated in anticipation of any such orders that they would refuse to lead their men against this force (now armed by the Larne gun-running (April)), only served to increase the ferment.

To balance this Ulster development, the *Irish Volunteers* were formed some months later, and they likewise indulged in gun-running; some of them, under the influence of Redmond, joined the British army within weeks of the outbreak of the War (4 August 1914); the rest were largely controlled by the IRB

But the leaders of the IRB had decided that their patience would not last the length of any European war, with which they were not concerned, and they planned a general rising in co-operation with Connolly's Citizen Army. In the event, this did not take place until **Easter 1916**. The Proclamation of the Irish Republic was signed by Thomas J. Clarke, Seán MacDermott, Patrick H. Pearse, James Connolly, Thomas MacDonagh, Éamonn Ceannt (Kent), and Joseph M. Plunkett. They were all shot for treason in Kilmainham Gaol, together with eight others, while many more implicated in the rising were interned in prison camps. The insurrection itself—lead by *Patrick Pearse* and Connolly—was unsuccessful, and in the aftermath, the government (with authoritarian *Lord French* as viceroy) overplayed their hand. The parliamentary party lost heart; while English sympathy for the Irish cause was lost by many who considered that such action in time of war was a stab in the back.

Among others, **Éamon de Valéra** (an Irish Volunteer officer) was elected as Sinn Féin candidate in 1917. An attempt by the government to enforce conscription had to be abandoned because of nationalist resistance. In the general election of December 1918 the Sinn Féin party won 73 seats, the Unionists 26, and the parliamentary party was left with only six. Redmond had died earlier in the year. Sinn Féin forthwith put into operation the policy outlined earlier by Griffith. De Valéra became leader of the *Dáil Éireann* (Assembly of Ireland), with Griffith as his deputy, and ably supported by *Michael Collins*, controlling the armed forces which might well be required to defend themselves against the almost certain attempt of the British to enforce 'order' by military means.

British government in Ireland ground to a standstill. The Dáil, declaring itself independent of Great Britain (21 January 1919), appointed ministers, set up courts, collected taxes, and in general commanded obedience throughout the island, except among the Ulster Unionists, who were determined to be no part of an independent Ireland.

The **Anglo-Irish War** lasted from early in 1919 until the truce of July 1921. Martial Law was proclaimed, and the *Royal Irish Constabulary* were reinforced by contingents recruited from British ex-servicemen familiarly known as the *'Black and Tans'*, who, returning fresh from the European War, treated Ireland as occupied territory. Ruthless extremists gained the ascendancy on either side. A further auxiliary division of the RIC was established, later condemned by their own commander as a drunken and insubordinate body. Attacks were followed by reprisals; a raid on police barracks would precipitate terrorisation and executions; towns were battle-scarred, and (as in Cork) deliberately burned by the English; ambushes and assassinations were the order of the day in the now too familiar course of guerrilla activity. Some of it was carried into England, where property was destroyed, and *Sir Henry Wilson*, long an opponent of Irish self-government, was assassinated (1922).

A compromise treaty was signed in December 1921, brought about by the realisation that government could not be imposed by force; and by pressure from abroad: the distaste of the majority of the English people for the continued dragooning of Ireland was also thus acknowledged. Great Britain patronisingly conceded Dominion status to the 26 counties, and still demanded allegiance to the British Crown, a condition which sowed dissension. Due largely to the machinations of Carson and *Lloyd George*, which further exacerbated its situation, the South was faced with a *fait accompli* in that the British government had already passed the *Government of Ireland Act, 1920*, providing for a partition and a separate parliament for the six counties of **Northern Ireland**, where the majority had elected to remain part of the United Kingdom. This parliament had been opened by *George V* on 22 June 1921. In his speech, the king expressed the hope at the very onset of this unnatural political division that it would prove to be merely a temporary measure, 'the prelude of the day in which the Irish people, north and south, under one Parliament or two, as those Parliaments may themselves decide, shall work together in common love for Ireland upon the sure foundation of mutual justice and respect'.

The new native government in Dublin was also preoccupied with resolving a brief but disagreeable civil war, in which Michael Collins was ambushed and killed (August 1922) by 'irregular' opponents of the Treaty settlement. Arthur Griffiths had died ten days earlier. Trouble continued to smoulder. The last political assassination of the 1920s was that of *Kevin O'Higgins*, one of the Free State's most competent leaders, admired among others by W.B. Yeats (now a Senator), who in his last speech suggested that it was more desirable and important to have able men than representative men in the House.

William T. Cosgrave, head of the first Irish Free State government, handed over office to De Valéra in 1932. De Valéra remained in power (apart from some six years in opposition) until 1959, later (1959–73) becoming President. In 1937 a new constitution was adopted by a plebiscite, and Douglas Hyde became the first President (1938–45).

The 26-county state preserved a precarious neutrality during the 1939–45 War. In 1948 a new government was formed by *John A. Costello*, and in the following year Ireland declared herself a Republic; but although thus abandoning the British Commonwealth, her constitution still contained the main provisions of the laws and customs of the British constitution.

Costello's government broke down in 1951, largely as a result of internal conflict over a health scheme sponsored by *Dr Noel Browne*, which the Catholic hierarchy considered would undermine the inviolability of the family. This hierocratic aspect of the politics of the Republic seemed to smack of 'Rule by Rome', which further alienated the unbigoted in Northern Ireland who were otherwise sympathetic to the growth of the young and vigorous independent state. Other indications of clericalism were censorship, and the episcopal ban on Catholics attending Trinity College. But in 1972, as a result of a constitutional referendum, the Catholic Church was placed on a footing of equality with, not of superiority to, other religions, its privileged position under Article 44 being abrogated, an œcumenical act which did much to moderate the obsessive fears of many Orangemen.

On 22 June 1921 *Sir James Craig* (later Lord Craigavon), the son of a Co. Down whiskey millionaire, became Prime Minister of the six counties which had contracted out of the proposed formation of an independent Irish state, and remained in virtually unchallenged control until his death in 1940, the *Special Powers Act* of 1922, made permanent in 1933, being consistently invoked to frustrate any attempt to upset the traditional Unionist ascendancy in this latter-day 'Pale'. Those in a position to do so in Northern Ireland, among them the Orangemen, vociferously insisted on the continuance of Union with Great Britain, since they were in a two-thirds majority. But they had to contend with internal 'troubles' fostered by the repression of minority views. A boundary commission had been set up in the early 1920s, but its proceedings were terminated by a tripartite agreement signed in 1925 ratifying the border between the Free State and the Six Counties. In 1932 provincial vanities were gratified by the opening of an imposing new parliament building at Stormont, near Belfast.

Craigavon was succeeded briefly by *J.M. Andrews*, who was followed in turn by *Sir Basil Brooke* (later Lord Brookeborough; 1943–63). The industrial depression of the 1930s was alleviated during the *1939–45 War*, in which large numbers of all faiths joined the armed forces or played their part in the production of ships, aircraft, and other weapons, since when Northern Ireland's industries have been largely diversified, particularly in the manufacture of synthetic fibres.

Recent Irish History. In the early 1960s the Republic experienced an apparent economic transformation, accompanied by considerable social and economic change. The frugal, rural Ireland of Éamon de Valéra's arcadian vision gave way—if indeed it ever existed—to a self-confident, outward-looking buoyant state. It was hardly fortuitous that the period of change coincided with de Valéra's departure from active politics in 1959 and with his replacement, as the country's leader and most important politician, by the brusquely pragmatic *Sean Lemass*. Lemass's accession to leadership had been long delayed and now, for seven short but significant years (1959–66), he presided over the Republic's belated economic modernisation.

A gifted public servant, Kenneth Whitaker, was the author of *Economic Development* which, published as a government White Paper in 1958, heralded the planned development of the Irish economy. The gloom and depression of the 1950s were dispelled and, benefitting from favourable world trends, the decade ahead saw falling unemployment, an increased marriage rate, decreased emigration, and even net immigration for a time. The huge exodus to England and elsewhere in previous decades had been regarded as a shameful reproach to the ideal of national self-sufficiency. It now seemed as if the doleful demographic trends dating from the Famine were to be reversed, with the 1966 census showing a population increase for the first time.

But this rosy picture began to fade in the 1970s. Though manufacturing output doubled between 1960 and 1973—manufactured exports taking over from agriculture—the Irish economy ran into trouble thereafter partly because of the oil crises of 1973 and 1979 and the ensuing global recession, but also because of domestic factors. Heavy taxation, over-generous pay settlements, serious inflation, poor management, and uncontrolled foreign borrowing darkly shadowed the economy into the 1980s when the national debt (£20,000 million in 1986) and unemployment (230,000 in 1986 out of a population of 3,500,000) both reached astronomical heights, and emigration reared its head again (31,000 in 1986), as successive governments appeared unable to provide a living for a huge young population. Perhaps the basic problem was that the Irish economy was an exceptionally marginal and vulnerable one in modern trading conditions: perhaps it was that the Republic aspired to First World living standards while her resources were those of an—admittedly well-off—Third World country. In addition, the prolonged Northern conflict put further strains on the Southern economy (see below).

There were great expectations from the country's membership of the European Economic Community in 1973. In the event, there were benefits in terms of diversified exports, Community-funded development projects and, for a period, remarkable agricultural prosperity. But the new arrangement also meant the end of the old economic nationalism with its tariff-protected industries. Together with the energy crisis and the world recession, EEC membership caused a disastrous slump in the Irish manufacturing sector, the oldest industries—textiles, footwear, car assembly—being hit the hardest.

Meanwhile, the Industrial Development Authority did trojan work in attracting foreign firms to Ireland, supported by government policies of liberal tax incentives. But the generosity of Irish taxpayers was not always requited: they were dismayed to find that multi-nationals tended to take their profits home, and to close down outlying branches of their empires once recession struck. In spite of difficulties and disappointments, however, a skilful and expert workforce was developed in the new 'sunrise' industries—pharmaceuticals and electronics—though these were not as labour-intensive as their 'traditional' predecessors.

The social and cultural changes of the 1960s were more enduring than the ephemeral economic boom, but no less remarkable in their development and in their transforming effect on society. Such changes were partly a reflection of economic resurgence, partly the result of such diverse factors as two-way tourism, Vatican II and, above all perhaps, the introduction of a national television service (1960) which set the nation talking to itself in popular chat shows. The cosy complacency of an insulated society was shattered, and erstwhile taboo subjects were given an uninhibited airing.

Irish Catholicism lost much of its morose ambience and took on an optimistic world (and other-world) view, as well as a critical attitude towards the Catholic clerical establishment. There was a new lay independence, particularly in matters of sexual morality, and something of an á la carte approach to what had been heretofore a no-choice menu of obligatory doctrinal and moral items. There gradually developed an unaccustomed tolerance towards other Christian denominations and even towards exotic non-Christian sects.

However, despite a relative relaxation in religious practice, Catholicism in Ireland still remained more fervent and committed than anywhere else in western Europe. By a two-to-one majority, the Republic's electorate voted in a 1983 referendum to insert a 'pro-life' anti-abortion clause in the Constitution. Three years later (June 1986) a majority of similar proportions rejected a government proposal which would have modified the absolute constitutional ban on divorce. Neither of these issues was a clear-cut religious one, yet it was evident that a large majority of the citizens, despite their apparent newfound flexibility and tolerance in other areas, wished the Catholic ethos of the State to continue and were reluctant to take public morality out of the constitutional and legal sphere, even though such a process seemed to be required by the imperatives of the Northern situation.

Nonetheless, there was no mistaking the public shift in moral and social concerns in the 1960s and 1970s. A puritanical obsession with sexual morality—which for economic and other reasons had preoccupied Irish Catholics from the Great Famine era—gave place to a continuing public debate on the social injustices endemic in Irish society (traditionally caste-conscious though nominally classless) and on how best to distribute the modest national cake. There was a substantial improvement in social welfare provision and in the quality of the public health services. In education, though equality of opportunity remained a visionary objective, second-level access was improved through the provision of free transport and the (partial, at least) abolition of fees; there were rapid developments in technological education; and, with the extension of grants to students, the universities were no longer the exclusive preserves of the affluent professional and commercial classes. All in all, the high levels of education which could be regarded as a heritage of British rule were well maintained.

Culturally, too, the country clung tenaciously to a certain distinctiveness in the face of global levelling forces. The 1960s saw a remarkable popular resurgence of Irish traditional music which showed no sign of abating twenty years afterwards. It seems safe to say that at no time in the past have there been so many excellent performers of Irish music playing to such enthusiastic audiences. Again, in the teeth of competition from other sporting codes, the distinctive games (hurling and Gaelic football) of the Gaelic Athletic Association maintained their popular appeal. On the other hand, the Irish language—the revival of which had been State policy since independence—continued to languish despite the sentimental good will of the great majority of citizens, and considerable literary activity through the medium. The Irish, however, continued to make the English language creatively their own, and the work of poets and dramatists, in particular, were especially distinguished in the 1970s and early 1980s.

The regenerated Republic of the early 1960s also saw a modest place for itself on the changing world stage. As a west European Christian nation with no murky imperial past and a tradition of anti-imperialist resistance, it aspired to the role of honest broker at the United Nations, helping to ease the path of acceptance of the new Afro-Asian states into the family of democratic nations. The negative and isolationist neutrality of the 26-County State in World War II was now developing into a positive, if modest, contribution to international peace and understanding through an independent (though never quite 'non-aligned') stance in the forum of the United Nations, and through what proved to be honourable and distinguished service under the UN peacekeeping flag in such troubled areas as Cyprus, the Congo and the Lebanon.

Irish Catholic missionaries had long played a major role in Africa and elsewhere. That missionary spirit took a radical turn in the 1970s and 1980s as many Irish priests and nuns espoused the cause of oppressed people suffering poverty and injustice under neocolonialist regimes. In turn, that development was perceived by many Irish people as the working out of Ireland's proper world-role of constructive neutrality—that of identifying and showing solidarity with the small and poor nations athirst for justice. The perception may have carried with it delusions of grandeur and self-importance but there was no doubting the reality of popular feeling on the part of a citizenry exceptionally well-informed on world affairs. These relatively new feelings, however, tended to come into conflict with Ireland's traditional affection and regard for the United States, according as Irish unease grew with American nuclear and Latin American policies in the early 1980s. In this respect, the contrast between the ecstatic Irish reception afforded John F. Kennedy in 1963 and the cool, not to say hostile, reaction to Ronald Reagan's visit in 1984 is instructive and revealing in the light it throws on the development of Irish worldviews in the interim.

But world-views may be a luxury for a small country whose economic self-interest must come first. The Republic's membership of the EEC, notwithstanding the singular position of its military neutrality, gradually involved it in the common foreign policy-making process and ultimately committed it, moreover, to participation in common defence in the event of European union. It remains to be seen how an apparent conflict between this development and 'traditional' neutrality can be resolved. Meanwhile, a happier and less contentious expression of Ireland's interest in the wider world is to be found in the presence of teachers, development workers, research experts, various instructors, and nurses in Africa and the Middle East. What Ireland can offer here is a certain temperamental affinity, a rapport based on similar ex-colonial experiences, and the special small-scale expertise developed under native government in such areas as peat production and rural electrification.

Whatever changes occurred in the Republic in society and the economy, the party political system looked remarkably durable and stable from the 1960s to the 1980s, given the fragmenting tendencies of the proportional representation electoral system, the increasing socio-economic pressures from within and the potentially destabilising effect of the Northern conflict. Apart from two successive shortlived governments in 1981–82, the life span of Irish parliaments compare very favourably with European norms. Public interest in the political process continues unabated, even if it is increasingly expressed in disenchanted form. Political observers describe Irish politics as a two-and-a-half party system, with the two large parties which historically derive from the Anglo-Irish Treaty split (1921–22) alternating in government, *Fianna Fail* forming single-party administrations (under *Jack Lynch*, 1966–69, 69–73, 77–79; *C.J. Haughey*, 1979–81; 1982) and *Fine Gael* in increasingly uneasy coalition with the small Labour party (FG's *Liam Cosgrave* heading such a coalition in 1973–77, and his successor *Garret FitzGerald* being Taoiseach in 1981–82, 1982–). Labour occasionally tries to change its role from 'half-party' Coalition prop to socialist standard-bearer but the Irish electorate has as little appetite, it seems, for politics of the left as it has for politics of violence. In the mid-1980s, a new party, the Progressive Democrats, aspired to break the traditional moulds by offering a platform of enlightened approaches to the North, liberalism on public morality and Church-State matters, and a private enterprise stand on the economy. There may be alarming noises off stage but Irish politics continue to be cautious, solidly parliamentary, extraordinarily (by English or American standards) intimate and personal, and an unrivalled spectator sport.

In the 1960s, the Republic found its own business so absorbing that nationalist rhetoric and emotion (both in terms of anti-partitionism and anglophobia) declined, despite the publicity attending the fiftieth anniversary commemorations of the Easter 1916 Rising. There was widespread public approval for the Lemass-O'Neill meetings of 1965 as evidence of a genuine attempt to break away from the stale irredentist rhetoric and the virtual cold war between North and South that had lasted for forty years. Captain *Terence O'Neill*, premier of Northern Ireland (1963–69), set out, in his own words 'to build bridges between the two traditions in our community'. But his moderate brand of Unionism exposed him to the charge, made by Protestant extremists like the Rev. *Ian Paisley* and by rebels within the unionist parliamentary party, that he was selling out to popery and to the Republic. In reality, his reformism was too timid and too late.

The Catholic minority in Northern Ireland, comprising more than a third of the population, organised itself in 1967 in the Northern Ireland Civil Rights Association (NICRA)—inspired particularly by the civil rights movement in the USA—to demand reform in local government, electoral boundaries, public housing, and other areas where Catholics were discriminated against and treated as second-class citizens. The leaders of the new movement were particularly incensed that the economic development of the 1960s should have favoured the Protestant east of the province rather than Catholic areas like Derry where unemployment was chronically high. The decisions to site a new town, Craigavon, in the Protestant area of Co. Armagh and to ignore Derry's valid claim for a university in favour of Coleraine, were also seen as rankly partisan.

Though republicans were involved in the NICRA movement, its demands were made within the existing constitutional framework. Full rights as British subjects, not a united Ireland, were its objective, 'We shall overcome', not 'A Nation Once Again', its anthem. But the course of events was to change all that. Civil rights marches were met with violent repression from the Unionist authorities and extremist Protestants, and television cameras brought the Royal Ulster Constabulary baton charges at Derry on 5 October 1968 into countless homes in Britain, the Republic and elsewhere. The determined minority was inspired in different ways by such able and articulate leaders as *John Hume* and *Bernadette Devlin*. Against a background of growing violence, reforms were conceded or promised, but by now, in classic historical fashion, the 'troubles' took on a momentum of their own. Fierce rioting took place in Derry and Belfast in August 1969, causing the London government to intervene in the North after decades of indifference and inaction. When British troops arrived they were hailed by Catholics as their protectors against Protestant extremists and the RUC. But the popularity was short-lived and within a year the British Army's role was seen by nationalists as bolstering up the discredited Stormont regime.

Meanwhile, the IRA—or rather its Provisional faction—began to regroup as the protective force of the Catholic population, and from April 1971 the Provisionals undertook a campaign of bombing, shooting and arson supported by Irish-American arms and money, and aimed at forcing a British withdrawal from Northern Ireland. (In 1969–70 the IRA and its political wing, *Sinn Féin*, had split into the 'Officials', representing the Marxist political activism developed dur ing the 1960s, and the 'Provisionals', standing for traditional nationalist militarism and non-recognition of the 'puppet Free State'.)

Though the Provisionals continued over the years to deny angrily that their campaign was sectarian and directed against civilians, this was the tragic, if unintended, outcome. The widespread destruction, and the killing and maiming of civilians bitterly polarised the already divided communities and resulted in savage retaliation by Protestant extremists. In fact, the great majority of the 2500 fatalities (by the mid-1980s) were Ulster-born men, women and children, while British soldiers comprised but a small minority·of the total. Thus the conflict had much more the character of a civil, sectarian one than of the liberation struggle depicted in IRA propaganda. This was especially so with the formation of such loyalist paramilitary groups as the Ulster Volunteer Force and the Ulster Defence Association. It became ever clearer that it was Ulster Protestant rather than British blood that would have to be spilt in abundance if the IRA was to attain its objective.

Meanwhile, the credibility of the Unionist regime was further undermined when the constitutional nxationalist group, the Social Democratic and Labour Party (formed in 1970), withdrew from the Northern Parliament at Stormont. The decision of the Unionist government to introduce internment in August 1971 was a fatal one, leading to a sharp increase in violence and uniting the whole Catholic population in a total rejection of Stormont. The shooting dead by British Army paratroopers of thirteen unarmed civilians during a civil rights march in Derry on 30 January 1972 ('Bloody Sunday') was interpreted by nationalists as an outrageous attempt to enforce the authority of a tottering Stormont government. It came as no suprise that *Edward Heath*'s government suspended—in effect, ended—the Northern Ireland parliament in March 1972 and replaced it by 'direct rule' from Westminster, administered by the holder of a newly-created cabinet post, the Secretary of State for Northern Ireland. The half-century of locally-based Unionist ascendancy was over for ever: what was to take its place became the subject both of constitutional and violent debate.

As violence continued and as British (and Southern Irish) public opinion began to tire of the seemingly insoluble conflict, the British offered the first of a number of 'initiatives', or compromise arrangements. For a few short months in 1974, a fragile power-sharing Executive (moderate Unionists, SDLP, and bridge-building Alliance party) operated with a precarious majority in a newly-elected Assembly, backed by a tripartite Dublin-London-Belfast agreement (the Sunningdale conference). A massive and successful loyalist agitation brought down the Executive, and further attempts to bring the conflicting groups together failed totally, with direct rule continuing.

In 1980, there was begun a long process of exploration by the British and Irish governments of 'the totality of relationships' within these islands with the purpose of achieving peace, reconciliation and stability. There were various setbacks to Anglo-Irish relations in the years that followed—the traumatic situation created in all of Ireland in 1981 by the deaths on hunger-strike of ten republicans in the H-Blocks at Long Kesh internment camp in the North; the refusal of the Dublin government to support the British in the Falklands war—but the common resolve endured that terrorism must be defeated, that the legitimate aspirations of the nationalist minority must be recognised and provided for, but that the unionist majority would not be forced out of the United Kingdom. (The New Ireland Forum, 1983–84—composed of constitutional nationalists—attempted to reappraise traditional nationalist positions generously.) Above all, the alienation of a substantial number of northern nationalists from the constitutional process, and their support for the IRA (albeit often intermittent and passive) had to be countered.

These were the objectives of the Anglo-Irish Agreement announced by the two governments at Hillsborough in Northern Ireland on 15 November 1985. This ingenious accord attempted to balance unionist claims and nationalist aspirations, established an Intergovernmental Conference to deal with a wide range of affairs in the North, and provided for the possibility at some future date of a devolved government 'on a basis which would secure widespread acceptance throughout the community'.

Northern nationalists gave the Agreement a guarded welcome, and adopted a wait-and-see policy; public opinion in the South was overwhelmingly favourable, especially since the Agreement seemed to make no demands on the Republic; and unionists of all shades in the North were unremittingly and intensely hostile, vowing to smash the Agreement, while the Dublin and London governments were adamant that the accord was there to stay. As 1986 drew to a close, one of the great unasked, let alone unresolved, questions was: what would the Republic settle for? From an initial position of support for the northern nationalists in 1969–72 (the burning of the British Embassy in Dublin in 1972 after Bloody Sunday expressed popular feelings), the Republic's citizens, accustomed to consensus and the stability of a homogeneous society, had become gradually baffled, frustrated and sickened by the North—by its irreconcilable stances and its atavistic hatreds. The South was thankful that the direct overspill of violence (for example, the deaths of innocent civilians caused by Loyalist car-bombs in 1974; the occasional murders of Gárdaí by republican paramilitaries; and their assassination of the British Ambassador in July 1976 and of Lord Mountbatten in August 1979) was mercifully limited, but it was ever fearful of bloodier involvement. There was also anger at the cost to an already beleaguered economy of border security and additional prison expenditure, of lost industrial investment and sadly diminished tourist revenue. But whether, or how, all this would affect the Republic's constitutional position on the North and on unity remained unclear.

Cross of The Scriptures, Clonmacnoise, Co. Offaly.

ANTIQUITIES IN IRELAND

Ireland is particularly rich in archaeological remains, both sepulchral and secular, and these monuments remain an important part of the cultural and artistic heritage of the country.

Once considered to be Druidic altars, or by the peasantry as 'giants' graves', what are somewhat loosely described as **Dolmens** are in fact megalithic tombs, of which there are over 1400 in Ireland. They generally consist of three or more unhewn stones supporting a flat and often huge roofing stone. This capstone is usually placed in a slightly sloping position forming an enclosure beneath, and would have been hauled into place up the side of an earthern mound once covering the sides of the tomb, but which with erosion has long since disappeared. Sometimes two standing stones have been symmetrically placed to form a *Portal*.

These dolmens, according to romantic legend, were the 'beds of Diarmuid and Grainne'. Diarmuid, having eloped with the betrothed wife of Finn MacCoul, was forced to flee from pursuit for a year and a day, and nightly erected these shelters over a bed of ferns or moss for himself and Grainne, which caused there to be—so it is said—366 throughout Ireland.

On present evidence, the earliest of these megalithic tombs, usually placed in commanding positions on hill tops, are a form of **Court Tombs**, gallery graves (from shortly after 4000 BC), being formed by a long compartmented chamber behind a space or court flanked by

Poulnabrone Dolmen, The Burren, Co. Clare

Dromberg stone circle, Co. Cork

standing stones, where some form of funerary rite took place. There are several variations of this type, the most frequent being the 'horned cairns', with a form of portico at one or both ends. The 'wedge-tombs', named from their ground plan, of which there are two forms, are later, dating from as early as 3000 BC.

A distinct and slightly later development was the **Passage Grave** (as at *Newgrange*; 2500 BC). The builders may have come from Brittany, while these graves also have similarities with examples in Portugal. Essentially they consist of a long narrow passage leading to cells round a burial-chamber, and are covered by a round mound of earth, often surrounded by a kerb of stones. The passage, constructed with upright slabs, is usually roofed with lintels, and the chamber by a corbelled dome. The more visible stones are often lavishly ornamented, the roofs and walls being covered with concentric circles, spirals, and other incised patterns executed with a chisel or punch.

In every tumulus yet excavated traces have been found of urn-burial, and sometimes skeletons have been discovered in a sitting position holding an urn. These were either food-vessels, usually associated with inhumation, or cinerary urns, holding the ashes of the dead. Stone or bronze implements, and occasionally ornaments among other objects, have usually been uncovered in excavating these sites.

Stone Circles are mostly Late Neolithic–Early Bronze Age in date; some in the SW may be as late as c 1200 BC. When associated with barrows they may have been erected to give additional eeffect to the tumulus, as at Newgrange where a circle surrounds the site; isolated enclosures may merely have marked off a spot of religious or judicial significance.

Pillar-stones are also found, marking the place of interment, commemorating some dead, or indicating some boundary, and belong to the same class as the continental *menhir*: they are also known in

Ireland as *Galláns*. See also Ogham Stones, below. In addition, three decorated stones of the La Tène culture have been discovered in Ireland, at *Turoe* (Co. Galway), *Killycluggin* (Co. Cavan; now in the National Museum, Dublin), and *Castlestrange* (Co. Roscommon). The curious formalised Early Christian figures on *Boa Island* and *White Island*, both in Lough Erne, although of a much later date, may be conveniently mentioned here.

The ancient Irish in the early historic period were not nomadic. They were settled and practised mixed farming, in which cattle were important. In times of danger they returned with their flocks or cattle to their entrenched villages and forts. Their shelters within the enclosure were constructed with wood, stone, and wattles daubed over with clay, and the site was surrounded by a rampart and other defences, as much to keep their livestock in as marauders out. These **Ring-forts** built of earth or clay are known as **Raths**; those of stone are usually designated **Cahers** (*cathair*) or **Cashels** (*caiseal*). The term 'rath' has been loosely used, and it applies not only to the simple circumvallation with a stockade and fosse, but also to places of assembly and residence. It has been estimated that about 30,000 structures of this class exist in Ireland, although a large number must have been swept away as the improvements of agriculture extended over the country, or have been eroded to comparative shapelessness even if they can be detected by aerial photography.

Often these forts contained long narrow passages or galleries of uncemented stone overlaid with flat stones. Known as **Souterrains**, they were used either as storehouses or for places of temporary refuge. These burrows are also found independently.

The earthwork was surrounded by a breastwork and a fosse, and there are sometimes three or more circumvallations, while in the centre of some enclosures was a huge flat-topped mound on which the main residence stood. Occasionally the latter type had a bailey similarly defended, and they are found not only within the Pale, but also in Connacht and Munster, as their settlements were rapidly extended after the invasion.

Some of the larger hill-forts were celebrated in the early annals of Irish history, such as those at *Navan Fort* (near Armagh), or *Tara* (near Navan, Co. Meath), with a rath inside, which accommodated chieftains or High Kings.

More ambitious and more permanent defence works, usually sited on commanding hills and cliffs, are the stone-built **Hill-forts**, *Lis*; *Dúns* or **Promontory-forts**. Among the more imposing examples extant are *Dún Aengus* and *Dubh Cathair* on the Aran Islands, the *Grianán of Aileach* in Co. Donegal (just W of Derry), a large cashel inside a hill-fort, and—more perfect—*Staigue Fort*, W of Sneem, Co. Kerry, a large cashel. Neither the use of the arch nor mortar was known to the builders of these primitive 'cyclopean' structures, which were made with a slight batter, being wider at the base than at the top. One is constantly reminded of these various terms for such fortified places by the frequently recurring prefixes to present place-names, such as *Dun*gannon, *Lis*more, *Caher*civeen, *Rath*drum, etc.

Another type of fortification is the palisaded island, artificially constructed or improved, known as **Crannógs**, found near the edge of lakes, or further offshore, and sometimes approached by a causeway. Their inaccessibility caused some to be used as recently as the mid 17C. Few crannógs have stood the test of time, but one of the best surviving is at *Fair Head*, Co. Antrim. A reconstructed example, part of the Craggaunowen Project, may be seen near Quin, Co. Clare.

Another curious primitive structure, seen frequently on the Dingle Peninsula and elsewhere, is the 'beehive' hut or **Clochán**, a small stone shelter, usually circular, shaped like a beehive, in which stones are piled up on each other in corbel principle, and which is then closed at the top with flat stone slabs.

The first ecclesiastical buildings constructed by missionaries in Ireland were mostly of wood, but none has survived: these were called '*Duitheachs*'; actual churches were built of stone, '*Daimlaig*', when available. Those that have survived were often small oratories in relatively poor monasteries in the W. Usually they were very small—an average of 3m by 4.5m—and were often erected in sequestered and almost inaccessible sites, one of the earliest now existing being perched on *Skellig Michael*, a steep rock 12km off the Kerry coast. More accessible are those on *Scattery Island*, *Bishop's Island* (near Kilkee), on *High Island* (off the Connemara coast), on *Inishmurray* (off Sligo), on islands in Loughs Ree, Currane, Erne; on *Mt Brandon*, and many other places. Perhaps the best preserved is the very singular and beautiful *Oratory of Gallarus* (near Dingle). This is of the rectangular type which, with their domed roofs formed by the gradual approximation of horizontal unmortared stones, closed at the top by a single stone, were an adaptation of the clochán.

In turn these developed into so-called 'houses', accommodating a room or croft between the stone roof and the coved ceiling of the oratory (such as *St. Columba's House* at Kells, *St. Kevin's* at *Glendalough*, and *St. Flannan's* at *Killaloe*), and are of particular interest in displaying in their barrel-vaulting the transitional stage from the false to the true arch.

Often found in the proximity of such early monastic sites are the elarge blocks of stone, artificially hollowed and probably used as mortars, and known as **Bullauns**.

In 1845 George Petrie's study 'On the Origin and Uses of the Round Towers of Ireland' was published, demolishing numerous suppositions of previous antiquarians—their Danish origin; their use as anchorite's eyries, or penitential prisons, etc. It is now accepted that these distinctive **Round Towers**, some 70 of which now survive in whole or in part, some dozen or so almost perfect, retaining their original conical cap, were designed for the double purpose of belfries (*Cloigtheach*) or campaniles from which to call the monks in from the fields to prayer; and also as places of retreat. This may be inferred from their small entrances, almost always placed at some height from the ground, an obvious mode of securing safety common in ancient castles. They could be entered with ease by a wooden or rope ladder, which could be pulled up in the face of marauders, whether Viking or fellow Irish, and they originally contained a number of wooden landings joined by flights of wooden steps. The earliest of these graceful tapering towers were built in Ireland c 900, and continued to be erected until the early 13C. Three are preserved in Scotland, and one on the Isle of Man.

Characteristic of many churchyards—as with Calvaries in Brittany, which are likewise the imperfect assimilation of pagan superstition with Christian rites—are the **Crosses** and **High Crosses** of Ireland, from the memorial cross inscribed on a plain slab of the 7C to the elaborately sculptured free-standing crosses that proliferated between the 8C and the 12C. The primitive form, in some cases copying a wooden prototype, perhaps with metal ornaments, was improved by the binding of the shaft and arms by a circle or wheel. They combined great intricacy of interlaced or serpentine patterns

The Round Tower at Glendalough

with accurate representations of costume of the period in their panels of scriptural or symbolic subjects, which were no doubt produced as aids to faith. At *Clonmacnoise* one may see fragments and almost perfect examples of numerous incised crosses from the 8–12C, but both here and at *Ahenny, Kells, Monasterboice, Durrow, Drumcliff, Dysert O'Dea,* and *Moone,* among many others, there are superb examples of the High Cross, a form of religious art which is peculiarly Irish.

Lastly, one must refer to the once mysterious **Ogham Stones**—called after Ogmios, the Celtic god of writing—the elucidation of which was long a favourite topic with antiquarians, and which are now considered to be of Christian date (300–800) rather than pagan. Over 270 have been found in Ireland, the majority of them in Cork and Kerry. The key to Ogham writing, a somewhat clumsy adaptation of a primitive Latin or Greek alphabet, and the first in Ireland, is found in the 'Book of Ballymote' and other MSS, and was confirmed by Bp Graves of Limerick by independent investigation. Ogham script consists of a series of notches arranged on either side or across the edge of an upright stone (which should be read from the bottom to the top, but may be continued down the other side), or of lines incised on the stone. The alphabet does not contain the letters J, K, P, V, W, X and Y. In almost every case the inscriptions consist merely of a man's name and that of his father, and it is contended that they mark either a grave, like the *galláns*, or a boundary. In the Cathedral of *Killaloe* is a unique example of a stone preserving both a Viking Runic inscription and the same in Ogham.

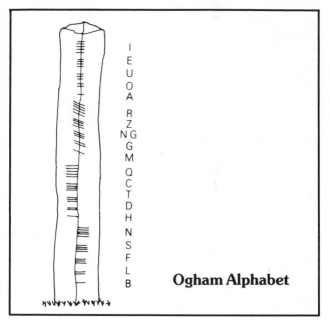

Ogham Alphabet

ARCHITECTURAL INTRODUCTION

By *Maurice Craig*

The first churches in Ireland, built soon after the coming of St. Patrick in the 5C, must have been of timber, and, like other wooden buildings of this and succeeding centuries, have disappeared. Ancient MSS speak of very small timber oratories only 4.5m by 3m (15ft by 10ft), and it is certain that among the surviving stone structures there are some which approximate to these dimensions and are primitive in type if not as early in date as has sometimes been presumed. There are ten or twelve very small churches, mostly along the western seaboard, whose internal dimensions are as little or even less. The two most celebrated and best preserved are the *Oratory of Gallarus*, near Dingle in Co. Kerry, and that on *St. MacDara's Island*, near Roundstone in Co. Galway.

The first of these is built on the corbel principle, each course of stones oversailing until they meet at the top: the result looks something like an upturned boat. The church on St. MacDara's island combines this technique with reminiscences of timber construction: these latter show in the *antae* (prolongations of the side walls at the front and back), which are continued upwards to the peak of the gable as 'barge-courses', where they terminate in a winged stone finial. The corbelled stone roof did in fact collapse, and has been re-erected only in very recent times.

The *clocháns* or beehive huts of the South and West are structurally similar to the Oratory of Gallarus, but circular: there are several on *Skellig Michael*, an early monastery in a stupendous situation out in the Atlantic, and many more on the Dingle peninsula. The corbelled construction was used right down to modern times for hen-houses in Kerry and for sweat-houses (a kind of primitive Turkish bath) in the northern half of Ireland, so that such buildings are difficult to date.

The typical early Irish monastery was a round enclosure dotted with beehive huts and containing a few very small churches, workshops, and miscellaneous buildings. Examples survive in a recognisable form on a few islands: *Inishmurray*, off the Sligo coast, *Inishcaltra* (or Holy Island) in Lough Derg (Co. Clare), and *Nendrum* on Strangford Lough (Co. Down). But there were very many others, of which the most famous to survive in something like recognisable form are *Clonmacnoise* (Co. Offaly), and *Glendalough* (Co. Wicklow), both of which show the tendency for small churches to multiply, to the traditional number of seven and indeed beyond. There are similar remains on the *Aran Islands*.

The primitive churches had square-headed doorways with massive lintels and inward-sloping jambs. The visible stones used in their construction are sometimes very large indeed (as in *Teampull Benen*, Inishmore). The first appearance of the round arch cannot be dated with precision. Small windows with round heads cut out of a single stone may be very early, but the true arch perhaps not before 1000 AD. Gradually the churches grew larger: the church of *Aghowle* (Co. Wicklow), which is c 18m by 7.5m (60ft by 25ft) is by Irish standards large.

Among the finest of the trabeated doorways are those at *Fore* (Co. Westmeath), *Clonamery* (Co. Kilkenny), and *Killevy* (Co. Armagh). The first two are decorated with architraves and crosses; the last-mentioned is plain but unusually massive.

The next development from the simple rectangular plan was to add a narrower and shorter chancel, as at *Mona Incha* (Co. Tipperary), where the chancel is an addition, or at *Trinity* and *Reefert churches* at *Glendalough*, where both parts were built together. But, save for a handful of exceptional examples (such as *Teampull Finghin*, *Clonmacnoise*; the larger church at *Raham*; or *Cormac's Chapel* at *Cashel*) there was no further elaboration of plan in the purely native buildings.

Some churches were roofed entirely in stone by a locally developed system. The corbelled stone roof was retained, steep in pitch to reduce the outward thrust, and braced by a barrel-vault lower down. In the smallest, and perhaps earlier, examples the void thus created served merely to lighten the superincumbent mass of stone; but in the larger examples the space is accessible and usable. *St. Mochta's House* (Louth), *St. Columba's House* (Kells), *St. Flannan's Oratory* (Killaloe), *St. Kevin's Kitchen* (Glendalough) are all note-worthy examples, all excelled in size and elaboration by *Cormac's Chapel*.

The Romanesque elaboration on early Christian themes showed itself in the decoration of W doorways, arcading, and chancel-arches. The W front of *St. Cronon's*, *Roscrea*, of perhaps 1150, similar work at *Ardfert* (Co. Kerry), and the doorways at *Killeshin*, *Freshford*, and above all *Clonfert Cathedral*, with their high gables, are distinctive of the Irish style. Although among the earliest buildings in the series, *Cormac's Chapel* (1134) combines in a unique way the high double stone roof, steeply gabled porches, wall-arcading, and in the chancel, the first cross-vault in Ireland, showing influence from several other countries.

The Round Towers are always found in association with an early Christian church-site: among the finest remaining examples are those at *Devenish*, *Ardmore*, *Cashel*, *Glendalough*, and *Antrim*. See also p 41.

The reforms initiated by St. Malachy in 1142 brought Ireland within the ambit of the European monastic system. The Augustinian and Cistercian orders were established in Ireland, and the latter in particular had an immediate and enduring influence on architecture. In place of the small cells and the small churches there arose, at *Mellifont* and its offspring (*Baltinglass*, *Boyle*, *Jerpoint*, *Ballintubber*, and others), large cruciform churches with conventual buildings regularly disposed round a rectangular cloister. At the same time the organisation of the Irish Church was brought into line with that in the rest of Europe.

Hard on the heels of the ecclesiastical reforms came the Anglo-Norman invasion of 1169, which quite rapidly had the effect of transferring the lordship of most of the richest lands of Ireland to Anglo-Norman hands, and though within less than a century the tide had begun to turn, the architectural change was irreversible. It was a change partly of scale and partly of materials. The great Norman castle, such as *Trim*, *Carrickfergus*, *Roscommon*, or *Liscarroll*, was not only built of stone (which no previous Irish buildings other than churches had been); it also reflected a political and military order new to the Irish scene.

The Norman castles divide naturally into two main types: those such as *Trim*, *Carrickfergus*, or *Adare*, which have a massive *donjon* or 'keep' (and with these can be grouped the slightly later and peculiarly Irish type in which the 'keep' has or had cylindrical turrets or 'flankers' at each corner, such as *Carlow*, *Ferns*, and *Terryglass*), and those which, inspired by Harlech and Beaumaris, consist essentially of a large enclosure with corner and intermediate·towers and a strong gate-house. *Roscommon, Ballintubber, Ballymote,* and *Liscarroll* are instances of the latter type, as are the town castles of *Limerick,* and *Dublin* itself, the latter completely transformed by 18C rebuilding. *Dundrum,* in Co. Down, stands almost alone with its cylindrical donjon, although that at *Nenagh* formed part of the outer defence, while that at *Waterford (Reginald's Tower)* was part of the town walls. Some other castles on rocks by the sea, such as *Carlingford* and *Dunluce,* are picturesque by virtue of their situation. So is the inland *Castleroche,* in Co. Lough, which as at *Athenry* (Co. Galway), has a substantial and spacious hall instead of a donjon.

There is little decoration in these castles: the elegant little chapel in one of the towers of Ferns is exceptional. In the abbeys there is naturally rather more. Thus at *Baltinglass* and *Jerpoint* we can study the interpenetration of Anglo-Norman architectonics and Irish Romanesque decoration; at *Boyle*—owing to the slowness of the building— observe the changes of style (mostly of English derivation) from the E towards the W; at *Mellifont* admire one of the latest essays in the round-arched style, and the lavabo very rare in Ireland; at *Athassel* notice the amplitude of the layout and the Augustinian feature of a NW tower (admittedly now reduced to a few metres only in height).

The 13C saw the building of a number of cathedrals which are still in being: notably the two in *Dublin, St. Patrick's* and *Christ Church,* the latter begun in the 12C, which are strongly English in character. The cathedrals at *Limerick, Killaloe, Kilkenny, Leighlin,* and *Cloyne* are all, like most Irish medieval buildings, small by English or Continental standards, but each has its individual beauty. The cathedral which keeps company with the Round Tower and Cormac's Chapel on the *Rock of Cashel* is also 13C, but was unroofed in the 18C.

Among the very few town churches of medieval origin still surviving and in use may be mentioned *St. Mary's, Youghal; St. Multose, Kinsale; St. Nicholas, Carrickfergus;* and *St. Nicholas, Galway.* There are substantial ruined remains of *St. Audoen's, Dublin; St. Mary's, New Ross;* and the churches at *Callan, Gowran,* and *Thomastown;* but on the whole the absence of such churches in Ireland is very marked.

The towns, which were effectively of Scandinavian foundation when on the seaboard (e.g. Dublin, Wexford, and Limerick) or of Norman foundation when inland (e.g. Kilkenny, Trim, and Kilmallock) bear evidences of their antiquity in their layout and atmosphere rather than in actual buildings. Even the town walls which most of them had are now very sparsely represented. *Fethard* has both walls and church.

Monastic remains, and those of the friaries (which are not in the strict sense monastic, but in Ireland are almost always loosely called 'abbeys') are much commoner. In fact Ireland is unique in Europe in possessing such a wealth of virtually intact though roofless friaries of the 14–15Cs.

The 14C had been almost a blank in Ireland where building was concerned, the result partly of the loss of impetus of the original invasion, partly of the devastations caused by the wars of Edward Bruce (1318), and partly of the Black Death, which reached the country in 1350. Almost the only building of any size assignable to this period is the very unusual square castle at *Ballymoon* (Co. Carlow), in which all the accommodation must have been in lean-to's against the massive outer wall.

Much the same must have been true of *Quin* (Co. Clare), where the Macnamaras founded a Franciscan friary within the walls of an earlier

Macnamara castle which had by then been ruinous for about 150 years. This is among the many Western friaries which, with their slender tapering towers and their tiny cloisters, are so typical of Sligo, Mayo, Galway, Clare, and Limerick. Among the most complete are *Sligo, Rosserk, Moyne, Rosserrily, Ennis, Askeaton*, and no less than three at *Adare*.

The same century saw the remodelling and adornment of some of the Cistercian and other abbeys. By their original rule they were forbidden to have towers or much in the way of decoration; but this limitation had been relaxed, in Ireland as elsewhere, and this coincided with the spectacular building-boom of the 15C.

As a result, the Abbey of *Holy Cross* (Co. Tipperary), although a 12C foundation, is now almost entirely a 15C fabric, restored for worship in the late 20C. It has, for Ireland, an unusually large amount of vaulting in its E end. At *Jerpoint Abbey* (Co. Kilkenny) the present massive tower was inserted, and the cloisters, with their fine decorative carvings, date from this time. The cloisters of the friaries are generally much smaller, and usually form an integral part of the buildings round the court. One of the most attractive, *Muckross* (Co. Kerry), is almost completely filled by a giant yew-tree.

There is much attractive carving and fine window-tracery to be seen in these buildings, but perhaps the most interesting work went into the wall-tombs with their canopies, such as those at *Dungiven* (Co. Derry), *Strade* (Co. Mayor), and *Kilconnell* (Co. Galway). A handful of monastic and friary churches are again in use for Catholic worship: besides Holy Cross, there are the Augustinian church at *Ballintober* (Co. Mayo), the great Cistercian church of *Duiske Abbey* (at *Graiguenamanagh*, Co. Kilkenny), the '*Black Abbey*' (Dominican friary) at *Kilkenny*, and churches at *Carrick-on-Suir, Ballyhaunis*, and *Meelick* near Eyrecourt, Co. Galway).

One of the minor mysteries of the Middle Ages is where the minor landholders and chieftains lieved before the 15C. The larger raths no doubt contained timber buildings which have perished, and in the S and E particularly there is evidence of moated sites which represent manorial units. But with the decay of the feudal system and the Gaelic resurgence which accompanied it, the individual proprietors felt the need of something more substantial: the tower-house.

These buildings, colloquially called 'castles', are very numerous, especially in counties Kilkenny, Tipperary, Clare, Galway, Limerick, and Cork. The earliest dateable examples are in Co. Down (between 1413 and 1441), but some small examples in the adjoining counties of Louth and Meath may be the fruit of a ten-pound subsidy introduced in 1429 for small towers in the Pale. At all events, vast numbers were built between 1400 and 1650, and they remain the most conspicuous class of antiquity in the Irish countryside. Some have been re-roofed in recent years, but only one (*Dunsoghly*, Co. Dublin) retains its medieval roof-framing. They are castles in the sense that they are defensible, with battlements, loops, bartizans, machicoulis, etc., and narrow stone staircases. Except at the very end of the period, they also have one or more stone vaults. They are generally small in area, and the units of accommodation are piled on top of each other. It can be taken as certain that they all had, originally, a bawn or stone enclosure attached to them, though in most cases this has been destroyed, through being used as a cheap source of stone. They vary in height between three and six storeys. Like earlier—and indeed also later—Irish buildings, they have in general a 'batter' or inward slope of the walls, often found with a more pronounced batter at the base, the latter to make projectiles bounce off to the discomfiture of the assailants.

Among the best examples are *Clara* and *Burnchurch* (both in Co. Kilkenny), *Derryhivenny* (which is dated 1643), *Fiddaun, Pallas, Dungory* (with a polygonal bawn), and *Aughnanure* (all in Co. Galway), *Rathmacknee* (Co. Wexford), *Ballynamona* (Co. Cork), *Knockelly* (Co. Tipperary), with a large rectangular bawn, and *Newtown* (Co. Clare), which like a few others, is round. Dunsoghly, already mentioned, and *Blarney* (Co. Cork) are among the largest of the towers.

The largest of all is *Bunratty* (Co. Clare), built c 1450, restored and partly modernised c 1600, only to fall into decay in the late 19C, and again restored in recent years. As in the smaller towers, there is one principal space per floor, but a multitude of smaller rooms in the four massive corner-towers ('flankers') and elsewhere. The plaster decoration of the chapel ceiling is amongst the earliest in Ireland, of about 1600.

Although the traditional tower-house continued to be built well into the 17C—one is known so late as 1683—an ampler, less military style of dwelling had already made its appearance. *Rathfarnham Castle* (c 1595; in Co. Dublin) is semi-defensible and has four flankers, but also large rooms, more than one per floor, and a plan which looks forward to the future. Similar buildings are *Kanturk Castle* (before 1609), *Portumna Castle* (before 1618; for the Earl of Clanricarde), *Raphoe Palace* (1636; for Bp Leslie), *Burntcourt* (c 1645; for Sir Richard Everard), and on a smaller scale *Glinsk* (in Co. Galway), and *Ightermurragh, Monkstown,* and *Mount Long* (all in Co. Cork). Of these only Rathfarnham remains roofed and occupied, while Portumna is the largest and grandest. In many cases large-scale domestic additions were made to pre-existing towers, sometimes exceeding in volume the original tower: good examples are at *Leamanegh* (Co. Clare), *Loughmoe* (Co. Tipperary), and *Donegal*.

At the same time some of the castles of the planters in the North show direct Scotch influence, as at *Burt* (Co. Donegal) or *Monea* (Co. Fermanagh), or are transplanted English manor-houses such as *Castlecaulfeild* (Co. Tyrone). An even more convincing 'English' manor-house is that added to the castle at *Carrick-on-Suir* by the Earl of Ormonde in about 1580: but this is exceptional. The long gallery contains plasterwork similar in date to that of Bunratty.

Semi-fortified houses of complex outline were built, such as *Ardtermon* (Co. Sligo), *Mallow Castle* (Co. Cork), and *Coppinger's Court* (also in Co. Cork). These were all semi-fortified, but the plan of the last-mentioned was used after 1660 for a quite unfortified house at *Richhill* (Co. Armagh), which is still roofed and has Dutch-style gables.

The names of the designers of these buildings are not known, and indeed many must be the product of the client's wishes (and his ability to make them comprehensible) crossed with the experience and skill of a master-mason. The most remarkable building of the early 17C, the huge (now ruined) palace built by the Earl of Strafford in about 1627 at *Jigginstown* near Naas, was no doubt largely directed by Strafford himself, though the names of John Johnston (as 'designer') and John Allen (as 'builder;) are associated with it. Here, for the first time in Ireland, brick was used on a large scale.

The Cromwellian wars were not a favourable time for building, yet very soon after 1660 there appeared a totally undefended type of house such as Richhill, already mentioned, *Beaulieu* (Co. Louth), and

Eyrecourt (Co. Galway), as well as many others now disappeared; with their steep roof, wide timber eaves and dormer windows, they were vulnerable to the Irish climate, and few have survived unaltered.

From 1660 onwards dates the great expansion of Dublin, which turned it in the space of a little over a century from a small untidy town bursting out of its walls, to the second city of the three kingdoms, without a rival after London. Four new bridges were built in rapid succession and many new streets laid out. The most notable public building from the period is the *Royal Hospital* at *Kilmainham*, laid out on the model of Les Invalides in Paris as an old soldiers' home, designed by Sir William Robinson and zealously promoted by the Viceroy, the Duke of Ormonde. The quays of Dublin, the Phoenix Park, and the large square of St. Stephen's Green all took their shape at this time.

Trinity College had been founded in 1592, but was effectively rebuilt on an ampler plan in the 1680s with a Dutch-baroque facade which was again replaced in the 1750s. The earliest building remaining in the college from about this time is the magnificent *Library* by Thomas Burgh, begun in 1712, an ambitious project for its time and place, which took a full twenty years to build.

In the country at large it took some thirty years for the economy to recover from the Williamite wars of 1688–92. One of the first surviving houses of the new century was *Shannongrove* (1709) in Co. Limerick, modest in size, but stately and with wings. Soon afterwards came *'Castle' Durrow* (Co. Leix), largely designed by its owner Mr William Flower, and built 1716–18. It has giant pilasters which had already appeared on the frontispiece to *Kilkenny Castle* (probably about 1685) but are otherwise not common.

The largest and most splendid of all Irish country houses is *Castletown* (Co. Kildare), begun for William Conolly, Speaker of the Irish House of Commons, in 1772. A massive block like an Italian town palazzo, it was designed externally by Alessandro Galilei, and internally by Sir Edward Lovett Pearce, the leader of the Irish palladians, who added the Ionic colannades and the wings. It cannot be considered separately from the almost contemporary rebuilding of the *Parliament-House* in Dublin, which was set in hand in 1729. Pearce was again the architect, but when he died in 1733 the building—the first purpose-built parliament-house in the world—was not quite finished. Later in the century it was enlarged to twice its original size, and after the Union of 1800 converted to the Bank of Ireland.

Provincial towns also were improved during this period, as witness the *Court-House* at *Kinsale*, the *Main Guard* at *Clonmel*, *Skiddy's Almshouse*, *St. Ann's Church*, *Shandon*, and the old *Custom House* (now part of the School of Art) in *Cork*, and the *Barracks* of 1706 in *Ballyshannon*. A great many towns and villages were regularly planned at this time, even when the embodiment was partly delayed until later. It is noteworthy that the splendid *Clock Gate* at *Youghal*, although not built until 1771, is a replacement of a very similar structure of at least a century earlier, which served the same dual purpose of gate-tower and prison. Many towns were provided with arcaded court-and-market houses; but most of the survivors, such as the *Tholsel* at *Kilkenny*, date from the second half of the century. Courthouses in county towns are mostly later (see below).

There was a wave of large country-house building from a little before 1730 to 1750. Pearce himself built *Bellamont Forest* (Co. Cavan) and *Cashel Palace* (Co. Tipperary), but his assistant and successor, the German-born Richard Castle, built many more, including *Hazelwood*

(Co. Sligo), *Westport* (Co. Mayo), *Powerscourt* and *Russborough* (both in Co. Wicklow), *Ballyhaise* (Co. Cavan), *Carton* (Co. Kildare), and *Bellinter* (Co. Meath). The most notable surviving early house in the SW is *Mount Ievers* (1736; Co. Clare), by Isaac and John Rothery. At the same time a large number of lesser houses in various versions of the pervasive palladian style, varied in scale and materials but, like the large houses, all tending towards severity, were built for minor landowners, farmers, clergy, and others. These have survived in fair numbers, though many have fallen into ruin. Like most Irish buildings before 1850 they are generally built of rubble-stone rendered with lime-plaster. A number of good minor houses by Nathaniel Clements date from 1750–65.

Other architects who worked in the provinces were John Aheron (Limerick and Clare), Francis Bindon, Michael Priestley of Derry, and a little later, Davis Ducart, a Piedmontese who worked in Cork and Limerick, and whose masterpiece is *Castletown Cox* (Co. Kilkenny), and John Roberts of Waterford, who built both cathedrals in that city and did some notable country-house work. The elder Morrison (John) in Cork had a more famous son (Sir Richard) and grandson (William Vitruvius), whose careers were based in Dublin and whose buildings belong to the next century. Thomas Ivory came from Cork to Dublin where two of his extant buildings, the *Bluecoat School* and *Newcomen's Bank* may still be seen, but he died prematurely at 54 in 1786.

In the coastal towns, and especially in Dublin, brick, much of it imported, was the favoured material. A handful of stone-face Dublin houses, mostly dating from the 1730s and 1740s such as *Leinster House*, *Tyrone House*, and *Clanwilliam House* (all by Richard Castle), with a few later examples such as *Charlemont House* (1767), *Powerscourt House* (1771) and the *Provost's House* in Trinity College (1759) stand out against the background of four-storey brick houses, plain externally but often lavishly decorated inside. These make up the fabric of 18C Dublin insofar as it still survives. They were designed mostly by master-builders or by builder-architects such as John and George Ensor, and decorated with rococo plasterwork by Robert West, or, later on, in the neo-classic style of Stapleton or Thorp.

The Royal Dublin Society's Drawing School, founded in about 1760, had Ivory for its first master and ensured a high standard in the many craftsmen and designers who passed through it.

Throughout the 18C and well into the 19C Dublin continued to grow. Before 1800 the houses were mostly built for the landed ruling class: after 1800 and the demise of the Irish Parliament they were increasingly occupied by, and built for, the professional and commercial classes. House for house, they tended to be larger than their London counterparts to which they bear a general resemblance. But the doorcases, at least before about 1790, are more varied, and many of the joinery details are different. The mysterious brass rail at breast-height just inside the front door seems to be peculiar to Dublin: explanations for its presence vary: not all are charitable.

The suburban houses of the early 19C are still in the same style, but on increasingly lofty basements. The flight of steps up to the front door is typical of the inner suburbs, and a special type of top-floor-entry house was developed, which is larger than it looks.

The year 1769 is a watershed. The competition for the Dublin *Royal Exchange* attracted 61 designs (24 from Ireland) and was won by Thomas Cooley from London. For the next twenty years the plum jobs tended to go to English architects, although like Cooley and his greater contemporary (and runner-up in the competition) James Gandon, some stayed in Ireland to make their career there. Gandon's great opportunities, the riverside *Custom House* (1781–91), and the *Four Courts* (1785–1802), the extensions to the Parliament House, the *King's Inns*, and *Carlisle Bridge*, are eclectic triumphs in which palladian baroque and neo-classic elements are harmonised, and set the seal on Dublin's character in the era of Grattan's Parliament.

In the country house field James Wyatt, in association with Cooley, figured prominently, as a little later, did John Nash. Wyatt's finest Irish house (and perhaps his finest work anywhere) is *Castle Coole* (Co. Fermanagh). Neither in town or country, nor even exactly a house, is the unique *Casino* at *Marino*, by Sir William Chambers for Lord Charlemont, only two miles from his own town house, also by Chambers, begun in 1761 or 1762, nearly thirty years earlier than Castle Coole.

Wyatt's Irish connexions included, besides Cooley, the Johnston brothers (Richard and Francis), who came to the fore especially after the death of Cooley in 1784, of Ivory in 1786, and the retirement of Gandon in 1808. Although Francis Johnston built one notable classical house, *Townley Hall* (in Co. Louth), most of his country houses after 1800 are in the castellated style, as are those of Sir Richard Morrison, James Sheil, and the Pain brothers, who had been Nash's assistants. This castellated manner had begun back in the previous century (*Castle Upton*; *Slane Castle*) and was to continue until the Famine.

Other practitioners of the manner were the Deanes of Cork, better known for their classical public buildings in Cork itself. As with the Darleys, Semples, and Morrisons, building ran in the Deane family. In the course of the 19C they produced three generations of architects, all three rather confusingly called Thomas; and all three still more confusingly being knighted as 'Sir Thomas'.

During the 16–17Cs most of the churches in Ireland lay ruined or at best in a patched-up state. A rare example of a 17C church is that built by Jeremy Taylor at *Ballinderry* (Co. Antrim). There is part of another at *Waringstown* (Co. Down), another at *Ballyconnell* (Co. Cavan), and another at *Kilbrogan* (in Bandon, Co. Cork). Among the earliest surviving post-Reformation Catholic churches are *St. Finbarr's South, Cork* (now spoiled), *St. Patrick's, Waterford* (unspoiled), and *Grange* (Co. Louth; well restored), all of the early 1760s. An exceptionally attractive example of an early 18C Church of Ireland (anglican) church is at *Timogue* (Co. Leix), of 1736. There are several good 18C and early 19C city churches in Dublin, Cork, Drogheda, and Wexford, while in *Belfast* the most remarkable still survival is the oval *Unitarian* (First Presbyterian) *Church* of 1782 by Roger Mulholland, who may also have done the beautiful example at *Dunmurry* (Co. Antrim).

But the majority of rural Church of Ireland churches were built in the fifty years before 1835 by the Board of First Fruits in a distinctive somewhat utilitarian gothic not without charm. At the same time the Catholic and Presbyterian bodies were building for themselves very attractive 'barn-churches' of simple rectangular or T-plan, of which a fair number still survive, as yet insufficiently appreciated. Too many have been ruthlessly modernised.

Many Irish towns and villages still bear the impress of the generous planning of the 18C and early 19C. Among the finest examples are Armagh, Birr, Roscommon, Tullamore, Ballyjamesduff (Co. Cavan), Mitchelstown (Co. Cork), Castlewellan (Co. Down), and Tyrrelspass (Co. Westmeath).

Francis Johnston, born in Co. Armagh in 1760, is the biggest name in the first quarter of the 19C. He left his mark on Dublin in *St. George's Church*, Hardwicke Place, and most conspicuously in the *General Post Office* in O'Connell Street. *Arus an Uachtaráin*, the President's House (formerly the Viceregal Lodge), owes its present form to him.

A number of admirable classical Catholic churches were erected in Dublin in the 1820s and 1830, such as *St. Audoen's*, *St. Andrew's*, *St. Nicholas of Myra*, *St. Paul's*, Arran Quay, by such architects as Patrick Byrne, John Leeson, and James Boulger. The impressive *Pro-Cathedral*, begun in 1816, is by an unknown architect. Churches of equal splendour were built in Cork, notably *St. Mary's*, Pope's Quay, by Kearns Deane, while in Belfast the church of *St. Malachy* by Thomas Jackson, finished in 1844, is a tour-de-force of picturesque gothick.

There are a few remaining bridges which are in part medieval, such as *Leighlinbridge* (Co. Carlow), or *Carrick-on-Suir* (Co. Tipperary), but the majority of xthe best masonry bridges are from the 18th and early 19Cs, and of these many of the best are over the rivers of the SE: the Slaney, the Nore, the Barrow, and the Suir. Many, such as those at *Graiguenamanagh* over the Barrow, and *Bennetsbridge* over the Nore, were rebuilt after great floods in the mid-18C. *Green's Bridge* in *Kilkenny*, by G. Smith, was built after a flood in 1764. *Wellesley (Sarsfield) Bridge* of 1824 in *Limerick*, by Alexander Nimmo, has been called Ireland's best stone bridge.

In the last quarter of the 18C the canals entailed some fine engineering work, as well as numerous graceful little bridges and many delightful lock-keepers' houses, often from a standard design by Rowland Omer.

The railway age enriched Dublin with several fine stations: notably *Kingsbridge (Heuston)* by Sancton Wood, *Broadstone* (now disused) by John Skipton Mulvany, and *Harcourt Street* (also disused) by George Wilkinson, in 1845, 1850, and 1859 respectively. There are some good provincial stations also by Mulvany and George Wilkinson, and two handsome yacht clubs by Mulvany in *Dún Laoghaire*.

The 19C was, in Ireland as elsewhere, a great age of church-building. The rising Catholic middle class, and the pence of the poor, combined to replace the cathedrals lost at the Reformation. Among those begun before the Famine are *Newry* (1825), *Carlow* (1828), *Ennis* (1831), *Armagh* (1838), *Longford* (1840), *Killarney* (1842), and *Enniscorthy* (1843). The last two are by A.W. Pugin, the others by Thomas Duff, Thomas Cobden, J.J. McCarthy, Dominick Madden, McCarthy and Joseph Keane respectively. Most of them took a long time to build: the names of the effective architects are given above, but in the case of Longford, for instance, Keane was followed by John Burke and George Ashlin. Begun after the Famine were *Limerick* (1856; by Philip C. Hardwick), *Monaghan* (1861) and *Thurles* (1865), both by J.J. McCarthy, *Cóbh* (1868; Pugin and Ashlin), and *Letterkenny* (1890; Hague and Macnamara). All those so far mentioned are gothic except Thurles, which is Lombardo-Byzantine, and Longford, which is classical. There were others, including some in the 20C which are mostly classical. During the same period three or four Protestant Cathedrals were built of which much the most notable is *St. Finnbar's*, *Cork*, in French gothic (1865–78) by William Burges.

Among the finest Catholic town churches of the mid-century is *St. Saviour's* Dominick Street, *Dublin*, by J.J. McCarthy. Two fine churches of 1851–58 in *Wexford* are by Pugin's pupil Robert Pierce.

Most Irish towns of any size have a handsome classical court-house of the early 19C, with a portico and often a dominating situation in the town plan. *Armagh*, by Francis Johnston, is one of the earliest (1805), and *Ennis* (1852) one of the latest. Others of note include *Dundalk* by Edward Parke and John Bowden (1813–18), *Derry* by John Bowden (1817), *Omagh* by John Hargrave (1820), *Carlow* by William Vitruvius Morrison (1828), *Tralee* by the same of similar date, and *Tullamore* and *Waterford* by Joseph B. Keane.

In many smaller towns there are court- and market-houses of a fairly standard plan by such figures as William Caldbeck and William Deane Butler. Sometimes the market-house is a separate building, and sometimes they are combined as in the very fine example of about 1790 at *Hillsborough* (Co. Down) by James McBlain.

The most original architect of the mid 19C was Benjamin Woodward, partner of Thomas Newenham Deane. In Dublin he built the *Engineering School* in Trinity College, the *Kildare Street Club*, and *St. Ann's Parochial Schools* in Molesworth Street, and his provincial work includes *Brownsbarn* (Co. Kilkenny), *Turlough* (Co. Mayo), and the *Long Gallery* at *Kilkenny Castle*. He died prematurely in 1861 aged 46. The northern architect William J. Barre died at the age of 37 in 1867: he had designed the *Albert Memorial, Belfast*; *Scrabo* tower; the *Ulster Hall, Belfast*; the *Crozier Memorial, Banbridge*, and much else. A longer-lived and more prolific architect was Sir Charles Lanyon (1813–89), whose best known work is *Queen's University, Belfast* (built as Queen's College; 1849), the *Northern Bank*, the *Custom House*, and the *Assembly's College*, all in Belfast. He also engineered the Antrim coast road.

This was a period of great expansion in Belfast: less so in Dublin, where, however, the *National Museum* and the *National Library* by Sir Thomas Manly Deane were built in the late 1880s.

From the very end of the century there are some very large buildings such as the *Scottish Provident Building* in Belfast (1899–1902) by Robert Young and John MacKenzie, and the *Belfast City Hall* (1896–1906) by Sir Brumwell Thomas, followed soon by the *College of Science* in Dublin (1911; now mostly occupied by Government offices) by Sir Aston Webb and Sir Thomas Manly Deane, and the *University College*, Earlsfort Terrace, Dublin (1918) by Rudolph M. Butler. The 'Art-Deco' buildings which appeared here and there soon afterwards are scarcely more inspiring. But a vein of eclecticism in the church work of William Scott and R.M. Butler has worn rather better, notably the latter's church at *Newport* (Co. Mayo; 1914).

The most conspicuous result of the building boom of c 1965–80 was to cover the countryside with bungalows built to designs taken from modern patternbooks, especially in certain favoured seaboard counties. But some modern buildings are worthy of mention. Earliest is the *Church of Christ the King* at *Turner's Cross*, Cork, of 1929–31, by Barry Byrne of Chicago. Ten years later came the orgonal building of *Collinstown airport, Dublin*, by Desmond Fitzgerald, followed in 1952–54 by *Busaras* (the bus station) in Store Street, by Michael Scott. Of the many new churches those of Liam McCormick, mostly in Co. Donegal (*Burt, Creeslough, Glenties* and others) are outstanding, as are *Garrison*, Co. Fermanagh, by J.J. Tracey; *Sion Mills*, Co. Tyrone, by Patrick Haughey, and *Athy*, Co. Kildare, by J.C. Thompson.

New university buildings at *Belfield, Dublin* (UCD) are by A. & D. Wejchert, by Scott Tallon Walker and by Basil Spence, and at *Trinity College* by Paul Koralek. The *Dublin Airport Hotel* and the conspicuous *Central Bank* and *City Offices* in Dublin are by Sam Stephenson. *Carrolls' Factory* just outside *Dundalk*, the *Broadcasting headquarters*

(RTE) at *Donnybrook* and the new *Bank of Ireland head office* in Baggot Street, Dublin, are from the office of Scott Tallon Walker.

Notable recent restorations are of the *Opera House, Belfast*, by Robert McKinstry, and the *Royal Hospital, Kilmainham*, by John Costello of Costello Murray Beaumont. The new *National Concert Hall* in Dublin is by Michael O'Doherty of the Office of Public Works, adapting pre-existing buildings. Most recently, a new *Theatre* at *Enniskillen*, Co. Fermanagh, is by Tom Mullarkey and Tony Easterbrook.

INTRODUCTION TO IRISH ART

By *Jane Fenlon*

Introduction. This very condensed account of Irish art cannot cover all aspects of the subject. It will endeavour to introduce the reader to main trends, materials used, sources of influence, and to illustrate these with examples from various periods. There is of course no documentary evidence for the earlier artefacts and it is not until the 11C that facts begin to emerge. This means that until then all stylistic judgements made are comparative with other European sources. From the 12C onwards, however, the names of craftsmen and patrons appear on some of the items made, and this of course helps to date them and gives some insight into patronage. After 1500 there is still a scarcity in documentation and it is not until the late 17C that more material is available to cast some light on the art of that period. In the 18C there is sufficient evidence available to show that travel to Europe and Italy in particular was quite common, with both artists and patrons making the journey. At this time many Irish artists worked in England and there was much artistic traffic between the two countries. In the first half of the 19C, however, the flow was heavily weighted towards England, but later in the century artists again travelled further afield to France and Belgium for their education. Despite their continental education many fine Irish artists had still to work in England, because of the poor financial situation at home. Later, 20C Irish Art follows the common experience of other countries; young artists travelling extensively, both to work and exhibit. It would now seem that art at many levels is once again flourishing in Ireland after the doldrums of the 1930s and '40s. There is much greater interest in exhibitions and sales of the work of emerging artists, established artists and those dating back to the fine landscape tradition of the 18C Irish school.

Pre-Christian Ireland (2500 BC–AD 450).

All the items mentioned in this introduction may be seen in the National Museum of Ireland, Dublin, unless otherwise stated.

The earliest objects made in gold can be dated to c 2000 BC. It is probable that the gold for these was found in Ireland and at a later date was mined in sufficient quantities to allow development of an export trade between Ireland and other European countries. Technical developments would seem to have been slow initially and for the first 500 years a limited range of objects in sheet metal was produced. After 1500 BC there is evidence of major advances in metalworking techniques.

Earlier Bronze Age (c 2500 BC–1200 BC). At this time objects were mainly made of sheet gold with punched and incised geometric motifs. The most commonly produced objects were *Lunulae* and '*Sun discs*'. Crescent-shaped lunulae usually have flattened terminals, and were probably worn around the neck. Relatively large numbers were produced and some were exported to Europe. 'Sun discs' are discs with cruciform patterns; these often have holes in the centre which may have been used to attach them to clothing.

Skilfully decorated pottery was also made for use at burials. An example of this is a large food vessel from Dunamase, Co. Laois (c 1600 BC), which is decorated with herringbone, chevron, and lozenge patterns. However within 200 years this custom of grave goods seems to have been abandoned and only plain, everyday ware was produced.

Later Bronze Age (c 1200 BC–c 300 BC). By now major technical advances are evident. The range of articles produced had increased considerably and various new metalworking techniques were introduced. Bar sections were used for the first time and with these, twisting, soldering and elaborate repoussé patterns were combined to produce many items of international artistic importance. This new expertise can be appreciated in the refined subtlety of *lock rings* (c 800 BC), rings of concentric circles of fine gold wire, either soldered or fused with exquisite finesse. These were probably used in the hair. Another fine piece is that known as the *Glenisheen gold collar* (c 700 BC). These pieces are uniquely Irish in design. Torcs made of twisted gold, both flat ribbon or bar sections, and dress fasteners were also made in large numbers, and a collection of these in various sizes and shapes can be seen at the National Museum of Ireland.

The Iron Age (300 BC–AD 450). It was during the Iron Age that objects decorated in the Celtic La Tène style first appeared in Ireland (the name derives from the Celtic site of La Tène in Switzerland). This style of abstract decorative motifs was common to Celtic Europe, north of the Alps. In Ireland these were modified into a characteristic form and were used to decorate objects in various materials, including stone, bronze and gold. An outstanding example is the *Turoe Stone* (c 300 BC; *in situ* at Turoe, Co. Galway), where early triskele and trumpet-end patterns swirl across the body of the stone, below which are bands of geometrical ornament. This monolith shows close links with similar stones in Britain. In bronze there is the remarkable decoration on a great curved trumpet (1C AD) found at Loughshade, Co. Armagh and in gold, the prime example is the fine *torc*, dated to the 1C BC, found at Broighter, Co. Derry. Here intricate repoussé patterns are raised on an incised background. The construction is a hollow tube with elaborate terminals and all elements show sophisticated metalworking skills.

Other important items from this time are carved stones, some of which are sculpted almost in the round as idols (e.g. the double-faced figure at *Boa Island*, Co. Fermanagh), while many others were carved as heads only. A fascination with the human head was a feature of Celtic art, often expressed in a very stylised form, as in the three-faced idol from *Corleck* in Co. Cavan.

Early Christian Ireland (c 400–c 1000).

The coming of Christianity to Ireland meant new outlets for the arts. In metalwork, sacred objects for use with the liturgy were required. Later, the scriptoria of many monastic settlements were to produce some of the finest examples of illuminated manuscripts in Europe. It is of interest that the decoration used on the pages of the illuminated manuscripts coincided with that used by the metalworkers, suggesting that the workshops were in close proximity to one another. An instance of this cross-fertilisation is the surcoat of the evangelical symbol of Man from the *Book of Durrow*, which is clearly based on millefiori glasswork. Similarly the various circular motifs used in the *Book of Kells* find their parallels in the colourful enamelled studs of the goldsmiths. The spread of Christianity also meant a new influx of artistic ideas, especially from the Mediterranean and from Anglo-Saxon England, and many of these are reflected in the decorative forms of the period. Irish artists showed particular skill in blending the naturalistic art of the Mediterranean with their own predilection for subtle abstract pattern making.

Metalwork. A diverse range of influences are apparent in metalwork of this period. For instance, chalices are Byzantine in form with adaptations of Saxon Frankish cloisonné work used in their decoration. Technical innovations in the use of enamelling, when added to the introduction of gold filigree, granulation and other advances, meant that Irish metalwork was of a very high standard of craftsmanship. All of these techniques were used with breathtaking precision and the minuteness of handling is extraordinary. Added to this was the use of cast bronze with champlevé enamel, and millefiori glass decoration. The motifs used were mainly in the ultimate La Tène style and there are a number of latchet brooches, toilet implements and other small mundane articles exhibiting these various skills. One of the more important items was the penannular brooch, originally an imported type, perhaps from the Romano-British world. Early examples are fairly plain with ultimate La Tène designs in cast bronze with enamelling. Later comes the remarkable 'Tara Brooch', a silver gilt pseudo-penannular brooch (8C), showing panels of cast mouldings with groups of motifs in the ultimate La Tène style, gold filigree, amber and polychrome glass ornament. All the surfaces are decorated and small areas of subtle artistry are combined in the overall design. In this brooch, as in the *Ardagh Chalice* (8C), and in the recently discovered *Derrynaflan Hoard*, Irish metalworking reaches a superb climax. Both chalices show Saxon influence in the adaptation of polychrome studs with inset metal grilles after the manner of cloisonné garnet work. The gold filigree panels on both are the best examples to be found in Irish art. The paten and paten stand from the Derrynaflan Hoard are unusual finds; only one other example is known in Ireland.

Shrines or reliquaries were another manifestation of ecclesiastical influence and reflect the cult of relics which Ireland shared with mainland Europe. They took many forms, shrines for bells, books and croziers being the most numerous (see below). In the 8th and 9Cs, house-shaped shrines, based on early Irish oratories, were popular, and there is also the splendid *Moylough belt shrine* (c 700), enclosing the remains of what was evidently the leather girdle of an early saint.

Illuminated Manuscripts. The majority of Irish illuminated manuscripts were copies of the Gospels or Psalms written in a beautiful Irish version of minuscule and majuscule script. Some have elaborately decorated pages showing pictures or symbols of the evangelists, before each set of gospels. In some cases these pages are followed by a richly illuminated carpet page and subsequently by ornamented initials. The production of Irish manuscripts was not confined to this island, but took place in monasteries of Irish foundation in Britain and Europe.

The manuscript illuminators exploited a variety of sources. Celtic La Tène motifs were united with elaborate interlace patterns, which in turn were combined with elongated animals of Germanic origin. Elements of Early Christian art and iconography from the Mediterranean world are also evident.

These manuscripts were not only beautiful, they were often held in reverence and were believed to be endowed with special powers. The earliest known manuscript, a Psalter called the 'Cathach' (battler; early 7C; Royal Irish Academy, Dublin), was carried into battle by the O'Donnell clan as a talisman. In another, the 'Book of Durrow' (late

7C; Trinity College, Dublin), was soaked in water which was then used as a cure for sick cattle.

The most famous of the manuscripts is the '**Book of Kells**' (c 800; Trinity College, Dublin), often described as 'the most beautiful book in the world'. A gospel book of 340 folios (680 pages), it is written in Latin using a majuscule script. Mention is first made of it in 1007, when it was recorded in the Annals of Ulster as being stolen from the Church in Kells, Co. Meath. During the Cromwellian wars it was sent to Dublin for safe-keeping and was presented to Trinity College, Dublin in 1661 by Henry Jones, Bishop of Meath. There is evidence of several different hands at work on this book, using many of the motifs already evident in the earlier MSS. It is, however, in the richness of decoration and in the combinations of the different motifs and styles that the Book of Kells outshines all other manuscripts of this kind. The Chi-Rho page shows wonderfully intricate combinations of interlace with La Tène motifs, and in less closely worked areas there are scenes of endearing domesticity, albeit with sacred connotations.

Stone Slabs and High Crosses are dealt with in the section on Antiquities. Here it is sufficient to note that in certain examples, like the High Crosses at *Ahenny* in Co. Tipperary, the craft of the metalworker was translated directly into stone. This is most obviously seen in the arrangement of the panels of ornament and in the raised stone versions of rivet bosses.

Viking Influence (c 1000) and the Later Medieval Period (to c 1500).

There has been much debate about the Viking influence on Irish Art. Many of their decorative forms, such as the *Ringerike* and later *Urnes* motifs, were used and adapted by Irish artists. It would also seem that craftsmen of Scandinavian origin were working in Ireland. Evidence for this has been found during the recent excavations of Viking sites in Dublin where many trial pieces in bone and also objects in wood have been unearthed, skilfully worked, some using the Ringerike decorative motif. Other items, such as the penannular brooches of the 9th and 10Cs and the cast metal panels on the book shrine of the 'Cathach' (11C) exhibit Scandinavian influence.

Later Medieval Period. By the beginning of the 12C it is notable that many items of metalwork were signed by the craftsman or were inscribed with the name of the donor. Inscriptions often combine both, as in the Gaelic text on the *Lismore Crozier* (c 1100): 'A prayer for Nial Mac Meic Aeducan who caused this to be made. A prayer for Neactain the craftsman who made the work'. These inscriptions not only allow pieces to be dated more accurately but also point to the fact that craftsmen were held in high esteem by the society in which they lived. Of those objects that have survived from the 11th and 12Cs, reliquaries of various types form the main part. The most important pieces are the *Cross of Cong* (c 1123) and the *Shrine of St. Patrick's Bell* (c 1100). Items from the Romanesque period often show a delightful combination of Scandinavian Urnes and Ringerike motifs with traditional Irish themes. However, the technical methods employed, among them champlevé enamel, millefiori glass studs and filigree work, often look back to the past.

During the late 14C and the 15C there was a period of Gaelic resurgance. This seems to have stimulated interest in older art forms, especially those found on the ancient reliquaries, many of which show evidence of extensive refurbishing at this time. Most of this work is crude in execution and does nothing to enhance the appearance of the objects. Attention was also focused on the ancient manuscripts, many of which were transcribed and preserved in large compendiums. This revived interest in manuscripts may have provided the impetus for making a copy of an 11C book satchel for the Book of Armagh.

Although the quality of work done at this time does not compare with that of the finest pieces of Irish metalwork produced in the 7th and 8Cs, it is still of interest and is comparable with examples from the rest of Europe. The items produced are a testimony to the vigour of the Gaelic revival. Many liturgical objects, however, followed more conventional European norms—the silver gilt *Limerick crozier* (1418) and the *Ballylongford* (Ballymacasey) *processional cross* (1479) both belong to the mainstream of Gothic art, neither exhibiting any particularly Irish features.

This final burst of artistic activity by the Irish metalworkers in the 15C was to mark the end of a long and illustrious tradition in this art form. Stretching back over 3000 years and culminating in the 'Golden Age' of the 7th and 8Cs, Irish metalworkers exhibited sophisticated skills, at times unrivalled elsewhere in Europe.

Painting and Sculpture (1500–1700).

Works by the artists mentioned below may be seen in the National Gallery of Ireland, Dublin.

The dissolution of the monasteries after the Reformation and subsequent dispersal of their contents may explain the scarcity of portable artefacts suriving from this period. The changes in form, noticeable in the items that have survived, may be seen as a result of the waning of Gaelic cultural influence when, towards the end of the century, land confiscation and resettlement were beginning. During the 17C colonisation continued, possibly accelerating a decline that had already commenced. The Cromwellian and Williamite wars during the 17C caused great unrest and specifically Gaelic Irish artforms disappear at this time. For the next 200 years artists looked towards England and Europe as sources of inspiration. New forms such as tomb sculptures in the English style were adopted and there are many examples of these to be found in the larger churches throughout the country. There are some portraits which have survived from the late 16C and first half of the 17C although these again are mainly in the style of Dutch and Flemish artists who had also worked in England. After the restoration of the monarchy in England in 1660, the Duke of Ormonde was appointed Lord Lieutenant of Ireland and an upsurge of artistic patronage was generated, due to the influx of courtiers and retainers.

Several minor foreign and English artists visited Ireland in the latter part of the 17C. These were, in the main, portrait painters and included the Flemish *Gaspar Smitz* (died c 1707), and *John Michael Wright* (1617–90/1700), an accomplished British artist. Although a Guild of Painters was founded in Dublin in 1670, only one native-born artist of note from this period can be traced, *Garret Morphey* (*Murphy*; died 1716). Several portraits by Morphey can be seen in the National Gallery. His style shows a number of influences, mainly Flemish and French. There were a number of great picture collections in the country at this time, for example, the Dukes of Ormonde had paintings in their many residences in Ireland and England. Other important collections were made by the Percival family and the Earls of Inchiquin. Remnants of some of these collections can still be seen at Kilkenny Castle, the National Gallery of Ireland and Malahide Castle.

Woodwork and Plasterwork. The most accessible examples of wood-carving and plasterwork of this period can be seen in the *Royal Hospital at Kilmainham* on the outskirts of Dublin. There are some fine wood carvings in the Chapel and Great Hall by *James Tarbary*, a French Huguenot refugee. Probably also by Tarbary are three superbly carved tympana over the arched entrance doors. The plaster-work ceiling of the chapel has a profusion of fruit and flowers arranged in geometrical sections.

The Eighteenth Century.

Painting.

Painting in the 18C begins with some dull portrait painters, mainly in the manner of Sir Godfrey Kneller. Also at this time some Irish-born artists made the Grand Tour. They were *Charles Jervas* (c 1675–1739), *Hugh Howard* (1675–1738) (who studied under Carlo Maratta) and *Henry Trench* (died 1726). On their return from Italy they practised mainly in London; Jervas was appointed Principal Painter to George I in 1723. *James Latham* (1696–1747), an accomplished portrait painter, is only known to have worked in Ireland. He was born, probably, in Co. Tipperary, of a landed family. He went to Antwerp where he was a member of the painters guild of St. Luke for one year (1724–25). His work, for various members of the landed gentry, shows a masterly handling of paint and colour. Other native-born portraitists who had successful practices in Ireland were *Phillip Hussey* (1713–83) and *Robert Hunter* (fl. 1750–1803). Among a number of Irish artists who had fashionable studios in London were the portraitists *Thomas Frye* (1710–62), and *Nathaniel Hone the Elder* (1718–84). The latter spent most of his life in England and had a successful career there, becoming a founder member of the Royal Academy in 1768. His most famous painting is 'The Conjuror', a satire on Sir Joshua Reynolds and his working methods.

The Dublin Society Drawing Schools. In the 1740s an event of great importance in Irish art took place with the founding of the *Dublin Society Schools*, set up by the Society to provide a centre where drawing and design could be taught, with the aim of improving and stimulating design in art and manufacture. This had application in many areas, and advertisements in the Dublin newspapers of the day indicate that woodcarvers, silversmiths and other craftsmen were encouraged to attend. The first master was *Robert West* (died 1770), an artist who had trained in France. He was assisted by *James Mannin* (died 1779) who may have been from Northern Italy, but who also trained in France. Many of the country's finest artists were pupils at the schools: *George Barret* (c 1728/32–84), the *Healy brothers* (*Robert* and *William*; fl. 1765–71 and fl. c 1769–74 respectively), *Thomas Roberts* (1748–78) and *Hugh Douglas Hamilton* (1739–1808) being perhaps the most outstanding.

Landscape Painting in Ireland can be said to begin with the work of the visiting artist *William van der Hagen* (died 1745), a painter of Dutch origin. He painted various port scenes and his 'View of Waterford', of 1736, is of the topographic type, but he also painted classical landscapes. Later in the century a distinct school of Irish landscape painting emerges. Two early examples of this are works by *Joseph Tudor* (fl. 1739–59) and *Susannah Drury* (fl. 1733–70) who were awarded premiums by the Dublin Society's Schools for their landscape painting in 1740. *George Barret*, born in Dublin, was a contemporary of Richard Wilson (1714–82), the prominent English artist. He painted some of his earliest and most outstanding landscapes in the Dargle Valley which runs through the Powerscourt demesne in Co. Wicklow. These introduce elements of later Romantic art to the Irish scene. They were influenced by Edmund Burke's essay on the 'Sublime and Beautiful', written at this time. Barret moved to England in 1763 and while there he travelled extensively, fulfilling commissions for patrons all over the country.

Around the middle of the century a number of Irish artists travelled to and worked in Italy. Among them were *Robert Crone* (c 1718–79), who remained in Italy for ten years and later worked in London; *James Forrester* (c 1730–76), who died in Rome in 1776, and others like *Solomon Delane* (1727–1812?) and *Hugh Primrose Deane* (fl. 1758–84). Later in the century another outstanding talent emerges in the landscapes of *Thomas Roberts* (1748–78), also a pupil of the Dublin Society's Schools. His work shows familiarity with Dutch and French painting and he exhibited some works painted entirely in the manner of Claude Vernet. During his short life he often exhibited at the Society of Artists and is regarded as the most brilliant landscape artist working in Ireland at that time. *William Ashford* (c 1796–1824) was an English-born artist who worked mainly in Ireland although he did exhibit in London. He enjoyed the patronage of many landowners and painted series of views of their various properties.

Pastellists. The known works of the brothers *Robert* and *William Healy* are exclusively in pastel and exhibit a remarkable mastery of that technique. Perhaps the finest example is 'The Castletown Hunt with Tom Conolly' (1768), which shows a frieze of horses with their riders and hounds. Another artist who excelled in this medium was *Hugh Douglas Hamilton*; his pastel portraits of male sitters are particularly fine. Hamilton also painted in oils, and when he visited Italy in 1778 he enjoyed the patronage of many of the visiting nobility there. Although justly famous for his portraits, he also painted subject pictures, the 'Cupid and Psyche' (now in the National Gallery of Ireland) is one of the few known examples of this kind of work by him. He had a long and extremely successful career and his work embodies the development of Irish 18C portraiture, from the early days of the Dublin Society's Schools with the emphasis on drawing, manifested in Hamilton's early pastel portraits, popular in both Dublin and London, through his development as a painter in oils during his visit to Rome, and his adoption of neo-classical composition for his portraits. *Henry Tresham* (1751–1814) also worked in a neo-classical vein and many of his works are of historical subject.

The giant of 18C Irish painting was *James Barry* (1741–1806). He was a friend of Edmund Burke and was influenced by his writings. Barry's work was usually on a large scale and he can be regarded as being in the mainstream of neo-classical painting. Various influences can be seen in his paintings apart from the obvious antique references. There are, for instance, many direct quotations from Michelangelo, and he was also known to have admired the early work of Poussin and some of Le Brun's paintings. He had travelled extensively and visited Italy, making careful study of sculpture and painting as he went. On his return to England he exhibited a variety of classical subject pictures. In 1777 he embarked on an ambitious series of six paintings to decorate the premises of the Society of Arts in London. This was to be the grandest historical cycle painted by an artist in Britain in the 18C.

At the time he also made engravings and some of these images were extremely powerful. A vivid self-portrait painted in 1803 can be seen in the National Gallery of Ireland.

Other artists of note in Ireland during the 18C were *Thomas Hickey* (1741–1824), an accomplished portrait painter; *Nathaniel Grogan* (c 1740–1807), who painted landscapes and genre scenes which usually include large groups of figures that give interesting insights into Irish life at the time; *George Mullins* (fl. 1756–75), who painted landscapes, and *James George Oben* (fl. 1779–1819) and *John Nixon* (c 1750–1818), who worked in watercolour.

Many artists visited Dublin during the century, most of them English, Italian, and Flemish. An important English visitor was the portrait painter *Stephen Slaughter* (1697–1765) who came here early in the century. Later came *Francis Wheatley* (1747–1801), *Gilbert Stuart* (1755–1828), *Tilly Kettle* (1735–86) and *George Chinnery* (1774–1852), who were also fashionable portraitists. *James Malton* (fl. 1785–1803) and his son are remembered for their very fine set of views of Dublin. Italian visitors included *Vincent Waldre* (1742–1814) from Faenza, who painted three canvases for the ceiling of St. Patrick's Hall in Dublin Castle, and *Filippo Zafforini* (working in Dublin 1798–1811), who painted a series of grisaille decorations at Aldborough House (1798). The Flemish artist *Peter de Gree* (1751–89) also specialised in grisaille paintings and came here at the invitation of David La Touche of Marly.

Applied Arts. Also working in Ireland during the 18C were the *Francini brothers*, Italian stuccadores, whose exuberant plasterwork decoration can still be seen at Russborough and Castletown House. Stucco decoration was popular in both country houses and city mansions from the late 17C until well into the 19C. Two outstanding Irish masters of this technique were *Robert West* (fl. 1744–90), famous for his exuberant birds and floral decorations, with fine examples of these still to be seen at his house at 20 Dominick Street, Dublin, and, later, *Michael Stapleton* (died 1801), some of whose work may be seen in Belvedere House, Dublin.

Irish Silver. Modern Irish silver dates from the charter of 1637 given by Charles I to establish the Dublin Goldsmiths' Company. Early 18C Irish silver is rather plain and robust, but after the 1750s the exuberance and rococo elements that are to be seen in plasterwork, for example, are also evident in this field. Towards the end of the century there is a return to more sedate pieces following the influence of the neo-classical and fashionable Adam style.

Irish Furniture and Woodcarving. Irish furniture and woodcarving generally followed the direction of English work during the early part of the century. Later, from the 1740s onward, a distinctly Irish style becomes evident. It typically uses dark mahogany with rich carving. A plainer style of furniture existed concurrently, which was often elegant, with a little subtle decoration. Splendidly decorated mirrors were popular and several looking-glass makers flourished in Dublin. The firm of *Francis and John Booker* of Essex bridge were responsible for some superb examples in an architectural style. Furniture styles again follow English trends from the end of the 18C onwards.

Sculpture. The influence of English sculpture continued well into the 18C. *William Kidwell* was an English sculptor who lived in Ireland from 1711–36 and whose most important monument was that to Sir

Donough O'Brien in Kinasoolagh Church, Co. Clare (c 1717). Kidwell's work seems to have been influential. It exemplified the need for good quality craftsmanship, and his naturalistic approach appears to relate to work done by *John Houghton* (died 1761) and *John Kelly* (fl. 1756). Both these craftsmen worked in the field of architectural ornament, notably on the elaborately carved chimneypieces and door cases popular in their day, as well as pedimental sculpture and' even furniture. Houghton's chimneypiece in the House of Lords is justly famous, as are his magnificent picture frames. As in painting, the advent of the Dublin Society's Schools also stimulated and improved the work of the wood carvers and sculptors: a number of the Schools' students later worked for famous masters. One of these was *Patrick Cunningham* (died 1774) who was apprenticed to *John van Nost the Younger* (died 1780).

Van Nost came to Ireland about 1750. He was the son of a Dutch sculptor of the same name, who had lived in England. The younger van Nost seems to have introduced the fashion for portrait busts to Ireland. He had a successful practice in official commissions and one of these was for the statues of Justice and Mars which still stand on the gates of Dublin Castle. Many tomb sculptures were also commissioned from him. Patrick Cunningham continued in the portrait bust tradition for a time but despite considerable help and encouragement from the Dublin Society he gave up sculpture and took to making small bas relief portraits in wax.

As with the painters, some sculptors travelled to Italy; *Christopher Hewetson* (c 1739–94), another of Van Nost's pupils, was perhaps the most accomplished of these. While in Italy his commissions included a papal bust, a cardinal's monument and work for many famous figures at the time. An impressive example of his style can be seen in a monument to Provost Baldwin in the Examination Hall of Trinity College Dublin. Of the sculptors who remained in Ireland all their working lives, *Edward Smyth* was the most important, and fine examples of his work are to be seen on many late 18C buildings in Dublin. Smyth attended the Dublin Society's Schools and was apprenticed to *Simon Vierpyl* (c 1725–1810), a sculptor of Dutch origin, who carried out commissions for Lord Charlemont. Among the better-known examples of Smyth's work are the masterly riverine heads that form the keystones on the ground floor arches of the Custom House in Dublin. He again worked for James Gandon at the Four Courts and at the new Houses of Parliament (now the Bank of Ireland, College Green). Outside Dublin his work can be seen on the Bishop's Gate in Derry and in the compelling figure of the crucified Christ at the RC Church in Navan.

The Nineteenth Century.

After the passing of the Act of Union with England in 1800, Dublin was no longer the seat of parliament. This resulted in an outflow of the nobility and gentry to London. The middle classes now became the major patrons and a change of taste is reflected in the type of commission. Portraiture still remained popular if somewhat duller. *Martin Cregan* (1788–1870), *William Cuming* (1769–1852) and *Robert Lucius West* (1774–50) were the principal portrait painters among those artists who remained in Dublin. Another portraitist, working on a very small scale, was *Adam Buck* (1759–1833) who later went to England and whose charming pictures in watercolour showed an interest in the work of Flaxman. *Martin Archer Shee* (1769–1850) had left for London

in 1788 where he developed a successful practice: in 1830 he succeeded Lawrence as President of the Royal Academy. Other Irish artists who worked in London were *Richard Rothwell* (1800–68) and
Nicholas Crowley (1819–57), both fashionable portraitists and specia-
lising in sentimental studies. The work of all these artists continued to
relate to English work of the same period. This was not so in landscape
painting where the influence of George Barret and the romantic
aspects of his landscapes can be seen in the work of *Thomas Sautelle
Roberts* (1760–1826) and the later work of *James Arthur O'Connor*
(1791–1841). O'Connor was a friend of *Francis Danby* (1793–1861)
who, though born and educated in Ireland, spent his career in England
and took Romanticism to new heights.

The use of watercolour was increasing in popularity about this time.
George Petrie (1789–1866) combined his use of this medium with an
interest in antiquities. He travelled about Ireland drawing atmos-
pheric views of various archaeological sites. He was to influence
Frederick William Burton (1816–1900) who had journeyed with him on
his painting trips and who was to become one of the most important
exponents of watercolour.

Subject pictures with a strongly sentimental vein were also much in
demand. *Joseph Patrick Haverty* (1794–1864) and *John George
Mulvany* (c 1766–1838) were the principal practitioners of this type of
painting in Dublin. A major figure working mainly in England was
Daniel Maclise (1806–70). Born in Cork, he had a practice there producing small pencil portraits. He moved to London in 1827 where his
pictures, many of them of historical subjects, soon gained great popularity. He also painted several famous scenes such as the 'Death of
Nelson' for the House of Lords. He continued to work on a large scale,
and his oil painting of 'The Marriage of Strongbow and Eva' also
shows his deep interest in correct antiquarian details of costume and
settings.

From the 1860s onwards Irish artists began to go further afield for
their education. After attending the Dublin Metropolitan School of Art
(formerly the Dublin Society's Schools) they often went to France and
Belgium, particularly Paris, Brittany and Antwerp. One such artist was
Nathanial Hone (1831–1917) (a descendant of the 18C artist of the
same name) who spent 17 years in France and who painted out of
doors in the manner of the Barbizon painters. Another was *Roderic
O'Conor* (1860–1940) who studied in Antwerp. His use of bold brush
strokes and vivid colours finds parallels in the work of his friend Gauguin and that of Van Gogh.

After a period of study in Antwerp, *Walter Osborne* (1859–1903)
returned to Ireland and settled in Dublin. His gentle landscapes and
society portraits now enjoy enormous popularity and are much sought
after by collectors. *John Lavery* (1856–1941) is perhaps best known for
his portraits. Born in Belfast, he went to Glasgow and later studied in
Paris at the Academy Julien. His early genre paintings show idyllic
scenes of the French countryside and have a sense of colour and
tonality that is lacking in his later work. Also working at this time were
a number of women artists who had studied abroad. Among them was
the remarkable *Sarah Purser* (1848–1943), who had a large portrait
practice in Dublin and whose works hang on the walls of most public
institutions in the city. *Rose Barton* (1864–1929) and *Mildred Anne
Butler* (1858–1941) both worked mainly in watercolour and their pictures have the same kind of appeal for collectors as those of Walter
Osborne.

Nineteenth Century Sculpture. Irish sculptors benefitted from increased interest in this art form and from the prevailing fashion for tomb sculptures throughout the century. Many sculptors went to England in search of commissions. While several established large practices there and at the same time continued to obtain commissions in Ireland, thereby ensuring that we have good examples of their work here. *Christopher Moore* (1790–1863) was one of these, and he is noted for his portrait busts (e.g. that of John Philpott Curran in St. Patrick's Cathedral, Dublin). Two exquisitely carved angels by *Peter Turnerelli* (1774–1839) are to be seen at the Pro-cathedral in Dublin. Born in Belfast, Turnerelli trained in London and was later acclaimed internationally. His work has a classic quality and some of his pieces show close study of 15C Italian sculpture. The Cork-born sculptor *John Hogan* (1800–58) was one of the few Irish artists of the period to produce religious works. He went to Rome and worked there for 24 years, before returning to Cork. While in Rome he had sent home a number of religious pieces, one of them a Dead Christ for the Carmelite Church in Dublin.

By the mid century many of the most famous figures working in England were in fact Irish. Two of them were commissioned to work on the Albert Memorial in Kensington Gardens, London. *Patrick MacDowell* (1799–1870) (from Belfast) carved the group of Europe at the base of the memorial, while *John Henry Foley* (1818–74) was commissioned to carve the statue of Prince Albert and was recognised as one of the finest sculptors of his day in England. A pupil of the Dublin Society's Schools, throughout his long and successful career Foley was inundated with work. In Ireland his best known works are the O'Connell Monument and the statues of Edmund Burke and Oliver Goldsmith which stand outside Trinity College.

Twentieth Century Art.

In the early years of the century there was an increasing interest in Irish subject matter shown by both painters and sculptors. This is of course understandable, given the renewed interest of the Celtic Revival in earlier artistic achievements. The very fine group, the 'Fall of Cuchulainn' by *Oliver Sheppard* (1864–1941), is a handsome illustration of this. The work is strongly influenced by the Art Nouveau style and yet manages to capture the tragic mood evoked by the theme. Another artist whose work portrays the tragedy of those times was *Jerome Connor* (1875–1943), for example his great monument to those who died on the Lusitania. The powerful works of *Andrew O'Connor*, which are to be seen in Dublin, show an awe-inspiring grasp of inner vision that is unsettling to see. Most of O'Connor's other works are still in America, where he was born and worked for much of his life.

Painting. The best known painters of the period, who stayed to work in Ireland, were *Jack B. Yeats* (1871–1957) and *Paul Henry* (1876–1958). Yeats chose as his subject matter specifically Irish themes of legend, with circuses and fairs included in his view of Irish life in general. Work in his early period is often in watercolour and is simply illustrative, whereas his late style is quite distinctive in its brilliant colour and free vigorous brushstrokes. The paintings of Paul Henry capture a much softer and gentler dimension of Irish life, and he is famous for his ability to paint the luminous quality of the western skies of Connemara. An artist whose Irishness was not so obvious in his work was *William Orpen* (1878–1931). Orpen was considered a prodigy and his draughtsmanship was much admired. He attended the Metropolitan

School of Art in Dublin and then the Slade School in London. His early works are particularly notable for the free handling of paint and the study of light on subject matter. Later, he became a fashionable portrait painter and he was much sought after in London. He had a number of Irish pupils, among them *Patrick Tuohy* (1894–1930) and *Sean Keating*, both of whom painted regularly in the west of Ireland. Their style followed that of their teacher with little recognition of the more abstract principles of modern art of that period.

Three artists who did move into the mainstream of modern art and who introduced Cubism into Ireland during the 1920s were all women. *Mary Swanzy* (1882–1978) was an intrepid traveller who sometimes painted in the manner of Gauguin. The others were *Mainie Jellet* (1897–1944) and *Evie Hone* (1894–1955), another descendant of that famous family of artists. Hone is now perhaps best known for her work in stained glass which marked a peak of magnificence in Irish stained glass making during the first half of the century. *Sarah Purser* founded the 'Am Túr Gloine' stained glass workshops which produced many fine artists, including *Wilhelmina Geddes* and Hone herself. But in many ways the finest and most imaginative work was by *Harry Clarke* (1889–1931), whose windows fill with colour and light the most unlikely parish churches throughout Ireland, from Ballinrobe to Castletownshend, and Dublin.

There was a lull in artistic production during the bleak 1930s and 40s, but the last 30 years have seen a new surge of energy and enthusiasm in this area. Abstract art became increasingly popular in the late 1950s and Irish artists moved through the various phases of 0p and Pop, some going on to Photo Realism. Recently, there has been a renewed interest shown in figurative art. As before many of our finest artists work in England and elsewhere, especially *William Scott* (1913–) and the sculptor *F.E. McWilliams* (1909–), both of whom are from the north of Ireland. *Louis le Brocquy* (1916–), from Dublin, now works mostly in France. At the moment there are comparatively large numbers of young artists working and travelling abroad to study and exhibit. Sculpture is also flourishing and its boundaries with painting overlap as they do elsewhere in the world. The Irish art scene is a healthy and thriving one, with frequent exhibitions of work by both emerging and established artists.

'Thatching,' by Jack B. Yeats. From The Aran Islands *(1907).*

TOPOGRAPHICAL INTRODUCTION

The large island known as Ireland is 84,421km² (or 32,595 sq. miles) in area, of which 14,139km² (or 5,459 sq. miles) is the extent of the Six Counties. Its greatest width is 275km (171 miles) and its greatest length 486km (302 miles). Its total population in 1981 was approx. 5,005,500 of which 1,562,100 (or 1,550,500 according to the mid 1984 estimate) live in the six counties which comprise Northern Ireland. The Republic, with approx. the same population as it had in 1891, is the least densely populated country in Europe, with 50 people per km² (and an average of only 25 in Connacht).

In 1841 the population of the island was 8,175,000 (and in 1845 probably approaching 8,500,000), which by 1851 had dropped to 6,552,000, largely due to death during the famine and emigration, the latter continuing throughout the second half of the century, and since. The census of 1961 recorded a population of only 2,818,000 for the Republic, since when it has shown a rapid increase. During the period 1871–91 some 1,400,000 emigrated; during the decade 1961–71 the total was approx. 205,000.

The earlier division of the country into the historic provinces of *Leinster* (SE), *Munster* (SW), *Connacht* or *Connaught* (W), and *Ulster* (NE), is no longer of any great significance: see map opposite, but for convenience the counties are described in these four sections of the island.

LEINSTER (1,790,500 inhab.) is probably the most fertile, and owing to its accessibility and the presence of the city of Dublin in its midst, of the four provinces it has been the most subject to outside influence. Its shores offered the richest prey to both Danish invaders and Anglo-Norman adventurers. It later absorbed the old province of Meath, and today is made up of the following twelve counties:

The small county of **Dublin** is divided roughly between the old districts of Cualann, the mountainous region bordering on Wicklow to the S, and Fingall, 'the tribe-land of the Gall' or foreigners (Danes) to the N. In Anglo-Norman times Co. Dublin was roughly co-extensive with the Pale (see p 92), the boundaries of which were guarded by the fortifications of the settlers.

To the N lies **Meath** (*Midh*), the fertile and largely level plain (nowhere rising above 260m) of heavy grassland and woods surrounding the valleys of the Boyne and Blackwater, with their slowly flowing streams. It was once the centre of the kingdom, and Tara was the seat of the High King.

Further N is **Louth** (*Lughbhadh*), the smallest county on the seaboard strip between the Boyne and Armagh; it is mostly flat, but mountainous in the N. It consists of part of the xancient lordship of Oriel, the patrimony of Cuchulainn, and the peninsula of Cooley (Cuailgne) or Carlingford, celebrated in the story of the 'Cattle Raid of Cooley' (a seven-year struggle between Ulster and Connacht).

Westmeath (*Iarmhidh*), likewise mainly level and, as its name implies, part of the kingdom of Meath, is another grazing county, extending W as far as the Shannon (to the country of Goldsmith's 'Deserted Village'), and encloses some charming loughs frequented by anglers. In the middle of the county is the Hill of Uisneach, another ancient royal residence.

Longford (*Longphort*), the county of the Edgeworths and of Goldsmith, prolonging Westmeath to the NW, and largely coinciding with the ancient district of Annaly, contains a good deal of bog; it borders

on Lough Ree to the SW.

Kildare (*Cill Dara*) lies to the SW of Dublin. It is the flattest part of Ireland—the grassy Curragh being famous—and contains the larger part of the great Bog of Allen. Its E border is fringed by the foothills of the Wicklow mountains, from the glens of which the clans of O'Byrne and O'Toole, driven thence by the Normans, harried their lowland neighbours.

Offaly (*Ua bhFailghe*), a long L-shaped area extending from the Bog of Allen to the Shannon, and S beyond the Slieve Bloom range, lies to the W of Kildare. The E part was originally in the province of Meath, while the SW was once in Munster. It was made shire land in the time of Philip of Spain and Mary Tudor, and was named King's County in honour of the former. Clonmacnoise, on the Shannon, was one of the more important religious foundations in the land. It is abutted to the S by **Leix** (or more usually **Laois**; pron. Leeish), formerly Queen's County, named after Mary (see above), bordered by two ranges of hills to the NW and SE, but the rest is flat and boggy. The O'Mores, whose land it was, had their headquarters at Dunamase, near Portlaoise (Maryborough).

Immediately S of Co. Dublin is Co. **Wicklow**, in Irish *Cill Mhantáin*, early occupied by the Danes. It is one of the most attractive counties in Ireland, its mountains extending to the sea, and within easy reach of Dublin. It was long a favourite retreat of fugitives from authority, while in Glendalough it possesses one of the most famous, and most beautifully sited, of Early Christian retreats.

To the SW of Wicklow lies **Carlow** (*Ceatharlach*), another small farming county, largely a plain on the E bank of the Barrow, with the Mt Leinster range a conspicuous feature to the SE.

Kilkenny (*Cill Chainnigh*), further SW, corresponds roughly to the ancient kingdom of Ossory. Its name comes from the sainted abbot Canice, who founded the first church in its county town. It is rolling countryside, the valley of the Nore being one of the richest and pleasantest stretches of Leinster.

To the E is **Wexford** (also with a Danish name, the Irish form being *Loch Garman*), well-tilled, and with orchards, but wind-swept. To the NW are mountains, with the Slaney valley, girt with low hills, in the centre, while in the extreme S are the level 'English baronies' of Forth and Bargy.

MUNSTER (998,300 inhab.), the largest province in Ireland, contains the cities of Cork, Limerick and Waterford, and also Killarney, the beautiful surroundings of which live up to their reputation. The whole of the W coast of the province is broken up into rias and peninsulas by the unremitting force of the Atlantic, while through its N half flows the Shannon to its broad estuary. It comprises the following six counties:

Waterford, to the SE, is the Danish-derived name of the county, known in Irish as *Port Láirge*, which was the first to be occupied by the Anglo-Normans. It is mainly a mountainous area, with the Comeragh and Knockmealdown ranges the most prominent, but is bounded on the N by the lower Suir valley and is traversed by the Blackwater. It was part of the kingdom of Ormond, and the central baronies of the Decies recall the ancient tribe of the Déisi that once occupied them.

It is abutted by **Cork** (*Corcaigh*), the largest county in Ireland, extending from the mouth of the Blackwater to Cape Clear, with fertile valleys alternating with tangled ranges, the refuge of fugitives throughout the ages. It corresponds more or less with the old kingdom of Desmond. S Cork was the patrimony of the O'Driscolls, who were driven further W when the O'Donovans fled from Limerick before the Geraldines; the extreme W was the home of the O'Mahonys; while NE Cork was early occupied by the Anglo-Norman Roches. It has a singularly mild climate.

This is shared by **Kerry** (*Ciarraighe*), occupying a series of peninsulas stretching out into the Atlantic between the mouth of the Shannon and Bantry Bay. Ciarraighe was originally the name given only to the district round Tralee, the rest being known as Iar Mumhan, or West Munster. The whole county is mountainous except in the extreme N; and in Carrantuohill, in the MacGillycuddy's Reeks, it possesses the highest summit in Ireland. Close to the foot of the Reeks is the Vale of Killarney, while to the NW, the Dingle Peninsula (co-extensive with the barony of Corkaguiny) contains a remarkable number of pre-Christian and Early Christian remains. Among Kerry families are the O'Sullivans, the O'Donaghues, the MacCarthys, and the MacGillycuddys.

Limerick (*Luimneach*) is the fertile strip bordering the S bank of the Shannon from above the city of Limerick to about half way down the estuary, rising gradually to the zone of hills which separate it from Co. Cork to the S. The E part was oreiginally the home of the O'Briens and the O'Connells. Limerick itself, famous for its siege, has the lowest bridge across the Shannon, while a short distance above is the power station of the 'Shannon Scheme', and not far to the NW in Co. Clare is Shannon Airport.

To the E is the inland county of **Tipperary** (*Tiobraid Arann*), extending from Lough Derg, the largest and the lowest of the great Shannon lakes, to the Knockmealdown mountains. It includes the rich land known as the 'Golden Vein' (between Cashel and Limerick). Further S are the Galty mountains; to the N rise the Silvermine mountains, and other lower hills. N Tipperary, with E Limerick and Clare, made up the ancient kingdom of Thomond; S Tipperary was the kingdom of Ormond—a name assumed later by the powerful Anglo-Norman family of Butler. The Rock of Cashel, in S Tipperary, was once the headquarters of the kings of Munster, and still preserves enough relics of antiquity to give a good idea of its former importance; an even older royal residence was at Cahir, where the 'cathair' of the kings stood on a rock washed by the Suir, flowing from N to S through the centre of the county.

Clare (*an Clár*) lies on the N bank of the Shannon; indeed until the 4C it was included in Connacht, later becoming part of the kingdom of Thomond. Fertile along the river estuary, it becomes more barren and hillier to the N, and the barony of Burren, overlooking Galway Bay, is made up principally of dessicated limestone hills, while the W Clare coast culminates in the imposing Cliffs of Moher. Among its ancient owners were the MacNamaras and the O'Deas, weith the O'Briens of Thomond in the northern baronies of Inchiquin and Corcomroe.

CONNAUGHT, now more usually **CONNACHT** (424,400 inhab.), the wild NW province of Ireland, contains on its Atlantic seaboard some of the most magnificent scenery in Europe, while thanks to its comparative remoteness and to the barrenness of its soil, which offered little to attract foreign marauders, it remains as a whole the most purely Irish part of Ireland. The proverbial expression 'To Hell or Connaught' recalls the days when the owners of the land in S and central Ireland were driven across the Shannon by Cromwell to make room for his subordinates who were awarded Irish land in lieu of pay for their sanguinary services. It was largely here that the Congested Districts Board did so much to alleviate the suffering of its inhabitants, when over-population brought many of them near to starvation, this, in spite of considerable depopulation by emigration since the decimating famine. It should be noted that the population (in round figures) of the following five counties—four of them in Connacht, and including Clare—have decreased between the years 1841 and 1981 to the following extent: Sligo—from 180,900 to 55,450; Roscommon—from 253,600 to 54,550; Mayo—from 388,900 to 114,750; Galway—from 440,200 to 172,000; and Clare—from 286,400 to 87,550, a total of 1,550,000 being reduced to 484,300.

It comprises five counties. **Galway** (*Gaillimh*), to the N of Clare, divided into two very different portions by island-studded Lough Corrib. Connemara, one of the most beautiful parts of Ireland, lies to the W; to the E, extending as far as the Shannon and Lough Derg, stretches a level plain, part bog, part good land.

Mayo (*Muigheo*), further N, contains some of the loveliest and some of the bleakest country in Ireland. E Mayo is a dull rolling upland, but further W, in the baronies of Murrisk and Burrishoole, surrounding Clew Bay, the scenery is magnificent, dominated by the cone of

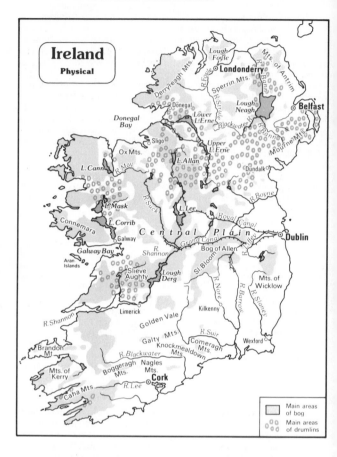

Croagh Patrick. Here also is Achill (the largest island off the Irish coast), and to the NW are the baronies of Erris and Tyrawley, practically uninhabited moorland with a grim and forbidding coastline, while in the extreme SE is the Plain of Mayo.

Sligo (*Sligeach*) is mountainous in the E round Glencar and Lough Gill, and in the centre, about Slieve Gamph; elsewhere it is undulating, especially in the MacDermott country to the S. To the W of the town of Sligo is an area rich in prehistoric remains, while just N, at Drumcliff, under Ben Bulben's head, lie the remains of W. B. Yeats.

To the E of Sligo is **Leitrim** (*Liathdruim*), representing the old district of West Breffni or Breffni O'Rourke. It is intersected by the Upper Shannon, which here flows through Lough Allen; and in the N part of the county are Lough Melvin and one end of Lough Gill. Towards the SE the county becomes less mountainous as it merges into the plain of Leinster, and **Roscommon** (*Ros Comáin*), the whole of the E side of which is bounded by the Shannon, which here includes Lough Ree. It is a dull plain, boggy in the S, but more fertile between Boyle and

Elphin. Roscommon is essentially a grass county, with hardly 'a sod turned'.

Of the nine counties which comprise **ULSTER**, those of Donegal, Cavan, and Monaghan are independent of the 'Six Counties' (see below), which, remaining part of the United Kingdom, are known as Northern Ireland; see below for a fuller background to the province, and also the Historical Introduction. Ulster has suffered from a very chequered past. Its tribes were powerful and its chieftains vigorous, and except for the incursions of the Danes and such freebooters as John de Courcy (late 12C) and Edward Bruce (early 14C), it was comparatively undisturbed by foreign invasions. Its total population is 1,792,250. That part other than the Six Counties has a population of 230,150.

Donegal (*Dún na nGall*), the northwestern county of Ireland—somewhat tenuously attached to Leitrim—with its deep glens, winding bays and rugged cliffs, has scenery hardly surpassed for wild grandeur. With the exception of the eastern baronies of Raphoe and Inishowen, it represents the ancient baronies of Tyrconnel, the land of the descendants of Conaill, son of Niall of the eNine Hostages.

Immediately E of Leitrim lies **Cavan** (*Cabhán*, the 'hollow place'), bisected by the meandering Erne. The W half, formerly called Breffni O'Reilly, was originally part of Connacht. To the N is a wild district of mountain and bog, the highest summit being the Cuilcagh, on the W side of which is the accepted source of the Shannon. In the N will be seen a type of two-storey thatched house with hipped roofs found in very few other places in the country. Between Dowra on the Leitrim border and Lough Allen are remnants of the Worm Ditch or Black Pig's Dyke, a boundary wall built by Ulstermen in the 3C AD.

Monaghan (*Muineachán*), part of the ancient lordship of Oriel (patrimony of the MacMahons), is a county of low hills and little lakes, lying as it does in the 'drumlin belt'. It is well cultivated, with 'potatoes and oats to the verge of the bog'. To the SE it is abutted by Louth.

The Six Counties. In the time of Queen Elizabeth I, Ulster was in a continual state of rebellion, and in 1607, following the flight of the Earls of Tyrone and Tyrconnel, most of the fertile land in Armagh, Tyrone, Derry, Fermanagh, Donegal and Cavan, with part of Monaghan, was confiscated by the crown. The patrimony of its Irish proprietors was occupied, or 'planted' by settlers, from England and, mainly, from Scotland. Extensive tracts were also granted to the London Guilds—the Drapers, Salters, Skinners and others. Apart from the Crown plantation scheme there were other waves of settlers, including Huguenots and Moravians, and it is still possible to detect their influence. Several of the 'bawns' or defended farms erected by these various settlers to protect themselves from the dispersed native population can still be seen, with their courtyard enclosed by battlements and corner towers. Inside stands the 'castle' of the squire or 'undertaker', so-called because he undertook, in exchange for his grant of land, to colonise it, and erect a castle and church.

The Scots spread through N Down and W through Derry as far as Donegal early in the 17C. In Antrim they settled thickly round Ballymena and pushed N as far as Ballymoney, driving the MacDonnels back into the Glens. The present-day dialect in these areas is still noticeably that of Lowland Scots. Here too may be seen the simple but well-proportioned Presbyterian 'barn' churches, with their round-headed windows and tall box pews. In the Crown scheme the planters who settled in Armagh, Fermanagh, and S Tyrone were mainly

English from Norfolk, Suffolk, and from the Midlands. The parish churches which the undertakers were obliged to build had usually a W tower with an oblong nave and chancel. Their style has been called 'Planters' Gothic', and embodies much Renaissance detail. The single spire or tower of the Church of Ireland, the classical portico of the Presbyterian meeting-house, and the twin spires of the 19C Catholic church or cathedral are still a characteristic of many Ulster towns.

Much is made of the Ulster ancestry of a high proportion of the Presidents of the United States of America, even if the descent is tenuous, and although only some of the more prominent connections are specified in the text, it may be of interest to mention that the following, at least, have some relationship with Ulster: Chester Alan Arthur, James Buchanan, Grover Cleveland, Ulysses Grant, Benjamin Harrison, Andrew Jackson, Andrew Johnson, William McKinley, James Monroe, James Knox Polk, and Woodrow Wilson. General James Shields, General Thomas Jonathan ('Stonewall') Jackson, and General Sam Houston were also of Ulster stock.

The six independent counties of 'John Bull's other island' still remaining politically part of the United Kingdom are Londonderry, Antrim, Down, Armagh, Tyrone and Fermanagh. Their population in 1981 was 1,562,100 (the mid 1984 estimate was 1,550,500), of which 28 per cent admitted at the census to being Roman Catholic. 18.5 per cent preferred not to commit themselves. Protestants are in the majority in the first four, and are more equally balanced by Catholics in Tyrone and Fermanagh. Electing by a majority to abide by the Union, under the Government of Ireland Act of 1920 they continued to be controlled by Westminster, although a local Parliament was set up in Belfast, the industrial capital of the North, to deal with a number of internal matters. This Stormont parliament was abolished in 1973; but see the latter part of the Introduction to Irish History.

Co. Down extends S from Belfast, its N half part of the drumlin country, a belt of curious hillocks of glacial origin crossing the island from coast to coast. The district has been aptly called 'the basket of eggs'; many of the drumlin hills are indeed ovoid in shape and testudinate in contour, and in Strangford Lough (as in Clew Bay), where the general land mass has been submerged, the tops of the drumlins rise above the water forming small round-backed islands giving the appearance of basking whales. In the centre of the county rises Slieve Croob and the Legananny Hills, while in the S are the much praised peaks of the Mourne Mountains.

Immediately to the N of Belfast, in the NE corner of Ireland, is **Antrim**, for the most part a land of high rolling moorlands dissected near the coast by wooded glens. To the W the hills gradually descend to the Bann valley and the flat shores of Lough Neagh, while on the remaining three sides the moors fall abruptly to the sea, forming in places sheer cliffs. The coast road, built in the 1830s, enables this fine stretch of coast to be seen to advantage. Running into the hills are the narrow valleys known collectively as 'the Nine Glens of Antrim', some, such as Glenariff, broadening out near their mouths. On the N coast is the famous natural curiosity of the Giant's Causeway. This was the country of the MacDonnells, while S Antrim belonged to the O'Neills.

To the W is **Londonderry**, familiarly known as **Derry**, taking its later official name from a charter of James I, who presented it to some of the city companies of London. Before the Plantation it was part of the territory of Tir Eoghain, 'the land of Owen', son of Niall of the Nine Hostages, and associated in early Christian days with St. Columba (or Columcille), who is said to have erected a church under an oak (doire) at Derry. The greater part is mountainous, the main ranges being the Sperrin mountains in the S, and the Carntoghers, a long bare ridge running N from Draperstown to the sea. The well-wooded Faughan valley, running SE from Derry, is one of the prettiest parts of the county.

Tyrone, a corruption of *Tir Eoghain* (see above), to the S, was part of the O'Neill earldom, which included also Co. Derry and the Donegal baronies of Inishowen and Raphoe. The county is broken up by hills, and in the N the Sperrin range extends across the border from Co. Derry. Its long low whitewashed farmhouses are often sheltered by a clump of trees, but the area tends to be open moorland, in spite of the popular description 'In Tyrone among the bushes', which originated in a poem by William Collins, born in Strabane in 1838, who later emigrated to America. In the 17C these districts were planted largely by settlers from the W Midlands of England, and the dialect of S Tyrone, like that of S Armagh, containing many words and expressions current in Elizabethan England, has thrown light on certain previously obscure passages in Shakespeare.

Fermanagh 'the country of the Man of Monach', to the SW of Tyrone, occupies the valley of the Erne, which with its chain of lakes with their densely wooded islets, divides the county into two. Before the Plantation of Ulster it was the country of the Maguires. Although Fermanagh is about half Catholic, Enniskillen, the capital (long a bastion of Protestantism) resisted the troops of James II. On both sides of the valley the ground is hilly, the escarpment on the Cavan border rising to over 600m. The dialect of S Fermanagh is distinct from that of neighbouring Tyrone, the amphibious natives of this district being separated from the English planters by lakes, and their mother tongue remained Irish until comparatively recently.

Armagh, between Tyrone and Down, is the main fruit-growing district of Ulster, and the county is best seen in May when the orchards are powdered with apple-blossom. In the S is the mountainous district round Slieve Gullion. The city of Armagh was long the ecclesiastical capital of Ireland, where St. Patrick founded his first cathedral, while at an earlier date neighbouring Navan Fort was the main base of the king of Ulster and the headquarters of the Red Branch Knights, the Irish equivalent of the Arthurian Knights of the Round Table.

BIBLIOGRAPHY

So many books are being published on Ireland that no attempt has been made to up-date the bibliography included in the last edition of this Guide. The brief list below includes comparatively recently published titles, some of which themselves contain comprehensive bibliographies for further or more specialised reading.

Mark Bence-Jones, Burke's Guide to Country Houses: Ireland; *Brian de Breffny* and *George Mott*, The Churches and Abbeys of Ireland; *A. Gwynn* and *R. N. Hadcock*, Medieval Religious Houses: Ireland; *Anthony Weir*, Early Ireland: a field guide; *Maurice Craig*, Dublin 1660–1860, and The Architecture of Ireland from the earliest times to 1880; *Maurice Craig* and the *Knight of Glin*, Ireland Observed; *Peter Harbison*, Guide to the National Monuments of Ireland; *Ann Hamlin* (ed.), Historic Monuments of Northern Ireland (1983 edition); *C.E.B. Brett*, Buildings of Belfast 1700–1914 (1985 edition); *W. A. McCutcheon*, The Industrial Archaeology of Northern Ireland; *Frederick O'Dwyer*, Lost Dublin; *Alistair Rowan*, The Buildings of Ireland, North West Ulster (the first of several volumes projected, published by Penguin, 1979); *Desmond Guinness*, Georgian Dublin; *Brian de Breffny* and *Rosemary FFolliott*, The Houses of Ireland; *Edward Malins* and the *Knight of Glin*, Lost Demesnes, Irish Landscape Gardening, 1660–1845; *Anne Crookshank* and the *Knight of Glin*, The Painters of Ireland, c 1660–1920; *J. S. Curl*, The Londonderry Plantation, 1609–1914; *Roger Stalley*, The Cistercian Monasteries of Ireland; *H. B. Clarke*, Medieval Dublin.

Maps

Both Bord Fáilte and the Northern Ireland Tourist Boards can supply general maps for the tourist; also available from the latter is a serviceable map and street index of Belfast at 1:10,000. Perhaps the best one-sheet map of the island as a whole is the *Michelin Map 405* at 1:400,000, although some may prefer the double-sided *A.A. Touring Map* at 1:350,000. The country is seen in more detail on the five sheets published by *Bartholomew* at 1:250,000 ('Quarter-Inch'). The *Ordnance Survey Road Atlas of Ireland* may be found useful. Other maps supplementing the *Atlas Section* of this Guide are listed below.

The *Ordnance Survey, Phoenix Park, Dublin* publish a general map at 1:575,000, and also cover the country in four overlapping sheets at 1:250,000, but those requiring more detail may obtain the series at 1:126,720 ('Half-Inch'), noting however that several sheets are no longer available, being superceded progressively with the new series at 1:50,000. Unfortunately the information on these is not always as detailed or accurate as it should be. They also publish District maps of the Dublin, Wicklow, Cork, and Killarney areas at 1:63,360 ('One-Inch'), of Dublin itself at 1:20,000, and of the Limerick area at 1:250,000, etc. Also of interest is their *Monastic Map* (1:625,000).

A map of 'medieval Dublin' from c 840–c 1540 was published in 1978 by the Friends of Mediaeval Dublin. Detailed maps of *The Burren*, and of the *Aran Islands*, produced by T.D. Robinson, are also of interest.

The *Ordnance Survey, Colby House, Stranmillis Court, Belfast BT9 5BJ* publish four sheets at 1:126,720 covering Northern Ireland only, which is also seen in more detail in 18 sheets at 1:50,000, replacing the series of nine sheets at 1:63,360. The first (Northern Ireland) of four sheets covering the island as a whole at 1:250,000 is also available.

Mention should be made here of the *Atlas of Ireland* published by the Royal Irish Academy in 1976. Both Dublin and Belfast publish a wide range of more detailed or specialised maps and plans, catalogues of which may be requested.

Those motoring from London to either Fishguard or Holyhead will find the *Michelin Map* 403 (and 404, if necessary) or the *AA Map of Wales and the West Midlands* convenient.

PRACTICAL INFORMATION

Approaches to Ireland and Transport in Ireland

Tourist Information. The **Irish Tourist Board (Bord Fáilte**; pron. Board Falcha), with their main offices at Baggot St Bridge, Dublin 2, will provide general information gratis, and book accommodation. Postal enquiries should be addressed to Bord Fáilte, PO Box 273, Dublin 8.

For Northern Ireland, see below.

Dublin Tourism have offices at 14 Upper O'Connell St, at the Bord Fáilte head office at Baggot St Bridge, and Trinity College. They also have public information offices during the summer, and can provide much useful information with regard to entertainment in the city, tours, etc.

Among Regional tourist offices in the Republic itself are the following, normally open from 9.00–18.00 Monday to Friday and 'til 13.00 on Saturday: 17 Church St, *Athlone*; Town Hall, *Cashel*; Grand Parade, *Cork*; *Dublin Airport*; Market Sq., *Dundalk*; 1 Clarinda Park North, and St. Michael's Wharf, *Dún Laoghaire*; Bank Pl., *Ennis*; Eyre Sq., *Galway*; Rose Inn St, *Kilkenny*; Town Hall, *Killarney*; Derry Rd, *Letterkenny*; The Granary, Michael St, *Limerick*; Dublin Rd, *Mullingar*; *Shannon Airport*; *Rosslare Harbour*; Main St, *Skibbereen*; Temple St, *Sligo*; Godfrey Pl., *Tralee*; 41 The Quay, *Waterford*; The Mall, *Westport*; Crescent Quay, *Wexford*.

Among branches elsewhere are the following: *Northern Ireland*—53 Castle St, Belfast, and Foyle St, Derry. *Great Britain*—150 New Bond St, London W1; 28 Cross St, Manchester; 6/8 Temple Row, Birmingham; 19 Dixon St, Glasgow.

USA—757 Third Av., New York; 230 N Michigan Av., Chicago; 625 Market St, San Francisco. *Canada*—10 King St E, Toronto. *Australia*—37th level, MLC Centre, Martin Pl., Sydney. *New Zealand*—87 Queen St, Auckland.

There are branches in *Europe* in Paris, Milan, Frankfurt, Amsterdam, Brussels, Copenhagen and Stockholm.

The **Northern Ireland Tourist Board** have offices at River House, 48 High St and 53 Castle St, Belfast, and Foyle St, Derry. They have branches at 11 Berkeley St, London W1, 142 Queen St, Glasgow, and 38 High St, Sutton Coldfield. Also at Neue Mainzerstrasse 22, 6000 Frankfurt am Main, West Germany, and 3rd Floor, 40 W 57th St, New York, NY 10019. *The British Tourist Authority* represent Northern Ireland elsewhere outside the UK, and also at the British Travel Centre; see below.

Travel Agents. General information may be obtained gratis from the Irish Tourist Board (Bord Fáilte) and the Northern Ireland Tourist Board offices in London and elsewhere abroad; see above. Any accredited member of the *Association of British Travel Agents* will sell tickets and book accommodation.

By Sea. Numerous and comparatively frequent **Passenger and Car Ferry Services** across the Irish Sea are operated by the Córas Iompair Eireann (CIE, or Irish Transport Board) or the Ulster Transport Authority (UTA) in conjunction with British Rail.

The main routes are: London–Holyhead–Dún Laoghaire

(Dunleary)–Dublin (B + I Line); Liverpool–Dublin (B + I Line); Liverpool–Belfast (Belfast Car Ferries); Stranraer–Larne (Sealink); Cairnryan–Larne (Townsend Thoresen).

There is also an *Ulsterbus Express* to destinations in Ireland from Victoria Coach Station, 164 Buckingham Palace Rd, London SW1, and also two Express buses from London to Galway via Dublin, and from Glasgow to Dublin.

The *British Rail Travel Centres*, can provide further information, travel tickets, sleeping-berth tickets, seat reservations, etc.; ferry bookings may be made through Sealink Car Ferry Centre, 52 Grosvenor Gdns, SW1.

For travellers from the Continent, there are also ferries (Irish Continental Line) from Le Havre to Rosslare; Le Havre to Cork (summer only), and Cherbourg to Rosslare; also from Roscoff to Cork (Brittany Ferries).

Regular **Air Services** between Great Britain and Ireland are maintained by *Aer Lingus* (see also below under Holiday Facilities), working in conjunction with *British Airways*. Full information about flights may be obtained from British Airways, 75 Regent St, London W1, and from Aer Lingus, 2/4 Maddox St, W1 (with branches at 150 New Bond St, London Tara Hotel, Wright's Lane, Kensington, W8 and 103 Kilburn High Rd, NW6.).

There are Aer Lingus offices at 40 Upper O'Connell St, and 42 Grafton St, Dublin, and also branches in Dún Laoghaire, Belfast, Cork, Shannon, and Limerick. British Airways offices are at 112 Grafton St; TWA at 44 Upper O'Connell St.

Dublin airport is at *Collinstown*, 8km N of Dublin (see Rte 31), and the Air Terminus is at the Busáras, Store St. *Belfast International* airport is 26km (16 miles) W of Belfast. *Belfast Harbour* airport is just NE of the city.

Regular flights are scheduled from London (Heathrow) to Dublin, Cork, Shannon, and Belfast.

There are also regular flights from Liverpool, Birmingham, Bristol, Cardiff, Leeds, Bradford, Manchester, Newcastle, Glasgow, and Edinburgh to Dublin, Cork, or Shannon, and to Belfast, and also a service from Luton to Dublin provided by *Ryan Air*. They may also be approached from the USA and Canada via Prestwick (or London).

From the Continent, there are flights to Dublin, some with intermediate stops, or to Cork or Shannon, from several European centres and also from further afield, with connecting flights with the above.

There are of course *internal flights* between Dublin and Shannon, Cork, Londonderry, and Belfast, etc.

From North America there are regular flights from New York and Boston to Dublin, and from Chicago and Montreal to Dublin or Shannon. There are connecting flights from Shannon to Belfast, apart from direct charter flights from New York and Canada.

There are regular bus services from airports to town terminals, and coach services between Dublin airport and some of the larger central hotels; taxis will also meet planes, and many car-hire firms have offices at the airports, all of which have the usual restaurants, shopping, exchange, and hotel-booking facilities, and Information Bureaux.

Holiday Facilities. *Aer Lingus* provide a number of interesting combinations in the way of tours, etc., which are well worth the considera tion of travellers wishing to reduce costs. Among these are the following, but Aer Lingus should be approached direct for the latest information.

A. A return flight from the UK; the use of a *self-drive car* for a week for two people, together with a generous free mileage allowance, for the price of their excursion air fare alone.
B. A *self-drive car* with unlimited mileage, *and seven nights accommodation*, booked in advance or otherwise; alternatively, seven nights in a cottage or farmhouse.
C. The use of a five-berth *horse-drawn caravan* in lieu of a car.
D. The use of a four- or six-berth *cruiser* on the Shannon.
E. Flights in combination with *coach tours* and accommodation.
F. Golfing or Fishing holidays.
G. Agricultural tours, etc.
H. Reductions for spouse, children, students, etc., full details of which may be gleaned from the Aer Lingus brochure issued in conjunction with their subsidiary, *CaraIreland Tours*, 52 Poland St, London W1.

Aer Lingus will provide prospective travellers with regard to any other facilities which may be available and which may assist in the planning of holidays, business congresses, conventions, etc.

Very similar facilities are also available for travellers sailing to Ireland with the **B + I Line**, 155 Regent St, W1, also in conjunction with CaraIreland Tours: further information may be obtained through branches of the Irish Tourist Board or members of the Association of British Travel Agents. The agents for B + I in the United States are Lynott Tours Inc, 350 Fifth Avenue, New York, NY 10118.

Sealink also offer inclusive rail and hire-car facilities in addition to their normal sailings.

Railways. The main lines in Ireland are: *Dublin (Heuston Station)* to Limerick and Cork; to Limerick, Mallow, Killarney, and Tralee; to Kilkenny and Waterford; to Athlone, Claremorris, and Westport or Ballina.
Dublin (Connolly Station) to Belfast; to Wicklow, Wexford, and Rosslare; to Mullingar, Athlone, and Galway; to Mullingar and Sligo.
From Cork to Tralee.
From Belfast to Londonderry.
There are interconnecting buses between Connolly and Heuston stations in Dublin, and from the latter to the city centre (by the O'Connell Bridge) or to the main Bus Station (*Busáras*, Store St).

Coastal commuter services are provided from Connolly, Tara St, and Pearse St Stations, Dublin. There is also the recently inaugurated DART service of fast trains connecting Bray to Howth via the centre of Dublin.

Buses. The routes of provincial bus services, maintained by the CIE and the UTA and their subsidiaries, cover a remarkably extensive area of the country, and although a comparatively small amount of luggage may be carried, many tours, even to remote districts, may thus be conveniently made. In addition, there are a number of principal and Express service radiating from Dublin (from the *Busáras*, Store St) and other main towns.

Excursions are also organised during the season from many centres through scenically attractive areas, with convenient stops for lunch and tea, etc. Seats should be booked in advance. Details of all such services and tours may be obtained from local bus-stations, or tourist offices; see p 78.

There are CIE offices at 59 O'Connell St and 35 Lower Abbey St, Dublin.

It should be noted that the destinations of some buses are still indicated on the vehicle *in Irish only*, which may well confuse the visitor, who should always check with the conductor or driver.

Motorists visiting Ireland will save trouble by joining either the *Automobile Association* (Fanum House, Basingstoke, Hants RG21 2EA), the *Royal Automobile Club* (83 Pall Mall, London SW1), the *Royal Scottish Automobile Club* (17 Rutland Square, Edinburgh), or the *American Automobile Association* (8111 Gatehouse Road, Falls Church, Virginia 22042). These organisations will provide any necessary documents, as well as information about rules of the road in Ireland, restrictions regarding caravans and trailers, arrangements for spare parts, insurance, etc. Although there are certain restrictions on the use of their vehicle while in Ireland, visitors may import and re-export their cars without any formality. Visiting vehicles other than those registered in Northern Ireland must carry a nationality plate while in the Republic. Motorists not the owners of their vehicle should possess the owner's permit for its use abroad. It should also be noted that in the towns of Northern Ireland there are areas to which vehicle entry is restricted, or in which unattended vehicles may not be parked.

Some *petrol stations* are closed on Sundays; motorists should not let their tanks become low too late in the evenings.

The *Royal Irish Automobile Club* is located at 34 Dawson St, Dublin; the *Ulster Automobile Club* is at 3 Botanic Av., Belfast. There are branches of the AA in Gt Victoria St, and of the RAC at 65 Chichester St, Belfast.

Most important towns, ports, and airports now provide *Car-hire* facilities; see also p 80.

The roads in Ireland, few of which are subject to heavy traffic, are particularly suitable for tourists, although in some of the narrower and winding roads in remoter districts there are occasional steep gradients. Often the road signs will indicate a sharp bend, for instance, which is in fact barely noticeable when being traversed, but this is not always so. In many areas cows, sheep, horses, and other livestock are liable to wander onto the highway. Most places are sign-posted, in both English and Irish, and in both miles and kilometres. It has been noticed, however, that the ends of a remarkable number of signs have been broken or knocked off, or the signs twisted in another direction, which can easily lead to confusion, if travellers are not referring to a map as well.

In the Republic, the roads are divided into three categories: the main network of National roads, e.g. N2; and those with the prefix R (R123, etc.), although some are still marked as Trunk roads (T2) or Link roads (L93), together with an extensive range of minor roads and tracks. In Northern Ireland the equivalent roads are marked A2, or B6 as in Great Britain, apart from the two main motorways driving SW and NW from Belfast, indicated as M1 and M2 respectively.

Most routes described in this guide have been arranged in a form radiating clockwise from Dublin, or fanning out from Belfast; others extend from such centres as Limerick—convenient for those visitors landing at Shannon—from Cork, Galway, and Rosslare, etc.

It should also be emphasised that it is not possible to cover some of the longer routes *and visit all* the monuments described along that route in a day, but they do suggest a general direction which it is convenient to follow. It is for the driver to decide which detours or sub-routes to follow, and to plan overnight stops.

Excursions into the immediate environs of Dublin are described in Rtes 1E–G, and the first parts of Rtes 2C and 19. Other rewarding excursions only slightly further afield are those to Trim (Rte 29), and thence along the Boyne valley to Newgrange (Rte 30; taking in perhaps Mellifont Abbey and Monasterboice). To the S of Dublin, the Wicklow Mountains offer a number of scenic drives, among the most attractive and interesting (although likely to be crowded at weekends) is that to Powerscourt and Glendalough (Rte 2B).

While it is recommended that travellers should on no account ignore the centre of Ireland—Kilkenny, Cashel, Caher, Kilmallock, Birr, Clonfert and Clonmacnoise, and numerous other towns and sites spring to mind—it is also appreciated that many tourists may wish to follow a coastal route round the island, and a list of these is given below in an order starting from Dublin. The Editor's preferences are given where there are alternatives.

The circuit of Ireland may be made by following routes 2B–5–11A–12B–13–16–15B (these last two in reverse)–part of 18A–18B (or the sub-route Ennis-Lahinch)–22A–24B–part of 27–28–(34B)–part of 33B–35–40–31 (in reverse).

Cycling. Much of Ireland is particularly suitable for exploration by bicycle, and visitors' bicycles are treated as personal effects and may enter the country free of duty. Bicycles may also be hired from any one of some 120 *Raleigh Rent-a-bike dealers*, a list of which is given in a leaflet, outlining conditions of hire, produced by the Irish Raleigh Industries Ltd (Broomhill Road, Tallaght, Dublin 2) in conjunction with the Irish and Northern Ireland Tourist Boards, and may be obtained at any tourist office.

Tourist offices can likewise advise on holiday transport by **Horse-drawn Caravan**, or **by Boat** on Ireland's canals, loughs, and rivers.

Formalities and Currency

Passports and **Identity Cards** are not necessary for British travellers entering the Republic of Ireland from British ports and airports, nor from Northern Ireland, but travellers arriving direct from the Continent or America, and elsewhere must be in the possession of passports.

The border between the Republic and Northern Ireland may *only* be passed at the authorised border-crossings. These are normally open 24 hours a day.

A note on recent 'troubles'. In view of suggestions to the contrary, the Editor feels justified in forewarning the readers that they may well be somewhat dismayed at first on crossing the unnatural frontier between the Republic and Northern of Ireland, where sporadic incidents will probably still occur until an unequivocal entente is reached, which is the urgent aim of the governments concerned.

It is always disturbing to cross borders under the scrutiny of armed guards and to pass military patrols. Burnt-out buildings are commonplace; while the sight of police stations incongruously surrounded by chicken-wire barricades tends to make the country look more beleaguered than it is.

Having been forewarned, it must be reiterated that reasonably prudent and circumspect visitors may, by avoiding certain specific districts, travel unmolestedly throughout the 'Six Counties', where they will receive the same warm welcome as elsewhere on the island, whatever their religious persuasion.

Custom House. Except for travellers by air, who have to pass customs at the airport of arrival, luggage is scrutinised at the port of disembarkation. Travellers between Great Britain and Northern Ireland are not normally subject to customs examination, but their luggage, packets, and parcels, are liable to be opened for reasons of security, and likewise when entering from the Republic, at the customs posts at the authorised crossings. Vehicles must stop if challenged by a Customs Patrol.

Currency Regulations. There is no restriction on the *importation* of currency into Ireland, although there are on the exportation of gold coins from the Republic to Northern Ireland/Great Britain. If travelling further afield after visiting Ireland, you may normally take Sterling area currency (including Irish notes) to a total value not exceeding £100 per person, and foreign currency, including travellers' cheques, to a total value not exceeding £500. Those resident outside the Sterling area may export, in addition, any foreign currency which they held on arrival.

The complicated regulations which lay down even what you may spend your money on in countries not subject to British law are set out in the leaflet 'Notice to Travellers', which may be obtained from most banks.

Money. The Irish pound (*punt*) no longer has parity with Sterling (since mid 1979). US dollars are also accepted. Irish coins, issued since 1928, are now identical in shape and size to the British coinage: e.g. ½p, 1p, 2p, 5p, 10p, and 50p. Irish currency notes are issued in denominations of £1, £5, £10, £20, £50, and £100. British coins and notes are also in circulation with the exception of the £1 coin and the 20p piece. Irish coins and notes are not generally accepted in Northern Ireland, nor in the rest of Great Britain, but may be exchanged at any bank. A £1 coin was minted for Northern Ireland in 1986, the reverse depicting the flax plant.

Banks in the Republic are open from Monday to Friday from 10.00–12.30, and from 13.30–15.00, and in Dublin remain open until 17.00 on Thursdays; the day for remaining open late varies elsewhere. Some agencies in the larger centres (such as at Thomas Cook Ltd and American Express, at 118 and 116 Grafton St, respectively) also provide foreign exchange facilities, while most hotels and larger shops accept travellers' cheques and credit cards, etc. The Dublin Airport bank is open every weekday except 25 December from 7.15–23.30 from Easter to the end of October; at other times from 8.15–21.00 (Saturday 8.15–21.30). *Travelling Banks* may occasionally be found in remote country districts.

In Northern Ireland banks are open from Monday to Friday from 10.00–12.30, and 13.30–15.30. At Belfast International Airport exchange facilities are available from May to September from 9.00–12.15; 13.15–15.00; 18.00–20.00 except Saturday and Sunday, when the bank is open from 10.00–12.00 only. At other times from 10.00–13.30. There are exchange facilities on the main Dublin/Belfast road at Newry, and at 68 Strand Rd, Londonderry, and at Thomas Cook, 11 Donegall Pl., Belfast.

Postal and other Services

Most **Post Offices** are open between 9.00–17.30 on weekdays, but may be closed between 13.00–14.15. Some may close at 13.00 on Saturday. In N Ireland they all close at 13.00 on Saturday. The GPO in O'Connell St, Dublin, is open for the sale of stamps, acceptance of telegrams, registered and express items, poste restante facilities, and with a *Bureau de Change*, from 8.00–20.00 Monday to Saturday, and from 10.30–18.30 on Sunday and Bank Holidays. Letters marked 'poste restante' and registered letters are only handed to the addressee on proof of identity. Bureau de change facilities are also available at the main POs in Cork, Killarney, Galway, Wexford, Waterford, Bray, Mallow and Skibbereen.

Irish postage stamps must be used on letters posted from the Republic; *letter boxes* are painted green. British stamps are used in Northern Ireland, where letter boxes are painted red, but the narrowed slit of the latter will not accept anything but the thinnest envelopes, and larger packets must be posted at post offices.

Telephones. Public call-boxes may be found at most post offices, railway stations, at hotels, some shops, and in kiosks (although too many of the latter appear to have been the target of vandalism, etc.). Ireland now has STD communications with Great Britain and the rest of the world. Kiosks are painted cream and green in the Republic, and red in the Six Counties.

In emergencies, dial 999 to call the Fire Brigade, Ambulance, or Police.

Police. In the Republic the police or Civic Guard are known as the *Garda Síochána* (or more simply, the Garda; plural Gardai; pron. Gardee). This force is an amalgamation (in 1925) of the Royal Irish Constabulary and the Dublin Metropolitan Police. Their headquarters are in Phoenix Park, Dublin. They are unarmed unless undertaking special duties.

In Northern Ireland the *Royal Ulster Constabulary* (RUC), recently supported by a reserve force, continue to pursue their objective of law enforcement.

Health Services. Travellers requiring medical attention may contact the *Eastern Health Board*, 1 James St, Dublin 8, or the *Irish Medical Association*, 10 Fitzwilliam Pl., 2; the *Irish Dental Association* is at 29 Kenilworth Sq., 6. There are reciprocal agreements between Britain and the Republic with regard to hospital and prescription charges, etc. In Northern Ireland, the advice of the nearest hospital may be sought.

Lost Property Offices. Dublin City bus services: Transport House, Bachelor's Walk; all train services, long-distance buses and coach tours: Connolly Station; Taxis; Carriage Office, Ship St. The Belfast Lost Property Office is at Musgrave Police Station in Ann St.

Useful Addresses

For those in Northern Ireland, see p 330.

The figure terminating each address refers to the postal district of Dublin.

Embassies and Consulates in Dublin: *British Embassy*, 33 Merrion Rd, 4; *American Embassy and Consulate*, 42 Elgin Rd, 4; *Canadian Embassy*, 65 St. Stephen's Green; *Australian Embassy*, Fitzwilliam House, Wilton Terrace, 2.

Among *Irish Embassies* abroad are those at: 17 Grosvenor Pl., *London* SW1; 2234 Massachusetts Av., *Washington* (with Consulates at 580 Fifth Av., *New York*; 681 Market St, *San Francisco*; and Rigley Bldg, 400 N Michigan Av., *Chicago*); 170 Metcalfe St, *Ottawa* 4; and Bank House, Civic Sq., *Canberra*.

A full list of other Consulates and Trade Delegations may be obtained from the *Department of Foreign Affairs*, Iveagh House, 80 St. Stephen's Green, 2.

Cultural bodies, etc.: *The Irish Arts Council* (An Chomhairle Ealaion), 70 Merrion Sq., 2; *The National Trust for Ireland* (An Taisce; pron. An Tashker), The Tailors' Hall, Back Lane, Dublin 8; *The Military Historical Society for Ireland*, 86 St. Stephen's Green, 2; *The Old Dublin Society*, 58 S William St, 2; *Royal Inst. of the Architects of Ireland*, 8 Merrion Sq. N, 2; *Royal Irish Academy*, 19 Dawson St, 2; *Royal Society of Antiquaries of Ireland*, 63 Merrion Sq., 2; *The Irish Georgian Society*, Castletown House, Celbridge, Co. Kildare; *Department of Lands*, 24 Upper Merrion St, 2; *The Ordnance Survey*, Phoenix Park, 8; *An Foras Forbartha* (Conservations and Amenity Advisory Service), St. Martin's House, Waterloo Rd, 4; *Office of Public Works*, 51 St. Stephen's Green, 2; *National Monuments Advisory Council*, Ely Place Upper, Dublin 2; *Royal Dublin Society*, Ballsbridge, 4; *Royal Society for Industrial Archaeology*, c/o the RDS; *Royal Horticultural Society*, 16 St. Stephen's Green, 2.

For information regarding the *Gaeltacht*: Gaeltarra Eireann, Na Forbacha, Gaillimh.

For **Sporting bodies**, see pp 88–9.

Hotels and Restaurants

Hotels. The art of hospitality is a gift natural to the Irish, and travellers will as a rule find a warm welcome at an Irish hotel, often more informal than in certain countries, and in general a high standard of service and cleanliness. The visitors' attention is drawn to the several country-houses and castles which have been adapted to accommodate guests, and one should ask for the latest list of 'Irish Country Houses, Manors and Restaurants' (ICHRA). Unfortunately it includes certain establishments which do not deserve to be there, while omitting several hotels of quality—the Dunraven Arms at Adare comes to mind—which merits inclusion. There are also a number in the modern stereotyped 'international' style, perhaps better equipped with amenities, which most clients will never use but all must pay for, and normally catering more for businessmen and groups than for the individual traveller.

Most hotels provide a full meal service; indeed in many places the only food available will be found at the hotel. The majority have bars, and a suprising number offer a baby-sitting service.

They are annually classified by the Irish Tourist Board, and are included in their *Official List of Hotels and Guesthouses*, a copy of which should be requested. They are graded as either A*, A, B*, B, and C. Most bedrooms in the scale A hotels have private bathrooms *en suite*, but not all.

Guesthouses, smaller in scale than hotels, and not open to non-residents, may give a more personal service, but frequently only provide breakfasts and evening meals. They are similarly graded from A to C, and should certainly not be overlooked.

The Board produces annually a list of approved *Town and Country Homes and Guesthouses*, in which a more traditional and homely way of life will be experienced. Evening meals will be provided if reasonable notice is given. A circular 'shamrock' sign, on which the current year and the words 'Approved Bord Fáilte' are printed, should be displayed on or in each house so listed. An illustrated guide to *Farmhouse Accommodation* is also available on request.

The Irish Tourist Board have a *Central Reservation Service* at 14 Upper O'Connell St, Dublin 1 (PO Box 273, Dublin; telephone 781200; telex 33125), which will endeavour to make reservations, not only in hotels and guesthouses, but also on river-cruisers, and for horse-drawn caravans. It will also give information about car hire. A small fee for these services is charged.

The Northern Ireland Tourist Board (48 High St, Belfast; tel. 0232 246609 for information) also produce a guide to places to stay in the 'Six Counties'.

Visitors to Dublin (or Belfast) in particular are recommended to book accommodation as far in advance as possible, for with the proliferation of Trade Fairs, Conferences, etc., not only the larger hotels get booked up *en bloc*, but also many of the smaller central ones, and they risk being accommodated at short notice some considerable distance from town.

Hilton Park, Scotshouse, near Clones

Complaints should be brought to the notice of the owners or management of the premises involved in the first instance. If full satisfaction is not obtained, the local tourist office should be advised, but it is preferable to write to the tourist board concerned. In the Republic, complaints should be addressed, without compunction, to the Customer Relations Unit, Bord Fáilte, Baggot St Bridge, Dublin 2, together with receipted bills in cases of alleged overcharging. Letters of commendation are also appreciated.

Where a service charge is included, no tipping is expected except in the case of exceptional service. VAT (Value Added Tax) is, by law, included in all Irish restaurant and hotel prices.

The Tourist Board, which encourages the use of approved accommodation only, can also supply lists of self-catering accommodation in rented *Cottages, Chalets, and Villas*, and likewise *Camping parks*, with details of their amenities and equipment for hire. A list of *Youth Hostels* in Ireland may be obtained from *An Oige* (or Irish Youth Hostel Association), 39 Mountjoy Sq., Dublin, and from YHANI (Youth Hostel Association of Northern Ireland), 56 Bradbury Pl., Belfast BT7 1RU. The Tourist Board publish an overprinted 'Youth Hostel' edition of their map of Ireland, showing the situation of hostels throughout the island.

Restaurants; Food and Drink. There has been a substantial increase in recent years in the number of restaurants in Ireland, even in remote areas, and the situation is improving. Tourist offices can supply lists of restaurants in their area, giving their capacity, price range and specialities; all have met the full requirements of Regional Health Boards.

No longer is the tasty potato basic to the Irish diet; many less familiar vegetables are being introduced. The home produce is usually of excellent standard, but only in comparatively recent years have many people become more knowledgeable, and have prepared the ingredients acceptably. Most forms of seafood, long ignored, are of superlative quality, and likewise Irish salmon and trout, etc. The butter and cream from the *Creameries* (a word used in preference to dairies) is also of good quality and abundant—unfortunately too many restaurants supply butter in small packaged pats. Few will resist the soda bread, made with buttermilk, and the bracks.

Some restaurants, which may easily be avoided, also assume that piped background music (even at breakfast) is conducive to a better appetite. A list of those which provide 'traditional' entertainment, and 'traditional' medieval banquets, may be requested; likewise of 'Singing Pubs' and similar convivial establishments.

Breakfast is usually a substantial meal, and therefore should be ordered early by those wishing to make an early start. Luncheon is usually served between 13.00 and 14.00. The traditional evening meal, served at any time after 17.00 followed by a light supper before retiring, has given way to dinner at 19.30.

At present some restaurants have only a *Wine Licence*; in these, wine only may be served with food from 12.00–14.30, and from 18.30–21.00, but it is expected that legislation will soon permit the sale of all drinks with meals in Bord Fáilte-approved restaurants.

Licensing Hours. The hours during which alcoholic liquor is legally on sale in the Republic are considerably more liberal than those applying in Great Britain (and Northern Ireland; see below). On weekdays its sale is officially permitted between 10.30 and 23.00 (or 23.30 in summer), although bars and pubs are ostensibly closed for an hour between 14.30 and 15.30 daily. On Sundays the opening hours are from 12.30–14.00, and from 16.00–22.00. Hotel residents can usually obtain a drink at any reasonable time, while non-residents may order refreshments with their meals. The sale of alcoholic liquor is prohibited on Good Friday throughout the island, nor is it on sale in Northern Ireland on Sundays, except in hotels and licensed restaurants when consumed with meals. Pubs in Northern Ireland are open between 11.30 and 23.00 from Monday to Saturday *only*, not that this much diminishes the proportion of the annual income spent on drink.

Perhaps the most ubiquitous of Irish drinks is a famous stout or porter known internationally as *Guinness* (see p 130), although there are a number of perfectly acceptable lighter beers, and they require no commendation.

Irish Whiskey, spelt with an 'e' to distinguish it from mere whisky, is bottled only after having been matured in wooden casks for at least seven years, and has a distinctive flavour unlike Scotch, Bourbon, or rye. When mixed with sugar and strong coffee and sipped through a layer of cream, it is known as 'Irish coffee': most people will prefer it neat.

Sports and Outdoor Activities

General information may be obtained from the Irish Tourist Board (see p 78), and in Northen Ireland from the *Sports Council*, 49 Malone Rd, Belfast. Among the many sporting associations, the following may be found useful in providing more detailed information: the *Gaelic Athletic Association*, Croke Park, Dublin; *Federation of Mountaineering Clubs of Ireland*, 7 Sorbonne, Ardilea Estate, Dublin 14; *Irish Yachting Association*, 87 Upper George's St, Dún Laoghaire; *Inland Waterways Association of Ireland*, Kingston House, Ballinteer, Dublin 14.

Golf is popular, and almost all clubs—there are over 200—will admit visitors on payment of moderate green fees. The championship courses and the better-known 18-hole links in the neighbourhood of Dublin, Belfast or Cork will satisfy the most exacting golfer, while much pleasure may be gained on any of the large number of 9-hole courses throughout the island, many of them surrounded by outstandingly beautiful scenery. A list of golf-links may be obtained from the tourist boards.

Shooting. Firearms certificates must be obtained (for shotguns) from the Secretary, *Department of Lands*, Forest and Wildlife Service, 22 Upper Merrion St, Dublin 2; (for rifles) from the *Department of Justice*, 72 St. Stephen's Green, Dublin 2. Visitors wishing to take *any form* of firearm into Northern Ireland should enquire in advance to the Northern Ireland Tourist Board (48 High St, Belfast) about the current regulations and restrictions, etc.

Anglers should also approach the tourist boards in Dublin and Belfast.

Bord Fáilte can also advise on where the game of '*Hurling*' (resembling hockey) may be watched.

Equestrian sports, etc. While the Irish Tourist Board can supply information concerning schedules of race meetings, horse shows, point-to-point meets, riding schools, horse and pony trekking, horse-drawn caravan holidays, beagling, hunting (despite Oscar Wilde's famous quip), and bloodstock and non-thoroughbred sales, the following addresses may be of help: *Royal Dublin Society* (RDS), Ballsbridge, Dublin (on whose grounds the Royal Dublin Show takes place in August); *National Stud*, Tully, Co. Kildare; *The Racing Board*, 9 Merrion Sq., Dublin 2; *The Turf Club*, 25 Merrion Sq. (and also at The Curragh, Co. Kildare); *Show Jumping Association of Ireland*, 34 Upper Fitzwilliam St, Dublin 2; the *All-Ireland Polo Club*, Phoenix Park, Dublin 8; and the *Bord na gCapall* (the Irish Horse Board), St. Maelruans, Tallaght, Co. Dublin.

The Irish Horse Board was established by the Irish government in 1971 to maintain and improve the quality of breeding of Irish horses and ponies, to develop equestrian sports, and promote the marketing of bloodstock. The breeding and sale of racing and thoroughbred horses are not controlled by this body. The lush grass from Ireland's rich limestone land, long the stronghold of Swift's noble *Houyhnhnm*, is ideal for horse-breeding, which has always been a traditional occupation. Connemara ponies may be seen at the Connemara Pony Show at Clifden, Co. Galway, each August. The board can advise on the whereabouts of Auction Sales, private sales, and Horse Shows; on transport facilities, and export regulations; and can provide a detailed list of approved and registered riding schools, stables, and other establishments, and what facilities they can offer—the latter is available in a booklet entitled 'Where to ride in Ireland'.

The *Sports Council* (49 Malone Rd, Belfast) can advise on similar facilities in Northern Ireland. The *Royal Ulster Agricultural Show* is held at the Balmoral Showgrounds, Belfast, in late May. The offices of the *Royal Ulster Agricultural Society* are at the King's Hall, Lisburn Rd, Belfast.

The Irish Tourist Board can also advise on *Agricultural Tours* (covering livestock production, sheepbreeding and dairying, etc.).

Forest Parks. In recent years there has been a proliferation of these sites throughout Ireland, many of them with their Nature-trails for the budding ecologist. A number of *National Parks* have also been inaugurated: at Killarney, Glenreagh, and in Donegal and Connemara. Full details of their whereabouts may be obtained from the *Forest Park and Wildlife Service*, Department of Lands, 22 Upper Merrion St, Dublin 2, who also publish a number of informative and tastefully produced booklets and leaflets on the Natural History of the island, together with lists of bird haunts, etc. *The Forest Service*, Department of Agriculture, Dundonald House, Stormont, Belfast, the *National Trust for Northern Ireland* (Rowallane, Saintfield, Co. Down), or the Northern Ireland Tourist Board, can provide comparable material for the 'Six Counties'.

The address of the *Irish Wild Bird Conservancy* is c/o The Royal Irish Academy, 19 Dawson St, Dublin 2; that of the *Royal Society for the Protection of Birds* is 58 High St, Newtownards, Co. Down. The *Ulster Society for the Preservation of the Countryside* is at 49 Malone Rd, Belfast.

General Information

Public Holidays. The main holidays in the Republic are: 1 January; 17 March (St. Patrick's Day); Good Friday; Easter Monday; first Monday in June; first Monday in August; Christmas Day; 26 December (St. Stephen's Day).

In Northern Ireland the first Monday in June and the first Monday in August are replaced by the 12 July (Orange Day) and the last Monday in August. 27 December is a Bank Holiday.

Climate and Season. The climate of Ireland is temperate; the winters mild. Only on the E coastal strip are there fewer than 200 rainy days a year. Snow falls rarely except on the highest ranges. May and June are the sunniest months. Waterproofs, or at least a light raincoat, may be required at any season, but it should be remembered that a period of continuous rain is the exception; what appears to be a persistent downpour may well be followed by a day of brilliant sunshine.

Ireland, or at least its more picturesque attractions, is likely to be comparatively crowded during July and August, when tourist facilities are in full swing, and accommodation should be booked well in advance. The latter half of May and June are more comfortable, but September and October are probably the months in which the country is to be seen at its best: the weather is at its most settled, the banks of fuchsia are in flower, and the colour of both valley and mountain is particularly striking—the only drawback being the comparative shortness of the evenings.

Admission to Antiquities, monuments, castles, etc. Rose Macaulay, in her 'Pleasure of Ruins', wrote: '$EWone cannot travel more than a few miles in Ireland without passing some broken abbey or church; they lie strewn along coast and river, hill and plain, island and lake-side, in ruinous profusion. Destroyed by Danes, by Normans, by Englishmen, by decay, by time, by poverty, vandalism and dissolution, their crumbling arches and portals and fragments of wall stand in reproachful witness to the passing of a murdered culture'.

The principal monuments of Ireland, frequently but by no means always indicated by *green* signposts, are under the care of a government commission (partially protected by the National Monuments Act of 1930, amended 1954); the majority are likewise 'in State care' in Northern Ireland. In a number of cases—as at Cashel, Clonmacnoise, Jerpoint, Holycross, Cahir castle, etc.—they are in the charge of an official guardian, in which case a small charge is made for admission. Where there is no regular guardian on the spot and the object of interest is behind locked gates, generally there is a notice announcing the whereabouts of the key, and there is rarely any difficulty or undue delay in obtaining assistance in gaining entry. Certainly, apart from a few areas given over to heavy tourist traffic, those offering help or advice do so disinterestedly, and a few pleasant words of thanks often goes at least as far as a gratuity. Indeed it is surprising the amount of information one can gain in the most unexpected quarters, even if it is somewhat embroidered.

One somewhat macabre sight noticed not infrequently among the ruins of churches and monasteries is evidence of their continued use as a cemetery, although the practice is officially deprecated. Often one will stumble across a recent burial mound, with its cross or wreath, plastic or otherwise$EW.Some families have the hereditary right of burial within monastic precincts, and prefer for private reasons to be interred in the most sanctified ground possible.

Travellers wishing to visit country houses and castles are advised to acquire from any office of the Irish Tourist Board the latest list produced by the *Historic Irish Tourist Houses and Gardens Association* (otherwise known as HITHA; 3A Castle St, Dalkey, Co. Dublin) and likewise the brochure produced by *The National Trust* in Northern Ireland (Rowallane, Saintfield, Ballynahinch, Co. Down BT24 7LH), or from local tourist offices in Northern Ireland, which will give the times of admission, etc. Although the privacy of owners should at all times be respected, in cases where admission normally applies only during the summer season, for example, the *seriously* interested visitor may be courteously granted permission to enter at other times. The local tourist office is usually in a position to advise on the local situation, but it is always preferable to apply in advance.

Several such mansions also hospitably accept guests, and tourist offices should be applied to for lists of such establishments and other similar guest houses.

Ruins. During the period 1919–23 alone, some 70 out of a total of at least 2000 country houses in Ireland were burnt. Although a number of these were subsequently rebuilt, the great majority of ruined buildings were merely dismantled and allowed to fall down. No trace remains of many more which were entirely demolished and their site ploughed over. As Mark Bence-Jones, editor of *Burke's Guide to Country Houses: Ireland* (1978) has emphasised, one should beware of approaching ruins too closely and to venture within their walls, for to do so 'is to court falling plaster on one's head and unexpected cellars opening up beneath one's feet'. He goes on to warn that should an accident occur, 'the ruin in question would almost certainly be bulldozed as being "dangerous"; so that in the interests of preservation, as well as in their own interests, country house enthusiasts should treat ruins with respect'.

Even a decade ago an alarming number of those surviving were described as 'now derelict' or with an uncertain future, largely caused by the introduction of capital taxes in the Irish Republic at a time when the cost of maintainance was rocketing, and the future of many more is increasingly precarious in spite of the strenuous efforts of preservation undertaken by the Irish Georgian Society, the Ulster Architectural Heritage Society, the Northern Ireland National Trust and Commissioners of Public Works, An Taisce, among other bodies.

Bogs. Approximately one-seventh of the land area of Ireland is covered by bogs, which, forming such a noticeable part of the landscape, require some brief explanation.

There are basically two types of bog: the 'raised' or 'red' bog; and the 'blanket' bog. The *raised bog*, mostly sited in the central lowlands, requires a climate with less than 100cm (40 inches) of rain a year, being more dependent on ground water than the *blanket bog*, which is found further to the W of the country and in regions over the 400m contour (c 1,300ft), including the Wicklow Mountains. The blanket bog thrives on higher rainfall—over 125cm (50 inches) annually—and general humidity. Intermediate conditions produce bogs with mixed characteristics.

The raised bogs develop above a fen, some having started to accumulate between 7,000 and 5,000 years ago (burying the skeletons of the Giant deer and tree trunks such as 'bog oak'), the rising dome of peat formed by the hummocky growth of *Sphagnum moss* being frequently 8m deep. Plants such as the Marsh andromeda, Bog asphodel, Deergrass, Beak-sedge, with lichens, ling, and heaths on drier sites, are often present.

The *blanket bogs*, as their name suggests, cover much more extensive areas, even whole regions, as in NW Mayo, developing directly on the mineral soil. By filling in hollows (and sometimes burying archaeological sites), and conforming to the contours, they also produce a general 'rounded' or streamlining effect. The peat formed is usually only 2–3m thick, although deeper in the hollows; Sphagnum moss plays a lesser role, and the vegetation is more grassy. Among the more common species are cotton grasses, and low shrubs such as heathers in addition to Deergrass and Bog asphodel, while in lower lying districts they contain more Purple moor grass and Black bog rush.

Peat, or *Turf* as it is more frequently called in Ireland, the natural resource thus produced, was long the only fuel available in rural areas, and until recently was cut by hand with the long-handled turf-spade. Only in 1934 did a State-directed board start machine-cutting, until superseded in 1946 by the State-sponsored *Bord na Móna*, which now employs some 5,000 people. Massive machinery is used, but apart from producing peat briquettes for domestic use, milled peat, and peat moss for gardeners and horticulturalists, etc., more than 25 per cent of Ireland's electricity is derived from peat-fired generating-stations, supplied with fuel from these mechanical cuttings. In 1970 some 55,000 hectares (135,000 acres), mostly from the raised bogs in level districts, were yielding 4,000,000 tonnes of peat per annum, although the undulating but shallower blanket bogs to the W were also being harvested. In remoter districts on the Atlantic Coast, the turf-spade, donkey-cart, and piles of peat on the road-side are still in evidence.

The Irish Language is officially the first language of the Republic, although the everyday language of most Irishmen is English, which is 'recognised' as the second language, a point brought home to visitors, who will see many public signs and placenames written up in both, although some confusingly will remain in Irish alone. Many, however contrived, such as *aerphort*, will be immediately recognisable; others—such as *Fir*, and *Mná* (Gentlemen, and Ladies)—less so.

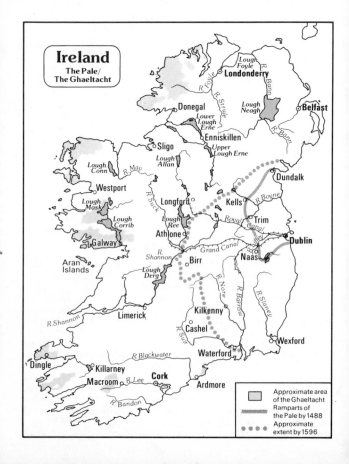

All Acts of Parliament and statutory instruments, Agenda and Proceedings of the Dáil and Senate are published bilingually, even if few use Irish in parliamentary debate. Some proficiency in the language is expected, even if standards are unexacting, in such bodies as the Police; but although it is obligatory in certain positions, since 1974 a knowledge of Irish has no longer been compulsory in the Civil Service.

Although the campaign initiated by Douglas Hyde to revive the language, which was on the verge of extinction late in the last century, and which led to the establishment of the Gaelic League in 1893, did much to foster interest in the vernacular—and indeed it was again taught in the primary schools—interest has generally declined in recent years. In the 1950s it was estimated that merely 30,000 people used Irish as a normal medium of speech, of whom only 3,000 were ignorant of English, while perhaps 3 or 400,000 had a reasonable knowledge of it as the standardised second language. The census of 1971 optimistically claimed that there were 789,000. These Irish-speaking districts, defined in 1956, are known as the **Gaeltacht** (see map), and the authority responsible for the Gaeltacht is now known as the Údarás na Gaeltachta. Its main enclaves are located as follows: NW of Donegal; NW of Mayo, and on Achill Island; much of Connemara, and immediately NE of Galway city itself, and on the Aran Islands; the Dingle peninsula; SW of Killarney, and between Killarney and Macroom; and a small enclave S of Dungavan. It covered an area of 4,800km^2, less that 6 per cent of the total surface of Ireland. The total population of the area was then 78,500, but the number actually at work in the Gaeltacht in 1961 was only 27,000, largely in agricultural employment. It was almost conterminous with what were known as the Congested Districts. Owing to the poverty of the soil and overpopulation—in spite of the inroads of actual starvation and emigration in the mid 19C—the economic problems here were so acute that the British Government set up a special administration to attend to them, which was thereafter known as the 'Congested Districts Board'. On the purely material side it effected many improvements, and later merged with the Department of Lands, but as far as the preservation of the Irish language was concerned, Government Commissions have been less successful, for while idealistic advocates for the revival live largely in English-speaking Ireland, those subsisting in the Gaeltacht often doubt its utility when it comes to their own economic survival. Indeed, the few numbers of native Irish speakers remaining brings it almost within measureable distance of extinction. It has been remarked that it is both ironic and symbolic that O'Sullivan's 'Twenty Years Agrowing', and 'Peig', by Peig Sayers—both with a wide circulation in their English translation—describe life on the Blasket Islands off the Kerry coast, which have been uninhabited for over a quarter of a century.

Irish is a language of Indo-European origin belonging to the *Goidelic* development of Celtic. Its idiom is profuse; its grammar difficult, although the irregular verbs are only nine. There are slight dialectical differences peculiar to Ulster, Munster, and Connacht respectively, but these are of no great complexity. Yet, such is its warmth of expression, that it has been described as 'the language for your prayers, your curses, and your love-making'! The language has passed through the transitions known to scholars as Old Irish, Middle Irish (900–1200), and Early Modern Irish (1200–1650), to Modern Irish. The first (c 600–900) is practically a closed book to all but philologists, although a considerable body of literature from that period survives; indeed that Irish was the oldest vernacular literature in Europe after Greek and Latin. Middle and Early Modern Irish has attracted more general attention. Its literature is largely devoted to a vast mass of mythological and heroic saga; narrative, lyrical, and elegiac poetry; hagiology, homilies, and translations of foreign works of devotion; medieval works of philosophy, medicine, and science; native annals, histories, clan records, and topographies; free Gaelic renderings of classical and medieval literature; and a mass of proverbial matter, epigrams, songs, and folklore in general.

Emblems, etc. The national *flag* of the Republic is a tricolour of green, white and orange, green being displayed next to the staff. It is said to have been introduced in 1848 as an emblem of the Young Ireland movement by Thomas Francis Meagher, and at Easter 1916 flew above the General Post Office, Dublin. The colours represent the Gaelic and Anglo-Norman stock, and the supporters of William of Orange, the Protestant planters; Meagher suggested that the white signified the lasting truce between the Orange and Green, beneath whose folds 'the hands of the Irish Protestant and the Irish Catholic may be clasped in heroic brotherhood'.

The standard of the President is a golden *harp* on an azure field; the harp being a symbol which replaced the earlier three crowns on Irish coinage in the early 16C.

The *shamrock* is said to have been used by St. Patrick to explain the idea of the 'Trinity' to the pagan Gaels, and it is still frequently displayed as an emblem of Ireland in general.

The *National Anthem* was written in 1907 by Peadar Kearney, who with Patrick Heeney, also composed the music. First published in the newspaper 'Irish Freedom' (1912), it was known as 'The Soldier's Song' (Amhrán na bhFiann), and its chorus, displacing the earlier Fenian anthem 'God Save Ireland'—which might have been disparagingly misinterpreted—was adopted in 1926.

The origin of the arms of the province of *Ulster*—shorn of legendary trappings—is that it was derived from those borne by De Burgo, Earl of Ulster at the period of the Norman invasion, with the addition of the O'Neill escutcheon, the '*Red Hand* of O'Neill'—argent a dexter hand gules. The right hand is severed at the wrist, from which no blood should flow. Some confusion has arisen in the past by the indiscriminate use of both dexter and sinister hands by the Order of Baronets of Ulster, instituted by James I, when 'a hand gules', otherwise unspecified, was adopted as their device.

Glossary of Architectural, Topographical, Political and Associated Terms

ANNAGH marshy ground
ARD a high place
ATH a ford
BAILE a settlement or townland
BALLA a wall
BALLAGH marshy ground
BALLINA an entrance, or ford
BALLY a town; it has been estimated that there are no less than 5000 townlands in Ireland with names commencing with this prefix
BAWN a fortified enclosure attached to a castle, or the yard of a tower-house
BEEHIVE HUT small stone edifice, shaped like an old-fashioned beehive, and vaulted by corbelled construction; also *Clochan*
BEN a peak
BOG; see p 91
BULLAUN artificially hollowed stone, probably used as a mortar
BUN end of a road; foot of a hill; mouth of a stream
CATHER, CAHER, or **CATHAIR** a fort of dry stone construction, usually so-called when the structure is larger than a *Cashel*
CAIRN a mound of stones heaped over a prehistoric tomb
CALP a dark limestone found principally in the Dublin region
CARRICK or **CARRIG** a stone walled enclosure encircling a church, monastery, or ring-fort
CASHEL a *Rath* of which the bank is supported by a stone wall
CASTLE in Ireland, often merely a semi-fortified house, or manor-house; not necessarily fortified in the normal sense of the term
CATHEDRAL in Ireland, often a church of unpretentious dimensions
CILL; see KILL
CLACHAN a small group of dwellings or farm-buildings, but smaller than a hamlet
CLARE a level; a plank bridge
CLOCHÁN a row of stepping-stones fording a river; also a *Beehive hut*
CLOGHER a stony place
CLON a meadow
CORRIE a circular hollow at a valley head, often holding water
CRANNÓG an island, often artificially built, in a lake or marsh, sometimes connected to the mainland by a submerged causeway; it was usually fortified by a palisade, and contained dwellings
CUL a back

CURRACH or **CURRAGH** a marsh or low plain; also a small boat or coracle, formed of hides stretched over a lath framework, later of tarred canvas
DÁIL ÉIREANN (pron. Dau-il airan) the lower house of the Irish Parliament; the *Oireachtas* or upper house being known as the Senate or *Seanad*. It is usually populated by members of Fianna Fáil or Fine Gael, as the two main political parties are named. Members of the Dáil (*Teachta Dala*) are known as TDs, not MPs. The Prime Minister is the *Taoiseach* (pron. Tee-shock).
DEMESNE enclosed park or garden surrounding a mansion; an estate
DERG or **DEARG** red
DERRY an oak-grove
DIOCLETIAN WINDOW large semi-circular window comprising three lights divided by two vertical mullions
DIAMOND in Ulster, the central square or market-place of a Plantation town
DOLMEN simple megalithic tomb formed of three or more upright stones covered by a cap-stone, and once enclosed by an earth mound
DONAGH a large church
DRUM or **DROM** a ridge or hillock
DRUMLIN a small hill, often oval in shape, formed by glacial action; a large part of Ulster is physically divided from the rest of the island by a belt of such drumlins; see p 72
DÚN or **DOON** fort
ENNIS, INIS, or **INCH** an island
ESKER an alluvial morain or deposit of sand or gravel, usually left by an ice-sheet, and forming a sinuous ridge, sometimes used anciently as a track
FENIAN member of the Irish Republican Brotherhood, founded in 1858, to undermine British 'ascendancy' in Ireland
FERT grave, tumulus, mound
FIR Men (on lavatory entrances)
GAELTACHT district in which the vernacular is still partially Irish; see p 92
GALLAN or **GALLAUN** standing stone
GALLOWGLASS mercenary soldier (Irish *gall óglach*, foreign warrior), usually from Scotland (13–15C)
GARDA; pl. Gordai policeman or guard (pron. Gorda or Gor*die*)

GLEN or GLAN   a valley or glen

HIBERNIAN-ROMANESQUE   Irish round-arched style of architecture used prior to the Norman invasion

IRA   Irish Republican Army; as with *Sinn Féin* (see below), too often the mask behind which extremist guerrilla agitators have hidden, and ostensibly outlawed in 1936

KEEL or KILL   narrow

KELP   type of seaweed, calcined for its properties as a fertiliser

KILL or CILL   early monastic site, cell, or chapel

KNOCK or CNOC   a hill; there are some 2000 townlands in Ireland with this prefix

LIS   earthen fort, or the green open space enclosed by a *rath*, on which livestock was penned

LIBERTY   suburban area once beyond the jurisdiction of a mayor

LOUGH   a loch or lake; sometimes an inlet of the sea

MNÁ   Ladies (on lavatory entrances)

MOR   big, great

MOTTE   flat-topped mound, once fortified (by the Normans)

MOY   a plan

MUCK   a pig

MULL   a rounded height

OGHAM   5C 'script' formed of notches or lines representing twenty letters of the Latin alphabet, marked on either side or across the angle between adjacent surfaces of standing-stones, where they usually indicate a name; see p 43

OUGHTER (uachtar)   upper

OWEN (less often *Avon*)   a river

PALE   district spreading westwards from Dublin during the 12th to 16C, its varying frontier, fortified by 'castles', circumscribing the area under effective Anglo-Norman control; the expression 'beyond the Pale' covering the unsegregated rest of the country, later having a depreciatory connotation; see p 92

PLANTATION   referring to the settlement of the English or Scots in Ulster after 1607

POTEEN   an illicitly distilled spirit usually made from potatoes

RATH   circular rampart, often palisaded, surrounding ancient dwellings; see *Cashel*

ROS   a promontory; also occasionally, a wood

SCELLIG or SKELLIG   lofty crag or rock

SEAN   old

SHEILA-NA-GIG   sculpted female figure in which certain sexual attributes are emphasised, and probably connected with a fertility cult, or to frighten off the Devil

SINN FÉIN (pron. Shin Fane)   'Ourselves Alone'; an influential political party or cult, originally founded to promote Home Rule, but later used by extremists to further their own ends, and which has periodically been pronounced illegal by the Establishment

SLIEVE (sliabh)   mountain

SOUTERRAIN   underground chamber

STRAD   a street

STRAND   the usual term in Ireland for a beach or shore

TEAMPULL or TEMPLE   a church

TEN-POUND CASTLE   one built under the act of 1429, subsidising the erection of small forts in the Pale (see above) by the grant of the then-substantial sum of £10

THOLSEL   Town Hall

TOBAR, TOBER, or TUBBER   a well, often claimed to be Holy

TOGHERS   cross-country tracks made by timber or brushwood thrown down across boggy ground

TOOME   a tomb

TULL, TULLY (Kulach)   hillock

TURF   peat or peat-fuel; see p 91

TYR or TER   territory

INDEX MAP OF ROUTES

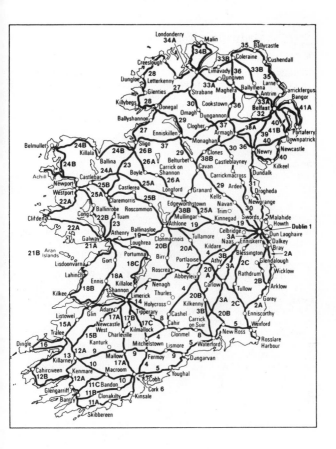

1 Dublin

A. Introduction

DUBLIN, its English name derived from a corruption of the Irish *Dubh Linn* (Dark Pool), and more recently associated with the name *Baile Átha Cliath* (the Town of the Hurdle Ford), is the capital of Ireland. Dublin County Borough has 525,900 inhabitants, with an additional 477,300 in the rest of the County, including the Borough of Dún Laoghaire, making a total of 1,003,150.

It occupies an attractive site at the head of Dublin Bay, protected by the hilly promontory of Howth to the N, and the headland of Dalkey to the S. Dublin itself is divided transversely from W to E by the river Liffey, embanked throughout its course within the city. Few of its surviving buildings, with the exception of its two cathedrals, date back further than the middle of the 18C, but its imposing Georgian squares and terraces (some unfortunately derelict), and many of its public buildings, are fine examples of late 18C civic architecture; indeed a remarkable amount still remains of Dublin as depicted in James Malton's 'Picturesque and Descriptive Views' of 1792–99.

Much is being done, somewhat belatedly, to improve the sad appearance of parts of the town, which over the years has been allowed to deteriorate in the hands of speculators. Considerable work still remains to be done in restoring damaged buildings and depressed areas. Regrettably, this is too often an uphill struggle, although several new buildings are themselves of quality architecturally, even if they are entirely out of context.

Not the least charm of the city is its surroundings, the neighbouring seaboard offering a variety of sandy strands and attractive scenery; to the N and W extends the fertile plain of Meath; while not far to the S rise the Wicklow Mountains, offering a pleasant haven from the city.

In the city itself are the outstanding collections of the *National Gallery of Ireland*, and—not far from the centre—the *Chester Beatty Library*; the cathedrals of *Christ Church* and *St. Patrick's*; the extensive sanctuary of *Trinity College* and its famous *Library*; and among the more important public buildings, those of the Old Parliament House (now *The Bank of Ireland*), the *Custom House*, the *Four Courts* (of Justice), *Dublin Castle*, and the *Royal Hospital* at Kilmainham, apart from numerous lesser known monuments. All these contribute to making it one of the more interesting European cities to visit. The importance of its cultural contribution over the centuries, particularly in the field of literature, need hardly be emphasised. Among sporting events, the Dublin Horse Show in August is world-famous; its stout, synonymous with 'Guinness', needs little commendation.

The **Tourist Office** at 14 Upper O'Connell will provide information on accommodation, restaurants, theatre bookings, etc. and details of cinema programmes, concerts, exhibitions, day tours and other entertainments.

AIRLINE OFFICES. *Aer Lingus* offices are at 40 Upper O'Connell St and 42 Grafton St. *British Airways* offices are at 112 Grafton St. *TWA* at 44 Upper O'Connell St. *Dublin Airport* is at *Collinstown*, 8km N of Dublin; the *Air Terminal* is at the *Busáras*, Store St.

RAILWAY STATIONS. The main railway stations of Dublin are *Heuston Station* and *Connolly Station*, W and NE of the city centre respectively; see Plans.

BUS STATIONS. There are offices of *CIE* (Córas Iompair Eireann; Irish Transport Board) at 59 O'Connell St and 35 Lower Abbey St, which can provide details of provincial and local services as can the *Busáras* (Bus Station, Store St; Pl. 4), where bus timetables and plans of routes in Dublin can be obtained.

GPO. On the W side of O'Connell St: see Pl. 3 and p 137.

For the addresses of *Embassies*, *Consulates* and *Cultural* bodies, etc. see p 85. See also pp 88–9 for details of *Sporting* and other organisations in Dublin.

The Irish name for Dublin, *Baile Átha Cliath*, confirms that there was long a crossing of the Liffey here, but its importance dates from the Danish invasion of the 9C, when Vikings settled near the estuary and built a defensive wall. Here they remained, harrying the surrounding country, and also trading, until their defeat by Brian Ború at Clontarf in 1014, which certainly curtailed their activities. In 1170/71 the Danes were driven out by the Anglo-Normans, Hasculf, their leader, being taken prisoner and executed when attempting to regain the place. In 1172 Henry II received the homage of several Irish chieftains where College Green now stands, and gave the city by charter to the men of Bristol. It became the seat of government in an area of varying extent, which was fortified by castles held by Anglo-Norman barons, and known as the *Pale*. This was in turn harried by tribes from the Wicklow Mountains, notably in 1209, and it was unsuccessfully assaulted in 1316 by Edward Bruce. In 1486 Lambert Simnel was crowned in Christ Church. Dubliners showed scant support for the rebellion of 'Silken Thomas' Fitzgerald in 1534. George Browne, Archbishop of Dublin in 1536–54, was largely responsible for introducing the Reformation into Ireland. In 1580 Edmund Spenser, the poet, arrived here to take up the post as secretary to the lord deputy.

At first, under the Marquess of Ormonde, Dublin held out for Charles I during the Civil War, in 1646 resisting Owen Roe O'Neill's army, but in the following year it surrendered to Parliamentary forces, and Ormonde was heavily defeated at Rathmines in 1649 in an attempt to regain the city. James II held his last parliament here in 1689, and caused the base coinage known as 'brass money' to be struck, which became a serious grievance. Public street-lighting had been introduced in 1697. The xpopulation of Dublin at the time was approx. 64,500; by 1750 it was between 130,000 and 150,000; by 1800 this had grown to 200,000, and by 1841 to 372,700. In 1757 the 'Wide Street Commissioners' were established, an organisation which did much to improve the town. The 'Paving Board' was set up in 1773.

The history of 19C Dublin was turbulent: in 1798 Lord Edward Fitzgerald died of wounds resisting arrest during the rebellion of that year; in 1803 Lord Chief Justice Kilwarden was murdered in the street, and Robert Emmet was executed for his part in a projected but abortive rising. The Repeal movement coincided with the founding of 'The Nation' newspaper in 1842 by Charles Gavan Duffy, Thomas Davis and John Blake Dillon, with whom John Mitchel later allied himself, before being tried for sedition and transported. In 1844 Daniel O'Connell, elected Lord Mayor in 1841, was incarcerated in Richmond Gaol on a charge of creating discontent and disaffection. In 1873 the first great Home Rule conference was held in the Rotunda, while a few years later (1881–82) saw the height of the Land League agitation in Dublin: its leaders, including Charles Stewart Parnell, were thrown into Kilmainham Gaol. Members of a secret society calling themselves 'The Invincibles' haunted the streets; Lord Frederick Cavendish, the new Chief Secretary, was assassinated in Phoenix Park. Home Rule activity increased during the next few years, and in 1905 the Sinn Féin movement was founded at a meeting at the Rotunda. In 1913 the life of the city was paralysed by strikes fomented by James Larkin, while labour organisations were defended by the Citizen Army. In 1914 the Irish Volunteers were enrolled, to counterbalance the illegal establishment of the Ulster Volunteers. The unfortunate 'Bachelors' Walk affair' followed an attempt at arming the Irish Volunteers by the Howth gun-running.

In 1916 took place the 'Easter Rising', in which the Post Office, City Hall, South Dublin Union, and other public buildings were taken over by the Irish Volunteers co-operating with the Citizen Army. The movement was partly crushed by spasmodically repressive measures, but in 1919 the first Sinn Féin parliament, under the presidency of De Valéra, met in the Mansion House, later deciding to support the guerrilla bands that were causing disturbances throughout the country. The assassination of Alan Bell, a magistrate, in March 1920, led to reprisals and counter-reprisals, culminating in 'Bloody Sunday' (21 November) and the burning of the Custom House (25 May, 1921).

A settlement was meanwhile under way, and the treaty establishing the Irish Free State was ratified by the Dáil in January 1922. England was now partially extricated from the 'troubles', but Dublin still suffered from fire and slaughter. The armed members of the reactionary faction objecting to Home Rule, shelled out of their strongholds in the Four Courts and in O'Connell Street, in June 1922 began a campaign of incendiarism which was gradually suppressed by the strong hand of the Dublin government. The murder of Kevin O'Higgins, the most vigorous administrator of law and order, in 1927, was the last outburst of anarchy. By 1931 most of the public buildings had been restored to their original use.

Although the Free State remained neutral in 1939, some suburbs of Dublin were mistakenly—or perhaps as a threat—bombed by German aircraft in 1940. In the following spring the fire engines of Dublin raced to the succour of Belfast.

The last 40 years have seen a growth of new industries in the outskirts of the city, and the erection of a number of new buildings, many of them of considerable architectural merit. Much work remains to be done to improve the appearance of some very central areas, apart from the demolition of derelict dwellings.

With the unfortunate recrudescence of 'troubles' in the 'Six Counties' in the late 1960s, some fanatics endeavoured to spread the conflict. The burning down of the British Embassy in Merrion Square on 2 February, 1972 was a spontaneous retaliatory reaction to the deplorable turn of events in Derry; the killing of Christopher Ewart Biggs, the British Ambassador, by a terrorist land-mine (28 July 1976) was an inexcusable action universally condemned.

Among the more famous citizens of Dublin the following may be listed. In the realm of scholarship and literature: Richard Stanyhurst (1547–1618); James Ussher (1581–1656); Sir James Ware (1594–1666); Sir John Denhaem (1615–69); William Molyneux (1656–98); Thomas Southerne (1660–1746); Jonathan Swift (1667–1745); Sir Richard Steele (1672–1729); Thomas Parnell (1679–1718); Edward Malone (1741–1812), the Shakespearean scholar; John O'Keefe (1747–1833); Richard Brinsley Sheridan (1751–1816); Thomas Moore (1779–1852); Charles Robert Maturin (1782–1824), author of 'Melmoth the Wanderer'; George Petrie (1789–1866), the antiquary; Samuel Lover (1797–1868); Anna Maria Hall (1800–81), author of 'Tales of the Irish Peasantry'; James Clarence Mangan (1803–49); Charles James Lever (1806–72); Joseph Sheridan Le Fanu (1814–73); W.E.H. Lecky (1838–1903), the historian; Bram Stoker (1847–1912), author of 'Dracula'; Oscar Wilde (1854–1900); George Bernard Shaw (1856–1950); Katharine Tynan (1861–1931); William Butler Yeats (1865–1939); John Millington Synge (1871–1909); Oliver St. John Gogarty (1878–1957); Seán O'Casey (1880–1964); James Joyce (1882–1941); James Stephens (1882–1950); Samuel Becket (born 1906); and Brendan Behan (1923–64).

The arts are represented by: George Barret (1732–84); Robert Carver (fl. 1750–91); Samuel Percy (1750–1820), the wax-modeller; William Mossop (1751–1805), the medallist; Nathaniel Hone (1718–84); Hugh Douglas Hamilton (1739–1808); Thomas Hickey (1741–1824); Sir Martin Archer Shee (1769–1850); Sir William Orpen (1878–1931); Albert Power (1882–1945), the sculptor; Evie Hone (1894–1955); and Francis Bacon (born 1909).

Among composers: John Field (1782–1837, in Moscow); Michael William Balfe (1808–70); and Sir Charles Villiers Stanford (1852–1924); and the singer and friend of Mozart, Michael Kelly 1764?–1826).

Among Irish patriots: James Napper Tandy (1740–1803); Henry Grattan (1746–1820); Theobald Wolfe Tone (1763–98); Robert Emmet (1778–1803); Thomas Clarke Luby (1821–1901); John Dillon (1851–1927); and Arthur Griffith (1872–1922).

And in their various fields: Sir Thomas Molyneux (1661-1733), and Robert Graves (1797–1853), physicians; Samuel Madden (1686–1765), the philanthropist; George Faulkner (c 1699–1775), the bookseller and printer; 'Peg' Woffington (1718–60), the actress; Edmund Burke (1729–97), statesman and orator; Arthur Wellesley, Duke of Wellington (1769–1852); Alexander Mitchell (1780–1868; died in Belfast), inventor of the screw-pile; F.M. Lord Wolseley (1833–1913); Lord Carson (1854–1935), the apologist of Union.

Note. The names of streets in Dublin are written up in both English and Irish. The numbering of houses in some of the older streets is consecutive, starting one side and returning down the other, so that No. 1 may be opposite No. 365.

Dublin and its immediate environs are covered in the following six sections. In addition to Rtes 1E, F, and G, the excursion to *Castletown House* at Celbridge (see Rte 19) may easily be made by car.

Hours of admission to the principal Monuments, Museums, and Collections.

CT = Conducted tour. All these times are subject to change, and one should check with Tourist Offices for the latest information.

	Open
Bank of Ireland	Mon., Tues., Wed., Fri. 10.00–12.30; 13.30– 15.00. Thurs. 10.00–12.30; 13.30–17.00
Chester Beatty Library	Tues.–Fri. 10.00–17.00. Sat. 14.00–17.00 CT Wed. and Sat. at 14.30
Christ Church cathedral	Oct.–Apr. Tues.–Fri. 9.30–12.45; 14.00–17.00; Sat. 9.30–12.45. May–Sept. Mon.–Sat. 9.30–17.00
Civic Museum	Tues.–Sat. 10.00–18.00; Sun. 11.00–14.00
Dublin Castle: State Apartments	Mon.–Fri. 10.00–12.15; 14.00–17.00. Sat.– Sun. 14.00–17.00. Check in advance by tel. 777129
Four Courts	Mon.–Fri. 9.30–17.00
James Joyce Tower, Dún Laoghaire	May–Sept. Mon.–Sat. 10.00–13.00; 14.00– 17.00. Sun. 14.30–18.00. Oct.–Apr. by appoint. Tel. 808571
Kilmainham Jail	Sun. 15.00–17.00. CT Wed. in June/July 10.00– 12.00; 14.30–16.00
Kilmainham: Royal Hospital	Sat. and Sun. Check by tel. 718666
Malahide Castle	Mon.–Fri. 10.00–12.45; 14.00–17.00. Apr.– Oct. Sat. 11.00–18.00. Sun. 14.00–18.00. Nov.–Mar. Sat. and Sun. 14.00–17.00
Marino Casino	Apr.–Sept. 10.00–19.00 daily. Oct.–Mar. Sat. 10.30–17.30. Sun. 14.00–17.00
Marsh's Library	Mon., Wed., Thur., Fri. 10.30–12.30; 14.00– 16.00. Sat. 10.30–12.30
Municipal Gallery	Tues.–Sat. 9.30–18.00. Sun. 11.00– 17.00
National Gallery	Mon.–Sat. 10.00–18.00. Thur. 10.00–21.00. Sun. 14.00–17.00
National Library	Mon.–Thur. 10.00–21.00. Fri. 10.00–17.00. Sat. 10.00–13.00
National Museum	Tues.–Sat. 10.00–17.00. Sun. 14.00–17.00
Royal Irish Academy	Mon. 9.30–17.15 (or 19.45 July–Sept.). Tues.– Fri. 9.30–17.15
St. Michan's	Mon.–Fri. 10.00–12.45; 14.00–16.45; Sat. 10.00–12.45
St. Patrick's cathedral	Mon.–Fri. 9.00–18.00. Sat. 9.00–16.00. Sun. 10.00–11.00; 14.00–15.00
St. Werburgh's	Mon.–Fri. 10.00–16.00 by arrangement; tel. 783710
Trinity College; Old Library	Mon.–Fri. 9.30–16.45. Sat. 9.30–12.45

The topography of Dublin can be best understood by taking the **O'Connell Bridge** (Pl. 3) as a point of reference, although it is no longer the focal point of the city. Formerly known as Carlisle Bridge, it was built in 1792–94 by James Gandon, rebuilt and widened in 1880, and is the principal bridge spanning the *Liffey*, here 42m wide. The

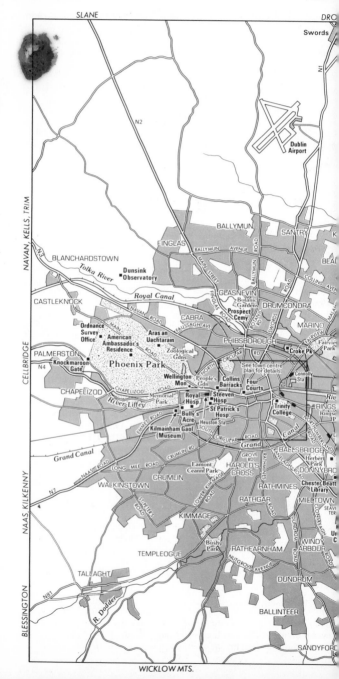

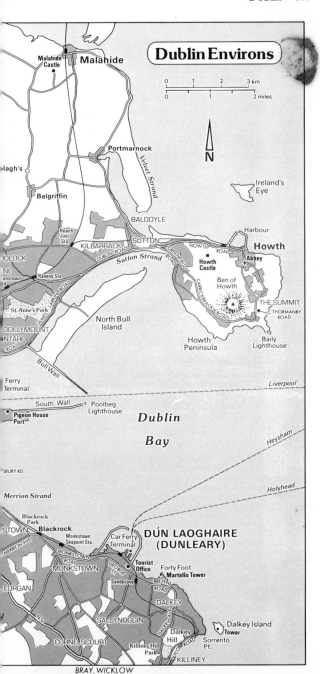

Dublin Environs

0   1   2   3 km
0   1   2 miles

N

Malahide Castle
Malahide
Portmarnock
Velvet Strand
Ireland's Eye
...lagh's
Balgriffin
BALDOYLE
Harbour
Howth Junc Sta.
KILBARRACK
SUTTON
HOWTH ROADS
Howth
...OLOCK
DUBLIN ROAD
Sutton Strand
Howth Castle
Abbey
...NE
...onstown
Raheny Sta.
GREENFIELD ROAD
Ben of Howth
St. Anne's Park
JAMES LARKIN ROAD
CARRICKBRACK ROAD
THE SUMMIT
DOLLYMOUNT
North Bull Island
THORMANBY ROAD
...NTARF
...ROAD
Bull Wall
Howth Peninsula
Baily Lighthouse

Ferry Terminal
Liverpool
South Wall
Poolbeg Lighthouse
Pigeon House Port
Dublin Bay
Heysham
...SBURY RD.
Holyhead
Merrion Strand
Blackrock Park
Blackrock
...STOWN
Monkstown Seapoint Sta.
Car Ferry Terminal
DÚN LAOGHAIRE (DUNLEARY)
MONKSTOWN ROAD
MONKSTOWN
GEORGE ST.
Tourist Office
Forty Foot
Martello Tower
Sandycove
BREFFNI ROAD
...LORGAN
N11
DALKEY
SALLYNOGGIN
DALKEY AVE.
Dalkey Hill
Dalkey Island
Tower
CORNELSCOURT
Killiney Hill Park
Sorrento Pt.
VICO ROAD
KILLINEY

BRAY, WICKLOW

river is crossed within the municipal boundaries by ten road bridges, two railway bridges, and one footbridge, and divides Dublin into two somewhat unequal parts; the southern half, being of more intrinsic interest, will be first described. For O'Conxnell St and North Dublin, see Rte 1D.

From the bridge itself, the main building in view looking E along the N bank of the Liffey, is the *Custom House*; see Rte 1D. This lies beyond the tower of *Liberty Hall* (headquarters of the trades unions), its less obtrusive predecessor being a centre of activity in fomenting the independence movement, and is partially obscured by the unsightly 'loop line' *Railway Bridge* (1889). The new *Matthew Talbot road bridge* (1978) spans the river not far beyond, while further E are the docks.

The construction of **Dublin Harbour** was begun in 1714 with the embanking of the Liffey and the construction of a quay known as *North Wall*. The Ballast Board, founded in 1707 to supervise the dredging and lighting of the channel, was succeeded in 1786 by the Port and Docks Board. Later developments were the building of the South Wall and the *Bull Wall*, the latter (to the NE) a mole to guard the harbour from the encroachment of a sandbank called the North Bull Island.

At the beginning of the South Wall is *Ringsend* (the end of the 'rinn' or spit of land between the Liffey and the Dodder), where Cromwell landed in 1646 with 12,000 horse, foot, and artillery to start his brutal subjugation of Ireland. The bridge here dates from 1803. The *South Wall*, a granite breakwater over 5km long, approaches the *Pigeon House Fort* (started in 1748; now a power station) rather more than half-way along it, with a little harbour, the landing-place of the Dublin packet before 1813. Both the power station and harbour were enlarged in 1933–39. The wall beyond leads (2km further) to *Poolbeg Lighthouse* (1762; view of the N shore).

B. Central Dublin South of the Liffey; East of College Green

Few buildings of any merit line the Liffey immediately W of the O'Connell Bridge (see above). From its S end two thoroughfares diverge: that bearing left (SE), D'Olier St, shortly meets the W end of Pearse St.

Patrick Pearse, a leader of the 1916 insurrection, was born in 1879 at No. 27 Pearse St, on the left of which, just beyond the railway bridge, stands *St. Mark's* (1758; deconsecrated).—To the right, a few steps further, is *Pearse St Railway Station*. *St. Andrew's Church* (1832–37; by James Boulger), with its Doric portico, is adjacent.—A short distance further along this otherwise uninteresting street is (right) the headquarters of the *Dublin City Library*, housing the Gilbert Library of MSS and books relating to the history of Dublin; The Dix Collection of early Irish printed books, including some fine Irish bindings; a set of the Cuala Press publications and books by W.B. Yeats, with associated items concerning the Irish Literary Revival; and rare series of Irish Almanacks, newspapers and periodicals, etc.—Pearse St approaches *The Tower* (1862), a former sugar refinery and later iron-foundary, now housing the workshops of the *Tower Design Guild*, where contemporary craftwork is for sale. The road then crosses the Grand Canal (commenced 1765) and the river *Dodder* before bearing SE towards the sea at *Sandymount Strand*.

Bear right at the S end of D'Olier St to skirt the N side of *Trinity College*, with a view ahead of the E front of the *Bank of Ireland*; see below.

Westmoreland St, running directly S from the O'Connell Bridge, also converges on this junction, passing (left) an inferior statue of

College Green in the early 19C, looking E towards Trinity College, with the Bank of Ireland in the centre

Thomas Moore. Immediately to the S is **College Green** (Pl. 5; previously Hoggen Green, the site of the *Viking Haugen* or *Thengmote*, the burial-ground and meeting-place levelled in 1682), a natural focal point of the city. In its centre is a statue of Henry Grattan by John Foley (1879).

A leaden equestrian statue of William III (1701), long an object of popular invective, was removed from here in 1929 after having been damaged by a landmine. It has been replaced by one of Thomas Davis, leader of the Young Ireland movement, by Edward Delany.

On the NW side of College Green stands the *Bank of Ireland, one of the most striking of Dublin's 18C buildings, begun in 1729 by Sir Edward Lovett Pearce to house the Irish Parliament, but in 1803, after the Act of Union, bought by the Bank of Ireland Company (incorporated in 1783) for £40,000.

The main S Front, with an Ionic portico at the back of a square court, is flanked by two semicircular wings with projecting columns and niches alternating. Above the pediment is Hibernia, with Fidelity and Commerce at either side, by Edward Smyth of Dublin (1809). The E Front (by James Gandon; 1785) is rendered effective by the use of Corinthian columns beneath an Ionic entablature; the statues here (1787; also by Smyth) represent Wisdom above, with Justice and Liberty below. The W Front has an Ionic portico of 1797 by Francis Johnston, surmounted by military trophies by Thomas Kirk.
    The interior has been largely rebuilt to accommodate offices, and the old *Court of Requests* is now the main banking hall. The former *House of Lords*, with its coffered ceiling, tapestries woven for the room by Jan van Beaver, with a fine glass chandelier of 1788, and the mace of the House of Commons (1765), can usually be seen on request; as can the *Directors' Dining-room*, with a decorative stucco ceiling taken from a demolished building.

No. 27 College Green was the home of George Chinnery before his departure for the Orient in 1802.

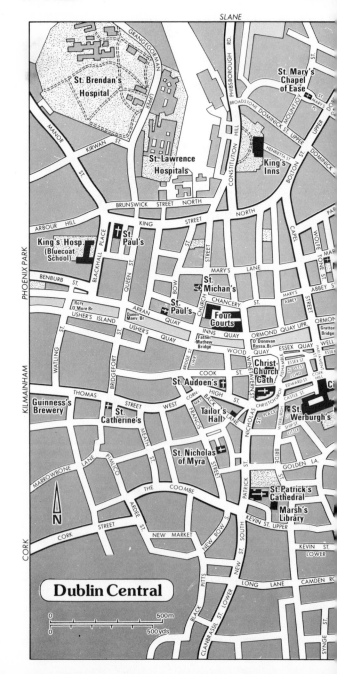

Dublin Central

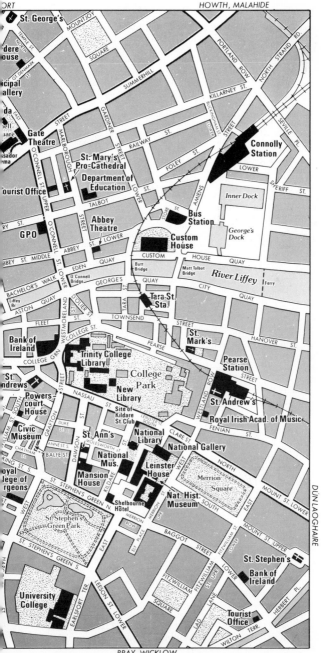

HOWTH, MALAHIDE

ORT

St. George's

dere
ouse

icipal
allery

da

Gate
Theatre

ourist Office

GPO

ABBEY ST. MIDDLE

BACHELOR'S WALK

ASTON QUAY

Bank of
Ireland

St.
ndrews

Powers-
court
House

Civic
Museum

oyal
lege of
rgeons

University
College

MOUNTJOY

SQUARE

TEMPLE ST. NORTH

GT. DENMARK ST.

SUMMERHILL

GARDINER STREET

RAILWAY ST.

KILLARNEY ST.

PORTLAND ROW

NORTH STRAND RD.

SEVILLE PL.

Connolly
Station

LOWER

SHERIFF ST.

Inner Dock

George's
Dock

Bus
Station

Custom
House

CUSTOM HOUSE QUAY

Butt
Bridge

O'Connell
Bridge

Matt Talbot
Bridge

River Liffey

Ferry

CITY QUAY

Tara St.
Sta.

St.
Mark's

HANOVER ST.

Pearse
Station

PEARSE STREET

St. Andrew's

Royal Irish Acad. of Music

FENIAN ST.

National
Library

CLARE ST.

National Gallery

St. Ann's

National
Mus.

Leinster
House

Merrion
Square

Mansion
House

Nat. Hist.
Museum

Shelbourne
Hotel

St. Stephen's
Green Park

BAGGOT STREET

MOUNT ST. UPPER

St. Stephen's

Bank of
Ireland

Tourist
Office

DÚN LAOGHAIRE

BRAY, WICKLOW

For Dame St, running W, see Rte 1C.

The E side of College Green is occupied by the main front of **'TRINITY COLLEGE**, 90m long, with a classical portico of the Corinthian order, built in 1755–59, possibly by Henry Keene (1726–76; only briefly in Dublin) and John Sanderson, supervised by Hugh Darley. It has also recently been attributed to Theodore Jacobsen, architect of the Foundling Hospital in London. In front are statues of Goldsmith and Burke, both by Foley (1863 and 1868 respectively).

The University of Dublin, or Trinity College, familiarly known as 'TCD', was founded by Elizabeth I in 1591 on the site of the Priory of All Hallows, possibly at the instance of Henry Ussher (uncle of James Ussher), Archbishop Loftus, the first provost, and Luke Challoner. It was long the preserve of members of the established Protestant Church, until freed of religious restrictions in 1873, although even in the 1940s it was still considered a pernicious place by the more devout Catholics.

Among its provosts were Richard Baldwin (c 1672–1758; for 41 years from 1717), Francis Andrews, John Hely Hutchinson (1724–94; 'the Prancer'), John Barrett (1753–1821; 'Jacky'), and the classical scholar and 'character', John Pentland Mahaffy (1839–1919).

Among those who have attended Trinity College were: James Ussher, Southerne, Farquhar, Congreve, Swift, Burke, Malone, Samuel Molyneux (the astronomer), William Molyneux (the philosopher), Thomas Molyneux (the physician), George Darley, Thomas Moore, Maturin, Lever, Le Fanu, Oscar Wilde, Synge, Gogarty, William Rowan Hamilton, Henry Flood, Henry Brooke, Goldsmith, Nahum Tate, George Berkeley, Charles Wolfe, John Wilson Croker, William Howard Russell, Thomas Davis, Aubrey de Vere, Samuel Ferguson, Sir Robert Kane (author of 'Industrial Resoures of Ireland'; 1844), Edward Dowden, John Mitchel, James Hannay, Grattan, Wolfe Tone, Robert Emmet, Isaac Butt, J.B. Bury, Bram Stoker, Edward Carson, Douglas Hyde, Samuel Beckett, and Thomas Prior (c 1682–1751; philanthropist, and founder of the Dublin Society).

The average number of students attending the college is 7,000; it distinguished itself by admitting female students to degrees as early as 1903.

The grounds are generally open to the public and provide a pleasant haven in the city centre. Above the main gateway is a hall known as the *Regent House*. The first cobbled quadrangle, called Parliament Square, was erected during the 18C from funds voted by the Irish Parliament. On the right is the *Theatre* (1779–91) or examination hall, with an Adam ceiling by Stapleton, a gilt oak chandelier from the Old House of Commons, and an organ said to have been taken by Ormonde from a Spanish ship at Vigo in 1702. Note also the monument to Provost Richard Baldwin, by Christopher Hewetson.

On the left is the *Chapel* (1798), similar in design, with good woodwork and stucco ceilings. The new organ (1969) preserves the original casework by George Green. In 1973 the chapel was opened to all Christian denominations who have chaplains at the University. Both the Theatre and Chapel were designed by Sir William Chambers, but erected by Graham Myers. Beyond the Chapel is the *Dining-hall* (1743) by Richard Castle (also known as Cassels; born in Hesse-Cassel c 1690, he came to Ireland in c 1727, where he died in 1751), containing portraits of eminent members of the University, restored after a recent fire.

The *Campanile*, by Sir Charles Lanyon, in the centre of the quadrangle, was erected in 1853 for Archbishop Beresford. A short distance beyond, reclining on the green sward, is a figure by Henry Moore. William Hartpole Lecky (1838–1903), the historian and a professor here, is commemorated by a statue.

The **'Old Library**, on the right of the second quadrangle, was begun by Thomas Burgh in 1712 and completed in 1732, and since 1801 has been one of the Copyright Libraries. The collection of books it contains was started in 1601; later acquisitions include the library of Archbishop James Ussher in 1661, and the Fagel collection, purchased in 1802. It now contains some 5,000 MSS and two million printed books (including the New Library; see below).

Interior of Trinity College Old Library

On the Ground Floor are book stores; until enclosed in 1892, this was an arcaded loggia (the 'Colonnades'; modelled on the Library of Trinity College, Cambridge). At the W end a staircase (1750, by Castle), with plasterwork by Edward Simple, ascends to the *Long Room* (60m long), its original flat plaster ceiling being replaced by a semicircular barrel-vaulted roof in 1856–62. Some of the busts here, including those of distinguished fellows, deserve attention, among them that of Swift, by Roubiliac, and Patrick Delany, by Van Nost.

Among the principal treasures of the library is the ***Book of Kells**, a magnificently illuminated copy of the Gospels designed by unknown hands in the monastery of Kells in Meath in c 800.

Rebound in four volumes in 1953, two are normally displayed in rotation. It comprises 340 profusely decorated pages. At the beginning of each Gospel is a sumptuous coloured illustration, while others, only slightly less so, embellish each chapter, and all the borders, capital letters, etc., are the classical standard of early Irish decoration. The *cumdach*, or metal shrine which once enclosed it, was stolen before the dissolution of the monastery, but the book passed into the possession of the Bishop of Meath, and was given to the college after 1660.

Other cases contain the *Book of Durrow (7C), the earliest of the collection, but no longer preserving its silver case, lost after 1677; the 8C *Book of Dimma (from Roscrea), with its cumdach of silver-plated bronze (c 1150); and the *Book of Armagh* (c 807), which contains the entire New Testament, with its satchel of stamped leather (early 11C). Lord Curzon had observed the custom of placing valuable books in such satchels in Greek and Coptic monasteries, and hanging them beyond the reach of rats.

Remaining cases exhibit a selection of autographs, etc. An Irish harp, also preserved here, misleadingly called that 'of Brian Ború', is nevertheless one of the oldest and most elaborate instruments of its type (c 1400). The carved Royal Arms of Elizabeth I near the exit are the only extant relics of the original college building. The *Manuscript Room* is also in the Old Library building, containing the MSS of J.M. Synge and William H. Lecky, the correspondence of Sir Arthur Chichester, the diaries of Wolfe Tone, etc.

By the E end of the Old Library, between the Fellows' Garden and the College Park, stands the *New Library* (1967; by Paul Koralek). Adjacent to the S, approached from a new entrance in Nassau St, are the functional *Arts and Social Science Buildings*, also by Koralek.

The so-called 'Magnetic Observatory' of 1837, by Frederick Darley, which stood here, has been re-erected at *University College* (cf.).

On the opposite (N) side of the Square is the *Graduates' Memorial Building* (1892), with a quadrangle of 1790–1806 called Botany Bay behind. On the E side is the red brick '*Rubrics*', the oldest range in the college (c 1690), but mutilated during restoration in 1894.—New Square, the third quadrangle, contains (left) the *Doric Printing House*, built by Castle in 1734 for John Stearne, Bishop of Clogher; and right, the *Museum Building* (by Benjamin Woodward), and other mid-19C structures. Behind extends the College Park, with sports grounds, beyond which are the medical and science faculty buildings. The geological collections, and the *Herbarium* of Trinity College, may be visited by prior appointment.

An exit at the SE corner of the grounds is the closest direct approach to the *National Gallery*; see below.

Turning left on making our exit from the main front of Trinity College, we pass (left) the ***Provost's House** (1760), built for Provost Andrews by John Smyth.

It contains plasterwork by Patrick and John Wall, and a collection of paintings bequeathed to the college by the Rev. Samuel Madden. In the great saloon is a portrait of the 4th Duke of Bedford, by Gainsborough.

Just beyond, Grafton St diverges right, a narrow but busy commercial thoroughfare which leads S towards St. Stephen's Green; see p 119.

Bearing left at this junction, follow Nassau St (widened 1834, and previously St. Patrick's Well Lane), flanking the grounds of Trinity College, and passing (right) the N end of Dawson St (see p 124).

A modern building houses the *Kilkenny Shop* (established by the government-sponsored Kilkenny Design Workshops), where a representative cross-section of recent Irish workmanship and design may be seen and bought.

Nassau St is prolonged by Leinster St, off which Kildare St leads S (see p 121). On the corner here, in a brick 'Venetian palazzo' of 1860 by Benjamin Woodward, was the former home of the prestigious *Kildare Street Club*, the traditional refuge of Dublin conservatism, and now of the Alliance Française.

Continuing E along Clare St, we shortly reach the NW corner of ***Merrion Square** (Pl. 6/8), a large quadrangle, 275m long and 165m wide, once Lord Fitzwilliam of Meryon's land, lined on three sides by dignified Georgian mansions (1762 *et seq.*; mainly by John Ensor). Formerly it was the abode of professional men, but many of the houses have now been divided up into offices. The central gardens were the site of kitchens dispensing soup to starving refugees in 1847–49.—

No. 1, on the corner, with its conservatory, was the home of Sir William and 'Speranza' Wilde; their son, Oscar Wilde, was born (1854) at No. 21 Westland Row, a short distance N, where the town house of Lord Conyngham (No. 36), built in 1771 by Nicholas Tench for his own use, has since 1871 housed part of the *Royal Irish Academy of Music.*

Other distinguished denizens of Merrion Square were Daniel O'Connell (No. 58); W.B. Yeats (at No. 82, from 1922–28); Sheridan Le Fanu, who died at No. 70; and 'AE' Russell, who lived at No. 84. No. 39 was the British Embassy until February 1972, when it was burnt out following a riot in reprisal for military brutality in Londonderry; No. 42 was the home of Sir Jonah Barrington, the diarist.

Lower Mount St prolongs the N side of the square, passing near *Sir Patrick Dun's Hospital* (1803; built from a design by Henry Aaron Baker, following a bequest of Sir Patrick Dun, 1642–1713, the physician). It is extended beyond the Grand Canal by Northumberland Rd; at No. 130 J.M. Synge died in 1909.

Opposite the W side of Merrion Square, with the restored *Rutland Fountain* (1791), is Leinster Lawn, with an 18m-high *Obelisk* commemorating Arthur Griffith, Michael Collins, and Kevin O'Higgins (among the more eminent founders of the 'Free State'). Beyond is the E front of *Leinster House*; see p 124. The first balloon ascent in Ireland, by Richard Crosbie, took place here in 1783.

On the N side of Leinster Lawn, entered from Merrion Sq., is the *NATIONAL GALLERY OF IRELAND. Designed by Francis Fowke, it was opened in 1864, owing its inception largely to William Dargan (1799–1867), prime mover of the Exhibition of 1853, held on the adjacent Leinster Lawn. The building was later enlarged, and further extended in 1968.

It is not generally appreciated that it is one of the larger galleries in Europe. Naturally, there is a generous representative collection of the Irish School, but much of its strength lies in its small Dutch masters and works of the 17C French, Italian, and Spanish Schools; it also contains two rooms devoted to Continental drawings and English watercolours.

The building also accommodates an extensive *Art Reference Library, Lecture Theatre* (where free public lectures are regularly given), and a good self-service *Restaurant* (open during gallery hours).

By the entrance is a statue (1927) of George Bernard Shaw by Paul Troubetzkoy (1866–1938); Shaw bequeathed one third of his estate to the gallery, which had given him so much pleasure in his youth. Among other benefactors have been Sir Hugh Lane, Sir Alfred Chester Beatty, and the Countess of Milltown. For other *Sculpture*, see p 118.

R8, adjacent to the Entrance foyer, contains a **Bookstall** selling publications on Irish art and architecture, etc. in general, apart from the much-improved illustrated summary catalogues of the collections of the National Gallery.

To the left of the entrance is **R1** (see plan), containing several particularly large canvasses, among them *David Wilkie*, Napoleon and Pius VII at Fontainebleau. From the far end steps ascend to **R14**, devoted to temporary exhibitions. **R1A** displays two 11–12C frescoes from St.-Pierre-de-Campublic (Beaucaire; near Avignon) representing Christ enthroned, and an Annunciation and Adoration of the Magi; also a collection of **Icons** (13–18C) purchased with money from the Shaw Bequest, and several works largely of the **early Italian Schools**, including *Fra Angelico*, The attempted martyrdom of SS Cosmas and Damian with their brothers; *anon. 15C Florentine* The Battle of Anghiara (1440), and The taking of Pisa (1405); *Master of*

Marradi, The story of Lucretia; *Uccello*, Virgin and child; *Andrea di Bartolo*, St. Galganus; *Giovanni del Biondo*, Virgin and child with angels; *Pseudo Domenico di Michellino*, The Assumption; *Giacomo del Pisano*, Virgin and child with SS Mary Magdalen and Peter; *Jacques Yverni*, Annunication; also a collection of 14–18C icons.

RR2–7; largely **Irish School**. Portraits by *John Butler Yeats*; several works by *William Leech*; *Francis Danby*, The opening of the Sixth Seal; *John Mulvany*, View of Kilmallock; *James Arthur O'Connor*, Ballinrobe House, and Gardens; *Thomas Hickey*, An Actor between the Muses of Tragedy and Comedy, An Indian girl, Col William Kirkpatrick with attendants; *George Chinnery*, Portrait of a Mandarin, Mrs. Conyingham, The artist's wife; *Hugh Douglas Hamilton*, several portraits including the Earl-bishop of Derry with his granddaughter; *Gilbert Stuart*, William Burton-Conyingham; *Hugh eHoward* (1675–1738), Arcangelo Corelli, the Composer; *Stephen Slaughter*, A lady and child; *Thomas Frye*, Sir Charles Kemeys-Tynte; *Garret Morphey*, William, 4th Viscount Molyneux of Maryborough and Bridget, Viscountess Molyneux; *Philip Hussey*, An interior with members of a family; *Robert Hunter*, A gentleman with gun and dog; *Nathaniel Grogan*, The river Lee approaching Cork; *Thomas Roberts*,

George Barret the Younger, Self-portrait (National Gallery of Ireland)

Landscapes; *James Latham*, Bishop Clayton and his wife. *John Lewis* (fl. 1750–57; scene-painter of Smock Alley Theatre), Portraits of Peg Woffington; *Nathaniel Hone the elder*, Self-portrait, The Piping Boy (Camillus, the artist's son), Horace Hone sketching, The conjuror; *William Ashford*, Views of Dublin from Clontarf, eand from Chapelizod, and of Dublin Bay; *Anon.* View of Leixlip castle (c 1750); *George Barret*, Landscapes, including Powerscourt waterfall; *Robert Carver*, Landscape; *John Comerford*, Mrs Dobbyn; *Martin Archer Shee*, Mrs Clementson; and several representative works by *Nathaniel Hone the younger*, *Walter Osborne*, and *Jack B. Yeats.*

From **R28** (see below), to the right of the entrance foyer, we may turn into R29, with a collection of Enamels, Miniatures, including examples of this genre by *Nathaniel Hone the elder*, and *Horace Hone*, and Objets d'Art. **RR 28 and 30** are devoted to the **French School**, including Still Lifes by *Desportes* and *Chardin*; *Chardin*, The young governess, The card-trick; *Greuze*, The Capuchin doll; *Roslin*, Portrait of the Marquis de Vaudreuil; *Perronneau*, Male portrait; *Courbet*, Portrait of Dr Adolphe Marlet; *Poussin*, Acis and Galatea, Entombment, Bacchante and Satyr, and The Holy Family; *Claude Lorraine*, Juno confiding Io to the care of Argus; *Louis Le Nain*, Adoration of the shepherds; *Rigaud*, Portrait of Philippe Roettiers; *attrib. Étienne de la Tour*, The image of St. Alexis; *Baron Gérard*, Julie Bonaparte and her daughters; *David*, The funeral of Patroclus; *Millet*, The stile; *Signac*, Lady on a terrace; Landscapes by *Daubigny*, *Harpignies*, *Corot*, *Sisley*, and *Monet*; Portraits by *Largillière* and *Nattier*; *Berthe Morisot*, Le corsage noir; *Alexis Simon Belle*, Portrait of Sir Carnaby Haggerston; *Nanine Vallain*, presumed Portrait of Letitia Bonaparte (Madame Mère); *after François Fabre*, John Henry, 2nd Marquis of Lansdowne; *Pissarro*, Flowers in a Chinese vase; *Meissonier*, Group of cavalry in the snow; *Nolde*, Woman in a garden. (R31, adjacent, now accommodates the Restaurant.)

Jonathan Swift, by Charles Jervas (left), and Esther Johnson, Irish School (right)

From **R28** we reach the foot of the spiral stairs, on the walls of which hang *Henry Munns*, Portrait of Francis Danby; *Thomas Lawrence*, John Wilson Croker, and John Philpot Curran; *George Barret the younger*, Self-portrait; *Charles Jervas*, Jonathan Swift; *René Berthon*, Lady Morgan; *George Watts*, Mrs Caroline Norton; *James Latham*,

Esther Johnson ('Stella'); *Francis Cotes*, Maria Gunning, Countess of Coventry; *Sydney Hall*, Charles Stewart Parnell; *Thomas Hickey*, Edmund Burke and Charles James Fox; *Walter Osborne*, Edward Dowden, and The Ward Hunt; *John Butler Yeats*, Lady Augusta Gregory, W.B. Yeats, George Moore, and Douglas Hyde; *Henry Jones Thaddeus*, John Redmond; *John Collier*, George Bernard Shaw; *Nathaniel Dance*, Arthur Murphy; *James Barry*, Self-portrait as Timanthes; *attrib. Romney*, Elizabeth Gunning, Duchess of Argyll; *Romney*, Mary Tighe; *George Mulvany*, Thomas Moore, and Daniel O'Connell; *Jacques-Émile Blanche*, James Joyce; *Sarah Purser*, 'AE' Russell, Roger Casement, and Jack B. Yeats; *Casimir de Markievicz*, Constance Markievicz (the artist's wife); *Sarah Harrison*, Sir Hugh Lane; *Hugh Douglas Hamilton*, Richard Lovell Edgeworth; *Martin Archer Shee*, Henry Grattan; *Tilly Kettle* with *William Cuming*, James Gandon; *Philip Hussey*, Presumed Portrait of Hester van Homrigh

Thomas Hickey, Edmund Burke in conversation with his friend Charles James Fox (National Gallery of Ireland)

('Vanessa'); *Richard Livesay*, James Caulfield, 1st Earl of Charlemont; *Pavel Tchelitchev*, James Joyce.

The stair passes **R33** on the mezzanine floor, the venue of occasional exhibitions of **Drawings and Watercolours**, of which the gallery preserves an exceptional collection (the illustrated summary Catalogue runs to 850pp), any of which may be seen on application. Among them are a series of 31 watercolours by *Turner*, bequeathed to the gallery in 1900.

R34 German School. *Cranach the elder*, Judith with the head of Holofernes; *Bernhard Strigel*, Count Montfort and Roetenfels; *Conrad Faber*, Heinrich Knoblauch and Katherina Knoblauchin; *Wolfgang Huber*, Anthony Hundertpfundt; *Georg Pencz*, Portrait of Georg Fischer.

Conrad Faber, Katherina Knoblauchin (National Gallery of Ireland)

RR21 and **35; Flemish and early Netherlandish Schools**; and **RR36–7, Dutch School**. *Brueghel the younger*, Peasant wedding; *Isembrandt*, Virgin and child in a landscape (? Rest on the Flight into Egypt); *School of Isembrandt*, Temptation of St. Anthony; *Jan de Cock*, The Flight into Egypt; *after Van der Weyden*, St. Luke painting the Virgin; *attrib. Ambrosius Benson*, Portrait of a lady (as the Magdalen) reading; *Pourbus the younger*, Portrait of a lady; *Jan Mandyn*, Christ in limbo; *Jan Siberechts*, The Farm cart; *Rubens*, Annunciation; and with *Jan Brueghel*, Christ in the house of Martha and Mary; *Van Dyck*, Portrait of Frederick Marselaer, Boy standing on a terrace; *Teniers the younger*, Farmhouse interior, The three philosophers; and with *Lucas van Uden*, Peasants merrymaking; *Willem Duyster*, A man and his wife, Interior with soldiers, Interior with figures; *Van Goyen*, View of Rhenen-on-the-Rhine; *attrib. Elyas Isack*, The five senses; *Johannes van Kessel*, The dam at Amsterdam; *Jacob van Ruisdael* and *Thomas de Keyser*, Soestdijk near the Hague; *Dirck van Delen* and *Dirck Hals*, Interior with ladies and cavaliers; *Jacob Duck*, Interior with woman sleeping; *Matthias Stomer*, The Arrest of Christ; *Jan Steen*, Village school; *Pieter de Molyn the elder*, Prince Maurits and Prince Frederik Hendrik going to the chase; *Wouvermans*, The cavalry halt; *Nicolaes Berchem*, Stag hunt; *Cornelis Troost*, The dilettanti (Jeronimus Tonneman, and his son playing a flute); *Jan Lagoor* and *Adriaen van de Velde*, The ferry-boat; *attrib. Gerrit van Honthorst*, A feasting scene; *Ludolf de Jongh*, Shooting party; *after Van de Velde the younger*, Man-of-war firing a salute; *Jacob van Ruisdael*, Wooded landscape; *after Jacob van Ruisdael*, Stormy sea; *Salomon von Ruisdael*, The halt; *Jan-A. Beerstraten*, The Heyligewegs Gate at Amsterdam; *Frans Post*, View in Brazil; *Van Ostade*, Boors drinking and singing; *Jan Molenaer*, Peasants teaching a cat and dog to dance; *Pieter Claesz*, Still life; *Willem Heda*, Still life; *Anthonie de Lorme*, Church interiors, including the St. Laurenskerk, Rotterdam; *Pieter de Hooch*, Tric-trac players; *Govaert Flink*, Head of old man and Portrait of Louis van der Linden; *Rembrandt*, Rest on the Flight into Egypt; *Studio of Rembrandt*, Portrait of a young lady; *Jan Lievens*, Portrait of an old man (? Rembrandt's father); *Jacob Cuyp*, Portrait of an old lady, and others; *Karel du Jardin*, The Ridingschool; *Abraham van den Temple*, Portrait of a lady; *Bartholomeus van der Helst*, Portrait of an old lady; *Hondecoeter*, Poultry; *Jan Weenix*, A Japanese crane and King vulture; *Paulus Moreelse*, Portrait of a child; *Jan Mytens*, Lady playing a lute, and Family group; *Michiel van Miereveld*, Portrait of a lady; *Pieter Codde*, Interior with figures; *Godart Kamper*, Violinist; *Dutch School* (1641), Male portrait.

R38 Spanish School. *Murillo*, Joshua van Belle, The Holy Family, Mary Magdalen; *Zurbarán*, Sta Rufina; *Ribera*, San Procopius; *Alonso Coello*, Prince Alexander Farnese; *Pantoja de la Cruz*, Juana de Salinas; *El Greco*, St. Francis in ecstasy; *Bernardo de Castro*, Gomez; *Navarrete*, Abraham and the three angels; *Goya*, The Conde del Tajo, Woman in a white shawl, Lady in a black mantilla, and El Sueño (The dream).

Adjacent are **RR 16–17; British School**. *Reynolds*, Robert Henley, 2nd Earl of Northington, A parody on Raphael's School of Athens, John Hely Hutchinson, Chearles Coote, 1st Earl of Bellamont, George Grenville, Marquis of Buckingham, and his family, and several chavicature portraits; *William Segar*, Robert Devereux, Earl of Essex; *Anon.* Portrait of Sir Walter Raleigh (1598); *Francis Wheatley*, The Dublin

The National Gallery

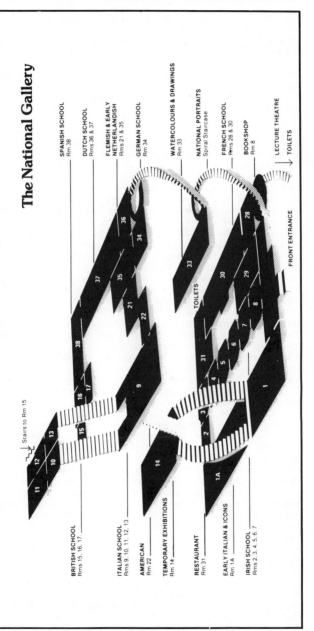

SPANISH SCHOOL
Rm 38

DUTCH SCHOOL
Rms 36 & 37

FLEMISH & EARLY
NETHERLANDISH
Rms 21 & 35

GERMAN SCHOOL
Rm 34

WATERCOLOURS & DRAWINGS
Rm 33

NATIONAL PORTRAITS
Spiral Staircase

FRENCH SCHOOL
Rms 28 & 30

BOOKSHOP
Rm 8

LECTURE THEATRE

TOILETS

BRITISH SCHOOL
Rms 15, 16, 17.

ITALIAN SCHOOL
Rms 9, 10, 11, 12, 13

AMERICAN
Rm 22

TEMPORARY EXHIBITIONS
Rm 14

RESTAURANT
Rm 31

EARLY ITALIAN & ICONS
Rm 1A

IRISH SCHOOL
Rms 2, 3, 4, 5, 6, 7

Stairs to Rm 15

FRONT ENTRANCE

Volunteers in College Green, 4 November 1779, Mr and Mrs Richardson, The Marquess and Marchioness of Antrim; *Hogarth,* Benjamin Hoadly, The Western family, The Mackinnon children; *Zoffany,* David Garrick; *Gainsborough,* the actor James Quin, Gen. James Johnston, Mrs Horton, afterwards Duchess of Cumberland, Duke of Northumberland, View in Suffolk; *Hoppner,* Self-portrait holding fish; *Allan Ramsay,* Sir John Tyrell, Bart.; *Reinagle,* Captain William Congreve with his son, and Mrs Congreve with her children; *Romney,* Portrait of a lady; *William Doughty,* Miss Sisson; *Lawrence,* Lady Elizabeth Foster, afterwards Duchess of Devonshire; *Kneller,* William Congreve; *Anon.,* The Fair Geraldine (Elizabeth Fitzgerald, 1527–89); *Anon.* Portrait of Sir Henry Sidney; *Stubbs,* Sportsmen at rest; *Richard Wilson,* Italian landscapes; *Reaburn,* Matthew Fortescue of Stephenstown.

RR 9–13 accommodate the **Italian Schools**. *17C Bolognese School,* St. John the Baptist in the wilderness; *Guardi,* The Doge wedding the Adriatic; *Moroni,* A widower with his two children; *Batoni,* Pius VI, Joseph Leeson, afterwards 1st Earl of Milltown, and Joseph Leeson, afterwards 2nd Earl of Milltown; *Veronese,* SS Philip and James the Less; *Lorenzo Lotto,* Portrait of a nobleman; *Titian,* Baldassare Castiglione, Ecce Homo; *Pensionate del Saraceni,* St. Peter denying Christ; *Anon.* Portrait of a young man of the Branconio family, c 1610; *Perugino,* Pietà; *Piombo,* Card. Ciocchi del Monte; *attrib. Bellini,* Two Venetian gentlemen; *attrib. Francesco Granacci,* Holy Family with St. John; *Mantegna,* Judith with the head of Holofernes; *Palmizano,* The Virgin enthroned between SS John the Baptist and Lucy; *Castiglione,* A shepherdess finding the infant Cyrus; *Lavinia Fontana,* Visit of the Queen of Sheba to Solomon; *Pordenone,* A Count of Ferrara; *Tintoretto,* A Venetian gentleman; *Longhi,* The artist painting; *Canaletto,* View of the Piazzo San Marco; *Bellotto,* two Views of Dresden; *Panini,* Fête in the Piazza Navona, Rome; *Studio of G.-B. Piazzetta,* A Pastoral Outing; *Filippino Lippi,* The musician; *Mengs,* Portrait of Thomas Conolly; *attrib. Hugh Douglas Hamilton,* Portrait of the Card.-Duke of York.

Sculpture. Among the more important sculptures displayed are the following: *attrib. Barthélemy Prieur* (c 1540–1611), Duc de Mercoeur; *François Duquesnoy* (1594–1643), Portrait of Card. Guido Bentivoglio; *Michael Rysbrack* (1694–1770), Male bust; *attrib. Patrick Cunningham* (fl. 1750–74), Jonathan Swift; *attrib. Juan Alonso Villabrille y Ron* (1663?–1732), The prophet Elias overthrowing the prophets of Baal; *Ferdinand Dietz* (1708–77), Chronos with one of his children; *Christopher Hewetson* (1739–98), Sir Watkins Williams Wynn; *Dalou,* The bather, and Head of a girl; *Rodin,* Brother and sister, Man with a broken nose, Head of Father Julien Eymard; *Renoir,* Pendule, Hymne à la vie; *Bourdelle,* Head of a man; *Maillol,* three female statuettes; *Jacob Epstein,* Head of a girl; *Thomas Kirk,* Bust of Richard Brinsley Sheridan.

Leave the *National Gallery* and turn right to skirt Leinster Lawn. Shortly looking along the S side of Merrion Sq., at the far end of Upper Mount St, the pepper-pot cupola of **St. Stephen's** (1825; by John Bowden, and completed by Joseph Welland) is seen. Although the exterior is in the Greek Revival style, the interior (containing a Snetzler organ-case designed for the Rotunda Chapel in 1754) is Victorian.

We now reach the entrance of the *Natural History Museum,* its interior preserved, like a fly in amber, as it must have been at its inauguration. Nevertheless it contains a remarkably complete collection of Irish fauna, including three perfect skeletons of the prehistoric Irish elk, or—more correctly— Giant Deer (*Megaloceros giganteus*), which became extinct in Ireland c 8000 BC.

Further S, on the opposite side of Upper Merrion St, No. 24, *Mornington House* (without any plaque) was the birthplace of Arthur Wellesley, first Duke of Wellington (29 April, 1769– 1852), the fourth son of Garrett Wellesley (1735–81), first Earl of Mornington, who held the chair of music at Trinity College on its establishment in 1764.

Passing (right) Government Offices and the *College of Science* (1911; by Sir Aston Webb and Sir Thomas Manley Deane), we soon reach Baggot St, which enshrines the name of Baggotrath Castle, the home of the Bagods and the Fitzwilliams, which disappeared early in the 19C. No. 67 Lower Baggot St was the home of Thomas Davis (1814–45), leader of the 'Young Ireland' party, and embellished with his bust. No. 134 was for many years the premises of the Cuala Press.

The SE extension of Baggot St leads to the residential suburb of *Ballsbridge* (see Rte 1F), passing (left), not far beyond East Fitzwilliam St, the administrative offices of the *Bank of Ireland*, a tower block designed by Ronald Tallon (1972), where a continuously changing exhibition of contemporary Irish art may be seen, one of the more impressive commissioned works being the Aubusson tapestry of Patrick Scott, entitled 'Blaze'.

Beyond, to the right, are the offices of *Bord Fáilte* (the Irish Tourist Board), with an information desk, overlooking the Grand Canal, here, in *Wilton Terrace*, pleasantly flanked by trees; while to the left is *Herbert Pl.*, leading to *Huband Bridge* (1791), one of the more attractive canal bridges remaining unaltered. *Portobello House* (1807; formerly the Grand Canal Hotel) has been well restored.

A short distance S is ***Fitzwilliam Square** (Pl. 8), the smallest, latest (1825), and best-preserved of Dublin's Georgian squares. It is now the 'Harley Street' of Dublin, being almost entirely occupied by the medical profession. W.B. Yeats lived in a flat at No. 42 in 1928–32.

Upper Merrion St is prolonged on the far side of Baggot St by **Ely Place** (Pl. 7; pronounced to rhyme with 'high'), a cul-de-sac preserving some interesting relics of Georgian Dublin (c 1770). Long associated with the Law, it was the home (No. 4) of John Philpot Curran (1750–1817) and of the unpopular Earl of Clare, an opponent of Catholic emancipation, derisively called 'Black Jack' Fitzgibbon (1749–1802). When Lord Chancellor he had to barricade his house (No. 6) against a hostile mob (1794).

No. 8 was known as *Ely House*, and is one of the finest Georgian mansions in the city, with a remarkable staircase depicting the Labours of Hercules, and Adam decoration by Michael Stapleton. Barry Yelverton, Lord Avonmore (1736–1805) lived at No. 3. No. 4 was also the residence of George Moore in 1900–11 and is described in 'Hail and Farewell'. No. 25, formerly the home of John Wilson Croker (1780–1857), and later of Oliver St. John Gogarty, now forms part of the art gallery of the *Royal Hibernian Academy*, a modern building out of harmony with the street. No. 36 was briefly the home of Mrs Felicia Hemans (1793–1835), the poetess, who later moved to 21 Dawson St, where she died; her grave is in St. Ann's Church in that street.

Turn W at the bottom of Merrion St into Merrion Row, passing (right) the disused *Cemetery* (1693) of Dublin's Huguenot colony, to approach the NE corner of **St. Stephen's Green** (Pl. 7), a park of 9 hectares. It was an open common until 1663, when it was enclosed, although not finally encircled by buildings until the late 18C. The gardens were laid out in 1880 as a public park at the expense of Lord Ardilaun (Sir Arthur Edward Guinness, 1840–1915).

The *Wolfe Tone Monument*, by Edward Delany, stands at the NE corner; it has lost its two wolfhounds. In the gardens is a memorial to W. B. Yeats by Henry Moore, and here also are busts of James Clarence Mangan (1803–49; by Oliver Sheppard); Thomas M. Kettle (1880–1916), poet and patriot; Jeremiah O'Donovan Rossa (1839–1915), the Fenian; and Countess Constance Markievicz (1884–1927; by Seámus Murphy). The statue of Lord Ardilaun is by Thomas Farrell.

Regrettably, few of the once dignified houses that once surrounded the green retain their charm, many having been converted to office use, or otherwise vulgarised. Whole sections of the square, particularly on the W side and at the SW corner, have been almost entirely demolished by speculators, or remain derelict.

St. Vincent's Hospital, until moved out of town, stood at the SE corner, occupying Meath House, largely rebuilt.

Lower Leeson St, leading SE from this corner, approaches the suburb of *Donnybrook* (see Rte 2A).

On the E side of Earlsfort Terrace (leading SW) is the *Irish Film Theatre*, and opposite stands *Canada House*, beyond which is a plain granite building reconstructed in 1978–81 to house the *National Concert Hall*.

It was formerly the home of *University College*, Dublin, incorporated in 1909 as one of the constituent colleges of the National University, succeeding the Royal University. The original edifice was erected in 1865 for the International Exhibition, and was rebuilt in 1914–18 by R.M. Butler.

A new University campus has been laid out at *Bellfield*; see Rte 2A. Among eminent members have been Douglas Hyde (Professor of Modern Irish, 1908–32) and Eóin MacNéill, co-founders of the Gaelic League, and Kevin O'Higgins, an outstanding member of the first Irish Free State cabinet.

George Borrow stayed briefly at No. 75 St. Stephen's Green South in the summer of 1859, prior to a walking tour in Ireland.—No. 80, the earliest house in Dublin by Richard Castle (1730), once the residence of Lord Iveagh, with extensive gardens behind, is now the *Department of Foreign Affairs*, incorporating No. 81. The Victorian ballroom (1863) was designed by Young of London. Just beyond, No. 85 (*Clanwilliam House*, by Castle; 1739, with stucco ceilings by the Francini brothers) and No. 86 (by Robert West; 1765) form *Newman House* (where Gerard Manley Hopkins was a Classics professor in 1884–89), now incorporated into University College. John Henry Newman was its first Rector (1853–58). Adjacent is the *Catholic University Church* (its bizarre neo-Byzantine interior recently restored), founded by Newman in 1854, and built by John Hungerford Pollen.

From the SW corner of the Green, Harcourt St curves S, many of its red brick houses retaining good 18C stucco work. No. 6, now a Celtic bookshop, became famous as the HQ of the Sinn Féin organisation; it and other houses in the street were occupied by various proscribed departments endeavouring to function surreptitiously with the government set up after the 1918 election had been 'proclaimed'. Edward Carson (1854–1935), the intransigent opponent of Home Rule, was born at No. 4. The former *Harcourt St Station*, at the far end of the street (left), built by George Wilkinson in 1859, has been converted to house the Agricultural Credit Corporation.

No. 33 (then No. 3) Synge St, four streets to the W of and parallel to the S end of Harcourt St, was the modest birthplace of George Bernard Shaw (1856–1950).

In Cuffe St, largely rebuilt, leading W from the SW corner of St. Stephen's Green, No. 35 was the home of 'Honest Jack' Lawless (1773–1837, the intimate of many United Irish leaders), where Shelley stayed on his second visit to Dublin (1813).

On the W side of the Green, the only remarkable building remaining is that of the *Royal College of Surgeons* (1806; by Edward Parke; and in 1825 extended by William Murray), which became the HQ of the Citizens' Army during Easter Week, 1916, with Constance Markievicz much in evidence. Nos 124–25, then one house, was probably the birthplace of Robert Emmet.—Charles Robert Maturin (1782–1824) lived and died at No. 37 York St, adjacent.

Leaving on the left the S end of Grafton St, one may turn E along the N side of St. Stephen's Green, once known as 'Beaux' Walk'. We shortly pass Dawson St (see p 124) to reach, on the corner of Kildare St, the **Shelbourne Hotel** (described in 'A Drama in Muslin' by George Moore, one of many celebrated figures to have resided there); it is still a convenient rendezvous. Its long history has been written up by Elizabeth Bowen. The present building dates from 1865–67; it was the earlier hotel on the site of Shelburne House (*sic*), opened in 1824, which had been patronised by Thackeray in 1842.

In Kildare St, leading N here—originally Coote Lane—stood Lady eMorgan's salon from 1821 until 1839. Born Sydney Owenson (?1783–1859), and daughter of the actor Robert Owenson, who in 1785 opened the Fishamble Street Theatre, she was the author of 'The Wild Irish Girl' (1806), etc.—We pass (right) a modern block of government offices to reach the main front of *Leinster House* (Pl. 5/6; see below), its quadrangle flanked by the *National Museum* and the *National Library*, two nearly symmetrical buildings by Sir Thomas Deane (1890), the main features of which are their massive colonnaded entrance rotundas.

The **NATIONAL MUSEUM** houses a remarkable collection of *Irish Antiquities*, among them some of the finest examples of Early Christian Art in Europe. They deserve a better setting, and attempts are being made to find alternative accommodation, perhaps in part of the *Royal Hospital, Kilmainham* (cf.). The greater part of the collection was made by the Royal Irish Academy, and transferred here in 1891. Certain important items may be on temporary exhibition elsewhere in Ireland or abroad, and some sections may be closed to the public while awaiting reformation.

From the Entrance Rotunda, with temporary exhibitions, we enter the Great Hall, containing some of the more notable items, among them the following:

In the central lower section: *Gold Ornaments* (mainly of the Bronze Age); lunules, torques, and gorgets; necklaces of hollow balls, and thin hammered discs; 'ring-money', a model boat, and amber beads. Of special interest is the *Feakle Treasure*, consisting of a gorget and other ornaments found in Co. Clare in 1948, the first 'associated' find of its kind in Ireland, datable to c 650 BC. One case shows the development of the penannular brooch or fibula (6–10C), a characteristic form of Irish ornament; others contain bronze articles (bucklers, cauldrons, trumpets, spear and axe-heads, etc), also a buckler of leather, and two of alder-wood; and another describes the development of the axe, spear, and sword from 2000 to 250 BC.

At the opposite end are the *Crosier-Shrines*, including those of St. Berach, St. Mura of Fahan, and St. Dymphna of Tedavnet (all 11C); those of Clonmacnoise (also 11C), and Lismore (c 1100), and the crosier of Cormac MacCarthy, king-bishop of Cashel (died 1138), of Limoges enamels (early 12C) are likewise displayed here.

Among outstanding items are the *Ardagh Chalice* (early 8C, found together with the adjacent cup and brooches, of a later date, in a ratxh at Ardagh, Co. Limerick, in 1868).

This two-handled cup of silver, heavily alloyed with copper, is decorated with a variety of Celtic ornamentation; its bands and bosses, gold filigree work, studs of cloisonné, and the names of the twelve apostles, should be closely examined.

The finest of a notable series of processional crosses and crucifixes, mainly 13–15C (including the large *Ballylongford Cross* made for Cornelius O'Connor of Kerry in 1479) is the *Cross of Cong* (1123), made of oak sheathed with silver and with panels of gilt bronze, richly adorned with interlacing patterns and jewelled bosses. It was made by order of Turlough O'Connor for the church at Tuam, and brought to Cong by Roderick O'Connor.

The iron bell of St. Patrick and its shrine

The *Shrine of St. Patrick's Bell* (12C), of bronze ornamented with silver-gilt, gold filigree, and gems, is the finest of numerous bell-shrines; it was made to enclose the bronze-coated iron *Bell of St. Patrick* (cf. p 280), the oldest example of Irish metal-work known to survive (?c 406). Other examples are the *Clogán Oir*, or Golden Bell of St. Senan, from Scattery, and the *Corp Naoimh*, another bell-shrine, preserving its leather satchel, from Temple Cross, Co. Meath.

Another case contains the *Breac Maodhog*, notable for details of costume, also with its leather satchel, made in the 11C for St. Moedoc of Drumlane (Co. Cavan); and the *Lough Erne Reliquaries* (8C), one inside the other.

Curious also are the shrines of *St. Lachtin's Arm* (1118–27); of *St. Brigid's Shoe* (1410; from Loughrea); the *Fiacal Phadraig* (1376; containing the tooth that fell from St. Patrick's head at Killespugbrone, near Sligo); the *Domhnach Airgid* (8C, with an outer case of 1350), and other book-shrines, including that of the Stowe Missal (1045– 52).

The raised Terrace surrounding this central area is occupied by a roughly chronological collection of classified antiquities from c 6000 BC to the 17C, including flint implements; incised bone implements from crannógs; reconstructed burials; vessels, querns (including a saddle quern from Newgrange); domestic articles and agricultural implements of all types; a yew-wood gaming-board (10C); weapons, including axeheads with applique silver ornament; bronze trumpets; bells (mainly 10C); *Viking* relics, and Roman relics imported by them; a huge 16C bronze brewing vat; medieval dress; Irish and imported religious sculptures (14–17C); and tubs of 'bog-butter' still in a remarkable state of preservation.

An important group on the far side of the terrace includes the *Tara Brooch* (700–750; found on the shore near Bettystown in 1850), the richest surviving example of the penannular type of brooch common in Irish art; it is of white bronze, decorated with patterns of great delicacy, and studded with glass and amber. Here too is the *Moylough Belt-shrine* (8C) from near Tubbercurry, of silvered bronze with applied enamel decoration.

Adjacent are a group of *Ogham Stones* (see p 42).

The collection of *Sheila-na-gigs* (see Glossary), hidden from public gaze in the basement, may be inspected by *bona fide* scholars, who should apply in advance to the Curator.

Off this hall is a series of rooms devoted to Historical Collections, concerned with the rebellions and wars of Ireland down to 1922; further exhibits of Viking material; and the Indian Collection.

Stairs ascend to the First Floor, to all appearances a Conservatory, with a surrounding gallery containing cases displaying Irish *Silver*, pewter, and other metal-ware; English and Irish *Glass*, including that of Waterford; textiles and costumes, etc.—Other rooms contain the *Ceramics Collection*, and in a gallery over the entrance rotunda, firearms, and Irish *Swords* (from the 14C).

The section devoted to *Musical Instruments* has recently been re-displayed after a fashion; other sections are still closed.

Temporary Exhibitions are held at 7–9 Merrion Row.

To the N is the **NATIONAL LIBRARY**. Temporary exhibitions of Irish Bookbindings, etc. may be seen in the entrance hall. The main *Library* or Reading-room, on the first floor, was opened in 1890 to accommodate the collections of the Royal Dublin Society (founded as the Dublin Society in 1731), previously shelved in Leinster House, and purchased by the State in 1877.

This included the *Jolly Collection* of some 23,000 printed books and 6000 pamphlets, containing among its rarities Thomas Carve's *Lyra* (Vienna, 1651). The library preserves a representative collection of first editions of 17C Irish authors, and of Swift, Goldsmith, Yeats, Joyce, etc.; a collection devoted to the Napoleonic period; and the archives of the Butler and O'Brien families, etc. Among its MSS are a 13C copy of Giraldus Cambrensis's *Topographia Hibernica* (c 1190); G.B. Shaw's early novels; a copy of Joyce's *Portrait of the Artist as a Young Man*; and the *Diary* of Joseph Holloway (from 1895–1944), minutely describing the Irish theatre during this period; and more recent donations. It also contains an unrivalled collection of old Irish maps, topographical prints, and drawings, etc., and among its newspapers is a run of the *Freeman's Journal* (1763–1924). Since 1927 the library has been a legal deposit library for all material published in Ireland.

A 35mm film is available, being a visual record from the 17–19C of Prints and Drawings in the National Library and of the *Lawrence Collection of Photographs of Ireland* (1880–1910; some 25,000 plates).

The *National College of Art*, successor to the Dublin Society's Drawing School, is temporarily accommodated behind the library building.

The sober mass of **Leinster House**, seat of the *Dáil Éireann* (House of Representatives) and the *Seanad Éireann* (Senate), which constitute the *Oireachtas* or National Parliament, was erected in 1745 from designs by Richard Castle as the town mansion of the Dukes of Leinster, and was originally known as Kildare House. In 1815 it was bought by the Royal Dublin Society, from whom it passed to the government in 1922.

The public is admitted when Parliament is *not* sitting, by applying at the Kildare St entrance, and the Superintendent or an usher will usually show visitors around. When either house is sitting, visitors should arrange, preferably in advance, with a member of the House they wish to visit, to obtain an admission card. In his last speech here W.B. Yeats suggested that it was more desirable and important to have able men than representative men in the House! The Upper House, or Senate, consists of 60 members; the Dáil at present consists of 166 elected members. The Prime Minister is known as the *Taoiseach*; the President as *an tUachtarán*.
   Since the Constitution of 1937, the office of President has been held by: Douglas Hyde (1938–45); Seán T. Ó Ceallaigh (1945–59); Éamon de Valéra (1959–73); Erskine H. Childers (1973–74); Cearbhall Ó Dálaigh (1974–76); and Patrick J. Hillery (1976–   ).

From the main hall a passage leads (right) to stairs ascending to the gallery of the *Dáil*, with its semicircular rows of benches, occupying an extension of the original building opened in 1897 as a lecture hall. Of more interest are the rooms of the *Seanad*, to the left of the entrance, with some good 18C mantelpieces, doorways, stuccoed and compartmented ceilings, etc.; the ceiling in the Senate chamber itself was designed by Wyatt in 1780.

Note at the foot of the stair near the Library door the ensign of the 69th Regiment of Meagher's Irish Brigade (who fought at Virginia and Maryland), presented to the people of Ireland by John Fitzgerald Kennedy, then President of the United States, on his visit to Leinster House in June 1963, only five months before his assassination.

Opposite the entrance to Leinster House, Molesworth St, retaining some typical 18C mansions, extends W.—On the left of the N half of Kildare St is the building of the *Royal College of Physicians*, incorporated in 1667. At the far end of Molesworth St is Dawson St.
   Turning left into Dawson St we pass *St. Ann's*, a well-designed church (by Isaac Wills; 1720) hidden behind an uncompleted mid-19C facade by Sir Thomas Deane, but containing good woodwork (including shelving of 1723 used for the distribution of bread to the poor of the parish).
   On the same side of Dawson St (No. 19) is the **Royal Irish Academy**, a society founded in 1785 for the encouragement of science and learning. It has occupied these premises, with charming stuccoes in the vestibule, since 1852.

The **Library** contains some 2,500 valuable MSS, either Irish or related to Ireland, including 58 leaves of the *Cathach* or MS Psalter of St. Columba, traditionally dating from 560; the *Leabhar Breac* ('the speckled book'; before 1411); and the 11–12C *Leabhar na hUidhre*, or Book of the Dun Cow; the *Stowe Missal* (early 9C, and probably originating at Tallaght), among material brought from the Buckingham collection c 1800–49; the *Book of Ui Maine* (c 1390); the *Book of Ballymote* (early 15C); and the *Annals of the Four Masters* (1632–36; from Donegal). These and others may be seen on special request, but facsimiles are available for inspection. The library also houses over 30,000 volumes, the majority relating to Ireland, and other collections including Thomas Moore's library, and Early Scientific books.

Adjacent is the **Mansion House** (1710, with a Victorian stucco front), residence of the Lord Mayor, and scene of many important public meetings held in the Round Room, or *Rotunda*, an addition by John Semple (1821) built to accommodate a banquet held in honour of George IV's visit. In 1919 the Declaration of Irish Independence was adopted here.

On reaching *St. Stephen's Green* (see above) we may turn right to approach the S end of Grafton St, returning thence to *College Green*.

Chatham St, the first turning left off Grafton St, leads past (right) Balfe St, in which Michael William Balfe (1808–70), composer of 'The Bohemian Girl' and other operas, was born (then No. 10 Pitt St; now demolished).

C. Central Dublin South of the Liffey; West of College Green

From *College Green* (Pl. 5; see p 105), the old High Street runs W under the successive names of Dame St, Cork Hill, Lord Edward St, and Christchurch Pl. **Dame St** was once the principal resort of the goldsmiths, as evidenced by its banks facing the *Bank of Ireland* building; see p 105.

Nos 2 and 3 were the premises of *Daly's Club*, which grew from a chocolate or coffee-house established here c 1750 by one Patrick Daly. By 1790 it had become so popular with the bucks and rakes, wits and literati of Dublin that a new building was erected at the expense of the convivial coterie that gathered there. By c 1823, however, it had all but expired, owing to its very exclusiveness, and it was superseded by the *Kildare Street Club* (cf.). Francesco Geminiani (1687–1762), the composer, lived and taught for several years in Dame St, in a house with a concert-room attached.

On the next corner (right) stood *Jury's Hotel*, until it moved to Ballsbridge in recent years; beyond rises a new tower block.—Some distance further W, set back from the street, is the *Central Bank*, beside which is the reconstructed facade of Edward Parke's *Commercial Buildings* (1796–99), passing which we reach (left) the **City Hall**, built in 1769–79 by Thomas Cooley as the Royal Exchange, and decorated in the Corinthian order. Since 1852 it has been occupied by the Dublin Corporation except during the suspension of that body in 1925–32. The central rotunda, supported by 12 columns, shelters statues of local worthies, including one of Dr Charles Lucas, by Edward Smyth, but it has been spoilt by the enclosure of the open aisles which originally surrounded it. The muniment room contains charters dating back to 1172 and the ancient regalia of the corporation.

Almost opposite, Parliament St, where No. 12 was the office of the Fenian journal 'The Irish People', and No. 27 the premises of George Faulkner (?1699–1775), the printer, descends to *Grattan Bridge*.

To the right is Essex St, the site (until 1815) of the *Smock-Alley Theatre*, founded in 1637 by John Ogilby, a Scottish printer. George Farquhar played his first part here in 1697 and Thomas Sheridan managed the theatre (rebuilt 1735) in 1745–59 (except for a brief interval).

Immediately to the W of the City Hall, and flanking Cork Hill, stands **DUBLIN CASTLE** (Pl. 6). The main court, or Upper Castle Yard, is entered from the street adjacent to a building of 1781 by Thomas Ivory, originally *Newcomen's Bank*, added to in 1888.

The building of the castle (1204–28) is ascribed to Myler FitzHenry, a grandson of Henry I, and its completion to Henry de Londres, Archbishop of Dublin. A rivulet

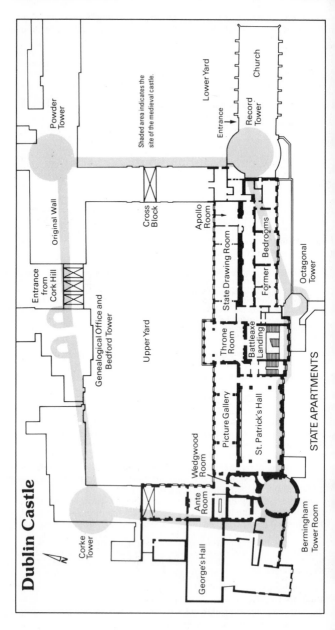

known as the *Poddle*, which supplied the moats, is now enclosed in a sewer. In the 16C the castle stood on the SE corner of the city, and in 1534 it successfully withstood a siege by Thomas Fitzgerald. The first Lord Deputy to make his residence here was Sir Henry Sidney (1565), and it remained the official seat of the lords lieutenant until the establishment of the Free State in 1922.

On Easter Monday 1916 it was attacked by insurgents, some 50 of whom who died being buried temporarily in Castle Yard. In 1941 the State Apartments were damaged by a accidental fire, but they have been well restored.

The entrance to the **State Apartments** is opposite the street entrance, immediately to the right of which is the *Genealogical Office* (see below). Groups are escorted round the principal apartments, furnished xthroughout with colourful Donegal or Killybegs carpets, and lit by modern Waterford glass chandeliers. Note the green Connemara marble floor to the left of the entrance. The Grand Staircase ascends to the landing, off which (left) is *St. Patrick's Hall*, the former scene of investiture of the Knights of St. Patrick, with a painted ceiling of c 1778 (by Vincent Waldré, brought over by the Marquess of Buckingham, the Viceroy, for whom he had worked at Stowe), and armorial bearings.—Hence we enter the *Round Drawing Room*, with its 'Gothick' windows, in the drum of the *Bermingham Tower* (1411; reconstructed 1775–77); as a State Prison, this tower has been the gaol of a number of famous Irishmen from Hugh Roe O'Donnell (1586) to those who were victimised during the 'troubles' of 1918–20.—We next traverse the blue *Wedgwood Room*, with plaques attributed to John Flaxman and paintings ascribed to Angelica Kauffmann. Off an anteroom opens *George's Hall*, added to the apartments for the visit of George V and Queen Mary in 1911. The regalia known as the 'Irish Crown Jewels' were mysteriously stolen from the Genealogical Office just prior to the state visit of Edward VII and Queen Alexandra in 1907, and have never been recovered.

Returning through the anteroom, we traverse the *Picture-Gallery*, with a series of 12 portraits of viceroys, to enter the richly gilt *Throne Room* (1740; redecorated by Francis Johnston), containing a throne possibly presented by William III. We next pass into the *State Drawing Room*, with its original furniture, re-upholstered; the paintings are by G.P. Panini (1740). The *State Corridor*, designed by Sir Edward Lovett Pearce, leads (left) to the *Apollo Room* or *Music Room*, with a ceiling of 1746 incorporated here in 1964–68 from a drawing-room in Tracton House, Merrion Row.

On the far side of the corridor is a series of drawing-rooms, formerly bedrooms, in the second of which is a ceiling transferred here in 1952 from demolished Mespil House (c 1751), displaying some outstanding stucco-work; note also the original door furniture. One of the rooms contains The Card Sharpers, by Matthew William Peters (1741–1814) and a Portrait of the Countess of Southampton, by Van Dyck. The last room visited was the bedroom in which James Connolly lay wounded (a bullet having fractured his ankle at the siege of the Post office; cf.) before being shot by a firing squad at Kilmainham Gaol (cf.) in 1916.

The **Genealogical Office**, with robust flanking gates by Sir Edward Lovett Pearce (one a dummy), and an elegant cupola, was previously the office of the Ulster King of Arms. It now accommodates a *Heraldic and Genealogical Museum*. The collections include the robes of a Knight of St. Patrick, the brass City of Dublin freedom box of St. John Davies (1626), probably the oldest such in existence; heraldic china and glass, and documents. A circular stair ascends to the *Reference Library*.

Turning left on making our exit, we may cross the Upper Yard and turn right under the *Cross Block* to the *Record Tower* (now the State Paper Office) and *Chapel*. The Record Tower, one of the four original towers (much altered in 1813), was once used as the Wardrobe Tower, but from 1579 for the state papers were stored there until their transference to the Record Office at the *Four Courts* (cf.), where they were practically destroyed in 1922.

The *Chapel* is a restored pseudo-Gothic edifice (1807–14) by Francis Johnston, built on the site of earlier chapels, with a curious external decoration of over 100 heads (among them Swift, Brian Ború, and sundry saints) carved in Tullamore limestone by Edward and John Smyth. Hence we may regain Cork Hill by crossing Lower Castle Yard.

In Cork Hill was the site of the *Eagle Tavern*, where the 'Hell Fire Club', founded in 1735 by the 1st Earl of Rosse, held its revels.

On the right of its continuation, Lord Edward St, is Fishamble St, in which stood the *Music Room* where on 13 April 1742 Handel's 'Messiah' was first performed 'for the relief of the prisoners in the several Gaols and for the support of the Mercer's Hospital \$EW and of the Charitable Infirmary'. His 'Judas Maccabaeus' was also first performed here, in 1748.

In the same street was born Henry Grattan (1746–1820), a pioneer of Irish liberty; the poet James Clarence Mangan (1803–49), who passed his last years in abject poverty in neighbouring Bride St, dying of cholera in Meath hospital; and Abp James Ussher (1581–1656), at No. 3, which survived until 1944.

Extending S from Fishamble St is Werburgh St, between which and Little Ship St stood the house (No. 7 Hoey's Court), where Jonathan Swift was born in 1667.—In Castle St, leading back towards Dublin Castle, was born the actor Thomas Doggett (died 1721), who provided the 'coat and badge' raced for by London watermen.

St. Werburgh's Church (entered through Bristol Buildings, 7–8 Castle St), an ancient foundation, was rebuilt in 1715 by Thomas Burgh, and remodelled after a fire in 1759. Of more interest is the interior, by John Smyth, well-restored in 1960, with a sumptuously carved pulpit by Richard Stewart, and an organ-case of 1767. The stucco in the chancel is by Michael Maguire. In the W vestibule is a 16C Fitzgerald tomb; in the vaults are the remains of Lord Edward Fitzgerald, who died of wounds received at his capture in 1798, while in the graveyard lies his captor, Major Henry Sirr (1764–1841).

Lord Edward St is continued by Christchurch Pl., once the heart of the old city, with the *Tholsel* (or Town Hall; demolished 1809) on the site of Nos 1–3, and the original 'Four Courts' (demolished 1796) at the W end of the cathedral.

CHRIST CHURCH (Pl. 6), the cathedral of the combined sees of Dublin and Glendalough (C. of I.), stands in a green churchyard at the corner of Christchurch Pl. and Winetavern St. Its external appearance is almost entirely due to the complete restoration of 1875, although the original design was followed to a large extent. On the S side of the transept are the slight remains of the old chapter-house (1230); further W was the cloister.

It is unique among the cathedrals of Ireland (and Great Britain) as being of Danish foundation. In 1038 Sigtryg or Sitric 'Silkbeard', chief of the Christianised Danes of Dublin, founded the establishment called Christ Church of the Holy Trinity, the crypt of which still remains. In 1163 St. Laurence O'Toole, the archbishop until 1180, superseded the secular clergy by a community of regular canons, and in 1173 Strongbow and his Anglo-Normans began building a new church on the site. O'Toole's successors, John Comyn and Henry de Londres, mistrusting the Celtic-Danish community, attempted to transfer ecclesiastical power to the church of *St. Patrick* (see below). Later archbishops appear to have divided their attentions equally, although Christ Church usually took precedence. Lambert Simnel was crowned as 'Edward VI' here in 1487, and until the 16C the Lord Deputy was sworn in here.

The S wall of the nave, which stood on a peat bog, collapsed in 1562 and, although it was roughly rebuilt, the mass of debris was not removed until 1875. On the disestablishment of the Church of Ireland, St. Patrick's was declared a national cathedral, while Christ Church became the mother church of the diocese. Henry Roe, a wealthy distiller (not to be outdone by Sir Benjamin Guinness; see St. Patrick's), commissioned George Edmund Street to undertake its restoration, and work was in progress between 1871–78. Of the older building little remains except the N wall of the nave, the transepts, and the W bay of the choir.

On entering the Nave from the SW porch we see ahead the N wall, a good example of Early English design of the Somerset type (c 1230); the arrangement of the clerestory and triplet triforium under one arcade is attractive. The sagging of the N wall out of the perpendicular due to subsidence is most obvious from the E end.—Off the N aisle opens the *Baptistery*, one of Street's additions, based on the foundations of a vanished N porch.

In the S aisle is the so-called tomb of Strongbow (Richard de Clare, 2nd Earl of Pembroke and Striguil; died 1176), but the armoured effigy is apparently that of an Earl of Drogheda. Strongbow's bowels may be buried here, and the probable visceral monument is the demi-figure beside the larger tomb, which—on no historical foundation—is pointed out as being one of Strongbow's sons cut in two by his own father for showing cowardice in battle!

The Transepts and Choir are separated from the nave by a screen designed by Street. The transepts and crossing, with their admixture of pointed and semicircular arches, are typical of the transitional work of c 1170. Note also the brass lecterns. In the S Transept is the magnificent tomb of the 19th Earl of Kildare (died 1734), by Sir Henry Cheere. Off the S transept opens the *Chapel of St. Laurence O'Toole*, containing two ancient effigies, one of a prior (1212) and the other of a lady reputed to be the wife or sister of Strongbow.

The Choir and E Chapel, dedicated to St. Laud (a 6C Norman bishop) contains the embalmed heart of O'Toole (who died at Eu, near Dieppe, in 1180), two old slabs, and a few surviving 13C tiles.

The **Crypt**, with its rough arches (and the wooden wedges used in its construction still in position), extends under the whole building, and is the original foundation of the Danish church. In one of the E chapels are the tabernacle and candlesticks used at the Mass of James II in 1689, and at the entrance to another are the figures of Charles II and James II (as Duke of York) by William de Keyser, from the old Tholsel. Here also is the *Sneyd Tomb*, by Thomas Kirk (1777– 1845).

The *Synod House*, connected with the cathedral by a bridge, preserves the original tower of the church of St. Michael the Archangel.

Immediately to the NW of *Christ Church* rise two towers of modern government offices, which have been the subject of controversy. In recent decades the derelict site had been dug over by archaeologists, and a large number of important finds of the Viking and Norman period, including a series of early dwellings, had been made in the peat-like deposits of centuries. These could have been preserved below the new buildings.

This area is crossed by High Street, which leads to Cornmarket, in turn extended by Thomas St, the main thoroughfare leading W from the city centre towards *Kilmainham*; see Rte 1E.

A short distance along High St we pass (right) steps descending to **St. Audoen's**, Dublin's only surviving medieval parish church, of which the 12C tower and W door and a 15C nave aisle remain intact; the ruins of the 15C nave and chancel may be seen on request. Beneath the tower is the tomb of Lord Portlester and his wife (1496), while the aisle contains a font of 1194 and some battered monuments of the Segrave family.

An alley below the church leads down to an *Archway* of the 13C *City Walls* (restored), in a room above which the 'Freeman's Journal' was founded in 1764.

A short distance S, on the opposite side of High St, in Back Lane, is the brick-built **Tailors' Hall**, dating from 1706, and the only remaining guildhall in Dublin. For many years in a sorry state of preservation, it is now being restored, and contains some interesting architectural details—the front door is dated 1770. It was used in 1792 by the Catholic Committee of the United Irishmen.—In Francis St, further W, stands *St. Nicholas of Myra* (1832, by John Leeson).

From Cornmarket, Bridge St leads downhill, near the bottom of which, to the left down an alley, stands *The Brazen Head* (1688), later the headquarters of the United Irishmen, where 15 of them were arrested in the same year. Beyond is the *Father Mathew Bridge* (1818, by George Knowles; previously Whitworth Bridge), replacing the first Dublin bridge (1210), and crossing the Liffey towards the *Four Courts* (see Rte 1D). The oldest surviving bridge is *Mellows Bridge* (1768), the next to the W.

At No. 22 Cornmarket Lord Edward Fitzgerald took refuge before his arrest (see St. Werburgh's) at No. 151 Thomas St.—Some distance along the S side of Thomas St rises deconsecrated *St. Catherine's Church*, a massive structure of 1769, by John Smyth, with an imposing facade, recently cleaned. The organ has also been restored, and the building is used for concerts and meetings. Robert Emmet was executed here in 1803, near the spot where his adherents had murdered Arthur Wolfe, Lord Chief Justice Kilwarden (1739–1803). A few steps beyond, at St. James's Gate, is the entrance to **Guinness's Brewery**, which covers an area of 26 hectares (64 acres) on both sides of the road.

In 1759 the small Rainsford's Brewery on this site was purchased by Arthur Guinness, who began brewing 'porter' as it was then known. Approx. 60 per cent of the beer sold in the Republic is now brewed here. Visitors may no longer tour the brewery, but are welcome to enter the Hop Store in Crane St (left), where during normal working hours they may see an explanatory film about the manufacture of this world-famous stout, and are courteously invited to sample their beers and stout, bottled or draught. A *Brewing Museum* may be visited by prior appointment with the curator.

A short distance S is the *Grand Canal Harbour* of c 1780.

Nicholas St and Patrick St lead S from *Christ Church*, running gradually downhill through a quarter of artisans' dwellings and housing estates, replacing what was once one of the most insalubrious slum districts in Dublin, to *St. Patrick's Cathedral*, adjoined by gardens laid out at the expense of Lord Iveagh on the site of some exceptionally squalid quarters.

In The Coombe, a street a few minutes' walk to the W, is the brick facade of the old *Weavers' Hall* (1745).—Patrick St is later prolonged to the S by Clanbrassil St, now largely a Jewish enclave. Further S to the right beyond the Grand Canal, in the suburb of *Harold's Cross*, is **Mount Jerome** (Protestant) **Cemetery**, where lie J.S. Le Fanu, William Lecky, William Carleton, Edward Dowden, 'AE' Russell, J.M. Synge, George Petrie, and Thomas Davis, among others.

***ST. PATRICK'S CATHEDRAL** (Pl. 6), the national cathedral of the

Church of Ireland (Protestant), is a statelier and larger building than Christ Church, which it was intended to supersede. Like its sister cathedral, it has been only too thoroughly restored, but in this case with slightly more respect for the historical development of the fabric. It is known for its long association with Jonathan Swift, who served as dean from 1713 to 1745, but it also contains one of the more interesting collections of funerary monuments in Ireland.

St. Patrick himself is believed to have baptised converts at the well on this site, and the ancient church of St. Patrick de Insula was chosen by Abp John Comyn in 1190 for elevation to collegiate rank as a counterblast to the favour shown by followers of Strongbow to the independent monastic establishment of Christ Church; see above. His successor, Henry de Londres (1212–28), raised St. Patrick's to cathedral status, and the building of the two churches went on concurrently.

Standing beyond the city walls, the new church had to be fortified against the marauding O'Byrnes and O'Tooles, whose haunts in the Wicklow Mountains were only too near, and over the 'Liberty' thus formed, with the adjacent Liberty of St. Sepulchre, the archbishops, as princes palatine, exercised supreme jurisdiction until 1860. Meanwhile, since Cromwell's visitation, when the building was used as stables, it had become progressively more ruinous, sections being walled off as separate churches, until in 1866–69 a general restoration was undertaken by Sir Thomas Drew, financed by Sir Benjamin Guinness (1798–1868), whose complacently seated commemorative statue, by Foley, is by the SW entrance porch. Further sums were expended in 1900 by Lord Iveagh in the repair of the aisles and choir, which did much to preserve at least the structure of what by then was an almost moribund church.

Steps descend from the entrance porch into the Nave, which, together with the choir and transepts, dates in general design from the time of De Londres, and is probably due to London masons. The W end of the N aisle was rebuilt after a fire in 1381 and the sturdy NW tower added, but curiously out of alignment with the rest of the building. The *Spire*—taller and more pointed than that of Christ Church—dates from 1739. In the time of Henry VIII the nave-vault collapsed and the original clustered piers were replaced by granite shafts, which were encased in stone in 1866.

At the foot of the second column—half-right from the entrance (see Pl. 1)—brass tablets mark the *Grave of Jonathan Swift* (1667–1745) and that of Esther Johnson (1681–1728; better known as 'Stella'), who lie side by side. On the left of the adjacent door is a fine bust of Swift by Patrick Cunningham (1775); on the tablet above is a Latin epitaph from his own pungent pen: 'He lies where furious rage can rend his heart no more'; while his simple record of Stella is on the other side of the doorway.

In the SW corner (left) is the dark Baptistery, possibly part of Comyn's building, with an old font. Against its outer wall is the huge **Boyle Monument** (Pl. 2), remarkable for its profusion of painted figures, but ill-lit. It was originally erected by the 'great' Earl of Cork (1566–1643) at the E end of the choir, and its removal thence in 1633 by Strafford (when Lord Deputy, and at the instigation of Abp Laud) led to the enmity of Cork, the primary cause of Strafford's later impeachment and execution.

The uppermost figures represent Dean Weston (died 1573), Lord Chancellor of Ireland; below him are Sir Geoffrey Fenton (died 1608) and his wife, the dean's

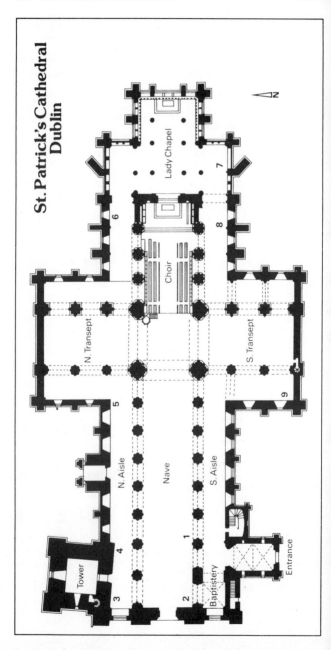

St. Patrick's Cathedral
Dublin

Lady Chapel

Choir

N. Transept

S. Transept

N. Aisle

Nave

S. Aisle

Tower

Baptistery

Entrance

daughter. Still lower are the Earl of Cork and his second wife (the latter a daughter of Fenton), with four sons, six daugxhters, and an infant supposed to represent the physicist Robert Boyle (1627–91; cf. St. Mary's, Youghal).

In the NW corner is an ancient recumbent stone cross that marked the site of St. Patrick's Well, and to the right is a bust of J.P. Curran (1750–1817; Pl. 3). In the N Aisle as we go E is the restored monument of Abp Thomas Jones (died 1619) and Sir Roger Jones (died 1620); then come memorials of Turlough O'Carolan (1670–1738; Pl. 4), the last of the Irish bards, erected by Lady Morgan, and—just near the transept—of Samuel Lover (1797–1868; Pl. 5), the novelist and miniaturist.

The N Transept, for many years serving as the parish church of St. Nicholas Without, lay in ruins until 1830, and has since then been twice rebuilt. Swift's pulpit stands in the NW corner.

The **Choir**, the best-preserved part of the ancient fabric, is also the Chapel of the Order of St. Patrick. Its knights were installed here from the institution of the order in 1783 until 1869, when the Irish Church was disestablished. Above the stalls hang the helmets, swords, banners, and paraphernalia of members of the order, which do not improve the appearance of the Choir.

In the Choir aisles are some of the most interesting monuments in the church: on the N side of the N Choir Aisle (restored 1902) is the marble effigy of Abp Fulk de Saundford (died 1271; Pl. 6), and opposite is a tablet marking the grave of Frederick Herman, Duke of Schomberg (1615–90), who fell at the Boyne. The epitaph, with its sarcastic reference to the indifference of Schomberg's family, is due to Swift. The *Lady Chapel*, built by Abp Saundford (a Londoner) in c 1256, resembles in the delicacy of its details the contemporary work in the Temple Church in London.

From 1666 to 1816 it was assigned to a Huguenot congregation, but by 1840 it was in ruins, since when it has suffered from over-restoration. By the SW window is a monument to Sir Benjamin Guinness's only daughter, who in her youth participated in charitable works to relieve the 'Bodily and Spiritual wants' of the poor. Immediately above her monument, in the stained glass is the text: 'I was thirsty and ye gave me drink'. The NE and SE Chapels retain Dutch brass candelabra (17C); in the latter is an effigy of Abp Tregury (died 1471; Pl. 7). In the wall of the S Choir Aisle are four interesting brasses (Pl. 8), a form of memorial rarely occurring in Ireland: those of Dean Sutton (died 1528), with an erasure probably due to a change of doctrine at the Reformation, and Dean Fyche (died 1537), with silver inlay, are especially noteworthy; that of Sir Henry Wallop (?1540–99, Lord Justice of Ireland) dates from 1608, and that of Sir Edward ffitton the Elder from 1579.

The S Transept was for many centuries used as a chapter house. Leaning against a pier is an old door, pierced with a rough hole. In 1492 a fierce dispute took place in the nave between the Earls of Kildare and Ormonde over a matter of precedence, each supported with a band of armed retainers. Ormonde took refuge in the chapter house, and a reconciliation having been effected, a hole was cut in the door so that the two earls might shake hands. Also in this transept is a monument to the poet Charles Wolfe (1791–1823). In its SW corner is the characteristic monument of Lady Doneraile, by Simon Vierpyl (c 1780: Pl. 9), and above (right) is a plaque to Swift's servant, McGee.

Turning left on making our exit from *St. Patrick's*, we pass (right; opposite the cathedral) the Deanery Garden, where a house stood (which had burned down, and was replaced by one dating 1781, perhaps over the original cellars) from which could be seen the midnight burial of 'Stella'. Swift's bedroom overlooked the cathedral, but the Dean moved to another room on that night so that he might not see the light in the church. It contains a portrait of Swift by Bindon in a carved frame by John Houghton.

The interior of Marsh's Library

A short distance along the street (left) is the entrance to **'Marsh's Library** (Pl. 8), founded by Abp Narcissus Marsh (1638–1713) and built in brick from 1701 by Sir William Robinson (its W facade faced in stone in 1863–69). It was the first public library (open then to 'All Graduates and Gentlemen') in Dublin, and remains one. It consists of two wings at right angles, and its charming and well-restored interior has remained practically untouched since the founder's time. In 'Ulysses', Joyce refers to the 'stagnant bay in Marsh's Library' where he read in October 1902. Note the three 'cages' in which readers were locked with their rare books to work undisturbed under the eye of the librarian. The library preserves some 80 incunabula (including a volume of Cicero printed in Milan in 1472) and 300 MSS.

Part of the collection originated in the library (c 9,500 volumes) of Edward Stillingfleet (1635–99), Bp of Worcester, acquired by Marsh, and many later scholars made bequests of their books to the library. Swift was a governor, and it contains his annotated copy of Clarendon's 'History of the Rebellion'. Only recently have funds been made available to renovate the building, and to conserve and repair

the 25,000 16C–early 18C books themselves, the bindings of which were previously unprotected from the sun.

From *Marsh's Library* continue up the street and turn left along Upper
Kevin St and Lower Kevin St. To the S stood Swift's walled garden
which he called 'Naboth's Vineyard'.

Aungier St, the next thoroughfare crossed, extends N towards
Dame St, and is prolonged to the S, with various changes of name, to
the suburbs of *Rathmines* and *Ranelagh*. No. 12 Aungier St was the
birthplace of the poet Thomas Moore (1779–1852).—Continue E along
Cuffe St (see p 120) to reach the SW corner of *St. Stephen's Green*.

By turning left off Cuffe St along Mercier St (Upper and Lower) we
approach South William St, with (right; No. 58) the **Civic Museum**,
occupying the Assembly House erected for the Society of Artists in
1765–71, and after 1791 used for a time by the City Assembly owing to
the ruin of the old Tholsel. In 1862 it was used to stable the Fire
Brigade! The main *Octagon Room* contains drawings, models, and
maps and plans of Dublin, a set of Malton's views, wax models, and
miscellaneous relics, including the shoes of the Irish giant, Patrick
Cotter O'Brien (c 1761–1806), 8 feet 7 inches tall (261cm).

The next building on the right is much-degraded *Powerscourt
House*, in 1835 converted into the offices and warehouses of a whole-
sale drapers, and recently adapted to accommodate shops and restaurants around its courtyard. Built in 1771–74 for Viscount Powerscourt
by Robert Mack, it preserves stucco work by James Stapleton and
woodcarving by Ignatius McCullagh, which may be seen in several
rooms.

College Green is reached a short distance to the N, first passing
(right) *St. Andrew's* (completed 1873; by 'Lanyon, Lynn and Lanyon'),
the successor of an elliptical building known as 'The Round Church',
rebuilt by Johnston (1803–4; burnt out in 1860).

D. Central Dublin North of the Liffey

From *O'Connell Bridge* (Pl. 3; see p 101) *O'Connell Street*, the widest
thoroughfare in Dublin, runs almost due N, and is described below.

Before ascending this street, turn E along Eden Quay, passing
below the unsightly railway bridge, to reach the *Custom House (Pl.
4), fronting the Liffey, and built here in the face of considerable opposition. Externally this is one of the most impressive buildings in
Dublin, and the first masterpiece of James Gandon (1743–1823), an
English architect of Huguenot extraction, born in London and invited
over to Dublin in 1781 by John Beresford. The main S Front—best seen
from the far bank—has a fine Doric portico, with statues by Edward
Smyth and Agostino Carlini, and masks of the Rivers of Ireland, also
by Smyth, on the 14 keystones. The N Front has a smaller portico
bearing statues of the Continents, by Joseph Bankes. Flanking each of
the wings is a pavilion with the arms of Ireland above. The central
copper dome is 38m high, topped by a statue of Commerce. Like most
of the principal buildings along the N bank of the Liffey, it suffered
during the 'troubles'. Set alight by a party of Republicans on 25 May
1921, it blazed for five days, and its extensive records were destroyed.
Restored, it now houses government offices.

For the *Docks* and *Harbour*, see Rte 1A.

Immediately NE of the Custom House, in Store St, is the central *Bus*

Station or *Busáras*, built in the early 1950s by Michael Scott and Partners. A short distance beyond, on the E side of Amiens St, is *Connolly Railway Station* (1844–46; previously *Amiens St Station*); Charles Lever, the novelist, was born in a house on its site.

NW of the Custom House are the imposing offices of the *Irish Life Assurance Co.* (1977; by Andrew Devane of Robinson, Keefe and Devane).

Hence we may make our way W along Lower Abbey St, passing (left) the new **Abbey Theatre**, opened in 1966 and designed by Michael Scott. Its predecessor was burnt out in 1951. It houses two auditoria, the *Abbey Theatre* proper (638 seats) and the *Peacock* (157 seats). The earlier theatre, standing partly on the site of the Morgue, had been erected at the expense of Miss A.E.F. Horniman (of the tea-packing family, whose father had founded the Horniman Museum, London), and opened in 1904. W.B. Yeats and Lady Gregory were its first directors.—We regain O'Connell St a few steps to the W.

O'Connell Street in the 19C, showing Nelson's Pillar, since demolished

Only a few doors away there stood, until largely destroyed in the Easter Monday Rising of 1916, the building of the *Royal Hibernian Academy*, one of the most tragic of the cultural losses of the rebellion.

O'Connell Street was originally laid out by Luke Gardiner in the mid 18C, when it was known as 'Gardiner's Mall'. It was widened and then called Sackville St, and was intended to be an elongated residential square rather than a main thoroughfare. It takes its present name from Daniel O'Connell (1775–1847), 'the Liberator', a statue of whom (1882; by Foley), with allegorical figures (Erin casting off her fetters, etc.), stands at the foot of the street.

It is no longer dominated by *Nelson's Pillar*, a Doric column designed by William Wilkins, with its statue by Thomas Kirk, built 32 years before its counterpart in Trafalgar Square, London. Severely damaged by an explosion in 1966, it was later demolished.

O'Connell St was not only devastated in 1916, but also in July 1922, when it was the scene of the last stand of the 'Irregulars' of the anti-treaty party against the Free State government. Almost the whole of the E side was destroyed by fire, and Cathal Brugha, a leader of the Irregulars, who counselled surrender, but with the courage of fanaticism refused to do so himself, was shot down as he rushed out at the government troops.

Rebuilt O'Connell St, flanked by shops, banks, and cinemas, no longer retains the cachet it once had, however many statues line the central walk, and in the late evening is not the pleasantest place to take a stroll. Among these monuments, other than that commemorating O'Connell, are those to William Smith O'Brien (1803–64), leader of the Young Ireland party; Sir John Gray (1816–75), proprietor of the 'Freeman's Journal' and organiser of Dublin's water-supply; Father (Theobald) Mathew (1790–1856), the 'apostle' of Temperance; and Charles Stewart Parnell (1846– 91), the advocate of 'Home Rule'.

Shelley lodged at No. 7 in 1812, where he wrote 'An address to the Irish People'. Later he moved to 17 Grafton St.

Half way up the W side of the street is the **General Post Office** (Pl. 3), preserving its facade and fine Ionic portico (1815–17) by Francis Johnson. This was the main stronghold of the Volunteers during the Rising of Easter, 1916, commanded by Patrick Pearse and James Connolly. Set alight by shelling, the building was abandoned by its garrison, and both Pearse and Connolly were executed at Kilmainham Gaol soon after, providing additional martyrs for the movement. The building was re-opened in 1929, and within the main hall is a small commemorative statue, the 'Death of Cuchulainn' (pron. Coo-hu-lin) by Oliver Sheppard (1934). The *Philatelic Office* is in adjacent Henry St Arcade.

From the opposite side of the street we may turn E to Marlborough St—parallel to O'Connell St—and then bear left, passing stone-built *Tyrone House* (right), built by Castle in 1741 for the Marquess of Waterford, and occupied since 1835 by the Education Department; it contains good stucco work by the Francini brothers. A replica of the house was later erected to replace the stable block.

On the left, a dull Doric edifice as seen from the street, stands **St. Mary's Pro-Cathedral**, the main Catholic church of Dublin (1816–25). Of interest is the architectural model of the building, with its fluted columns and coffered dome, by John Sweetman, which may be inspected on request. It was the scene of Newman's public profession of the Catholic faith before Cardinal Cullen in 1851; its Palestrina choir was endowed by Edward Martyn; the high altar is by Peter Turnerelli.

Regaining O'Connell St, we pass at No. 14 the *Dublin Tourist Information Office*. At No. 59, opposite, are the offices of CIE (the Irish Transport Board), while a few steps further N (No. 40) are those of *Aer Lingus*.

At the end of the street (left) is the *Ambassador Cinema*, occupying the **Rotunda** of the since vulgarised Assembly Rooms designed by John Ensor and embellished by Gandon and Smyth in 1786. The roof of the Rotunda was rebuilt in 1932 and a new ceiling substituted. Among those who performed here in its heyday were John Field, Michael Kelly (?1764–1826, the singer, and a friend of Mozart), and Franz Liszt.

Immediately behind it is the *Gate Theatre*, accommodated in an extension of the Assembly Rooms built in 1784–86 by Richard Johnston (the elder brother of Francis). The theatre was founded in 1928 by Hilton Edwards and Micheál Mac Liammóir, and transferred to these premises in the following year.

Adjoining the Assembly Rooms to the W is the **Rotunda Hospital** (1751–55), designed by Castle just before his death, and later much extended. This, the first 'lying-in' or maternity hospital in the British Isles, was founded by Dr Bartholomew Mosse (1712–59), who had already started one on smaller premises in 1745. He also established the Assembly Rooms, the profits of which were devoted to the hospital. Of particular interest is the *Chapel, reached from the central doorway of the building, with its exuberant plasterwork (1757–58) by Barthelemy Cramillion, who greatly influenced Irish exponents of his craft. The gallery on the floor above affords a better close view of the ceiling.

Passing behind the *Gate Theatre* (see above), we skirt Parnell Sq. (formerly Rutland Sq.; left), with a *Garden of Remembrance* (1966) embellished with a monument to the 'Wild Geese' by Oisin Kelly (1971) and dedicated to those who gave their lives to the cause of Irish freedom. Here, until destroyed in 1942, stood two shelters of sedan-chair-men.—At No. 5, opposite, Oliver St. John Gogarty (1878–1957), the poet and author of 'As I was Going down Sackville Street' (1937), etc., was born. Among other dignified mid-18C mansions, many of them designed by John Ensor, No. 11 was once the town house of the Earls of Ormonde.

On the N side of the Square is *Charlemont House*, externally a graceful building of 1762—with an incongruous porch added in 1930—designed by Sir William Chambers and the 1st Earl of Charlemont as a residence for the latter.

It accommodates the ***Municipal Gallery of Modern Art**, founded in 1908 largely through the generosity of Sir Hugh Lane (1875–1915; a nephew of Lady Gregory), and containing a number of paintings from the Lane Bequest: others may be seen in the National Gallery of Ireland.

The original home of the Lane Collection was 17 Harcourt St, but after Lane's death by drowning when the 'Lusitania' was torpedoed, the collection was held in safe-keeping in London pending a pettifogging decision on the 'legal' interpretation of the codicil to his will. Agreement between the British and Irish governments was reached only in 1959, since when half the collection has alternated quinquennially between the two capitals.

In the Entrance Hall are a few portrait busts, including that of Michael Collins by Seámus Murphy, while also among the collection of sculpture is a small reclining figure by Henry Moore.—Notable among the paintings are: *Patrick Tuohy*, Mayo peasant boy; *William J. Leech*, The Cigarette; and examples of the work of *John Lavery*, including a Portrait of Arthur Griffith; *Kokoschka*, Portrait of Mr Isepp, and Pigeons; *Rouault*, Christ and the Soldiers; *Utrillo*, Rue Marcadet;

Bonnard, Boulevard de Clichy; *Vlaminck*, Flowers; *Vuillard*, Interior; and representative works by *Picasso* and *Gris*.

Fantin-Latour, Still Life; *Courbet*, The Pool, and The Diligence in the Snow; *Alfred Stevens*, The Present; *Manet*, Music at the Tuileries; *Daubigny*, Portrait of Honoré Daumier; *Pissarro*, View from Louveciennes; *Berthe Morisot*, Summer Day; *Puvis de Chavannes*, Toilet (an unusually small work); *Monet*, Winter Scene, and Waterloo Bridge; *Degas*, Beach Scene.

Vuillard, The Mantelpiece; *Boudin*, The beach at Tourgéville; *Corot*, Palace of the Popes, Avignon, and Woman meditating; *Daumier*, Don Quixote and Sancho Panza; *Renoir*, Les Parapluies; *Jongkind*, Skating in Holland; and *Manet*, Portrait of Eva Gonzales.

Other rooms contain *Burne-Jones*, Sleeping princess; *Sarah Purser*, Portrait of Edward Martyn; and several portraits by *Augustus John*; *W.J. Leech*, Sunshade, and Convent Garden; *Roderic O'Conor*, Self-portrait, and Breton Girl; *Jack B. Yeats*, The Liffey Swim, Jockey Act, and others; and works by *Louis Le Brocquy* (1916–), and other Irish artists of the period.

From the NE corner of Parnell Sq. we may walk along Great Denmark St, where *Belvedere House* (1785) contains stucco-work by Michael Stapleton. James Joyce attended the Jesuit school here between 1893 and 1898, as recorded in 'Portrait of the Artist as a Young Man' (Joyce being a pupil of whom the Fathers are not too proud).

Temple St North, the next left-hand turning, leads to *St. George's Church*, built by Francis Johnston (from 1802), with a fine steeple over 60m high, adapted from the design of that of St. Martin-in-the-Fields, London. Here in 1806 the future Duke of Wellington and Kitty Pakenham were married; her father, the Earl of Longford, lived in Parnell Sq. (then Rutland Sq.).—To the NW the street is prolonged by Eccles St, in which No. 64 was the home of Francis Johnston, and later of Isaac Butt; No. 7 (demolished in 1982) *was* that of 'Leopold Bloom', in James Joyce's 'Ulysses'.

Parallel to and E of Temple St is Gardiner St, the centre of an uninviting if not dangerous warren of tenements, in which stands the Jesuit church of *St. Francis Xavier* (1832), by Joseph Keane, with a redecorated interior and a tetrastyle Ionic portico.—Off Gardiner St opens **Mountjoy Square**, the centre of a fashionable quarter of Dublin during the greatest period of the British 'Ascendancy', but no longer so, although idealistic attempts have been made to effect some improvement in the sad condition of its remaining mansions.

In his 'Excursions through Ireland' (1820), Thomas Cromwell described this district, as seen from St. George's Church, as one which 'taste and opulence have united to embellish; the streets in the vicinity are all built on a regular plan; the houses are lofty and elegant; and neither hotels, shops, nor warehouses, obtruding upon the scene, the whole possesses an air of dignified retirement—the tranquillity of ease, affluence and leisure. The inhabitants of this parish are indeed almost exclusively of the upper ranks ...'.

Some distance NW of Mountjoy Sq., between the N Circular Rd and the Royal Canal (commenced 1789), lies *Mountjoy Prison*, scene of the incarceration of many insurgents in 1916–21 and of armed members of the faction opposing the setting up of the Free State government in 1922–23.

From the NW corner of Parnell Sq. we may follow Granby Row before turning left along Dorset St, an important but undistinguished thoroughfare leading NE to commence the N1 (the road out to the airport; see Rte 31).

In Mary Place, opposite Granby Row, is the deconsecrated 'Black Church' or *St. Mary's Chapel of Ease* (1829–30), the ingenious masterpiece of John Semple, built of black Dublin calp, and covering one huge parabolic vault.—No. 12 Dorset St was the birthplace of the dramatist Richard Brinsley Sheridan (1751–1816); No. 85 stands on the site of the birthplace of Seán O'Casey (1886–1964).—Arthur Griffith (1872–1922), architect of Irish independence and first president of the Dáil, and Sir William Rowan Hamilton (1805–65), the mathematician, were born in Dominick St, the next cross street, in which stands *St. Saviour's* (1858), by J.J. McCarthy. Plasterwork by Robert West (1755) may be seen at No. 20 Lower Dominick St.

Dorset St is prolonged downhill to the SW by Bolton St, off which leads (right) Henrietta St, one of the first in Dublin to contain large houses. Among them may be seen Nos 9 and 10 (Blessington House), both by Sir Edward Lovett Pearce, retaining relics of their original decoration, but sadly defaced by more recent occupiers. Others were gutted of their staircases, etc. by a Dublin alderman earlier this century and converted into tenements.

At the end of the street stands **'King's Inns** (Pl. 2), the Dublin Inns of Court, an impressive classical building designed by Gandon in 1795, begun seven years later, and completed by Henry Aaron Baker. Its cupola was added by Francis Johnston in 1816. It contains a fine Dining-hall (restored), an extensive Library, with Gothic Revival plasterwork by Frederick Darley (1827), and some pleasant gardens. Wings were added in the mid-19C. For its history, see under *Four Courts*, below.

To the NW is *Broadstone Station* (disused since 1937), by J.S. Mulvany (1850).

From Bolton St we may bear S along Capel St towards the Liffey.

In St. Mary's St, to the left, is *St. Mary's Church* (from 1697), by Thomas Burgh, where in 1747 John Wesley preached his first sermon in Ireland (in which he was later to travel some 40,000km); its interior is of some architectural interest, and it contains an organ by Renatus Harris, deserving restoration. Richard Brinsley Sheridan, Lord Charlemont, and Wolfe Tone were baptised here.—Adjacent is Wolfe Tone St (formerly Stafford St), where Theobald Wolfe Tone (1763–98), founder of the United Irishmen, was born.

The next left-hand turning off Capel St leads to *St. Mary's Abbey* (caretaker at No. 18), preserving part of the chapter-house and slype (late 12C) of the Abbey of St. Mary Ostmanby (Ostman=Danes), a Benedictine foundation transferred to the Cistercians in 1147. Here 'Silken Thomas' Fitzgerald, appointed Lord Deputy, threw off his allegiance to England in 1534, only to be captured, and in the following year, executed.

A few steps to the right in Upper Ormond Quay brings us to the **'FOUR COURTS** (Pl. 4), seat of the High Court of Justice of Ireland, and the second masterpiece of James Gandon, who, incorporating work by Thomas Cooley (1776–84), completed it in 1786–1802. The central block, entered through an imposing Corinthian portico (with weather-worn statues of Moses and the Legal Virtues, by Edward Smyth) is surmounted by the copper-covered drum or lantern dome which gives the building its distinctive outline. The upper rotunda provides a fine view over the city. It is flanked by two wings enclosing quadrangles. Off the circular central hall open the halls that contained the original 'four courts': Exchequer, Common Pleas, King's Bench, and Chancery.

The original Law Courts stood on the S side of the Liffey, to the W of Christ

The Four Courts

Church. A society of lawyers, or Inn of Court, was established in the time of Edward I in Exchequer St, and known as Collett's Inn. It was succeeded by Preston's Inn, on the site of the present City Hall. On the assumption of the title of King of Ireland by Henry VIII in 1541, the Society took the name of King's Inn, and the confiscated lands of the Dominican convent of St. Saviour (founded 1224), where the Four Courts now stand, were granted to it. It was in the building erected here that James II held his last parliament in 1689.

In the 18C it was arranged to transfer the Law Courts to their present site, and the Society of King's Inn took a new site in Henrietta St (see above); the old Law Courts were finally abandoned in 1796. In 1916 the Four Courts were temporarily occupied by the insurgents, with little damage being caused.

In 1922 the building was put in a state of defence and garrisoned by 150 anti-treaty men under Rory O'Connor, a civil engineer. On the 28–30 June it was heavily shelled by Michael Collins, thoughtless of the priceless archives in the adjoining Record Office, which were largely destroyed, although the shell of the Four Courts stood up to the explosions. The Law Courts were eventually re-installed here in 1931 and the restoration was completed the following year, with a number of minor but noticeable variations in the facade.

Behind the Four Courts is the *Green Street Courthouse* (1792), by Richard Johnston.

Immediately W of the Four Courts, opposite the *Father Mathew Bridge* (see p 130), Church St leads away from the Liffey to (left) **St. Michan's Church** (Pl. 3/4; pron. Mikan). It was founded in 1095, although the present building, except for its medieval battlemented tower and the tomb of Bp O'Haingli, is an early 19C restoration of a church rebuilt in 1685–86. Some of the furniture, including a movable litany desk, dates from 1724; a wreck of a keyboard is pointed out as that of an organ used by Handel, whose 'Dettingen' Te Deum was performed here; the carving of the organ-case has been ascribed to Cuvilliès. Burke was probably baptised at the font.

In the sheltered graveyard, near the path, lie Dr Charles Lucas (1713–71), founder of the 'Freeman's Journal', and, according to one tradition, Robert Emmet (1778–1803; but comp. below).

In the vaults lie the brothers Henry and John Sheares (1753–98, and 1766–98 respectively), executed as rebels, and the repellent mummies of so-called 'crusaders' (but probably 17C) preserved by the moisture-absorbing magnesian limestone of the vault, which do not merit their vulgar exploitation.

No. 12 Arran Quay (demolished), to the W of the Four Courts, was the birthplace of Edmund Burke (1729–97); *St. Paul's* (R.C.), just beyond, is a striking building of 1835–37, by Patrick Byrne.—To the N is the district of *Oxmanstown*, or 'Ostmen's Town', the Danish quarter. For the *Bluecoat School* here, and *Phoenix Park*, further W, see below.

We may make our way back from the Four Courts to the O'Connell Bridge by following the line of quays flanking the N bank of the Liffey, passing *Grattan Bridge* (1874) and the *Metal Bridge* (1819; officially *Liffey Bridge*; previously Wellington Bridge). It must be admitted that most of the buildings here remain in a sorry state of dilapidation. Beyond the footbridge we reach Bachelors' Walk, known for the affray that took place there on 26 July 1914 after the Howth gun-running (see p 150); a party of British troops (the King's Own Scottish Borderers) fired incontinently on a crowd of jeering and missile-hurling citizens, killing three and wounding 38.

Plasterwork in Lower Dominick Street

E. Western Environs

Phoenix Park may be approached from the O'Connell Bridge (from which it may be reached by bus) by following the quays along the N bank of the Liffey to the *Four Courts* (see above). Not far beyond, on the S bank, on a quay called Usher's Island, is the *Mendicity Institution*, a sad relic of Moira House (1752), residence of the Rawdon family until 1808; Pamela Fitzgerald was here when Lord Edward was arrested.

Blackhall Pl., a turning to the right, leads to (left) the **Bluecoat School** (Pl. 3)—properly the *King's Hospital, Oxmanstown*—a pleasant building (1773–1803) by Thomas Ivory, now belonging to the Incorporated Law Society. It contains wood-carving by Simon Vierpyl and restored stucco-work by Charles Thorp.

Slightly further N (right) is *St. Paul's* (C. of I.), which contests with St. Michan (see above) as being the probable last resting-place of Robert Emmet.—Beyond (left) is the strangely named Stoneybatter, assumed to be part of an ancient highway, from the English *stony* and the Irish *bóthar* (a road).

Continuing W along the river bank we pass (right) *Collins Barracks*, formerly the Royal Barracks (1704, by Thomas Burgh), the central blocks of which were demolished in the late 19C.—On the S bank is *Heuston Station*, a striking building (1845–6) by Sancton Wood, previously known as Kingsbridge Station.

For the *Royal Hospital*, Kilmainham, a few minutes' walk SW, approached by turning left up Military Rd, see below.

S of the station are the buildings of *Steevens' Hospital* (1720–33), by Thomas Burgh, named after its chief founder, Dr Richard Steevens (1653–1710). This, the oldest public hospital in Ireland, with a chaplaincy endowed by Esther Johnson ('Stella'), preserves the valuable *Library* of Dr Edward Worth (1678–1733). It was completed by Sir Edward Lovett Pearce.
    Just beyond is *St. Patrick's Hospital* (usually known as *Swift's Hospital*), with its rusticated stonework, founded in 1746 with a bequest from Swift. Built by George Semple, it was opened in 1757 and enlarged by Cooley in 1778. It is now a psychiatric centre, and contains some relics of Swift.

We now approach the main entrance to ***PHOENIX PARK**, one of the largest and most attractive enclosed public parks in Europe (1,750 acres, or 808 hectares), with a wall c 11km long.

The name of the park is believed to be a corruption of *Fionn Uisage* or *Fhionnuisce* (clear water), from a spring that rises not far from the *Phoenix Column*, erected by Lord Chesterfield in 1747. The layout of the park is mainly due to Chesterfield during his viceroyalty, although the original grant of crown land confiscated from the priory of St. John at Kilmainham was made by Charles II at the suggestion of the Duke of Ormonde.

Immediately to the right of the entrance is the *People's Garden*, a colourful flower garden, adjoining buildings of the Irish *Department of Defence*, designed by Gandon, but carried out from 1787 by W. Gibson. Near by are the *Garda Síochána Headquarters*, containing a small *Police Museum*.
    This SE corner of the park is dominated by the **Wellington Testimonial**, a 60m-high obelisk, the largest in Europe, designed by Sir Robert Smirke in 1817. A short walk to the W brings one to the *Islandbridge Gate*; see below.

To the right of the Main Road further N are the *Zoological Gardens*, opened in 1830 and famous for their lions and other large carnivora. The cottage orné near the entrance is by Decimus Burton; the grounds contain two natural lakes and numerous waterfowl, pelicans, flamingos, etc.

Beyond the Polo Ground is the *Áras an Uachtaráin* (Residence of the President), the former Viceregal Lodge, of 1751–54, by Nathaniel Clements (1705–77; who built it for himself). The Ionic portico was added in 1816 by Francis Johnston, and the lodge preserves a fine plaster ceiling from Mespil House. Opposite, in the Main Road, Lord Frederick Cavendish, the new Chief Secretary, and his under-secretary Mr Thomas Burke, were stabbed to death in 1882 by members of the 'Invincibles'.

To the left of the Main Road, which crosses the park from SE to NW, is the *American Ambassador's Residence* (formerly the Chief Secretary's Lodge, 1776; for Sir John Blaquiere), while some distance beyond the central *Phoenix Column*—with its phoenix perpetuating the misconception that the park is named after that fabulous bird rather than its spring (see above)—are (right) the former Under-Secretary's Lodge, appropriated by the *Apostolic Nunciature*, and (left) the offices of the *Irish Ordnance Survey* (previously the Mountjoy Barracks). Near the centre of the S side of the park is *St. Mary's* (Chest) *Hospital*, formerly the Hibernian Military School, with a chapel by Thomas Cooley (1771). It was the erection of the *Magazine Fort* (1734) on a hillock between this point and the main entrance that caused Swift to write his quatrain: 'Lo, here's a proof of Irish sense. Here Irish wit is seen. Where nothing's left that's worth defence, they build a magazine'.

An interesting return to the city centre may be made by leaving Phoenix Park by the *Knockmaroon Gate* (SW corner), and bearing left through the now suburban village of *Chapelizod*, traditionally taking its name from Isolde (or Iseult), daughter of Aengus, King of Ireland, and beloved of Tristan. It was also the scene of Sheridan Le Fanu's story 'The House by the Churchyard', and the birthplace of the autodidact newspaper magnate Alfred Harmsworth, later Lord Northcliffe (1865–1922).

For the road hence to *Celbridge*, see Rte 19.

From Chapelizod the centre may be regained by skirting the S wall of Phoenix Park, later passing the *Islandbridge Gate*.

From a point just E of the Islandbridge Gate, one may turn S along the South Circular Rd to approach the 'New' **Kilmainham Gaol**, designed by Sir John Traile, and ready for occupation in 1792. In 1866 it accommodated the Fenians; in 1881, the Land League agitators (including Parnell, Dillon, and Davitt); in 1883, the Invincibles; and in 1916, Republicans, where many were shot for treason, including Patrick H. Pearse, Seán MacDermott, Thomas MacDonagh, Éamonn Ceannt (Kent), Joseph M. Plunkett, Thomas J. Clarke, and James Connolly; among the exceptions were Sir Roger Casement, later hanged in London. In 1922 it lodged anti-Free State prisoners, but from 1924 to 1960 it remained untended to the elements. It is now being restored by volunteers as an *Historical Museum* in memory of these martyrs. Wilfred Scawen Blunt described his incarceration here and in Galway in 'In Vinculis' (1889). Note the carved panel of serpents known as 'the Five Devils of Kilmainham' above the rusticated entrance.

More historically edifying is the *Royal Hospital* at Kilmainham, a view of which may be glimpsed along the avenue immediately E of the gaol, adjacent to *Bully's Acre*, an ancient burial ground with a 10C sculptured cross-shaft. The Gothick *W Gatehouse*, the work of Francis Johnston, was moved here in 1846 from its former site beside the Liffey. The best approach to the hospital is by following Kilmainham Lane to the main entrance in Military Rd. The ***ROYAL HOSPITAL** (1680–87), recently scrupulously restored after decades of neglect, was founded by Charles II for 300 disabled and veteran soldiers at the instance of the Duke of Ormonde, then viceroy, who laid the foundation stone, and whose arms are above the exterior entrance to the Dining-hall. It was designed by Sir William Robinson in the Franco-Dutch Classical style. The Baroque *Chapel* contains some outstanding wood-carving by James Tabary, and a papier-mâché replica of the only florid Caroline ceiling in Ireland; the original, being unsafe, was dismantled in 1902. The clock-tower was added in 1701, and the Great Hall preserves pine panelling. The building is said to occupy the site of the cell of St. Maighnen (*Cill Maighneann*: Kilmainham), which was succeeded by a priory of the Knights of St. John, founded by Strongbow in 1174. It survived into the 1920s as a hospital, and was Police Headquarters from 1930–50. Restoration started in 1980. It is intended that the building, one of the more impressive in Dublin, and at present known as the National Centre for Culture and the Arts, will be used as an extension of the National Museum. Meanwhile one may apply to the Department of Works for permission to visit the interior.

Hence we may continue E, passing *St. Patrick's Hospital* (see above), to approach the extensive premises of the *Guinness Brewery* facing James St and Thomas St and *Christ Church*, see pp. 130 and 128, respectively.

A pendant to the above excursion is that to the *Botanic Gardens*, best approached by driving due N along Church St (Pl. 4) and its extension through the suburb of *Phibsborough*, and taking the right-hand fork shortly beyond the Royal Canal.— The **National Botanic Gardens** at *Glasnevin*, some 20 hectares, are skirted to the N by the river *Tolka*.

From their opening in 1790 until 1899, when the Department of Agriculture took charge, the gardens were under the care of the Royal Dublin Society; before that the demesne belonged to Thomas Tickell (1686–1740), the poet; and Swift, Steele, Delany, and Thomas Parnell all at one time lived in the vicinity; the yew walk in the garden is still known as 'Addison's Walk', although his connection with the district is not based on fact. Note the cast-iron *Palm House* (1842–50) by the Dublin ironfounder Richard Turner. The Rev. Patrick Delany's home, 'Delville', together with its plasterwork, was demolished in the 1940s.

Immediately to the SW is *Glasnevin* or *Prospect Cemetery*, in which are buried many of the advocates of Irish liberty, among them J.P. Curran (translated hence from London in 1834), Daniel O'Connell (from Genoa, where he died, and who was reburied in 1869 in the crypt under the Round Tower; he had also founded the cemetery, in 1832), C.S. Parnell, Arthur Griffith, Michael Collins, Thomas Ashe, William Dargan, James Larkin, Jeremiah O'Donovan Rossa, and (since 1965) Sir Roger Casement; also (in the Jesuit plot) Gerard Manley Hopkins.

Headquarters building of the Meteorological Service

On Glasnevin Hill, at the junction of Ballymun Road and the Old Finglas Road, is the pyramidal building housing the headquarters of the *Meteorological Service* (1980), designed by Liam McCormick and Partners. Clad in Ballinasloe limestone slabs, the building is surrounded by a moat.

F. South-eastern Environs

Lower Mount St (leading SE from Merrion Sq.) and Lower Baggot St (near the NE corner of St. Stephen's Green), with their extensions, converge a short distance beyond the Grand Canal near *Jury's Hotel* at **Ballsbridge**, one of the pleasantest residential suburbs of Dublin.— On the right is the cylindrical *American Embassy* (1964).

Crossing the river Dodder by a bridge of 1791, we reach the premises (right) of the **Royal Dublin Society**, behind which are their extensive *Show Grounds* (1881), where the Spring Show is held in early May and the Horse Show takes place in August. Visitors are courteously allowed to inspect the buildings, which accommodate a restaurant, bar, library, and concert-hall, etc.

The *Society*, founded in 1731 by 14 Dublin gentlemen (among them Thomas Prior and Sir Thomas Molyneux), and incorporated in 1750, occupied Leinster House from 1815 until 1925. It has specialised in the application of the arts and sciences to the country's use, among its activities having been the establishment of the Botanic Gardens (at Glasnevin; see above), the National Library and Museum, and the School of Art. Since 1877 it has been more particularly concerned with the encouragement of scientific agriculture and stock-breeding. Among early members of the Society were Samuel Madden, Henry Brooke, Patrick Delany, Lord Orrery, and Thomas Sheridan.

Opposite the RDS are the headquarters of the *Hospitals' Trust*, and the modern offices of the *Allied Irish Banks*.

We now follow Merrion Rd, shortly passing (right) the *British Embassy*, transferred here after the previous premises in Merrion Sq. were burnt out.—W.B. Yeats (1864–1939) was born at 'Georgeville', Sandymount Av., a short distance NE.

Shrewsbury Rd diverges immediately to the right, where at No. 20, set back from the road, is the ***CHESTER BEATTY LIBRARY** and **Gallery of Oriental Art**, one of the world's more important collections of Oriental art and MSS—and of Western books and MSS—donated to Ireland by Sir Alfred Chester Beatty (1875–1968), a Canadian mining millionaire, who in 1953 cehose to make Dublin his home. The collections were assembled over a period of 60 years, agents throughout the world assisting in the accumulation of materials descriptive of the w propagation of the written word.

The building nearest the entrance houses the *Garden Library*, containing European MSS displayed in furniture designed by Hicks of Dublin (1950–53). Among the illuminated works are a 12C Bible from Walsingham; a 'Speculum Historiale' (French; 1360–80) of the Duc de Berry, and numerous fine 15C examples, among them the Coëtivy Book of Hours (before 1445) and a prayer-book belonging to Philip II of Spain, with miniatures attributed to Simon Bening. Here too are the early printed books, and representative *bindings* of every period, notably an 18C Irish masterpiece (bound by Michael Wills), and icons.

On the far side of the garden is the *New Gallery* (1957), housing a Public Library and Lecture Theatre (seating 100). It accommodates the Oriental treasures, only a selection of which are on display at any one

The Simurgh rescues the infant Zol; from the Shah-Nama (Iran, 1590)

time, being periodically changed. To the left of the vestibule is the *Far Eastern Gallery*, with a selection of the 800 Chinese snuff-bottles in the collection; hand-scrolls; Chinese Rhinoceros-horn cups (11C); Chinese carved seals; two (of 18) Chinese imperial robes; and Jade books.

In an adjacent section are shown Japanese woodblock colour-prints—the collector had scruples at the inclusion of any of an erotic nature—Japanese and Chinese lacquer (the sap of the *Rhus*

Venicifera tree); Nara-e (paintings); Tsuba (sword guards); Inro (pill-boxes, etc.); and Netsuke.

Stairs ascend to the *Islamic Collection*, with a representative selection of Korans, largely from Persia, Egypt, and Turkey; Arabic bindings; Sanscrit MSS (12–13C) on palm-leaves; Persian lacquer-work; Indian miniatures, with a particularly fine collection from the Mughal period; Tibetan miniatures; Batak MSS from Sumatra; Burmese Parabaiks (18–19C) and 'concertina' books, 90m long, a curious example of folk art.

Among other precious items in the collections are the Babylonian clay tablets (2500–2300 BC); and Egyptian and Greek papyri, notably the Biblical texts. Here also are the near-Eastern MSS—Arabic, Syriac, Coptic, Hebrew, Turkish, Persian, Armenian, and Ethiopic—and medieval Greek, Serbian, and Bulgarian texts.

Anthony Trollope lived at No. 5 Seaview Terrace, a short distance to the S, in 1854–59.

Regaining the main road, the shore at *Merrion Strand* is soon reached, opposite the site of *Merrion Castle*, anciently the seat of the Fitzgeralds.—At *Blackrock* (*An Charraig Dhubh*) we pass (right) the site of the villa of 'Frascati', built for Provost Hely Hutchinson of Trinity and occupied in 1793–99 by Lord Edward Fitzgerald and his beautiful Pamela as their first Irish home; most of the demesne has been built over. Blackrock was the birthplace of John Dillon (1851–1927), the Nationalist politician; Kevin O'Higgins (1892–1927) the statesman, was assassinated there.

At contiguous *Monkstown* is an eccentric *Church* by John Semple, with its chessmen-like turrets, and remains of its castle.

DÚN LAOGHAIRE (as it is usually spelt), or *Dunleary* (as it is pronounced; 54,500 inhab.), was known as *Kingstown* from the embarkation of George IV (who had disembarked at Howth in an undignified state of inebriation) in 1821 until the establishment of the Free State a century later, when all such memorials of the British 'Ascendancy' were as intemperately swept away. Its harbour, long the Irish terminus for the mail-boat, and now of the Sealink ferry to Holyhead, was designed by John Rennie, and was under construction from 1817 to 1859, being connected with Dublin by rail in 1834. The artist Sarah Purser (1848–1943) was born here.

Dún Laoghaire is Ireland's principal yachting centre and the HQ of several clubs, of which the Royal St. George and the Royal Irish are the oldest (designed by J.S. Mulvany; 1832 and 1846 respectively). A *Maritime Museum* has been installed in the *Mariners' Church*, containing a number of historical models, including one of 'The Great Eastern', the cable-layer (cf. Valentia Island), and a ship's boat of 1796.

At **Sandycove**, to the E, the birthplace of Sir Roger Casement (1864–1916), is a *Martello Tower* in which James Joyce (with Oliver St. John Gogarty; 'Buck Mulligan') resided briefly in September 1904, and which is described in the first chapter of 'Ulysses'. It now houses a small *Joyce Museum*, opened in 1962, initiated by Sylvia Beach, the first publisher of his masterpiece in Paris 40 years previously. These martello towers are characteristic of this stretch of the coast, when they were erected in anticipation of Napoleonic invasion.—Near by is the 'Forty-Foot Hole', a cove popular with strong swimmers.

From Sandycove the road passes restored *Bullock Castle* (with a small museum), an old battlemented house above a little harbour, and enters **Dalkey** (pron. Dawky), a residential resort beneath the N slope of Killiney Hill. It has been claimed that John Dowland (?1563–1626), composer and lutenist, may have been born here. In the main street are remains of fortified mansions (15–16C) and a ruined church (St. Begnets), relics of its earlier importance, when Dalkey roadstead was the principal landing-place of passengers from England.

From the town centre one may ascend to *Sorrento Point* for the view S towards Bray Head and the two Sugar Loaf hills (see Rte 2B).—Hence the Vico road follows the coast, skirting the Killiney hills before descending to *Killiney* itself; see Rte 2A.

Below is *Dalkey Island*, with a small ruined Benedictine church and martello tower. It was a stronghold of Danish pirates, and in the 18C notorious for the periodical elections of the 'King of Dalkey', originally a student prank, but later invested with political significance until suppressed by Lord Clare in 1797. The last 'king' was a bookseller, named Armitage.

Dalkey Av. climbs S to *Dalkey Hill*, with its park, whence a path lead to the summit crowned by an old telegraph tower (*View*). *Torca Cottage*, on the hill, was the boyhood home of G.B. Shaw in 1866–74.—On the E side is a quarry which supplied granite for the construction of Dún Laoghaire harbour. On adjacent *Killiney Hill* is an obelisk erected as a famine relief work in 1742.

G. North-eastern Environs

A round trip of c 40km (25 miles).

From the *Custom House* (Pl. 4; see p 135) we follow Amiens St NE.— To the left in Portland Row stands *Aldborough House* (Pl. 2), once an imposing building (1792–98) in the style of Sir William Chambers, and now a Post Office store.—The road crosses the Royal Canal and the river Tolka. On the N bank, to the W, is the sports ground of *Croke r Park*, named after Abp Croke (1824–1902), a strong advocate of athletics and temperance. The road skirts (right) *Fairview Park*, on land reclaimed from the sea.—For the *Casino* at *Marino*, a suburb a short distance up the Malahide road; see p 151.—Just E of this junction one o may take either the Howth Rd, passing in the suburb of *Killester* the ruins of an old church and abbey, or bearing right, skirt Dublin Bay and *Clontarf* (*Cluain Tarbh*, bull's meadow), the scene of the battle of Good Friday, 1014, when the Irish under Brian Ború, mortally wounded in the combat, broke the power of the Danes. *Clontarf Castle* (1835) was built on the site of an ancient fortification of the Pale, which had belonged successively to the Templars and to the Knights of St. John.

Beyond *Dollymount* we pass (left) *St. Anne's Park*, and (right) *North Bull Island*, accommodating the Royal Dublin and St. Anne's golf links. The two roads to Howth converge at *Kilbarrack*, with a ruined 13C church said to be a votive chapel of the mariners of Dublin Bay, and a short distance beyond, at *Sutton*, we reach the narrow isthmus of the **Howth Peninsula**. Whistler occupied a villa here in 1900, and caused consternation by papering over half its north-facing windows!

The road skirts the N shore of the peninsula, passing (right) the main entrance to *Howth Castle* demesne; see below.

The peninsula was acquired in 1177 by Sir Almeric Tristram, a Norman noble, and the lands have remained without a break in the possession of his family. The change of name to St. Lawrence is attributed to a vow of Sir Almeric's, made at a battle fought on St. Lawrence's Day, to assume the name if victorious.

Howth itself, a resort of steep streets, has an unexpectedly large harbour, and commands a view of Ireland's Eye.

The name of Howth is derived from the Danish 'hoved' (head) and is pronounced to rhyme with 'both'; the Irish name, *Binn Eadair*, recalls the legendary hero, Edar. It was the Dublin packet-station from 1813 until it was superseded by Kingstown (cf. Dún Laoghaire) in 1833. Its harbour, constructed in 1807–09, and frequented by both yachts and fishing-boats, was the scene of the gun-running incident of 26 July 1914 (following the success of the Larne gun-running shortly before, arming the Ulster Volunteers). Only 900 rifles and 25,000 rounds of ammunition were landed here from Germany in Robert Erskine Childer's yacht the 'Asgard' to similarly arm the Irish Volunteers. The sequel to this was the reprehensible Bachelors' Walk affair; see p 142.

The offshore quartzite rock of *Ireland's Eye*, now a bird sanctuary, bears the ruins of an old chapel, the successor of one built in the 7C by the sons of St. Nessan. On its N-facing cliff nest the peregrine falcon, shearwater, guillemot, fulmar petrel, puffin, and other sea birds; many species of tern frequent the Malahide estuary.—*Lambay Island* (p 324) is seen beyond.

The *Abbey Church*, above the harbour, and surrounded by a wall, is in part a Danish foundation of 1042, perhaps built by Sigtryg, but the main part of the church, with rude square piers, dates from c 1245, and the E end was added in the 15C. Near the SE corner is the tomb of Christopher, Lord Howth (died 1430) and his lady, with the St. Lawrence and Plunkett arms.—Facing Abbey St is the so-called *College* (16C).

Howth Castle, a few minutes' walk W of the town, is an irregular battlemented structure dating from 1564, but much restored (probably by Francis Bindon in 1738, and by Morrison and Lutyens since), and the seat of the Earl of Howth until the death of the 4th Earl and 30th Baron in 1909.

For many years the castle door was open to all comers at mealtimes, a custom dating, it is said, from 1575, when Grace O'Malley, the uncrowned queen of the West (cf. Clare Island), passed by on her return journey to Ireland after visiting Queen Elizabeth. Inhospitably refused admittance to the castle on the excuse that the family was at dinner, she abducted the heir of Howth to her castle of Carrigahowley, and retained possession of him until she had wrung a promise from Lord Howth to keep his gates open at mealtimes in the future. The story is apocryphal.

The *Gardens are famous for their rhododendrons and for the early 18C formal garden with its 9m-high beech hedges. In the demesne are the ruins of *Corr Castle*, a tall square 16C edifice, and a dolmen.

The road climbs SE from the village centre to make the circle of the peninsula, now being regrettably over-exploited: villas and housing estates continue to proliferate. From *The Summit* one may climb to the *Ben of Howth* (171m), with a cairn said to cover the remains of King Crimhthan Niadhnair (AD 90). A cliff walk approaches the *Baily Lighthouse* (1814) on the SE point, erected on the site of an old stone fort or baile, and replacing the older hill-top beacon.—The road returning to Sutton round the S side of the peninsula, providing extensive views towards Dublin, passes (left) the ruined church of *St. Fintan* (9C, but altered) in a graveyard.

From Sutton we may bear NW, and then turn N, skirting the coast near a sandy peninsula known as the *Velvet Strand*, and soon enter the village of **Malahide** (9,150 inhab.), a resort on the estuary of the Broad Meadow river, with a parish church preserving some of the few hatchments in Ireland, and the villa of *Emsworth* (c 1790), by Gandon.

SW of the village is the demesne of *Malahide Castle, seat of the Talbot family (except during the years 1653–60, when it was tenanted by the regicide Miles Corbet) since Richard Talbot received a grant of land here in the reign of Henry II, and until the late Lord Talbot's decease in 1975, when it was acquired by the Dublin County Council.

Considerably altered over the centuries, the present building is flanked by two slender drum towers of c 1765. Between 1928 and 1948 many of the papers of James Boswell (great-grandfather of Emily Boswell, who married the 5th Lord Talbot) came to light in the castle, including the original version of the 'Tour to the Hebrides' and an early draft of the 'Life of Johnson', which were acquired by Yale University, as described in 'The Treasure of Auchinleck' by David Buchanan (1975). It is said that on the morning of the Battle of the Boyne some 14 Talbots, all first cousins, breakfasted at Malahide before sallying out to their death in that contest, which is depicted in a painting by Jan Wyck hanging over the fireplace in the Great Hall. The hall is the only surviving medieval Great Hall in Ireland to retain its original form and, until recently, to remain in domestic use.

Among the more notable paintings on display here in the spring of 1986 were: after Van Dyck, The Concert; after Maratti, Luke Wadding (founder of the Irish College in Rome; cf. Waterford); Kneller, Portraits of General Godert van Ginkel and of Richard Steele; after Batoni, the Earl-bishop of Derry; George Barret, several landscapes; anon. Irish School, William Conolly and Adam Loftus; Lely, James Butler, 1st Duke of Ormonde; Longhi, Portrait of General Christopher Nugent; attrib. Thomas Hickey, Portrait of Joseph Hickey; Romney, The artist's wife; John Lewis, Portrait of Thomas Sheridan; Frank Reynolds, Coursing enthusiasts; Hogarth, Portrait of Lord Wade; after Hogarth, 2nd Viscount Boyne.

The 14–15C Abbey beside the castle was unroofed by Corbet (see above), but contains the 15C tomb of Maud Plunkett, 'maid, wife, and widow in one day', who survived to marry Sir Richard Talbot as her third husband.

A Railway Museum is being installed in the old Corn Store at Malahide, with a collection of model trains, etc.

Swords (see Rte 31) lies 4km to the W.—The return road to Dublin from Malahide (R107) leading S, shortly passes (right) Feltrim Hill, crowned by a mill, and the old seat of the Fagans, where James II spent a night on his flight from the Boyne.—3km St. Doolagh (or Dulough), a hamlet with a * Church which is one of the oldest still in use in Ireland (c 1230), with a high-pitched roof and sturdy square 15C tower with stepped battlements, and 19C additions. Inside are two chambers lighted by Gothic windows with trefoil heads; in the smaller is the so-called tomb of St. Doolagh; and three staircases lead to vaulted upper chambers. To the N is an octagonal stone-roofed building which probably served as a baptistery; on the roadside is a stone cross.—Nathaniel Hone, the Younger (1831–1917), the landscape painter, lived near by during the latter part of his life.

We soon enter the NE outskirts of Dublin, after passing through Artane, where the partisans of 'Silken Thomas' murdered Abp Allen, Wolsey's nominee, in 1534. We shortly see on our right, in the grounds of Lord Charlemont's old estate of Marino (the house of which was demolished in 1921), a charming little Palladian *Casino (1762–71, but not entirely completed until some years later), by Sir William Chambers. Its roof urns are chimneys; its sculptures are by Simon Vierpyl and Joseph Wilton; and the whole building has recently been the object of the overdue restoration it deserved. Four carved stone lions by Wilton crouch at the corners of the terrace. Both Arthur Young and (two years later, in 1778) John Wesley visited the demesne, which delighted them.

We regain the Howth road at Fairview Park, immediately to the SW, to re-enter the city near the Custom House.

2   Dublin to Wexford

A. Via Wicklow

146km (91 miles). N11. 21km *Bray*—27km *Rathnew*, 2km NW of
Wicklow—26km *Arklow*—17km *Gorey*—17km *Ferns*—12km
Enniscorthy—24km **Wexford**.

The direct road leaves Dublin by Leeson St (SW corner of St. Stephen's
Green), soon crossing the Grand Canal, and traversing the suburb of
Donnybrook, on the river *Dodder*. Donnybrook was famous for its fair,
founded by King John in 1204, the noisy mirth and pugnacity with
which it was conducted leading to its suppression in 1855. (Barrington
was told by a priest that more marriages were celebrated in Dublin
during the week after the fair than in any two months of the rest of the
year.) Its place has been taken by the *Irish Radio and TV Centre*.

Sir Edward Lovett Pearce (c 1699–1733), the architect, is buried in
Old Donnybrook churchyard.

The improved road passes (right) the extensive *Bellfield Campus*,
dotted with the modern buildings of *University College*, in construction since the mid-1960s.

Stillorgan, birthplace of Sir William Orpen (1878–1931), with the
slight remains (left), including an obelisk of 1727 by Sir Edward Lovett
Pearce, of the demesne of the Viscounts Allen, shortly beyond which
we pass (right) *Galloping Green* and a road leading to the
Leopardstown racecourse, with the Wicklow hills rising beyond.

Further S, to the right, is the village of *Carrickmines*, with a ruined church said to
be of Danish foundation; at *Brenanstown*, nearer the main road, in the private
grounds of *Glendruid*, is a fine portal dolmen.

We next traverse *Loughanstown*, with a 12–13C church and a tall cross
in a nearby field, and as the road descends the Shanganagh vale the
Sugar Loaf (see Rte 2B) comes into view on the right front.

To the E lies *Killiney*, a small resort below Dalkey Hill to the N (see Rte 1F), with a
strand extending all the way to Bray. The old *Church* on the hill, possibly 11C, is
of the Glendalough type, retaining a W doorway with inclined jambs, with a
primitive cross under the lintel, and a semicircular chancel arch; the N nave wall
had openings which led to an added aisle.

On the flank of *Carrickgolligan Hill* (left; 278m) are the ruins of the old
church of *Rathmichael* and the stump of a *Round Tower*.—We pass the
ruins of *Kilturk* church (left), and crossing the river Dargle, enter
BRAY (*Bré*; 22,850 inhab.), an attractively sited dormitory town and
resort, popular since the mid 19C. It was James Joyce's family home
from 1888 to 1891. The town is sheltered by *Bray Head* to the SE (rising
further S to 240m), its summit commanding a close view of the Little
and Great Sugar Loaf.

BRAY TO WICKLOW BY THE COAST ROAD (25km). Following the R761 S, we
pass (right) *Kilruddery*, the Tudor-revival seat (c 1820, by Sir Richard Morrison)
of the Earls of Meath, famous in hunting annals. It preserves *Formal Gardens
dating from the late 17C, with twin canals and pond; above it rises the *Cnoc
Gilspir* or *Little Sugar Loaf* (341m). A little further S the Great Sugar Loaf comes
into view again, while to the left are the ruined church and castle of *Rathdown*.—
After 6km we pass (right) the remains of *Kindlestown*, a 13C halled castle.—To
the E lies the resort of **Greystones**; to the SW is *Delgany* (together 7,450 inhab.),
the latter with a prominent church of 1789 containing the imposing monument to

David La Touche, by John Hickey (1751–95).—We traverse *Newcastle*, named after a fort of the Pale, before regaining the main road at *Rathnew*.

From *Little Bray*, on the N bank of the Dargle, we ascend the valley, shortly entering *Kilbride*, at the confluence of the Dargle and Glen-cullen streams, just to the SW of which, in the grounds of *Killcroney*, are the remains of the old church.—Hence a by-road climbs due W up the deep wooded *Dargle Glen* in the Powerscourt demesne, the grey shell of the great house (see Rte 2B) being seen from *View Rock*, backed by the distant mass of Kippure.

Better views are provided by taking the improved road (R761) forking right in Bray, which rejoins the main road near the demesne of *Hollybrook*, with its holly, arbutus, and ilex shrubs. A former house here was the home of Robin Adair (c 1737), made famous by the song set to the old Irish air 'Eileen Aroon'. Hence the road passes *Kilmacanoge*, at the foot of the *Rocky Valley*, through which a lane leads up to join the R755 W of the *Great Sugar Loaf* (503m; for its ascent, see Rte 2B). We now enter a defile between the Great and Little Sugar Loaf known as the *Glen of the Downs*, the ancient bed of a displaced river now a wooded ravine, and descend through a series of demesnes to *Newton Mount Kennedy*, including *Mount Kennedy* itself, designed in 1772 by James Wyatt and built in 1782 by Thomas Cooley and Richard Johnston, and containing elaborate plaster-work by Stapleton. Beyond *Dunran*, in its rocky glen, we by-pass (right) the village of *Ashford*, on the Vartry.

Hence a by-road ascends the valley near the *Devil's Glen*, a romantic defile with its waterfall, and the remains of *Glenmore*, a castellated pile erected by Francis Johnston for Francis Synge, a great-grandfather of J.M. Synge, and partially rebuilt.

Just beyond Ashford are the *Gardens of Mount Usher*, laid out in 1868 by the Walpole family, and preserving some rare plants. Also to be seen here is an extensive collection of carriages, traps, carts, etc.— At *Rathnew* (1,350 inhab.) the R752 diverges SW to (14km) *Rathdrum*, see Rte 2B, and SE to adjacent *Wicklow*.

The county town of **WICKLOW** (5,200 inhab.), of Viking foundation, lies on a long creek or 'wick' through which the Vartry enters the sea, flanked by a grassy strip of land known as *The Morrough*. Near the town entrance are the ruins of a *Franciscan friary* founded in 1279 by the O'Byrnes and O'Tooles after defeating the Fitzgeralds; a statue in the town commemorates Miles Byrne (1780–1862) and leaders of the 1798 insurrection. The 18C *Church*, with a square tower and dome, preserves a Romanesque door of a medieval church.—On the cliffs to the S are remains of *Black Castle*, begun c 1175 by Maurice Fitzgerald.

Beyond *Wicklow Head* and as far as *Brittas Bay* and *Mizen Head*, extends the *Silver Strand*, spoilt by caravans, and seen only intermittently from the road.

We may regain the main road (N11) SW of Wicklow, to approach **ARKLOW** (8,650 inhab.), a boat-building centre at the mouth of the Avoca, with an imposing stone domed church of c 1840, and the tower of an old castle. It was the scene of General Needham's defeat of the insurgents in 1798.

From Arklow we drive SW, passing (left) the isolated hill of *Tara* (253m; not to be confused with that in Meath) before entering **Gorey** (2,600 inhab.) with its long main street, once an important cattle market.

Hence there are two direct roads S to Wexford, that nearer the coast (R742) passing through (6.5km) *Courtown*, a small resort on a sandy strand backed by dunes, some 6.5km S of which a track leads left to *Glascarrig Abbey*, with ruins of a Benedictine house.

The parallel road (R741) traverses uninteresting pastoral country, after 22km passing (right) *Oulart Hill*, the scene of an insurgent victory on 27 May 1798 under Fr John Murphy, before the disaster of Vinegar Hill (see below). We cross the Slaney by an iron bridge some 19km beyond, to enter *Wexford*.

The main road from Gorey continues SW parallel to a range of hills, among them *Slieveboy* (421m) to (18km) **FERNS** (800 inhab.), once the capital of the Kingdom of Leinster, and still sharing a bishop with Ossory and Leighlin. Ferns was many times plundered by the Danes, and suffered similarly at the hands of Dermot MacMurrough's rivals, being a refuge of that chieftain. The first monastery here was built after 598 in memory of St. Mogue (Maedoc-Edan) of Clonmore. The *Cathedral* (1816–17) incorporates the central part of the chancel of an older building (1223–43; burnt in 1577) containing the monument of an ecclesiastic, perhaps Bp St. John (died 1243). To the E are the remains of the *Austin Priory*, founded by MacMurrough c 1160, where a cross-shaft covered with a key pattern is said to mark his grave. The tower (23m high), with a square lower stage, is round above. There are some plain High Crosses in the churchyard. On the hill outside the village are the ruins of *St. Peter's* (17C), apparently reconstructed with fragments from two older buildings. The *Castle* (early 13C), on the site of the stronghold of the Kings of Leinster, was partially dismantled in 1641 by Sir Charles Coote, but retains a cylindrical angle-tower and a beautifully vaulted oratory. The *Bishop's Palace*, near the cathedral, is 18C. The village also preserves a few old cottages, and has a modern pyramidal-shaped church. A hill just to the W commands a good view of Mt Leinster (surmounted by a wireless mast) and the Blackstairs range.

Shortly beyond Ferns we meet the N80 (see Rte 2C), where we bear left for **ENNISCORTHY** (5,000 inhab.), built at the head of the navigable reach of the Slaney. It retains its four-storey *Castle-keep* with corner towers in excellent preservation, having been rebuilt in 1586–95 by Sir Henry Wallop on the site of the mid-13C original, and restored by his descendant the Earl of Portsmouth in the 19C. It was taken by Cromwell in person in 1649. Since 1963 it has housed a small local museum of bygones. *St. Aidan's Cathedral* (1843–48), by A.W. Pugin, has a later tower built with stones from an old Franciscan monastery. There is a ruined church, *Templeshannon*, at the N end of the town.

Over the E bank of the Slaney rises *Vinegar Hill* (121m), with the shell of its windmill, the final position occupied by the Irish insurgent forces after the capture and sack of the town in 1798. Here on 21 June some 500 were killed when the hill was assaulted by General Lake with 13,000 men; the remainder of the motley army rapidly dispersed.—*Monart*, a Georgian mansion with a Venetian window, lies some 4km W of the town off the R702.

ENNISCORTHY TO NEW ROSS (32km). Veering W, and then SW, the N79 traverses the foothills of the Blackstairs range, and 3km before entering *New Ross* (see Rte 5) by-passes (right) *Mountgarret Bridge*, and the old keep of *Mountgarret Castle*. For the road hence to Waterford, see Rte 8.

Skirting the E bank of the Slaney, after 4km we pass (right) *Black Castle*, once a Franciscan Abbey, the lands of which were later held by Edmund Spenser.—At the next main junction we may either bear right to cross the river by the *Ferrycarrig Bridge*, the scene of a skirmish in 1798, and overlooked by the ruined *Castle* of Robert

Fitzstephen (the first built by the Anglo-Normans in Ireland, in 1169), or left through *Castlebridge*, to approach Wexford from the N, passing near (left) the wildfowl reserve of *North Slobs*—that of *South Slobs* lies on the far bank of the wide harbour. The estuary is crossed by a new bridge commanding a pleasant view of the town.

WEXFORD (11,400 inhab.), an old county town traversed by a long narrow meandering main street flanked by innumerable bars, and running parallel to the quays overlooking the harbour, is a manufacturing centre for agricultural machinery. Since 1951 it has also been the venue of a Music Festival in late October.

Associated in legend with the pre-Christian Queen Garman (its Irish name is *Loch Garman*), Wexford (*Waesfjord*) first appeared in history in the 9C as a Danish Viking settlement, which seems to have maintained its independence until 1169, when MacMurrough and his Anglo-Norman allies Robert Fitzstephen and Maurice Fitzgerald captured it. In 1174 Strongbow here celebrated the marriage of his sister Basilia de Clare and Raymond 'le Gros' Fitzgerald. In 1649 Cromwell took Wexford, destroyed the churches, and massacred the garrison. Some 80 'Defenders' were killed here in July 1793; in 1798 it was held by the United Irish insurgents.

The landscape painter Francis Danby (1793–1861) was born here; also, in what is now part of 'White's Hotel', Sir Robert McClure (1807–73), discoverer of the NW Passage; Jane Elgee, later Lady Wilde (1826–96; who wrote under the pseudonym of 'Speranza') and mother of Oscar, was born in the old rectory, Main St.

At the NW end of the town are the ruins of *Selskar Abbey*, a priory founded by the Roches, Lords of Fermoy, at the end of the 12C. The square battlemented *Westgate Tower* survives of the town gates, and the 19C church adjoining it stands on the spot where the first treaty between the Anglo-Normans and the Irish was ratified in 1169. In the garden above the Bull Ring, towards the centre, are the ruins of *St. Mary's*, on the site of a commandery of the Knights Hospitallers. Further S, off the Main St, are the conspicuous ruins of *St. Patrick's*. Cromwell occupied No. 29 South Main St in 1649. A plaque marks Thomas Moore's residence in 1851 in the Cornmarket, while on *Crescent Quay* is a statue of Commodore John Barry (1745–1803), born at Ballysampson (near Tacumshin; see below). Commanding the 'Lxexington' in taking H.M.S. 'Edward', Barry effected the first capture of the US Navy (although he subsequently suffered defeat and lost his ship). The so-called *Twin Churches* (1851–58) are by Robert Pierce.

For the cross-country roads from Wexford to Athlone via Carlow and Portlaoise, and via Kilkeeny, Rosscrea, and Birr (for Galway), see Rtes 20A and B.

WEXFORD HARBOUR, an extensive bay over 13km wide and 6.5km long, famous for its swans, is safe but shallow, and cross-channel ferries from Fishguard and Le Havre now berth at **Rosslare Harbour**, c 19km SE by the N25. The resort of *Rosslare*, with a sandy strand, is approached from *Killinick*, about half-way between Wexford and Rosslare Harbour.

Some 4km S of Rosslare Harbour stands *Ballytrent House*, birthplace of John Redmond (1856–1918), for many years leader of the Irish Party in the British parliament after the eclipse of Parnell. A ring-fort lies within the grounds.—Out to sea rises the *Tuskar Rock*, with a lighthouse built in 1815 and improved in 1885.—To the N are the cliffs of *Greenore Point*; to the S is *Carnsore Point*, the sandy SE extremity of Ireland. Near by are remains of *St. Vogue's Church*, built by St. Veoc, who died in Brittany in 585.

6km SE of *Killinick* (see above) is *Tacumshin*, where one of the few remaining windmills in Ireland may be seen (1846; reconstructed 1952). To the E of Tacumshin is a lagoon known as LADY'S ISLAND LAKE; the island itself, connected by a causeway with the mainland, preserves the ruins of a monastery and castle keep (both c 1237) and a later tower.

EXCURSION FROM WEXFORD TO KILMORE QUAY (23km). 7km S of Wexford we fork to the right off the Rosslare road, shortly passing (right) *Rathmacknee Castle*, probably erected by John Rosseter in 1451. It has a five-sided bawn and a five-storey tower with stepped battlements.—A short distance beyond (right) lies *Mayglass*, with a church ruined in 1798, retaining Norman arches, and further S (left) *Bargy Castle*, another tower- house (converted to a hotel), once the property of Bagenal Harvey (see below).

The so-called 'English Baronies' of Bargy and Forth were colonised by Anglo-Norman adventurers from South Wales in the 12C, and may be reckoned as the part of Ireland where the English language has been spoken the longest. At adjacent *Tomhaggard* is a late-14C church near the Tacumshin Lake.—Continuing SW, at *Forlorn Point* is the hamlet of *Kilmore Quay*, known to deep-sea fishermen for its bass and pollack.

Boats may be hired to visit the offshore reef-girt **Saltee Island**, once the terror of navigators. Beauchamp Bagenal Harvey (1762–98) and John Henry Colclough (1769–98), two leaders of the Wexford insurrection, were discovered after the rout of Vinegar Hill hiding in a cave on the outer *Great Saltee*, and were escorted thence to Wexford, where they were beheaded. The island is now a bird sanctuary.

The return trip may be made by driving due N past (right) *Ballyteige Castle* (15–15C), and after 6km forking right for *Murntown*, shortly beyond which (right), we pass *Johnstown Castle*, a massive pile designed by Daniel Robertson in a Norman and Gothick-revival style, encasing the 13C stronghold of the Esmonde and Fitzgerald families; it now accommodates an agricultural college.

For *Coolhull Castle* and the district between it and Waterford Harbour, see p 172.

B. Via Enniskerry and Laragh (for Glendalough)

146km (91 miles). R117. 21km *Enniskerry*—R755. 25km *Laragh* (for **Glendalough**)—11km *Rathdrum*—R752 and 747. 19km *Arklow*—N11. 17km *Gorey*—17km *Ferns*—12km *Enniscorthy*—24km **Wexford**.

DUBLIN TO ROUNDWOOD VIA THE SALLY GAP: an ALTERNATIVE but more mountainous route to Glendalough. At *Terenure* (see Rte 2C) we turn due S along the R115 across the Dodder, passing (left) *Rathfarnham Castle*. Built by Abp Loftus in c 1580–95, it was later the residence of the Marquess of Ely, who erected the triumphal arch at the N entry.—W.B. Yeats's last home, from 1932, called 'Riversdale', is not far S of *Rathfarnham*.—3km further S we fork right and commence the ascent, passing (left) *Mt Venus*, with a large dolmen, probably never roofed.—Higher up we cross the flank of *Killakee*, behind which rises *Glendoo Mountain* (587m). To the right lies the Glenasmole valley (entered by a road circling the W of the one described), with its reservoir.

Crossing the shoulder of a ridge ascending S to *Kippure* (752m), the highest peak in Dublin County, we descend to *Glencree*. On the left is a *Cemetery* (1961) in which are interred c 100 German servicemen whose bodies were washed up on the Irish coast in both World Wars.—Two roads descend the Glencree valley: one to the N of the river—with a view of *Powerscourt*—leading directly to *Enniskerry* (see below), passing at *Parknasilloge* a small but perfect dolmen; the other road, bears left further S (along the flank of *Tonduff*), from which we may approach the Powerscourt waterfall; see below.—The road continues S from Glencree, shortly passing (right) LOWER and UPPER LOUGH BRAY, and climbs to the *Sally Gap*. For roads hence, see Rte 2C.

From Dame St (Pl. 6) we turn S into Great George St, and shortly fork left through the suburb of *Ranelagh*, the site of the 'Bloody Fields', scene of a massacre of the early English colonists by the men of Wicklow on Easter Monday, 1209; it was later the site of a pleasure-garden like its London namesake. The R117 soon turns right through

Milltown, on the Dodder, and *Dundrum*, with the ruins of a castle in the demesne of *Dundrum Castle*, home of William Dargan (1799–1867) largely responsible for laying the Irish railways; Roebuck Lodge, at *Clonskeagh*, was the home of Maud Gonne MacBride (1866–1953), the Nationalist, and friend of Yeats. We continue through *Stepaside*, at the foot of the *Three Rocks Mountain* (450m), with a tall (12C?) *Cross* by the roadside at *Kilgobbin*, its church in ruins. Some distance to the right of the next village, *Kiltiernan*, with a curious little church, is a large dolmen with a capstone almost 7m long.

The road now ascends a hill to the defile of *The Scalp* before climbing down into the Glencullan valley past the site of a monastery (left) to **Enniskerry**, a charming village (1200 inhab.), with a copper-spired church, and a good centre for excursions into the hills. An additional attraction are shops supplying clothes designed by Donald Davies, although their manufacture is no longer a local industry. Until recently these were produced in the out-houses of neighbouring *Charleville House*, rebuilt by Whitmore Davis c 1820 after a disastrous fire in 1792; the interior may have been designed by Sir Richard Morrison.

Less than 1km S is the entrance (right) to the demesne of **Powerscourt House**, magnificently situated, the gardens of which are open to the public. A beech avenue leads up to the house, an imposing granite building (1731–41) by Castle, encasing an earlier house, with two arcades connecting the central block to two-storeyed pavilions. At present the shell of the main block stands desolately in its gardens,

The gardens of Powerscourt House

for in November 1974 it was virtually gutted by fire, which destroyed many of its valuable contents.

The *Gardens, although laid out in the 18C, were radically trans-formed between 1843 and 1875, and are entered through fine wrought-iron *Gates* (c 1770) brought here from the Cathedral of Bamberg, Bavaria. The *View* from the 244m-long *Terrace* looking across the Dargle valley towards the Great and Little Sugar Loaf, is very striking.

Maurice Craig informs us that Daniel Robertson, designer of the upper terraces—but as far as is known no relation of the present Editor—'was wheeled about the place in a wheelbarrow grasping a bottle of Sherry. When the Sherry was finished Mr Robertson ended his designing for the day'.—Also of interest is the *Armoury.*—Plants may be bought at nurseries near the entrance.

A walk of c 6km through rhododendron woods will bring one to the Powerscourt waterfall, but this is also easily approached by car from the main road; see below.

On regaining the main road, turn right. After crossing the Dargle by the *Tinnehinch Bridge*, one of the more attractive spots in the district, and passing (right) the entrance to *Charleville House* (see above), the next right-hand turning leads to the entrance of the Deer-park (left) in which the *Powerscourt Waterfall*, the highest in the British Isles, hurls itself obliquely across a rock-shelf 120m high. Above it rise the summits of *War Hill* and *Douce Mountain* (724m).

Tinnehinch House replaces one presented to Henry Grattan by the Irish Parliament in 1782.

Returning to the main road, we bear right towards (11km) *Roundwood*, also approached by a minor road parallel to it to the W. To the E rises the **Great Sugar Loaf** (503m), a steep but simple climb from the highest point of the main road, and rewarded by one of the finest *Views* in the area.

Inland is the great mass of the Wicklow Mountains, with Douce, War Hill, and *Maulin* in the foreground, and *Tonduff* behind, while away to the SW is *Lugnaquilla*, 924m. To the NE, the coast can be followed from Bray to Howth, with the Mourne Mountains in the far distance, while on a clear day the Welsh hills are visible to the E.

Before entering *Roundwood* we pass (left) the VARTRY RESERVOIR, part of Dublin's water supply.

A lane to the right beyond Roundwood leads to (3km) *Oldbridge*, from where the Lough Dan area can be explored. In the hills above the Lough, Joseph Holt, the insurgent, held out for three months after the disasters of 1798 before surrendering to Lord Powerscourt and being transported to Botany Bay, returning in 1813. To the N is LOUGH TAY, situated in a cliff-girt basin, which may also be approached from the Sally Gap road; see Rte 2C.

We descend the Annamoe valley. **Annamoe** itself was the scene of the remarkable escape from death of Laurence Sterne, who at the age of seven, when staying at the parsonage, fell unharmed through the mill-race while the mill was working. Hence the road winds steeply down to *Laragh*, a small village at the confluence of the Annamoe and Avonmore, where we turn right for the important Early-Christian site of *Glendalough*, 3km distant.

The *VALE OF GLENDALOUGH* ('glen of the two lakes') soon splits up into two valleys, the *Vale of Glendasan*, to the N, being followed by a road from the Wicklow Gap (see Rte 2C); the left-hand fork continues along Glendalough itself, its Lower and Upper Lakes being flanked to the S by *Mullacor* and *Lugduff*, and to the N by

Camaderry. The best view up the valley, with the flat-topped mass of *Table Mountain* in the distance (699m), may be obtained from the hillside above the neighbouring hotel.

A lane hence continues up the valley to a car-park close to the shore of the Upper Lake.

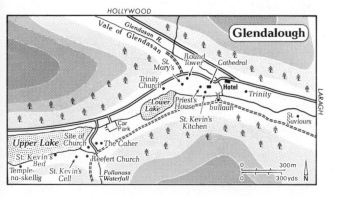

The foundation of Glendalough as an ecclesiastical site is ascribed to St. Kevin (*Coemhghen*, the fair-born), a scion of the royal house of Leinster, who built a church on the S bank of the upper lake some time in the 6C. Later he removed to the opening of the valley and died there at an advanced age in 618. The monastery which his disciples built flourished until the 11C, when it was ravaged by the Danes. In 1398 the English of Dublin sacked it, and by the 16C the destruction was almost complete.

The first group of old buildings lies in a cemetery enclosure approached through a plain ruined gateway of two arches above which once stood a tower, standing just behind the hotel.

The *Cathedral*, the nearest ruin, was probably erected at the beginning of the 9C, although the chancel, constructed of less massive masonry than the nave, is 11–12C. The chancel arch has been partly rebuilt. Note the clustered shafts of the N doorway, the ornamental E window (of an oolite foreign to the neighbourhood), and the grave slabs.—To the S is St. Kevin's Cross (c 1150), a granite monolith 3.3m high, perhaps unfinished, for the wheel enclosing the cross is unpierced.—Near it is the *Priest's House* (12C), partly reconstructed in 1875–80, above the door of which is a carved figure of St. Kevin (?) between two ecclesiastics (damaged).

The most interesting building is slightly further down the slope, and is known as *St. Kevin's Kitchen*. It is in fact a fine example of a two-storeyed oratory, 7m by 4.5m in area, with a steeply pitched stone roof. Within, it consists of a barrel-vaulted lower chamber and a loft above. A chancel (since demolished) and sacristy were later added at the E end, and a round bell-turret at the W. The present entrance is the chancel arch, the original square-headed W entrance having been blocked up. Note that the 'arch' is in fact formed merely by cutting away the horizontal courses of stone. A collection of stone cross-slabs and other remains may be seen.

To the NW rises the *Round Tower*, 33.5m high, its conical cap having been reconstructed with the original stones. The doorway, over 3m from the ground, is without ornament.—To the W, outside the

St. Kevin's Church or 'Kitchen', Glendalough

enclosure, is *St. Mary's Church*, believed to have been the first building in the lower valley, and marking the site of St. Kevin's grave.

Also of interest, and best approached by crossing the stream S of St. Kevin's Kitchen and following a path to the left, is St. Saviour's. At this point is an artificially hollowed stone or *bullaun*, into which—according to legend—St. Kevin used to milk a mysterious white doe, to provide food for a child he had found abandoned at his hermitage. *St. Saviour's Church* (12C) preserves the best Irish Romanesque decoration in the valley, but some stones were incorrectly replaced when the building was restored in 1875.—Returning to the ballaun, we may continue E, skirting the bank of the LOWER LAKE, to approach the Upper Lake.

A few steps up to the left, overlooking the UPPER LAKE, are the remains of *Reefert Church*, later the burial-place of the O'Tooles, behind which a path ascends the *Lugdaff Glen* to the *Pollanass Waterfall*.

In a cliff on the S bank of the Upper Lake is the so-called *St. Kevin's Bed*, a rocky ledge only approached by boat. It was visited by Sir Walter Scott and Lockhart in 1825, among earlier tourists. Legend relates that the hermit chose this inaccessible haunt as a refuge from the persistent attentions of a beautiful colleen, until one morning, awaking to find her standing beside him, St. Kevin pushed her into the lake, which presumably cooled her ardour.—Further W are the slight remains, partly reconstructed, of *Teampull na Skellig* (the 'church of the rock'), probably the earliest building in the glen. *St. Kevin's Cell* is traditionally associated with the foundations of a beehive hut between his 'Bed' and Reefert Church.

Between Reefert Church and the carpark to the N are five 'termon' or boundary crosses. The *View* from this point up the valley is outstanding.—Hence we may return to the hotel via the road skirting the N side of the Lower Lake. On the road returning to Laragh we pass (right) *Trinity Church* (11–12C), with a round-headed E window and chancel arch.

From Laragh the main road veers SE down the *Vale of Clara*, and through the hamlet of Clara Bridge, to **Rathdrum** (1250 inhab.), a pleasant village perched on the steep side of the wooded Avonmore valley.

Just S of Laragh a 'Military Road', constructed at the beginning of the 19C to prevent a recurrence of the 'troubles' of 1798, climbs to the right across the E flank of the hills into the Avonbeg valley, and ascends again before reaching *Aghavannagh*, see below.

THE GLENMALUR VALLEY. Bear right just S of Rathdrum to *Ballinaclash*, there turning right and following the road parallel to the Avonbeg river. The valley, remarkably straight, lies along the line of a large fault, and contains numerous glacial moraine-boulders, which lie in piles on either side. Here in 1573 took place the crushing defeat of Lord Grey de Wilton by Fiagh MacHugh O'Byrne. In later years it was the resort of fugitives from the English, such as Hugh Roe O'Donnell (1591) and Michael O'Dwyer (1798). It was the setting of Synge's play 'In the Shadow of the Glen' (1903). We skirt the demesne of *Ballinacor* (left) and continue to *Baravore Ford* at the head of the valley, a base for the ascent of *Lugnaquilla* (924m), the loftiest summit of the Wicklow Mountains.

The ascent may be made by bearing left up the side of *Clohernagh*, its E spur, a fatiguing climb, often boggy, and dangerous in misty weather. An indistinct track leads over the head of the *Glenmalur valley* into that of *Imail*, and to *Donard*, see Rte 2C.

RATHDRUM TO BUNCLODY (54km). This minor cross-country road, forking right just S of the village, traverses *Ballinaclash* (see above), and from *Aughrim*, pleasantly situated in a valley just below the confluence of the Ow and Derry, roughly follows the Derry valley.—From Aughrim, the old 'Military Road' leads NW to *Aghavannagh*, where a group of barracks was built in the post-1798 period; one was later used as a shooting-box by both Parnell and Redmond.— After 8km a by-road leads right to *Moyne*, birthplace of Edwin L. Godkin (1831–1902), founder of the New York 'Nation' in 1865.—Shortly beyond this turning we fork left for *Tinahely*, whence we follow the R749 past *Colattin Park* demesne (left) to enter *Shillelagh*, famous for its oak-wood, which gave its name to the Irishman's cudgel; in later years the name was applied to the more modern 'blackthorn'. The King of Leinster is said to have sent oak hence to William Rufus for the roof of Westminster Hall; it was also used in St. Patrick's Cathedral, Dublin.—A turning (left) off the Tullow road, leading NW behind a hill, approaches *Aghowle*, where the primitive *Church* (early 12C?), well preserved but for the S wall, has a massive doorway like that at *Fore*, in Westmeath.—The road from Shillelagh continues down the valley before bearing left and then right for *Bunclody*, on the N80, where we turn left for *Enniscorthy*, 14km SE; see Rte 2A.

The main road from Rathdrum (R752) passes (left) *Avondale House* (1779, possibly designed by Wyatt, and built by Samuel Hayes), birthplace of Charles Stewart Parnell (1846–91), now a forestry school. Some distance beyond (left) is *Castle Howard* (early 19C), finely placed, with a view down the *Vale of Avoca*, near 'The Meeting of the

Waters' (the confluence of the Avonmore and Avonbeg), immortalised in the lines of Thomas Moore (1807). Unfortunately some stretches of the valley are now marred by mine workings (gold-bearing and sulphur-bearing pyrites, etc.; in 1745 a gold nugget of 22 ounces was discovered, but the mother lode has never been found).

A good view of the Wicklow Mountains is commanded by the ridge of *Cronebane*, above Castle Howard, reached by a road from *Lion's Bridge*; on the summit is the 4m-long *Motta Stone*, traditionally reputed to be the 'hurling-stone' of Finn MacCoul.

Another meeting of the waters—those of the Aughrim and Avoca rivers—takes place at *Woodenbridge*, among pinewoods. Beyond, passing (left) the demesne of *Shelton Abbey* (1770, but transformed into a Gothic Revival mansion c 1819), spoilt by industrial encroachment, and (right) *Glenart Castle*, the residence of the Earls of Carysfort, and now a convent, we enter *Arklow*. The road hence is described in Rte 2A.

C. Via Blessington and Tullow

141km (88 miles) N81. 31km *Blessington*—30km *Baltinglass*—18km *Tullow*—after 8km turn left onto the N80 for 32km *Enniscorthy*—22km **Wexford**.

From Dame St turn left down Great George St and take the right-hand fork before crossing the Grand Canal, traversing the suburb of *Rathmines* (scene of Ormonde's defeat by Michael Jones in 1649) and *Rathgar*, there bearing right along Terenure Rd E.

The first street to the right, Brighton Rd, leads to Brighton Sq., where at No. 41 James Joyce (1882–1941) was born.—J.M. Synge (1871–1909) lived from 1872–90 at No. 4 Orwell Park, to the left of Orwell Rd, leading SE from this junction at Rathgar; his birthplace was No. 2 Newton Villas, on the far side of the Dodder.

Continuing SW through *Terenure*, we traverse *Templeogue*, once the home of Charles Lever, and the Wicklow Mountains come into view on the left. After 3km we reach *Tallaght*, a favourite place of residence in the 17–18Cs, and the birthplace of Sir William Howard Russell (1820–1907), war correspondent for 'The Times'. By the church is a crenellated tower, part of an abbey which stood here until the 13C; the house of *Oldbawn*, built c 1635, was demolished in 1970; on a hill to the SE, *Mt Pellier*, are the ruins of what was the country headquarters of the 'Hell Fire Club' (see p 128). The road circles to the W before climbing the valley to *Brittas*, beyond which a branch road (left) affords access to the E side of the LACKEN RESERVOIR (1938).

BRITTAS TO ROUNDWOOD (31km). 3km beyond Brittas, the R759 turns through *Manor Kilbride* and climbs steadily parallel to the headwaters of the Liffey, with the *Kippure* massif to the N (752m; with a TV mast) to *Sally Gap*, a mountain cross-road a short distance S of a bog forming the source of the Liffey. The Dargle, which descends towards Powerscourt, has its source in the same bog.—From Sally Gap there is a rough road—part of the 'Military Road' constructed after 1798—which bears S along the flank of the main range and descends past the *Glenmacnass Waterfall* before following the river to Laragh. The main road, affording magnificent plunging views of LOUGH TAY (on the shore of which, at *Luggala*, St. Kevin is said to have had a cell, and now graced by a rebuilt Gothic 'cottage') and towards *Lough Dan*, skirts the S flank of *War Hill*, and *Douce Mountain* (724km). Crossing over into the Vartry valley, it reaches the R755 just N of Roundwood.

From Brittas we get a fine view of the mountains to the SE as we approach **Blessington** (1000 inhab.), with one long street and a church built by Abp Michael Boyle in 1669. Austin Cooper's late 17C house, with its important gardens, was burnt and demolished in the 'troubles' of 1798. Ninette de Valois (1898–), creator of the Sadler's Wells Ballet, was born at neighbouring *Baltiboys*.

A turning (right) not far short of the village leads to *Kilteel*, where the re-erected chancel arch of its church preserves figure sculpture; there is a tower-house near by.—To the left of this junction is one of three castles in the neighbourhood dating from the early 14C. Gravel works in the area have scarred the landscape.

A short distance beyond Blessington, a left-hand turn leads up to the LACKEN RESERVOIR, where the Liffey used to descend in a series of cataracts. At the foot of the principal fall was the 'pool of the Pooks', the haunt of the malicious water-sprite or kelpie of Irish fairy-tale. Both have been much reduced by the construction of the dam at Poulaphuca, further S.

To the right before reaching *Poulaphuca*, is ***Russborough**, the former Palladian seat of Joseph Leeson, later the Earl of Milltown. Built in 1741 by Castle and Francis Bindon, and its ceilings richly decorated by

Marine scene by Joseph Vernet, commissioned for Russborough

the Francini brothers (Paul and Philip), it was described in 1748 as 'a noble new house forming into perfection'.

Alfred Beit (1853–1906), uncle of the present owner, founded with Cecil Rhodes the De Beer Diamond Mining Company at Kimberley, and started collecting works of art in the 1880s. Sir Alfred Beit acquired the house in 1952, and it now accommodates the treasures of the Beit Foundation. Unfortunately it has twice been the object of theft. In 1974 some 16 paintings were stolen in an armed raid (organised by Bridget Rose Dugdale, in an attempt to raise funds for the IRA), but they were recovered undamaged. In May 1986, only a few weeks after having been visited by the Editor, art thieves struck again.

The list below includes some of the more important works of art seen prior to the latest robbery: Dining-room, with a notable marble fireplace; *Murillo*, The prodigal son series.—Hall; paintings by *Oudry*, and *Magnasco*, and two busts by Pajou.—Drawing-room; four Marine scenes by *Joseph Vernet* commissioned for this room; *Van Steenwijk the elder*, Church interior.—Bedroom, with a Soho chinoiserie tapestry by John Vanderbank of 1720; a bed of 1790; works by *Bonington*, and *Boucher*; *W. van der Velde*, Marine view; *Sargent*, copy of a section of Velázquez's The tapestry weavers.—Music Room, with a mantlepiece depicting Leda and the swan, probably by Thomas Car-

Vermeer, Woman writing (Beit Collection)

ter; *Vestier*, Portrait of the Princesse de Lamballe; *Raeburn*, Sir John and Lady Clerk of Pennycuik; *Gainsborough*, Sketch of the dancer Giovanna Bacelli, and Jack Hill (not a girl) with a puppy and pitcher; two small Views of Florence by *Bellotto*; two paintings by *Guardi*, etc. Note the Serpent clock.—Saloon, with its original floor; *Jacob van Ruisdael*, Landscape and Schloss Bentheim; *Jan Steen*, Feast of Cana; *Vermeer*, Woman writing (the only other of his major works in private hands is in Buckingham Palace); *David Teniers*, Village dance; *Palamedez*, Musical party; *Hobbema* and *A. van der Velde*, Landscape; *Hals*, The lute-player (note repainting of hat); *Rubens*, Head of an abbot; *Metsu*, Man writing, and Woman reading; note the chairs by Pluvinet with Gobelins tapestries, and the blue ceramic water-spaniel once belonging to Mme du Barry.—Library; *Goya*, The actress Antonia Zarate (later than the portrait in Leningrad); *Reynolds*, Thomas Conolly of Castletown; *Morelsee*, A Huguenot lady; and a microscope and its case (1772; by Gozzi of Parma).—The plasterwork in the Staircase is attributed to Irish pupils of the Francini brothers.

From *Hollywood*, 5km S of Russborough, the R756 crosses the mountains via the *Wicklow Gap* to *Glendalough* and *Laragh*; see Rte 2B. From the Gap one may easily ascend *Tonelagee* (816m), to the N, for the splendid comprehensive panorama of the Wicklow Mountains.

N of Hollywood lies *Ballymore Eustace*, an old Pale town on the Liffey, burnt in 1572, but there are some old houses to be seen in the district. On nearby *Broadleas Common* is a large stone circle known as the *Piper's Stones*.

The road begins to descend into the upper Slaney valley, passing (left) *Donard*, with a number of minor antiquities in the neighbourhood, including the ring-fort on a mound known as *Ball Moat*.

9km SE in the *Glen of Imail*, near the foot of Lugnaquilla, at *Derrynamuck*, is a cottage reconstructed in the traditional style and containing a folk museum, commemorating Michael O'Dwyer's refuge here in 1798.

Descending through *Castleruddery* with its Druidic circle we shortly by-pass (up on the right) the village of *Stratford-upon-Slaney*, founded for a weaving community before 1780 by Edward Stratford, Earl of Aldborough, to enter *Baltinglass* (1,050 inhab.), preserving remains of the Cistercian Abbey of *Vallis Salutis*, founded by Dermot McMurrough in 1148. The square tower was added in 1830. The estate of the Eustaces, viscounts Baltinglass, were forfeited under Elizabeth I and later passed to the Earls of Aldborough.—The bivallate hilltop fort of *Rathcoran*, to the NE, with its chambered cairn, commands a view.

Hacketstown, 14km SE, was the scene of two battles in 1798.—3km further S, at *Clonmore*, a monastery was founded by St. Maedhoc (or St. Mogue; 6C); the NE tower, known as 'the Six Windows', of the late 13C castle of De Lacy, is well preserved.

Leaving two roads leading to the right for Carlow (see Rte 3A), we cross the Slaney to reach *Rathvilly* (*Ráth Bhile*, the fort of the trees), where the large rath represents the royal stonghold in which the King of Leinster was in residence on the arrival of St. Patrick, by whom he was baptised. The summit of the rath (171m) commands a view extending from Lagnaquilla to the NE to Mt Leinster to the S, to distant Slievenamon (SW), and to the Slieve Bloom range to the NW.— *Haroldstown Dolmen*, 5km SE, was inhabited until the last century.

Tullow (2,300 inhab.), a pleasant agricultural town on the Slaney, preserves only a battered cross (in the Abbey burial ground) of its Austin priory. Fr John Murphy, a leader of the 1798 rising, was hanged at Tullow, and his body burned in a tar barrel.—There is a large rath at *Castlemore*, 1.5km W; and 5km E, at *Rathgall*, another of three concentric stone walls.

A by-road leads SW from Tullow to (20km) *Leighlinbridge* (see Rte 3A) on the main road to Kilkenny, 24km further SW.

8km S of Tullow we turn left onto the N80, and descend past the confluence of the Slaney and Derry, and at 13km enter *Bunclody* (also known as *Newtownbarry*).

An older road, further E, passes the once-beautiful riverside demesne of *Ballintemple* (house demolished), famous for its rhododendrons, and *Clonegal*, with a tree-lined street, commanded by the castellated pile of *Huntington Castle* (partly 17C).

To the right *Mt Leinster* (793m) is conspicuous, as we descend the valley to (19km) *Enniscorthy* and **Wexford**, 22km beyond; see Rte 2A.

3   Dublin to Waterford

A. Via Carlow

153km (96 miles). N7. 30km *Naas*—N9. 11km *Kilcullen*—38km **Carlow**—at 20km the N10 forks right for (17km) **Kilkenny**—20km *Thomastown*—8km *Knocktopher*—26km **Waterford**.

From Dame St we drive due W to *Kilmainham* (see Rte 1E) shortly after bearing SW, passing near (left) *Drimnagh Castle*, with a well-preserved moat and bawn, and by-passing (right) *Clondalkin*, with remains of a medieval church, and a *Round Tower*, 25.5m high with its original conical cap; the staircase is an 18C addition. The episcopal see of Cluain Dolcáin was established in the 7C by St. Mochua, but the only traces remaining are the tower and a granite cross in the churchyard.

At **Rathcoole** (2,950 inhab.) we skirt foothills of the Wicklow Mountains rising to the SE.

Newcastle, 3km NW, has a 15C church with a fortified tower, and an attractive mid-18C rectory; *Lyons House* (1797), to the W, with a large artificial lake, lies in the valley through which the Grand Canal runs. It was the home of Lord Cloncurry (1773–1853), a United Irishman, and a friend of Lord Anglesey, lord-lieutenant of Ireland in 1828. It is now part of the University College, Dublin, and an arch from Browne's Hill has been re-erected at one of its entrances.

After 6.5km a right-hand turn leads shortly to *Oughterard*, where a stump of a *Round Tower* is all that remains of a 6C monastery burnt in 1094; the ruined 16–early 17C church was the burial-place of the Ponsonbys of Bishopscourt (see below) and of early members of the Guinness family. On the hill to the SW was fought the famous duel between O'Connell and D'Esterre (a Dublin merchant who challenged him and was fatally wounded) in 1815.

We traverse *Kill*, adjacent to *Bishopscourt House* (c 1788), possibly designed by Gandon, and the site of an important bloodstock establishment.—S of Kill lie the remains of *Hartwell Castle*.

NAAS (8350 inhab.; pron. Nāce), the county town of Kildare, is a very ancient centre (*Nás na Riogh*, meeting-place of the kings), and once the residence of the Kings of Leinster, while the States of Leinster formerly assembled in a rath outside the town. At *Oldtown*, in the N suburbs, is one pavilion remaining from the first Palladian house built in Ireland, designed by the architect Thomas Burgh (1670–1730) as his country seat. Naas is now a hunting and horse-racing centre; *Punchestown Racecourse* is particularly attractive at the April meeting when the gorse is in bloom.

NAAS TO CLANE (8km). The R407 leads N to (3km) *Sallins*, a village on the Grand Canal. 1.5km W of Sallins is the *Leinster Aqueduct*, by which the canal crosses the Liffey. We traverse *Bodenstown* (right), where a monument marks the grave of Theobald Wolfe Tone (1763–98), commemorated by a pathetic ballad by Thomas Davis.—After 3km we pass (right) *Blackhall*, birthplace of Charles Wolfe (1791–1823), the poet.—At *Clane*, where a six-arched bridge crosses the Liffey, the ruins of a *Franciscan Friary* founded in the 13C by Sir Gerald Fitzmaurice are preserved.—To the right of the Maynooth road, some 3km N, is the Jesuit College of *Clongowes Wood*, containing stained glass by Evie Hone and of the school of Sarah Purser in its chapel.—*Celbridge*, see Rte 19, lies some 8km NE of Clane.

At Naas we fork left for (11km) *Kilcullen* (1,550 inhab.), a rambling village, where the Liffey is crossed by a bridge of 1319.

Some 3km SW (by-passed) are remains of the old walled town, with parts of an *Observantine abbey*, a *Round Tower*, and shafts of 9C crosses.—For *Dún Ailinne*, and the N78 to Athy and Kilkenny, see Rte 3B.

Dunlavin, 10km SE, has a notable domed *Court-house* of 1743 (restored) and a church of c 1816.

16km *Ballitore*, a village just W of the road, was founded by the Quakers. Edmund Burke received his early education at the hands of Abraham Shackleton (1697–1771), a Yorkshireman, who founded the school here in 1728. Mrs Mary Leadbeater (1758–1828), the authoress of 'Annals of Ballitore' (1862), etc., and his grand-daughter, also lived here.

Nearby is the *Rath of Mullaghmast* (171m), once a stronghold of the Kings of Leinster, and the scene in 1577 of the treacherous massacre of the chiefs of Leix and Offaly by the English and their allies the O'Dempseys, who had invited them to a friendly conference. The 'Wizard Earl' of Kildare (see below) is said to be buried in the rath in an enchanted sleep.

The road next traverses the villages of *Timolin* and *Moone*, the former with a 12C effigy of a knight in its churchyard. In the garden of *Moone Abbey* are the ruins of a 14C *Franciscan Friary* and a re-erected 9C *Cross* over 5m high, with sculptured panels of stylised and naive figures. *Moone House* is also of interest.

We soon enter **Castledermot**, a straggling village (800 inhab.), taking the second half of its name from St. Diarmuid, who founded a monastery here in c 800. The castle was that of Walter de Riddlesford, built in 1182, where Sir Edmund Butler defeated Edward Bruce in 1316. A parliament was held here in 1499. Among other remains are a *Round Tower* (20m high), erected by Abbot Cairbre (died 919), two fine sculptured *High Crosses*, and a Romanesque doorway (of which the modern church's doorway is a copy). Further S, on the other side of the main street, are the relics of a *Franciscan Friary*, founded in 1302, with a curious early 16C tomb, adjoining a square building known as the *Abbey Castle*.—N of the village is the so-called *Pigeon House*, the square tower of a house of Crutched Friars, built by Riddlesford in c 1200.

4km NW stands *Kilkea Castle*, a seat of the Fitzgerald family and now an hotel, notorious for being haunted by the 'Wizard Earl' (Gerald, 11th Earl of Kildare; died 1585), who rides every seventh year into his former study on a white charger

The Cross at Moone Abbey

shod with silver. Battered in the 1798 rebellion, the castle was restored in 1849. Hermione, Duchess of Leinster (then Marchioness of Kildare), bored with her husband and her home, composed the couplet: 'Kilkea Castle and Lord Kildare Are more than any woman can bear'. Sir Ernest Shackleton (1874–1922), the Antarctic explorer, was born at *Kilkea House*.

CARLOW (11,700 inhab.), the county town, is in Irish *Ceatharlach*, the four-fold lake, perhaps the meeting of the Burren and the Barrow.

Standing on the edge of the Pale, it was a place of great strategic importance, and was walled by Lionel, Duke of Clarence, in 1361, but taken and burnt in 1405 by Art MacMurrough, and again by Rory Og O'More in 1577. On 25 May 1789 several hundred Irish insurgents were ambushed and killed in a fierce battle in its streets, and buried in the gravel-pits at *Graiguecullen* on the opposite bank of the river. Some 200 more were hanged or shot in retribution.

The *Castle*, originally Anglo-Norman (early 13C), preserves two of its flanking towers. Although it suffered during the sieges, much of its ruinous condition is due to the enterprising Dr Middleton, who fixed upon the old fortress as being a suitable site for a lunatic asylum, and in using an excessive charge of gunpowder with the idea of reducing the thickness of the wall, succeeded in demolishing a good part of the structure.

The *Cathedral*, designed in the Gothic style (1828) by Thomas Cobden, contains the tomb of its builder, Bp James Doyle (of Kildare and Leighlin; 1786–1834), a champion of Catholic emancipation. Its sculptor, John Hogan, gained election to the Institute of the Virtuosi of the Pantheon in 1837, being the first native of the British Isles to win admission to that learned Roman Society.

Adjoining *St. Patrick's College*, a seminary founded by Bp Keefe and opened in 1795, was among the first in Ireland in which Catholic teaching was tolerated by English law; see also Maynooth.—The *Court House* in Dublin St is a dignified building of 1828–30, with an ionic portico, by W.V. Morrison.

In the demesne of *Browne's Hill* (with a stone house of c 1763), 3km NE, is an imposing *Dolmen*, its capstone, weighing 100 tonnes, being the largest in Ireland.—At *Sleaty* (*Sleibhte*), 3km N on the W bank of the Barrow, are the ruins of a monastery founded by St. Fiach, a disciple of St. Patrick, and a 5C cross.

Killeshin, 4km W of Carlow, within a girdle of limestone hills which surrounds the disused Leinster coalfield, retains a remarkable if ruined Romanesque *Chapel (park beyond the modern chapel on the left). Its particoloured doorway with four recessed arches has sculpted heads as capitals; above runs a votive inscription in Irish, its decoration in part obliterated. The E window is a late-Gothic insertion.

Leaving Carlow, we pass near the site of *Clogrenan Castle*—on the far bank of the Barrow—built by Sir Edward Butler and held by eight men against the besieging force of Sir Peter Carew in 1568.

At 10km the new by-pass veers to the right across the Barrow just before **Leighlinbridge**, where the first bridge over the river was constructed in 1320. On its E bank lie the ruins of the *'Black Castle'*, erected by partisans of Hugh de Lacy in 1181, and later the residence of Sir Peter Carew. Not much more than a 16C tower remains. The physicist and mountaineer John Tyndall (1820–93) was born in the village. To the S is the *Dinn Righ* rath, marking an ancient seat of the Kings of Leinster.

3km due W is **Oldleighlin**, site of a monastery founded in the 7C by St. Laserian, and the see of both a Catholic and Protestant bishop (combined with Kildare, and with Ossory and Ferns respectively). The Protestant *Cathedral*, built after 1248 and altered and enlarged in 1529–49, preserves a late-12C font and curious 16C grave-slabs. The 14C *Bridge* has been widened.

LEIGHLINBRIDGE TO WATERFORD VIA NEW ROSS (43km). Follow the E bank of the Barrow (R705) past (left) *Dunleckney Manor*, former seat of the Bagenal family, who settled here in the 16C. We enter *Muine Bheag* (or **Bagenalstown**; 2,500 inhab.), with sandstone and granite quarries, and retaining its court house and an imposing *Railway Station* of c 1850.—3km E is the massive square ruin of *Ballymoon*

Hiberno-Romanesque doorway of Killeshin church

Castle (early 14C), preserving some interesting features.—After 12km
we turn to cross the Barrow, leaving on the left the demesne of the
Kavanagh family, the lineal descendants of the MacMurroughs, Kings
of Leinster; while from the Georgian village of **Borris**, further E, we
may reach the *Sculloge Gap* in the *Blackstairs Mountains*, the highest
of which is *Mt xLeinster* (793m).

Borris House (late 18C, and modernised by R. and W.V. Morrison c
1820) was formerly the home of Eleanor Butler (1739–1829; later one
of the 'Ladies of Llangollen'). It then became the residence of Arthur
MacMurrough Kavanagh (1831–89), the politician and sportsman—
although born with only stumps of arms and legs. On visiting Abbey
Leix he remarked to his hostess: 'It's an extraordinary thing—I haven't
been here for five years, but the station-master recognised me'.

We follow the R705 via *Ullard*, with a 9C Cross and a 12C Romanesque church in ruins, to enter **Graiguenamanagh** ('the granary of
the monks'; 1,530 inhab.), a little town on the W bank of the Barrow,
here crossed by a mid-18C seven-arched *Bridge* by George Semple.

Tinnahinch Castle, on the far bank, was a Butler fortress. The town, overlooked to the S by gracefully shaped *Brandon Hill* (516m), is built among the ruins of the Cistercian abbey of *Duiske*, founded in 1207 by William le Mareschal. The *Catholic Church* consists of the choir, transepts and part of the nave of the abbey church (badly restored), and contains a 13C effigy of an armoured knight. The original octagonal tower fell down in 1774.

Hence the main road runs parallel to the W bank of the river via *Ballyogan*, with the ruins of *Galmoy Castle* and a churchyard cross with spiral ornaments.

A more interesting road follows the E bank, passing (right) *St. Mullins*, named after St. Moling, Bp of Ferns (died 696), who is buried here in the monastery he founded, a plan of which is drawn in the 7C MS 'Book of Mulling'.—Adjacent to the present church are the ruins of several older churches, a 9C *High Cross*, and a Norman motte.—Hence we continue S, at 12km entering *New Ross* (see Rte 5) via *Mountgarret Bridge*, defended by an old keep.

The N25 leads SW from New Ross to (23km) *Waterford*, briefly skirting the well-wooded bank of the Barrow, and with retrospective views of Brandon Hill and the Blackstair range before making the descent into the Suir valley.

EXCURSIONS to the S may be made conveniently from New Ross, or alternatively from Wexford. Take the R733 along the E bank of the Barrow, shortly forking right, and passing (right) *Dunganstown*, a hamlet whence the late President John Kennedy's grandfather emigrated to Boston; a *Memorial Park* was opened here in 1968.—13km *Dunbrody Abbey*, a picturesque ruin, was founded in 1182 by Hervé de Montmorency, seneschal of Strongbow, but not built for some 30 years. The cruciform church (almost 60m by 42.5m), a plain but graceful building in the Cistercian manner, is fairly complete (although the S wall of the nave fell in 1852), and preserves a massive low 15C tower. The chapels opening off the transepts and the E window in the Early English style are its most noteworthy features. A tower to the E, and an archway to the W, are the chief remains of the conventual dependencies.

We continue to skirt the estuary opposite *Passage East* via *Duncannon*, with an old fort taken by Lord Castlehaven in 1645 and held by him against Ireton in 1649. James II sailed hence for Kinsale after his defeat at the Boyne, and later William III embarked here for England.—Towards the end of the peninsula is *Slade*, a fishing village with a well-preserved late-15C or early-16C *Castle* with a 17m-high tower and adjoining an early 17C house.—Beyond lies *Hook Head*, with a lighthouse surmounting a circular keep of 1170–84.

Returning along the same road, we fork right past *Baginbun Head*, where the first Anglo-Norman expeditionary force landed in May 1169, 300 men under Robert FitzStephen and Maurice FitzGerald. The earthworks on the neck of the headland are probably of Celtic origin.—Keeping to the right through *Fethard* and *Saltmills*, we shortly reach *Tintern Abbey*, in a pleasant demesne running down to a creek of *Bannow Bay*. It was founded in 1200 by William le Mareschal, Earl of Pembroke, in thanksgiving for his rescue from drowning on the coast, and peopled by monks from Tintern in Gwent. The E end is a ruin, but the W end, tower and transepts have been restored, having been used as a dwelling from the mid 16C until recently. Bearing NW hence we may return directly to *New Ross*.

The excursion may be extended to include *Bannow*, on the far side of its bay, founded by the Normans, but later buried by drifting sand. It was a ruin as early as the 16C, although it returned two Members of Parliament until 1798, when the Earl of Ely was paid £15,000 in compensation for the loss of the seat! A ruined church survives above the bay. It may be approached by by-roads circling the N side of the bay via *Clonmines* (or *Wellington Bridge*), another 'rotten borough' disfranchised in 1798. It was a Danish settlement of some importance; nothing remains except the towers and walls of a *Dominican abbey* founded by the Kavanaghs in the 14C; ruins of churches, one fortified, and other fortifications abound.—There is a charming little late 16C *Castle* at *Coolhull*, some 5km SE, a crenellated two-storey structure.

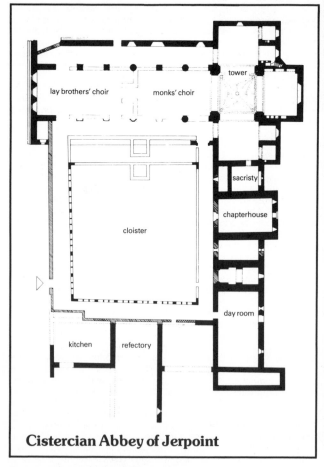

Cistercian Abbey of Jerpoint

From just W of Leighlinbridge, the main Waterford road (N9) continues SW. The N10 shortly diverges (right) for *Kilkenny*; see Rte 3B. After another 7km we traverse *Gowran* (pron. Gawran), one of the chief seats of the Lords of Ossory. The chancel of the old collegiate *Church* (c 1275) has been restored; it retains a massive square tower and contains a marble font and interesting 14–17C tomb-slabs, including that of the 1st Earl of Ormonde (died 1327).—Immediately W of the next village of *Dungarvan* is *Tullaherin*, with a ruined church and *Round Tower*, 22m high. The name (*Tulach Chiarain*) signifies that it was the burial-place of St. Kieran. We pass (left), 8km beyond, the church of *Kilfane*, which preserves the *Effigy* of a mailed knight of the Canteville family.

Thomastown (1,300 inhab.), named after Thomas FitzAnthony Walsh, Seneschal of Leinster, who built a castle and the town walls, is entered shortly. It preserves few remnants of its former importance except the defence towers near each end of the bridge spanning the Nore, and a large ruined church (13C) within which a modern church has been erected. The Catholic church contains the old high altar from Jerpoint (see below). Below the town, on the opposite bank of the river, is ruined *Grenan Castle*. George Berkeley (1685–1753), Bp of Cloyne and philosopher, was born at *Dysert Castle*, 3km SE of Thomastown.

Crossing the Nore, we bear right, and soon reach (left) the ruins of *Jerpoint Abbey.

Founded in 1180 (possibly 1160) for Cistercians, probably by Donal MacGillapatrick, Lord of Ossory, the abbey gained renown under its first abbot, Felix O'Dullany (died 1202), founder of St. Canice's Cathedral, Kilkenny. At the Dissolution in 1540 its lands passed to the Ormonde family.

The *Cloister*, restored in 1953, dating from a 15C rebuilding, preserves some interesting carving, including a St. Christopher. The S side of the *Nave* has vanished, but on the N a row of six wide pointed arches on low piers separates it from the aisle. The clerestory windows and the triple W window are round-headed. There is no W door, the only entrance to the church having been a fortified porch on the N side of the nave. The nave appears to be of a later date than the choir and transepts, which are in the Irish Romanesque style, the former retaining its stone barrel vault, but the E window is a 14C insertion.

The tower, with its characteristic Irish battlements, is probably 15C. The S Transept contains Walsh and Butler tombs of the late 15th and early 16C, and in the choir is the early 13C tomb of O'Dullany, with his crosier gnawed by a serpent. There are two more carved tombs in the N Transept. The Chapter-house contains objects found among the ruins.

At *Newtown Jerpoint*, to the NW, is a ruined church with an unusual gallery, and a 15C tower.

Our road shortly joins that from Kilkenny at *Knocktopher* (*Cnoc an Tóchair*, the hill of the causeway), still preserving traces of an ancient causeway crossing the marshy valley, and a medieval tower and other remains of its Gothic church. To the right as we turn S are the considerable remains of a *Carmelite priory* founded by the 2nd Earl of Ormonde in 1356.—To the W, at *Sheepstown*, is a very primitive (11C?) church.

Passing *Ballyhale*, we cross the *Slieve Brenach* hills before descending into the valley of the Suir, briefly skirting its N bank to approach the bridge spanning the river, providing a view across to Waterford.

WATERFORD (38,450 inhab.; Post Office on the Quay), an ancient city, preserves few buildings of any great interest. It is nevertheless admirably placed on the S bank of the Suir, Spenser's 'gentle Shure', which unites with the Barrow some 10km E of the town, and expands into the estuary of *Waterford Harbour*.

Part of the restored cloister, Jerpoint Abbey

Danish Vikings settled here perhaps as early as 853, the best-known of their chieftains being Reginald, son of Sigtryg. It has been claimed that he built the first church here on the site of Christ Church c 1050. In 1170 Raymond le Gros defeated the Danes, and Strongbow occupied the town in the following year in preparation for the landing of Henry II (1172). In 1171 Strongbow was married at Waterford to Eva, daughter of Dermot MacMurrough, King of Leinster. King John, when Earl of Morton, established a mint at Waterford, which continued to issue coins for 200 years. It showed its loyalty to Henry VII by refusing to admit the pretender, Lambert Simnel, and by sustaining a siege of 12 days by Perkin Warbeck and the Earl of Desmond. Accordingly, in 1493, it was given the right to the device 'Intacta manet Waterfordia'. An enviable distinction was won in 1649 when the town forced Cromwell to abandon its siege, but in 1650 it was stormed by Ireton. James II received a welcome on his flight from the Boyne (1690), but the town surrendered soon after to William III.

In the early 19C Waterford was famous for the manufacture of glass. The finest examples date from 1780–1810, but the excise duty imposed in 1825 hampered its production and by 1851 the trade was virtually dead; it was not revived until 1947.

Waterford was the birthplace of Luke Wadding (1588–1657), Franciscan scholar, historian and professor of theology at Salamanca; Michael Wadding (1591–1644), missionary to the Mexican Indians; Dorothy Jordan (1762–1816) and Charles Kean (1811–68), actors; Vincent Wallace (1813–65), the composer of 'Maritana'; Thomas Meagher (1823–67), a member of the Young Ireland party, who, transported to Tasmania, escaped to fight in the American Civil War at Fredericksburg; and William Bonaparte-Wyse (1862–92), the philologist, and grandson of Lucien Bonaparte. John O'Donovan (1806–61), topographer and historiographer, was born at *Slieveroe*, to the NE. Lord Roberts (1832–1914), although born in India, came of a distinguished Waterford family. John Redmond, who succeeded Parnell as leader of the Home Rule party, was MP for Waterford for 26 years.

The broad Quay flanking the Suir is the centre of activity (with the Tourist Office at No. 41), at the NW end of which is a bridge of 1913, the successor of that built in 1794 by Lemuel Cox of Boston, Mass., for a sum *less* than his original estimate. In O'Connell St, parallel to this end of the quay, are the tower and ruins of *Blackfriars* priory, a Dominican foundation of 1226 dissolved in 1541; from 1617 it served for a time as the assize court. Walking down this street we pass (right) a small local *museum*, and the *Chamber of Commerce* (1795), by John Roberts (1749–94; grandfather of Lord Roberts). In an alley to the right is the interesting galleried church of *St. Patrick* (1764). On reaching Broad St turn left to regain the Quay, passing (right) *Holy Trinity Cathedral* (R.C.), also designed by Roberts in 1793–96, with a late 19C facade added.

Turn right further along the quay to reach the ruined Franciscan *Friary* with its spire, called the 'French Church', founded by Sir Hugh Purcell c 1240. Its choir was used in 1695–1819 as a chapel for a Huguenot colony; the nave served as a hospital chapel from 1693 to 1815.

Higher up the hill is the *Cathedral of Christ Church* (1773; C. of I.), again by Roberts (on the foundations of a medieval building demolished in 1770), but damaged by fire in 1815, and altered by Sir Thomas Drew in 1891. The structure is undergoing restoration and is at present closed to the general public, although a request for permission to enter may be made to No. 17 Cathedral Sq. The recently vandalised interior contains the curious Rice Monument (1469), with a 'memento mori' representing a decomposing corpse, and the Fitzgerald monument of Carrara marble.

Opposite the S side of the cathedral is the 18C *Bishop's Palace*, built by Bp Foy, restored and refaced in 1975 for Corporation use. Beyond it is The Mall.

A few minutes' walk down Catherine St, on the far side of the Mall, brings one to the *Court House* (1849), a dignified design by J.B. Keane, adjoining a pleasant park, through which the noisome John's River meanders.

Also in the Mall is the *Town Hall* (1788). At the junction of the Mall and Quay stands **Reginald's Tower**, a sturdy pepper-pot, and the most obvious antiquity in Waterford, probably 12C, on the site of an earlier fort, and restored in 1819 to house a police-station. It now contains a small exhibit of civic insignia and historical relics, including King John's sword and mace. The marriage of Strongbow is said to have been celebrated here; see History.—Other fragments of *City Walls* survive at the top of Castle St, to the right of the Cork road, and among private gardens, etc.

To visit the **Waterford Glass Factory**, some 2km down the Cork road, apply at the Tourist Office, 41 the Quay. Tours take place on weekdays, when one may see certain stages in its manufacture, cutting, and polishing, etc. Children are not admitted, nor is photography allowed. Glass is not sold at the factory, although most shops in the town sell it.

Mt Misery, overlooking the transpontine suburb of *Ferrybank*, commands a panoramic view of the town, which is also well seen from *Cromwell's Rock*, doubtfully identified as the post of the Protector during his unsuccessful siege.

Some 12km SE of Waterford, approached by the R683, passing *Little Island*, with an old castle of the Fitzgeralds, lies *Passage East*, with a 15–16C castle, whence a passenger ferry crosses the estuary. Perkin Warbeck took ship here after his failure to storm Waterford in 1491.—On the coast further S is the site of *New Geneva*, a colony of Genevese established here in 1785 by Lord Temple with a grant of £50,000 from Parliament. They were unreasonable in their demands, however, and soon returned to their own country. Their dwellings were converted into barracks, and in 1798 used as a prison.

Further S, opposite Hook Head, is *Dunmore East* (750 inhab.), named from the 'great dun', remnants of which can still be traced. It was formerly of importance as the terminus of the mail-packet service from Milford Haven to Waterford, and still possesses a long pier.—To the S is the cliff of *Black Knob*, beneath which is the so-called *Merlin's Cave*.—For *Tramore*, 17.5km W see Rte 5.

B. Via Athy and Kilkenny

157km (97 miles). N7. 30km *Naas*—N9. 11km *Kilcullen*—N78. 22km *Athy*—28km *Castlecomer*—19km **Kilkenny**—T14. 20km *Knocktopher*—N9. 27km **Waterford.**

For the road from Dublin to *Kilcullen*, see Rte 3A. Immediately beyond Kilcullen we fork right, passing (right) the large circular royal fort of *Dún Ailinne*. Beyond (13km) *Fontstown* is *Ardscull*, with a conspicuous old fort or motte almost 17m high and planted with trees, beside which Edward Bruce defeated Sir Edmund Butler in 1315.—To the S is *Inche Castle*, enlarged by the Earl of Kildare c 1420.

   ATHY (4,900 inhab.; pron. with the accent on the last syllable: *Baile Átha h-Í*—town of the ford of Í, a Munster chieftain slain here in the 2C) is a busy agricultural centre in the fertile valley of the Barrow, where a branch of the Grand Canal joins the navigable river. It has a modern *Dominican Church* (1965) and a pleasing *Market House* (c 1780) in its square (where in 1798 the first wooden triangle was set up on which United Irishmen were spreadeagled and flogged by the militia). Standing on the borders of Kildare and Leix, it was the scene of many battles. Defending the bridgehead is *White's Castle*, built by the 8th Earl of Kildare in c 1500 and repaired in 1575 by a certain William White; while in a field N of the town is *Woodstock Castle*, of c 1290, remarkable for the thickness of its walls, but which was severely damaged during a siege by the Confederates under General Preston in 1649.

5km NW lies *Kilberry*, with peat-moss factory and ruined abbey, while on the opposite bank of the Barrow stands *Reban Castle*, a fortress of Richard de St. Michel, builder of Woodstock Castle.

At 10km we cross the Carlow–Portlaoise road; see Rte 20A.—18km **Castlecomer** (1,550 inhab.), an elegant little town built by the Wandesforde family after 1637, and the centre of the defunct Leinster coalfield (once noted for the production of smokeless anthracite). The motte of the first Anglo-Norman castle which gave the town its name lies to the E. A later castle was besieged in 1641–42, and the town suffered at the hands of the insurgents in 1798.

   Some 7km beyond, we pass (left) **Dunmore Cave**, a series of limestone caverns opening from one to another, the second of which contains a huge stalactite pillar known as 'the Market Cross'. Here, according to legend, the monster Luchtigern, 'Lord of the Mice' was slaughtered; it may possibly be the site of a massacre of some hundreds trapped here by Vikings on a plundering expedition in 928.—We continue to descend the Dinin Valley, which shortly joins the Nore, and enter Kilkenny, the county town.

KILKENNY (9,450 inhab.), one of the oldest and most interesting towns of Ireland, is attractively situated on the Nore (Spenser's 'stubborn Newre'): it has been called the 'Marble City' from the fine and long-quarried limestone in the neighbourhood. Not much is visible of the once-famous posting-inns except their yards and passages, but many houses hide pleasant interiors behind unimposing facades. It also preserves a large castle and a cathedral of distinction, while among its industries are the Kilkenny Design Workshops.

Cill Chainnigh (the church of St. Canice) was the ancient capital of the Kings of Ossory. A fortress seems to have been established here by Strongbow as early as 1172, and the episcopal see of Ossory was transferred here from Aghabo in 1202. In the 14C Kilkenny was at the height of its fame, and was the scene of many parliaments, that of 1366–67 passing the notorious 'Statutes of Kilkenny', penalising the descendants of the Anglo-Normans for excessive Hibernisation, making it a treasonable offence for them to marry any man or woman of the Irish race! The lordship was purchased from Strongbow's descendants c 1400 by James Butler, 3rd Earl of Ormonde.

In 1642–48 it was the headquarters of the Confederates, and a great assembly of Catholic clergy was held here in 1645, presided over by Lord Mountgarret and Rinuccini, the Papal Legate. The former came to terms with his relative Ormonde, the viceroy, after the Irish victory at Benburb in 1646, but the intransigent legate issued an edict of excommunication on all who desired peace with Cromwell. In 1650 the Protector himself succeeded in storming Kilkenny, and the garrison under Sir Walter Butler marched out with full military honours.

The novelists Michael and John Banim (1796–1874, and 1798–1842 respectively) were born here, as was James Stephens (1825– 1901), the Fenian; and also the 'matchless actress' Catherine Raftor, commonly known as 'Kitty' Clive (1711–85), but she was not the Kitty responsible for the expression 'fighting like Kilkenny Cats'. The usually accepted version is that Cromwell's troops diverted themselves here by tying together the tails of two cats, which like tow, they then set alight, leaving the cats to claw their way free.

The important buildings of Kilkenny are all on the W bank of the Nore. On the E bank, that approached by the Dublin road, is *St. John's*, a parish church incorporating part of a hospital founded by William, Earl of Pembroke c 1220, preserving a beautiful Lady Chapel, although the choir is in ruins.—Adjacent and in Maudlin St are traces of *Town Walls*; these may also be seen in the grounds of *Kilkenny College* (1780), to the left, nearer the modern bridge in John St. This is the successor of St. John's College, founded in 1666, where Swift, Congreve, Berkeley, Farquhar, and many other eminent men were educated.

Crossing the river, with an oblique view of the Castle to the left, and passing (right) a particularly attractive bar (Tynan's), we ascend Rose Inn St, on the right of which are *Shee's Almshouses* (1594), to reach The Parade. Turn left here to approach Kilkenny Castle, which occupies a prominent position overlooking the Nore.

The **Castle**, under restoration, occupies three sides of a quadrilateral; the fourth side was destroyed in 1659. With its grey stone round

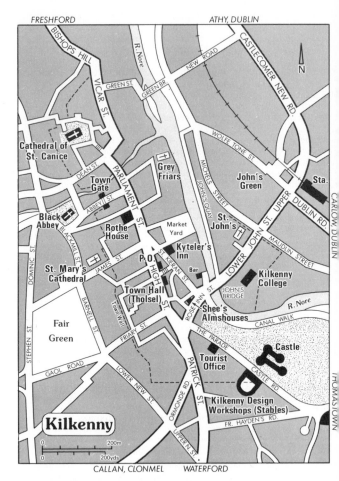

towers and battlements, it still maintains a martial air, although it was almost entirely rebuilt in 1826–35 by William Robertson.

The castle originated in 1192, being erected by William le Mareschal, Earl of Pembroke, son-in-law of Strongbow, probably on the site of an earlier fortress commanding this river crossing. In 1392 it passed by purchase to James, 3rd Earl of Ormonde, the descendant of Theobald FitzWalter, who had received lands from Henry II and the appointment of Chief Butler of Ireland; his son took the title of Butler or Botiler as a surname. The Butlers played a prominent part in Irish history and waged a bitter feud with the Fitzgeralds of Kildare. The Dukes lost lands and fortune in defence of the Stuart cause, and the 2nd Duke was attainted in 1715. The earldom was revived in 1791 in favour of John Butler, and survived until 1935. In 1967 the castle was given to the town, and now houses a picture gallery.

The main entrance is a classical composition of 1685. Although the

Butler archives have been transferred to the National Library, and its contents dispersed, the castle contains a number of Butler family portraits, a self-portrait by Van Dyck, a portrait of Strafford, and works by Rubens, Kneller (of James, 12th Earl and 1st Duke of Ormonde; 1610–88), and Lely. A tapestry factory was once at work in the building. From the kitchens a long passage leads under the main road to the stables.

These *Stables*, opposite the entrance, now accommodate the showrooms and offices of the *Kilkenny Design Workshops*. Some of their studios and workshops are in a semi-circular range of buildings to the rear, beyond which stands a restored house of the Butler family.

The Parade is continued to the SE by Castle Rd, at the far end of which is *St. James's* or *Switsir's Hospital* (1803), an almshouse embellished with an agreeably pompous statue of its founder.

From the Parade, the High St runs uphill, passing (right) the **Tholsel** (1761), by the amateur architect William Colles, a curious and rather ungainly building with an arcade over the pavement, and an octagonal clocktower (reconstructed).—Behind it stands *St. Mary's* (13C; disused), containing the fine monument of Richard Rothe (1637), and in the churchyard the tombs of John Rothe (N side; 1612), and Sir Richard Shee (1608), with sculptured figures at the base.—Stepped lanes descend to St. Kieran St, in which stands *Kyteler's Inn*, associated wih witchcraft trials in 1324, but recently reconstructed and housing a restaurant.

Beyond the Tholsel, on the left of Parliament St, is ***Rothe House** (1594; restored in 1966), containing a collection of local antiquities, and with an atttractive courtyard.—Almost opposite, a tablet marks the site of the Confederation Hall, where the Irish Confederation Parliament met in 1642–48.—Towards the end of the street, a lane to the right leads to the ruins of a *Franciscan Friary*, retaining a beautifully graduated seven-light window, and a graceful tower.

Crossing the stream of the Bregagh into Irish Town, we ascend a short flight of steps to approach the ***Cathedral of St. Canice**, which, despite the damage done by Cromwell's troops, is one of the finest unruined churches in Ireland.

The present edifice—69m long by 37.5m broad—was begun probably by Bp Hugh de Mapilton in 1251–56, and completed by Bp Geoffrey St. Leger after 1260. The central tower fell in 1332, but was reconstructed by Bp Ledrede (died 1360), who also installed the stained glass, while the fan-vault was designed by Bp Hacket in 1465. The havoc committed by the Cromwellians was temporarily repaired, but the church remained in a deplorable state until the time of Bp Richard Pococke (1756), when the choir was refitted and the monuments rearranged. The bishop himself (1704–65), who in 1741 'discovered' Chamonix, has been described as 'the dullest man that ever travelled'—unlike his younger contemporary the Earl-Bishop of Derry. The internal stonework was somewhat injudiciously stripped during a restoration of 1866.

The most notable features of the exterior are the low and massive central tower, the characteristically Irish stepped battlements of the parapet (a restoration except on the transepts), and the unusual quatrefoil windows of the clerestory. The quatrefoil motif recurs on the W front, where the doorway is well designed. It is abutted by a *Round Tower*, 30m high, capless, but otherwise in good preservation.

The aisled Nave, of five bays, is noteworthy mainly for its monuments and other furniture. The traceried gallery above the W door was probably used for the exhibition of relics. The first tomb in the S Aisle is that of Bp Hacket (1478); the second is of Honorina Schorthals (née Grace; died 1596). Next comes a female effigy wearing the old Irish or

Kinsale cloak. The 12C Font of black marble has incised patterns in the corners. Against the wall beyond the S door are the tombs of the 1st Viscount Mountgarret (1571), with a good armoured effigy, and of Bp Walsh (1585).

In the N Aisle, between the pillars opposite the font, is the grave-slab of the son of Henry de Ponto of Lyra, perhaps the oldest memorial in the church (1285). By the wall is the fine figure of James Schorthals (1508). In the floor further E, opposite the mutilated effigy of Sir John Grace (1552), is the gravestone of Edmund Purcell (died 1549), captain of Ormonde's gallowglasses, with a mailed half-figure, the Emblems of the Passion, and St. Peter's cock crowing on the edge of the High Priest's pot in which he was cooking it. In the next bay are the tomb of Adam Cottrell (1550), with a base appropriated from a 13C monu-ment, and the wall-slab of the Bourchier brothers (1584–87), with an elaborately carved escutcheon.

The central lantern is roofed with Bp Hacket's vault. In the W corner of the N Transept is *St. Kieran's Chair* (13C; seat modern), and on the N wall is a large aumbry adorned with heads; here also are the tombs of the Pack family, including that of the Peninsular War veteran, Sir Denis Pack (died 1823). In the *E Chapel* is a piscina of curious design, possibly a survival from the earlier church. The S Transept may be regarded as the Ormonde Chapel, as it contains numerous tombs of the Butler family: in the centre lies the 2nd Marquess of Ormonde (died 1854); to the S, the 8th Earl (died 1539) and his wife; and against the S wall, the 9th Earl (?; died 1549), with a remarkably good effigy bearing a sword.

The *Choir*, flanked by chapels, has a modern floor of Irish marble. The E window (in memory of the 2nd Marquess of Ormonde) replaces the magnificent stained-glass representation of Gospel history for which the papal nuncio Rinuccini offered £700 only a few years before it was smashed by Cromwell's philistines. By the N wall is an episcopal crosier, probably that of Bp Ledrede, gnawed by a serpent.

Adjacent is *St. Canice's Library*, containing some 3,000 16–17C volumes, bequeathed by Bishops Otway and Maurice, including among its rarities the MS Red Book of Ossory. The *Bishop's Palace* is of 1735–36.

To the NE, the Nore is spanned by *Green's Bridge* (1765), a Palla-dian design with five arches.

On regaining Parliament St turn right along Abbey St and under the sole surviving *Town Gate* to reach the *Dominican Church*, incorpo-rating the slender tower and several fine early 14C windows of the ancient *Black Abbey*.—Hence Blackmill St ascends towards the *Cathedral of St. Mary's* (R.C.; 1843–57), a commonplace building, its grey limestone tower (60m high) a conspicuous feature of the landscape.—Hence James St returns to the High St.

6.5km NE of Kilkenny stands the five-storey tower-house of *Clara Castle*.

KILKENNY TO CLONMEL (50km). The N76 leads SW, passing near (right) *Desart*, birthplace of James Hoban (1762–1831), who emigrated to America in 1785 and was the architect of the White House, Washington.—1.5km to the left of the main road is the tower-house of *Burnchurch* (15–16C).—16km *Callan* (1,450 inhab.), an ancient town whose present fame is mainly derived from its ruins, most notable among which is the *Austin Friary*, founded in the 15C by Sir James Butler, to the NE. On the riverbank are traces of a castle, bombarded by Crom-well in 1650. The choir of the parish church has survived S of the centre.—9.5km SW is *Mullinahone*, home and burial-place of Charles Kickham (cf. Tipperary).—We pass at *Killamery* a richly sculptured 9C *Cross* of the local type, before skirting (right) *Slievenamon* (719m; see Rte 8) and descending into the Suir valley (near *Kilcash*, to the right, with a Romanesque door to its ruined church). The road bears W for *Clonmel*; see Rte 8.

From Kilkenny, follow the N10 S to cross Kings river at (11km) *Stonyford*. 3km W is **Kells**, formerly known as *Ceanannus Caraighe* (Kenlys-in-Ossory) to distinguish it from the greater *Kells* (*Ceanannus Mór*) in Meath. It preserves important remains of an *Augustinian priory* erected by Geoffrey FitzRobert (c 1193), protected by an extensive walled enclosure with rampart towers.

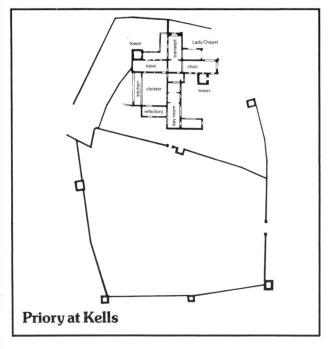

Priory at Kells

Further W is *Newton Castle* (early 16C).—3km S of Kells, at *Kilree*, is a *Round Tower*, 29m high, which has lost its cap. The monolithic Cross, in a field beyond, similar to those at Ahenny, is said incorrectly to commemorate Niall Caille, King of Ireland (845) drowned trying to save a henchman who had fallen into Kings river.

SE of Stonyford is *Mount Juliet*, with a house of c 1780, and a fox-hunting centre, with stud farm and the kennels of the Kilkenny hunt.—*Jerpoint*, see Rte 3A, is a short distance beyond.

7km S of Stonyford we enter *Knocktopher*, and follow the road described in Rte 3A to **Waterford**.

4   Dublin to Cork via Kildare, Portlaoise and Cashel

250km (155 miles). N7. 52km *Kildare*—32km *Portlaoise*—N8. 14km *Abbeyleix*—29km *Urlingford*—9.5km (*Thurles* lies 10km W) 22.5km **Cashel**—18km *Cahir*—24km *Mitchelstown*—14km *Fermoy*—35km **Cork.**

For the road from Dublin towards and for **Naas**, by-passed, see Rte 3A. From Naas we continue on the N7, shortly passing (left) the remains of *Jigginstown House* (c 1627), a huge unfinished brick-built mansion with a frontage of 115m, erected by Strafford as a residence for Charles I.—A bypass is under construction S of **Driochead Nua** (or *Newbridge*; 5,800 inhab.), on the Liffey. It arose round a cavalry barrack built here in 1816, and now has a cutlery factory and the Peat Board's experimental station; see pp 91–2.

Downstream on the right bank of the river are the ruins of *Great Connell Abbey*, built in 1202 by Myler Fitzhenry, and peopled with Austin Canons from Llanthony. Part of the tomb of Walter Wellesley (died 1539), Bp of Kildare and Prior of Connell, is preserved in the graveyard.

We shortly reach **The Curragh** (*Currach*, a racecourse), one of the finest stretches of turf in Ireland (2,000 hectares). Although mainly devoted to pasturage—St. Brigid's flocks are said to have ruminated here—it has been known as a military training centre since 1646, and as a racing tract for centuries before that. In March 1914 it came into prominence when General Hubert Gough and 57 other British army officers stationed here threatened to disobey *if* ordered to fire on Carson's 'Ulster Volunteers', a decision euphemistically referred to as 'The Curragh Incident'. It has several training stables, and its *Racecourse* is the venue of the 'Irish Derby' in late June or early July, when the district is entirely given over of the racing fraternity.

KILDARE (4,000 inhab.; in Irish *Cill Dara*, the church of the oakwood) is a small but ancient town, owing its origin to St. Brigid, who in 490 founded the first of several religious houses here. Her 'Fire' was kept burning in her church despite Danish and other raids until the Reformation, except for one short break in 1220 when it was extinguished by order of De Londres, Abp of Dublin.

The present *Cathedral* was begun by Bp Ralph de Bristol in 1229, which, enlarged and embellished by Bp Lane in 1482, was ruined in the Confederate war in 1641, when the N transept and choir were razed. In 1683–86 Bp Morton rebuilt the choir in the prevailing classical style, while in 1875 G.E. Street (who also 'restored' the cathedral of Christ Church in Dublin) undertook what amounted practically to a rebuilding, although keeping to the old design.

The W front, Choir, and N transept are entirely new, but the remarkable buttresses of the nave walls, connected by arches, and the simple but effective S transeptal facade are on the original 13C plan. At the W end is a primitive font, and in the S transept and choir are old monuments, one of a 13C bishop, and sculptured stones.

To the SW is an old *Cross* (reconstructed); to the NW, the foundations of a 'firehouse'.—The *Round Tower* (31m high; 12C?) is notable for its unusually elaborate doorway, 4m from the ground; the incongruous battlements are a 19C addition.

A castle here had been erected by De Vesci in the 13C on the site of an earlier fortress of Strongbow's; its history is that of the Fitzgeralds, earls of Kildare, a family founded by Maurice Fitzgerald in 1169.—To the S of the town are the ruins of a *Franciscan friary*.—1.5km S, at *Tully House* is the *National Stud*, a flourishing horse-breeding establishment presented to Britain in 1916 by Lord Wavertree. It retained extra-territorial rights until 1944 when the British establishment was moved to Wiltshire, and the Tully stud was vested in the Irish government.—A fine *Japanese Garden*, laid out in 1906–10, may also be visited here.

Conspicuous from their position on the edge of the great central plain are the *Red Hills*, a low sandstone range to the N of Kildare. The highest of them is *Dunmurry Hill* (231m; just to the right of the Rathangan road); adjoining that on the NE is *Grange Hill* (with the curious outcrop known as the 'Chair of Kildare'); while on the Robertstown road, to the NE, is the *Hill of Allen*, where a monument—the erection of which damaged the old fort—marks the site of a residence of the Kings of Leinster.

The road past the latter soon enters the dreary expanse of the **Bog of Allen**, a vast peat-bog which is now playing its part in the economic development of the country. In 1946 the *Bord na Móna* (the Turf, or Peat Board) was set up, a corporation devoted to the production of machine-cut peat for use as fuel in power stations, and elsewhere; see pp 91–2. Its experimental station is at *Droichead Nua*, and 'turf villages' have been built near the bogs to house both permanent and seasonal workers.

At **Robertstown** is the former *Grand Canal Hotel*, erected for the accommodation of 'express' canal passengers, and now again commercialised; there is a small canal museum here, and a '*Falconry*' in the neighbourhood.—Further NW, at *Allenwood*, is a turf-actuated power station of the Electricity Supply Board, while at *Lullymore*, beyond, is a large turf-processing works; others are located near *Rathangan*, 9.5km NW of Kildare.

10.5km **Monasterevin**, a small canal-town (2,150 inhab.), retains a square-towered church adjoining *Moore Abbey* (18C; once the home of the singer John McCormack, 1884–1945), commemorating a monastery founded in the 12C on the site of an older foundation, by Dermot O'Dempsey, Lord of Offaly. It had the reputation of being a very cold house, and the story is told that when the 4th Earl of Clonmel visited the place, an abnormally heavy portmanteau among his luggage burst open when being carried up the stairs, and was found to be full of coal! It is now a hospital. Beside the canal is a warehouse originally the *Charter School* (c 1740).—At *Kildangan*, SE of the town, is an extensive demesne, and an old tower.

MONASTEREVIN TO PORTARLINGTON AND TULLAMORE (37km). We follow the R420 to the W, crossing the Grand Canal, and shortly pass (right) *Lea Castle*, the remnant of a De Vesci stronghold of which the gateway and a round bastion have survived. Slighted by Cromwell's order in 1650, it was last inhabited by a noted horse-stealer, 'Cathal na gCapall' ('Charles the Horse'), who used the vaults as stables, and carried on a flourishing trade.

10km **Portarlington** (3,400 inhab.) takes its name from Sir Henry Bennet, afterwards Lord Arlington, to whom the neighbouring country was given after having been confiscated from the O'Dempseys in 1641. The tall dignified houses and extensive orchards and gardens are due to a colony of Huguenot settlers established here by General Ruvigny, Earl of Galway, who had founded the town in 1667. There is a well-proportioned *Market-house* (c 1800) in the main square. The first Irish power-plant to be driven by peat was built here in 1948.—15km NW is the village of *Geashill*, preserving remains of *Digby Castle*, an O'Dempsey fortress, which was later occupied by the Lords Digby, and an Anglo-Norman motte. *Tullamore*, see Rte 19, lies 12km beyond.

To the right beyond *Ballybrittas* lies *Emo Park*, (or Court) the seat of the Earls of Portarlington (see above), with a domed porticoed mansion designed c 1790 by Gandon, completed c 1810 by Sir Richard Morrison, and recently restored.—In the church at adjacent *Coolbanagher* is a remarkable sculptured font from a vanished church which stood in the park.—To the S of the main road is *Morretta Castle*, an ancient stronghold of the Fitzgeralds, on a stretch of open moorland known as the *Great Heath of Maryborough*.

PORTLAOISE (pron. Portleesha, and sometimes spelt as two words, but still also known as *Maryborough*; 4,050 inhab.), is the county town of Laois (Leix), formerly Queen's County. The original name of the settlement, established here in the reign of Mary I, was Fort Protector; this was changed to The Fort of Leix, but nothing remains of the castle erected to hold in check the powerful O'Mores except part of the curtain-wall. Bartholomew Mosse (1712–59), initiator of the Rotunda Hospital in Dublin, was born here.—At nearby *Ivyleigh* is the *Irish Car Museum*, with some 200 exhibits.

For the *Rock of Dunamase*, 5km E, see Rte 20A; for the road from Portlaoise to Limerick, see Rte 5.

From Portlaoise turn SW onto the N8, shortly passing near (left) *Bally knockan House*, the site of the *Pass of the Plumes*, the marshy level where Essex was defeated in 1599 by Owen MacRory O'More, its name is said to derive from the plumed helmets left on the battlefield.

14km **Abbeyleix** (1400 inhab.), a charming village of tree-lined streets, takes its name from an abbey founded by Conogher O'More in 1183, of which nothing remains. The tomb of Melaghlin O'More, a 13C Prince of Leix, may be seen in the demesne of *Abbeyleix House*, built in 1773–74 for the 1st Viscount de Vesci by Wyatt, and refaced in the 19C; the *Gardens* are open to the public. Sir Jonah Barrington (1760–1834) was born here.

At *Ballinakill*, 6km SE, are fragmentary remains of a castle that stubbornly resisted Cromwell in 1649. A by-road regaining the N8 passes (left) *Rosconnell*, with a 13C church rebuilt in 1646. The Empress Elisabeth of Austria was entertained at the late 18C mansion of *Heywood*—now demolished—near Ballinakill, when she visited Ireland to hunt in 1879 and 1880.

9km *Durrow*, built round a large green, lies at the crossroad from Kilkenny to Roscrea; see Rte 20B.—To the W is the demesne of *Castle Durrow* (1716–18), which we pass (right on leaving the village). It was built by the Fitzpatricks, who likewise erected the ruined priory and castle of *Aghmacart*, to the right some 6.5km beyond.—After 6.5km we pass (right) the *Round Tower* of *Fertagh* (restored), 27.5m high, burnt by O'Loughlin, King of Ireland, in 1156, beside which is a chapel surviving from a 14C Austin priory.—*Johnstown* is soon entered, to the W of which is *Foulkscourt Castle* (c 1450) in the demesne of a ruined mansion of 1715.—*Urlingford*, in a boggy district.

5km S of Urlingford stands *Kilcooly Abbey, which is approached by a long drive. The ruins of the Cistercian church, rebuilt after 1445, founded from Jerpoint by Donal Mór O'Brien in 1182, are unusually well preserved, especially the choir and transepts; the aisleless nave has lost its roof. We enter by the N Transept, which retains its vault and contains a font with a curious interlaced pattern. In the *Choir* is the tomb of Piers Butler of the Cantwell family, with good examples of the floreated cross motif. Over the fine doorway of the S Transept (late 14C?) are a Crucifixion, with St. Christopher on the right, and lower down a vigorous figure of a bishop surmounted by a censing angel, all in high relief; note also the *Mermaid panel on the doorway. On the W piers of the tower are two unusually-placed sedilia, one elaborately decorated. The tracery of the E window was added at the 15C restoration. The cloister arcade has almost disappeared, while some of the monastic chambers have been fitted up with fireplaces and ceilings. The dovecot survives NE of the church.—Some 3km S, at *Clonamicklon*, is a 17C gabled Butler castle with a fortified bawn.—Close by rises *Slieve Ardagh* (333m).

8km beyond Urlingford we pass (left) the two churches of *Leigh*, or

Liathmore Mochoemog, one an 8C structure with a high-pitched roof (partly restored); the other a 12–15C building containing 13–14C tomb slabs. A monastery was founded here before 650 by St. Mochoemog.

The main road continues SW direct to (22.5km) **Cashel** (see below), passing at the next crossroad, the *Turnpike*, *Grallagh Castle* (left), with a 16C towerhouse, but the following DETOUR via Thurles to visit *Holycross* is recommended.

Forking right, we shortly pass a ruined tower before entering **Thurles** (7,350 inhab.), an ancient episcopal and market town, where in 1174 Strongbow met his match at the hands of Donal O'Brien and Roderick O'Connor. The *Castle* (12C) guards the bridge over the Suir, and there is another smaller fort near the square. The *Cathedral*, in an ugly bastard Lombardic style (1865–72) by J.J. McCarthy, contains the original tabernacle from the Gesù in Rome adapted for this setting.— 3km N of the town is *Brittas Castle*, the remains of a moated medieval-revival edifice by W.V. Morrison, on the site of an earlier fortress; its completion came to an abrupt halt in 1834 when the owner was killed by a piece of falling masonry; the barbican tower is impressive.

THURLES TO LIMERICK (65km). We follow the R503 almost due W, keeping to the left on passing the racecourse (right) and at *Rosmult*, bear right to ascend the Owenbeg valley, with *Knockalough* (457m) on our left, and continue to climb through desolate scenery until just beyond (22km) *Milestone*.—After another 12km we pass, above *Rear Cross*, a remarkable two-chambered dolmen on the flank of *Mautherslieve* (542m). The road descends the valley of the Clare, with its cascades, with (left) *Cullaun* (463m), one of the Slievefelim Mountains, and the more distant *Slievekimalta* (693m) to the N.—30km *Limerick*; see Rte 14.

From Thurles we drive SW on the R660 via (6km) **Holycross**, with its ruined *Abbey, a Cistercian house attractively placed on the bank of the Suir. Its church, its masonry in a fine state of preservation, was restored in 1971–77.

The Abbey of Holy Cross was founded in 1180 by Donal O'Brien, King of Thomond, as a shrine for a relic of the True Cross given to his father Murtogh O'Brien in 1110 by Pope Paschal II. It was almost certainly enlarged in the 15C, but luckily it has not been disconcertingly spoilt by 19C or more recent additions, which is too frequently the case.

The most striking feature of the exterior of the church is the beautiful reticulated window-tracery, that of the E and W windows and the S transept being especially notable.

We enter through the *Cloister*, partly restored, with the *Cellarium* and *Dorter* on the W side, and the *Sacristy*, *Chapter House* (with a doorway of unique design), and *Monk's Parlour* on the E.

The *Nave*, with its wooden roof, of grey stone set off by white-washed walls, with one row of round-headed and one of pointed arches, is a good example of transitional work. Note the sculpted owl on the wall near the crossing. The S transept is the finest thing in the church, with its two E chapels, one with an interesting vault, separated by a narrow platform, above which is an elaborately groined roof borne on twisted columns, and probably designed for the exposition of the relic. The vaulted *Choir*, extended at a later date some distance W of the squat central tower, is remarkable for its carving, strongly Celtic in style, and excellently preserved owing to the durable quality of the local limestone. Noteworthy is the late 14C *Sedilia*, bearing the arms of Ormonde and Desmond, with foliated crockets and elaborate carved valance.—The N transept also has two chapels, and traces of painting.

We later skirt *Boherlahan*, where Charles Bianconi (born in 1786 in

Lombardy, died 1875), the Irish transport entrepreneur, is buried. His home from 1850 was at *Longfield House* (c 1760), a short distance to the W. Now a hotel, it is also in the care of the Irish Georgian Society, and open to the public.

CASHEL (2,450 inhab.), in Irish, *Caiseal* (stone fort), 30km from the turning for Thurles, was the ancient capital of the Kings of Munster, and long a famous ecclesiastical centre. The Rock of Cashel, rising above the town, is crowned by the ruins of a cathedral, beside which shelters Cormac's Chapel, an outstanding example of Irish-Romanesque architecture.

The Rock of Cashel; aerial view from the East

Cashel was fortified at a very early date, and was certainly a stronghold of Brian Ború (926–1014). The first church was founded here by St. Declan, a 6C disciple of St. Patrick: the bishop's see, founded soon after, is now united with Emly, Waterford, and Lismore. In 1171 Henry II here received the homage of Donal O'Brien, King of Thomond, and lesser nobles, and in 1315 Edward Bruce summoned a parliament here. In 1495 the cathedral was set alight by Gerald, Earl of Kildare, who, when he was arraigned by Henry VII for his action, alleged in extenuation that 'he thought the archbishop was in it'. Enchanted by the candour of the reply, Henry immediately re-appointed him in the office of Lord Deputy. In 1647 the town was plundered by Lord Inchiquin ('Murrough of the Burnings'). The lead roof of the cathedral was probably removed in 1749 by Abp Arthur Price (died 1752)—or his successor—who, it was said, was too lazy to climb the hill to his church. The Protestant archbishopric was reduced to a bishopric in 1839; the Catholic archbishop's cathedral is at Thurles.

The conspicuous **Rock of Cashel**, rising abruptly to c 30m above the plain, is stated in legend to be due to the Devil, who, in some great hurry to cross the mountains to the N, bit out a huge block and spat it onto the plain below, the measurements taken of the gap in the Devil's Bit Mountain (of Silurian grits) corresponding exactly—it is said—to the dimensions of the Rock! Glacial scratchings on the rock offer the

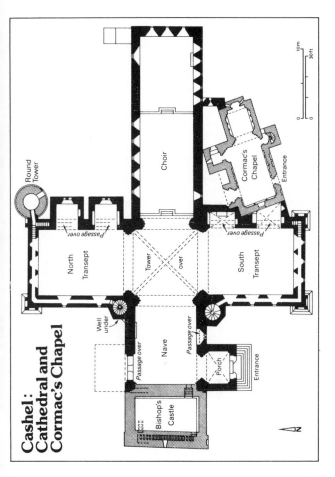

**Cashel:
Cathedral and
Cormac's Chapel**

Round Tower

North Transept

Passage over

Tower

over

South Transept

Passage over

Choir

Cormac's Chapel

Entrance

Well under

Nave

Passage over

Passage over

Porch

Entrance

Bishop's Castle

N

less Milesian explanation that it is a monoclinal fold of carboniferous limestone penetrating the ubiquitous glacial drifts.

The largest building on the summit, which commands panoramic *Views*, is the shell of the **•Cathedral**. Erected in the 13C, it was restored following a fire in 1495, and again after its desecration in 1647. The *Castle* of the archbishops was added to the W end by Richard O'Median, archbishop in 1406–40, at the same time as the central tower was raised and the parapets battlemented, giving it a defensive character.

It is entered on the S side by a massive porch with a Gothic doorway. The Transepts, containing some good 16C tombs, have well-designed windows, and in the N transept is a series of sculptures representing the Apostles and sundry saints, and the Beasts of the Apocalypse, with the Butler and Hacket arms. The long *Choir* is flanked by lancet windows, but the large E window has vanished. On the S side is a recum-

bent figure of Abp Myler Magrath (?1523–1622), the notorious pluralist, who apart from being archbishop for 52 years, held four bishoprics
and no less than 77 other livings! An octagonal staircase turret ascends
beside the central tower to a series of defensive passages in the thickness of the transept walls, those on the N side affording access to the
Round Tower (see below).

The view from the top of the central tower is even more extensive: to
the N is seen the Devil's Bit; to the E, Slievenamon, with the Comeragh
range further S; to the SW are the Galty Mountains; to the NW towards
Limerick rises the dark mass of Slievefelim; while to the W lies Tipperary and the 'Golden Vale'.

Directly abutting the S side of the cathedral, but not structurally
connected with it, is *Cormac's Chapel* (*Teampull Mór Chormaic*), the
most remarkable feature of which is the retention of the 'high stone
roof', the traditional covering of the early saints' cells (as at Glendalough, Kells, and Killaloe) with highly developed formal decoration in
the Romanesque manner.

The chapel, of a browner stone that the cathedral, was built in 1127–
34 by Cormac MacCarthy, King of Desmond and Bp of Cashel. Its plan
is peculiar, having a square tower on either side at the junction of nave
and chancel; the N tower is 15m high to the top of its pyramidal roof;
the other, which is slightly higher, has lost its roof, and has been
finished by a later battlemented coping. The present S entrance is
notable for its carving, while the later W door, giving access from the
cathedral, has been blocked. Bands of blind arcading surround the
exterior, including the towers, which themselves are decorated by
string-courses. There are certain strong resemblances to contemporary work at Murbach, in Alsace. The main entrance on the N side is
now obstructed by the cathedral, but one can see its elaborate arch-
mouldings, and the tympanum displays vigorous sculpture of a cen-
taur shooting a lion.

The dark and somewhat dank interior is likewise embellished by
blind arcading. The ribbed barrel-vaulted roof of the nave rests on
massive pilasters, the bases of which are level with the capitals of the
chancel arch, which is not quite central. The chancel arcading is surmounted by round-headed triplets. The square altar recess is decorated with twisted columns, and lighted by two oblique windows; the
arch above it bears a curious row of heads. An 11C stone tomb-chest,
decorated in the Scandinavian style, has been placed at the W end, but
its original polychrome, and that of the church itself, has long perished. Above the vault are two lofts approached by a stair in the S
tower, that over the nave having a fireplace.

Adjoining the N transept of the cathedral is a *Round Tower*, 24m
high (11C).—The much-worn shaft of a *High Cross* (c 1150), with a
figure (?St. Patrick) on one side and the Crucifixion on the other, which
formerly stood in the entrance enclosure, is now preserved in the
adjacent *Hall of the Vicars-Choral* (c 1420; altered in the 17C). It has
recently been restored, and its vaulted undercroft contains fragments
from the site, and also a tomb depicting armed knights (from Athassel;
see below).

Just below the Rock are the ruins of *Hore Abbey*, founded for Cistercians (on a Benedictine site) in 1272 by Abp MacCarville, and at one
time fortified.

The town preserves considerable but fragmentary remains of antiquity, often put to commercial account, including *Quirke's Castle*, a
fortified residence (15C) in the main street, and the *Bishop's Palace*, a
fine early Georgian mansion of c 1731 by Sir Edward Lovett Pearce

(now an hotel), from which a winding walk following a path used by the more agile archbishops, leads to the Rock.

The Protestant *Cathedral* dates from 1784, with a spire added in 1812; its chapter-house contains a notable library (mainly 16–17C), presented by Abp Bolton in 1743; a museum of local interest is housed in the vestry. The churchyard is bounded on two sides by the *Town Walls* (*temp.* Edward III), in which are inserted four tomb-effigies of members of the Hacket family (c 1260).—The *Catholic church* preserves some relics of *Hacket's Friary*, a Franciscan house of c 1250; while also of interest are the ruins of the *Dominican Priory* (1243), founded by Abp MacKelly.

CASHEL TO TIPPERARY (19km). The N74 runs W, after 7km passing (c 2km left) at *Golden*, just beyond the *Suir Bridge*, with its defensive tower, ***Athassel Priory**, founded for Austin canons in 1192 by William Burke (or De Burgh). The important and extensive ruins include a very fine doorway and the tomb of the founder; also a cloister and fortified outer works. Richard de Burgh (died 1326) is buried here. Nothing remains of the town, burnt in 1319 and again a decade later.

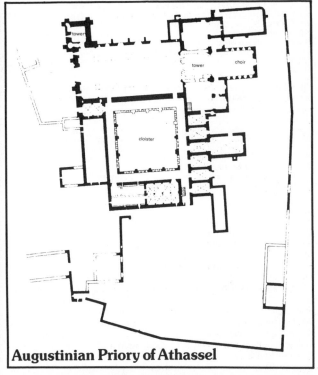

Augustinian Priory of Athassel

Regaining the main road, we shortly pass *Thomastown Castle*, a 17C house refaced and embellished by Sir Richard Morrison in the Gothick taste in 1820, and now an ivy-clad ruin. It was formerly the seat of the earls of Landaff, and the birthplace of the advocate of temperance, Fr

Theobald Mathew (1790–1856). Swift was an earlier visitor to the house, which once had extensive gardens.—For *Tipperary*, see Rte 8.

From Cashel we drive due S, with occasional views of the Galtee or Galty Mountains to the SW, after 9km traversing *Newinn*, immediately beyond which a lane leads right to *Knockgraffon*, where the Norman motte succeeded a stronghold of the Kings of Munster.

We descend the valley to **Cahir**, (*Cathair*, a fortified town; 2,100 inhab.), a pleasant village of great antiquity on the crossroads Dublin–Cork and Waterford–Limerick. Its imposing *Castle commanding the Suir bridge was built in 1142 by Conor O'Brien; largely rebuilt in the 15C; restored in 1840, and again since 1964, it now contains a small museum. It was besieged by Essex (1599), Inchiquin (1647), and Cromwell (1650). Relics of an early 13C Priory of Augustinian Canons, abutted by a 17C tower, lie off the Tipperary road.

For *Ardfinnan*, 9.5km SE, see Rte 8.

CAHIR TO LISMORE OVER THE KNOCKMEALDOWN MOUNTAINS (c 37km). Driving due S on the R668 immediately W of the town, we shortly pass (left) *Tubbrid*, where the historian Geoffrey Keating (c 1570–c 1644) is buried, to *Clogheen*, to the E of which is *Castle Grace*, a fine ruin; *Shanbally Castle*, by Nash, demolished in 1957, lay to the NW.—The road climbs steeply SE into the hills in a series of hairpin bends to reach the *Gap* at 339m between *Sugarloaf Hill* (655m) to the W and, to the SE, *Knockmealdown*, the summit of the range (793m), in Irish *Cnoc Mealdomhnaig*, or Mealdowney's Hill. Samuel Grubb, once owner of Grace Castle, chose to be buried here in an upright position, which has since been known as 'Grubb's Grave'. Hence the road descends S to *Lismore*, on the N72 from Dungarvan to Fermoy, 23km W, where we may regain the Cork road; see Rte 9.

From Cahir, the N8 turns SW along a wide valley commanding superb views, flanked to the N by the *Galty Mountains*, and with the Knockmealdown range to the S (see above).

The **Galty Mountains** (Galtymore, 917m) or *Galtee Mountains*, are among the loftiest in S Ireland, occupying a triangle between Tipperary, Cahir and Mitchelstown, and are prolonged to the W by the *Ballyhoura* range. On every side they rise abruptly, and on the S side the Old Red Sandstone is cut up by deep gullies into bold escarpments. The usual ascent is via *Mountain Lodge* (see below) and the saddle between *Galtybeg* and *Galtymore*. The ridge walks command extensive *Views*, including the mountains above Killarney (SW), the distant Slieve Bloom range (NE), and the nearer Knockmealdown and Comeragh ranges to the S and SE.

After 9km we pass (left) the remarkably complete shell of the late Elizabethan mansion of *Burncourt* or *Burntcourt* (1641–45), built for Sir Richard Everard, and in 1650 set alight by Cromwell, or perhaps by Lady Everard to prevent it falling into his hands.—On the right at the next bridge is the approach road to *Mountain Lodge* (see above); beyond and NW of *Kilbeheny* is a ruined castle.

MITCHELSTOWN (3,100 inhab.) preserves a large market square, where police fired on a crowd in September 1887 during the Home Rule agitation, killing three. The vanished castle, founded by the White Knights of Desmond, passed by marriage c 1660 to the Lords Kingston, and was replaced in 1823 by a mansion later demolished, its masonry being used to construct the church at *Mount Melleray* (cf.). The almshouses for Decayed Gentlefolk to the NE, known as *Kingston College* (founded in 1771), built by John Morrison of Cork, is of interest.

The town is known for its *Caves, perhaps the finest group of limestone caverns in Ireland, best approached via *Ballyporeen*, 11km to the E, where a turning N leads to a house marked 'The Caves'. The guide will provide lights, but a certain amount of rough scrambling is involved. They are divided into two groups, the *Old Caves* and the *New*, the latter only discovered in 1833; the former (for spelaeologists only), described by Arthur Young in 1777 (when agent for Lord Kingston), were known long before that, as it was here that Sugán Earl of Desmond, was hiding when run to ground by Edmund Fitzgibbon, the last of the White Knights, in 1601. The rock formations, stalactites and stalagmites, are impressive.

Mallow, see Rte 9, lies some 29km SW of Mitchelstown, approached via the N73, traversing *Kildorrery*, near which stood *Bowen's Court* (1776), home until 1959 of the novelist Elizabeth Bowen (née Cameron, 1899–1973). It was demolished in 1961.—About 5km beyond is the castle of *Ballynamona*.

The main road (N8) to Fermoy ascends due S across the *Kilworth Mountains*, a prolongation of the Knockmealdown range, rising to 297m, with fine retrospective views, leaving on the right the lonely tower of *Caherdrinney*, and further down (left) the village of *Kilworth*, with the desecrated demesne of *Moore Park*, traversed by the river Funshion.

An older road leads SW from Mitchelstown past *Killeenemer*, with a 12C church, before turning left to *Glanworth*, with a ruined castle of the Roche family, the 13C church of a Dominican priory founded by them, and a 13-arched bridge.— Turning SE, the road passes, at *Labbacallee*, a wedge-shaped passage-grave.

FERMOY (3,100 inhab.), long a British garrison town, owes its origin to the enterprise of John Anderson, a Scottish merchant, who in 1789 built a hotel and some houses here and entered into a contract with the government for the erection of barracks, which lie on the N bank of the Blackwater. The *College* was formerly a military school. *Fermoy House* (now demolished), in the town centre, dated from c 1790; *Castle Hyde*, an imposing late-Georgian house by Abraham Hargrave overlooking the river to the W of the town, was the ancestral home of Douglas Hyde (1860–1949; first President of Ireland), although he was born at *Frenchpark* (cf.).

A left-hand turn off the N8 just S of Fermoy leads shortly to **Castlelyons**, preserving ruins of two castles and a 14C priory. The *Barrymore chapel*, adjoining the parish church, contains an 18C monument.

Beyond (8km) *Rathcormack* we pass (left) the fine Georgian mansion of *Kilshannig* (1765; by Davis Ducart), with some outstanding plasterwork by Paul and Philip Francini and with a fine cantilevered staircase.

Climbing out of the valley we reach *Watergrasshill*, where Francis Mahony (cf.) was parish priest, and descend towards Cork. In the NE suburbs we pass *Riverstown House* (rebuilt 1734), restored by the Irish Georgian Society, and preserving fine plasterwork by the Francini brothers, who were employed here 20 years before their embellishment of Kilshannig (see above).

Shortly beyond, we meet the N25 and turn right into the E suburbs of **Cork**; see Rte 6.

5   Wexford to Cork via Waterford, Dungarvan, and Youghal

179km (111 miles). N25. 37km *New Ross*—23km **Waterford**—46km **Dungarvan**—31km **Youghal**—42km **Cork.**

From *Wexford* (see Rte 2A), the New Ross road bears almost due W, after 8km leaving on the left the road to *Taghmon*, where a rude cross in the churchyard is all that remains of the monastery founded in the 6C by St. Munna (*Teach Munna*). The hymn-writer Henry Francis Lyte (1793–1847) was curate here in 1815.—After 15km we pass (right) *Carrickbyrne Hill*, with a monument to Sir Ralph Abercromby (1734–1801), benevolent commander of the all-too-brutal British troops in Ireland prior to March 1798; and (left) *Scullabogue House*, scene of the massacre of c 200 Protestants that June, when a barn in which they had sought shelter was set alight.

NEW ROSS (5,400 inhab.), a small port on the Barrow, is said to have been founded by Isabella de Clare, a daughter of Strongbow. Due to its strong fortifications, it was long a rival of Waterford.

Originally called *Ros Mhic Treocin*, in the 16C it took the name Rossponte, and was so known to Spenser. The bridge was destroyed by its Irish defenders in 1643, but in 1649 it was replaced with a bridge of boats by Cromwell, the first to be seen in Ireland. In 1798 the Irish insurgents under Bagenal Harvey made a determined attack on the town, and were only repulsed after a stubborn struggle, in which Lord Mountjoy was killed. Charles Tottenham (1685–1758) was MP for New Ross from 1727 until shortly before his death. He is said incorrectly (by Sir Jonah Barrington) to have ridden 60 miles overnight to Dublin, entering Parliament House in his muddy boots in time to give a casting vote against an unpopular measure.

Today, the most attractive feature of New Ross is the river, crossed by a swing-bridge of 1869. The *Tholsel* was rebuilt in 1806; of the fortifications little is left but a tower and fragments of gates, while a Protestant church (*St. Mary's*) occupies the site of a *Franciscan friary* (13C), some walls of which have survived; in the ruins is the tomb of Peter Butler (died 1599), and in the graveyard a slab claimed to be the cenotaph of Isabella (see above).—All trace of the great Dominican abbey of *Rosbercon*, on the W bank of the Barrow, has vanished.

For roads to *St. Mullins* (14km N), and *Inistioge* and *Jerpoint* (16km and 25.5km NW), see pp 264 and 173 respectively.

Leaving behind the old warehouses and more recent petrol installations of the town, the main road to Waterford first skirts the well-wooded banks of the Barrow. Beyond *Glenmore* a steep ascent commands fine retrospective views of *Brandon Hill* (left) and the *Blackstairs* range, before the road descends into the Suir valley to *Waterford*; see p 274.

THE COASTAL ROUTE THROUGH TRAMORE (53km) is an alternative to the main road from Waterford to Dungarvan. The R675 drives due S (passing near *Knockeen*, to the right, with a perfect Portal Dolmen) to (13km) **Tramore** (5,650 inhab.), a popular resort on a sandy but exposed bay between *Brownstone Head* and *Great Newton Head*, both surmounted by old towers; on the latter is a cast-iron figure of a sailor known as 'The Metal Man'. Immediately E of the town a sand spit known as *The Burrows* almost cuts off the lagoon of *Back Strand* from the sea. The road W reaches the sea again at *Annestown*, behind which are the ruins of *Dunhill Castle*, the original stronghold of the Le Poers. Some 14km further W, at *Drumlohan* (right) several Ogham stones may be seen (re-erected).—*Stradbally*, on the coast, was once the site of an Austin friary.—We regain the main road at *Dungarvan*.

The N25 leads W from Waterford, skirting the *Glass Factory*, towards the *Comeragh Mountains*, after 7km passing (right) the demesne of *Mount Congreve*, an early 18C mansion ostentatiously re-faced and remodelled in 1965, when some of its interesting decoration was wantonly destroyed. Its gardens may be visited.—Shortly beyond (right) are the ruins of *Kilmeaden*, a castle of the Le Poers taken by Cromwell in 1649, who in anger at having to raise the siege of Water ford, hanged the owner out of hand.—We cross the river Mahon at *Kilmacthomas*, birthplace of the Irish comedian Tyrone Power (1787–1841; Tyrone Power, the film star, and the theatrical producer Sir Tyrone Guthrie were two of his great-grandsons). Beyond Kilmacthomas the road winds round the S side of the Comeragh range, commanding a good view of Dungarvan on the final descent.

DUNGARVAN (6,650 inhab.), a busy market-town partly built on a regular plan, lies at the head of its fine harbour, and is the capital of the district of *The Decies*. It retains the ruins of a *Castle* erected by King John. It was saved from Cromwell's bombardment in 1649, it is said, by the Protector's pleasure at seeing a woman affecting to drink his health at the town gate.—At *Abbeyside*, a suburb on the E bank of the Colligan, spanned by a bridge of 1815, are the ruins of the *MacGraths' Castle* and an *Austin friary* founded by the same family in the 13C and now incorporated in the Catholic church.

For the road hence to *Killarney* via Lismore, Fermoy, and Mallow, see Rte 9.

The R672 from DUNGARVAN TO CLONMEL (40km), leading NW from the town, is the best approach to the *Comeragh Mountains* (789m), the highest in Co. Waterford, and their S extension above Dungarvan, known as the *Monavullagh Mountains* (725m); it commands a fine view of the Galty range to the NW on the descent into the Suir valley.

Skirting Dungarvan harbour, the N25 bears SW, leaving to the left a lane leading to *Helvick Head*, its name betraying its Danish origin, between which and Ardmore is a small enclave of the Gaeltacht (cf.).

Beyond the summit of the *Drum Hills* (14km from Dungarvan) a road forks left for (8km) **Ardmore**, a small resort where a monastery is said to have been founded in the 6C by St. Declan. His *Oratory*, with its original door blocked and with a slate roof added in 1716, is still standing. The *****Cathedral**, or its remains, is a very ancient structure many times repaired and altered, with an 11C nave in the Irish-Romanesque style, and a Gothic choir, probably 13C.

Note the capitals of the chancel arch. The N wall of both nave and choir show traces of much earlier craftsmanship, including a course of rude cyclopean masonry and some unusual arcading; the N door, originally round-headed, has a pointed arch inserted. Two Ogham stones may be seen within the church.

More remarkable is the W Front, where within two blind arches below a blind arcade are some curious weathered sculptures, including Adam and Eve, the conversion of a pagan prince by St. Declan, the Judgement of Solomon, and the dedication of the Temple, etc.— Adjacent is a tapering *****Round Tower**, 29m high, one of the latest in Ireland (late 12C), unusual in having its floors indicated by decorative string-courses.

To the E is another group of buildings, including *St. Declan's Well* and ruined *Temple Disert* (?12–14C). The vanished Castle, near by, was occupied by Perkin Warbeck, and destroyed after a siege in 1642 when 117 of its defenders were summarily hanged.—To the S stands *Ardo*, a turreted 18C 'folly' house near the cliffs, abandoned c 1918 and now derelict.

Regaining the main road, we turn due W, and cross the estuary of the

Blackwater N of the long iron bridge of 1880 before bearing S to Youghal. Near the N entrance of the town we pass some fragments of *St. John's Abbey*, a 14C Benedictine house converted into an ammunition store by Charles II, and remains of *North Abbey* (Dominican) founded in 1268; *South Abbey* (Franciscan), of 1224, has entirely disappeared.

YOUGHAL (pron. Yawl; 5,850 inhab.), a market-town and fishing-port, exhibits some dilapidation, although with a sandy strand on the open sea to the SW, it is a popular resort during the season. Its Irish name is *Eochaill*, the yew-wood.

Although of more ancient foundation, little is known of Youghal before the Norman invasion. It was long a Fitzgerald stronghold, and in 1579 was besieged by Ormonde during the Desmond rebellion. On entering it, according to some reports, Ormonde hanged Coppinger, the mayor, for failing to protect the place. It was (very briefly) the residence of Sir Walter Raleigh, and of Sir Richard Boyle, later Baron Youghal and Earl of Cork. Edmund Spenser married Elizabeth Boyle, a kinsman of Sir Richard, in 1594, as idealised in his 'Amoretti' and 'Epithalamion'. Cromwell, well-received here, established his headquarters in the town in 1649; General Michael Jones, his lieutenant, died of fever here, and is buried in the Cork transept of the church. Hence William Lithgow, the traveller, embarked for St. Malo and Spain in 1620. William Congreve spent his infancy here.

Tomb of the 'Great' Earl of Cork, St. Mary's, Youghal

The long Main Street runs S parallel to the harbour, and is extended by the Strand. From the N end of this artery a lane ascends right past some old almshouses to **St. Mary's Church**, formerly collegiate; rebuilt in 1461 and over-restored in the 1850s after lying in partial ruin since the rebellion of the 15C Earl of Desmond in 1579. It preserves a detached belfry, 19m high; another at the W end was demolished in 1792. The W front is a good example of the Early English style.

The interior is notable for the nave roof, the provost's stall, the pulpit, and the font cover, all of old oak; and the font itself, unusually elaborate in design. In the nave hangs a rare example of a carved cradle (1684) for holding the sword of the Corporation. In the S aisle are the tombs of the 8th Earl of Desmond (1468), who founded the college, and Matthew Le Mercier (13C). The S Transept contains the tomb, with painted figures (restored by the Earl of Cork in 1619), of Richard Bennet and his wife, founders of the chantry that stood here. Here also is the *Tomb (comp. his monument in St. Patrick's Cathedral, Dublin) of the great Earl of Cork himself (1566–1643) with his two wives and nine of his 16 children, presenting with its copious inscriptions 'a series of heraldic and genealogical memoirs'. It is said to have been designed by the earl himself, and executed by Alexander Hills of Holborn. The choir contains the 15C tombs of the Flemings, and a good E window. The churchyard is abutted by part of the Town Walls (15–16C), with its round towers.

Just NE of the church stands Myrtle Grove, a much-altered Elizabethan mansion preserving carved oak wainscoting and contemporary chimneypieces. There is little justification for assuming that it was ever the actual residence of Raleigh in 1584–97 after he had been presented with 17,000 hectares (42,000 acres) of the confiscated Desmond estates, which he sold to the Earl of Cork in 1602. Statements suggesting that Raleigh 'drunk tobacco' and read over the MS of Spenser's 'Faerie Queene' under the yewtree, or that he planted the first potato in Ireland here, should be disregarded.

To the SE is New College House (1781–82), preserving a fine 17C chimneypiece.

Regaining and walking the length of Main St, we pass (left) the derelict remains of Tynte's Castle, and (right) Uniacke House (1706–15; by Leuventhan, a Dutch builder), known as the Red House. Eventually we reach the massive four-storey **Clock House** (1771; replacing an earlier tower), spanning the street, one of the more attractive features of the town, containing a small local museum.—On the opposite side of the harbour lies Ferry Point, from which Lord Castlehaven tried to bombard Youghal in 1645.

YOUGHAL TO LISMORE (26km). A pleasant excursion may be made by following lanes more-or-less skirting the W bank of the Blackwater, by turning left at the W end of the Bridge N of the town, and round Rincrew Hill, where Raymond le Gros built a preceptory for the Templars.—We next pass Templemichael, with a keep of the Fitzgeralds, at the mouth of the Glendine, and facing ruined Molana Abbey, approached by a causeway; an urn in one of the chapels commemorates Raymond Fitzgerald ('le Gros'), possibly buried here in 1186.—Some distance upstream on a crag stands Strancally Castle, blown up by Ormonde in 1579; New Strancally Castle, further N, near the mouth of the Bride, is a large castellated building by Pain of Cork.—Higher up, on the opposite bank, is **Dromana Castle**, in beautiful grounds, with a curious 'Hindu' Gothick lodge topped by a green onion dome (c 1830; recently refurbished by the Irish Georgian Society). Here are also the ruins of a keep of the Fitzgeralds of Decies, the birthplace of the 'Old' Countess of Desmond (?1500–1604). For Lismore, see Rte

9; the return journey may be made by following the N72 to *Tallow*, and then the R634.

From Youghal the Cork road (N25), circling round the harbour entrance, bears due W towards Killeagh and Midleton; see below.

An ALTERNATIVE road (R633) forks left shortly after leaving Youghal, bearing SW directly to (c 25km) Cloyne. On approaching Cloyne the road passes the pleasant demesne of *Ballymaloe*, now a hotel.—**Cloyne** (in Irish *Cluain Uamha*, the meadow of the cave), now only a village (600 inhab.), was the seat of an ancient bishopric, founded by St. Colman in the 6C and now joined to Cork. Its most famous incumbent, from 1734, was George Berkeley (1685–1753). Its *Cathedral* is a plain building of the 13C, deprived of most of its character by restoration. Interesting features are the rude carvings on the small N door representing pagan symbols of life, and the heavy cubic masonry blocks from which the nave-arches spring. The house in which the philosopher resided was burned down in 1870. Opposite is a *Round Tower*, used as the cathedral belfry, 30.5m high including the castellated top added in 1683 after it had been struck by lightning; it displays an almost entire absence of taper.

SW of Cloyne are a number of sandy strands and small resorts frequented for their sea-fishing, among them *Ballycotton*, reached via *Shanagarry*, where the ruined castle, once the home of the Penn family, was visited by Willaim Penn in 1666 and 1698.

The main road may be regained at Midleton, 8km NW of Cloyne.

10km *Killeagh* (pron. Killa) lies at the foot of Glenbower, in which, on the Dissour, is the demesne of *Aghadoe*, which was known until 1932 as the 'maiden estate', having remained in the hands of the Capell family for almost 700 years; it is now a forestry centre.—5km *Castlemartyr*, the home of Henry Boyle, 1st Earl of Shannon (1682–1764), and of Roger Boyle, 1st Earl of Orrery (1621–79), who died here.—Some 3km SE stands the castle of *Ightermurragh* (c 1640).

8km **Midleton** (3,200 inhab.) founded c 1670 by the Brodrick family, preserves an 18C *Market-house* and the college at which J.P. Curran was educated. *Ballinacurra*, on a creek to the S, was the scene of Raleigh's exploit, when he claimed to have held the ford here single-handed against an insurgent band until rescued by his own men!—We shortly traverse *Carrigtohill*, with its limestone caves, and (left) *Barryscourt Castle*, with its rectangular keep.

CARRIGTOHILL TO CÓBH (9km). Immediately beyond, the R625 (and then 624) leads left onto *Fota Island*, on which *Fota House* contains a good collection of Irish landscapes, etc. The road then crosses a strait to *Belvelly*, with a 14C castle and martello tower, circles the W side of *Great Island*, the largest in *Cork Harbour*, which it overlooks, to (9.5km) **Cóbh** (pron. Cove; 6,600 inhab.), still the most extensive harbour on the S coast of Ireland. Well-sited and enjoying a mild climate, it was known originally as *The Cove* of Cork, but between 1849 (when Queen Victoria disembarked here) until 1922, it was called Queenstown.

The land-locked harbour first attracted notice in the 18C, being a convenient naval base and place of concentration for the huge convoys of transport required during the French and American wars. In 1838 the 'Sirius', the first steamer to cross the Atlantic, set sail from here, taking 18½ days. During the famine years it was the last Irish soil trodden by many thousands of emigrants before being crowded onto the waiting hulks known as 'Coffin Ships', too often unseaworthy, among other vessels. It was at the approaches to the port that, intercepted by the Royal Navy, the 'Aud', with a cargo of arms ordered from Germany by Sir Roger Casement in readiness for the Easter Rising, was scuttled (22 April 1916). The Royal Cork Yacht Club, with its clubhouse here, was founded in 1720. In the old graveyard N of the town are buried the Rev. Charles Wolfe (1791–1823), author of 'The Burial of Sir John Moore', and numerous victims of the 'Lusitania' disaster (cf. Old Head of Kinsale).

A good view of the harbour is gained from a terrace at the top of East Ferry Rd. The quay is dominated by *St. Colman's Cathedral*, by E.W. Pugin and G. Ashlin (from 1868), built of Dalkey granite in a Gothic style, decorated with Irish marble, and surmounted by a 90m spire. There is a picturesque terrace of 23 houses near by in Barrack St, known as the 'Pack of Cards'.

Immediately opposite the beach at *Haulbowline Island* are the headquarters of the Irish Navy, with steelworks, and *Rocky Island*; and further S, *Spike Island*, a convict prison in 1847–85, and now a military camp. **Cork harbour**, in which trans-Atlantic and other steamers now only occasionally lie, is approached by a curved channel, c 3km long and 1.5km wide, with a lighthouse at *Roche's Point*; at the inner entrance are two old forts.

Continuing due W from Carrigtohill, we shortly enter the NE outskirts of Cork, below the wooded suburbs of *Tivoli* and *Montenotte*. *Tivoli House*, with folly-studded garden, was largely gutted by a fire in the 1820s, and recently demolished; it succeeded a residence of Sir Walter Raleigh. Nearby *Woodhill*, now a ruin, was often visited by Sarah Curran, the betrothed of Robert Emmet, whose tragic romance inspired the pen of Thomas Moore and Washington Irving.—For **Cork** itself; see below.

6 Cork and its Environs

A. Central Cork

CORK (in Irish *Corcaigh*, a marsh; 136,350 inhab.), the third city of Ireland, and the second in the Republic, is one of marked contrasts, equally characteristic of some others, in that off its broad main thoroughfares open nasty and near-derelict alleys. Since Spenser's day, when he described the site and 'The spreading Lee that, like an island fayre, Encloseth Corke with his divided flood', the city has overflowed the island and extends far up its steep banks, with which it is connected by a series of bridges. One can but agree with an architectural authority that because of the sad state of so much of the fabric of the city, 'to walk about it on a bad day can be a very depressing experience'. Few houses of great architectural interest will be seen, although the colourfully painted facades of some terraces act as a foil to the adjacent grim and grey warehouses and other commercial buildings. Cork carries on a busy trade in agricultural produce, and is a prosperous centre of distilling, brewing, and bacon-curing; there are also tanneries, woollen mills, shipbuilding and motor works, etc.; in January 1977 the Verolme shipyard launched a vessel 225m-long of 70,000 tonnes.

Tourist Office, Grand Parade.

The *Airport* is c 6.5km S at *Ballygarvan*.

The *Railway Station* (*Kent* or *Ceannt*) is adjacent to the river, a short distance NE of the Brian Ború Bridge; it preserves a curious old 'Bury' locomotive of 1848.

Bus Station, Parnell Pl.

St. Barr or Finbarr, a native of Connacht, founded a monastic establishment on the S bank of the main channel of the Lee in the 6th or 7C. It attained a sufficient degree of wealth and learning to attract the covetous eyes of the marauding Danes, who after repeatedly plundering it, settled there and carried on a flourishing trade. In 1172 Diarmuid MacCarthy, Lord of Desmond, who had ousted the Danes, did homage to Henry II, but the Anglo-Norman colonisers lived in a constant state of siege and harassment from neighbouring tribes. In 1491 Cork supported the claim of Perkin Warbeck to the English throne, an inept move for which the mayor, John Walters, was hanged. It was the English headquarters during the Desmond rebellion of 1590–1600. In 1649 it offered no resistance to Cromwell, but held out for five days against Marlborough and the Duke of Wurtemburg in 1690; during the siege the Duke of Grafton (born 1663; an illegitimate son of Charles II) received a mortal wound.

The later 18C was a prosperous period, and Cork was noted for its glass manufacture c 1750–1839. During 1920 much of the city centre was deliberately set alight by the brutal 'Black and Tans'; Lord Mayor Thomas MacCurtain, an ardent Sinn Feiner, was deliberately murdered by members of the constabulary; his successor, Terence MacSwiney, died in Brixton gaol after a hunger strike of 75 days.

Among natives of Cork are Sir William Morrison (1767–1849), the architect; Richard Milliken (1868–1815), and the poet William Maginn (1793–1842) who edited 'Fraser's Magazine' and was the original of Thackeray's 'Captain Shandon'; Thomas Crofton Croker (1798–1854), the antiquary; James Sheridan Knowles (1784–1862), dramatist and actor; Mary Aikenhead (1787–1858), founder of the Irish Sisters of Charity; Francis Mahony (1804–66), humorous poet and journalist, better known as 'Father Prout'; the artists James Barry (1741–1806), Robert Fagan (1767–1816), and Daniel Maclise (1806–70); and in the world of letters, Edward Dowden (1843–1913), Daniel Corkery (1878–1964), Michael O'Donovan ('Frank O'Connor'; 1903–66), and Seán O'Faoláin (1900–). Sir Arnold Bax, the composer (1883–1953), died here.

From Youghal or Fermoy, the main approach to the city centre is by turning left across *St. Patrick's Bridge* (1860), its far end dominated by Foley's statue of Fr Mathew (see below), and traversing bow-shaped Patrick St to Grand Parade. The curve of the street is due to the fact that it has been constructed over a branch of the Lee; on the right towards its W end is *SS. Peter and Paul*, by E.W. Pugin. À short distance to the N is the *Crawford Municipal School of Art*, with a picture gallery containing works by Barry, Lavery, Orpen, and others, and a portrait of Sarsfield, by Kneller.—Adjacent, on Lavitt's Quay, is the *Opera House* (1965), by Michael Scott, replacing one burnt down in 1955.

Grand Parade, laid out in 1790–1801, also covering an arm of the Lee, runs S to the South Channel, whence a good view is obtained towards the Protestant Cathedral to the SW, perhaps better seen from a distance. Oliver Plunkett St leads left halfway down the Parade, while further S is the parallel South Mall, with the principal offices and banks. At the far end of South Mall, *Parnell Bridge* crosses to the *City Hall*, with its domed clock-tower (1936), while further E, on the 'prow' of the island, stands the classical *Custom House* (1814–18), by William Hargrave the Younger.

The return to Grand Parade may be made by following the N bank of the South Channel, passing *Holy Trinity Church*, also known as the *Fr Mathew Memorial Church* (1832), by G.R. Pain, with a graceful lantern spire, the church of the Capuchin convent of which Theobald Mathew (1790–1856), the 'apostle' of Temperance, was superior.

From the W end of the Fr Mathew Quay, *Parliament Bridge* (1806) crosses to the S bank, where, at the far end of Mary St a lane to the left leads to the *Red Abbey Tower*, sole relic of an Augustinian abbey which served as Marlborough's headquarters in 1690. Near by is *St. Finbarr's South* (also known as the *South Chapel*; 1766, with a S transept added in 1809), containing original fittings, and monuments.

From the S end of the bridge, O'Sullivan Quay and its prolongation leads W past *South Gate Bridge* (1713), by Coltsman, and with a view

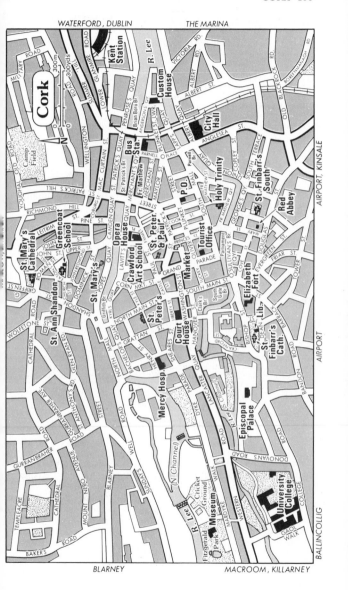

of the remains of *Elizabeth Fort* (17C) on the left, to approach **St. Finbarr's Cathedral** (C. of I.), a curiously sited pile in the French Gothic style by William Burges, completed in 1878, with a central spire 40m high.

It replaced another in a Doric style (1734), demolished in 1864, which had itself succeeded the original cathedral, severely damaged by bombardment in 1690. Of the latter (in which Spenser was probably married in 1594) only a few 12C fragments survive.

The interior is aesthetically unappealing. Its bells date from 1751.

The return to the centre may be conveniently made by descending the hill and bearing left towards *Clarke's Bridge* (1776), by Samuel Hobbs. A short distance N of the bridge is Washington St with, opposite, the imposing *Corinthian portico* of the **Court House**, by James and G.R. Pain (1835; its interior rebuilt after a fire in 1891). Turning right here, we soon regain Grand Parade.

From Liberty St, behind the Court House, Sheares St leads W. Prospect Row turns right to *Mercy Hospital*, previously the Mayoralty House (1765–73), by Davis Ducart, preserving a fine staircase, and plasterwork by Patrick Osborne.

The extension of Sheares St, a dull 10-minute walk to the W, will take us along the Mardyke—described in previous editions of this Guide as 'a fine public promenade shaded by old elms', but certainly no longer so—to reach (right) *Fitzgerald Park* and the *Cork Museum*, with historical and regional collections.— A short walk to the S brings one to the entrance of *University College*, where the Doric-porticoed *Gaol Gate* (1823, by the Pains) survives. It was started by Michael Shanahan, the builder of Downhill (cf.). The first University buildings, a quadrangle in the Tudor style (1849), contain a *Library* preserving many old locally printed books, and a room with memorials of Arnold Bax. Here also is a group of Ogham stones. In the grounds to the E are the *Honan Collegiate Chapel* (1915), in a bastard Irish-Romanesque revival style, with windows by Sarah Purser and Harry Clarke, and the *Institute of Dairy Science*.—Hence Western Rd brings us back to Washington St.

B. North Cork

Following North Main St, the first right-hand turning in Washington St from Grand Parade, we shortly pass (left) *St. Peter's Church* (C. of I.; 1783–88), with an octagonal tower base which has lost its spire, and cross to the N bank of the Lee, leaving on our left Bachelors' Quay, on which a few Georgian houses survive. Bearing half-right we ascend Shandon St, shortly turning right along Church St to **St. Ann, Shandon**, immortalised in the lines of Fr Prout in praise of its bells, cast at Gloucester in 1750; Francis Mahony himself lies in his family vault near the N foot of the tower. The church was built in 1722–26 on the site of an older church destroyed in 1690, and is remarkable for its particoloured steeple, faced on two sides with white limestone, on the other two with red sandstone. The name Shandon (*sean dún*, old fort) recalls a castle of the Barrys that stood on the site of the porticoed Dominican church of *St. Mary's* (1823–39, by Kearns Deane) on Pope's Quay.—In the churchyard is the *Skiddy's Alms House* (1718–19); the *Greencoat School* has been demolished.

Further up the hill stands *St. Mary's Pro-Cathdral* (R.C.), also known as the

North Chapel, a not-very successful Gothic building of 1808 with a conspicuous 'wedding-cake' tower.

Turning steeply downhill, we regain the quays, and may turn back into the centre by *St. Patrick's Bridge*.

Immediately E of central Cork, approached from Albert Quay (by the City Hall), is the riverside walk known as the Marina, beyond which it is prolonged to *Blackrock Castle*, reconstructed in the early 19C as a castellated residence, but damaged by fire in 1872. Conspicuous from the river, it is now a restaurant.—The ruin of nearby *Dundanion Castle* (in private grounds) is said to mark the spot from which William Penn sailed to America on his second voyage in 1699.

C. Environs of Cork

9km NW of Cork, approached by forking left off the N20 onto the R617, is the village of *Blarney*, with woollen mills, but charmingly situated in wooded country. It is famous for the 'Blarney Stone', the sill of one of the machicolations of its large 15C *Castle*, built by Cormac Laidhir MacCarthy, lord of Muskerry, on a rock overlooking the river Martin. It consists of a tall tower and a stouter and later battlemented keep, and preserves some Jacobean brickwork. It is apt to be crowded during the season, being a popular excursion on the track beaten by organised tours.

Legend does not relate how this particular piece of masonry came to be invested with its garrulous and grandiloquent properties, which were unknown at the beginning of the 19C. However, the association of the name Blarney with persuasive talk possibly dates from the protracted negotiations between Queen Elizabeth I (or her Lord Deputy, Sir George Carew) and the MacCarthy *Mór* of that time, concerning a mundane matter of land tenure. The queen herself is said to have coined the phrase, exclaiming petulantly after a succession of evasive answers from MacCarthy: 'This is *more* Blarney!' The well-known lines of Fr Prout describing the stone are a supplementary verse to Richard Milliken's song 'The Groves of Blarney'. Mrs Carter Hall's play of the same name was first produced in 1797.

   Difficult of access, the 'stone', when kissed, is said to endow the speaker with extraordinary powers of eloquence, but to perform this osculatory feat properly the candidate must be hung head downwards over the battlements on the S side of the castle. The guides trafficking in this mummery may very well point out other more accessible stones alleged to be equally efficacious!

CORK TO KINSALE VIA PASSAGE WEST AND CARRIGALINE (44km). The direct road to Kinsale is described in Rte 11A. Driving SE via Anglesea St and Southern Rd, we follow the R609, shortly crossing the Douglas river.

   Hence the R610 circles a peninsula to the E via (7km) **Passage West** (3,600 inhab.), a decayed town extolled by Fr Prout, and once famous for its dockyard on the S shore of LOUGH MAHON. We may regain the main road by skirting the narrow estuary to *Monkstown*, with ruins of a fortified mansion (1639); to the SW, at *Ringaskiddy*, opposite *Cóbh*, is a martello tower.—Turning left on reaching the R611, we enter *Carrigaline* (4,150 inhab.) on the Owenboy river and at the end of a long creek. Its old castle was long considered impregnable.—A road skirts the S side of the creek and *Drake's Pool* (where Sir Francis Drake took refuge with his ships when hard-pressed by a superior Spanish fleet in 1587), to (7km) *Crosshaven* (1,400 inhab.), a popular resort with good bathing at *Church Bay* to the E or at *Myrtleville Bay*, SE on the Atlantic.—The R611 continues SW over a range of low hills, and at *Ballyfeard* bears W to meet the R600 at *Belgooly*, some 6km NE of **Kinsale**; see p 210.

7 Dublin to Limerick via Naas, Portlaoise, Roscrea, and Nenagh

193km (120 miles). N7, bypassing *Naas* to 51km *Kildare*—32km *Portlaoise*—38km *Roscrea*—32km *Nenagh*—40km **Limerick**.

For the road from Dublin to *Naas*, see Rte 3A, and from Naas to *Portlaoise*, Rte 4.

9km NW of Portlaoise lies *Ballyfin House* (1821–26), perhaps the grandest early Classical mansion in Ireland, designed by Sir Richard Morrison for Sir Charles Coote; it now houses a school.

From Portlaoise we drive W across rather boggy country, shortly bearing SW parallel to the extensively reafforested *Slieve Bloom Mountains*, the highest summit of which is *Arderin* (527m), to the SW. At 7km we pass *Concourse Bridge*, where a few mounds are the only trace of the *Churches of Clonenagh*, a once-famous monastery founded by St. Fintan.—We traverse (7km) *Mountrath* (1,350 inhab.), a decayed town on a tributary of the Nore, and the village of *Castletown*, built round a green, before reaching the *Pike of Rushall*, above which rises the ruined castle of *Rushall*, also built for Sir Charles Coote.—*Roundwood House*, an 18C Palladian villa, recently restored by the Irish Georgian Society, lies 5km NW of Mountrath.—5km SE of Rushall is *Aghaboe*; see Rte 20B.—Just beyond the Pike we meet the R434 from Kilkenny (see Rte 20B) before entering *Borris-in-Ossory*, with its long main street, once a place of importance and known as 'The Gate of Munster', defended by a castle of the Fitzpatricks, the ruins of which still stand.

12km **ROSCREA** (4,200 inhab.), pleasantly situated on a tributary of the Bosna, preserves the fine ruins of its **Austin Priory*, founded c 1100 on the site of a 7C foundation of St. Cronan. The main doorway of the church, with its typical steep gable, is flanked by arched and gabled niches; within is a mutilated image, and in the churchyard is a cross with a rude carving of the Crucifixion. The *Round Tower* opposite has lost its cap, but is otherwise well preserved. It is said to have been reduced in height by the English in 1798 after a sentry had been sniped at.—The square *Keep* of the castle (c 1285; once moated) of the Butlers until the end of the 17C, was in Ormonde hands until 1703, and still retains its stone roof. It stands within an older curtain wall of the time of King John, preserving one of its round towers. Also within the enceinte is *Damer House*, with 17C gables and chimneys, under restoration. It was purchased by John Damer in 1722.

On the S side of the town, at the approach to a modern church, is the square tower and part of the church of a *Franciscan Friary* of 1490.

SE are remains of the abbey of *Mona Incha*, notably a cross, damaged and repaired, and a ruined church with a fine Romanesque archway and 13C S and E windows. According to Giraldus Cambrensis, no one could die on the island on which the abbey was built in the midst of a lake, now drained.

Some 6km N is *Leap Castle*, an ancient and much-haunted stronghold of the O'Carrolls. Rebuilt, it was burned in 1922; The ruin commands a good view of the *Slieve Bloom* range to the NE.

Birr (see Rte 20B) lies 19km NW.

ROSCREA TO THURLES (33km). The N62 leads due S, with a range of hills to the left rising to the *Devil's Bit Mountain* (479m), to (19km) **Templemore** (2,400 inhab.), where in the demesne of *The Priory* are the ruins of a castle of the

Templars (?) and a gable-end of their church. George Borrow, as a boy, spent a few months here in 1816, and recorded the scenery later in 'Lavengro'.—10km SW, at *Borrisoleigh*, is another ruined castle.—The road descends the Suir valley, passing (left) *Loughmoe*, with a ruined castellated mansion (15 and 17C) of the Purcells to the E of the railway, and 8km beyond, enters *Thurles*; see Rte 4; likewise for the road hence via *Holycross* to *Cashel*.

The N7 continues SW, with the *Devil's Bit Mountain* (see above) rising to the left. After 21km, at *Toomyvara*, with a ruined 15C church, the main road bears right.

The left-hand fork leads to (16km) *Silvermines*, recalling the old mines of silver-bearing lead once worked here, and lying beneath the *Silvermine Mountains* (489m), beyond which rises *Slievekimalta* (693m).

11km **NENAGH** (5,700 inhab.), an important agricultural centre, preserves one of the three large cylindrical *Keeps* of the castle of the Butlers (early 13C), dismantled in the 17C. Also of interest is the octagonal Governor's House of the former *Gaol*, now a convent, and remains of a *Friary*, S of the centre.

At *Rathurles*, to the NE, is a trivallate ring-fort, in the centre of which is a 15C church.—*Dromineer*, 10km NW, on LOUGH DERG, is a favourite snipe-shooting centre.

The road skirts the S slope of the *Arra Mountains*, off which a right-hand turning leads to (5km) *Killaloe* (see Rte 18C), while some 12km beyond this junction we pass (right) **Castleconnell**, a village on the Shannon and a spa in the 18C. The *Castle*, standing on an isolated rock, was a seat of the O'Briens, Kings of Thomond, and was later granted to Richard de Burgh, the Red Earl of Ulster. It was blown up by General Ginkel during the siege of Limerick. The salmon fishing was adversely affected by the 'Shannon Scheme' (see p 253), but has since been improved. The river forms some rapids a little downstream.

We shortly bear W and on the outskirts of **Limerick** pass (right) the entrance to the *National Institute for Higher Education*, with its museum; see Rte 14.

8   Waterford to Limerick via Clonmel and Tipperary

125km (78 miles). N24. 26km *Carrick-on-Suir*—21km **Clonmel**—(*Cashel* lies 24km NW)—16km *Cahir*—22km *Tipperary*—40km **Limerick**.

For the road from Wexford to Waterford, see Rte 5.

Leaving Waterford, we pass (left), just after the Kilkenny road diverges right, the ruined Ormonde keep of *Grannagh Castle*, where the Suir makes a bend to the S. We rejoin the river at *Fiddown*.

A long bridge crosses an islet to the far bank below wooded *Mt Bolton*. Just S of this hill, and W of *Portlaw*, (1,250 inhab.) once a busy manufacturing village, lies **Curraghmore**, the imposing seat of the Marquesses of Waterford, with its forecourt commanded by a remodelled medieval entrance tower surmounted by a stag, the crest of the Le Poers. It was built by John Roberts of Waterford in 1742–50, and contains interior decoration by Wyatt. To the right of the mansion is a *Shell House* sheltering John van Nost's statue of Lady Catherine Power. It was the birthplace of Admiral Lord Charles Beresford (1846–1919). The demesne is regarded as one of the most beautiful in Ireland.

Shortly beyond Fiddown we traverse *Piltown*, an attractive village with the seat of the Earl of Bessborough, restored since burnt in 1923.—A lane leading uphill to the right ascends to the *Leac an Scáil* dolmen at *Kilmogue*, the largest in the region; other prehistoric remains are scattered around the village of *Owning*, to the W of this lane.—Nearby stands *Castletown (Cox) House*, built for Abp Cox by Ducart in 1767–71, containing fine plasterwork by Patrick Osborne.

CARRICK-ON-SUIR (5,550 inhab.) is a market-town situated at the foot of a beautiful stretch of the river. The *Castle* of the Butlers (13C), E of the town centre, was supplemented by the erection of an

The Castle, Carrick-on-Suir

Elizabethan mansion (before 1584) by the 10th Earl of Ormonde. It preserves some of its original decoration, including an impressive fireplace, but deserves another thorough restoration. It has been claimed that Anne Boleyn (1507–36; grand-daughter of the 7th Earl) was born there.—In the Main St is the *Tholsel*, with a clock tower and lantern. A street opposite leads to the Suir, here crossed by a medieval *Bridge*, approaching, in the suburb of *Carrickbeg*, the remains of a large *Friary*, its church partially rebuilt.

At *Ahenny*, 7km N, on the monastic site of *Kilclispeen*, are two 8C *High Crosses*, carved with spirals and reticulated patterns, instead of the panels more usual at a later date; remains of similar crosses may be seen at *Kilkeeran* on the right of the same road, before it starts to climb.

The R676 from CARRICK TO DUNGARVAN (37km) climbs steeply onto the lower slopes of the Comeragh Mountains.—After some 9km we reach a col, whence an ascent to the right brings us to LOUGH COUMSHINGAUN, a gloomy tarn set in a deep corrie with rock walls 300m high. Above it the mountains rise to 789m. Further N is CROTTY'S LAKE, in a smaller corrie, named after a local 'Robin Hood' of the 1750s. The road soon joins the N25, bearing right for *Dungarvan*; see Rte 5.

Between Carrick and Clonmel the Suir makes its way between *Slievenamon* to the N and the *Comeragh Mountains*: the views on both sides are attractive.

The minor road, skirting the thickly wooded S bank, passes the demesnes of *Coolnamuck* (house demolished), *Glen Poer* (a seat of the De la Poer family), *Gurteen Le Poer* (formerly the home of the statesman Richard Lalor Sheil, 1791–1851), with a mansion of 1830–66 in a mixture of 'Revival' styles, and *Tikinor* (17C), built for Sir Richard Osborne.

The main road traverses *Kilsheelan Bridge*, to the E of which the ruined church preserves a 12C arch with traces of delicate carving.— NW of the village lies late Georgian *Newtown Anner*, a seat of the Duke of St. Albans.

KILSHEELAN BRIDGE TO CASHEL VIA FETHARD (30km). The R706 leads NW, with *Slievenamon* (719m; view) rising steeply from the valley on the right. The name of this sandstone hill is a corruption of *Sliabh na nBán Fheimheann*, the mountain of the women of Feimhinn. Legend relates that the redoubtable Finn MacCoul, unable to choose a wife, seated himself on the summit, while all the suitably nubile *and* agile who wished to do so, raced up the slope, the winner securing his hand. The race was won by Grainne, daughter of King Cormac, who then eloped with Diarmuid: see pp 38 and 300. The hill is also celebrated by Ossian as the hunting-ground of the Fianna, the hero-army of Finn.

At 9.5km we pass (right) *Kiltinain Castle*, a fortified quadrangle with corner towns, and shortly beyond, enter **Fethard** (1000 inhab.), an old-world town deriving its name (*Fiodh Ard*, high wood) from the forests with which it was once surrounded. The Protestant Church occupies the nave of a 14C building, while the Catholic incorporates part of an Austin friary dating from the reign of King John. Slight remains of the ancient *Ramparts*, which were assailed by Cromwell in 1650, are still standing.—4km NE stands the 16C tower-house and extensive bawn of *Knockelly*.—About 2km W of *Lisronagh* (5.5km S of Fethard, on the Clonmel road) is *Donaghmore*, where the ruined church of St. Farannan has a fine *Doorway* carved with elaborate Romanesque patterns.—From Fethard we continue NW (R692), after 6km passing (right) *Knockbrit*, the birthplace of Margaret Power, Lady Blessington (1789–1849), the authoress, and friend of Byron.— For *Cashel*; see Rte 4.

CLONMEL (12,400 inhab.), a busy and well-sited town, with pharmaceutical works, is known in Irish as *Cluain Meala*, the Honey Meadow.

A place of ancient importance, it received its charter as a borough and its fortifications from Edward I. As an Ormond possession it was besieged by Kildare in 1516. In 1650, under Hugh Duff O'Neill, it withstood for a time the assaults of Cromwell.

Laurence Sterne (1713–68), the author of 'Tristram Shandy', was a native of Clonmel, and Margaret Power (see above) lived here intermittently from childhood. Charles Bianconi (cf.) ran the first public car service, from Clonmel to Cahir, in 1815, in which year George Borrow was a pupil at the old grammar school, near the West Gate (now the County Engineering HQ). Here his young friend Murtagh taught him Irish in exchange for a pack of cards! Anthony Trollope lived here in 1844–45, after his marriage.

Perhaps the most charming feature of the town is the Suir, here flanked by riverside walks and old warehouses. Some relics of the siege may be seen in the *Museum*, on the N side of Parnell St; in Abbey St, to the S, is the *Franciscan Church*, retaining a tower (altered) and some 15C tombs from the 13C friary church. The *Tholsel* (1674), or *Main Guard*, at the E end of O'Connell St, is a handsome building in the style of Wren, and possibly by Sir William Robinson. The W end of this main street is arched over by the turreted *West Gate* (1831), rebuilt on the site of one of the four town gates. Part of the rampart wall may be seen to the N from the churchyard of *St. Mary's*, an interesting 13C building spoilt by 15C and 19C restoration, the best features of which are the octagonal steeple and the fine tracery of the E window.— *Powerstown Park*, to the NE, is the venue of race-meetings; Clonmel is also the home of the Tipperary foxhounds.

Cashel is 24km to the NW.

Some 14km SW, passing (left) *Knocklofty* (seat of the Earl of Donoughmore), lies *Ardfinnan*, the site of a monastery founded in the 7C by St. Finan the Leper; the castle, built by King John when Earl of Morton, stands on a steep rock overlooking the Suir. Two of the square towers are well preserved; the rest was battered down by Cromwell. Crossing the river by a three-arched bridge, we may regain the main road at Cahir by shortly turning right.

The N24 bears NW beyond Clonmel, with good views ahead of the *Galty Mountains*, and of the *Knockmealdown range* to the left.—16km **Cahir**, whence the road to *Cork* turns SW; see Rte 4.—Turning right immediately beyond Cahir, we ascend the Ara valley, shortly passing *Toureen Peakaun*, a monastic site with a 12C church. To the left is the *Glen of Aherlow* (views), the hiding-place of Geoffrey Keating (cf.). The road crosses the wooded outlying ridge of *Slievenamuck* (rising further W to 368m) before descending into the rich plain known as the 'Golden Vale' or 'Vein'.

TIPPERARY (5,000 inhab.), made famous by the marching song, and taking its name (*Tiobraid Arann*, the well of Ara) from the nearby source of the river Ara, is a manufacturing and dairying centre preserving hardly any remains of antiquity, except a gateway of a 13C Austin priory. A statue (1898, by John Hughes) commemorates Charles Kickham (1826–82), the scholar, novelist, and patriot.

Tipperary played a prominent part in the 'Land League' agitations, when the tenants of Mr Barry Smith established a temporary settlement ('New Tipperary') outside the town. The scheme, called 'The Plan of Campaign', was unsuccessful as a boycotting measure, and was soon abandoned. James O'Neill, father of the American dramatist Eugene O'Neill, was born on a farm on the outskirts of the town; and the Fenian leader John O'Leary (1830–1907) was also a native.

The outbreak of the Anglo-Irish war in 1919 is commemorated by a monument at *Sollohod Cross*, N of Tipperary (where Brian Ború beat the Munster Danes), while at (8km) *Donohill*, just beyond, is a fine Anglo-Norman motte.

Kilmallock (see Rte 17B) lies 32km to the W on the R515.

The N24 continues NW, passing (left) the Tipperary racecourse, to (9km) *Oola*, to the SW of which Patrick Sarsfield surprised and destroyed William III's siege-train destined for Limerick, at the same time blowing up the fortified Tudor castle of Oola.—To the N rise the *Slievefelim Mountains* (*Cullaun*, 463m being conspicuous), on the W foothills of which stands *Glenstal Abbey* (now a school), a 19C building with a cylindrical keep, a modern church (1956), and an old terraced garden, recently restored.—A church with a Romanesque doorway and later additions lies further W, at *Clonkeen*.

For **Limerick**, see Rte 14.

9   Dungarvan to Killarney via Lismore, Fermoy, and Mallow

148km (92 miles); c 7km more to include the detour to Kanturk. N72. 24km *Lismore*—26km *Fermoy*—30km *Mallow*—(at 21km *Kanturk* lies 4km to the N— 45km **Killarney**.

We join the N72 NW of Dungarvan, later passing (left) *Affane*, where the cherry tree is said to have been first cultivated in the British Isles, having been brought from the Canaries by Raleigh, to approach **Cappoquin**, a village charmingly placed at a bend of the Blackwater as it turns S towards the sea.—Note the 'Indian' folly gates on the Villierstown Rd, c 3km S.

5km to the N, some 200m up on the flank of the *Knockmealdown Mountains*, is the Trappist monastery of **Mount Melleray**, founded in 1832 after the expulsion from France of foreign members of the Order. Sir Richard Keane presented them with 240 hectares of land, and a heavy Gothick building was later erected in the wooded demesne.

Beyond Cappoquin the road follows the ***Valley of the Blackwater**, a beautiful stream reputed for its trout and salmon, which we shortly cross by a *Bridge* of 1775 by Thomas Ivory, largely rebuilt after floods in 1853, with a fine view of Lismore as we enter.

Lismore (900 inhab.) remains a pleasant village, even if of less importance than in the past.

The monastery and bishopric founded by St. Carthach in the 7C became a centre of monkish learning, and the retiring-place of kings, despite the incursions of Danes and the men of Ossory. The Papal Legate was visited here by Henry II in 1171. The castle (originally built by King John when Earl of Morton, in 1185) was the residence of the bishops until Bp Magrath generously presented it to Raleigh in 1589. In 1602 he sold it to Richard Boyle, the 1st or 'Great' Earl of Cork (1566–1643), one of the more successful of the English adventurers who sought their fortune in the exploitation of Ireland in the 16–17Cs. His sons Roger Boyle (1621–79; later Earl of Orrery), the statesman, and Robert Boyle (1627–91), 'father of British chemistry', were born here. According to Aubrey, the latter was 'nursed by an Irish Nurse, after the Irish manner wher they putt the child in a pendulous Satchell (instead of a Cradle) with a slitt for the Child's head to peepe out'. Roger Boyle held the castle for the king in 1641, but it fell to Lord Castlehaven in 1645, and in 1753 passed by marriage to the Duke of Devonshire.

The *Castle*, overlooking the river, was largely rebuilt in 1812–21 by the 'Bachelor Duke', and in 1850–58 remodelled by Sir Joseph Paxton and Henry Stokes. There is, however, a fine yew walk, said to be 800 years old, and the *Gardens* may be visited.—The *Protestant Cathedral* was almost entirely destroyed by Edmund the White Knight c 1600, and rebuilt in 1679–80 by Sir William Robinson; the spire was added in 1827, possibly by G.R. Pain. In addition to many tomb-slabs of the 9–11Cs, there is in the nave, with its Georgian glass and 'Gothick' vaulting, a sumptuous monument to the Magrath family (1557), and the grave of Abp Myler Magrath (?1523–1622; cf.). The *Catholic Cathedral* is a neo-Lombardic edifice of 1888.

To the E is the *Great Rath* (*Lios Mór*), which gives Lismore its name.

The R666, running 23km due W along the N side of the valley, passes near (right) the remarkable early 19C Gothick gates and bridge of *Ballysaggartmore*, the house of which was never erected due to lack of funds!—Beyond *Ballyduff*, with a fortified manor of 1628, we pass (left) *Mocollop Castle*, a ruined drum-tower of the Desmonds, and further W, the ruins of *Carrigabrick Castle*.

The main road runs SW from Lismore to (7km) *Tallowbridge*, where *Lisfinny*, a square tower of the Desmonds, is incorporated in a modern house.— *Tallow*, just to the S on the far bank of the Bride, was the birthplace of the sculptor John Hogan (1800–58; see Carlow).—From Tallowbridge we bear W, shortly passing near (left) the tall tower of *Conna*, to enter *Fermoy*; see Rte 4.

From Fermoy, the N72 follows the N bank of the Blackwater, passing (left) *Castle Hyde* (see Fermoy entry) and *Ballyhooly*, with an ancient tower of the Roches, restored in the 19C.—To the S rise the *Nagles Mountains* (427m).—We now make a turn to the N through *Castletownroche*, in the Awbeg glen, where the old keep of the Roches, incorporated in the later *Castle Widenham*, was gallantly defended by Lady Roche against the Cromwellians in 1649, but her outlawed husband was neglected by Charles II and became dependent on the charity of the Duke of Ormonde. At the mouth of the

Awbeg is *Bridgetown Abbey*, founded by FitzHugh Roche in the reign of King John.

   Mallow (6,550 inhab.), an old-fashioned town once with a reputation as a spa, retains a number of elegant 18C houses, and is now frequented by anglers. The *Castle*, part of which are the stables of its predecessor (1584) burned in 1689, has a fragment of the older Desmond fortress in its grounds. It has been in the Norreys and Jephson families for 350 years; Sir John Norris (c 1547–97) died here. Thomas Davis (1815–45), the poet and patriot, and William O'Brien (1852–1928), the Nationalist leader, were natives of Mallow. The rebuilt railway viaduct over the Blackwater to the W of the town was blown up by 'Irregulars' in 1923.

   The N72 continues W up the river valley, passing (left on the far bank) the burnt-out Tudor residence of *Dromaneen*, belonging to the O'Callaghans. Behind it we see the *Boggeragh Mountains*, a stony and uncultivated range which rises further W to 644m (*Musheramore*).

   The DETOUR may be made N to the old town of **Kanturk** (2,000 inhab.; in Irish *Ceann Tuirc*, the boar's head), with an attractive market-house, and the birthplace of Barry Yelverton, 1st Viscount Avonmore (1736–1805), the lawyer.

7km further NW is the village of *Newmarket*, birthplace and residence of John Philpot Curran (1750–1817), patriot, orator, and wit, who lived in the *Priory*. His daughter Sarah, betrothed to Robert Emmet, lies in the churchyard.—To the N rise the desolate *Mullagharierk Mountains* (408m).

The main road is regained to the SW of Kanturk, passing (right) the huge uncompleted Elizabethan *Castle known as *MacDonough's Folly* (before 1609); so grandiose were the plans that the government took alarm, and placed a veto on its continuation.

Some distance S at this junction, near **Millstreet** (1450 inhab.), stands *Drishane Castle*, a tower-house of 1450, with later additions and a modern top.—S of Millstreet is *Kilmeedy Castle*, a ruined O'Keefe fortress.

The N72 crosses the Blackwater for the last time at *Duncannon Bridge*, on the boundary of Co. Cork and Kerry, beyond which the scenery improves. To the S rises *Caherbarnagh* (682m), and further W, the prominent and characteristically shaped hills known as *The Paps* (694m and 691m).—On the next descent we have a good view of (left) *Crohane* (657m) and *Mangerton* (838m), the mountains overlooking the Vale of Killarney, and shortly join the N22 from Cork, to enter **Killarney** itself; see Rte 13.

10   Cork to Killarney via Macroom

87km (54 miles). N22. 38km *Macroom*—49km Killarney.

An ALTERNATIVE road to Macroom is the R618, which follows the N bank of the Lee and its reservoir, after some 13km passing the ruined church of *Inniscarra*, founded by St. Senan. Above it is the main dam (244m long) and hydro-electric station; there is another dam and power station at *Carrigadrohid*, further W.—To the NE on the first dam is the demesne of *Ardrum*, while on the far bank of the reservoir stands the square keep of *Inch Castle*. We ascend a side valley at *Inishleena*, with another church founded by St. Senan, before reaching *Dripsey*, on a cliff, above which perches *Carrignamuck Castle* (15C).
   Carrigadrohid is named from a ruined castle ('the rock of the bridges') built on an islet in midstream on a site said to have been chosen to gratify the whim of the

beautiful Una O'Carroll by her lover Diarmuid MacCarthy. In 1650 it was besieged by Lord Broghill and taken by a strategem. An attempt at persuading the captured Bp of Ross to exhort the garrison to surrender was unsuccessful, the choleric cleric on the contrary urging them to hold out at all costs, for which act he was hanged on the spot. The entrance to the castle from the bridge was built by Cromwell's order.

We pass (left) the 16C tower of *Mashanaglass Castle* before meeting the N22 just short of Macroom.

The new main road from Cork now keeps to the S side of the Lee valley through *Ballincollig*, with old barracks, SW of which is the 14C keep of a stronghold of the Barretts, and other ruins. To the N of the village, on a cliff overhanging the Lee, are remains of *Carrigrohane Castle* (14–17C).

Beyond *Ovens*, with several limestone caves, we pass (left) *Kilcrea*, preserving the ruins of a *Franciscan friary* (1465), with a lofty tower and the grave of its founder Cormac MacCarthy (died 1494), and also the *Keep* of a castle of the MacSweeneys.—The road continues to skirt the river past (left) *Crookstown*, near which are two more MacSweeney strongholds.

At *Bealnablath*, 4km SW, an unworthy monument marks the spot where in August 1922 Michael Collins was ambushed and murdered by 'Irregulars' of the Republican army.—Near *Templemartin*, 5km SE, at *Garranes*, is a large fort, 106m in diameter, revealing on excavation the workshop of 6C bronze-smiths and enamel workers; it has been identified with *Rath Raithleann*, the birthplace of St. Finbar.

Beyond Crookstown the road bears NW into the Lee valley with its reservoir. 3km short of Macroom, the R584 turns off to the left for *Ballylickey*, on Bantry Bay; see Rte 11C.

Macroom (2,500 inhab.), a small one-street town of no great interest, preserves some late Georgian houses, and an early 19C markethouse; the *Castle*, the demesne of which is entered by a castellated gate in the middle of the main street, dates from c 1200. Unsuccessfully defended by the Bp of Ross (see above) against Lord Broghill, it is said to have been the birthplace of Admiral Sir William Penn (1621-70), father of the founder of Pennsylvania. The 15C castle, later enlarged, and admired by Swift, was burnt in 1921.

See Rte 11C for the road hence to *Bantry*.

The Killarney road ascends the Sullane valley, passing (right) *Carrigaphuca Castle*, a ruined MacCarthy tower, 'the rock of the pooka', the haunt of a malicious elf.—We now traverse a Gaelic-speaking enclave.—*Ballyvourney*, preserving a number of early Christian remains, a Sheila-na-gig, and three Ogham stones, is overlooked to the N by *Mullaghanish* (648m), the E summit of the *Derrynasaggart Mountains*, which the road shortly crosses at its summit level of 291m, entering Co. Kerry. The descent provides a good view to the right of *The Paps* (see above), and (left) of *Crohane* (657m).—At *Poulgorm Bridge*, where we cross the Clydagh, a road to the left (R569) leads down via *Kilgarvan* to *Kenmare*, some 27km SW.—We soon enter the valley of the Flesk, and descend alongside the stream to **Killarney**; see Rte 13.

11 Cork to Bantry

A. Via Kinsale and Skibbereen

124km (77 miles). R600. 26km *Kinsale*—35.5km *Clonkilty*—N71.
30.5km *Skibbereen*—33km *Bantry*.

We follow the airport road to the S, shortly passing (left), in the suburb
of *Turner's Cross*, the concrete *Church of Christ the King* (1925; by
Barry Byrne, of Chicago). We climb over a ridge before making our
descent to *Fivemilebridge*, there crossing the Owenbeg river to skirt
the river Stick to *Belgooly* at the head of Oyster Haven. On the E side
of the estuary are the ruins of *Mount Long Castle* (1631), built by Dr
John Long, hanged for his part in the rising of 1641.

KINSALE (1,750 inhab.), a picturesque little fishing harbour on the
estuary of the Bandon, has a long history.

It dates at least from Anglo-Norman times, Miles de Courcy having been created
Baron of Kinsale in 1223. The Barons Kingsale (as the title is now spelt) are the
premier barons of Ireland and had the right of remaining covered in the presence
of the sovereign, a privilege won by John de Courcy, who entered the lists as a
champion on behalf of King John against the representative of Philippe Auguste
of France in some wrangle over the Duchy of Normandy; the French champion,
overawed by De Courcy's martial appearance, did not wait to do battle and,
breaking through the lists, fled precipitately to Spain.
    Kinsale was the scene of the landing of Don Juan del Aguila with a Spanish
force in 1601; the Spaniards, assisted by the Earls of Tyrone and Tyrconnel, held
out for ten weeks against Mountjoy and Carew, but when the time came for a
united attack only the Irish took the field. They were routed, and their allies
surrendered. It then became a naval station and was colonised with English
settlers.
    In the Parliamentary War Kinsale declared for Cromwell, but in 1689 it wel-
comed James II when he landed in an attempt to regain his crown. Defeated, he
sailed hence the following year, and it was shortly after occupied by Marlborough. Admiral Sir William Penn was Governor of James (or Old) Fort and Captain of the Foot Company in 1660–69; Lord Ligonier was Governor in 1739–42.
Neither Irish nor Catholics were allowed to live within its walls until the close of
the 18C, and the first post-Reformation Catholic church was not built here until
1809.

The great attraction of Kinsale is its position, the charm of which is well
appreciated from *Compass Hill*, ascended by crooked streets behind
the *old* church. On the S bank opposite is the ruin of *Ringrone Castle*.
On the E side, lower down, is the village of *Summer Cove*, with good
bathing, overlooked by *Charles Fort* (1677), opposite the remains of
Old Fort (1601–3).

A number of smaller houses in the decaying town, many of them
slate-faced, have been tastefully restored; a prominently placed new
hotel has a less pleasant facade. The most interesting building is **St.
Multose**, erected after 1179, with a massive W tower. The N transept,
and a font probably contemporary with the foundation, are notable.
The ruined *Galway Chapel*, adjoining the S transept, was added in
1550, the sculptured reredos and tombs from which are in the S aisle.
Some hatchments, rare in Ireland, have also been preserved. The N
nave arcade and roof were rebuilt in 1835, and in 1951 a more judi-
cious restoration took place.

A small *Museum* (in the restored *Tholsel* of 1706) contains relics of
the siege of 1601 and other objects of local interest.—Near by is
Desmond's Castle, also known as the 'French Prison', a good example

of a 16–18C town house. The slate-hung *Fish-market* dates from 1784.

Our road skirts the Bandon river, shortly crossing the estuary by a new bridge, to *Barrel's Cross Road*.

The left-hand fork here leads to the *Old Head of Kinsale*, a promontory which, although only 80m high, commands a fine coastal view, especially of *Seven Heads* and *Galley Head* to the W. It was off the Old Head that on 7 May 1915 the 'Lusitania' was torpedoed by a German submarine, with the loss of 1,198 lives; 190 were drowned here in 1816 when the troopship 'Boadicea' was wrecked. In 1973 an extensive field of natural gas was discovered offshore.

The main road continues to *Ballinspittle*, SW of which is a prehistoric fort with triple ramparts. Passing S of the partly restored castle of *Kilbrittain*, Gothick-Revival around a 16C MacCarthy tower, we follow the attractive tree-skirted inlet to (25.5km) **Timoleague** (*Teach Molaga*, St. Molaga's House), taking its name from a church founded by a 7C disciple of St. David. This was replaced in the 14C by a *Franciscan Friary*, founded by Donal Glas MacCarthy, Prince of Carbery (died 1366) and added to by Bp Edmund de Courcy (died 1518). The friary was famous for its Spanish wine, which its position on the shore of a creek made it easy to land. The best features of the ruined church are De Courcy's graceful tower, the S transept, and the E and W fronts, all with lancet windows, and the S nave arcade. Two tomb recesses survive, and. in the extensive ruins of the friary, three bays of a cloister.

We cross the neck of a peninsula to (10km) **Clonakilty** (2,700 inhab.), a market-town of no great interest, founded by the Earl of Cork in 1614, and the birthplace—at *Woodfield*, c 5km W—of Michael Collins (1890–1922), C-in-C of the Irish Free State Army at his death; see *Bealnablath*.

Some 9.5km SW is *Galley Head*, a conspicuous promontory with a lighthouse and the ruined castle of *Dundeady*, whence we may regain the main road beyond the ruins of *Castle Freke* (Gothick-Revival), the former demesne of the Barons Carbery.

At (13km) **Ross Carbery** we again meet the sea. The village contains a small *Cathedral*, rebuilt in the 19C, with a re-set 13C window and a tower of 1612; it was the site of St. Fachan's monastery, and the slight remains of his church lie to the S. To the E are relics of a commandery of the Templars. Jeremiah O'Donovan Rossa (1839–1915), the Fenian, was born here.

Hence the main road to Skibbereen—17.5km W—turns inland via *Leap*, picturesquely situated on a narrow ravine.

The more interesting *coast road* forks left just W of Ross Carbery, passing (left) the tall, gabled, and machicolated ruin of *Coppinger Court* (mid 17C) to *Glandore*, a sheltered village, whence a bridge crosses the harbour to *Unionhall*, where—or at *Castletownshend*, further SW—Swift stayed during the summer of 1723 (after Vanessa's death), occupied in writing a Latin poem describing the scenery of the district.—The O'Donovan fortress of *Rahine Castle* lies ruined to the S.

On the W side of the next inlet is **Castletownshend**, formerly guarded by a castle of the O'Driscolls. This was the scene of a naval engagement in 1602 between English and Spaniards. Edith Somerville (1858–1949), who collaborated with her cousin Violet Martin ('Martin Ross'; 1862–1915) in writing 'Some Experiences of an Irish R.M.' and 'The Real Charlotte', etc., lived much of her life at *Drishane House*, and died at *Tally House*; both were buried in the churchyard here. The Church contains windows by Harry Clarke. In 1936 Admiral Somerville, Edith's brother, aged 72, was assassinated here by IRA gunmen.—The views from the cliffs at the harbour mouth are very fine.

Hence we pass (left) *Knockdrum Fort*, with a stone wall 29m in diameter, and *Lissard*, the former seat of the O'Donovan, before entering Skibbereen, 9km NW.

Skibbereen (2,150 inhab.), a small market town of slight interest in itself, but attractively situated on the Ilen just above its estuary, is a good centre from which to explore the neighbourhood.

EXCURSION TO BALTIMORE (3km, one way). The R595 skirts the S bank of the Ilen, in the estuary of which are the islands of Inishbeg and Ringarogy. **Baltimore**, the ancient seat of the O'Driscolls, whose ruined castle crowns a rock overlooking the pier, is a small fishing port with a good harbour protected from the Atlantic by Sherkin Island. Contrary to some assumptions, the American city is not named after this village, but after the Earl of Baltimore's estate in Co. Longford. In 1537 it was burned by the men of Waterford in revenge for the seizure of one of their vessels in the harbour, and in 1631 it was sacked by Algerian pirates, who carried into slavery over 100 of its inhabitants. Its fishing industry was revived in 1887 by Baroness Burdett-Coutts, who founded a fishery training school.—There is a fine view of Cape Clear and the Fastnet from the headland with the sea-mark S of the town.

On **Sherkin Island**, 8km long and 3km wide, reached by motorboat from Baltimore, are the ruins of *Dunalong Castle* and of a *Franciscan Friary* founded by the O'Driscolls in 1460.—We may likewise approach **Clear Island**, similar in size, once fortified by a castle of the same family, with a church of 1200 on the site of an earlier monastery. *Cape Clear*, at its SW end, is the extreme S point of Ireland, except for *Fastnet Rock*, further SW, a lonely reef with a lighthouse 45m high, familiar in the past to trans-Atlantic passengers, and to yachtsmen as the turning-point of long-distance races. The cliffs on the S side of *Clear Island* are imposing. A sea-bird observatory has been established here.

On the return from Baltimore, we may fork right to pass LOUGH HYNE, an inlet of the sea with an entrance just wide enough to admit a boat. There is a marine biology station here. The islet in the middle bears a ruined tower.

On leaving Skibbereen we pass (right) the ruin of a *Cistercian Abbey*, and shortly skirt the head of *Roaringwater Bay*, with its many islets (*View), and with (left) *Ballydehob*, once a copper-mining centre, at the head of the longest creek. Hence the main road turns due N over low hills to (33km) *Bantry*; see Rte 12A.

The LONGER DETOUR, skirting the shores of the two peninsulas jutting out into the Atlantic, may be made from Ballydehob, following the R592 to the SW via (7km) **Skull** or **Schull** (500 inhab.), a fishing-harbour at the foot of bleak *Mt Gabriel* (407m), also with several old copper-mines in the vicinity. Continuing W past (left) *Spanish Cove*, we reach *Crookhaven*, well-described as the 'Ultima Thule' of civilisation in S Ireland, but with a safe harbour, its entrance facing E and protected from Atlantic gales.—Hence a track goes on to *Mizen Head*, the extreme SW point of the mainland. The signal tower, at the cliff edge, is approached by a bridge over an impressive chasm, while the summit of the head (233m) commands a view of the two other capes in which the peninsula of West Carbery ends: *Brow Head* to the S, and *Three Castle Head*, the latter named from the ruined forts of the O'Mahonys.

Hence we may follow the S shore of Dunmanus Bay, with the lower Seefin hills on the parallel peninsula to the N, passing ruined *Dunmanus Castle* and *Dunbeacon*, yet another stronghold of the O'Mahonys. At *Durrus*, at the head of the inlet, we may either turn W, or continue NE to *Bantry* direct.

The detour may be extended by following the N shore of Dunmanus Bay from Durrus to (15km) *Kilcrohane*.—*Sheep's Head* at the extremity of the peninsula, lies 10km beyond.— From Kilcrohane we turn N over the flank of *Seefin* (345m), the summit of which enjoys some of the finest *Views in the area, with a splendid panorama of the Caha Mountains on the N side of Bantry Bay. Hence we skirt the N side of the peninsula to *Bantry*.

B. Via Bandon

91km (56½ miles). N71. 31km *Bandon*—R586. 30km *Dunmanway*—
30km *Bantry*.

We follow the N71 SW from Cork, at the summit of the first ascent
passing (right) the ruins of *Ballymacadane Abbey*, an Augustinian
house founded c 1450. To the left as we bear W in the next valley is
Ballyhassig, scene of a desperate fight between Florence MacCarthy
and the English in 1600. We skirt and soon cross the Owenboy river.—
Inishannon, once a fortified town, stands at the upper limit of navigation of the Bandon river; the ruined castle of *Poulnalong*, built by the
Roches, lies on the E bank, on the road to Kinsale road 14km SE; see
Rte 11A. Crossing to its S bank, we briefly bear W, passing on its
opposite bank the ruins of *Dundaniel* and *Kilbeg* castles, before entering Bandon.

Bandon (2,050 inhab.), founded by the Earl of Cork c 1608, was until
1688 strongly walled, but its ramparts were then dismantled, although
remains may still be discerned. The town had been 'planted' with
English and Scottish settlers, and in 1649 Cromwell visited it on
several occasions. William Hazlitt (1778–1830), the essayist, spent 3½
years of his early childhood here. The church of *Kilbrogan* (N bank)
was among the first Protestant churches to be built in Ireland, in 1610.
Shippool Castle, a 17C tower-house, lies to the NE.

From Bandon the N71 continues SW to (21km) *Clonakilty* (see p 211), whence we
may follow Rte 11A.

We re-cross the river and skirt the demesne of *Castle Bernard*, with a
Gothick-Revival mansion on the far bank, burned in 1921.—To the
right on approaching *Enniskean* stood the noble 17C house of *Palace
Anne*, recently demolished except for the dilapidated right-hand
wing, together with its old garden.

4km NW of the next village is *Kinneigh*, where the *Round Tower* (almost 21m
high) is unique in that its lowest 5.5m are hexagonal, not round. The doorway is
some 3m up, and the interior has been fitted up with iron ladders.

The main road continues past (right) *Fort Robert*, residence of Feargus
O'Connor (1794–1855), the Chartist, and, 11km beyond Enniskean, the
interesting and well-preserved ruins (left) of *Ballynacarriga
Castle* (1585), a seat of the MacCarthys.—**Dunmanway** stands at the
entrance of some hilly country.—Hence a road runs directly W to Ban-
try, but the better route runs parallel to it to the S via (13km)
Drimoleague, 13km beyond which we reach the N71 and turn right for
Bantry (see Rte 11A), with *Whiddy Island* to the W.

C. Via Macroom

90km (56 miles). N22. 37km *Macroom* crossroads—R584. 53km
Bantry.

For the roads to *Macroom*, see Rte 10.—Just short of the town turn left,
passing (left) the upper part of the reservoir, and *The Gearagh*, a
marshy area covered with dwarf oak, and cross *Toon Bridge*. We meet
the river Lee again at *Inchigeelagh*, with the commanding tower of

Carrynacurra or *Castle Masters* to the left, a former O'Leary stronghold. The village is frequented by anglers on LOUGH ALLUA, a
winding extension of the Lee, the N bank of which we now skirt,
before crossing and climbing S. To the right below the pass lies
*LOUGH GOUGANEBARRA, the source of the Lee, a small deep tarn
walled in on three sides by precipices which after rain are veiled by
cataracts. Here, on an island, was the oratory of St. Finbar, who
drowned in its depths a hideous dragon that had been unaccountably
overlooked by St. Patrick (cf. *Croagh Patrick*). An 18C courtyard with
eight cells surrounds a plain wooden cross; there is also a small
modern oratory. The summits around the lake—among them *Conicar*
(572m)—commanding fine views towards Glengarriff and Bantry Bay,
are best reached from the mountain road between Glengarriff and
Kilgarvan; see Rte 12A.

The *Pass of Keimaneigh* (201m; in Irish *Céim ab Fheidh*, pass of the
deer) is a savage defile between (left) *Doughill Mountain* and
Foilastockeen, where many unusual ferns and alpine plants grow in
the rock crevices. From here we descend the wild valley of the
Owvane, later passing (right) *Carriganass Castle*, an O'Sullivan
stronghold.—At *Ballylicky* we reach the head of Bantry Bay (*Views*),
and turn S for (5km) *Bantry*; see below.

12   Bantry to Tralee

A. Via Kenmare and Killarney

111km (69 miles). N71. 18km *Glengarriff*—27km *Kenmare*—32km
Killarney—N22. 16km *Farranfore*—18km **Tralee**.

BANTRY (2,850 inhab.) is a small town at the head of Bantry Bay (in
Irish *Beanntráighe*, hilly strand), with a large market square, and once
with flourishing fisheries. Tim (Michael) Healy (1855–1931), the first
governor-general of the Free State (1922–28), was born here.

Bantry House (1740, with a S front of 1840), stands in Italianate gardens just W of
the town. It commands a fine view of the bay and contains a few paintings of
interest and four Aubusson tapestries.—To the N of the town is ruined
Reenadisert, an early 17C house.

Offshore in Bantry Bay (see below) lies *Whiddy Island*, on which stand
the battered remains of *Reenabanny Castle*, built by the O'Sullivans,
and relics of some 19C redoubts. Regrettably the island has been
disfigured by an unsightly petrol dump established in the face of considerable criticism by Gulf Oil in 1968, taking advantage of the depth
of the bay to accommodate their giant tankers. Following the explosion of the tanker 'Betelgeuse' in January 1979 operations were
suspended, but the site *may* again be developed as a distribution base.

Bantry Bay, some 34km long and 6.5km broad, being free from rocks and sand-
banks, and thus providing secure anchorage, has from its remoteness twice
attracted invading fleets. In 1689 a French squadron was engaged here by
Admiral Herbert in an indecisive battle, after which he was created Earl of Tor-
rington; and in 1796 Général Hoche attempted a landing with 43 ships and
14,000 men, but owing to adverse weather only 16 vessels (without Hoche) got as
far as the bay. A scouting party that landed was captured, and the ships, seeing

no hope of an improvement in the weather, cut their cables and returned to France. Among those on the 'Indomptable' was Wolfe Tone.

The S side of the bay is described at the end of Rte 11A.

From Bantry we drive N, to circle the head of the bay, crossing the Mealagh river at a charming little cascade, and traverse *Ballylicky* (*views*). At *Snave Bridge* we turn sharp left; the right-hand road, a winding mountain road, leads up the Coomhola valley, rising to 355m near LOUGH NAMBRACKDERG, before descending to *Kilgarvan;* see p 213.

Passing (left) the demesne of *Ardnagashel*, we veer NW, skirting *Glengarriff Harbour* (*Views*), backed by the Caha Mountains. In the bay lies *Garinish* (or *Ilnacullin*) *Island* (15 hectares), accessible by boat, with its beautiful gardens with their tropical plants, landscaped in 1910–13 by Harold Peto for the then owner, Annan Bryce. G.B. Shaw visited the place in 1923, and here wrote part of 'Saint Joan'.

We pass (left) *Glengarriff Castle* before entering the village. **Glengarriff** has a particularly mild climate (mean annual temperature 11° Celsius), making it a pleasant winter resort. Arbutus, fuchsia, yew, and holly luxuriate here, their foliage extending down to the water's edge, and the sea, warmed by the Gulf Stream, affords excellent bathing, boating and fishing. At the back of Glengarriff is the 'rough glen' (*Gleann Garbh*), where trees and shrubs fill the crevices between the tumbled glaciated boulders; and above rise the bare summits of the *Caha Mountains*, the graceful *Sugarloaf* prominent to the W.

Just beyond the village on the left is *Cromwell's Bridge*, a half-ruined structure built, it is said, by order of Cromwell at an hour's notice. Exploration of the numerous creeks, further on, off the Castletownbere road, makes a pleasant excursion. The best of the nearer climbs are *Cobduff* (E; 376m), reached from the Bantry road, and the *Sugarloaf* (W; 574m), reached either from the coast road at *Furkeal Bridge* or by a track on the N side of *Shrone Hill*. To the N of the Sugarloaf, between it and the Glengarriff river, is a wilderness of tiny lakes (alleged as usual to be 365 in number), and the larger BARLEY LAKE.

From Glengarriff to Kenmare via the 'Tunnel Road' (N71; 27km); see below.

The LONGER ALTERNATIVE DETOURS via the *Healy Pass* (55km), or via *Castletownbere* (82km), also known as the 'Ring of Beara', in emulation of the more promoted 'Ring of Kerry' (see Rte 12B), are first described. Driving SW from Glengarriff, we pass below the *Sugarloaf* (see above) to skirt Bantry Bay and the S side of the *Bere* or *Beara Peninsula*, the rocky ridge of the Caha range worn smooth by glaciation.

At (19km) *Adrigole Bridge* (see below) we may turn right for the winding ascent of the ***Healy Pass**, begun as famine relief work and completed in 1931 under the aegis of Tim Healy (see Bantry), at the summit of which (330m) we enter Co. Kerry, with *Knockowen* (659m) to the E. Below (left) lies the dark green islet-studded GLANMORE LOUGH, and further N an extensive and beautiful ***View** embracing the Kenmare river, the *Iveragh Mountains*, and the *MacGillycuddy's Reeks*.—At *Lauragh Bridge* we turn right into the Glantrasna valley, and descending again to sea level we pass (left) *Ormond's Island* and (right) the lower of the CLOONEE LOUGHS, the upper lakes and LOUGH INCHIQUIN being approached by a lane to the right of *Cloonee*. Beyond this village we skirt the narrowing estuary before turning left across the suspension bridge for *Kenmare;* see below.

Continuing W beyond Adrigole, we pass beneath the cliffs of

Hungry Hill (684m; the highest of the Caha range) with a cascade over 200m high, most impressive after heavy rain; to the left lies *Bere* (or *Bear*) *Island*, 9.5km long, once strongly fortified to protect the natural harbour and former naval base of *Bear Haven*. **Castletownbere** (850 inhab.) is the only village of any size on the peninsula, with a sailing school and fishing port.

Dunboy Castle, to the SW, the ancient seat of the O'Sullivan Bere, is famous for its stubborn resistance under MacGeoghegan to the asault of Sir George Carew after the surrender of Del Aguila at Kinsale (1602), when he tried unsuccessfully to blow up the fortress before it was stormed; the survivors of the garrison were hanged on the spot, but O'Sullivan Bere contrived to escape to Ulster and died in exile in Spain.

The excursion should be continued further W towards **Dursey Island** (24km from Castletownbere), with some impressive cliffs, beyond which rise the rocks called the *Bull*, *Cow*, and *Calf*.

Hence, crossing a ridge, we descend (*View*) to *Ballydonegan Bay*, and over another rocky ridge to skirt *Coulagh Bay*, with a fine strand. The road leads NE along the N side of the peninsula to *Eyeries*, passing (right) *Knockoura* (489m) in the *Slieve Miskish* range.

From Castletownbere we ascend N before climbing down to *Eyeries*, passing (right) below *Maulin* (621m). To the left on a hillock is an Ogham stone over 5m high, the tallest known; beyond is *Ballycrovane Harbour*. We approach the sea again beyond a low bridge at *Ardgroom Harbour*, before meeting the 'Healy Pass' road at *Lauragh Bridge*.— To the left is the wooded demesne of *Derreen*, with ancient oaks, exotic tree ferns, and rhododendrons, etc. The house has been rebuilt since burned down in 1922. Here in 1867–68 J.A. Froude wrote most of his history of 'The English in Ireland in the 18C'. There is an old church and a cell of St. Cinian at adjacent *Kilmakillogue* village. For the road hence to *Kenmare*; see above.

The MAIN ROAD FROM GLENGARRIFF TO KENMARE is impressive, providing extensive *Views* as it climbs out of the thickly wooded rock-strewn valley, and winds up its E side and over heather-covered hills. At the summit level (304m) we cross the watershed into Kerry through a tunnel. To the E rises *Knockboy* (706m). We traverse three more short tunnels on the descent into the Sheen valley before bearing round to the W and crossing the Kenmare river by its suspension bridge (1934).

Kenmare (1,100 inhab.), an attractive village at the head of its long inlet, was founded in 1670 by Sir William Petty (1623–87), ancestor of the Marquesses of Lansdowne and responsible for the 'Down Survey'; it is a good centre for excursions, and frequented by anglers.

Energetic walkers may approach Killarney by following the old track (c 30km), which climbs due N from Kenmare via *Windy Gap*, descending to *Galways Bridge* on the new road; see below. On the descent to the bridge we may bear right, keeping on the old road, over another high pass into the *Esknamucky Glen*, and along the W side of *Mangerton* mountain to *Torc Waterfall*, 7km from Killarney.

The well-engineered *Road* to Killarney ascends the Finnihy valley (NW), crossing the stream at *Sahaleen Bridge*, with superb retrospective views. At *Moll's Gap* (263m), between *Boughil* (left; 627m) and *Derrygarriff*, we begin the descent. *MacGillycuddy's Reeks* are seen across the valley to the N, while beyond (right) LOOSCAUNAGH LOUGH the **Vale of Killarney** suddenly comes into view, in striking contrast to the bare uplands we have been traversing. The *Prospect* on the left shortly beyond is one of the finest in Ireland, with the *Gap of*

Dunloe on the left behind the UPPER LAKE, and MUCKROSS LAKE and
LOUGH LEANE closing the vista ahead. Passing between the *Long
Range* and *Torc Mountain*, we enter the woods on the lake shore.

For **Killarney** and its environs, see Rte 13.

The road leading N hence via *Farranfore* to (34km) *Tralee* is of little
interest apart from its retrospective views on leaving Killarney. The
short detour to *Aghadoe* (see p 223) is worth making.—At Farranfore
the N23 diverges NE direct to *Limerick*; see Rte 15B in reverse, and a
minor road (R561) leads due W via *Castlemaine* towards the *Dingle
Peninsula*; see Rte 16.

B. Via Kenmare and Cahirciveen: the 'Ring of Kerry'

190km (118 miles). N71. 18km *Glengarriff*—27km *Kenmare*—N70.
22.5km *Parknasilla*—40km *Waterville*—15km *Cahirciveen*—27km
Glenbeigh—14km *Killorglin*—(**Killarney** lies 21km to the E)—9.5km
Castlemaine—16km **Tralee**.

This fine scenic road round the *Iveragh peninsula* is apt to be overcrowded at the
height of the tourist season, but is nevertheless well worth following. Such
detours as those to Valentia Island, etc. will of course add to the distance.

For the road from Bantry to *Kenmare*, see the first part of Rte 12A.

Immediately N of Kenmare we turn left onto the N70, skirting the
thickly wooded N bank of the estuary, with only intermittent glimpses
of the water, passing (right) *Dunkerron Castle* (1596) near an old keep
of the O'Sullivan Mór, and, further on, the demesne of *Dromore
Castle*, with the ruined stronghold of the O'Mahonys, before reaching
Blackwater Bridge.—Hence a minor road climbs up through the beautiful and densely wooded Blackwater valley to the *Ballaghbeama Gap*
(259m).

The main road, skirting the flank of *Knocknagullion* (412m) and
passing *Ross Island*, shortly traverses *Tahilla* and *Parknasilla*, the
latter a small resort established in the former demesne of Dr Charles
Graves (1812–99), Bp of Limerick. The wooded grounds of the main
hotel are intersected by a labyrinth of salt-water channels; the
bathing is good both in the sheltered waters here and from the open
strand beyond. The village lies in the parish of Kilcrohane, the priest of
which, Fr Michael Walsh, was the original of 'Fr O'Flynn' in the song of
Afred Percival Graves (1846–1931, son of the bishop and grandfather
of the poet Robert Graves). To the S lies *Rossdohan Island*, on the
mainland facing which is the burnt shell of *Derryquin Castle*. On the
far side of the bay is *Garinish*, the island demesne of the Earl of Dunraven. The island's sandy coves are a haunt of the Atlantic seal.

At the head of the estuary lies **Sneem**, a charming village ranged
round its green, below an amphitheatre of mountains, with
Mullaghanattin (772m) to the NE, and the peak of *Coomcallee* to the
W. Crossing a ridge, we descend towards the sea and enter
Castlecove.

A narrow lane (right) beyond the church climbs 3km NE to •**Staigue
Fort**, the most perfect example in Ireland of a prehistoric stone fortress. It is a circular dry-stone wall 34.5m in diameter, and originally
5.5m high, varying in thickness from 4m to 1.5m, the only entrance to
which is on the S side. Within are two small chambers; a series of steps

in the walls ascend to a defence platform providing splendid seaward views. We return on our tracks to the main road.

At adjacent *West Cove* are some old copper mines and the ruined church of *Kilcrohane*, beyond which we turn away from the *Kenmare River*—as the estuary is named—and enter *Catherdaniel*, a village with (left) a stone fort; closer to the sea lies *Derrynane*, with an Ogham stone found below the waterline and re-erected here. **Derrynane House**, dating back to c 1702, was long the residence of Daniel O'Connell (1775–1847), and preserves some personal relics of 'the Liberator', who inherited it in 1825 (see also Cahirciveen, below).

On offshore *Abbey Island*, reached dryshod at low tide, are the battered ruins of a small abbey founded in the 6C by St. Finan Cam; it commands a good view of *Deenish* and the *Scariff Islands* to the W, and of *Dursey Island* to the S; see Rte 12A.

We shortly climb N over the *Coomakesta Pass* (208m), with a retrospective view of the *Slieve Miskish* range S of the Kenmare River, and N across *Ballinskelligs Bay*, and W—very briefly—of the *Skelligs* themselves; see below. The road now winds downhill round the mountain backbone of the Iveragh Peninsula, passing a stone circle and two huge menhirs and (right) the ruined church of *Templenakilla*, before entering **Waterville** (500 inhab.), a small resort between LOUGH CURRANE and Ballinskelligs Bay.

The lough, c 27km round, provides good fishing, while further up the valley of the Cummeragh river are several mountain lakes abounding in sea-trout and brown trout. On *Church Island*, in Lough Currane, are ruins of the house (6C) and church (12C) of St. Finan Cam; the former is almost circular without and rectangular within; the latter is a good but defaced specimen of Irish Romanesque.— In the parallel valley of the river Inny to the N, a minor road ascends NE to *Bealalaw Bridge*; see p 225.

WATERVILLE TO CAHIRCIVEEN VIA VALENTIA ISLAND. On crossing the *Inny Bridge* turn left, circling the bay to *Ballinskelligs*, a sheltered village on a fine strand, with remains of an abbey practically eroded by the sea, and a castle.—To the SW rise *Bolus Hill* (410m) and *Bolus Head*, which we leave on our left as we bear NW to *St. Finan's Bay*.—A lane to the right leads to *St. Buonia's Chapel*, a very primitive oratory, with a well, several cells, and two standing-stones.—Following the line of the bay we shortly zig-zag uphill, passing (left) the small Romanesque ruin of *St. Finan's Chapel* (12C), with views out to sea towards *Puffin Island*, and the *Skelligs*; see below. We may regain the main road 11km to the E, or alternatively by taking the ferry from Knightstown to Reenard.

Valentia Island—also *Valencia*—in Irish *Daibhre* (the oak-wood), or *Béal Inse*, is 11km long and 3km broad, with a population of c 700. It is separated from the mainland by a tortuous sound with narrow entrances. Its once-famous slate is no longer quarried. The original Atlantic cable was laid from here.

After several more-or-less unsuccessful attempts to lay the cable between 1857 and 1865, it was finally laid by the cable ship 'The Great Eastern', the departure point being near the SW end of the island; the landing point was at Trinity Bay, Newfoundland.

A road on the N side of the island skirts *Glanleam*, the demesne of Lord Mounteagle, with its subtropical gardens and enormous fuchsias. Offshore is the island of *Beginish*, obstructing the N entrance of Knightstown harbour. Beyond it rises the abrupt cliff of *Doulas Head* (107m sheer).—To the W of Glanleam is *Geokaun* (268m), the highest point on the island, which ends in the *Fogher Cliff*, providing a good view of the Dingle mountains and the Blaskets.—The cliffs of *Bray Head* (241m) at the SW end of Valentia are also worth visiting.

The village capital of *Knightstown* takes its name from the Knights of Kerry, a branch of the Fitzgerald family, whose ancestral seat is at Glanleam.

In calm weather boats may be hired here for trips to the Skelligs, the Blaskets, and for deep-sea fishing, etc. There are curious early Christian remains on both Beginish and adjacent *Church Island*.

The route to the Skelligs passes *Lemon Rock* and the higher *Little Skellig* (134m; the haunt of some 18,000 gannets). *Great Skellig* or *Skellig Michael*, 12km from land, is a huge double peak of rock (186m and 217m high) with two lighthouses (the upper one disused) and a small landing-place on its NE side.

On the N side, approached by a flight of over 500 steps, is the monastery of *Sceilg Mhichíl* (under restoration), possibly founded by St. Finan in the 7C,

The Skelligs

consisting of a group of cells, two oratories, all of dry rubble, and two rude crosses, together with the ruins of a more recent church, all enclosed by an unmortared wall of perfect construction although on the edge of a dizzy precipice. For many years a visit to the Skelligs was a penitent's pilgrimage; after visiting the ruins, he had to ascend to the summit, a feat involving several rock-traverses of great difficulty to the inexperienced. Although considerably more inaccessible than the associated Mont St.-Michel in Brittany, it was raided by Vikings in 823, and its monks are said to have emigrated to *Ballinskelligs* in the 12C.

Cahirciveen (1,450 inhab.), 15km N of Waterville, is a busy agricultural centre famous as the birthplace of Daniel O'Connell (1775–1847), 'the Liberator'. The ivied ruin where he was born is E of the town to the left of a bridge on the bank of the Carhan river; see *Derrynane*, above. On the opposite side of the narrow estuary and to the W is the ruin of *Ballycarbery*, a MacCarthy castle. Near it, to the right of the road, is a well-preserved cathair.—About 3km NW is *Leacanabuaile Fort*, accessible only from the E, preserving one (of three) beehive huts occupied in the 9–10C.

Further up the wide valley we turn N between the isolated hill of *Knocknadobar* (689m) and a range to the E, the highest peak of which is *Coomacarrea* (772m). Regaining the sea at *Dingle Bay*, we round *Drung Hill* and skirt the coast 'en corniche', with extensive *Views towards the Dingle mountains, from Baurtregaum to the E to Mt Eagle to the W, with the Blaskets beyond. To the E, the head of the bay is almost closed by two ridges of dunes behind sandy strands, the nearer one at *Rossbeigh* with a signal tower for guiding ships into Castle maine harbour.—We descend into the glen of the Behy, enclosed to the S by a mountain amphitheatre called the 'Glenbeigh horseshoe', the river taking its source in three lakes—COOMNACRONIA, COOMAGLASLAW, and COOMASAHARN, the last and southernmost lying in a gloomy cirque at the foot of *Coomacarrea*.

Passing (right) *Wynne's Folly* (1867), we traverse the village of *Glenbeigh*, a small resort with excellent fishing in the neighbourhood and reputed for its seafood, before crossing the Caragh.

A road to the right skirts LOUGH CARAGH, a long sickle-shaped lake fringed with woods below steep hills, before opening out into a wider valley around *Glencar*; it continues S to *Bealalaw Bridge*; see p 225.

The main road continues NW across dull bog-land to **Killorglin** (1,300 inhab.), a salmon-fishing centre with a 'Puck Fair' in mid August, nominally for goats, but in fact for all kinds of cattle. It preserves the shell of a castle which belonged at various times to the Knights Templar and the Fitzgeralds. There are good views towards the *MacGillicuddy's Reeks*, rising in echelon to the SE.

Some 5km SE of Killorglin, at *Kilcoolaght East*, are six Ogham stones (some broken; a seventh has been stolen!).

From Killorglin the R582 leads 21km E to **Killarney** and near the right bank of river Laune, after 7km passing (right) the fine ruin of *Ballymalis Castle* (16C; of four storeys), and with an increasingly closer view of the Reeks, dominated by *Carrantuohill* (1,038m; 3,414ft), Ireland's highest peak.

From Killorglin we drive NE, passing (left) in the demesne of demolished *Kilcolman Abbey* the ruins of *Killagh Priory* (known also as the 'White Church'), an Austin priory founded in the reign of King John; a huge tomb of the Godfrey family stands outside the S wall.—Further S is the plain church of *Kilcolman*, with well-designed windows.—Traversing *Milltown*, we shortly cross the Maine by an old bridge once defended by a castle, giving its name to *Castlemaine*, now a derelict port, ruined by the silting up of its estuary and river.

The R561 to (or from) the S side of the Dingle peninsula leads W from the village; see Rte 16.—We ascend over the E end of *Slieve Mish*, and descend (awkward curves) to *Tralee*, see Rte 15A.

13 Killarney and Environs

KILLARNEY (7,700 inhab.) owes its reputation entirely to the beauty of its surroundings; the town itself, where the local industry of lace-making has been largely replaced by the wider net of commercialised tourism in the area, has few attractions. Its climate is mild; its vegetation rich; and for the energetic (and less agile) there are innumerable walks and climbs in the adjacent mountains, among them the highest in Ireland. Not only will anglers delight in the neighbouring loughs and rivers, which have been praised by travellers in search of the sublime and beautiful since the mid 18C. Among several earlier visitors who have brought the luxuriant scenery to the notice of the world have been Bp Berkeley, Sir Walter Scott, and Thackeray. Sir Julius Benedict's opera 'Lily of Killarney' was first performed in 1862. See map on pp 14—15 of Atlas.

Those without their own transport will be at a disadvantage, for most of the more interesting excursions are at some distance from the town, although the so-called 'Jaunting Cars', horse-drawn, with lateral back-to-back seating, may be hired, and the routes they follow are the outcome of generations of experience. By taking the advice of the jarvey or guide, who by-and-large apply the art of genial guidance without that excessive show of interest so noticeable in some countries, one *may* economise in both time and money. The importunate demands of plausible touts and gypsies should be politely but firmly ignored.

Jaunting cars charge a minimum per person, or per car for, say, 2½ hrs. The *Tourist Office*, at the S end of the main street, can advise on the current rate, and also for the day's excursion to the Dungloe Gap by jaunting car, by pony and trap through the gap, and the return by boat through the lakes, among other diversions. Cars and boats (at Ross Castle) may also be hired. Any imposition should be reported to the Tourist Office.

Killarney, in Irish *Cill Áirne* (the church of the sloe), stands in the valley of the Flesk on the NE side of Lough Leane, the lowest of the three lakes. The only building of importance in the town—described as a 'miserable village' in 1749—is the Catholic *Cathedral*, an elaborate Gothic-Revival edifice of 1842–55, perhaps the best designed by A.W. Pugin. In the early 1970s, at the cost of £278,500, the structure was restored and adapted to the modern liturgical practice, and the damaged plasterwork removed to expose the natural stone.

Opposite is the demesne of *Killarney* (or Kenmare) *House*, the former residence of the earls of Kenmare, accidentally destroyed by fire in 1913, with a new house built on the site in 1956, and another further W in 1974.—Facing the *Franciscan Church* (1860) in College St is a memorial by Seámus Murphy to four Kerry poets of the 17–18Cs: Pierce Ferriter (died 1653), Geoffrey O'Donoghue (died 1677), Aodhagan O'Rahilly (died 1728), and Eoghan Ruadh O'Sullivan (died 1784).

The most obvious natural feature in the immediate vicinity of the town is LOUGH LEANE, the largest of the *Lakes of Killarney*, approximately 2,000 hectares in extent and 8km long by 3km wide. Also known as the *Lower Lake*, it is divided into roughly equal parts by a wooded peninsula known as *Ross Island* (see below). In the lake are over 30 small islands, of which the largest is *Innisfallen* (8.5 hectares), densely covered by trees, particularly ash and holly. Its exploration may be combined with Excursion B; see below. Perhaps the best general view of the lake may be had from *Aghadoe*; see Excursion A.

Close to the landing-place on Innisfallen are the ruins of an *Abbey*, founded in the 7C by St. Finan Lobhar (the Leper), famous for the 'Annals of Innisfallen', an historical compilation of the 13C, the only copy of which is now in the Bodleian. The abbey church is of no architectural beauty, but the smaller church to the N, once ivy-mantled, has a good Romanesque W door.

A number of the islets between here and the landing at Ross Castle are associated in name with O'Donoghue, a chieftain who holds eternal court beneath the water, and—with luck—may be seen emerging every year just before sunrise on May Day.

E of Ross Island, and S of the town, the lough is entered by the river Flesk, descending from the Derrynasaggart range to the SE. Beyond is *Castlelough Bay*, overlooked by the ruins of the small castle of Mac-Carthy Mór, while on the shore is Muckross Abbey, also approached direct from Killarney by a turning right off the N71. The outflow of Lough Leane is the Laune river, at its extreme N end, which itself flows NW through Killorglin into Dingle Bay.

Entering the extensive Muckross demesne, presented to the nation in 1932, and also known as the *Bourne-Vincent Memorial Park* after its donors, we reach after 1km the Franciscan foundation of **Muckross Abbey** (1340), refounded by Donal MacCarthy in c 1440, to which period most of the present building belongs. Suppressed by Henry VIII, it was revived for a while in 1626 only to be ruined by General Ludlow in 1652. Its best features are the strong square tower and its E window, but it is principally interesting as having been for centuries the burial-place of four notable Kerry families: the MacCarthys, Mac-Gillycuddys, O'Donoghues, and O'Sullivans; the modern tomb in the centre of the choir commemorates MacCarthy Mór, created Earl of Clancarty by Elizabeth I in 1565.—On the N side are the *Cloisters*, a vaulted quadrangle surrounding a large yew-tree, the arches of which are round-headed on the S and W sides and pointed on the other two. On the sill of the central arch on the N is a sundial; at the corners, staircases ascend to the domestic apartments above.

From the abbey we may cross part of the gardens with their fine rhododendrons to *Muckross House*, and descend to the peninsula between the Lower and MIDDLE LAKE (or MUCKROSS LAKE; 275 hectares), to the S. The mansion of 1843, built for Henry Arthur Herbert by William Burn, contains an amateur 'folk museum' preserving a number of bygones, an interesting panorama of 1837 by C.K. Farrelly, and engravings of Killarney (published 1770) by Jonathan Fisher.

To the W rises *Sheehy Mountain* (557m); to the S beyond the Middle Lake is *Torc Mountain* (538m). Continuing W we pass tiny DOO LOUGH and cross *Brickeen Bridge* onto thickly wooded *Dinis Island*, and regain the mainland at the so-called 'Meeting of the Waters'.

For the *Upper Lake*, see below.—We may return from this point by bearing SE along the far shore of the Middle Lake.

From beside a bridge across the Owengarriff a path ascends to the *Torc Waterfall*, a cascade 18m high between wooded banks, beyond which we get a beautiful view from the summit.

We next traverse the village of *Muckross*, where Professor Rudolf Eric Raspe (1737–94), the creator of 'Baron Munchausen' died (to the end masquerading as a mining expert, and employed in investigating local copper lodes on behalf of the Herbert family). Beyond Muckross (right) is the old ruined chapel of *Killeaghy*.

The **Upper Lake** (175 hectares), the smallest but perhaps the most beautiful of the three—on the shores of which the Kerry arbutus (Arbutus unedo) flourish; best seen in October and November when its red fruit is at its prime—may be approached by the N71, narrow in places, ascending SW to the S of the 'Meeting of the Waters' roughly parallel to the LONG RANGE. Its banks are likewise covered with arbutus and royal fern. Above their far side rises the *Eagle's Nest* (335m), where until a century ago the Golden eagle was a common sight.—Further W is *Purple Mountain* (835m), beyond which rear the **MacGillycuddy's Reeks**, the highest mountain group in Ireland, with *Carrantuohill* rising to 1,038m (3,414ft), a confused mass of sandstone, among which the last wild wolf in Ireland was killed in 1700. Their fastnesses were also the haunt of the clan whose name they bear, the head of which holds the title of The MacGillycuddy of the Reeks (pron. Máclicuddy).—To the left of the road rises *Mangerton* (838m), while further SW the N71 climbs to *Moll's Gap* (263m), some 9km NW of *Kenmare*; see latter part of Rte 12A.

Among walks from Killarney the following four may be recommended, although—depending on the amount of time available—expeditions may be made in almost any direction S of the town, but preferably in clear weather.

An Ogham Stone at Dunloe

A   The Gap of Dunloe (32km; much of this route is also followed by organised tours or routine excursions; see above). Leave the town by the Tralee road bearing N, and ascend a steep lane to the left as the main road turns right. The first turning on the left leads up along a ridge overlooking the N bank of the Lower Lake to **Aghadoe** (120m; *Achadh-da-eó*, the field of the two yews). A church built here in the 7C by St. Finan the Leper soon after became the seat of a bishopric now united with Limerick and Ardfert. The present *Church* perhaps retains part of the original building in the nave, which has a fine but damaged W door; the choir, an addition of the 13C, has an Ogham stone built into its S wall. To the NW is the stump of a *Round Tower*. Below the graveyard is a round *Castle*, with walls over 2m thick, perhaps once part of the episcopal residence, and possibly as early as the 9C.—The *View* from hence towards Lough Leane is very fine; above its glistening surface rises an amphitheatre of mountains from the Reeks to the SW to Mangerton to the SE.

We continue W and make our way downhill to the main road from Killarney (R582), there turning right before forking left parallel to the lakeside, and crossing the Laune just below its outflow. On the right is *Dunloe Castle* (now a hotel), once a stronghold of the O'Sullivan Mór (1215). In the grounds is a group of Ogham stones, mostly discovered in a souterrain (since destroyed).—We now turn S towards the savage defile known as the *Gap of Dunloe*, passing so-called *Kate Kearney's Cottage*, where a bar replaces the cabin of an early 19C beauty who dispensed 'mountain dew' (poteen) to the thirsty tourist. Ponies or traps may be hired here.

Hence the track shortly crosses the stream and skirts BLACK LAKE, CUSHVALLEY LAKE, and AUGER LAKE, beyond which the pass narrows between the steep slopes of *Purple Mountain* (835m; left) and the *MacGillycuddy's Reeks*.

The boulder-strewn gorge is fabled to have been cleft by Finn MacCoul with a blow of his sword, while the absence of fish in an adjacent tarn is said to be due to the fact that St. Patrick there drowned the last snake in Ireland (comp. pp 214 and 280).

Just beyond the *Head of the Gap* (242m) there is a splendid view of the Upper Lake (see above).

On the right is the so-called *Black Valley* or *Cummeenduff Glen* (*Cum ui Dhuibh*, O'Duff's Valley), which penetrates into the heart of the Reeks and ends in a series of tarns, beyond which a fine walk ascends (right) to CURRAGHMORE LOUGH, below the S slope of *Carrantuohill* (see below).—*Purple Mountain*, on the left of the road, is an easy but boggy climb from the Head of the Gap, rewarded by a fine view.

The road zig-zags down into the Gearhameen valley, where we turn left and, keeping to the left, follow the N bank of a stream. After 1.5km cross to skirt the S shore of the Upper Lake, gaining the N71 c 13km SW of Killarney, not far N of *Galway's Bridge*, and adjacent to the cascade of *Derrycunnihy* ('oak-wood of the rabbits').

B   A much shorter excursion is that to **Ross Castle**, 3km SW of Killarney, at the neck of the peninsula of *Ross Island*, with its disused copper-mines. Its graceful 14C *Keep* (restored) is surrounded by outworks with cylindrical corner-towers; a spiral stair of 94 steps ascends to the top of the keep. This principal residence of O'Donoghue Mór, the chief of one of the three septs of his clan, was the last place in Munster to be taken by the Cromwellian forces (1652), being gallantly defended by Lord Muskerry. General Ludlow, reminded of the tradition that 'Ross Castle could not be taken until a ship should swim upon the lake', had ships bearing ordnance sent up the Laune from Castlemaine, and the garrison, when they saw them, surrendered. Shelley spent a few weeks in a cottage here with Harriet in 1813.

C Glenfesk and Lough Guitane (c 27km). Following the N22 SE, after c 3km we pass (left) a stone circle at *Lissivigeen*, known as *The Seven Sisters*. Further on we cross the railway and the river Flesk, and pass (right) the ruins of *Killaha Castle*, seat of The O'Donoghue of the Glens. Shortly beyond this at *Glenfesk Chapel* we turn right to skirt the N shore of bleak-looking LOUGH GUITANE, famous for its trout. It is overlooked to the SE by *Crohane* (657m) and to the SW by *Stoompá* (693m). We shortly descend to meet the N71 at *Muckross* village (see above) and turn right to regain Killarney.

A pendant to the above is the **Ascent of Mangerton**. This rounded peak (838m), which dominates the lakes from the S, is an easy climb from Muckross. Take the Lough Guitane road from Muckross, after 1.5km ascending S by a bridlepath, which later commands a good view of LOUGH GUITANE on the left. After about three-quarters of the ascent we strike the crater-like hollow in which lies the tarn known as the DEVIL'S PUNCH BOWL, the principal feeder of the Torc Waterfall and source of Killarney's water-supply. Charles James Fox is said to have swum round it when on a visit to the Earl of Kenmare in 1772. As we approach the summit we see on the left a large and deeper combe, *Gleann na gCapall* (the *Horse's Glen*), at the bottom of which there are three gloomy tarns: LOUGH ERHAGH, LOUGH MANAGH, and LOUGH GARAGARRY. The *View from the summit is magnificent. Due W are Torc and Purple Mountains, and the Reeks beyond; further NW, beyond Lough Leane, is the distant Slieve Mish range, above Tralee; the silver thread of the Shannon can be seen to the N; to the E are Stoompa and Crohane close at hand, with The Paps, Caherbarnagh, and the distant Galty Mountains beyond; to the S and SW are the Caha Mountains, and the mass of confused hills above Kenmare, with Kenmare River on the right.

D KILLARNEY TO (29km) BEALALAW BRIDGE. Skirting the N side of Lough Leane, we fork left across the Laune, as if approaching the Dunloe Gap (see A, above), but then bear W along the N slope of the Reeks, cross the river Gaddagh, and ascend the valley of the Cottoners river. On the left is seen the corrie of *Coomloughra* at the W end of the Reeks.—From (25.5km) the upper end of LOUGH ACOOSE, an alternative ascent of Carrantuohill can be made; but see below.

The **Ascent of Carrantuohill** (1,038m; in Irish *Corrán Tuathail*, the Left-handed reaping-hook), the highest mountain in Ireland, should not be attempted in bad weather, as mists are frequent. The usual approach is via the Gaddagh valley, see above. The ascent, easy at first, follows the Gaddagh to its head in a deep combe (the *Hag's Glen*) in which are two unattractive lakes (LOUGH GOURAGH and LOUGH CALLEE). Some rocks on the mountainside on the right are known as the *Hag's Teeth*. A very steep climb leads up the W side of the combe to the topmost ridge, a narrow horseshoe covered with slippery grass. The view is disappointing (comp. Mangerton), except for the fine silhouette of the mountains above Dingle to the NW, and the coasts of Dingle Bay and Kenmare River. LOUGH CARAGH is well seen immediately below to the NW.—The descent may be made into *Glen Cummeenduff* on the S side, and down the valley road to the Upper Lake, or W by the summit of *Caher* (973m) and the S ridge of Coomloughra corrie to LOUGH ACOOSE.

A right-hand turning W of Lough Acoose leads to *Glencar Hotel*, delightfully situated among woods near the S end of LOUGH CARAGH, see p 220, and a favourite angling centre.—Continuing SW we shortly reach *Bealalaw Bridge*, on the Caragh.

Hence a mountain road climbs SW over the *Ballaghisheen Pass* (304m) between

Knocknacusha (left; 547m) and *Knocknagapple* (686m), beyond which, at *Lissatinnig Bridge*, the road divides, the left-hand branch descending the Inny to *Waterville*, and the right fork crossing a pass towards *Cahirciveen*, see Rte 12B.

The road ascending to the left at Bealalaw Bridge is the approach for two mountain excursions. The first, a very rough track, keeps to the left up the *Bridagh Valley* (the upper valley of the Caragh) and crosses a high pass into *Glen Cummeenduff*.—The other route S from Bealalaw Bridge (rough but improving) turns sharp right at (6km) the entrance to the *Bridagh Valley*. Leaving on the right the track to CLOON LOUGH, the road ascends the N side of *Mullaghanattin* (right; 772m), and crosses the ridge at the *Ballaghbeama Gap* (259m), a wild and stony defile, beyond which a track on the left leads to LOUGH BRIN. Our road skirts the W side of the Kealduff valley and strikes the inland road (R568) from Sneem to Killarney at *Gearha Cross*.—Thence we may descend through *Derreendarragh* to *Blackwater Bridge*, about half-way between Parknasilla and Kenmare (see Rte 12B); or alternatively turn left (* Views) to join the Kenmare–Kilarney road at *Moll's Gap*.

14 Limerick

LIMERICK (60,750 inhab.), the fourth largest city in Ireland, stands mainly on the S bank of the Shannon just above the beginning of its estuary. The old centre is divided into three districts; *English Town*, to the N of the confluence of the Abbey River with the Shannon, and the old fortified port; *Irish Town*, on the S bank of this stream, but not contained by the original walls; and the 18C suburb of *Newtown Pery*, further S. Always of importance, Limerick regained its prominence in the 1920s after the construction by a German syndicate of Ireland's first hydro-electric power station at Ardnacrushna, a short distance to the N, harnessing the energy of the Shannon (see Rte 18C). The opening in 1945 of the Shannon International Airport at *Rineanna*, 24km NW, with its trading estates, further increased its material prosperity. Its industries include bacon-curing, milling, tanning, the manufacture of clothing, 'guipure' lace-making, the curing of tobacco, and the packaging of dairy products, etc.
Tourist Office in The Granary, SE of the Mathew Bridge.

Of Danish foundation, like most Irish seaports, Limerick (probably a corruption of the Irish *Luimneach*, the name of a part of the Shannon, was taken by Brian Ború when he assumed the overlordship of Munster, and became the capital of the Munster kings. A strong castle was built here by King John, who entrusted it to the stewardship of William de Braose; Irish Town was not included within the walls until the time of Edward II. The city was occupied for some months by Edward Bruce in 1316.

In the Civil War it sustained two sieges; in 1641, when it was taken by the Irish, and in 1651, when Hugh O'Neill held out for six months against Henry Ireton, who died here of the plague in the same year. Anthony Hamilton (c 1646, probably in Roscrea–1720), the satirist, and author of 'Mémoires du Comte de Grammont', was governor of Limerick in 1685; he spent the last 30 years of his life at St.-Germain-en-Laye.

The most famous siege of Limerick was that of 1690. Held by Tyrconnel as the last Jacobite bastion in Ireland, it had already been unsuccessfully assaulted by William III with 26,000 men. Lauzun, the commander of James's French troops, abandoned it to its fate, and the unhappy defenders were waiting for the arrival of William's siege-train from Dublin when Patrick Sarsfield (the titular Earl of Lucan), slipping with a small band between the besiegers' piquets, crossed the Shannon at Killaloe, surprised the siege-train from the rear, blowing it up and

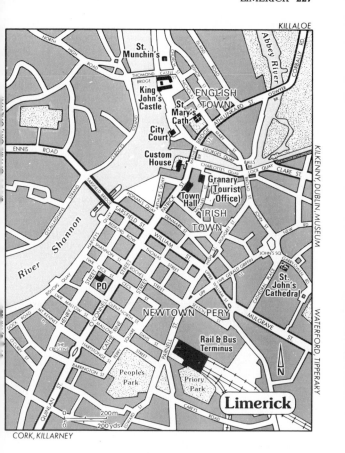

capturing the cannon and ammunition. The delay was momentary, as more ordnance was brought up from Waterford and a breach made in the walls; but the defenders, both men and women, repulsed the assault with heavy loss. Tyrconnel succumbed to an apoplectic stroke and the command devolved on Sarsfield and D'Usson, but a violent attack by Godert de Ginkel (later created Earl of Athlone), William's commander, carried the Thomond bridgehead-fort, and five-sixths of Limerick's garrison were butchered. To save further slaughter, Sarsfield surrendered on honourable terms, and on 3 October 1691 a treaty was signed on the notorious Treaty Stone. Under the treaty Catholics were promised that the privileges they had enjoyed under Charles II would be honoured. Through no fault of William's, the treaty was repudiated, and some thousands of Irish soldiers—later known as the 'Wild Geese'—left the country to enlist abroad. Sarsfield himself died in 1693 at the battle of Landen (c 60km E of Brussels).

The fortifications of Limerick were dismantled in 1760. Bp Edward O'Dwyer, at least, condemned the repressive measures of the military authorities during the period of the Easter Rising of 1916.

Among natives of the town were the dramatist and novelist Gerald Griffin (1803–40) and the artist and architect Francis Bindon (c 1690–1765).

The word 'Limerick', first used at the turn of the century to denote a form of nonsense-verse (and erroneously applied to verses composed by Edward Lear) is said to come from the chorus 'Will you come up to Limerick' following an extemporised 'nonsense-verse' sung at convivial gatherings, not necessarily at Limerick.

The main hotels and principal shops are in the planned 'Georgian' quarter of Newtown Pery, which takes its name from Edmond Sexton Pery (1719–1806; Speaker of the Irish House of Commons from 1771–85), its founder, who was a brother of the first Lord Glentworth, the ancestor of the earls of Limerick. Regrettably, modernisation has already made serious destructive inroads in this area, where both Charlotte's Quay and Arthur's Quay have been lost to posterity. The *Crescent* (with a statue of O'Connell, by Hogan) at the S end of O'Connell St, the main throughfare, is undergoing the restoration it deserves. Mallow St, slightly further N, contains a number of 18C buildings in a reasonable state of preservation.

A short distance to the right here is the People's Park, with a small *Art Gallery* and *Museum* (preserving the pedestal called 'The Nail', which once stood in the Exchange in Nicholas St, on which the city merchants paid their debts, whence perhaps came the expression 'to pay on the nail' in imitation of the Bristol custom).

Sarsfield St, further N, leads from O'Connell St to balustraded *Sarsfield Bridge* (1824–27; previously Wellesley Bridge, by Alexander Nimmo, following Perronet's design for the Pont de Neuilly, Paris), the main approach to Co. Clare and from Shannon Airport. *Our Lady of the Rosary*, on the Ennis Rd, is one of the rare successful examples of contemporary ecclesiastical architecture in Ireland.

The restored Granary, Limerick

O'Connell St is extended to the N by Patrick St, with (right) the *Town Hall* (1805) and (left) the *Custom House* (1769; by Davis Ducart), its more imposing pilastered front facing the river. A short distance E (right) at this point is the recently restored 18C **Granary**, housing the *Tourist Office*, a restaurant, and library. To the N, the *Mathew Bridge* crosses the Abbey River to English Town. To the left is the *City Court* (18C), and ahead (left) the entrance to the churchyard of **St. Mary's**

Cathedral (C. of I.), founded by Donal O'Brien in 1172 but many times altered since and extensively restored in 1857–60. The most prominent external features are the square W tower (36.5m high), the upper part restored after 1690, the parapet battlemented in the Irish style, and the 12C W doorway.

The plain interior contains several monuments of interest. At the W end of the S aisle is the Pery or St. George's Chapel, with tombs of the earls of Limerick above the Pery vault; in the S transept are the Bullingfort and Galway tomb (1414) and the Budstone tomb (c 1400). To the left of the altar is the elaborate polychrome monument of Donough O'Brien (died 1624), Earl of Thomond, and his wife. The *Choir* is notable for its 23 *Misericords, a rare feature in an Irish church, and for its tomb-slabs, including that of the founder (died 1194). The misericords probably date from c 1490, when the cathedral was enlarged by Bp Folan. The N transept contains the arcaded monument of Geoffrey Arthur, treasurer (died 1519). In the next chapel is an original stone altar-table, with five consecration crosses. The brass candelabra date from 1759.

Nicholas St, behind the cathedral, leads to Castle St, with the ancient entrance to **King John's Castle** (c 1200), its N side still bearing traces of the bombardment of 1690, with walls 3m thick and drum-towers 15m in diameter, the latter providing a view of the town and the Shannon. The castle's appearance was considerably marred by its use later as barracks and the recent philistine erection in the enceinte of council houses.

N of the castle in Church St is *St. Munchin's*, a 7C foundation rebuilt in 1827, with a fragment of the *Town Wall* behind it; it is believed to occupy the original cathedral site, and the bishop's throne is still preserved there.

W of the castle is *Thomond Bridge*, the old Shannon bridge, 152m across, rebuilt by James Pain in 1836–39.

At its far end, on the site of Thomond Gate, is the *Treaty Stone*, a limestone block raised on a pedestal, on which it is alleged that the violated treaty of 1691 was signed. Here also, on the adjacent river bank, Sarsfield's troops were given the opportunity of enlisting in the English army, of which barely one-tenth took advantage.

Regaining the cathedral, one may turn left up Athlunkard St, where there are remains of a fortified house (*O'Brien's Castle*).—Mary St leads SE from here to *Barrington's Hospital* (1829), on George's Quay. Hence one may cross the Abbey River by *Balls Bridge*, following Broad St and John St to *St. John's Hospital*, inside the entrance of which are massive gateways which were part of the city's defences.

St. John's Cathedral (R.C.) is a neo-Gothic church by Philip C. Hardwick and Maurice Hennessy (1856-61), with a tower and spire 85m high; its Treasury contains a mitre of 1418 and other cult objects.—To the NW is St. John's Square (1751), preserving some houses perhaps designed by Francis Bindon. Hence Gerald Griffin St and Roches St bring us back to O'Connell St.

A rewarding EXCURSION—by car—may be made by following the Dublin road (N7), turning left after 3km just beyond a ruined tower on the right. We shortly approach, at *Plassey*, the buildings (by Arthur Gibney, 1972) of the *National Institute for Higher Education*. Since 1977 the *Hunt Collection, the result of 40 years of collecting by the late John Hunt in the fields of Early Christian art and archaeology, has been housed here. It is well worth visiting both for the quality of the exhibits and for the way they have been displayed: see also the *Graggaunowen Project*, Rte 18A.

By the entrance is an early 17C Mannerist statue from Augsburg of the 'Genius of the Arts', an interesting anon. painting of Kilmallock (c 1800), and an early 17C map of Limerick. Section 1, Flint scrapers, daggers, and spearheads (Danish); 4, Bronze spearheads; 5–6, Swords and axes; 7, Greek pottery candlestick in the shape of a hand; 8, Late Bronze Age shield; 9, Bronze buckler, with repoussé design; 10, Bronze cauldron; 13, Tyrolean pottery (15C), and from Sicily (18C); 16, Irish ware, some with a blue glaze from the Delamain factory (Dublin, 18C); 25, Irish silver, including the Midletown mace (18C); 22, Sweetmeat set; 23, Beleek ware, including a stags-head candelabra; 26, Glass chamber-pots, one with a lid, now rare; 27, Molds.

Section 34, Falcon's leather hood and hawk's call; 30, 16–17C two- or four-handled drinking vessels of wood, or *methers*; 31, Keys and metalwork; 33, Spurs, etc.; 35, Bronze Age gold torque, and earrings, etc.; 36, Cloak-pins; 37, Late Bronze Age brooch displaying a cross as part of the enamelled decoration; 38, Ivories, including a comb, and a linen and ivory abbess's belt; 39, Portuguese Instruments of the Cross, showing eastern influence; 44, a large Irish monastic bronze bell; 42, Limoges enamels (13C); 45, Irish sanctuary bells; 46, 7–8C Irish Crosses with enamel inlays (Durrow period); 50, Ivory box (Sicilian, 13C); 52, Irish processional cross, Statue of the Virgin (12C German), and a collection of bronze, wood, and ivory crucifixes; 54, 17C Irish ecclesiastical silver; 55, Silver pyx (13C; note greyhound); 56, Communion cup of 1697. Near the exit are a collection of rosaries and crosses of the Penal period, a Roman colander, and an Irish silver-plated necklet of the Viking period.

15   Limerick to Killarney

A. Via Glin, Listowel, and Tralee

137km (85 miles). N69. 28km *Askeaton*—24km *Glin*—6km *Tarbert*—18km *Listowel*— 27km **Tralee**—38km **Killarney**.

Leave Limerick by Dock Road, at first skirting the S bank of the Shannon, after 8km passing (left) at *Mungret*, the ruins of a monastery founded by St. Patrick and placed in charge of Nessan the Deacon. Despite repeated Danish raids it was regularly rebuilt and flourished until the Dissolution, first under Canons Regular and then under Dominican rule. Besides the 15C church, with its square battlemented tower, there are remains of two older churches and, nearer the road, a castle.

On the right are seen the isolated towers of *Carrigogunnell* ('the Rock of the O'Connells'), a castle built on a crag near the Shannon in the 14–16C and blown up by General Ginkel; it deserves restoration. We cross the Maigue and pass more ruins: *Court Castle* on the right, and, beyond *Kildimo*, *Cullan Castle* on the left. On the right are the minute 10C church of *Killulta* and the demesne of *Dromore Castle*, a fantastic Victorian Gothick-Revival confection (1867–70), including a Round tower, by E.W. Godwin, now dismantled.

Shannongrove (1709), an imposing mansion, lies near the river beyond *Pallaskenry*, 3km NW.

On the left further on is *Curragh Chase*, burned accidentally in 1941, and the birthplace of Aubrey de Vere (1814–1902), the poet, who was visited here in 1848 by Tennyson; his grave is in the Protestant churchyard at Askeaton.—Beyond, to the left, we pass the ruined tower of *Derreen*, and S of *Kilcornan*, the fortified 15C church of *Killeen Cowpark*.

Askeaton (1,000 inhab.; in Irish *Eas Geíphtine*, Gephtin's waterfall) was defended by a strong *Castle* (1199) of the earls of Desmond, the ruins of which stand on an island in the Deel. The great hall (27.5m by 9m) is well preserved, but the rest was slighted in Cromwell's wars. It was the last home of Gerald Fitzgerald, the last great earl of Desmond, who fled here after the failure of his revolt against Ormonde in 1570; the castle surrendered in 1580, but the earl held out for four years in the Kerry hills. The *Parish Church* preserves part of a commandery of the Templars (13C). The *Franciscan Friary*, on the E bank of the Deel N of the town, retains its *Cloister, completed c 1420, with black marble arcading. This was the burial-place of James Fitzgerald, 14th Earl of Desmond (died 1558), the Lord Treasurer of Ireland. The Limerick 'Hell Fire Club' is said to have met at Askeaton.

At *Foynes* we regain the S shore of the Shannon estuary, where the former trans-Atlantic seaplane base has been superseded by Shannon airport, on the far bank.

2km S as we turn towards the Shannon lies *Shanagolden*, 3km E of which are the tree-lined ruins of *Old Abbey*, an Augustinian house preserving its dovecot and a fine W door in the ruined church.—Over 2km S (on the Ardagh road) is the ruin of 13C *Shanid Castle* (*Seanad*, or Council), a former Desmond fortress. *Knockpatrick* (172m), the hill between Foynes and Shanagolden, commands one of the more comprehensive views of the estuary; it is named from a ruined church said to have been built by St. Patrick.

The village of **Glin** (650 inhab.) is adjacent to the seat of the 29th Knight of Glin, a scion of the Fitzgerald clan, whose family has held it in succession for 700 years. During the Desmond rebellion the old castle was besieged by Sir George Carew and surrendered after a fierce hand-to-hand fight; the then Knight survived, only to fall at Kinsale a year later. The ruined keep stands by the stream. The present *Castle* (1789–1812), with later Gothick embellishments and 'folly'- lodges, lies to the left of the road just W of the village.

We enter Co. Kerry before reaching *Tarbert* (700 inhab.), a village protected by a wooded hinterland but now disfigured by a power station, and the S terminus of the car-ferry to *Killimer* on the Clare coast.

The ferry, which normally sails every hour on the hour from 10.00–18.00 or 19.00 may cross more frequently between May and September from 9.00–22.00. The crossing averages 20 minutes.

TARBERT TO TRALEE VIA BALLYBUNION (59km). A rather dull road leads W. 8km *Ballylongford*, at the head of its creek, was the birthplace (at *Crotto House*; demolished) of Earl Kitchener (1850–1916). To the N are the ruins of a Franciscan monastery, *Lislaughtin Abbey* (1477), with three finely carved sidilia and a good E window; and at the mouth of the creek, protected by *Carrig Island*, stands *Carrigafoyle Castle*, once a stronghold of the O'Connors of Kerry and inhabited until a century ago, with a vaulted Tower, 26m high.—We continue W, passing *Knockanore Hill* (267m), also with views across the Shannon estuary, to **Ballybunion** (1,350 inhab.), a popular seaside resort with good bathing and surfing and 4km of sandy strand, divided by a rocky promontory bearing the ruins of a castle, beneath which is a curious cave. To the N are more caves and the rock-scenery of *Doon Bay*, with *Lick Castle* beyond, among other old cliff forts presumably erected to guard the entrance to the Shannon.—To the S the road circles the Cashen estuary to *Ballyduff*.—Just beyond this village a lane on the left is the approach to the *Round Tower of Rattoo*, 28m high, one of the most perfect extant (cap restored); near by is a 13C Austin Priory church.—On the coast W of Ballyduff are the ruins of the Cromwellian fort of *Ballingarry*.—From Ballyduff roads continue S to *Tralee*, and SW via *Causeway* and *Ardfert*; see below.

The direct road leads SW from Tarbert to (11km) **Listowel** (3,550 inhab), in Irish *Lios Tuathail* (the fort of King Tuathal), a thriving country town, but of slight interest. Two ivied towers are all that remain of the *Castle*, the last to surrender in the Desmond rebellion. It fell in 1600 to Sir Charles Wilmot, who put the entire garrison to death.

A straight road leads NW hence to the coast at *Ballybunion* (see above), which once ran parallel to the only monorail track in the British Isles, worked on the Lartigue system, opened in 1888 but abandoned in 1925.

Leaving Listowel, we turn right at the Feale bridge and shortly reach a fork and bear left for Tralee, skirting the NW slope of the *Stack's Mountains*, rising to 356m.

The right-hand road, following the railway, offers a slightly longer alternative, passing *Lixnaw*, with the old *Castle* of the Earls of Kerry, and *Abbeydorney*, where there are ruins of a 14C(?) *Franciscan friary*.

TRALEE (16,500 inhab.), although the busy county town of Kerry, is devoid of any trace of antiquity, largely due to its unhappy history.

As the headquarters of the earls of Desmond, it suffered when their estates were forfeited and the 15th earl was murdered in the mountains (see below). The castle was awarded to Sir Edward Denny, but in 1641 it was retaken by the Irish. Its citizens themselves set fire to the place on the approach of Lord Inchiquin (to deny him his usual pleasure) in 1643, and the Jacobites followed their example in 1691 when the Williamite troops were advancing on the town.

The *Court House*, by William Vitruvius Morrison, has a typical Ionic portico. Some Georgian houses are preserved in Day Place. In the Park is the *County Hall* (1928), unexpectedly built of red sandstone in this limestone country (although it was also used for the ancient church of *Ratass*, c 2km E).—*Tralee Harbour*, at the mouth of the little river Lee (Tralee, *Tráigh Li*, the strand of the Lee) is so shallow that the town was connected by a ship-canal with *Blennerville*, to the SW.

For the Dingle Peninsula, see Rte 16; for the 'Ring of Kerry' road, see Rte 12B, in reverse.

12.5km due W of Tralee is *Fenit*, the birthplace of St. Brendan (483–578).

9km NE of Tralee is **Ardfert**, famous as the episcopal see founded by St. Brendan (now united with Limerick and Aghadoe). Here are the imposing ruins of a 13C *Cathedral*, of red and grey stone, the choir of which is lighted by a good E triplet, while in a niche beside the altar is the effigy of a bishop. The W door is a good example of Irish Romanesque; the S transept and sacristy are of the 14–15C. To the NW is part of a much older building. Adjacent are two small churches; *Temple-na-Hoe* (12C) and *Temple-na-Griffin* (late Gothic); a round tower near them fell in 1771. The cathedral was finally abandoned in 1641, when the *Castle*, to the E of it, was destroyed. In the grounds of *Ardfert Abbey*, the former seat of the Crosbies (described in 1785 as 'an old-fashioned place in a very bleak country'), are the ruins of a *Franciscan Friary*, founded by Thomas Fitzmaurice in 1253, with a good choir, a S chapel of 1453, and part of a cloister and refectory.

Sir Roger Casement landed from a German submarine on Ardfert sands on Good

Friday, 1916, to be arrested some hours later in the rath called *MacKenna's Fort*; he was hanged at Pentonville on 3 August.

The main road (N22) from Tralee to Killarney runs SE to (18km) *Farranfore*, where it is joined by the direct Limerick road, see below. The view SW towards the *MacGillycuddy's Reeks*, as we approach them, is imposing.

For a spectacular * **View** of the LOWER LAKE (Lough Leane) and the amphitheatre of hills beyond Killarney, turn sharp right at 14km, just N of the town, and then along the ridge towards the church on *Aghadoe Hill*; see p 223.

For **Killarney** and environs, see Rte 13.

B. Via Adare and Newcastle West

111km (69 miles). N20 and then N21. 17km *Adare*—25km *Newcastle West*—21km *Abbeyfeale*—22.5km *Castleisland*—(*Tralee* lies 19km W)—9.5km *Farranfore*—16km *Killarney*.

We drive SW from Limerick to (10km) *Patrickswell*, just beyond which the N20 bears left for Mallow and Cork; see Rte 17A.—The right-hand fork leads shortly to **ADARE** (800 inhab.), an unusually neat village, with several thatched cottages, probably a 19C 'improvement'. It stands on the river Maigue, and is noted for its trees (*Ath Dara*, ford of the oaks), and for its monastic remains. Ancestrally associated with the O'Donovans and with the Fitzgeralds, earls of Kildare, it is now presided over by the Earls of Dunraven, whose seat is *Adare Manor* (see below).

To the left ,on the river bank is *Desmond Castle*, approached for a close view through the demesne of the Manor.

We cross a long *Bridge* of 14 arches of c 1400, and pass (right) the *Austin Friary*, probably built by John, 1st Earl of Kildare, in 1315. On the N side are the cloisters converted into a mausoleum by the Earl of Dunraven in 1826, and in the church (restored 1852) are memorials to other members of the Wyndham-Quin family; the school-house occupies the old refectory.

Opposite the *Dunraven Arms Hotel* is the entrance to Adare Manor (see below). Further down the main street (right) is the *Catholic church*, occupying that of the *White Abbey*, a Trinitarian friary founded in 1230, and saved from being turned into a market-house in 1811 by the then Earl of Dunraven.

The well-wooded demesne of **Adare** contains in addition to the mansion itself both the *Desmond Castle* and a Franciscan Friary. The castle (built by the O'Donovans and rebuilt by Thomas, 2nd Earl of Kildare, died 1328) consists of a keep within a moated inner ward, the whole surrounded by a spacious quadrangle. In the adjoining churchyard are the ruins of the parish church and a 14C chapel.—The beautiful ruins of the * *Franciscan Friary*, founded in 1464 by Thomas, 7th Earl of Kildare (died 1477), who is buried in the choir, have a graceful tower, two attractive little chapels in the S transept, and, in the choir, some carved niches sheltering the tombs of the Fitzgeralds. On the N side are the well-preserved cloisters, with an old yew in the centre of the garth, and the refectory, and infirmary, among other conventual dependencies.

The 18C mansion of *Adare Manor* was enlarged in the Tudor-

Revival style between 1832 and 1876, A.W. Pugin being responsible for some of the 19C reconstruction.

The road now passes through a district once known as 'The Palatine', owing to the settlement here of a colony of Lutherans from the Rhenish Palatinate, expelled by the French in the early 18C; traces of them survive in some local surnames.—4km *Croagh* has a ruined tower (right), and the remains of an old church, beyond which we traverse **Rathkeale** (2,000 inhab.), a straggling village with a tall church spire, preserving fragments of a 13C Austin priory and a 15C keep of the Desmond's known as *Castle Matrix*, repaired by Sir Walter Raleigh, and recently restored.

8km SE, at *Ballingarry*, is a ruined Franciscan friary and the fortified mansion known as *Parson's Castle*. At Ballingarry there was a serious 'affray' during William Smith O'Brien's 'rising' in July 1848.

4km beyond Rathkeale the right-hand fork leads direct to *Listowel* (see Rte 15A) via *Ardagh* (where the 'Ardagh Chalice' was found in a neighbouring rath, and now in Dublin).

We bear left for **Newcastle West** (3,400 inhab.), with a restored castle built by the Knights Templar in the 12C. Beyond, the road climbs *Barnagh Hill*, passing, 5km S, *Glenquin Castle*, a tower-house of 1462, restored in the 19C. The road descends through beautiful but desolate country to **Abbeyfeale** (1,400 inhab.), to the SE of which is the amphitheatre of the *Mullaghareirk Mountains*; part of a Cistercian abbey is incorporated in the Catholic parish church.—Hence the road climbs up the Owveg valley before descending to **Castleisland** (2,250 inhab.), to the E of which rise *Mt Eagle* and, beyond, *Knockanefune* (438m), near the source of the Blackwater.

Tralee is 19km to the W, the road passing below *Desmond's Grave*, the burial-place of Gerald Fitzgerald, 15th Earl of Desmond (died 1583), murdered in his mountain refuge by the soldiers of Ormonde.

After 9.5km we reach *Farranfore*, to the W of which lies *Castlemaine*, the approach to the 'Ring of Kerry'; see Rte 12B. *Killarney* is 16km S; see Rte 13, and also the last paragraph of Rte 15A.

16   The Dingle Peninsula

The promontory of **Dingle**, or *Corkaguiny*, is the most northerly of the five peninsulas that extend into the Atlantic from the SW of Ireland like the fingers of a hand, each with its ridge of mountains. The Dingle peninsula is particularly notable in that, apart from possessing the highest peak in the country after MacGillycuddy's Reeks (and some of the most magnificent coastal scenery in Munster), it preserves an une-qualled series of Early Christian monuments, Iron Age fortifications, beehive huts, etc., most of which are now in state care. Its W half is part of the Gaeltacht, noted for the purity of its idiom.

From Tralee, the direct road (R559) leads to the town of Dingle, 50km SW.—Beyond *Blennerville* is the ruined church of *Annagh*, to the right, with a sculptured stone in its enclosure. To the S the *Slieve Mish Mountains* rise steeply from the coast.—At *Camp*, 15km from Tralee, the main road starts to climb diagonally across the peninsula (see below).

This village is a good base for the ascent of *Caherconree* (825m), the track climbing Glen Fas before bearing left to the summit. The cathair or fort of King Curol MacDaire that gives the peak its name stands at 625m, and is probably the most elevated in Ireland; to the N on the ridge is a dolmen called 'Finn MacCoul's Table' or 'Chair'. Further to the E is the highest summit of the Slieve Mish Mountains, *Baurtregaum* (850m).

The coastal road continues to skirt the N side of the peninsula, passing (right) the little resort of *Castlegregory*. Here in 1580 Raleigh and Spenser were entertained in a castle by Black Hugh, son of Gregory Hoare. Beyond, a sandy headland divides *Tralee Bay* from *Brandon Bay*, ending in the rocks of *Rough Point.*—Offshore are the *Magharee Islands*, otherwise known as the *Seven Hogs*; on *Illauntannig*, the largest, are the ruins of a small monastic establishment built within a cashel.

Passing beneath the double peaks of *Beenoskee* (825m), between which, in a crater-like hollow, lies gloomy LOUGH ACUMMEEN, and with the peak of *Mt Brandon* (251m) ahead, we bear SW away from the sea, climbing steeply to the *Connor Pass (456m; Views), below which three lakes lie in the Owenmore valley. To the left, in an amphitheatre of rocks nestles tiny LOUGH DOON. The rapid descent to *Dingle* (see below) provides extensive views of the Iveragh peninsula to the S beyond Dingle Bay.

From Camp, the main road climbs above the valley of Glenagalt ('the valley of the madmen', so called from a healing spring that was alleged to cure madness), to the top of the pass. The more gradual descent to *Anascaul* provides good views across the bay. The road bears W parallel to the coast, on which stood *Minard Castle*, a stronghold of the Knights of Kerry largely destroyed in 1650 by Cromwell's troops. Above us on the right boldly rises *Croaghskearda*. We traverse *Ballintaggart*, where in a circular burial-ground nine Ogham stones are preserved, three of them bearing incised crosses, before entering *Dingle*.

Dingle (1,350 inhab.) enjoys a superb situation on its almost landlocked harbour at the foot of *Ballysitteragh* (623m). The town itself preserves no trace of antiquity except the Desmond tomb of 1540 in its churchyard, although it was once walled (*Daingean ui Chuis*, the fortress of O'Cush). It still possesses a fishing-fleet.

While the archaeologist may profitably spend many days exploring the vicinity, only a few of the more interesting and important antiquities are described in the following excursions. The roads, even if narrow, are better than might be expected in a district remote until comparatively recently.

THE CIRCUIT OF SLEA HEAD (42km by road). The R559 leading due W from Dingle passes (right) three standing stones before reaching *Ventry* (*Fionn Trágha*, white strand), standing at the head of its harbour, more exposed to Atlantic gales than that of Dingle. This area is traditionally the last occupied by the unassimilated Danes in Ireland, and legend tells of a homeric battle fought here by Finn MacCoul.

Beyond, to the left, is the cliff-edge promontory-fort of *Dunbeg* (approach dangerous), guarded by a massive stone rampart 4.5m to 7.5m thick, and provided with a subterranean passage to allow a safe exit for the defenders in case of surprise. Between Ventry and Slea Head, on the lower slopes of *Mt Eagle* (516m) over 400 clochans or 'beehive' huts have been discovered in various states of preservation, the best of which are at *Fahan*. Indeed, it is said that some are still

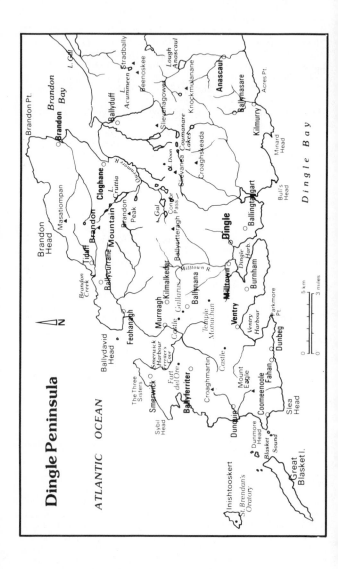

being built by local people with an eye to attracting silver from the curious but less discriminating tourist.

17km **Slea Head** commands a magnificent *View of the Iveragh peninsula to the S, with the Skelligs (see Rte 12B) in the distance, and of the Great Blasket due W. Rounding the promontory (viewpoints) we approach the hamlet of *Coomeenole*, beyond which protrudes *Dunmore Head*, the furthest W point of the Irish mainland, once defended by a rampart almost 400m long; on the summit is an Ogham stone with an usually long inscription. A little further N is the village of *Dunquin*, where *corraghs*, light but seaworthy boats of tarred canvas stretched on a frame, are still occasionally to be seen.

The Blaskets (reached by boat from Dunquin or Dingle) are a group of iron-bound islands, uninhabited since 1953. Life there earlier in the century has been graphically described in Maurice O'Sullivan's 'Twenty Years agrowing' and Peig Sayers's 'Peig'; and also in Tomás O'Crohan's 'The Islandman' and Robin Flower's 'Western Island' (both the first two translated from the Gaelic into English). On the *Great Blasket* stood the castle of Piaras Ferriter, the last Irish chieftain to surrender to Cromwell. His safe-conduct after his capitulation was dishonoured, and he was later hanged. On the N side the cliffs rise to a height of 293m. The westernmost is *Tearaght Island*, with a lighthouse 83m high; and to the N is *Inishtooskert*, with a ruined oratory of St. Brendan.

The road continues N before turning away from the sea along the N slope of *Croaghmartin*, passing an attractive little cove below, and with a fine view across to the cliff ridge of *Sybil Head* and *The Three Sisters*, and of *Ballydavid Head* across *Smerwick Harbour*. Beyond looms the mass of Mt Brandon.—From just beyond *Ballyferriter* the Dingle road turns S, passing by a low ridge the castle of *Rahinnane* (right) before regaining *Ventry*.

A lane running NW from Ballyferriter and passing the remains of the castle where Piaras Ferriter (see above) was born, leads to *Ferriter's Cove*, where in 1579 a Spanish force landed, accompanied by Dr Nicholas Sanders, the Papal Nuncio.—Crossing the isthmus to the W side of *Smerwick Harbour*, they built a fort, the *Fort del Oro*, or *Dún an Oir*, as a base of operations against England. Although reinforced in the following year, this fortified settlement was taken by Lord Deputy Grey and the garrison was butchered, as was common practice at the time, on the orders of Mackworth and (perhaps) Raleigh. Sanders escaped, but died a fugitive in 1581; Mackworth was murdered by the O'Connors of Offaly. The episode has been described in Kingsley's 'Westward Ho!'.

An alternative road back from Ballyferriter is that continuing E, which shortly climbs the far side of the valley to a small hamlet where it bears left. At the next crossroads, at the hamlet of *Ballynana*—having first visited the *Oratory of Gallarus* (on the right of the lane descending to the left; see below)—we turn right over a ridge and drive SE towards Dingle Harbour.

TO THE ORATORY OF GALLARUS, KILMALKEDAR, AND MOUNT BRANDON (c 25km by road). Immediately beyond *Milltown* (just W of Dingle) we turn right and shortly ascend a low pass, and at the hamlet of *Ballynana* we fork left downhill along a lane. After a short distance the road widens (parking space), and a path leads across to the field in which stands the *Oratory of Gallarus*, one of the most perfect relics of early Irish Christianity (?8C). This curious little building, resembling in part an upturned boat, is a development of the clochan or corbel-roofed style of construction, but rectangular instead of circular in plan (6.5m long, 5.5m wide, and almost 5m high). The dry rubble masonry is almost perfect, except for a slight sag in the roof-line. It is entered by a low square-headed doorway with slightly inclined sides, and is lighted by a small semicircular window cut out of a single stone in the E wall, and deeply splayed. The two-holed flagstones above the door were doubtless sockets for wooden door-posts. In the churchyard is an inscribed cross.

The Oratory of Gallarus, Dingle

Continuing down the lane, a right-hand turn approaches (right) *Gallarus Castle* (15C), just short of which is a group of ruined beehive huts, one restored.

Regaining the main road at Ballynana, we turn left to the hamlet of *Kilmalkedar*, where there is an interesting 12C church, consisting of a roofless nave with a good doorway and ornamented chancel-arch; inside is the 'Alphabet Stone', on which the letters of the alphabet are incised. In the churchyard is an Ogham stone, several inscribed stones, a cross and sundial.—To the N beyond a lane is *St. Brendan's House*, a rude 12C structure, showing some 'batter', and probably a priest's residence.

Hence the road descends towards *Smerwick Harbour* and the village of *Murreagh*, where we turn right for *Feohanagh*, from which

the cliffs of *Ballydavid Head* (244m) may be explored. The road bears NE towards *Mt Brandon* and the hamlet of *Ballycurrane*, to the left of which is *Brandon Creek*, the starting-point for the steep ascent of (6km) *•Brandon Head*, where the cliffs rise to 377m.

Cars may continue a short distance (right) to the hamlet of *Tiduff*, whence may be made the easy ascent of **Mount Brandon** (951m; the second highest peak in Ireland) rising directly from the sea. A broad green path leads up to the crest of the ridge, where we turn right to reach the summit, on the N and S sides of which are small stone circles. The superb •View extends from Loop Head (NE beyond the mouth of the Shannon) to the MacGillycuddy's Reeks (SE), and S towards the Iveragh mountains beyond Dingle Bay. Immediately to the SE is the slightly lower *Brandon Peak* (840m), below which nestles LOUGH CRUTTIA.—The descent of the E side, down a wild and precipitous glen towards *Cloghane* at the head of *Brandon Bay* is very impressive but not easily found without a guide.

Descending to Tiduff, we regain the road, and drive almost due S, crossing a low col and down the Milltown valley to Dingle.

Other points of interest in the neighbourhood are *Temple Monachan* (5km NW), where there are remains of an oratory and the well of St. Monachan, with an Ogham stone, and a 'Killeen' (a cemetery for suicides and unbaptised infants); and the COOMANARE LAKES (8km NE). These are approached by a road ascending *Connor Hill*, and bearing E for c 1.5km a little before reaching the summit of the pass (see p 235). The number of arrow-heads found on the hillside bears out the tradition of a great battle fought here in ancient times.

The return from Dingle to Tralee (or to Castlemaine, for *Killarney*) may be made by following the R559 E towards *Annascaul*, just before which we bear right to skirt *Dingle Bay*, with a good view ahead of the sandy 'inch' or peninsula, 4.5km long, separating and sheltering *Castlemaine Harbour* from the Atlantic. We traverse, on passing this magnificent strand, the village of *Inch*, with the *Slieve Mish Moun tains* rising on our left, and the *MacGillycuddy's Reeks* prominent to the SE.—At *Castlemaine* (see Rte 12B) we strike the N70 from *Tralee* (16km N) to *Milltown* and *Killorglin* (9.5km SW), and the start of the 'Ring of Kerry' (see Rte 12B, in reverse). The R563 leads directly from Milltown to *Killarney*, 17.5km SE; see Rte 13.

17 Limerick to Cork

A. Via Croom, Charleville (Rath Luirc), and Mallow

93km (58 miles). N20. 18km *Croom*—16km *Charleville*—24km *Mallow*—35km **Cork**.

From Limerick (Rte 14) we bear SW past *Patrickswell*, before forking left. Shortly passing (left) the tower of *Fanningstown*, we enter **Croom** (850 inhab.), an ancient fortress of the Fitzgeralds; their *Castle* (late 12C) was modernised by the Croker family early in the 19C.

To the W (across fields) is the *Round Tower* of *Dysert*, 20m high and lacking its two top storeys; the adjoining church is built of very rude masonry.

At *Monasteranenagh*, or (simply) *Monaster*, 4km E on the Camoge, are the ruins of a Cistercian monastery founded in 1148 by Donal O'Brien, King of Munster, in thanksgiving for his defeat of the Danes at *Rathmore Castle*, further E. Beside the ruins of the church, which shows some good carving, are remains of the abbey mill and an old bridge.

9.5km S of Croom are crossroads: 3km to the E lies *Bruree*, with the remains of a fortress of the De Lacys and of a castle of the Templars; *Kilmallock* lies 6.5km beyond (see Rte 17B). It was at the home of his mother, Katherine Coll, at Bruree, that Éamon de Valéra spent much of his childhood.

6.5km **Charleville** (or **Rath Luirc**; 2,850 inhab.) was founded c 1659 by Roger Boyle, first Earl of Orrery, and named in honour of Charles II. Boyle's mansion was burnt down by the Duke of Berwick in 1690. A charming little 18C market-house remains, but it has lost its cupola.

12km W is ruined *Kilbolaine Castle* (early 16C; but in an earlier style), partly moated, and with two circular towers.

Continuing S, we skirt the *Ballyhoura Hills* to the E before entering **Buttevant** (1,150 inhab.) on the Awbeg (called the Mulla by Spenser), which is supposed to derive its name from the cry 'Boutez en avant' (push forward) used by David de Barry in an encounter with the Mac-Carthys. It gave its name to a viscounty borne by the Barry family. The ruins of the Franciscan *Abbey* (late 13C) are interesting; the nave contains some good canopied tombs of the 14C, while on the E side of the S transept is a small chapel with Barry, Fitzgerald, and Butler monuments; beneath the choir is a crypt vaulted from a single massive pier of four columns. A tower of the Desmonds has been incorporated in the Catholic church. The earlier fortifications of *Buttevant Castle*, overlooking the river, the old seat of the Barrys, was made into a home in the early 19C by John Anderson (cf. Fermoy). The Protestant *Church* (1826), by the Pains, is notable.

Liscarroll, 11km NW of Buttevant, was the scene of a battle in 1642, when David, first Earl of Barrymore, was fatally wounded. A later notable was Sir John Purcell of Highfort, who, armed only with a carving-knife, slew eight armed robbers single-handed as they forced their way into his bedroom. The massive *Castle keep* probably dates from shortly after the Anglo-Norman invasion.

7km E of Buttevant is *Doneraile* (pron. Dunerale; 900 inhab.), once owned by Edmund Spenser, whose son sold it to William St. Leger, ancestor of the Viscounts Doneraile. Their seat, *Doneraile Court* (rebuilt c 1730) is being restored by the Irish Georgian Society. The tomb of the first Viscount (died 1727), by Sir Henry Cheere, can be seen in the church.

Some 4.5km NW of the village stand the ruins of **Kilcolman Castle**, Spenser's home—or in an adjacent house—for several years, where he wrote the first three books of the 'Faerie Queene'. The castle is ruined above the ground floor, but the top of the walls can be reached by a turret stair. The demesne is now part of a wild-fowl refuge, and access is normally restricted. Spenser, as secretary to Lord Grey de Wilton, the Lord Deputy, came into possession of the property in 1586 after the forfeiture of the Earl of Desmond's estates, and took up residence in 1588. In the following year a visit of his friend Raleigh (cf. Youghal) decided him to publish his poem, and he moved to London. He stayed there until 1591, when he reluctantly returned to Kilcolman—the period of 'Colin Clouts come home againe'—and remained here until 1598, when the house was burned during Tyrone's rebellion. In 1594 he married Elizabeth Boyle, daughter of a gentleman of the neighbourhood.

About 1.5km S of Buttevant we pass (left) the ruins of *Ballybeg Abbey*, founded 1229 by Philip Barry, now incorporated in a farmhouse, and soon after begin the gradual descent into the Blackwater valley to *Mallow* (see Rte 9).—Hence the Cork road ascends the Clyda valley, passing (left) *Mourne Abbey*, a preceptory of the Knights Templar, and (right) the mid 13C tower of *Castle Barry*, built by John de Cogan. It was in Fitzgerald hands in 1439–1601, when a Barrett purchased it, and it was also known as Castle Barrett. After briefly climbing, we descend the valley of the Martin towards **Cork**; see Rte 6.

B. Via Lough Gur, Kilmallock, Charleville (Rath Luirc), and Mallow

103km (64 miles). R512—20km **Lough Gur**—14.5km **Kilmallock**—
R515. 9.5km *Charleville (Rath Luirc)*—N20. 24km *Mallow*—35km
Cork.

We leave Limerick by the N24 (for Tipperary), immediately diverging
right to approach the NW corner of *Lough Gur**, a pretty lake where
the last of the Desmonds, according to legend, holds eternal court
beneath its waters, emerging every seventh year on a silver-shod
steed. Of more historical interest is the remarkable concentration of
stone circles and other rude stone monuments to be seen on its banks,
from Neolithic dwellings (2000 BC) to those of the Early Christian
period. An *Interpretive Centre* has been set up on its NE bank,
approached by the R514; see Rte 18C. Among these sites are those
between the road and the NW corner of the lake, including—as we
walk away from the road—two stone circles, a large standing stone
(leaning slightly), a crannóg (not a good example, and now too close to
the shore) a small stone circle, and a ring-fort.

If we chose to make our way round the lake (in a clockwise direction), we pass at
its NE extremity the foundations of huts joined together to look like spectacles; to
the SE of the latter, two stone forts probably in occupation until the 10C; and on
the hill (*Knockadun*) beside the lake, a Stone Age house, burial-place, and enclosure. Skirting the SE corner of Lough Gur, we reach the ruins of *Black Castle*, and
may return to the main road by following the S bank, passing a wedge-shaped
gallery-grave.

14.5km **KILMALLOCK** (1,300 inhab.), now a small country town, was
once one of the most important places in Munster, and the headquarters of the earls of Desmond.

Its history is interwoven with the annals of the earls, a branch of the great Fitzge-
rald family which dominated the greater part of Munster from the 14C to the 16C.
Maurice FitzGerald, or FitzThomas, the 1st Earl, died in 1356, and Gerald Fitzgerald, the 15th Earl, was killed in 1583, a fugitive from the Earl of Ormonde backed
by the power of Queen Elizabeth. The first of the White Knights, a sept of the
Fitzgerald family that made its headquarters at Kilmallock, won his nickname at
Halidon Hill (1333), where he was knighted by Edward III for services against the
Scots, his glittering armour being conspicuous in the fray. Lord Blakeney (1672–
1761), the defender of Stirling Castle and Minorca, and Sir Eyre Coote (1726–83),
who defeated Hyder Ali, were natives of Kilmallock.

The town presents a picture of fallen greatness. Of its fortifications
(slighted by Cromwell's order) *Blossom's Gate* remains, on the Charleville road; and, on the N approach, the so-called *King's Castle*—
used by a blacksmith in the 19C—survives in Sarsfield St. The church
of *SS. Peter and Paul* has a ruined nave and transepts; its tower is part
of an old *Round Tower*, considerably altered.
  On the banks of the Loobagh rivulet, NE of the centre, is the beautiful *Dominican Abbey**, founded late in the 13C by Gilbert Fitzgerald
of Offaly. The finest part of the ruins is the church choir, with a well-
restored E window; here also are several interesting tombs, including
that of Edmund Fitzgibbon (?1552–1608), the last White Knight, who
in 1604 defeated James FitzThomas Fitzgerald, the 'Sugan' (i.e. straw)
Earl of Desmond, who had assumed the title. There is another good
window in the transept; over the crossing is a tower over 27m high,
supported by unusually narrow arches.

1.5km W lies *Ash Hill Towers*, a mansion of 1781 with one facade rebuilt in the

Gothick-Revival style in 1833; it contains Wyatt-type plasterwork (adm. by appointment).

8km SE and 6.5km S of Kilmallock respectively lie *Kilfinane*, with a trivallate rath 9m high, and *Ardpatrick*, with remains of a *Round Tower* and traces of a monastery founded by St. Patrick (?). SW of the latter, overlooked by *Seefin* (528m), is the demesne of *Castle-Oliver*, birthplace of Lola Montez (Marie Gilbert, 1818–61), the dancer and adventuress.

Leaving Kilmallock through *Blossom's Gate*, we bear SE to (9.6km) *Charleville (Rath Luirc)*; see Rte 17A, and for the route hence to *Cork*.

C. Via Hospital and Mitchelstown

102km (63 miles). R512. 14km—R514. 6.5km—R513. 7km *Hospital*—25.5km. *Mitchelstown*—N8. 14km. *Fermoy*—35km **Cork**.

Our road passes little of interest until we reach (left) the ruins of Elizabethan *Kenmare Castle*, on the outskirts of **Hospital**, a village which once belonged to the Knights Hospitallers; the early 13C church preserves a figure of a knight.—*Knockainy*, to the W, at the foot of the isolated hill of the same name, preserves remains of a Fitzgerald castle and traces of a 13C Austin priory. Further W, on either side of the Bruff road, are the mansions of *Baggotstown* (left; early 17C) and (right) *Kilballyowen*, rebuilt, and incorporating an old tower of the O'Gradys.

Emly, 7km to the E, is a village of ancient importance. The see founded here by St. Ailbhe (Albeus), a shadowy contemporary of St. Patrick, was amalgamated with Cashel in 1568, and the old cathedral was demolished in 1828; a large rude *Cross* survives in the churchyard.

Continuing S from Hospital, we traverse *Knocklong*, with the ruins of a castle of the O'Hurly's, and an old church on a hill to the W. The road approaches the Galty Mountains to the SE and the Ballyhoura range, their western outliers.

At *Pinker's Cross*, a lane to the left leads shortly to *Galbally*, beautifully situated at the head of the *Glen of Aherlow*, where the pass from Tipperary into N Cork was for many years in dispute between the Fitzpatricks and the O'Briens. Near the bridge rises the lofty tower of *Moor Abbey* (15C), a Franciscan house founded in the 13C by Donough Gairbreach O'Brien.—At *Duntryleague* (or *Cush*), near by, is a fine Passage-grave.

Continuing S from Pinker's Cross, we reach *Ballylanders*, with a ruined church and abutting 17C tower, before traversing the upland below the Galty range, to descend to *Mitchelstown* (see p 190), whence we follow the road described in Rte 4, through *Fermoy* to *Cork*.

18 Limerick to Galway

A. Via Ennis and Gort

103km (64 miles). N18. 16km. *Hurlers Cross.* (*Shannon Airport* lies 8km W)—19km *Ennis*—31km *Gort* (for *Kilmacduagh*, and *Thoor Ballylee*)—19km *Kilcolgan*—18km **Galway**.

A more interesting, and only slightly longer ALTERNATIVE to the main road—regained at *Ennis*—is that through *Quin*, which is described first.

For the first 9.5km we follow the N18 from the Sarsfield Bridge, passing *Cratloe Castle* (right), and *Cratloekeel Castle* and *Castle Donnell* (left), before turning right onto the R462 at *Cratloe*, with *Woodcock Hill* (307m) rising on the right.

4km *Sixmilebridge*, just to the E of which is the charming doll's-house-like Georgian mansion of *Mount Ievers* (c 1736–37), by Isaac and John Rothery, with an entrance front of ashlar stone, and a garden front of brick.—We continue N across a plain studded with small lakes, with here and there the ruined castles of the Macnamaras and the Fannings, and after 4.5km fork left onto the R369.

The second turning to the right soon reaches the entrance (left) of the *Craggaunowen Project*, centred around the *Castle* of c 1550, restored in the 19C, and acquired in 1965 by the late John Hunt, who initiated the project.

Since then a number of authentic replicas of ancient dwellings have been constructed in the grounds, among them a Late Bronze Age *crannóg*, and a *ring-fort*. They dramatically bring to life aspects of the Irish past which are not always easily envisaged; the erection of a megalithic tomb and an Early Christian church are also projected.

The entrance lodge preserves early 19C cottage furniture and utensils (and incidentally serves tasty traditional scones). The *Castle* contains a good representative collection of Irish, English and Continental furniture and sculpture from the 14th to the 17Cs. In display cases, also forming part of the Hunt Collection, are examples of metalware, pottery, reliquaries, etc.; the rest of the collection is now accommodated at the *National Institute for Higher Education*, Limerick (see latter part of Rte 14).

Regaining the main road, we turn right, and shortly pass (left) *Knappogue Castle* (1467; over-restored since 1966), vying with Bunratty (see below) in providing pseudo-medieval banquets.—There are remains of an early monastic foundation at *Finlough* or *Fenoe*, to the S.

The village of **QUIN** (Irish *Cuinche*, arbutus), which we next enter, contains one of the best-preserved abbeys in Ireland. This is the country of the Macnamaras, whose fortresses abound in the vicinity, and the *Franciscan Abbey* here was founded by Sioda Macnamara in 1402 within the four towers of the Norman *Castle* (destroyed 1286), three of which still partly exist. The abbey church consists of a nave and chancel with a tower between them, and contains tombs of the Macnamaras, including that of the notorious duellist 'Fireball' Macnamara. The cloister, with coupled columns and later buttresses, is in better condition than most.

Quin Abbey was suppressed in 1541. In 1584 Donough Beag O'Brien was brutally executed here by Sir John Perrot, lord deputy. The Franciscans returned however, and although their community was officially disbanded in 1651 the last monk, Fr John Hogan, died only in 1820 and is buried in the NE corner of the cloister.

Near by is the early 13C church of *St. Finghin*.

About 3km NE is the mound of *Magh Adhair* (7.5m high), the ancient inaugura-tion-place of the Kings of Thomond.

From Quin we soon bear W and cross the river Fergus, to enter (10km) *Ennis* by the Railway Station; see below.

The main road from Limerick as far as (9.5km) *Cratloe* is described above, beyond which is the imposing late 15C *Castle of **Bunratty**, with its four square angle-towers, joined on the narrower fronts by lofty arches. It is the venue for candlelit 'medieval' banquets. Adjoining is a 'Folk Park', where traditional dwellings have been erected and furnished.

Once the residence of the earls of Thomond, the castle was conti-nuously inhabited until the 19C when it was for a time used as police barracks; it was acquired by Viscount Gort in 1954, and has been restored to its 15–16C condition. It contains good 14–17C furniture, tapestries, etc., while in the banqueting hall above the stone-roofed guard-room some 17C stucco work is preserved; off it opens a chapel.

In 1276 Brian O'Brien, King of Thomond, was expelled from his dominions, which were granted to Sir Thomas de Clare (who built the first *stone* castle here), but in the next year De Clare was forced to ally himself with Brian against the rebellious Turlough O'Brien. The alliance was unsuccessful, and De Clare, in mortification at his defeat, arrested Brian in the castle and had him dragged to death by horses. Bunratty reverted to the O'Briens, however, and was restored by Donough O'Brien, Earl of Thomond (died 1624). In 1646 it was taken by the Irish Confe-derates inspired by the presence of Cardinal Rinuccini.

Shortly beyond Bunratty, the road to the **Shannon International Airport** bears left.

Opened in 1945, it has the distinction of being the most westerly air-base in Europe, and was also the first custom-free airport in the world. All the usual facilities are provided in the way of overnight accommodation, restaurants, shops, etc. During the last three decades an industrial estate established by the Shannon Free Airport Development Co. (with factories producing precision tools, electronic equipment, industrial diamonds, etc.) has grown up alongside the airport; the population of the adjacent 'new town' is now 8,000.

We pass near (left) *Urlanmore Castle*, where the main tower room preserves medieval outline paintings of animals, before traversing **Newmarket-on-Fergus** (1,350 inhab.) to the W of which is the church of *Kilnasoolagh*. This has an important *Monument of c 1717 by Wil-liam Kidwell (1662–1736), a recumbent figure of Sir Donough O'Brien, ancestor of Lord Inchiquin, for whom *Dromoland Castle*, to the NE of Newmarket, was built. This mansion, by the Pain brothers (1826) replaced an 18C house; in the elaborate formal gardens designed by John Aheron are a Doric rotunda and a 17C gate, moved here from Lemaneagh earlier this century. Now a hotel, it was the birthplace of William Smith O'Brien (1803–64), a leader of the 'Young Ireland' party. Near the SE entrance of the demesne is a large stone fort, where in 1854 the great Clare Gold Hoard was discovered.

Passing (left) *Carnelly House* (c 1740; probably designed by Francis Bindon), we cross the river Fergus, a broad tributary of the Shannon, at *Clarecastle*, named after a fortress of the O'Briens that stood on an island in the river. The mid 18C bridge has recently been destroyed.

Beyond, to the right, are the ruins of *Clare Abbey*, an Austin priory, founded by Donal O'Brien, the last King of Munster, in 1195. The lofty central tower, a later addition, is its most conspicuous feature; there are fragments of a cloister and other conventual dependencies on the S side.

ENNIS (6,200 inhab.), the busy county town of Co. Clare, has little changed since it was described in the mid 19C, with its suburbs and outskirts as 'ill-defined, and scattered' and not presenting a single good street.

Among its eminent natives were the artist William Mulready (1786–1863), the precocious poet Thomas Dermody (1775–1802), and the actress Harriet Smithson (1800–54), who married Hector Berlioz in 1833. Monuments in the town also commemorate Daniel O'Connell, MP for Clare in 1828–31, and the 'Manchester Martyrs' (Allen, Larkin, and O'Brien), executed in 1867 for the violent rescue of a Fenian prisoner in Manchester gaol. Éamon de Valéra represented the county from 1917–59.

To the N of the narrow streets of the old town stands the *Court House*, a Classical building of 1850–52; also of interest is the ruined *Friary*, nearer the centre by the river, founded by Donough Cairbreach O'Brien in 1242, and suppressed in 1543. The slender tower has received an incongruous top storey with ugly spirelets. The S transept, with its stepped gable and graceful window tracery, and the row of twin and triplet windows in the choir, are attractive. The choir shelters (N side) the MacMahon monument (c 1470), altered in 1843 and restored in 1953; the Inchiquin tomb on the S side, and other good sculpture. There is a vaulted sacristy or chapter room on the N side but other conventual dependencies are fragmentary.

The *R.C. Cathedral* dates from 1831–43.

Ennis is connected by direct roads with all parts of Co. Clare, the W seaboard of which is covered by Rte 18B, while the area near Lough Derg is described in Rte 18C. One of the more interesting monuments in the neighbourhood may be seen at *Quin*, 10km SE; see above.

Beyond Ennis the N18 bears NE through a wide lough-studded valley, passing (right) LOUGH INCHICRONAN, on a peninsula jutting out into which is a ruined 12–15C abbey, to *Crusheen*. Not far N of Crusheen the N18 enters Co. Galway at a bridge between two small lakes. We pass (left) *Ardamullivan*, a 16C tower of the O'Shaughnessys, and (right) the demesne of *Lough Cutra Castle*, a handsome Regency residence built from the designs of Nash by the Pain brothers c 1816 (adm.). Its Victorian accretions have now been removed. Views of the lough may be enjoyed through the trees. On the right further on is the 'Punchbowl', a deep wooded chasm at the bottom of which is seen part of the stream that flows underground from Lough Cutra to Gort.

Gort (1,100 inhab.) is a rather dull former garrison town with a triangular market-place.

At **Kilmacduagh**, 5.5km SW, is a very interesting group of ecclesiastical ruins. It was here that St. Colman MacDuagh founded an episcopal see c 610 (now united with Killaloe, Kilfenora, and Clonfert), and the original church was built for him by his kinsman Guaire Aidhne, King of Connacht. The present *Cathedral*, a 14–15C rebuilding, incorporates the 10C W doorway (now closed) with its massive lintel. The N chapel contains 16–18C O'Shaughnessy tombs, a figure of St. Colman, and two Crucifixions. More interesting is the church of *O'Heyne's Abbey*, to the NW, a 13C foundation with evidences of earlier occupation (?10C). The piers of the chancel arch and the two-light E windows are in the mature Irish Romanesque style (c 1266); the vaulted sacristy and chapter house remain on the S. The *Oratory of St. John*, N of the cathedral, may date from St. Colman's time. Beyond it is the 14C *Bishop's Castle*. The restored *Round Tower*, 34m high, with its doorway 8m from the ground, leans 60cm out of the perpendicular. *Teampull Muire*, E, beyond the road, preserves two round-headed windows and a doorway.

Fiddaun Castle, 4km S, is a well-preserved stronghold of the O'Shaughnessys.

Some 5km NE of Gort, reached by a turning left, and left again off the N66 to Loughrea, is ***Thoor Ballylee**, intermittently the residence of W.B. Yeats (1865–1939) between the years 1921–29. The derelict tower was saved and restored by the Kiltartan Society, presided over by Mrs Mary Hanley. It was once known as Islandmore Castle, and in 1617 was the property of Richard de Burgo, Earl of Clanricarde. In 1896 Yeats and Arthur Symonds, when guests of Edward Martyn at Tullira Castle (c 3km N; see below), were introduced to Lady Gregory, and the poet had visited the place some years before purchasing it in 1916 from the Congested Districts Board for £35. He commenced converting it the following year.

In 1948 a stone was set up here, inscribed with his words:
'I, the poet William Yeats
With old millboards and sea-green slates
And smithy work from the Gort forge
Restored this tower for my wife George.
And may these characters remain
When all is ruin once again.'

Thoor Ballylee

By then the tower—depicted on the cover of his volume of poems of that name in 1928—was already in a sorry state of dilapidation, as he predicted.

Now restored, the interior of Thoor Ballylee, the tower well-seen from across the adjacent mill-stream, or from its small walled garden—note the sculpted head high up on the wall—may be visited from March to late October.

Much of the original oak furniture made on the spot and designed by W.A. Scott—note the bookshelf over the bed-head—and china is preserved (indeed the former could not be moved down the stair!), together with a complete set of broadsheets illustrated by Jack Yeats, and a collection of 1st editions of W.B. Yeats. One will see the 'narrow winding stair, a chamber arched with stone A grey stone fireplace with an open hearth'. The walls have been repainted in their original colours, some dark blue; and a stair ascends to the flat roof, passing a huge jackdaw's nest.

A small bookshop, also selling Cuala Press prints, has been installed in the Kitchen, an abutting thatched cottage; there is a tea-room serving appetising 'bracks' in the stable across the lane.

Further NE, the road leads past (left) *Isertkelly*, a mid 16C house, with a ruined church nearby, on the NW slope of the *Slieve Aughty Mountains* (*Cashlaundrumlahan*; 367m), towards *Loughrea* (24km from Gort; see Rte 18C).

Returning to Gort, we may continue N on the N18, shortly passing (left) **Coole Park**, from 1880 the home of Augusta, Lady Gregory (1859–1932), and a centre of the Irish literary revival, of which Yeats wrote in 1929:

'Here, traveller, scholar, poet, take your stand
When all those rooms and passages are gone,
When nettles wave upon a shapeless mound
And saplings root among the broken stone...'.

Lady Gregory's home at Coole Park before demolition

The only physical reminder is the *Autograph Tree*, a copper beech in the overgrown garden belatedly undergoing clearance, inscribed with the initials of W.B. and J.B. Yeats, G.B. Shaw, J.M. Synge, Seán O'Casey, John Masefield, Violet Martin, Augustus John, Katharine Tynan, and others. It stands to the N of the demolished house, which, brought by the Free State government in 1927, became progressively more derelict until pulled down in 1941 by a building contractor for the value of the stone.

We traverse *Kiltartan*, with a ruined 13C *Castle* and church, and shortly pass (right) *Tullira Castle*, a 17C tower-house encased by a mock-Tudor rebuilding of 1882, and the home of Edward Martyn (1859–1923), the dramatist and patron of the arts, in particular that of stained glass.—We soon veer NW through *Ardrahan*, with the shattered remains of its keep, *Kiltiernan*, with an early church surrounded by a stone enclosure, and *Kilcolgan*, with a ruined castle and church.—At the head of the creek of *Dunbulcaun Bay* lies *Clarinbridge* (where an Oyster Festival is held in September). We bear round the head of Galway Bay, meeting the N6 E of *Oranmore* (bypassed), and veer W for *Galway* itself; see Rte 21A.

B. Via the Coast: Kilrush, Kilkee, Lahinch, and Lisdoonvarna

217km (135 miles). N18 to (35km) **Ennis**—N68. 43km *Kilrush*—N67. 13km *Kilkee*—47km *Lahinch*—18km *Lisdoonvarna*—43km *Kilcolgan*—N18 and N6. 18km **Galway**.

Several alternative routes may be followed—shorter or longer; a recommended compromise is that to *Kilfenora*, and then SW through *Ennisyimon* to *Lahinch*. Thence follow the coast road to the *Cliffs of Moher* and to *Lisdoonvarna*, before crossing the *Burren* to *Ballyvaughan*.

For the road from Limerick to *Ennis*, see Rte 18A.

ENNIS TO LAHINCH DIRECT (30km). The N85 drives NW via *Inagh*, where the R460 bears W across the N slope of *Slievecallan* (390m), a flat-topped limestone hill, to *Milltown Malbay*; see below.—We descend the Cullenagh valley through **Ennistymon** (1,100 inhab.), well-sited above a cascade, and dominated by a ruined church and cemetery.—*Lahinch* (see below) lies on the coast 4km to the W.

ENNIS TO LISDOONVARNA VIA KILFENORA (35.5km). At *Fountain Cross*, 4km NW of Ennis, we fork right onto the R476, passing (right) the ruins of *Ballygriffy Castle*.

Of more interest is the next turning to the left, which leads in 2.5km to the ruins of **Dysert O'Dea** (right), which consists of a *Church*, 32m long, with 13–14C windows and a 12C *Doorway* with a semi-circle of sculptured heads; the stump of a *Round Tower* (12m high); and in the adjacent field, a *High Cross* with interlaced and zoomorphic patterns and a Crucifixion (E side) above a figure said to represent St. Tola, founder of the church (8C); the penultimate stone of the cross appears to be missing.

Inscriptions record its repair in 1683 by Michael O'Dea, a member of the family that owned the adjoining *Castle* (15C; to the N), re-erected in 1871. Dysert was the scene of a battle in 1318, when Sir Richard de Clare and his son were killed and Anglo-Norman control of Thomond brought to an end.

Leamanah Castle, Co. Clare

We may regain the road just S of *Corofin*, a village lying beween
LOUGH ATEDAUN (right) and *LOUGH INCHIQUIN, backed by wooded
hills, the E shore of which we skixrt, passing the old castle of *Inchiquin*
(a former residence of the O'Quinns). In the lough is the island (*Inis Ui
Chuinn*) that gave its name to the whole district and a title to the
O'Brien family.—*Killinaboy*, beyond the N end of the lough, has two
ruined churches, one preserving a good Sheila-na-gig over a door,
the stump of a *Round Tower*, an ancient Tau-shaped boundary cross,
and the tower of a castle said to have been occupied by the deans of
Kilfenora.

The low hills that rise to the N between this point and the coast
abound in ruined churches and cahers; the finest of these rock-forts is
at *Ballykinvarga*, 3km NE of Kilfenora, with a limestone 'Chevaux de
frise'; that at *Cahercommaun*, 6.5km N of Killinaboy, has been
excavated to reveal the interior chambers.—We pass on the right the
ruined 17C mansion of *Lemaneagh* or *Leamanah*, incorporating an
earlier tower (c 1420) of the O'Briens, before reaching **Kilfenora**, a
place of ancient importance and an episcopal see now joined with
Killaloe. The *Cathedral* of St. Fachan is a small 12C building with a
stepped square tower; the nave has been tastelessly fitted up as a
parish church, but the roofless choir has a fine E window and a monument believed to be of St. Fachan. In the graveyard is an imposing 12C
*High Cross, 4m high, with a Crucifixion on one side and a bishop and

Detail of the High Cross at Kilfenora

two other clerics on the other; also fragmentary crosses of a like date.

The small *Burren Display Centre* (open mid-April to mid-September) provides an audio-visual description of the area (see below), and its varied botany and wildlife.—We enter *Lisdoonvarna* 8km to the NW; see below. *Ennistymon* lies 9km SW, and *Lahinch*, 4km beyond.

Although the direct road (N68) from Ennis to Kilrush is 18km shorter, it is of less interest than that skirting the Shannon estuary, described below.

ENNIS TO KILRUSH VIA THE R473 (61km). From Ennis, turn back along the Limerick road for c 2km before forking right. The road passes (right) between two lakes in the ground of *New Hall* (c 1764; probably by Francis Bindon), the ruins of *Killone Abbey*, founded by Donal O'Brien in 1190; it is said that his granddaughter Slaney (died 1260) was abbess. It has several unusual features, including a passage through the central pier, a curious corbel at the SE angle, and a crypt, the burial-place of the MacDonnells.

The road keeps near the shallow estuary of the Fergus, studded with low islands, and passes (right) ruined *Dangan Castle*; on offshore *Canon's Island* are the ruins of another of the Donal O'Brien abbeys (early 13C), surrounded by a circular wall. We skirt the demesne of *Cahiracon*, and then follow the Shannon shore, with views across the estuary towards Glin, before turning NW round the head of *Clonderlaw Bay*.— *Killimer* is the N terminus of the car-ferry to *Tarbert* and the Kerry bank of the Shannon. The ferry normally sails every hour on the half-hour from 9.30–17.30 or 18.30, but may cross more frequently between May and September from 9.30–21.30. The crossing averages 20 minutes.

In the churchyard of Killimer is buried 'Colleen Bawn', Eily or Ellen Hanley, whose beauty led to her tragic end at the hands of her secretly-married husband, who drowned her in the Shannon in a fit of jealousy (1819).

Kilrush (2,750 inhab.), a small market town with a harbour, is of slight interest. At *Cappagh Pier*, to the SW, boats may be hired for visiting offshore Scattery Island.

Scattery (*Inis Cathaigh*) was the retreat of St. Senan (died 554). Remains of five churches survive, among them the 9–10C *Cathedral*, with a good W door and later windows. Near it are the *Oratory* (11C; rebuilt) and *Round Tower*, 38m high, the tallest and perhaps the oldest surviving in Ireland, unique in having its entrance at ground level. *Temple Senan*, to the NW, with the alleged site of the saint's grave, has been much rebuilt; to the W of it is the Moenach inscribed stone. Near the E shore at *Templenamarve* (14–15C) and the vaults of a *Castle*, erected probably by the burghers of Limerick, to whom the island was assigned by Elizabeth I in 1582; while to the SW is *Knocknanangel*, with fragments of a primitive church and a later attached building.

St. Senan, like St. Kevin at Glandalough, excluded all women from his retreat. Legend states that St. Cannera, a sociable female saint, wished to share the island with him; but, more tractable than Kevin's admirer, she returned to the mainland at his express command. The saint was born at *Moylougha*, 7km E of Kilrush, where a lake and a ruined church mark the site.

13km NW of Kilrush is **Kilkee** (1,400 inhab.), a small resort with splendid coastal scenery in the neighbourhood, and good bathing, the inlet called *Moore Bay* being protected from the full fury of the Atlantic by a reef known as *Duggerna Rocks*. On the S shore is a natural amphitheatre of terraced limestone, and the *Puffing Hole*, a blow-hole through which the spray bursts in stormy weather.

KILKEE TO LOOP HEAD (c 27km, one way). Following the coast road, we pass *Bishop's Island*, with a beehive oratory and house ascribed to St. Senan (see above), beyond which the road climbs past *Green Rock*, a bold stack, to *Castle Point*, with the ruins of *Doonlicky Castle*, a MacMahon stronghold. On the cliff beyond is another ruined fort. Keeping to the right we eventually reach *Kilbaha*, the last village, and the Mouth of the Shannon.—Further W lies *Loop Head*, with its lighthouse (84m high).

The *View hence is superb, extending from MacGillycuddy's Reeks to the S, rising behind the Slieve Mish Mountains, and Brandon Head and Mt Brandon to the SW; to the N beyond the Aran Islands, is the coast of Connemara, with the Twelve Bens, and Slyne Head to the NW.—Just offshore is a stack called the *Lover's Leap*, fabled to have been Cuchulainn's refuge from an importunate lady, who pursuing him with some precipitation, perished in an intervening chasm.—An alternative road back follows the S shore of the peninsula through *Carrigaholt*, with a castle of the O'Briens, and *Doonaha*, birthplace of Eugene O'Curry (1796–1862), scholar and topographer.

Driving NE from Kilkee we pass cliffs increasing in height as far as Baltard Bay, beyond which we pass the Doonmore sandhills, and *Doonbeg Castle*, another O'Brien fortress, and bear left near LOUGH DONNELL, cut off from the sea by a shingle bar.—Off *Lurga Point*, on the headland of which is *Tromra Castle* (another O'Brien seat) lies *Mutton Island*, which may be visited by corragh from the fishing-village of *Quilty*, with a seaweed-processing factory. It is said to have been torn off the mainland by a storm in c 800, and preserves an oratory of St. Senan; on the landward reef a ship of the Armada was wrecked.

A left-hand fork just N of Quilty leads to *Spanish Point*, a landmark in the centre of *Mal Bay*, dangerous to shipping, as its name implies.

At Spanish Point were buried numerous bodies washed ashore from the

Armada. Many Armada vessels were wrecked off the Clare coast in September 1588, when its cliffs were manned by followers of Sir Turlough O'Brien of Liscannor (who favoured the Protestant party) to prevent any survivors actually landing.

The main road continues NE to the village of *Milltown Malbay*, with a turf-burning power station. To the E rises *Slievecallan* (390m), on the S flank of which is a huge dolmen.

We pass (left) the ruin of *Freagh Castle*, near a curious blow-hole, before entering **Lahinch**, a small resort on *Liscannor Bay*, beyond which we bear round towards *Hag's Head* (124m), passing the ruins of *Dough Castle, Kilmacreehy Church* (15C), and the square tower of an O'Brien fort at *Liscannor*.

The road now climbs the landward ridge of hills which form the *Cliffs of Moher*, a sheer precipice 8km long and rising to a height of 203m, one of the most impressive stretches of the coast in the W of Ireland, remarkable especially at nesting season for the quantity and variety of seabirds there, among them Guillemots, Razor-bills, Puffins, Kittiwakes, Shags, etc. The best view is enjoyed from *O'Brien's Tower*, approached by a track (parking) leading left from the main road. Steps climb to the right to a walled path running parallel to the cliff edge, built by Cornelius O'Brien, proprietor of the land, in 1835. Beware of gusts of wind. From the path and tower (restored) the junction of the limestone flags with the black shale above them in the stratified cliff is well seen, in between which is a calcareous band rich in fossils. Just below the tower is the spire-like stack of *Goats Island*; out to sea are the *Aran Islands* (Inisheer, Inishmaan, and Inishmore beyond; see Rte 21B), with the Galway coast on the right; Croaghaun, on Achill, over 100km NW, is visible on a clear day, beyond the Twelve Bens.

The Burren, Co. Clare

The road descends to *Lisdoonvarna* (600 inhab.), a spa with sulphur and Chalybeate springs rich in iodine and radioactive properties. The springs and the curious scenery of this wild glacio-Karsitic plateau known as **The Burren** (cf. *Kilfenora*, 8km SE), are due to its position at the junction of the porous Carboniferous limestone and shale systems. The whole area is the haunt of geologists and botanists, who will here find thriving in the crevices of its natural rock-garden of flagstones a remarkable number of calcium-loving plants, including blue Spring gentians, Mountain avens, Bloody cranesbill, white anemones, and yellow primroses, etc. It has the appearance of being so barren that Cromwellian troops claimed that there was neither wood to hang a man, water to drown him, nor earth to bury him. Caves and potholes (many dangerous, and only to be entered with a guide, or by experienced spelaeologists) are numerous, *Pollnagollum*, 5.5km to the N, being the longest cave known in Ireland (over 11km.).

The coast road (R477) hence to Ballyvaughan passes (right) *Ballynalackan Castle* on a crag, and turns N along the shore, with *Inisheer*, the nearest of the Aran Islands out to sea (see Rte 21B), and *Slieve Elva* (345m) inland. Passing several ruined churches and stone forts, we reach *Black Head*, a bleak and barren headland commanding a good view of *Galway Bay*, and turn E along the N flank of the terraced limestone cliffs, with (left) the 16C tower of *Gleninagh Castle*.

Ballyvaughan, 16km NE, an old seaside village, is approached direct from Lisdoonvarna by the N67, traversing the Burren plateau and passing (right) *Cahermacnaghten*, a stone fort known as 'O'Davoren's House' in 1675, where old Irish Brehon laws continued to be studied although previously abolished. Descending 'Corkscrew Hill', we pass (left) the prominent five-storey cylindrical tower (with a square base) of *Newtown Castle* (16C). Some 3km S of Ballyvaughan is the entrance to *Aillwee Cave*, representative of many in the region.

Bearing NE, we round a spur of the plateau, passing a ruined church preserving a lancet window and 16C N door, and (left) the castle of *Muckinish*, with its tall slender tower.

At this junction, a lane turning left off the right-hand fork approaches **Corcomroe Abbey** (an offshoot of Furness Abbey), founded for Cistercians in 1194 by Donal O'Brien. In the choir are mouldings recalling Killaloe, and some capitals repaying study, and there are traces of painting on the N wall, below which is the tomb of Conor O'Brien, King of Thomond (died 1267), grandson of the founder.

Returning to the road and turning left and left again, we pass near (right) *Oughtmama*, where three churches remain of an early monastic settlement, the westernmost with a pre-Romanesque nave and Romanesque chancel; note the interlaced antlers of two stags on the font.—Continuing on this minor road we shortly descend to regain the N67.—6.5km *Kinvarra*, a small port, with the well-restored 16C tower and bawn of *Dunguaire* (or *Dungory*; serving 'medieval banquets').

The road bears NE to *Kilcolgan*, just short of which we pass (left) the church of *Drumacoo* (13C), with a finely-carved S door, and near the burnt-out ruin of *Tyrone House* (1779), home of the St. George family, and the 'Big House of Inver' described by Somerville and Ross.—For the road hence to *Galway*; see last paragraph of Rte 18A.

C. Via Killaloe and Portumna

147km (91 miles). R463. 23km *Killaloe*—15km *Tuamgraney*—R352.
40km *Portumna*—N65. 32km *Loughrea*—N6. 37km **Galway**.

Leave Limerick via Athlunkard St. After crossing the Shannon, we
pass (left) at *Parteen* (or **Ardnacrushna**) the site of the great industrial
enterprise of harnessing the Shannon, usually referred to as 'The
Shannon Scheme', which was the first and is the largest hydro-electric
installation in Ireland.

In 1925 the Siemens-Schuckert company undertook the regulating of the tre-
mendous supply of water-power provided by the 30m fall in the river between
Lough Derg and Limerick; this included the construction of a dam near the foot of
the lough, a 12km-long Power Headrace Canal, the provision of a hydro-electric
power station and navigation locks, at Ardnacrushna, which came into operation
in 1929.

We shortly turn right, traversing *Cloonlara* and *O'Briensbridge*, the
only bridge between Limerick and Killaloe, where Ireton forced a
passage in 1651. Above the bridge the dam constructed in connection
with the Shannon Scheme has so widened the river as to make it an
extension of Lough Derg.
  KILLALOE (1,000 inhab.), a riverside village beautifully situated at
the S end of Lough Derg, frequented as the terminus of thex Shannon
cruiser run from Carrick-on-Shannon (see Rte 26A), is famous in Irish
annals. A long narrow bridge of 13 arches connects it to the Tipperary
village of *Ballina*. To the NW rises *Slieve Bernagh* (*Glenmagalliagh*,
531m); to the NE are the *Arra Mountains* (461m).

It occupies the site of a church founded by St. Dalua or Molua (*Cill Dalua*), known
also as Luanus, who died in c 622, and was succeeded by St. Flannan; and also (in
the vicinity) the palace of Kinora, the headquarters of BrianBorú (926–1014),
later destroyed by the men of Connacht. Thomas de Clare took the town in 1276.
Sarsfield crossed the Shannon here in 1690 to surprise William III's siege-train at
Oola, near Tipperary. It was to Dr Thomas Barnard, Bp of Killaloe from 1780, that
Dr Samuel Johnson remarked: 'The Irish are a fair people;—they never speak
well of one another'.

The **Cathedral of St. Flannan** was probably built by Donal O'Brien in
1182 on the site of an earlier church; its diocese has now absorbed
those of Clonfert, Kilmacduagh, and Kilfenora. The cruciform building
was restored in 1887; the upper part of the tower is modern. The zig-
zag mounding above the E window and the corbels on the N side of the
choir should be noted, while the E window of the S transept is unusual.
The most notable feature of the church is the interior of the blocked * S
Doorway, of earlier date, adorned with richly carved ornamentation
and grotesque heads, and said to be the entrance to the tomb of Murtogh O'Brien, King of Munster (died 1120). Beside it is the *Thorgrim's
Stone*, the granite shaft of a cross, with an inscription (c 1000) in both
runes and Ogham, the only bilingual one known, which was found
built into the churchyard wall in 1916. Against the W wall is a Celtic
Cross, 4.5m. high. The adjoining font has floreated decoration; that in
the choir is of 1752.
  In the churchyard are the well-preserved nave and chancel of a
* *Church* or Oratory, said to have been erected by St. Flannan. Its
steeply pitched stone roof is similar to those at Glendalough and Kells;
the doorway has two curious but worn capitals, one like a rough Ionic
scroll, the other with two lambs.

Next to the Catholic church stands *St. Molua's Oratory*, reconstructed here after its removal from Friar's Island when the level of the lough was raised (see above).

Lough Derg, the largest of the Shannon lakes (40km long; 3–5km wide), like Lough Ree further up the river, is studded with islands, and has a very irregular shore probably due to the slow decomposition of its limestone bed. It is noted for its rapid rise after rain, sometimes as much as 30cm in 24 hours, and it provides a natural reservoir for the Ardnacrushna hydro-electric station.

KILLALOE TO BIRR (62km). Crossing the Shannon, we turn N along the banks of LOUGH DERG, passing (left) *Derry Castle*. On the right rises *Tountinna* (461m), the highest of the Arra range, with some barrows known as the 'Graves of the Leinster Men' on its N flank. We turn E away from the lough and traverse the slate-quarrying village of *Portroe*.—23km *Nenagh* (see Rte 7), where we turn NE onto the N52.
The direct minor road to Birr via *Modreeny* (and near adjacent *Cloghjordan*, birthplace of the poet Thomas MacDonagh, 1878–1916) turns right off the N52 just N of the town and skirts a range of low hills. The highest we pass (21km; right) is *Knockshigowna* (213m), famous in the fairy legends of Ireland, its summit commanding a view of Lough Derg and the surrounding hills. 9.5km *Birr*, see Rte 20B.
The slightly longer but better road (N52) runs N to *Borrisokane* (850 inhab.), where we turn right for *Birr*.—The road beyond this village forks left via (8km) *Carrigahorig* for (6.5km) *Portumna*; see below.
A minor road (K493) diverges left off the N52 just N of Nenagh to skirt the E bank of Lough Derg, passing a number of pleasant demesnes, to regain the main road at *Carrigahorig*, among them *Terryglass Castle* (early 13C), of quatrefoil plan, near the site of an early monastery.

The beautiful road (recently improved) on the Clare bank of LOUGH DERG commands an even better view than that from the lake itself.

We bear NE from Killaloe, passing on the right a large fort, *Beal Ború*, which may represent the palace of Kinora; when excavated, it revealed remains of a rectangular timber house of the 11C. A lower road follows the lough-side before ascending, with a view of the fortress of *Castlelough* on the far bank; the newer road diverges left, with wider view on its descent towards *Tuamgraney*, with a ruined castle and 10C church.

Hence the R352 leads W to (33.5km) *Ennis*; see Rte 18A.—From adjacent *Scarriff*, two minor roads lead NW towards *Gort*, skirting LOUGH GRANEY; one passing near *Feakle*, where Brian Merriman (1757–1805), author of 'The Midnight Court', lies in the old churchyard.

We traverse **Scarriff** (850 inhab.), charmingly situated above the head of its bay, in which are several islets, and the demesne of *Woodpark*, before entering *Mountshannon*, a village nestling on the shore below the *Slieve Aughty* range (*Knockeven*; 378m), and frequented for trout and pike fishing.

Offshore to the SW lies **Inishcaltra**, or *Holy Island*, the seat of a monastic establishment founded by St. Caimin in the 7C, destroyed by the Danes in the 9C, and rebuilt by Brian Ború. There are remains of four churches: *St. Caimin's*, an early rectangular building with a Romanesque chancel added and an inserted W door; *St. Brigid's* (the smallest), with an elaborate Romanesque doorway; *St. Mary's*, much altered in the 16C, containing a monument to Turlough O'Brien and his wife (died 1626, and 1625); and *St. Michael's*, almost totally ruined. In St. Caimin's are the *Cross of Cathasach*, with inscriptions on its edges (c 1094), and another remarkable cross with nearly straight sides to its 'wheel'. The adjacent *Round Tower* (10C) is 24m high. To the NE, beyond the 'Saint's Graveyard', in an enclosure containing a well-preserved collection of early grave-slabs and the so-called 'Temple of the Wounded Men', is a very ancient structure, perhaps pagan, called the 'Anchorite's Cell'.

Beyond Mountshannon bear NE for some 23km before turning E at a T-junction for Portumna.—4km NW of this point stands the well-preserved tower-house of *Pallas*; at *Abbey*, 5km W, are ruins of a 14C Carthusian monastery, later Franciscan.

Portumna (1,100 inhab.), lying at the N end of Lough Derg, pres-erves the imposing ruins of a huge semi-fortified *Castle* (before 1619), accidentally burnt in 1826, and formerly the seat of the earls of Clanricarde; it is undergoing some restoration. The main approach (from the N) is through three aligned gates and formal gardens. Also in the demesne are arches of an early 13C Dominican convent, with two walks of a cloister, and the shell of the last earl's residence, burnt in 1922, six years after the death of that unpopular and reactionary land-lord. Among earlier visitors were the Duke of Berwick and Patrick Sarsfield.

Derryhivenny Castle, 6.5km NE, retains its four-storey tower of 1643 and most of its bawn.

We turn NW from Portumna for (32km) **LOUGHREA** (3,400 inhab.), attractively sited on the N bank of its Lough, with the ruins of a Car-melite *Friary* and a *Castle*, both built by Richard de Burgh c 1300. There is some good early 20C stained glass by Evie Hone and Sarah Purser, etc. in the *Catholic Cathedral* (1897–1903), an otherwise unim-pressive building by William Byrne; the surviving town gate is adjacent.

On the summit of a hill to the N is a good stone circle, while several crannogs have been discovered in LOUGH REA itself.

About 5km N, W of the village of *Bullaun*, is the *Turoe Stone*, with its richly ornamented carving in the La Tène style (Late Iron Age), moved here from a nearby ring-fort.—At *St. Cleran*'s, right of the Galway road 6.5km from Lough-rea, was born Robert O'Hara Burke (1820–61), the explorer of Australia. There are a number of ruined mansions in the area, including *Roxbrough House*, off the Gort road, the birthplace of Lady Gregory (cf. Coole Park), and *Dunsandel House* (6.5km NW of Loughrea), dismantled in the 1950s. At *Craughwell*, on the Galway road, are the kennels of the 'Galway Blazers' hunt (cf. Birr).

From Loughrea we gently descend towards the head of Galway Bay, after 37km entering **Galway** itself, for which see Rte 21A. For *Athenry*, to the N of this road, see the latter part of Rte 19.

19   Dublin to Galway via Athlone

215km (133 miles). N4. 13km *Lucan*—(*Celbridge* lies 5km to the W)—11km *Maynooth*—18km *Innfield*—19km *Kinnegad*—N6. 31km *Kilbeggan*—16km *Moate*—17km **Athlone**— 22km *Ballinasloe*— 31km *Loughrea*—37km **Galway**.

Following the N4 skirting the S wall of *Phoenix Park*, drive due W from Dublin, forking left over the Liffey at *Chapelizod* (see Rte 1E), and bearing to the right through *Palmerstown*, the suburban village giving its name to the Temple family, among whom the 3rd Viscount, Foreign Secretary in 1840–51, was the most famous. The steep slopes of the N bank of the river here are known as 'The Strawberry Beds'.

Lucan (11,750 inhab.) was much frequented after 1758 when the medicinal properties of its waters were discovered; it was also the venue for meets of the Kildare and Meath foxhounds and the Ward Union staghounds. The extensive riverside demesne of *Lucan House*

(since 1944 the residence of the Italian ambassador), was known as
Sarsfield House, after Patrick Sarsfield (born in Lucan; died 1693),
titular Earl of Lucan (created by James II in 1691). The present mansion, containing very fine decoration by James Wyatt and Michael
Stapleton, was not built until c 1776.—James Gandon, the architect,
died in 1824 at *Canon Brook*, to the SE; he is buried at Drumcondra.

A worthwhile DETOUR, and a recommended excursion from Dublin
(also approached from the centre by bus No. 67), may be made by
turning left immediately W of Lucan onto the R403 for (5km)
Celbridge, via the hamlet of *St. Wolstan*, where a 14C bridge spans the
Liffey, and with slight remains of an abbey founded by Adam de
Hereford c 1202. **Celbridge** (4,600 inhab.) was the residence, inherited from her father (the Williamite mayor of Dublin of Dutch descent;
cf. Drogheda), of Esther Vanhomrigh (1690–1723), Swift's 'Vanessa'.
Her unrequited passion for the dean is said to have hastened her
death. A seat by the riverside below her home, *Celbridge Abbey*, is
erroneously pointed out as her favourite retreat, which in fact was on
an adjacent island. Also of interest is *Oakley Park* (1720), and
Celbridge College (1730), both possibly by Thomas Burgh; while in
the disused Protestant church is the splendid monument to Speaker
Conolly and his wife, by Thomas Carter the Elder (1730). A house on
the left of the Clane road was the boyhood home of Adm. Sir Charles
Napier (1786–1860) and his brothers.

To the NE of the village stands the imposing mansion built for William Conolly (c 1660–1729), Speaker of the Irish Parliament from 1715,
and known as *Castletown House. It was built in 1722–32 by Alessandro Galilei and (internally) by Sir Edward Lovett Pearce, and consists of a central block flanked by curved colonnaded quadrants. It
remained in the Conolly family (through the female line) until 1965. It
is now the headquarters of the *Irish Georgian Society* (founded by
John Pentland Mahaffy in 1908), which has done so much to preserve
and restore Ireland's architectural heritage; the building is open to the
public.

Plasterwork of 1759–60 by the Francini brothers embellishes the

Castletown House

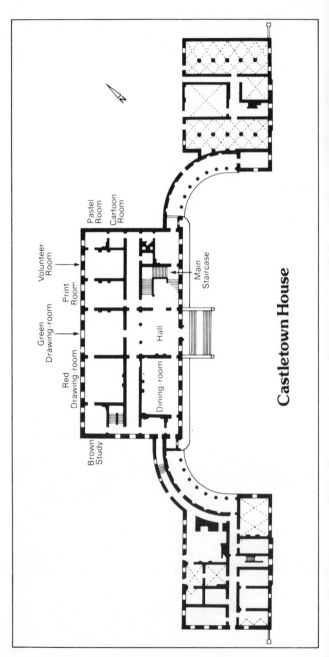

Castletown House

walls of the slightly later cantilevered staircase, with brass banisters. The *Long Gallery* on the first floor is decorated in the Pompeian manner, the work of Thomas Riley, and contains a portrait of 'Squire' Thomas Conolly by Mengs. Among other portraits in the house are those of William Conolly by Jervas, of 'Speaker' Boyle, Ginkel, Charles James Fox, etc. Also noteworthy is the 'print room' (c 1770), and a number of old views and maps of local interest, etc. At the end of a vista N of the house is a *Folly* of superimposed arches topped by an obelisk, probably designed by Castle in 1740; to the E is the so-called '*Wonderful Barn*', an equally curious conical structure with an external stair (1743).

About 2.5km to the N stands *Luttrellstown Castle*, elaborately gothicised in the early 19C by Luke White, in its beautiful demesne washed by the Liffey.

The main road from Lucan re-crosses the Liffey at **Leixlip** (9,300 inhab.), a large village on one of the most attractive reaches of the river. Above the modernised *Castle*, built for Adam de Hereford after 1170, was the famous Salmon Leap (Danish, *lax hlaup*), replaced by a 24m-high dam, part of the Liffey hydro-electric works, but provided with an ingenious fish-pass.

We continue W between the Royal Canal and the river Rye, before skirting (right) the demesne of **Carton**.

Regrettably the former seat of the Fitzgeralds, dukes of Leinster and earls of Kildare, is no longer open to the public. Richard Castle rebuilt the earlier mansion in 1739–45 (and died there in 1751, being buried in Maynooth church), and in the early 19C it was radically re-modelled by Sir Richard Morrison, who added a Regency dining-room. Other rooms retain stucco work by the Francini brothers, including, in the great saloon, the Courtship of the Gods (1739).

Maynooth (3,400 inhab.) retains its *Castle*, probably built in 1176 by Maurice Fitzgerald, a companion of Strongbow. It remained a Fitzgerald stronghold until 1535, when the rebel Lord Thomas Fitzgerald (known as 'Silken Thomas' from the silk fringes worn on the helmets of his retainers) was betrayed to Sir William Skeffington by his foster-brother Christopher Paris. Although restored to the 11th Earl in 1552, it was taken by Owen Roe O'Neill in 1647 and dismantled. A massive *Keep* remains, surrounded by several other towers, and fragments of outworks.

Adjacent is *St. Patrick's College*, founded in 1795, largely through the good offices of Edmund Burke, as a seminary for the Irish priesthood, whose continental schools were inaccessible during the Napoleonic wars. Thackeray condemned it for its 'lazy squalor'.

It succeeded a previous establishment of 1521, endowed by the 8th and 9th Earls of Kildare, suppressed in 1538. Of the two quandrangles, the first dates from 1795; the second, by A.W. Pugin, from 1845; the chapel, with its tall spire, was designed by J.J. McCarthy (1875). The Library contains some illuminated MSS, old Irish printed books and MSS, and books from Burke's library; the Museum of Ecclesiology contains church plate and vestments (including Geoffrey Keating's) used during 'Penal' times.

Taghadoe Round Tower, 4km S, although imperfect, is of unusually large dimensions.

Traversing *Kilcock*, we pass the ruined church and barrow of *Cloncurry*, before reaching *Innfield* (or Enfield).

INNFIELD TO TULLAMORE (R402; 53km). We traverse the BOG OF ALLEN to *Carbury*, the conspicuous ruined castle of which was the original stronghold of Sir Pierce de Bermingham (early 14C), enemy of the O'Connors. The existing 16C building has moulded chimneys and mullioned windows, and belonged to the Cowleys or Colleys, ancestors of the Duke of Wellington.—*Newbury Hall*, E of the town, dates from 1760.—*Mylerstown Castle*, a ruined tower to the N, was another fort of the Berminghams.—The road continues across the Bog to **Edenderry** (3,450 inhab.), on the edge of the Pale, defended by a castle of the Blundells, whose descendant, the Marquess of Downshire, was lord of the manor.

4km N, on a *Carrick Hill*, are the ruins of the church and castle of *Carraig Fheorais*, where Sir Pierce de Bermingham treacherously killed 32 of the O'Connors of Offaly who were his guests.—To the W of Edenderry lies *Monasteroris*, with a ruined church, dovecot, and monastery founded by Sir John de Bermingham c 1325; its Irish name, *Mainistir Fheorais* signifies the 'monastery of Pierce', founder of the family (see above); beyond lies another of their strongholds, *Kinnafad Castle*.

The next village of any importance on the road is (24km) **Daingean** (550 inhab.), formerly *Philipstown*, with remains of a castle erected in the 16C by Lord Justice Sir William Brabazon (died 1552). It was once the main town of Offaly (King's County), named after Philip II of Spain (husband of Mary Tudor) in whose reign Offaly became shire land. In an otherwise dull landscape, *Croghan Hill* is prominent to the N.—At *Geashill*, 3km S of the adjacent village of *Ballinagar*, is an Anglo-Norman motte and the slight remains of *Digby Castle*; see Rte 4.

10km **TULLAMORE** (7,900 inhab.), the county town of Offaly and an important agricultural and distillery centre, was the original terminus of the Grand Canal, and some interesting canal architecture remains. The principal Irish radio transmitting station has been established here, largely replacing that at Athlone. Tullamore also preserves an 18C *Markethouse*, a porticoed *Court House* of c 1835, by J.B. Keane, and a *Protestant Church* (1818) by Francis Johnston, containing the Charleville monument by Van Nost.—Castellated *Charleville Forest* (to the right of the Birr road, leading SW), of 1800–12, also by Johnston, preserves some interesting Gothic Revival details, and has recently been restored.—*Srah Castle* (1588) and *Ballycowan Castle* (1625), both W of the town on an extension of the canal (1804) are typical of the many fortified houses in the vicinity.— Some 20km to the S rises the *Slieve Bloom Mountains*.

From Tullamore we may regain our route in a variety of ways, the most rapid being at *Kilbeggan*, 12km N, via *Durrow Abbey* (see below), or alternatively by driving NW through **Clara** (2,600 inhab.), with flour mills and jute works, to (22km) *Moate*.

An interesting DETOUR is that from CLARA TO CLONMACNOISE, 24km W via (7km) the church at *Boher*, where is preserved the *Shrine of St. Manchan*, probably made at Clonmacnoise c 1130 for the abbey of Lemanaghan; the gabled yew-wood box is adorned with metalwork and cloisonné enamel, with later crude copies of figures from European Romanesque models.—The lane continues due W via the *Doon crossroads* to *Clonmacnoise* (see Rte 20A), while *Athlone* lies 12.5km NW.

TULLAMORE TO BALLINASLOE VIA CLOGHAN (55km). At 9.5km SW of Tullamore turn right off the N52 onto the R357.—At *Rahan*, 5km N of this junction, are the remains of an abbey founded in the 6C by St. Carthach, Bp of Lismore, the 12C *Church* of which still survives. The piers and capitals of the chancel arch are perhaps earlier; the rose-window, unique in Ireland, is late-Romanesque. Near by are a small ruined church (15C), with details from an older building.—19.5km *Cloghan* (500 inhab.), a neat village, 6.5km NE of which lies **Ferbane** (1,400 inhab.), with a peat-powered generating station, and *Gallan Priory*, a Georgian building 'gothicised' and retaining only slight relics of the former monastery said to have been founded in the 5C by St. Canoc. To the E is *Kilcolgan House* (Jacobean), and to the S ruins of a 15C church; remains of a monastery survive at *Lemanaghan*, 5.5km further NE.

Birr, see Rte 20B, lies 18km S of Cloghan.—3.5km NW of Cloghan we pass the keep and bawn of *Clonony Castle*, in a fair state of preservation.—To the SW lies *Shannon Harbour*, once important as standing at the junction of the Grand Canal and the navigable Shannon, with old warehouses, barracks, and a *Grand Hotel* of 1806.—9.5km *Shannonbridge*, 5.5km SW of *Clonmacnoise* for which, and for *Clonfert*, to the SW beyond the canal, see Rte 20B. We regain the main road at *Ballinasloe*, 13km NW of Shannonbridge.

Beyond Innfield we twice cross the Royal Canal before entering (13km) **Clonard** (*Cluain Ioraird*, or Erard's meadow), once the most famous bishopric in Meath, founded by St. Finian (520), an immediate successor of St. Patrick.

It was the seat of a school that numbered St. Kieran and St. Columba among its pupils, but nothing remains of its buildings except the curious panelled font of grey marble in the church and two mounds near by, one sepulchral, and the other (further NW) of military origin.

To the left of the road 3km SW is a large earthwork of low profile known as *Ticroghan Castle*, the defenders of which made a stubborn resistance to the Roundheads in 1650. *Ballyboggan*, further S, preserves the large plain church (near the river) of an Austin priory founded in the 12C.

At (6km) *Kinnegad* we enter Westmeath. Hence the N4 continues NE via Mullingar and Longford; see Rte 25A.

We bear left onto the N6, and skirting the N edge of the Bog of Allen (cf. p 183), traverse (15km) *Rochfortbridge*, named after Robert Rochfort (1652–1727), MP for Westmeath, Speaker of the Irish Parliament, and a friend of Swift, and 8km beyond, *Tyrrellspass*, laid out round a semi-circular green, where the church contains a monument by John Bacon, Jr, to the Countess of Belvedere (died 1814).—Just beyond is *Killavally*, birthplace of General Wade (1673–1748), the road-builder, with a 15C castle.

Kilbeggan, at the crossroads between Mullingar and *Tullamore* (12km S), has an old harbour on the Grand Canal, a market-house and court-house, and a distillery dating from 1757.

The mansion of *Newforest*, 5km NE, was built in 1749, while to the N stands *Middleton House*, nearer *Castletown Geoghegan*, with remains of a medieval priory and an Anglo-Norman motte and bailey.—Further NW rises the hill of *Uisneach* (or *Ushnagh*, 181m), the summit of which was an ancient Druidic assembly-place, and which commands a good view over the undulating plain.— Adjacent, to the S, is the lower hill of *Knockcosgrey*, considered the geographical centre of Ireland, on the W slope of which are the ruins of *Killeenbrack Castle*. Between the two hills, but slightly to the W, is *Killare*, the site of a 12C motte and bailey, and of an ancient monastery.

4km S of Kilbeggan, to the right of the Tullamore road, is *Durrow Abbey*, founded by St. Columba, where in the 7C was written the 'Book of Durrow', a copy of the Gospels now in Trinity College Library, Dublin. The late 10C *High Cross* and St. Columba's Well may be seen in the churchyard, and the present house, formerly occupied by the earls of Norbury, stands on the site of a castle built by Hugh de Lacy, who was murdered in 1186 by one of the workmen.

Immediately W of Kilbeggan the R436 diverges left to *Clara*, for *Clonmacnoise*, see above.

6.5km *Horseleap*, said to take its name from an exploit of Hugh de Lacy, 9.5km beyond which we enter **Moate** (1,850 inhab.), SW of which rises the *Motte of Grania*; some 8km NE, on the hill of *Knockast*, is preserved a large cairn, probably a pre-Celtic cemetery (c 2000 BC).

17km **ATHLONE** (9,450 inhab.), a market and manufacturing town, and road junction (by-pass under construction), sited astride the Shannon just below its outflow from Lough Ree, was long a military station. It may still be described (as it was in the 1840s) as 'an inconvenient, ill-built, irregular town, and not containing a single street fitted either for a general thoroughfare or business...'.

Baile Átha Luain, the Ford of Luan, was of little importance until the construction in 1210–13 of the castle by John de Grey, Bp of Norwich and Justiciar of Ireland. As the key to Connacht, Athlone was strategically important, and in 1641 Viscount Ranelagh was besieged here for almost six months by the men of Connacht. In 1690 it was held successfully for James II by Colonel Richard Grace; but in the following year, after a violent bombardment of ten days, Godert van Ginkel, William's Dutch commander, took the town by assaulting the bridge, despite a brave defence by the Irish army under Colonel Nicholas Fitzgerald and General St. Ruth. Ginkel was rewarded with the Earldom of Athlone. This bridge was replaced by the present structure in 1844. Thomas Power O'Connor (1848–1929), a prominent figure in 19C politics and journalism, and the singer John MacCormack (1884–1945) were natives of the town.

On the W bank, the *Castle*, repaired in 1547 and defaced since, but incorporating earlier work, and mutilated sections of the *Town Walls* of 1576, in spite of the bombardment of 1691 and the explosion of a magazine in 1697, still stood until recently supplanted by a housing estate.—On the E bank are the remains of a *Franciscan Abbey*, built by Cathal O'Connor and completed in 1241. A house at the corner of Church St and Northgate St is said to have been the residence (now modernised) of Ginkel after the siege. Other buildings of slight interest are the detached tower of *St. Mary's Church* and the ruins of *St. Peter's Abbey*.

3km E at *Moydrum*, in the demesne of Lord Castlemaine, whose mansion was destroyed in the 'Troubles', was the principal broadcasting station of Radio Eireann until superseded by that a Tullamore.—3km further E, at *Bealin*, is a 9C sculptured and inscribed *High Cross* of the Clonmacnoise type; note the hunting scene.

For the road from Monaghan to Athlone, see Rte 38B; and for that between Athlone and Roscommon (for Westport), Rte 25B.

A view of LOUGH REE (25.5km long and 11km across at its widest) may be obtained from a small promontory 4km N on the E bank, with wooded *Hare Island* offshore, on which are the ruins of a church said to have been built by St. Kieran before Clonmacnoise; this is one of many islets in the lough, some of them preserving ecclesiastical ruins, such as on *Saints' Island* (in fact a peninsula) near the head of the E lobe of Lough Ree.

From Athlone, the N6 bears SW to (22km) **BALLINASLOE** (*Beal Átha na Sluiaghe*, mouth of the ford of the hosts; 6,350 inhab.), a busy agricultural centre on the river Suck, a tributary of the Shannon. The town is known for its sheep fair, held in early October partly on the Fair Green, and partly in the demesne of *Garbally Court*, W of the town, built in 1819–24 by Thomas Cundy, and now a school.

In 1856, a peak year, almost 100,000 sheep and 20,000 head of cattle were sold here; it was also Ireland's largest horse fair before the advent of the internal combustion engine. It was the terminus (abandoned in 1961) of a branch of the Grand Canal.

Ivy Castle, a modern residence, has been built round the shell of the original fortress guarding the river crossing. Several 18C buildings survive, and a *Hospital*, with its domed tower (1839, by Francis Johnston) is impressive. *St. Michael's Church* (1852–58) by J.J. McCarthy (revised by Pugin) contains windows by Harry Clarke.

TO GALWAY VIA ATHENRY (62.5km). The R348 drives due W from Ballinasloe through (13km) **Kilconnell**, with a charming ruined abbey, founded in 1400 by William O'Kelly for Franciscans on the site of an earlier church of St. Canal. Its best features are the slender tower, the fine window-tracery, and part of a little *Cloister*, only 14.5m square, with arcades springing from a low wall. It contains some interesting monuments, and was probably the burial-place of St. Ruth (see below).—The country becomes bleaker and stonier as we approach (27km) **Athenry** (*Baile Átha na Rí*, ford of the kings; 1,500 inhab.), a decayed town on the Clarin preserving a number of memorials of its past importance.

The town was walled in 1211 and became the principal seat of the De Burghs and the Berminghams, and in 1316 it was held by those families against Phelim O'Connor, King of Connacht, a partisan of Edward Bruce. In 1596 it was burned by Hugh Roe O'Donnell, from which destruction it never recovered. Of the *Walls*, considerable although shattered fragments survive, including the *N Gate-Tower*, while the *Castle* preserves a rectangular keep (1238; restored) with outworks. The *Dominican Priory*, founded in 1241, dates mainly from the 15C, and contains tombs of the Berminghams, De Burghs, and other Galway families. Of the *Franciscan Friary* (1464), the Protestant parish church occupies the site of the chancel and crossing; the nave and transepts are ruinous. There is part of an old cross in the market-place.

The Galway road passes square *Derrydonnel Castle* on the left, and later meets the N6.—At (14km) *Oranmore*, by-passed, we reach *Galway Bay*. Its *Castle*, built by the Earl of Clanricarde in the 17C, surrendered to Sir Charles Coote in 1651. We shortly enter the E suburbs of *Galway* itself; see Rte 21A.

The main road veers SW through (8km) **Aughrim** (*Each Dhruim*, horse hill; 650 inhab.), where on 12 June 1691 General St. Ruth was defeated and killed by the Williamites under Ginkel.

Although the Jacobites were superior in position and numbers, the day was lost owing to the unwillingness of St. Ruth to take Sarsfield, his lieutenant, into his confidence, and to the fact that his troops in the castle of the O'Kellys had been supplied with ammunition which would not fit their muskets!

22.5km beyond, we enter *Loughrea* (see Rte 18C) and bear NW for (37km) **Galway**; see Rte 21A.

20 Wexford to Athlone

A. Via Carlow and Portlaoise

182km (113 miles). N11. 22km *Enniscorthy*—5km N80. 46km *Carlow*—36km *Portlaoise*—11km *Mountmellick*—23km *Tullamore*—39km **Athlone**.

For the road from Wexford to *Enniscorthy*, see the latter part of Rte 2A; from Enniscorthy to the road junction 8km S of *Tullow*, see the latter part of Rte 2C; both in reverse.—At this point, 32km NW of Enniscorthy, we bear left through *Ballon*, where a Bronze Age cemetery was excavated in the 19C, and after 19km enter **Carlow**, see Rte 3A. From Carlow, we continue NW, after 14km crossing the N78 10km SW of Athy.

5.5km beyond this junction a right-hand turn leads 2.5km to *Ballyadams*, with a large 17C monument of the Bowens in its churchyard.—The left-hand turn here leads shortly to *Clopock*, beneath a curious isolated rock, once fortified, S of which is *Lugacurren*, and the nearby dolmen known as the *Ass's Manger*.—3.5km W of Clopock lies **Timahoe** (*Tigh Mochua*, the house of St. Mochua), where the *Round Tower*, probably late 10C, is one of the best-preserved in Ireland. It is 29m high, and the doorway, 4.5m from the ground, has human-headed capitals and an arch richly moulded like that at Kildare. To the S of the Protestant church may be seen some ruins, perhaps of the monastery of St. Mochua.—Hence we may regain the road at *Stradbally*, 6.5km NE, or at *Portaoise*, 3.5km NW.

The N80 climbs over *Windy Gap* before traversing the long main street of **Stradbally** (i.e. Street-town; 1,000 inhab.), with the *Museum* of the Irish Steam Preservation Society (traction-engines, veteran cars, etc.), and the demesne of *Brockley Park* (1768; demolished 1944). *Stradbally Hall* was remodelled by Lanyon in the 1860s. Kevin O'Higgins (1892–1927), one of the more promising of Irish statesmen, was born at Stradbally.

We shortly pass (right) the *Rock of Dunamase* (the Fort of Masg), a very ancient fortress, recorded by Ptolemy under the name of Dunum. The steep rock, 60m high, is crowned by the extensive ruins of the castle of Dermot MacMurrough, King of Leinster, which passed by marriage into the possession of Strongbow. It was later the stronghold of the O'Mores of Leix, and after changing hands frequently during the Civil War it was blown up by Colonel Hewson in 1650.—On the opposite side of the road are the ruins of *Dysert Enos* Church, raised on the site of a hermitage of St. Aengus.

Portlaoise, see Rte 4, 11km beyond which we enter **Mountmellick** (2,950 inhab.) once a busy manufacturing town founded by the Society of Friends, but now only its 18C houses recall its prosperous past.— 3km W stands the demesne of *Summer Grove* (c 1760), and some 5km beyond, a charming stretch of the river Owenass known as *Cathole Glen*, with cascades and troutpools.

MOUNTMELLICK TO BIRR (43km). This pleasant road (R422 and R421) skirts the afforested N slopes of *Slieve Bloom*, traversing (5km) *Rosenallis*, a pretty village preserving the oldest Friends' burial-ground in Ireland (c 1700).—c 13km beyond lie the ruins of *Castle Cuffe*, one of the strongholds of Sir Charles Coote— 12km *Kinnitty*, an attractive village. On its outskirts is the demesne of *Castle Bernard* (1833, by the Pain brothers) preserving the shaft of a High Cross, a relic of St. Finan's 6C monastery, destroyed in 839.—At *Sierkieran*, 3km S, are remains of a monastery founded by St. Kieran (5C), with some curious sculptures includ ing a Sheila-na-gig on the church.—13km *Birr*; see Rte 20B.

From Mountmellick, the N80 continues NW via (14.5km) *Killeigh*, with the church of a Franciscan friary and an old churchyard, to *Tullamore*, for which and for the road hence to *Athlone*, 39km NW, see Rte 19.

B. Via Kilkenny, Roscrea, Birr, and Clonmacnoise

215km (134 miles). N25. 37km *New Ross*—R700. 24km *Thomastown*—17.5km *Kilkenny*—N77. 25.5km *Durrow*—R434 and N7. 33km *Roscrea*—N62. 19km *Birr*—36km *Clonmacnoise*—23km **Athlone**.

An ALTERNATIVE route as far as (79km) *Kilkenny* is that via *Enniscorthy*, 22km NW of Wexford on the N11, where we turn left onto the R702 towards (16km) *Kiltealy*, at the entrance of the *Scullogue Gap* (240m), the main and once the only pass across the Blackstairs Mountains, with *Mt Leinster* (793m) to the N and *Blackstairs* (732m) to the S. We make a winding descent to *Ballymurphy*, and keep right for *Borris*, crossing the Barrow at *Goresbridge* for *Gowran* (see Rte 3A); *Kilkenny* lies 14.5km further W.

For the road from Wexford to *New Ross*, see Rte 5. At New Ross we turn N to *Mountgarret Bridge*, with its old keep, before veering NW, skirting heather-covered *Brandon Hill* (516m), providing extensive views. As we descend towards the Nore through *Clonamery*, with an

11–12C church preserving a massive W door, we see on the left a hill crowned with an ornamental tower. Beneath is the wooded demesne of *Woodstock*, where a house by Francis Bindon was destroyed in 1922, once the seat of the Tighe family·

16km **Inistioge** (Teoc's or Tighe's island; pron. Inisteeg) is charmingly situated on the W bank of the Nore, here crossed by a ten-arch *Bridge* (18C). The village square is planted with lime trees, and two ancient towers, one incorporated in the parish church, recall the Austin friary that was founded here in 1210; in the neo-Classical mausoleum are some Tighe monuments, including the effigy by Flaxman of Mrs Mary Tighe (1772–1810), the author of 'Psyche'. A Norman fort in ruins stands on a rock overhanging the river.

8km *Thomastown*, just to the W of which lies **Jerpoint Abbey**; for both see Rte 3A.—We continue NW via *Bennettsbridge* to (17.5km) **Kilkenny** (see Rte 3B). The N77 ascends the Nore valley, shortly forking left, after 11km passing (right) *Foulksrath Castle* (16C on 13C foundations; now a Youth Hostel).

Some 6.5km W is **Freshford** (750 inhab.), with a central square, and the ancient *Church* originally built by St. Lactan (died 672), but rebuilt early in the 12C, with a richly decorated porch; over the inner arch are some early Irish inscriptions.—4km further SW is *Rathealy*, a trivallate ring-fort with a souterrain and foundations of both round and rectangular buildings. Nearby *Ballylarkin* church (13C), has good carved stonework.

6.5km *Ballyragget*, with a large square, preserves the 15–16C castle which was the headquarters of the Mountgarret branch of the Butler family, but which was used as barracks in 1798. Beyond Ballyragget we traverse *Ballyconra*, a seat of Viscount Mountgarret.—We cross the Portlaoise–Cashel road at *Durrow*, and turn NW just N of the village.

14.5km **Aghaboe** (*Achadh Bhó*, the land of the cow), where St. Canice founded a monastery c 550. Of the church preserving the saint's relics little remains, although it served as the cathedral of the see of Ossory c 1050–1200, when it merged with Kilkenny; but a small chapel and part of one aisle have survived from the *Dominican church* founded at the end of the 14C by the Fitzpatricks. Attached to the *Protestant church* is an old tower of the cathedral, and the walls and barns in the area are largely made up of re-used material.

We shortly cross the railway and join the N7 at *Borris-in-Ossory*, 8m. E of **Roscrea**; for both see Rte 7.

Hence we bear NW, descending the Little Bosna valley towards the Shannon, with the *Slieve Bloom* range to the E, and passing (right) after 8km the demesne of *Gloster*, where in 1749 Wesley preached in the mansion of Sir Laurence Parsons. Beyond, we pass (right) *Rathmore Castle*, before entering Birr.

Birr (3,700 inhab.), known formerly as *Parsonstown* from an earlier Laurence Parsons to whom the land was granted in 1620, was described from its very approximate central position as 'Umbilicus Hiberniae' in Sir William Petty's 'Survey of Ireland'. It is regularly built, and has a couple of attractive 'malls'. Both Catholic and Protestant churches are large early 19C Gothick buildings. A statue of the Duke of Cumberland (1721–65) formerly surmounted the column in the main square.

It was a previous Dooley's Hotel here that was burnt to the ground after a riotous invitation Meet party, which gave the Galway Hunt their nickname 'The Blazers'. An Ionic temple (1828), designed by Lord Rosse, serves as a school house.

Birr Castle and Gardens

Birr Castle, on the NE side of the town, the seat of the Earl of Rosse, was built in 1620–27 by Sir Laurence Parsons on the site of the keep of the O'Carrolls (the foundations of which survive). It was twice besieged in the 17C, in 1643 and 1690, and the fortified outworks were removed in the 18C. The facade was altered after c 1801 by John Johnston (died 1812) and his successors for Sir Laurence Parsons, 2nd Earl of Rosse, who added a battlemented third storey after a fire in 1832. The Vaubanesque outworks were constructed in 1846–48 as a famine relief project.

The *'Gardens* are open to the public daily. These were laid out by the 2nd Earl (1757–1841), and are not only noted for their box and yew hedges, but also for their magnolias, maples, conifers, and Eucryphia (from Nymans, Sussex), among a large variety of trees, shrubs and flowers, both common and rare, which make a visit to these gardens a rewarding experience. An informative booklet is available at the entrance lodge. A number of species are propagated for commercial purposes.

An additional interest is the shell of the **Rosse Telescope** (1845), 16.5m long, which stands half-left from the entrance. Built by the 3rd Earl (1800–67), the instrument was used by the 4th Earl (1840–1908) to make the first accurate measurement of the heat of the moon and to survey the spiral nebulae; the 183cm-diameter speculum was dismantled and removed to the Science Museum, London, in 1914. A small exhibition of optical flats, lenses, eyepieces, etc. is on display.

Sir Charles Parsons (1854–1931), the engineer younger brother, known for his development of the steam turbine, spent much of his boyhood at Birr; his turbine-propelled vessel, which made rings round the British fleet at the naval review of 1897, led to the general adoption of this method of propulsion for ships.

BIRR TO PORTUMNA, FOR GALWAY (25.5km) Immediately SW of Birr we turn right onto the R489, after 13km passing near (left) *Lackeen Castle*, a 16C tower-house standing in its bawn, and further W, to the left, the ruins of the abbey of *Lorrha* (13C). The *Protestant church* and *St. Ruadhans* (15C), E of the village crossroads, are also of interest. We cross the Shannon by a long bridge before entering *Portumna* for which, and the road beyond to (69km) *Galway*, see Rte 18C.

The Hiberno-Romanesque doorway of Clonfert Cathedral

BIRR TO BALLINASLOE VIA CLONFERT (45km). We follow the
R439 NW, passing (right) before (9km) *Taylor's Cross, Hill House*,
where the Rev. Arthur Nicholls, husband of Charlotte Brontë, died in
1898. They spent their honeymoon at neighbouring *Cuba Court*
(1845), recently demolished.—4km beyond lies **Banagher** (1,400
inhab.), celebrated for its fairs, its distillery, and its *Bridge* (1843)
across the Shannon. It was Trollope's first residence in Ireland as a
Post Office surveyor, and here he wrote some early unsuccessful
novels (1841–44).—*Cloghan Castle* (1249) 5km SW, slighted in 1595
and with a Georgian wing added in 1800, is now being restored.

Crossing the river, we fork right, and at 7km reach crossroads,
where the right-hand turn leads in 1.5km to **Clonfert**, which although
now no more than a hamlet, still appears as the title of the bishop of the
united sees of Killaloe, Clonfert, Kilmacduagh, and Kilfenora. The
partly ruined *Cathedral*, the successor of the monastery founded by
St. Brendan in 558 at *Cluain Fhearta* (the field of the grave), is notable
for its very fine Irish Romanesque *Doorway*, with its six recessed
orders and grotesque capitals, below a tall triangular pediment, as at
Roscrea. The chancel (early 13C) has quaintly carved corbels and

beautiful twin lancets at the E end; the S transept and slender tower were added after 1414.

7km SW of the crossroads stood *Eyrecourt Castle*, a Dutch-inspired house (late 17C), which is now a ruin, having been allowed to decay since 1920. 3km beyond to the SE, at *Meelick*, are a ruined castle of 1229 and the re-roofed church of a Franciscan friary founded in 1479.

Continuing NW from the crossroads, at 8km we leave *Laurencetown* on the left, with a tower-house, and after 6.5km pass (right) the well-preserved ruins of **Clontuskert Abbey*, an Augustinian house on the site of a monastery founded in the 9C, with a remarkable W Door of 1471, on which St. Michael, St. Catherine, and St. John the Baptist are depicted, together with a carved mermaid, pelican, and griffin, etc. *Ballinasloe* lies c 5km beyond; see p 262.

From Birr there are two routes to Athlone, the direct road via *Cloghan* (see Rte 19), *Ferbane*, and *Ballynahown*, and the more interesting road via Clonmacnoise, best approached by turning left at (16km) Cloghan for (13km) e*Shannonbridge*, with a power-station, and some massive 18C fortifications on the W bank, and there turning right for 7km.

   *CLONMACNOISE, or *Cluain Moccu* (or *Mhic*) *Nóis*—the meadow of the sons of Nós—is one of the most rewarding ecclesiastical sites in Ireland to visit. Entrance through the house near car-park.

The first church here was founded by St. Kieran in 548 on ground given by King Dermot. The saint died the following year, but the abbey grew in importance, and was sent a present by Alcuin on behalf of Charlemagne in 790. It continued to flourish in spite of the incursions of Danes, the men of Munster, and the Normans, and here Abbot Tigernach (died 1088) composed his Annals, and Maelmuire (died 1106) the 'Book of the Dun Cow' (in the Royal Irish Academy Library, Dublin). In 1552 it was plundered by the English from Athlone, and in 1568, on the death of Bp Peter Ware, the see was merged with that of Meath.

Clonmacnoise: aerial view, with O'Rourke's Tower in the centre, and the Shannon beyond

From the entrance we first follow a walk between two parallel walls on which a large number of incised grave-slabs (8–12C) have been tastelessly encrusted, to approach 'O'Rourke's Tower', a large roofless *Round Tower*, almost 19m high, with a doorway x1.5m from the ground, and eight bell-windows. It was erected a little later than the Cathedral and was large enough to contain the whole community in times of danger, but was struck by lightning in 1134.—*Teampull Conor*, to the N on lower ground, founded c 1010 by Cathal O'Connor, was converted into a parish church c 1780 and preserves only one round-headed doorway.—Beyond stand *Teampull Finghin*, on the N edge of the enclosure, believed to have been erected by Fineen Mac-Carthy Mór, preserving its chancel and the round *MacCarthy Tower* (1124), an unusually perfect example, retaining its conical top, but with its entrance at ground level, and with only two bell-windows.— Ascending towards the Cathedral we pass the much-worn shaft of the *North Cross*, while opposite the W door stands the *Great Cross* (early 10C), a monolith over 4m high, with votive inscriptions, now illegible, but said to commemorate Flann and Colman (see below). Of the elaborate sculptures, those on the E side depict the foundation of Clonmacnoise by St. Kieran, who is represented with King Dermot holding a maul. On the W side are Passion scenes, from which are derived Tigernach's alternative name for the cross—*Cros na Screaptra* (Cross of the Scriptures).

The *Cathedral* or Great Church (*Daimhlaig Mór*) was built in 904 by King Flann and Abbot Colman Conailleach, and rebuilt in the 14C by Tomultach MacDermot, from whom comes its later name of *Teampull Dermot*. The sandstone capitals of the W doorway, different in style and material from the rest of the building, were probably incorporated from the original 10C church; the choir vault and the elaborately ornamented N doorway, surmounted by a figure of St.

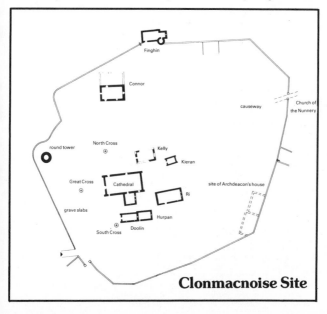

Clonmacnoise Site

Patrick between SS. Francis and Dominic, were built c 1460 by Dean Odo.

To the S is the *S Cross* (9C), with a Crucifixion, and floral and zoo-morphic ornamentation, beside the entrance to *Teampull Doolin* (12C or earlier), restored in 1689, and abutted to the E by *Teampull Hurpan* (17C).—Behind the latter stands *Teampull Righ* (Ri; or Meaghlin's Chapel; c 1200), to the N of which lie *Teampull Kieran*, with a good two-light E window, and, nearer the Cathedral, fragmentary *Teampull Kelly* (12C).

From the former, a causeway leads out of the enclosure to a track off which (after 275m), by crossing a stile (right) we approach the ruined *Church of the Nunnery*, founded by Devorguilla O'Meaghlin, wife of O'Rourke, Prince of Breffni, in 1167, with a good Romanesque door and chancel arch (restored 1867).

To the SW is the *Castle* (c 1212), built by John de Grey on the site of the Abbot's House (burnt 1135), and destroyed by the Cromwellians.

Turning E at Clonmacnoise, after 6.5km we pass (right) *Esker Hill*, on which is a slab with carvings related to the Neolithic wall-paintings of Spain, with conventional figures perhaps engaged in battle, before meeting the N62 at *Ballynahown*, where we bear NW for *Athlone*, see Rte 19. For the road NW from Athlone to **Westport**, see Rte 25B.

21   Galway and the Aran Islands

A. Galway

GALWAY, (Gaillimh) the largest town in Connacht (or Connaught; 37,850 inhab.), retains few relics of its antiquity, although a number of old merchant's houses and warehouses survive in the back streets laid out after a disastrous fire in 1473. Owing to the proximity of the 'Congested Districts', these became pullulating tenements during the later 19C, and exhibit a wretched state of dilapidation. Recent decades have brought industry to the area, and harbour facilities have been improved; indeed the town shows unusual activity, material prosperity being also apparent.

Galway claims to represent a city called *Magnata* mentioned by Ptolemy, but the first authentic account of the place occurs in the 'Annals of the Four Masters', who record a fort built here by the men of Connacht in 1124. In 1232 Richard de Burgh (or de Burgo) took this from the O'Connors, and colonised the district with fourteen families, later known as 'The Tribes of Galway', the opprobrious name given to them by the Cromwellians, mainly on account of their clannishness, which has since been regarded as a mark of distinction. Among the more prominent of this oligarchy—one might call them the lynch-pins—were the Lynch family, who are said to have provided the town with 84 mayors between the years 1485 and 1654.

In 1652 Galway was taken by Ludlow, and barbarously treated by the Parliamentary army. Its once-flourishing seaborne trade with France and Spain declined and the town decayed, in 1691 surrendering on honourable terms to Ginkel after his victory at Aughrim (cf.). Galway was the base of the old 88th Regiment, the Connaught Rangers, from the domestic annals of which Charles Lever drew numerous stories for his 'Charles O'Mally'.

John Wilson Croker (1780–1857), the politician and essayist, was a native of

Galway, as was Frank Harris (1856–1931), and Nora Barnacle (1884–1951), the wife of James Joyce. Wilfred Scawen Blunt was jailed here in 1887 for exhorting tenants of the Marquess of Clanricarde to resist eviction; he was later transferred to Kilmainham Gaol, Dublin. Stephen Gwynn (1864–1950), the author, was MP for Galway City from 1906 to 1918. Lady Gregory (1852–32) was buried here.
   The oysters of Galway are palatable, while during the spring run the river between neighbouring Lough Corrib and the sea is often packed with salmon.

Enquire at the Tourist Office, just SW of Eyre Sq., about transport to the Aran Islands; see Rte 21B.

The centre of activity is Eyre Square, in which is a monument commemorating the Gaelic writer Pádraic Ó Conaire (Patrick O'Conor; 1882–1928). In the *Bank* at No. 19 are displayed the silver Sword of Galway (early 17C), and the Great Mace (1710). The *Railway Station* is just S of the square, from the NW corner of which leads William St, extended

Lynch's Castle, Galway City

by Shop St, the main thoroughfare, although narrow. On the right of Shop St, at the corner of Abbeygate St, stands *Lynch's Castle (c 1600), the best-preserved of the mansions erected by the prosperous merchants of Galway, but degraded to house a bank. Noticeable are the mullioned and transomed windows surmounted by ornamental dripstones; medallions bear the lynx, the family crest.—In Abbeygate St are the slight remains of *Joyce's Mansion*.

Further on, in a turning to the right off Shop St, stands *St. Nicholas, founded in 1320 and many times altered since, although without marring its uniformity of design. The central tower is crowned by a curious pyramidal steeple. Its architecture is plain, although the W doorway and the decoration of the S porch is worth a glance. In the S transept is the late Gothic *Joyce Tomb*, with elaborate carving, and against the S wall a large tomb covers the remains of James Lynch FitzStephen, mayor of Galway in 1493, commemorated by the *Lynch Stone* embedded in a wall behind the church, said to record his summary 'act of Justice' in condemning his own son to death for murder and then personally hanging him when none of the citizens would serve as executioner. (The modern concept of 'Lynch Law' has no connection with this incident.)—Here also are the remains of *Burke's Mansion*, with a good doorway of 1602.

High St diverges left at the end of Shop St towards the *Wolfe Tone Bridge* (formerly Claddagh Bridge), which used to lead towards a picturesque settlement of thatched cottages known as *The Claddagh* (the beach), which were replaced by modern tenements in 1937. Further SW is the suburb and resort of *Salthill*.

There is no longer a 'king' of the Claddagh, nor are its red petticoats to be seen, and its festivals have degenerated into the realms of folklore. 'Claddagh rings', a small amulet shaped by two hands holding a crowned heart, of a type that used to be handed down as heirlooms in the female line, are reproduced for sale in the shops.

To the SE of the bridge is a fragment of *Wall*, known as the '*Spanish Arch*' (on the supposition that it protected Spanish ships trading in wine with Galway prior to 1584, when their privileges were removed). There is a local museum adjacent.

Eglinton St leads NW off William St (see above) and is continued by St. Francis St, where a church erected on the site of a Franciscan friary founded in 1296 by Sir William de Burgh, and damaged by the Cromwellians, contains the 16C tomb of Sir Peter French.—Turning left at the dull *Court House* (1812–15), by Sir Richard Morrison, we shortly cross the river by the *Salmon Weir Bridge* (1818). The lower *O'Brien Bridge* dates in part from 1342. On an island site, formerly that of the gaol, has been erected a *Catholic Cathedral* (1957–65; designed by John J. Robinson), with a copper dome, which is little less than an architectural disaster, however costly and well-intentioned.

On the far bank of the Corrib is the 'Gothic' quadrangle of *University College*, together with several modern buildings.

The college was founded in 1849 as Queen's College, and inherited the tradition of a 16C foundation which briefly gained for Galway the reputation of being 'the intellectual capital of Ireland'. It is still an important centre for the study of Gaelic language and its literature. Among Galway scholars were the historians John Lynch (c 1599–c 1673) and Roderick O'Flaherty (1629–1718).

For the roads hence to Westport via Clifden, and via Cong and Ballinrobe, see Rtes 22A and B, respectively; to Sligo, Rte 23; to Limerick, Rte 18, in reverse.

B. The Aran Islands

The *ARAN ISLANDS lie c 45km (28 miles) SW of Galway, and may be approached by regular ferries from the harbour to Kilronan on Inishmore, or from *Rossaveel* (near Costelloe, 36km W of Galway).

There are also daily flights. For details and for accommodation, apply to the Tourist Office, immediately SW of Eyre Sq., Galway; the air terminus is in Dominick St (to the W of Shop St).

The three islands are formed by a ridge of carboniferous limestone, like the Burren region (cf.), and present an almost unbroken cliff-face to the SW. The smallest island, *Inisheer* (Eastern island) lies only 8km from the Clare coast NW of the Cliffs of Moher; *Inishmaan* (Middle island) (5km long by 2km broad), is followed in alignment by *Inishmore* (Great Island, or *Aranmore*; 14.5km by 4km), by far the largest, which lies some 11km S of the Galway coast. They are in general barren and stony, most of the soil being produced by a compost of sand and seaweed. A striking feature of the landscape is the maze of dry-stone walls separating the small holdings. The vegetation is peculiar, trees being absent except in the most sheltered spots, while maidenhair and other rare ferns and rock-plants proliferate in the limestone crevices. The islanders (c 1,350 inhab.), mostly Irish-speaking, still often wear heel-less rawhide sandals or *Broga Urleathair*, commercially known as 'pampooties', and their fishing boats are the tarred canvas 'corraghs', an adaptation of the ancient coracles of stretched skin. The past life of the once unsophisticated community has been portrayed in J.M. Synge's 'The Aran Islands', first published in 1907; and in the film 'Man of Aran', by Robert Flaherty (1934); there are a number of more recent descriptions. Perhaps the most remarkable feature of the islands is the quantity—some 40 odd—of pre-Christian and early Christian remains preserved there.

Ara Naoinch, 'Ara of the Saints', owes its name to St. Enda, who obtained a grant of the archipelago from Aengus, King of Munster in c 490, and evangelised the inhabitants (the Firbolgs). He founded ten convents, which flourished, even if the islands themselves were disputed by the O'Briens and O'Flaherties. In 1587 the English subdued the latter and the monks were dispersed. In 1651 the castle of Arkyn, fortified by Clanricarde, held out for a year after the surrender of Galway, and when it fell the church of St. Enda was demolished by the Cromwellians to construct a fort, which was garrisoned for many years after the second capture of Galway in 1691.

Kilronan, the principal village on **Inishmore**, lies on the N side of *Killeany Bay*, on the S side of which is the hamlet of *Killeany*, once the headquarters of St. Enda (Einne or Eany); adjacent is the airstrip. The remains of *Arkyn Castle* are on a headland.—Passing the remains of a *Round Tower* S of Killeany, we may ascend to the diminutive but well-preserved hilltop church of *St. Benignus* (*Teampull Benen* or *Bheanáin*; 6C) with gables 4.5m high. The neighbouring cashel encloses some clocháns, probably monk's cells.—Further S, near *Iararna*, are the ruins of *St. Edna's Church*, and at the extreme SE point is a dry-stone *Round Tower*, said to mark the grave of St. Gregory.— One may return to Kilronan on foot by a track along the SW coast (a round of c 13km in all) passing *Dubh Cathair* (*Black Fort*), a promontory fort somewhat difficult of access.

The important remaining antiquities of the island can be visited from the road leading NW from Kilronan. At 1.5km we pass *Teampull Chiarain* (St. Kieran's) on the right, and a little further on (left)

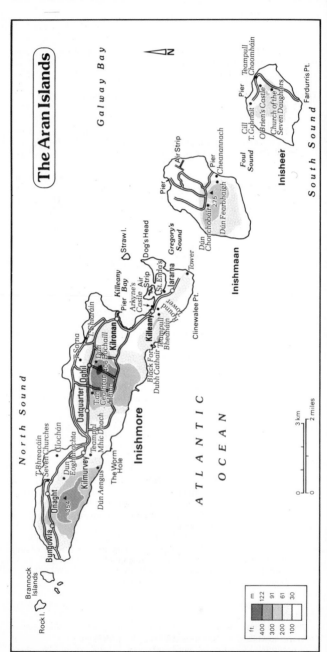

The Aran Islands

Galway Bay

N

North Sound

Brannock Islands

Rock I.

Bungowla
T-Bhreacáin
Seven Churches
Clochán
Dún Eoghanachta
Onaght
Kilmurvey
Dún Aengus
The Worm Hole
354

Inishmore

Oatquarter
Cowrugh
T.Soirbhe
Teampull Mhic Dhach
Teaghlach Dún Éinne 406 Eochaill
Dún
Aonghasa
Black Fort
Dubh Cathair
Killeany
Teampull Bheadáin
Round Tower
Clinewalee Pt.

Kilronan
Killeany
Bay
Pier Arkyne's
Castle Air
Strip St. Enda's
Iararna
Round Tower
Straw I.
Dog's Head
Gregory's Sound
Tower

ATLANTIC OCEAN

Inishmaan

Pier
Dún Chorchobair
Dún Chonchobhair 275
Dún Feárbhaígh
Pier
Cheánannach
Air Strip
Pier

Foul Sound

Inisheer

Teampull Chaoimhdin
Pier
Cill T.Gobnáit
O'Brien's Castle
Church of the Seven Daughters
Fardurris Pt.

South Sound

ft.	m
400	122
300	91
200	61
100	30

3 km
2 miles
0
0

Teampull Sorna (St. Sorney's).—On the hill to the left above *Oghil*, is *Dún Eochaill*, a fine circular fort (restored). Further W is *Teampull an Ceathrar Álainn* (the Church of the four Beautiful Saints), also restored.—Still further W, to the left, is *Kilmurvey*, with the well-preserved **Teampull Mac Duach*, dedicated to Colman MacDuagh, founder of Kilmacduagh. The original windows have sloping lintels; the round-headed E window is a later addition.

On the coast, 1.5km S, is ***Dun Aengus**, a huge prehistoric fort built on the edge of the cliffs, and which (according to some authorities) may well have been oval in shape prior to a cliff fall. It has three concentric lines of ramparts, of which the inner and middle are well preserved, while beyond the outer line is a ring of pointed stone stakes stuck in rock fissures serving as an antique Chevaux de frise; cf. *Ballykinvarga*.

S of *Onaght*, 9.5km from Kilronan, is another circular fort, *Dún Eoghanachta*, and on the N side of the road a perfect clochán, 2.5m high. Near the shore are the mis-called 'Seven Churches'; of which *Teampull Bhreacáin* (St. Brecan's) has been rebuilt and restored; the saint's grave, to the W, is marked by a richly carved cross-shaft.

The principal sight of **Inishmaan**, divided by a strait 1.5km wide (Gregory's Sound) from Inishmore, is the well-restored oval fort of *Dún Chonchobair* (Dún Conor or Chonchúir), together with *Teampull Cheanannach*, an oratory built of cyclopean blocks. To the W of the latter is *Dún Fearbhaigh*, a well-preserved fort. This island, visited by J.M. Synge sporadically between 1898 and 1902, was the scene of his play 'Riders to the Sea' (1905).

Foul Sound separates Inishmaan from **Inisheer**, on which is preserved *St. Cavan's Church* (Teampull Chaomháin); also the *Church of the Seven Daughters*, and *Dún Firmina* (or Formna), a medieval stronghold of the O'Briens, and the ruins of *Kilgobnet Church* (Teampull Ghobnait).

22 Galway to Westport

A. Via Clifden: Connemara

145km (90 miles). N59. 27.5km *Oughterard*—16km *Maam Cross*—35.5km *Clifden*—35.5km *Leenane*—30.5km **Westport**.

Connemara is the name given loosely to the beautiful but barren mountairous region bounded on the S by Galway Bay, to the E by Lough Corrib and Lough Mask, and to the N by Clew Bay, although Connemara proper (named after *Conmac*, the son of Fergus and Maeve; or from *Cuain na Mara*, harbours of the sea) is almost identical with the Barony of Ballynahinch, and is approximately that part W of a line from Killary Harbour along the Maamturk range to Gortmore, including the Twelve Bens and a wilderness of tiny lakes to the S.

Near Galway is *Iar Connacht*, a wilderness of granite; to the N of Maam Cross are the mountains of *Joyce's Country*, named after a family of Welsh extraction that settled here after the Anglo-Norman invasion, while N of Killary Harbour, in Co. Mayo, is an equally mountainous district known as *The Murrisk*. The scenery of the whole area is austerely beautiful, with some spectacular peaks and glens; its rivers team with fish; it is the country of the hardy Connemara ponies; and its tweeds are well-known. The roads are fair, and accommodation is generally good.

GALWAY TO CLIFDEN VIA THE COAST, the longer alternative road through this Gaeltacht region, is first described. Traversing the suburb of *Salthill*, the R338 skirts *Galway Bay* to (9km) *Barna*, with the slight remains of a castle of the O'Hallorans. A submerged peat-bog, c 3m below high-water mark, lends probability to the legend that Galway Bay was once a freshwater lake invaded by the Atlantic. Beyond *Furbogh* the country grows more desolate, but with good views across to the Clare coast.—9km *Spiddal*, at the mouth of the Owenboliska, preserves a few fragments of the hospice after which it is named. We continue due W through what was once part of the notorious 'Congested Districts', where crofters subsisted on the harvest of the sea—fish, and seaweed to fertilise their pocket-handkerchief fields. Some 13km beyond, the road veers NW, leaving the rock-bound peninsula of *Carraroe* to the left.

At (8km) *Costelloe* a lane forks left to *Bealadangan*, from which bridges—often built as famine relief schemes during the mid 19C—cross to the islands of *Annaghvane*, *Lettermore*, and *Gorumna*, the last only 11km N of the Aran Island of Inishmore (which, in addition to the Galway ferry, may be approached by boat from *Rossaveel*, just S of Costelloe).

From *Costelloe* (or *Casla* in Irish; also headquarters of the radio service for the Gaeltacht) we drive N to (10km) *Screeb* (9km beyond which we may regain the main road at *Maam Cross*; see below), where we turn W onto the R340 through *Gortmore*. Near by is the *Pearse Memorial Cottage*, used as a summer retreat by the patriot poet Patrick Pearse (1879–1916).—Beyond Gortmore, the road circles the hilly peninsula to the remote fishing village of (24km) *Carna*, to the E of which lies LOUGH SKANNIVE, with two crannóg-like islands; offshore is *St. MacDara's Island*, with important remains of an ancient *Oratory. To the W of Carna, on the far side of an inlet, stands the lonely tower of *Ard Castle*. From Carna we turn N, with a good view ahead of the Twelve Bens (see below), before turning left onto the R342 through *Cashel*, another angling resort at the head of land-locked *Bertraghboy Bay*, briefly patronised by Géneral de Gaulle after his retirement. At *Toombeola Bridge* we cross the Owenmore; downstream are the scanty remains of a Dominican priory founded in 1427 by the O'Flaherties.

Hence we may make a second circle (R341) seawards to **Roundstone**, a lobster-fishing village, laid out by Alexander Nimmo (1783–1832; see Sarsfield Bridge, Limerick) in the 1820s. Its environmental development' is planned. In the bay opposite is the island of *Inishnee*; while to the SW, on *Inishlacken*, are remains of a Franciscan monastery. The road passes the white shelly strand of *Dog's Bay* (formed by microscopic foraminifera) and bears round the conspicuous height of *Errisbeg* (300m). On the W slope of this isolated hill the Mediterranean heath flourishes, and it commands a curious view over the numerous small lakes of this flat waterlogged district. We reach *Ballyconneely*, with its so-called 'Coral Strand' (its grains being produced by a calcareous seaweed known as 'lithothamnion'), leaving to the W *Bunowen Castle*, beyond which are the rocks of *Slyne Head*. The exhilarating quality of the air between Roundstone and Clifden has given this route the name of the 'brandy and soda' road!

We skirt *Mannin Bay*, E of which the first aeroplane to cross the Atlantic landed in 1919 after a non-stop flight (of 16½ hours), piloted by Sir John Alcock and navigated by Sir Arthur Whitten-Brown. At *Ballinaboy* we cross the head of *Arbear Bay*, and passing a monastery, enter *Clifden*; see below.

GALWAY TO CLIFDEN VIA OUGHTERARD. The main road (N59) turns NW after crossing to the W bank of the Corrib, briefly running parallel to the river and LOUGH CORRIB (see Rte 22B) and the granitic wilderness of *Iar Connacht* (W Connaught), the ancestral home of the O'Flaherties; ahead rise the mountains of *Joyce's Country*. Beyond (right) BALLYCUIRKE LOUGH we see the lonely tower of *Caisleán na Caillighe* (or Hag's Castle). We next pass ROSS LAKE, a narrow sheet of water with a small ruined castle on an islet; to the W the bleak moors rise to *Knockalee Hill* (290m). We see to the right the ruins of the tall square keep of *Aughnanure Castle* (16C; restored), the main O'Flahertie fortress, before entering **Oughterard** (750 inhab.), an angling village on the Owenriff. Here boats may be hired to reach in Lough Corrib the 'Isle of the devout foreigner', *Inish an Ghoill Craibhthigh*, or *Inchagoill*, with the ruins of two churches, the earlier

Aughnanure Castle, near Oughterard

of which, *Templepatrick*, contains an early inscribed stone; *Teampull na Naoimh* is a good example of Irish Romanesque, restored.—Beyond Oughterard the road traverses a desolate waterlogged region, skirting (left) LOUGH BOFIN, to *Maam Cross*.

MAAM CROSS TO LEENANE (22km). Travellers wishing to drive direct to Westport may turn N here, ascending through a pass between *Leckavrea Mountain* (left; 612m) and the lower *Lackavra* before crossing *Maam Bridge*, there turning left.

In the long W arm of LOUGH CORRIB (right) stands the ruin of *Hen's Castle* (*Caisleán na Circe*), an O'Flahertie island stronghold; the present ruins date from the 13C rebuilding by the sons of Roderick O'Connor. The name is said to derive from a wonderful hen, a witch's gift to the O'Flahertie, which would lay enough eggs during a siege to feed a garrison; perhaps a more likely story is that the castle was saved from the Joyces by the prowess of Grace O'Malley (cf.), O'Flahertie's wife.—We ascend Joyce's River, a salmon and trout stream, with *Lugnabricka* rising on our right, into the heart of *Joyce's Country*. On the left rises the *Maamturk Mountains* (701m); on the right beyond *Kilmeelicken* church, a track diverges right for *LOUGH NAFOOEY (dangerous descent) and LOUGH MASK (see Rte 22B). We pass the lonely *Joyce's Graveyard* and descend the shoulder of the *Devil's Mother* (right; 648m) to *Leenane*, see below.

From Maam Cross the main road continues W, skirting the S bank of LOUGH SHINDILLA, with rugged *Leckavrea* (or *Corcogemore*; 612m) rearing up to the right. The valley soon opens out to the right, flanked by the *Maamturk range* (701m), the boundary between Connemara and Joyce's Country.—We traverse the hamlet of *Recess*, with an ugly church, an angling resort between *Glendollagh* and DERRYCLARE LOUGH (beside which the finest green Connemara 'marble' is quarried), with LOUGH INAGH further N.

Immediately N of Recess rises *Lissoughter*, commanding a fine *View* both of the Maamturk Mountains (NE), the most conspicuous peak of which is *Letterbreckaun* (667m; although the highest summit is 701m). To the W rise the group of mountains known as ***Twelve Bens** (sometimes corrupted to the 'Twelve Pins'), named in Irish *Benna Beola* (see below).

The road continues W, skirting the N bank of BALLYNAHINCH LOUGH, and below the Twelve Bens. From the central peak, *Benbaun* (728m), a series of ridges radiates in a roughly star-shaped formation, each rising in a number of quartzite peaks, all over 520m. Much of their beauty lies in their symmetrical cone-like forms, the colour of the heaths and lichens covering them, and the glint of the quartz on a sunny day, which adds much to the enchantment of the scene.

On the SE ridge, extending towards DERRYCLARE LOUGH, are *Bencollaghduff*, *Bencorr*, and *Derryclare*, with *Bencorrbeg* an irregular offshoot towards LOUGH INAGH. On the S ridge are *Benbreen*, *Bengower*, and *Benlettery*, with *Benglenisky* a little W. The W ridge has as its summits *Muckanaght* and *Bencul/lagh*; and on the N ridge is *Benbrack*.

Benlettery (580m), immediately above the road, offers the most rewarding ascent, owing to its more isolated position. From the summit we see Bertraghboy Bay to the S, with Errisbeg on the right and Cahel Hill on the left. To the SW is the labyrinth of lakes towards Clifden; to the NW Inishark and Inishbofin are seen out to sea; and to the E is the long ridge of the Maamturk Mountains, with the melancholy *Pass of Maumeen* that separates them from the Corcogemore.

On the S bank of the lough stands *Ballynahinch Castle* (now a hotel), once the residence of Richard Martin (1754–1834, at Boulogne), or 'Humanity Martin', known as the 'King of Connemara', and the founder of the RSPCA (1824).

Some 9km W of the lough we enter **Clifden** (800 inhab.), a good centre from which to explore the area, with a wide main street on a long ridge and a parallel street, standing at the head of the N arm of its bay. It has a flourishing lobster fishery, and is reputed for its Connemara tweeds. The derelict ruin of its *Castle* (1815), built by John D'Arcy, who then developed the town, is on the shore to the W.— *Gortrummagh Hill*, NW of the castle, offers panoramic views of the neighbourhood, including the Twelve Bens and the lake-studded district to the SE towards Roundstone (see above).

Climbing N from Clifden we have a brief view of the narrow inlet of *Streamstown Bay* on our first descent, on the N side of which is *Doon Castle*, a ruined O'Flahertie stronghold.

The next left-hand turn leads to (5km) *Cleggan*, a small fishing-village, whence boats may be hired to the offshore islands of *Inishbofin* (NW) and *Inishark*, with fine coastal scenery. *High Island* or *Ard Oilean* (off *Cleggan Head* to the W) preserves the considerable remains of a 7C monastery established by St. Fechin, but inaccessible except in fine weather. Inishbofin has a good harbour guarded by a 17C castle, and traces of a monastery founded by St. Colman in c 660.

The N59 bears NE and descends towards the broad hill-girt fjord of *Ballynakill Harbour*, with *Tully Mountain* (356m) rising boldly to the N. At the head of the bay is the village of *Letterfrack*, originating in a Quaker colony. The fuchsia hedges confirm the mildness of the climate. *Diamond Hill*, to the S, commands a fine view of the coast and of the Twelve Bens to the SE.

A by-road leads N to *Renvyle*, with several sandy strands. Ludwig Wittgenstein spent the summer of 1948 at Rosro Cottage, in the neighbourhood. What is now the *Renvyle House Hotel* was long the residence of Oliver St. John Gogarty, who here entertained Shaw, Yeats, and Augustus John.—*Renvyle Castle*, a ruin to the W, was held successively by the Joyces, O'Flaherties, and the Blakes. Beyond it are a dolmen and a ruined church. On *Crump Island* (offshore to the NW) is a ruined church, while on *Inishturk*, some 11km out to sea, with its twin peaks, are remains of a church built by St. Columba.

From Letterfrack the main road runs inland skirting an area of c 2000 hectares designated the *Connemara National Park* to the S, and traversing the *Pass of Kylemore*, bounded to the left by *Doughruagh*, and by the Twelve Bens to the S. We shortly pass, on the N side of LOUGH POOLACAPPUL, amid a forest of rhododendrons, the mock-Tudor residence of the Manchester merchant and Irish politician Mitchell Henry (1826–1910). Known as *Kylemore Abbey* (1866), since 1920 it has been a convent of the Benedictine Dames Irlandaises (whose house in Ypres was destroyed in 1914). Below *Garruan* (600m) we skirt the N side of KYLEMORE LOUGH, the E end of which commands a fine close view of the Twelve Bens.

To the right, beyond the lake, a 'famine road' built in the 1840s ascends SE up the glacier-scored valley, its lower end retaining numerous morain boulders, to LOUGH INAGH and to *Recess*, see above.

The main road skirts the S end of hill-girt LOUGH FEE (beyond the N end of which is *Salrock*, with its ruined church and graveyard) before descending (Views) towards the shore of *Killary Harbour*, 16km long, one of the most impressive of the Connemara inlets, a true fjord with deep water between steep mountains. On the N side rise *Muilrea* (*Mweelrea*) and *Ben Gorm* (817m and 700m respectively), separated by the defile of Delphi; due E stands the *Devil's Mother* (648m). At the far end of the estuary lies *Leenane*, a centre for fishing and for the exploration of this wild mountain region.

LEENANE TO WESTPORT VIA LOUISBURGH (53km), the longer but more interesting road (R335) turns left at Aasleagh church, and bears round the head of the fjord, skirting Ben Gorm. *Aasleagh* is the centre of the Erriff salmon-fishery. At *Bundorragha* we turn due N up the narrow valley dominated to the W by *Muilrea*, best ascended from the shore of Killary Harbour further W.

The easiest route is by a cut in the face of the hill and bearing over a saddle onto the main ridge. The *View* of the coast extends from Slyne Head to Achill, while immediately NE is the ridge overhanging the Delphi valley. An alternative descent is to cross the depression on the N between *Benbury*, connected to a third peak (*Benlugmore*) by a finely scarped ridge. From the summit of the former we strike N to avoid the precipitous NE face, to regain the road N of GLENCULLIN LOUGH, a heavy and boggy route not to be attempted after wet weather.

Passing (left) LOUGH FIN, we reach *Delphi*, a fishing lodge near the S end of sombre DOO LOUGH (3.5km long), well-deserving its name of 'Black Lake' in stormy weather. Skirting its N side, flanked by the *Sheeffry Hills* (761m), we climb out of the valley and descend past *Cregganbaum*, with a megalithic tomb, and across a desolate moor to the village of **Louisburgh**, taking its name from Louisburgh, Nova Scotia, at the capture of which in 1758, Henry Browne (uncle of the 1st Marquess of Sligo) was present as a young officer. There are some good beaches in the neighbourhood, at *Cloghmoyle* to the N, and at *Old Head* (NE). To the SW, also approached direct from Cregganbaum, are the extensive sands of *Carrowniskey Strand*, to the W of which is *Caher Island*, the haunt of wild geese, with *Inishturk* behind it; see above.

NW of Louisburgh, offshore from *Roonah Quay*, lies **Clare Island** (1,993 hectares); a mountainous but fertile island rising to 461m at *Knockmore* on the NW side, commanding a good view of the S coast of Achill. In the centre of the island are the ruins of a Carmelite *Friary* founded in 1224, on the N side of which is the tomb of Grace O'Malley or some member of her family. The *Castle*, at the E end of the island, was the stronghold of Grace O'Malley (Grainne ni Mháille; c 1530–c 1600), the Amazonian queen of the island, as famous for her piratical forays as for her modern way of treating her husbands, the first of whom was the O'Flahertie of Connemara. It is said that her castle in Lough Corrib was saved from the Joyces by her bravery. On her death she married Sir Richard Burke of Mayo (called MacWilliam Oughter), on condition that at the end of a year either party might end the union by merely dismissing the other. In due time she closed the doors against MacWilliam as he was approaching Carrigahowley Castle, having first astutely garrisoned all his castles with her partisans. Also well known is the story of her interview with Elizabeth I in London, from whom she refused all favours, proudly regarding the English queen as her equal; for her exploit at Howth, see Rte 1G.

From Louisburgh we drive E, skirting the S side of island-strewn *Clew Bay* (see Rte 24A), with **Croagh Patrick** (*Cruach Phádraig*; 763m) on the right.

The ascent of the 'rick' of St. Patrick may be made from the church of *Leckanvy* or (better) from *Murrisk Abbey*, further E, a house of Austin friars founded by the O'Malleys in 1457, with an aisleless church retaining a fine E window.

The summit, which appears to be conical from a distance, is in fact a small plateau crowned by a chapel. Here, it is said, St. Patrick banished with the tintinnabulation of his bell all the noisesome reptiles of Ireland, each time he rang the bell hurling it down the precipice of *Lugnanarrib* (to the S), its trajectory being accompanied by an avalanche of toads, serpents, and other repellent beasts. The bell was conveniently returned to him by fielding spirits. The *View extends S to the Twelve Bens (see above), and to the N across Clew Bay to the mountains of Achill; to Nephin (NE), and beyond to Slieve League in Donegal. Clare Island is prominent out to sea.

9km E of Murrisk we enter *Westport*; see Rte 24A.

The main road from Leenane ascends the Erriff valley under the lee of the *Partry Mountains*, rising to *Benwee* and *Maumtrasna* (681m and 671m respectively). Beyond *Erriff Bridge* the country opens out. Passing (left) LOUGH MOHER, we get a good view of *Croagh Patrick* (see above) and *Clew Bay* as we descend the wooded Owenwee valley towards *Westport*; see Rte 24A.

B. Via Cong and Ballinrobe

85km (53 miles). N84. 26km *Headford*—R334. 15km *Cong*—11km *Ballinrobe*—N84 and R330. 33km **Westport**.

Boats may be hired from Galway for the excursion to Cong through Lough Corrib.

A short DETOUR may be made immediately N of Galway by forking left past the slight remains of *Terryland Castle*, built by the De Burghs in the 13C, and *Menlough Castle*, a 16C mansion burnt in 1910, to the S shore of Lough Corrib and the black marble quarries of *Anglihan*, to the E of which we regain our road.

*Lough Corrib (17,400 hectares), 43.5km long and very irregular in outline, is one of the largest lakes in Ireland. For the most part it is very shallow and studded with islets and shoals, but it narrows considerably some 16km N of Galway, and towards its N end a depth of 45m has been recorded. It also divides Co. Galway into two unequal and very diverse parts: to the E is comparatively fertile grazing country extending towards the Shannon, while to the W is the barren, mountainous *Joyce's Country* and *Connemara*; see Rte 22A.

The N84 bears NE, passing *Ballindooly Castle*, before veering almost due N across the Clare river, with the towers of *Claregalway* conspicuous to the right; see Rte 23.

At 12km a road leads left to *Annaghdown* (*Eanach Dúin*, the marsh of the fort), 5.5km W on the shore of Lough Corrib, once the seat of the oldest bishopric in Co. Galway. A monastery and nunnery were founded there by St. Brendan, who died there in 577 after appointing his sister Brigid head of the latter. The extant ruins are those of a Franciscan church and friary, a Norman castle, and the bishop's house; in the graveyard are the ruins of a later church, with a fine E window transferred from the friary church. We may regain the main road by a lane leading N from the abbey.

Headford (750 inhab.), a village sheltered by the woods of *Headford Castle*, lies 2.5km S of the Black River, separating Galway from Mayo.

Hence the main road bears NE via (6.5km) *Shrule*, with the ruins of an abbey and the tower of a castle. The bridge was the scene of the treacherous ambush in which a party of Parliamentarian troops and others, under Sir Henry Bingham (retreating from Castlebar under safe-conduct), were set upon and massacred by one Edmund Bourke, a clansman of the Earl of Mayo.

Killursa Church, some 3km W of Headford, marks the site of a 7C monastery, later enlarged, founded by St. Fursa, a disciple of St. Brendan.

Our route follows the R334 NW, shortly passing (left) the ruins of ***Ross** (or *Rosserrily*) **Abbey**, founded in 1351 and refounded by Franciscans in 1498, but not finally abandoned until 1765. The church is of the usual aisled cruciform plan with a central tower, but has round-headed arches in the S aisle and the transepts, an uncommon feature at so late a date. On the N side of the church are small but nearly perfect cloisters, and its dependencies, among them the kitchen and guest-house, are particularly well preserved.

After crossing the Black River, we pass between (left) the ruins of *Moyne Castle*, with a church site enclosed by a cashel, and (right) the ruins of *Kinlough Castle* (16C) and a 13C church. To the W we have a view of Benlevy, with its flat top (see below), and, beyond, the mountains of Joyce's Country. Further NW, on the far side of Lough Mask, are the Partry Mountains.

At *Cross* we diverge left, passing near *Moytura House*, built by Sir William Wilde in 1865, to approach **Cong**, a small village deriving its name (*cunga*, a neck) from its position on an isthmus between Lough Corrib and Lough Mask, near the mouth of a swift stream flowing into the former (see below). It was one of the locations for the film 'The Quiet Man'. In the village is a 14C cross with an inscription to Nicol and Gilbert O'Duffy, abbots of Cong. Below the village is *Ashford Castle* (now an hotel), an ostentatious 'baronial' pile erected c 1870 by James Franklin Fuller for Arthur Edward Guinness, Lord Ardilaun (the title also being the name of an adjacent islet). Beside the entrance is an ugly prefabricated modern church (containing stained glass by Harry Clarke) abutting the beautiful little ruin of *Cong Abbey. This was founded for Augustinians in 1128 by Turlough O'Connor, King of Ireland, probably on the site of a 7C establishment of St. Fechin. It was further endowed by Roderick O'Connor, his son, the last native king, who spent his final 15 years in the abbey, dying there in 1198. The ruins preserve several fine doorways of a type transitional between Romanesque and Gothic and showing French influence, and a tall early Gothic E window. The cloisters were partly rebuilt in 1860, displaying the work of Peter Foy, a local mason employed by Lord Ardilaun's father.

The stream connecting Lough Mask and Lough Corrib has three parts of its course of 6.5km underground, the porous limestone being easily penetrated. The subterranean channel is accessible from above at a number of places including the *Pigeon Hole* (1.5km N) among other cavities, each with its fanciful name and legend. A curiosity of a different kind is the *dry Canal* between the two lakes, dug in the 1840s as a famine relief work with the idea of extending navigation; when completed, it was found quite to be incapable of holding water, owing to the porous nature of the rock!

The R345 leads W from Cong across the isthmus between the loughs to *Clonbur*, there bearing S, skirting the N end of LOUGH CORRIB below flat-topped *Benlevy* (416m; views) to *Cornamona*. Beyond *Claggan* we pass (left) *Hen's Castle* (see Rte 22A) before reaching (20km) *Maam Bridge*, the junction for roads leading NW to *Leenane* and S to *Maam Cross*.

Between Cong and the Westport road continuing N from Cross there are remains of several stone circles and cairns. Some have assumed that the battlefield of Southern Moytura was near here, the scene of the first great defeat of the Firbolgs by Tuatha dé Danaan, seven years before they were finally crushed at Northern Moytura.

From Cong we bear NE via *Neale*, in the demesne of which is a curious ornamental monument incorporating medieval sculptures and an inscription of 1757. The house was demolished c 1939.—A minor road nearer Lough Mask passes *Loughmask House*, on the shore beside a ruined castle, notorious as the residence of Captain Charles Boycott (1832–97), Lord Erne's agent, the reaction of the local tenantry to his inconsiderate treatment during the Land League agitation adding a new word to the English language. The neighbouring island of

Inishmaine has remains of a monastery burned in 1227, where the church preserves a late-Romanesque chancel arch, a good E window, and an archaistic square-headed doorway.

Ballinrobe (1,450 inhab.) is a convenient village from which to explore the E bank of LOUGH MASK (16km long by 6.5km wide). On the far shore is an Irish-speaking district backed by the Partry Mountains, the most prominent peak of which is *Maumtrasna* (671m). Beyond Ballinrobe the road passes between Lough Mask and LOUGH CARRA to (10km) *Partry*, where we turn left, leaving the N40 to continue N to (19km) *Castlebar*; see below. Circling the hills to the W, after 19km we pass (left) the church of *Aille* and the remains of *MacPhilbin's Castle* crowning a mound.—About 2.5km SW of the next crossroads is *Aghagower* (*Achadh-fhobhair*, field of the spring), where there is a *Round Tower* of rude workmanship 18m high wanting its conical cap, and a ruined church and oratory.—4km beyond this turning we enter **Westport**, see Rte 24A.

6km N of Partry (1.5km to the right of the Castlebar road), lies *Ballintober Abbey* (also *Ballintubber*). The over-restored church was founded by Cathal O'Connor, King of Connaught, for Austin canons in 1216, and largely rebuilt in 1270 after a fire. The main doorway surmounted by a lofty gable is early Gothic work; the rest of the nave; the choir, which preserves an unusual vault, has purely Romanesque windows at the E end. In a chapel S of the choir is a 16C altar-tomb with remains of a row of weepers incorporated. The cloister has likewise been restored.—The same road bears round the N end of Lough Carra to the shell of *Moore Hall*, the birthplace of George Moore (1852–1933), described in his novel 'The Lake' (1905); his ashes lie beneath a cairn on an offshore islet.— For *Castlebar*, see Rte 24A.

23 Galway to Sligo

141km (87 miles). N17. 33km *Tuam*—29km *Claremorris*—34km *Charlestown*—46km **Sligo**.

The much-improved Tuam road quits Galway by *Prospect Hill* and runs NE.—11km *Claregalway*, on the Clare river, preserves the massive square *Castle* of the De Burghs that saw so much fighting in the Cromwellian wars, and a *Franciscan Friary*, founded in 1290 and endowed by John de Cogan. Ostensibly suppressed at the Reformation, it was described by Bp Pococke in 1765 as still 'used as a Romish masshouse'. The most attractive feature of the ruins is the graceful tower, 24m high; the choir contains a De Burgh tomb.

We shortly leave on the left a road to Headford that passes *Cregg Castle*, the home of Richard Kirwan (1733–1812), the chemist, and his brother Dean Walter Blake Kirwan (1745–1805), the preacher.

The main road continues NE across the plain, with the isolated hill of *Knockma* (the 'Hill of the Fairies') rising prominently to the NW.

The right-hand fork leads to (77km) *Roscommon* via (45km) the demesne of *Mount Bellew* (landscaped by Hely Dutton), shortly passing the battlefield of *Knockdoe*, where in August 1504 Gerald Fitzgerald, the Great Earl of Kildare, defeated his son-in-law Ulick de Burgh.—*Knockmoy Abbey*—to the left 15km beyond this turning—was founded for Cistercians by Cathal O'Connor 'of the Red Hand' to commemorate his victory over the English under Almeric St. Lawrence in 1189 (*Cnocmuaidhe*, hill of the slaughter); there is a Romanesque triplet in the Choir, and traces of murals on the N chancel wall, and elsewhere.

We re-cross the Clare river before entering **TUAM** (pron. Chum; 4,350 inhab.), the ecclesiastical capital of Connacht, the seat of a Catholic archbishop and a Protestant bishop (until 1834 an archbishop), the see of the latter being united with Killala and Achonry. The see was founded by St. Jarlath (died 540), the master of St. Brendan and St. Colman of Cloyne, while in 1049 Aedh O'Connor, king of Connacht, established his residence here.

The most interesting building in the town is the spired *Protestant Cathedral* (St. Mary's), W of the centre, founded c 1130 (probably by Turlough O'Connor) and largely rebuilt in 1861–63 in an attempt at reproducing the original style. (If shut, apply at the drapers to the E of the Tuam Cross.) The only part of the earlier structure which has survived, the chancel, is unexpectedly of red sandstone. The main *Chancel Arch*, long used as a doorway, is one of the finest examples of 12C Romanesque work in Ireland, with its six recessed orders, elaborate mouldings, and richly sculptured capitals. There is a fine triplet E window with round-headed arches, and beyond that a 14C Gothic church, erected when the nave was demolished. Recently restored, it is now used as a synod hall. Note the marquetry of the Italian Baroque choir stalls (c 1740).

The *Cross of Tuam* in the Market Square, once taller, bears inscriptions in honour of Turlough O'Connor and Abbot O hOisin, archbishop in 1152.—The *Catholic Cathedral*, to the E, in the late Gothic style of 1827–37, is over-decorated both without and within. A *Museum* has been installed in *Farrell's Gate Mill* (17C), describing the processes of milling.—*Bermingham House* (1730), 3km E, may be visited.—At *Kilbannan*, c 3km NW, is a ruined *Round Tower*.

From Tuam, a more direct road (N83) to *Charlestown* (55km N) traverses (14km) *Dunmore*, with a ruined abbey founded in 1428 on the site of an alleged monastery of St. Patrick, and (17km beyond; see Rte 25B) *Ballyhaunis*.

We continue N before bearing NW to traverse (29km) *Claremorris* (see Rte 25B), 11km beyond which we veer NE through *Knock*. Apparitions seen in 1879–80 in the Catholic Church followed by miraculous cures brought the village temporally into the limelight. A modern basilica with a spiky spire has been erected, which was visited by Pope John Paul II (the first Pope to visit Ireland) in 1979. A huge hill-top runway has also been laid out. The road beyond is of slight interest; another 23km brings us to the Longford-Castlebar road at *Charlestown* (see last para of Rte 25A), which we cross, and shortly enter Co. Sligo.

11km **Tobercurry** (or *Tubbercurry*; 1,150 inhab.) is a small market town with one long street.

9km to the E lie the ruins of a castle and church at *Bunnanaddan*, near which was found the Moylough Belt (a belt-shrine, now in the National Museum, Dublin). The *Slieve Gamph* or *Ox Mountains*, are prominent to the NW.

The Sligo road rounds an isolated hill on the right beyond which a lane leads right to (2.5km) *Achonry*, the seat of a bishopric founded in the 7C by St. Nathy, a disciple of St. Finian of Clonard. It is now a mere hamlet with formless ruins of a church near the present one.—On the opposite side of the main road, at the foot of *Knocknashee*, is the ruined Franciscan *Court Abbey*, with a square tower over 27m. high.

We descend into the valley of the Owenmore, with *Templehouse* demesne and TEMPLEHOUSE LOUGH on the right; in the demesne are the ruins of a castle said to have belonged to the Knights Templar.— Beyond the bridge a road leads left to (5km) *Coolaney*, where a curious bridge spans the Owenbeg; *Moymlough Castle*, near by, is a ruined O'Hara stronghold; their more recent seat is at *Annaghmore*, an attractive demesne on the Owenmore left of the main road, beyond

which we meet the N4 at *Collooney*; for the road hence to Sligo, 11km
N, see latter part of Rte 26A; for **Sligo** itself, Rte 26B.

24 Westport to Sligo

A. Via Castlebar and Charlestown

104km (63 miles). N60. 18km **Castlebar**—N5. 29km *Swinford*—11km
Charlestown—N17. 35km *Collooney*—N4. 11km **Sligo**.

WESTPORT (3,400 inhab.), laid out in 1780 for Peter Browne, 2nd Earl
of Altamont (who had married a sugar heiress), possibly by a French
architect, still preserves some of its elegance. The canalised river Car-
rowbeg, flanked by tree-lined malls, is crossed by attractive old
bridges. To the S is the *Octagon*, once containing a statue of a later
benefactor of the town, the banker George Glendenning, but this was
demolished and the inscription obliterated in 1922. It was the scene of
the influential meeting in June 1879 at which Davitt and Parnell organised the Irish Land League. Canon James Owen Hannay (1865–
1950; the novelist 'George A. Birmingham') was rector here between
1892 and 1913.

To the W of the town, reached by a turning to the right of the main
road climbing S from the Octagon, is the entrance to the demesne of
*Westport House.

The seat of the Marquess of Sligo was built by Castle in 1730–34
round an earlier house (the walls of which were lapped by the waters
of Clew Bay), and additions were made c 1778 by Thomas Ivory and
James Wyatt. De Quincey was a guest here in 1800. From the
imposing *Entrance Hall*, to the left of which is the *Library*, we may
enter a series of rooms including the *Long Gallery*, containing family
portraits by Opie, Beechey, and Reynolds; the *Dining-room*, preserving good plasterwork and a fine set of four sideboards; a smaller
dining-room decorated with equestrian paintings, and a further gallery. Marble stairs ascend to the First Floor; on the walls are an interesting series of local views by George Moore and James Arthur
O'Connor (1792–1841), the latter responsible also for two landscapes
in the hall; notice also the Holy Family, by Rubens. The violin of J.M.
Synge is preserved here; note the naval prints, and Chinese wall-
papers of c 1780.

Further W is *Westport Quay*, preserving some late 18C warehouses.
Westport Bay leads into the much larger *Clew Bay, 24km long and
9.5km wide. Its E end is occupied by a host of small islands having the
appearance of stranded whales, formed by submerged drumlins, and
rendering navigation difficult. Beyond rises *Clare Island* (cf.). To the
SW is the cone of *Croagh Patrick* (cf.), to the NW the *Nephin Beg* range
and the *Corraun peninsula* (rising to 521m), with *Achill* beyond; see
Rte 24B.

Climbing E from Westport, and passing (left) a series of small
loughs, we approach (18km) **Castlebar** (6,400 inhab.), the uninteresting county town of Mayo, with a tree-bordered green; its ham,
however, is worth tasting.

The town was founded by Sir John Bingham and incorporated in 1613. In 1641 Sir

Henry Bingham was forced to surrender to the Irish Confederates under the Earl of Mayo, and although he marched out with a safe-conduct his party was massacred at Shrule Bridge. In 1798 Géneral Humbert's invading French army put to flight a stronger force under General Lake at the engagement known as the 'Castlebar Races', and entered the town in triumph; comp. Ballinamuck.

From Castlebar a minor road (R310) bears NE to (15km) *Pontoon*, skirting the long slopes of *Croaghmoyle*, rising to the left to 429m. This small angling resort takes its name from the *Pontoon Bridge* (near a perched block of granite, one of many in the vicinity) crossing the stream between LOUGH CONN, to the N (14.5km long, 5km wide) and LOUGH CULLIN (5km square), known for their 'gillaroo' or white trout, as well as the common brown trout. Their waters rise and fall at different times, in consequence the stream connecting them flows in either direction alternately. Crossing the bridge, we may turn left, briefly skirting Lough Conn before veering away towards *Ballina* (see Rte 24B), some 17.5km N.—The W bank of the lough is followed to (20km) *Crossmolina*, passing (left) *Nephin* (804m; easily ascended), and (right), on the peninsula of *Errew*, a fragmentary abbey on the lough shore; see Rte 24B.

The main road from Castlebar bears NE through (9km) *Turlough*, with a well-preserved *Round Tower*, and, 4km beyond, *Bellavary*.

BELLAVARY TO BALLINA (27km). The N58 turns NE through *Strade*, the birthplace of the influential Fenian leader Michael Davitt (1846–1906), with a museum of momentoes, and with the interesting remains of **Strade Abbey**, founded originally for Franciscans, but transferred in 1252 to the Dominicans. Much of the building is 15C work; note the fine sculptured *Tomb on the N wall of the chancel.—We shortly bear N through *Foxford* (1,000 inhab.), birthplace of William Brown (1777–1857), an admiral in the Argentine service, and with flourishing woollen industries. *Cromwell's Rock* marks the spot where the Protector and his army are said to have forded the river Moy. Continuing N on the N57, with the SW end of *Slieve Gamph* (or *Ox Mountains*) on our right, we follow the W bank of the Moy.— Some 5km E, beyond the Moy, part of the 12C church of *Kildermot* stands on the shore of LOUGH BALLYMORE. We pass (left) the demesne of *Mount Falcon* (now a hotel) before entering *Ballina*, see Rte 24B.

Continuing E from Bellavary, after 11km passing (left) at *Meelick* a *Round Tower* 21m high, we traverse the agricultural town of *Swinford* (1,350 inhab.) 5km beyond.—At *Charlestown*, (see Rte 25A) 11km further E, we turn NE and follow the road thence to Sligo described in Rte 23. For **Sligo** itself, see Rte 26B.

B. Via Newport, Mulrany, Achill Island, Belmullet, Killala, and Ballina

217km (135 miles), not including the excursion to **Achill**. N59. 12km *Newport*—19km *Mulrany* (for the *Corraun peninsula* and Achill)—32km *Bangor*—R313. 19km *Belmullet*—R314. 64km *Killala*—12km *Ballina*—N59. 59km **Sligo**.

The main road from Belmullet to Ballina is only 13km shorter than the route circling the coast.

Between Westport and Newport we traverse a broken drumlin district, without obtaining much of a view of Clew Bay to the W. The village of **Newport** (450 inhab.), an angling resort, both for sea-fishing in Clew Bay and for sea-trout in LOUGHS BELTRA (NE), FURNACE, and FEEAGH, is dominated by an old railway viaduct and an ungainly *Church* in the Irish Romanesque style (1914; by R.M. Butler).—Beyond the village we veer W at *Burrishoole*, crossing the river that drains Lough Furnace, leaving on the right the old road with its many-arched bridge.

On the E bank of the river (left) are the remains of *Burrishoole*

Abbey, founded for Dominicans by MacWilliam in 1486. The church preserves a solid central tower, the vault of which survives, supported by Romanesque arches leading into the S transept. The four-light E window remains, and there are traces of stone stalls; relics of dependencies lie to the N.

We continue due W, with *Cushcamcarragh* (712m), dominating the SW part of the *Nephin Beg* range to the right, but the road only allows intermittent views of *Clew Bay* and the Murrisk ranges beyond. We pass (left) the square tower of Grace O'Malley's castle of *Rockfleet* (15–16C; formerly *Carrigahowley*, scene of her defiance of her husband; cf. *Clare Island*), and 6.5km further W, *Rossturk Castle* (19C).

Mulrany (or *Mallaranny*), a village standing on the narrow isthmus that joins the Corraun peninsula to the mainland, enjoys a mild climate; fuchsias, rhododendrons, and Mediterranean heath abound. To the N it is dominated by *Claggan* (382m). The main road turns due N here, but the circuit of the *Corraun* (rising to 521m) and the excursion to Achill is recommended.

ACHILL ISLAND (3,100 inhab.) is approached by following the R319 across the isthmus and circling the N side of the Corraun peninsula, then crossing to the island by a swivel bridge of 1888. It is said that there were no foxes there before the bridge was erected, and that the islanders were then forced to protect their poultry with fences. The village of *Achill Sound* lies on the far bank of a narrow strait some 9.5km long and 1km wide, connecting *Clew Bay,* where its entrance is guarded by *Achillbeg Island,* with *Blacksod Bay,* its S part almost landlocked by *Inishbiggle.*

Achill is the largest island off the Irish coast (c 147km^2), and is largely covered with wild heather or bog. Its Irish-speaking inhabitants barely subsisted, relying on remittances from abroad until comparatively recently, when a modest prosperity was gained from tourist traffic and the development of cottage industries. Shark-fishing is extensively practised (April–July), which one would think might prejudice its strands, but the sharks are of the harmless basking variety.

The main road runs NW across the island through rhododendron plantations and the village of *Cashel* towards its summit level, with a view of *Slievemore* ahead, with *Croaghaun* further to the W, and *Minaun* to the S.

A road shortly leads right to *Dugort* on the N coast, where below the older cluster of cabins is 'The Settlement'.

Now a small tourist resort, it was founded in 1834 by a well-meaning Protestant clergyman, the Rev. E. Nangle, who erected schools and a printing-press. This aroused the rancour of the Catholic clergy with whom he waged a bitter war in the columns of the 'Achill Herald'. His efforts to proselytise the poverty-striken islanders were unsuccessful, although he eventually purchased three-fifths of the land of the island.

Slievemore, a 670m peak of quartzose and mica, rises steeply on all sides, especially towards the sea, below which are the *Seal Caves*, which may be visited by boat from Dugort in calm weather. On its S slope is a dolmen with a circle at each end, to the W of which is a 'booley' village of primitive cabins occasionally used during summer cattle-pasturing.

The main road descends to *Keel,* beyond its lough and at the far end of a 3km-long strand. At its E end rise the *Cathedral Rocks,* where the cliffs have been fretted into a series of caverns and columns, forming part of the *Minaun,* which may be ascended from the hamlet of *Dookinelly,* commanding a fine view of Clare Island from its summit (464m).

W of Keel is the village of *Dooagh,* with workshops of the St. Colman knitting industry. Higher up, on the W side of an amphitheatre of hills, and on the E flank of **Croaghaun** (666m) is *Corrymore Lodge*, once occupied by the unfortunate Captain Boycott (cf.); below lies *Keem Bay* with its deserted coastguard station. On the S side of the mountain amethysts are found; on the NW sheer and overhanging cliffs rise almost 600m above the sea, and care should be taken when nearing their edge. To the W it ends in the razor-like ridge of *Achill Head*; to the N is *Saddle Head*, on the shoulder of which is a tarn known as the 'Mermaid's Looking Glass'.

The summit of *Croaghaun* is best approached from LOUGH ACORRYMORE, above Boycott's lodge, bearing to the left beyond the lake; while from Dugort (or Keel) one may follow a ridge rising NW of Slievemore from a signal tower, soon overlooking LOUGH NAKEEROGE (right) on a curious rock shelf raised slightly above the sea. The *View is superb: to the N are the islands of Duvillaun and Inishkea, and the Mullet; to the S in echelon lie Clare Island, Inishturk, Inishbofin, and Inishark. From S to SE rise the Twelve Bens, Muilrea, and Croagh Patrick; to the E is the Nephin Beg range, while to the W extends the boundless Atlantic.

On returning to Cashel, the SE of the island may be explored by taking the second turning to the right for *Dooega*, there bearing left and following the 'Atlantic Drive', which circles the S point of Achill, returning along the *Sound* and passing the old graveyard and 15C *Tower* of *Kildownet* (or *Carrick Kildavnet*), the latter once a stronghold of Grace O'Malley.

From Mulrany the road drives due N along the bank of *Bellacragher Bay*, an extension of Blacksod Bay, with, after a few km, a view to the E of the summits of *Cushcamcarragh* (712m), *Nephin Beg* (628m), which gives its name to the range, and to the NE, *Slieve Car* (720m). Beyond *Ballycroy*, a lane leads seaward to *Doona Castle*, another of Grace O'Malley's possessions. The road shortly veers NE across the extensive bog to *Bangor*.

BANGOR TO BALLINA DIRECT (41km). The N59 ascends the bleak Owenmore valley to the E to *Bellacorrick*, with a power station. Beyond, we traverse the desolate barony of Tyrawley before descending to *Crossmolina* (1,350 inhab.), with another power station, and a good centre for pike and perch fishing in LOUGH CONN.
    On a promontory some 8km S are the remains of *Errew Abbey* (founded 1413), with a 13C church, while near by is the oratory of *Templenagalliaghdoo* (the 'Church of the Black Nun'), probably the site of a 6C monastery founded by St. Tighernan.
    The N59 continues E past the demesne of *Castle Gore*, in which is the well-preserved ruin of *Deel Castle*, to enter *Ballina*, see below.

The R313 leads NW from Bangor, briefly skirting the S bank of CARROWMORE LOUGH and a range of hills abutting its W bank, to (19km) *Belmullet*, at the narrowest part of the isthmus joining the Mullet peninsula to the mainland, here crossed by a *Canal* 365m long. **Belmullet** (1,000 inhab.) lies at the N extremity of *Blacksod Bay*, where in 1588 was stranded the flagship of Don Alfonso de Leyva, who was rescued by the O'Rourke and entertained at Dromahair (cf.), only to lose his ships and his life at Port-na-Spania (cf.).
    The *Mullet* is a curious mattock-shaped peninsula, its wild coastline sheltering the N reaches of Blacksod Bay from the Atlantic. To the E and NE is *Broad Haven*. At *Doonamo Point*, 8km NW, is a fine promontory fort with a wall 5.5m high in places, built across the neck of its headland, and enclosing three clochans and a circular rath.

The road leading S from Belmullet traverses the hamlet of *Binghamstown* (*An Geata Mór*), *Bingham Castle*, and (16km) *Aghleam*, beyond which is *Blacksod Point*, with Achill 9.5km S.
    Off the W coast opposite Binghamstown is the island of *Inishglora*, with the

ruins of a chapel built by St. Brendan. The few inhabitants of the *Inishkea* islands, further S, were transferred to the mainland in 1927 after a storm had overwhelmed the fishing-fleet; on both islands are engraved pillar-stones of the 7C type.

Leaving Belmullet, we shortly fork left onto the R314, skirting the S shore of *Broad Haven*, beyond which driving parallel to the N side of CARROWMORE LOUGH to (22.5km) *Glenamoy Bridge*, with a bog reclamation station.

A road to the left here leads to (14km) *Portacloy*, a tiny harbour shut in by high cliffs, to the W of which, past the detached headland of *Doonvinallagh* and a cave, is *Benwee Head* (250m), a stupendous cliff buttressing the NW corner of Mayo, and commanding views SW towards Achill and NE to the Donegal coast.—Offshore are a group of seven rock-stacks 90m high known as the *Stags of Broadhaven*.—Some 5km E, at *Porturlin*, is another little harbour near some curious rock-formations. There is a megalithic tomb at *Ross Port*, SW of Portacloy, facing Broad Haven itself.

The main road bears NE to *Belderg* parallel to the ridge between *Slieve Fyagh* (331m) and *Maumakeogh* (379m); the wild cliffs here, dominated by *Glinsk* (305m), may be visited by foot or by boat. Beyond Belderg we skirt the coast, where the dark rocks are pierced by a number of blow-holes, while inland rise the desolate moors of the Barony of Erris. There is a megalithic tomb on the hillside to the right of the road here and two more immediately to the W of *Ballycastle*, the next village, near the mouth of the Ballinglen river. Hence the R315 leads almost due S to (10km) *Crossmolina* (see above). To the NE is *Downpatrick Head*, off which is seen the detached fort of *Doonbristy*. Traversing a low pass, the road descends to *Palmerstown*, where the Cloonaghmore is crossed by an imposing bridge.

A road to the left here passes (right) *Rathfran Abbey* (1274), a ruined Dominican house, and leads N, through a district rich in ancient remains, including an Ogham stone at *Breastagh*. At (9.5km) *Kilcummin*, close to the shore on which the French landed in 1798 (see below), is a ruined church dedicated to St. Cuimin, with his well and gravestone marked with an incised cross.

We shortly enter **Killala** (600 inhab.), with a bishopric which is claimed to have been founded by St. Patrick himself.

The see, held at one time by the pluralist Myler Magrath (cf.), was joined in 1607 to Achonry, and in 1834 to Tuam. Killala Bay was the scene on 22 August 1798 of the landing of 1,100 French troops under Général Humbert, who invaded Ireland with the intention of assisting the Confederates. They were initially successful, but were forced to surrender on 8 September to Cornwallis at Ballinamuck (cf.).

The *Cathedral*, with a fine steeple, dates from a rebuilding of c 1670, except for a Gothic doorway (blocked) on the S side. Walter Blake Kirwan (1754–1805), the famous Dublin preacher, became Dean of Killala in 1800. Near it is a *Round Tower* (25.5m high), repaired since struck by lightning in 1800. An underground chamber or souterrain in the churchyard is the only other relic of antiquity. The Castle was demolished to make room for a housing estate in the 1950s.

The road hence to (12km) Ballina is not particularly interesting, but a minor road forking left immediately S of the town and running parallel to the main road and the Moy estuary passes (left) **Moyne Abbey**, in a field (entrance by farm) overlooking the sandhills of *Bartragh Island*, and founded by MacWilliam Burke in 1460. The entrance is by steps to the upper chambers of the ruined monastic buildings, of which several lower rooms retain their vaults. The church has a lofty tower and good tracery in its windows, while the cloisters are almost perfect.—4km further S (left) lies **Rosserk Abbey**, founded for Franciscans by the Joyce family in 1400, with an imposing tall tower and also with well-preserved cloisters. We regain the main road at the demesne of *Belleek*, immediately to the N of Ballina.

BALLINA (6,850 inhab.), although of no great interest, is one of the more important towns in the area, and is a centre for anglers on the Moy and its tributaries. It was the first town captured by the French after landing at Killala (see above). Its Catholic *Cathedral*, a 19C edifice, is adjoined by remains of an Austin Friary of 1427.

About 1.5km SW of the town on the road to LOUGH CONN is the Dolmen of the *Four Maols*. It marks the grave of four foster-brothers (whose names all began with 'Maol') who murdered their master Ceallach, Bp of Kilmoremoy, and were hanged by his brother at *Ardnaree* (*Ard na Riaghadh*, 'hill of the executions').

The direct road to Sligo crosses the Moy NE of Ballina and runs parallel to *Slieve Gamph* or *Ox Mountains*, the highest summit of which is *Knockalongy* (453m), to the NE, to meet *Sligo Bay* at *Dromore West*, a pleasant village on a brawling stream.

An ALTERNATIVE road (R297) keeps closer to the sea, traversing *Enniscrone* (or *Inishcrone*), a resort between dunes and low cliffs, some 3km N of which is *Castle Firbis* (left), the ruined stronghold of the MacFirbises, a family of poets and annalists. Duald MacFirbis (1585–1670) was the last of the hereditary 'Sennachies' or genealogists of Ireland.—Bearing E we reach *Easky*, a fishing village, near which are several ruined castles of the O'Dowds, before regaining the main road at *Dromore West*.

Hence we skirt the N flank of *Knockalongy* past *Skreen* (right), the birthplace of the mathematician and physicist Sir George Stokes (1819–1903). There is a neglected well of 1591 here, and on adjacent *Red Hill*, a large ring fort.

Between Red Hill and *Knockachree* to the S is LOUGH ACHREE, known as 'the youngest lake in Ireland', having been formed by an earthquake in 1490. The Dartry Mountains are well seen to the NE across Sligo Bay.

N of Skreen are the ruins of *Ardnaghlass*, another O'Dowd stronghold, and later of the MacSweeneys. We descend through woods to the shore of *Ballysadare Bay* and pass several old cottages, and at *Ballysadare* itself (see latter part of Rte 26A) turn left for (8km) **Sligo**, see Rte 26B.

25   Dublin to Westport

A. Via Mullingar and Longford

259km (161 miles). N4. 61km *Kinnegad*—18km **Mullingar** (by-pass under construction)—43km **Longford**—N5. 34km *Tulsk*—28km *Ballaghaderreen*—28km *Swinford*—29km **Castlebar**—18km **Westport**.

For the road to *Kinnegad*, see Rte 19.

At Kinnegad we bear NW.—After 6.5km a right-hand turning leads 6.5km to *Killucan*, preserving three 16–17C wayside crosses; nearby are remains of *Rathwire Castle* and traces of a Bronze Age barrow.

11.5km **MULLINGAR** (7,850 inhab.), the county town of Westmeath, and long a garrison town, is still an important agricultural and angling centre, retaining its 18C *Town Hall* and *Court House*. Its former *Cathedral* (of 1836), of which the clock is a survival, has been superseded by an unsuccessful building of 1936–39 by Ralph Byrne, embellished with mosaics by Boris Anrep and sculptures by Albert Power. Its twin towers dominate the surrounding countryside, which in the 17–19Cs was almost the exclusive domain of the Rochforts.

LOUGH ENNELL (4.5km S on the Tullamore road), LOUGH OWEL (4.5km NW on the Longford road), and LOUGH DERRAVARAGH (8.5km N on the way to Castlepollard), all provide good fishing.

Between the main road and Lough Ennell are the former mid 18C mansions of the Rochfort family: *Belvedere*, with splendid stucco ceilings of 1745, and with a remarkable sham ruin (1760; known as the 'Jealous Wall') in the grounds to screen it from another, *Tudenham Park* (formerly Rochfort), now a ruin, which belonged to a brother of Lord Belvedere (formerly Bellfield—whose wife had run off with another brother) with whom he had quarrelled. She was later incarcerated for almost 30 years at his seat at Gaulston.

1.5km E of *Crookedwood* (10km NE of Mullingar on the R394), is the 15C fortified church of *St. Munna*. Just SW of **Castlepollard** (10km further N), a small village, is the wooded demesne of **Tullynally Castle** (formerly 'Pakenham Hall', a grey castellated pile, originally a 17C house, classicised in 1775–80 by Graham Myers, and in 1803–6 transformed into a Gothick castle by Francis Johnston. Additions were made by James Shiel in 1825 and further extensions by Sir Richard Morrison (1842); it contains relics of the Duke of Wellington, whose wife was Catherine (or Kitty) Pakenham. It is the home of the Longford family.

At **Fore**, in a valley 5km E of Castlepollard, are the remains of an *Abbey* founded by St. Fechin in 630 and refounded early in the 13C as a Benedictine house by Walter de Lacy. The ancient cell, on the hillside, was occupied by a hermit as lately as 1764, while lower down are remains of fortifications and the church, remarkable for its massive doorway.—3km N of Castlepollard a well-preserved bawn with motte and bailey is seen on the right; to the left, a ruined church crowns a height; while further N, to the E of the road to *Finnea*, on LOUGH SHEELIN, is the abrupt crag of the *Hill of Mael*.

Beyond Mullingar the N4 skirts LOUGH OWEL, in which it is said that Máel Sechnaill, King of Meath, personally drowned the Danish chieftain Thorgestr (845). On the N bank is the demesne of *Clonhugh*, long connected with the Nugent family.

A DETOUR may here be made to the N to visit (3km) **Multyfarnham**, a village noted for the partial ruins of a once-powerful Cistercian abbey, founded in 1306 by William Delamere. Its most remarkable feature is the slender tower 27m high. It was saved from spoliation by the Nugents at the dissolution of the monasteries, but the friars were driven out in 1641 during the Civil War; the precincts are now occupied by Franciscans.—NE is LOUGH DERRAVARAGH, 9.5km long, with low and boggy banks except at its SE end. It is overlooked (just N of the abbey) by the demesne of *Donore*, another seat of the Nugents. On the far bank is *Faughalstown*, a retreat of Mortimer, 5th Earl of March, in the reign of Henry IV.

The road traverses *Bunbrosna*, where to the right are the grounds of *Wilson's Hospital*, a Protestant boarding- school founded in the 18C.

At *Ballinalack* (16km from Mullingar) we cross the Inny, to the SW of which is LOUGH IRON, with the remains of the 12C abbey of *Tristernagh*, destroyed in 1783, and *Templecross* church (15C).

13km **Edgeworthstown** (also known as *Mostrim* or *Meathas Truim*; 700 inhab.), on the Cavan–Athlone crossroads, has long been associated with the Edgeworth family, who became established in the neighbourhood in 1583 when the first Irish Edgeworth was appointed Bishop of Down and Connor.

Richard Edgeworth (1744–1817), father of the novelist, was a benefactor to the village, and *Firmount*, to the N, was the residence of the Abbé Edgeworth (1745–1807), who attended Louis XVI to the scaffold as his confessor. The Edgeworth's house is now a convent; it was the home of Maria Edgeworth (1767–1849) from 1782 until her death; she is buried in *St. John's* churchyard. She was visited here by Scott in 1825, and by Wordsworth in 1829. Some of her admirers in Boston, Mass., sent 150 barrels of flour during the famine of 1846, addressed to 'Miss Edgeworth, for her poor'.

Oliver Goldsmith attended school in Edgeworthstown in 1741–45 (building demolished).

Currygrane, 9.5km NW, was the birthplace of General Sir Henry Wilson (1864–1922), assassinated in London for his part in attempting to crush the Irish independence movement.

Ardagh, 8km SW, an ancient bishopric united to Kilmore and Elphin in 1833, shows little trace of antiquity. It is fabled as being the scene of an adventure of young Goldsmith, who mistaking the manor house for an inn, later founded the plot of 'She Stoops to Conquer' (1773) on his error.

14km **Longford** (4,000 inhab.), the capital of the county, and described by Frank O'Connor as 'a really terrible town', was once a fortress (long-phort) of the O'Farrels, but no trace remains either of their castle or of the priory they founded in 1400. The present *Castle*, adjoining the barracks, dates from 1627; and *St. Mel's Cathedral*, by Joseph B. Keane, with its lofty belfry, is in the Italian Renaissance style of 1840–93. The Clinton family, famous in Longford annals, included George Clinton (c 1686–1751), first governor of New York, and his nephew De Witt Clinton (1769–1828).

5km NE is *Carrigglass Manor* (1837), a Tudor-Revival house by Daniel Robertson, with stables and entrance arch by Gandon.

The N63 leads SW from Longford to (31km) *Roscommon*, crossing the Shannon at (17km) *Lanesborough*, a fishing centre at the N end of LOUGH REE, where boats may be hired.

For the road from Longford to *Sligo*, see Rte 26.

Our route continues W and then NW on the N5, through *Cloondara*, western terminus of the old Royal Canal, crossing the Shannon at *Termonbarry*, before veering N over the ridge of *Slieve Bawn* (263m).—22.5km *Strokestown* (600 inhab.), a planned market-town with a wide tree-lined street, to the E of which is the mansion of the Mahon family, the 17C building being extended c 1730, possibly by Castle, and altered c 1819.

10.5km NW is **Elphin** (500 inhab.), the seat of a bishop since the time of St. Patrick, claims (with *Pallas*; see Rte 38B) to be the birthplace of Oliver Goldsmith (?1730–74), who was educated at the diocesan school here before moving on to Athlone. His grandfather, the Rev. Oliver Jones, curate of Elphin, lived at *Smith Hill*, NE of the village.—We may regain the main road at *Tulsk*, 9.5km SW.

11.5km **Tulsk**, once a place of importance, has slight remains of an abbey founded in the 15C, perhaps by Phelim O'Connor. The road goes on, passing (left) the *Hill of Rathcroghan*, the site of the palace of the pagan kings of Connacht. The curious enclosure to the S is known as the *Reilig-na-Riogh* (Cemetery of the Kings); near it is a small sandstone pillar said to mark the grave of Dathi, the last pagan king of Ireland.

16km **Frenchpark**. The Protestant rectory was the birthplace of Douglas Hyde (1860–1949), the poet and Gaelic scholar, and first President of the Irish Republic (1938–45); he is buried in the churchyard here (cf. Fermoy). The mansion of *French Park* (c 1729), possibly built by Castle, and now roofless, was the former seat of the Lords De Freyne; near by are the remains of the Dominican abbey-church of *Cloonshanville* (1385).

We continue NW through (13km) *Ballaghaderreen*, birthplace of John Blake Dillon (1814–66), the politician and joint-founder of the

'Nation', a small market town preserving several Georgian houses, but spoilt by an ugly Gothic-Revival church, and 16km beyond, traverse **Charlestown** (700 inhab.). For the road hence to *Westport*, 58km SW, see the first part of Rte 24A, in reverse.

B. Via Athlone, Roscommon, Castlerea, and Claremorris

257km (160 miles). N4. 61km *Kinnegad*—N6. 31km *Kilbeggan*— 33km **Athlone**—N61. 19km *Roscommon*—N60. 30km *Castlerea*— 20km *Ballyhaunis*—18km *Claremorris*—27km *Castlebar*—18km **Westport**.

For the road to *Athlone*, see Rte 19.

From Athlone (by-pass under construction) we turn NW, skirting the W bank of **Lough Ree**, one of the larger of those irregular island-studded lakes that are characteristic of the Shannon valley. It is 25.5km long from N to S, and 11km across at its widest, and provides trout fishing in the may-fly season, and coarse fishing at all seasons.— After 8km we pass (left) *Moyvannan Castle*, and after another 8km reach (right) *Lecarrow*. From here a lane turns towards Lough Ree to (3km) the fortified promontory on which rises *Rindown Castle*, built by John de Grey in 1214 on the legendary site of a stronghold of Thorgestr the Dane. It is sometimes called *St. John's Castle*, having at one time passed into the possession of the Knights of St. John. The massive keep, 15m in diameter, is thickly clad with ivy.

8km *Knockcroghery*. On the summit of a hill to the W is a ruined Observatory.—To the E is *Galey Castle* (14C).

In the middle of LOUGH REE at this point is the island of *Inchcleraun*, or *Inis Clothrann*, named after Clothra, sister of that Queen Maeve who is said to have been killed here, when bathing, by a stone from the sling of Forbaid, Prince of Ulster. Its alternative name of *Quaker Island* recalls a 19C resident of that persuasion. The church here is notable as having a square tower of pre-Gothic date.

8km **Roscommon** (1,650 inhab.), an old wool-town, derives its name (Coman's wood) from a monastery founded here by St. Coman in 746. The most conspicuous building is the huge *Castle*, immediately N of the town, to the left of the road. It was erected by Sir Robert de Ufford, justiciar of Ireland, in 1278, but suffered considerably in the wars of the 16–17Cs. It was partially dismantled by General John Reynolds in 1652, but is thought to have been inhabited as late as 1691. The mullioned windows were added c 1580. The outer enclosure, entered through a fortified gateway, is defended by a drum-tower at each angle; in the inner court is the building that contained the state apartments.

The *Dominican Priory*, in the lower part of the town, founded by Phelim O'Conor, King of Connacht, in 1257, and rebuilt in 1453, has a very long and narrow church with a fine W window. On the N side of the choir is a tomb with a mutilated figure, said to be that of the founder; the four armed gallowglasses that guard it appear to be of later workmanship.—The classical *Court House* (1736) in the town centre, has a tower and dome.

About 5km NE is the demesne of *Hollywell*, taking its name from a well dedicated to St. Brigid. The Gunning sisters, daughters of James Gunning of *Castlecoote*

(6.5km W of Roscommon), whose beauty was the toast of London c 1750, are said to have owed their complexions to its water.

At *Athleague*, 9km SW of Roscommon, is the 'Fort of the Earls', divided by a trench across the middle after a series of indecisive contests between two rival nobles.—The *Castlestrange Stone*, 2.5km NW of Athleague, is a good example of Late Iron Age decoration.

The N61 leads N from Roscommon to (18km) *Tulsk*, see Rte 25A, and 26km beyond, to *Boyle*, see Rte 26A.

Our route continues NW on the N60, passing at 11km (right) the remains of a *Round Tower*, to (10km) *Ballymoe*.

6.5km S are the ruins of *Glinsk Castle* (17C), while 6km NE at *Ballintober*, is a huge *Castle* built before 1315, and the headquarters of the O'Conors of Connacht until the 18C. The plan is similar to that of Roscommon, but the towers are polygonal instead of cylindrical.—1.5km W of Ballymoe, in the churchyard of *Ballynakill*, is a fine effigy of a 15C armoured gallowglass.

The road turns N to (9km) **Castlerea** (1,850 inhab.) on the sluggish river Suck, where the Victorian *Clonalis House* (1878–80; by Pepys Cockerell) preserves the papers of the 18C antiquary Charles O'Conor in its large library, together with other family relics, portraits, and furniture; Turlough O'Carolan's harp stands in the billiards-room. Castlerea was the birthplace of Sir William Wilde (1815–76), the amateur antiquary and surgeon, and father of Oscar Wilde.—Bearing W, after 20km we enter **Ballyhaunis** (1,350 inhab.), preserving remains of an *Austin Priory*, its church restored.—8km to the NW is *Loughglinn*, with an 18C mansion and circular fort.

18km **Claremorris** (2,050 inhab.), a railway junction, is of slight interest. We continue NW over the plain, after 10km by-passing to the W the village of *Mayo*. Only traces of its abbey survive, where in the 7C St. Colman founded a once famous school, leaving his cell at Lindisfarne for that purpose; there is a legend that Alfred the Great attended a course of instruction here.

3km *Balla* owes its origin and name (*Ball Aluinn*, beautiful wall) to St. Mochua (7C), who built a church and sank two wells here, enclosing the whole with a wall. Some fragments, probably of the church, remain, near a small *Round Tower*, 15m high.

After another 14km we enter *Castlebar*, for which and for the road hence to *Westport*, 18km SW, see Rte 24A; *Newport* lies 17.5km NW of Castlebar; see Rte 24B.

26 Longford to Sligo

A. Longford to Sligo

92km (57 miles). N4. 37km *Carrick-on-Shannon*—15km *Boyle*—40km **Sligo**.

From *Longford* (see Rte 25A) we drive NW roughly parallel to the E bank of the Shannon, after 5km passing *Newtown Forbes*, which is separated from LOUGH FORBES, an expansion of the river, by *Castle Forbes*, the estate of the Earl of Granard, with a castellated mansion of c 1830 replacing that built after 1619 by Sir Arthur Forbes.—A right-hand fork just beyond the village leads 16km NE to *Ballinamuck*, where Géneral Humbert's invading force finally surrendered to Cornwallis on 8 September 1798. Some 884 French officers and men were then transported back to France, but c 400 of some 900 Irish rebels then cornered at Killala were killed, and another 90 (including Wolfe Tone's brother) were later executed.—14km *Dromod*, on the shore of LOUGH BOFIN, was once noted for its ironworks; it is now frequented for trout fishing both on this lough and its W extension, LOUGH BODERG.

DROMOD TO ENNISKILLEN (70km; 44 miles). The R202 runs NE via (9km) **Mohill** (1,050 inhab.) at the head of LOUGH RINN, 12km N of which is *Fenagh*, with two old churches remaining of an earlier monastery, and a megalithic tomb. Beyond Fenagh we traverse **Ballinamore** (850 inhab.) to (25km) *Swanlinbar*, just short of the border crossing, with the *Iron Mountains* to the NW (*Cuilcagh*, 665m, on the frontier) and likewise *Slieve Rushen* (405m) to the E.

Entering Co. Fermanagh on the A32, after 6.5km turn left for the demesne of *Florence Court, built for Lord Mountflorence in 1751–64, with wings added some years later by Davis Ducart. A well-proportioned residence (NT) containing rococo plasterwork by John West, it has been opened to the public since its restoration after a fire in 1955, when the ceiling of the sitting-room was destroyed. The fireplace in that room is notable. The *Library*, to the right of the entrance, containing prints of local views, and a portrait of the 2nd Earl of Enniskillen, by Lawrence, the collection of Meissen ware, and the so-called *Venetian Room* (named after its Venetian window) on the First Floor (ceiling restored) are of interest. The gardens contain numerous fine trees including the parent tree from which the Florence Court Yew has been propagated.

5km W is the *Cladagh Glen*, with a footpath ascending to the *Marble Arch Caves*, where the stream issues from an underground channel and flows beneath a detached archway. Further up the hillside are several swallow-holes. The caves, visited by La Tocnaye in 1796/7, may now be seen on a conducted tour in March–October.

We shortly meet the A4 from Sligo, and bear NE to *Enniskillen*; see Rte 37.

The N4 continues NW from Dromod, shortly passing (left) on the lough shore, *Derrycarne*, the scene of a skirmish between the troops of James II and William III in 1689.—We cross a loop of the Shannon at *Drumsna*, where stands the so-called *Doon of Drumsna*, an extensive range of earthworks and ramparts, before re-crossing the river at *Jamestown* (founded by Sir Charles Coote in 1625), with its defensive town gate, and the scene of an unsuccessful raid by Sarsfield in 1689.

18km **Carrick-on-Shannon** (2,050 inhab.) is the county town of Leitrim, and an angling centre for the Shannon and neighbouring lakes and streams. Carrick was given its charter by James I, but preserves few remains of interest except the old gaol and a *Court House* of c 1825. As the upper limit of navigation on the river, it has in recent years grown into an important base for the hiring of boats for excursions down the Shannon.

The length of the navigable river from here to *Killaloe* (see Rte 18C) is c 225km; six locks are passed, and up to nine leisurely days may be spent on its waters, although the journey can be made in 36 hours. The pleasantest months are from June to early September. For details of the types of boat (from 2–8 berth) which may be hired, tariffs, etc., apply to Tourist Offices.

CARRICK-ON-SHANNON TO BUNDORAN (75km). We drive N on the R280 through (6.5km) the village of *Leitrim*, which gives its name to the county, formerly the residence of the bishops of Liathdroma, and the site of a castle of the

O'Rourke, Prince of Breffni, a few ruins of which still remain.—7km *Drumshanbo*, an angling resort at the S end of **Lough Allen**, the third largest of the lakes formed by the Shannon (11km long, and 5km broad at its N end).

A minor road (R207) skirts the E bank of the lough below *Slieve Anierin* (586m) and *Slievenakilla* (543m), further N, part of the *Iron Mountains*, to *Dowra*, whence we may circle the lough by turning W, or continue NE, passing near (right) the source of the Shannon, to meet the N16 from Sligo immediately W of the border crossing of *Blacklion-Belcoo*, on LOUGH MACNEAN, see latter part of Rte 37.

The R280 skirts the W bank of LOUGH ALLEN, off which a left-hand turn leads shortly to *Keadew*, the last home of blind Turlogh O'Carolan (1670–1738), the 'last' of the Irish bards, and composer of the tune of 'The Star-Spangled Banner'. He is buried in *Kilronan* church (to the NW), preserving a 12–13C doorway.—The next left-hand lane leads to *Arigna*, with former iron-mines, and collieries. There is a power station on the lough-side. Further N we pass the ruins of St. Patrick's church at *Corglass* (or *Tarmon*) and veer NW to *Drumkeeran* and away from the lough between ranges rising to c 450m to the W, and to the NE. The road skirts BELHAVEL LOUGH and bears N, ascending the Bonet valley to the mountain-girt village of *Manorhamilton*, on the Enniskillen-Sligo road; see Rte 37.

An ALTERNATIVE road hence (R282) to Bundoran leads NE, over *Saddle Hill*, descending to (11km) the ruins of *Rossinver Church*, probably built by St. Tigernach, beyond which we turn left to skirt the S bank of LOUGH MELVIN.—A minor road to the right leads to the *Black Pig's Race* earthworks, a border dyke erected by Ulstermen in the 3C AD.—**Lough Melvin**, partly forming the frontier, is 12km long and 2.5km wide, and abounds in salmon, trout, and gillaroo, and contains a number of small islands. Towards its W end, below *Aghabohad* (410m), on an artificial island near the shore, are the ruins of *Rossclogher Castle* (15C), the stronghold of The MacClancy, where De Cuellar (cf.) eventually found refuge, and from which he made his way to Dunluce and back to Spain. *Rossclogher Abbey* is on the mainland. At *Kinlough* we turn right for *Bundoran*, see Rte 27.

The main road from Manorhamilton leads NW up the narrow valley past GLENADE LOUGH, between the precipitous mountain masses of *Truskmore* (644m, to the W), the highest of the Dartry Mountains, and another range rising to 523m.—We descend to *Kinlough*, at the W end of Lough Melvin (see above), and shortly enter *Bundoran*.

The Sligo road bears NW away from the Shannon at Carrick, and keeps above the S bank of the Boyle river, in fact a chain of lakes, passing (right) *Woodbrook House*, described in loving detail by David Thomson is his autobiographical study of life there in the 1930s, and beyond (right) near the site of *Rockingham House*, remodelled by Nash in 1810, but burnt out in 1863 and again in 1957, and since demolished; its demesne, somewhat mutilated, is now known as the *Lough Key Forest Park*.

15km **BOYLE** (1,750 inhab.) was the home of the King family, and here was born Edward King (1612–37), whose death by drowning inspired Milton's 'Lycidas'. Their dilapidated town residence, with a heavily pedimented front facing the river, was built to a design of Sir Edward Lovett Pearce or William Halfpenny, his assistant.

Their burial-place was the Cistercian *Abbey, founded by Maurice O'Duffy in 1235 and despoiled by Cromwell's troops in 1659, whose well-preserved ruins lie near the river. The long nave is notable as having early Gothic arches on the N side and Romanesque arches on the S; the details of the windows, pillars, and corbels are notewothy. There survive considerable remains of the monastic dependencies.

Lough Key, to the NE, studded with wooded islets in a sylvan setting backed by distant mountains, justly deserves the enthusiastic praise of Arthur Young, who visited it in 1766. On one of the islands are the remains of the *Abbey of the Trinity*, where the 'Annals of Lough Cé' (now in Trinity College Library) were written. Here too is the grave of

Sir Conyers Clifford (see below). On the river bank near the lough is the ruined church of *Asselyn*.

Some 8km W of Boyle is LOUGH GARA, with the ruined *Moygara Castle* on its W bank. Several crannógs have been excavated by the lake, while on the right of the road to it is a very large dolmen.—*Frenchpark* (see Rte 25A), lies 14.5km SW.

The Sligo road ascends NW across the *Curlew Mountains*, which although not rising over 264m, are a striking feature of the landscape.—7km *Ballinafad* is charmingly placed at the S end of LOUGH ARROW (8km long). Its *Castle* preserves three cylindrical towers, and around it was fought a bloody battle (1599) between Hugh Roe O'Donnell and the English forces of Sir Conyers Clifford, in which the latter was killed.

To the W of Lough Arrow rises *Bricklieve Mountain* (321m) on the slope of which (c 1.5km SW of *Tower Hill House*) is the *Carrowkeel* group of passage-graves, dating from 2100–2000 BC.

Further NW is *Keshcorran Hill* (361m; 5km from Ballymote), having on its W slope some caves to which many obscure legends are attached: one relates the birth here of Cormac MacArt and of the she-wolf that suckled him; another that it was a refuge of Diarmuid during his flight (having eloped with Grainne, the betrothed wife of Finn MacCoul).—On the E bank of the lough are the ruins of the Dominican abbey of *Ballindoon* (1507), and further SE, above *Kilmactranny* (on the Ballyfarnan road), are a number of cairns that are said to mark the site of the legendary battle of Northern Moytura, where the Firbolgs were defeated by the Tuatha dé Danaan (cf. *Cong*).—LOUGH NASOOL, c 2km N of Ballindoon Abbey, went suddenly dry for about a month in 1933, and local tradition states that this phenomenon occurs every 100 years, in memory of Balor 'of the Evil Eye', slain at Moytura.

From *Castlebaldwin*, just NW of the lough, a minor road leads 9km W to *Ballymote*, famous for its strong castle, built in 1300 by Richard de Burgh, the 'Red Earl' of Ulster. It was a bone of contention in the Civil War, when it was occupied by the Irish in 1641, but did not fall until 1645, before the united attack of Ireton and Coote. The ivied ruins are flanked by six corner towers. Here also are the remains of a *Franciscan friary*, where the 'Book of Ballymote' (early 15C) was compiled.—Hence we may regain our route at *Collooney*, c 12.5km to the N.

15km *Drumfin*, 2km E*of which, at *Riverstown*, is the demesne of *Coopershill*, its imposing mansion attributed to Francis Bindon.—We later pass (right) *Markree Castle*, the fine demesne of the Cooper family, with a huge castellated pile rebuilt at various times, after 1802 by Francis Johnston, before traversing *Collooney*. Here in 1798 a skirmish between a detachment of Limerick militia and Géneral Humbert's troops ended in the retreat of the former to Sligo; a monument commemorates the gallantry of Humbert's aide-de-camp.

3km *Ballysadare* (in Irish *Baile Easa Dara*, the town of the cataract of the oak), on the Owenmore, is reputed for its salmon fisheries. On the river bank are seen the ruins of an abbey founded by St. Fechin c 645. The road commands a view to the NE of the hills above Lough Gill (see Rte 26B) as we approach (8km) *Sligo*, see below.

B. Sligo and Environs

SLIGO (17,250 inhab.; Post Office in Wine St), attractively situated in the centre of a wooded plain, lies mainly on the S bank of the Garavogue, connecting Lough Gill to the sea; its Irish name is *Sligeach*, 'the shelly river'. It is a busy market town and road junction, and an important depot for Galway homespuns and Donegal tweeds. The area has also strong literary associations with W.B. Yeats, who as a boy spent many holidays with his maternal grandparents here, and was buried at Drumcliff, 8km N.

First heard of in 537 as the scene of a battle between the men of Connacht and those of the North, Sligo was plundered by Norse pirates in 807, and in 1245 became important as the residence of Maurice Fitzgerald, Earl of Kildare. His castle later became a bone of contention among the local septs, in particular the O'Connors and O'Donnells. In 1641 the town was sacked by Sir Frederick Hamilton, and the abbey burned, and in 1645 it fell to Sir Charles Coote after a battle in which Malachy O'Kelly, the martial archbishop of Tuam, was killed.

Adjacent to the Tourist Office in Stephen St, on the N side of the Garavogue, is the **County Library**, above which (opened on request) is a *Collection* of paintings and drawings by Jack B. Yeats (1871–1957) and his family, including John Butler Yeats (1839–1922), his father; his sisters Susan Mary (Lily) Yeats (1866–1949) and Elizabeth Corbet (Lolly) Yeats (1868–1940); and his niece Anne Yeats (born 1919). Among the portraits are those of Susan and Jennie Mitchell, W.B. Yeats, a Self-portrait, and John O'Leary; also portraits of Jack B. Yeats by Estella F. Solomons (1882–1968), and Seán O'Sullivan; and of W.B. Yeats by 'AE' Russell, and Seán O'Sullivan.

In the adjacent 'Museum' (open on request) is an extensive *Collection* of first editions of W.B. Yeats and other Yeatsiana, including autograph letters, and the Irish tricolour which draped his coffin at Drumcliff. Also works by Jack B. Yeats, including illustrated broadsheets, etc.; photographs and diaries; examples of the publications of the Dun Elmer Press and the Cuala Press; and drawings by 'AE'. In another room are local collections, including the violin of Michael Coleman (1887–1945).

Almost opposite is Bridge St, leading across the river, where the second turning to the left approaches **Sligo Abbey** (key near by), the only ancient building in the town, founded for Dominicans by Maurice Fitzgerald in 1252, and destroyed by fire in 1414. The ruins now standing date mainly from the subsequent rebuilding, although the deeply-splayed windows on the S side of the choir are evidently of 13C workmanship. The present ruinous condition dates from 1641.

Little remains of the nave except three arches on the S side and the N wall, in which is the elaborate tomb of Cormac O'Crean (1506). The tower is supported by lofty arches and fragments of its vault. Beneath the fine 15C E window is a carved altar of nine panels of a slightly later date, and on the S wall is the monument of O'Conor Sligo (died 1609) and his wife Lady Eleanor Butler (died 1623). The *Cloisters* are perfect on three sides, and retain some ornamented coupled pillars; on the N side is a lector's pulpit on a projecting corbel, once approached by a flight of steps above the cloister. The dormitory wall extends to the N; on the E side is the dark little chapter-house.

Walking W along Castle St and its extension, we reach (left) *St. John's Cathedral* (C. of I.; elevated to that rank in 1961), founded in the 17C, rebuilt to a design by Castle in the 18C, and remodelled in 1812 and 1883. It has a massive W tower, and contains the mutilated tomb of its founder Sir Roger Jones (1637) and his wife.—The near by *Catholic Cathedral* (also of St. John) dates from 1869–74.—Hence we may regain the town centre by turning left up O'Connell St (at the E end of John St).

8km W of Sligo, on the S side of the estuary, is the resort of *Strandhill* (600 inhab.).

On the shore to the N is the church of *Killespugbrone* ('church of Bp

Bronus'), named after a disciple of St. Patrick. A curious feature of this little ruin is that the round-headed doorway of normal type is on the S side instead of at the W end. Long-preserved here, and a goal of pilgrimage in the 17C, was the Shrine of St. Patrick's Tooth, now in the National Museum, Dublin.

To the S of Strandhill, but clearly visible from Sligo, rises Yeats's 'cairn-heaped grassy hill' of *Knocknarea* (328m), on the summit of which an enormous cairn is conspicuous, 180m round. It probably covers a passage-grave. Called *Misgaun Meaghbh* or *Miosgán Meva*, it is a monument to Maeve, Queen of Connacht (the 'Queen Mab' of English folklore), who reigned in the 1C AD, and is probably buried at *Rathcroghan*; see Rte 25A.

The * View from the summit extends from Slieve League and the Donegal Mountains to the N and NE to Nephin (and even Croagh Patrick on the Mayo coast) to the SW, while nearer are Ben Bulben and Truskmore (NE), the Curlew Mountains (E), and the Ox Mountains to the SW.
On the SW side is the *Glen of Knocknarea*, a chasm in the limestone c 1.5km long, bounded by steep cliffs. From the SE side one may return to Sligo by a minor road passing (right) *Carrowmore*, a low hill possessing the largest group of megalithic remains in Ireland. Many of the monuments, some dating back to 4,000 BC, have been partially or entirely destroyed by gravel quarrying, but three small well-preserved dolmens—the largest 2m high—and a rough stone circle are within easy reach of the road.

THE *CIRCUIT OF LOUGH GILL (c 37km). **Lough Gill**, only 3km SE of Sligo, rivals Killarney for sheer natural beauty, and is much less frequented. The lake is 8km long and 2–3.5km wide, abounding in trout, salmon and pike, and is connected with the sea by the Garavogue.— Driving NE from Sligo we shortly turn off the N16 onto the R286, passing (right) the wooded demesne of *Hazelwood*, with a house of 1731, one of the earliest Palladian buildings designed by Castle (for General Owen Wynne; now offices) on the N bank of the lough. We soon pass (left) charming LOUGH COLGAGH.

Above is the *Deerpark Monument*, a group of stones in a rough oblong (45m by 15m), a double tomb of a type related to the 'horned cairns', and still partly roofed, although the large central chamber was probably always open to the sky. The enclosures at either end are undoubtedly burial cists. To the S are a fine cashel and other stone monuments, partly destroyed.

The road descends to the shore and passes *Newtown Castle*, a well-preserved 16C ruin, on the point beyond which is a fragment of a stronghold of the O'Rourkes. At the E end of the lough is *Doonie* (or *Dooney*) *Rock*, a viewpoint that inspired a poem by Yeats, as did the tiny 'lake isle' of *Innisfree*, near the SE bank. Bearing round below the former we skirt the bank of the river Bonet to **Dromahair**, a pleasant village 21km from Sligo.

The *Old Hall*, on the river bank, built in 1626 by Sir William Villiers, occupies the site of *Breffni Castle*.

Hence Devorguilla, wife of Tiernan O'Rourke, eloped with Dermot MacMurrough, King of Leinster, in 1152. The subsequent combination of chieftains against MacMurrough led him to seek help from Henry II in return for vassalage (1166); Henry refused direct intervention, but allowed Strongbow to go to his assistance, the initial step in the Anglo-Norman invasion of Ireland. Here in 1588 Sir Brian O'Rourke entertained the shipwrecked Spanish captain De Leyva before his disastrous re-embarkation at Killybegs (cf.).

On the opposite bank are the imposing ruins of *Creevelea Abbey*, founded for Franciscans by The O'Rourke and his wife in 1508. It is notable for its large S transept, E window, and tiny cloister.

The return to Sligo is made by turning right onto the R287, after 6.5km bearing right between *Slish Mountain* (right) and *Slieve Daeane* to the S bank of Lough Gill. Offshore lies *Cottage Island*, and to the NE, *Church Island*. Bearing away from the lough we pass (right) *Cairns Hill*, an eminence crowned by two cairns, two cashels, and a stone circle, before meeting the N4, where we turn right for *Sligo*.

Another attractive excursion is to GLENCAR LOUGH, 8km NE of Sligo, described at the end of Rte 37.

27   Sligo to Derry via Donegal and Strabane

135km (84 miles). N15. 35km *Bundoran*—6.5km *Ballyshannon*—21.5km *Donegal*—29km *Ballybofey*—22km *Strabane*—A5. 13km **Derry**.

Driving N from Sligo, we leave the R291 to the left, which leads to (9km) *Rosses Point*. With a fine view ahead of Ben Bulben (see below) we reach (7km) **Drumcliff** (also *Drumcliffe*; *Droim Chliahb*, ridge of baskets), with a fine but weathered *High Cross* (c 1000), with elaborate sculptures of figures and animals, and scroll-work, marking the site of a monastery traditionally founded c 575 by St. Colmcille (or Columba). The stump remains of a *Round Tower*, struck by lightning in 1396. In the graveyard of the *Protestant Church* (where his grandfather was rector) William Butler Yeats (1865–1939) was buried in 1948, having died at Roquebrune in the South of France; his grave is just N of the porch.

At *Cooladrummon*, near Drumcliff, was fought the so-called 'Battle of the Books' between the followers of St. Columba and those of St. Finian of Movilla. The

Ben Bulben, seen from the South

latter claimed the copy St. Columba had made from his own copy of the psalter. The case was brought before Dermot, King of Meath, who (?according to Brehon Law) decided that 'as to every cow belongs its calf, so to every book belongs its copy', a ludicrous decision against which Columba appealed to his tribe. They won the ensuing skirmish, in which 3,000 of their rivals (it is said) were slain. It was in penance for this that Columba was sent by St. Molaise to convert the heathen in Scotland.

To the N rises 'bare Ben Bulben's head' (526m; *View from its table-topped limestone summit), the scarped side of which is at present defaced by prominent graffiti. **Ben Bulben** is the most westerly of the *Dartry Mountains*, which run inland to *Truskmore* (644m), and preserves some unusual flora. It was here that the final scene of the pursuit of Diarmuid and Grainne took place, when the hero was killed by the followers of Finn MacCoul.

A lane leads W from Drumcliff to (left) **Lissadell House**, the demesne of the Gore-Booth family. The house was built in 1834 by Francis Goodwin for the grandfather of the militant Countess Constance Markievicz (1884–1927), who was the first woman elected to the British House of Commons, but preferred to take her seat in the Dáil instead, and her poet sister Eva Gore-Booth (1870–1926), both friends of W.B. Yeats.

On the shore here are the scanty ruins of *Dunfore Castle* and, further on, the remains of a cashel with souterrains, a dolmen, and a stone circle.—Beyond is the fishing-village of *Raghly*, on the N point of *Sligo Bay*, with *Ardtermon Castle* (17C), once the seat of the Gore family. Hence we may regain the main road to the NE near Grange.

8km *Grange*.

A lane descends 2.5km W to the slight ruins of *Staad Abbey*, built (perhaps by St. Molaise) on *Streedagh Strand*, where three vessels of the Armada were wrecked, leaving 'eleven hundred dead corpses' on the shore. It was here that De Cuellar, a captain of the Armada, first sought refuge, but he found it already in ruins.

Hence a boat may be hired to visit **Inishmurray**, a small island to the NW, inhabited until 1948. It is named probably from St. Muiredach, a follower of St. Patrick, and is remarkable for the extraordinary number of its antiquities. The most important is a large cashel (53m by 41m), a pagan fort converted by St. Molaise into a small monastery in the 6C. It contains a beehive hut and three oratories: *Teach Molaise*, with thick walls of very large stones (c 9C); *Teampull Molaise*, much larger; and *Teampull-na-Teinidh* (Church of Fire; ?14C). The whole was amateurishly restored in 1880. Other remains include inscribed gravestones, three pillar-stones, two bullauns, and two wells.

8km beyond Grange we reach the *Creevykeel* crossroads, to the E of which is one of the finest *Court Cairns* in Ireland; excavations in 1935 revealed artifacts dating back to the Late Stone Age (c 2500 BC).—A lane leads 5km NW to *Mullaghmore*, with its harbour built by Lord Palmerston in 1842, to the SW of which is *Classiebawn Castle* (1842–72), which had been inherited by the late Countess Mountbatten. It was offshore here that Admiral Louis Mountbatten (1900–79) was blown up by members of the IRA.

We traverse *Tullagham*, with an ancient cross, before entering **Bundoran** (1,600 inhab.), a popular seaside resort 4km NW of LOUGH MELVIN (see Rte 26A), and commanding a good view N towards the Donegal coast, terminating with Slieve League to the W, and also with fine retrospective views of Ben Bulben. To the N of the town the cliffs, rich in fossils, have been worn into curious shapes, among which is the natural arch known as the *Fairy Bridge*.

We shortly enter **Ballyshannon** (2,650 inhab.), properly *Ballyshannagh* (*Béal Átha Seanaigh*, mouth of Shannagh's ford), on the steep N bank of the river Erne. It is now the site of a military camp;

its earlier *barracks* date from 1700, probably to the design of Colonel Thomas Burgh. Its *Castle* has almost disappeared.

It was the scene of a victory in 1597 of Hugh Roe O'Donnell, who drove off the besieging English force under Sir Conyers Clifford, inflicting great slaughter among them. Among its natives were 'Speaker' William Conolly (c 1660–1729), and the poet William Allingham (1824–89).

The house called 'The Abbey', NW on the Kilbarron road, marks the site of the abbey of *Assaroe* (*Eas Aedha Ruadh*, the falls of Red Hugh), called after an early king who was drowned there. Founded in 1178, it has almost vanished, except for the graveyard, with the tomb of the O'Clerys, and some fragmentary walls.— Some 3km beyond, on the shore, are the ruins of *Kilbarron Castle*, a fortress of the O'Clerys: Michael O'Clery (1575–1643) was chief of the Four Masters of Donegal (see below).

The R230 leads E to the frontier at (6km) *Belleek*, skirting the ASSAROE LAKE, formed in 1948–52 when the Erne was dammed to make a reservoir. LOWER LOUGH ERNE, 6km beyond, is described on p 315.

We now traverse, as far as Donegal, a belt of drumlins, an area called *The Pullans*. To the E of (9.5km; right) *Ballintra*, in the demesne of *Brownhall*, is a curious limestone ravine through which the Ballintra river flows, intermittently penetrating a subterranean cavern.— Beyond *Laghy*, we veer NW to (11km) *Donegal*, at the head of shoal-girt Donegal Bay, and at the mouth of the river Eske, with the *Blue Stack* mountains rising beyond.

DONEGAL (1,950 inhab.), in Irish *Dún na nGall*, the fort of the foreigners (i.e. the Vikings), is an ancient and historic town, the head-quarters of the O'Donnell clan, Cinel Conail, and the capital of their territory, Tirchonaill or Tyrconnel. The **Castle** (under restoration), N of the principal square (in fact a Plantation 'Diamond', laid out by Sir Basil Brooke), rebuilt by Sir Basil in 1610, is a fine Jacobean structure with a tall gabled tower and projecting turrets, and imposing chimney-piece.

The ruins of a *Franciscan Monastery* stand on the shore, protected by a sea-wall. It was founded in 1474 by Hugh O'Donnell and his wife Fingalla O'Brien, and both the founders and their son Hugh Og were buried in the precincts. The principal remains are those of the choir, the S transept, and two walls of the cloister. The rest was destroyed in 1601 by the explosion of several barrels of gunpowder, when Hugh Roe O'Donnell was besieging his cousin Niall Garbh (see below) and an English garrison.

Niall gained little by his desertion; having lost the confidence of the English, he was imprisoned in the Tower of London from 1609 until his death in 1626. Hugh died in Spain in 1602 on a mission to seek further assistance for Ireland.—The historical compilation known as the 'Annals of the Four Masters' was written within the abbey, or adjacent, during 1632–36, covering the history of the world up to 1616. The four masters were Michael O'Clery and his assistants, Fearfeasa O'Maolconry, Peregrine O'Duigenan and Peregrine O'Clery, a monument to whom stands in the Diamond.

E of the town is *St. Patrick's Church* (1934), incorporating traditional Irish motives, by Ralph Byrne.

For the road hence to Letterkenny via the Donegal coast, see Rte 28.

From Donegal we drive NE, after 6.5km passing (left) LOUGH ESKE, fringed with the groves of partly gutted *Lough Eske Castle* (1866), and backed to the N by the *Blue Stack* or *Croaghgorm* range (672m), to the E of which rise three 500m mountains. On an island in the lough is ruined *O'Donnell's Tower*, once used as a prison by that powerful clan. The road ascends the Lowerymore valley, once infested by highwaymen, with a fine retrospective view, and traverses the narrow *Barnesmore Gap* between *Croaghconnelagh* (left) and *Barnesmore*. Descending past (right) the melancholy tarn of LOUGH MOURNE we approach *Ballybofey*, where in the Protestant churchyard lies the founder of the Irish Home Rule Party, Isaac Butt (1813–79). Its population, together with *Stranorlar* on the far side of the Finn, crossed by a many-arched bridge, is 2,950.

From Ballybofey the R252 climbs over the hills to the W to *Glenties*, see Rte 28. For *Letterkenny*, 19km N, see p 308.

An alternative DIRECT ROUTE TO DERRY (38km) follows the N56, off which we shortly bear right onto the R326 for the village of *Convoy* on the Deela, a stream rising on the flank of the *Cark Mountain* (366m) to the W. There is a fine Stone Circle on a hilltop at *Beltany*, some 4km downstream. The next village, **Raphoe** (1,050 inhab.), was once the seat of a bishopric joined to the see of Derry in 1835. A monastery founded here by St. Columba was converted into a cathedral by St. Eunan in the 9C, it is said, but the present *Cathedral* is a plain Gothic building with transepts of 1702 and a tower of 1738; some curious carvings of an earlier date are preserved, however. The neighbouring *Bishop's Palace* or *Castle* (1636), with four bastion-like towers, still occupied in the 1830s, is now a ruin. Isaac Butt received his early education at the Royal School here.—We shortly cross the Strabane–Letterkenny road and descend into the Foyle valley to *St. Johnstown*, some 3km S of which is the square tower of *Montgevlin*, all that remains of a castle where James II held court during the siege of Derry. We soon fork right towards the frontier-post at *Carrigans*, to approach *Derry*, see Rte 34A.

Crossing the Finn, we bear right at *Stranorlar*, and drive down the valley via (12km) *Castlefin*, formerly a fief of the O'Donnells, and just short of *Clady* (in Tyrone) we turn NE parallel with the border to **Lifford** (1,450 inhab.), the scene of a battle in 1600 between Hugh Roe O'Donnell and the English garrison of Derry under his cousin Niall Garbh O'Donnell, who had deserted to the English side in resentment at Hugh's appointment as Earl of Tyrconnel. *Port Hall* (1746), and the courthouse, were designed by Michael Priestley. The *Clouleigh* Parish church (1622, and late 18C) contains part of a monument to Sir Richard Hansard and his wife, kneeling figures in Jacobean costume.

A bridge crosses the border to **STRABANE** (10,350 inhab.), an important agricultural centre situated just above the junction of the Mourne with the Finn, their united course being known as the Foyle; all three are noted salmon streams. The town was never of great architectural interest, and even in the 1840s was described as 'far from being neat, well arranged, clean, or orderly', and it has since suffered in the recent 'troubles'.

The main building of interest—now that the Courthouse has been demolished—is *Gray's Printing Shop* (NT), still in operation at 49 Main St, with several 19C presses.

It is possible that John Dunlap (1746–1812, in Philadelphia), a native of Strabane, was an apprentice here before emigrating to America, where in 1771 he issued the 'Pennsylvania Packet', which (from 1784) was the first American daily paper; he was also the first printer of the Declaration of Independence (1776). Another apprentice was James Wilson, employed here before 1807, when he also emigrated; he was the grandfather of President Woodrow Wilson, and was born at *Dergalt*, 3km to the E, where his farmhouse home is preserved (NT).

Another native of Strabane, which is remarkable for the number of men it has produced who have distinguished themselves in trans- Atlantic affairs, was Guy Carleton, Lord Dorchester (1724–1808). He was governor of Quebec for most of the period 1766–96. He defended Quebec and defeated the Americans on Lake Champlain in 1775–76, and was commander-in-chief in America in 1782–83. Among those who have distinguished themselves in Ireland are George Sigerson (1838–1925), Fenian, poet, and physician; and Brian O'Nolan (1911–66; better known as 'Flann O'Brien'), the author.

From Strabane the A5 runs above and parallel to the E bank of the Foyle, its river-meadows being subject to flood, veering closer to the stream as we approach **Derry**, which looks tranquil from a distance. We turn left across the 365m-long *Craigavon Bridge* towards the centre; see Rte 34A.

28 Donegal to Derry via the Coast Road: Glenties, Dungloe, Dunfanaghy, and Letterkenny

194km (121 miles). N56. 48km *Glenties*—27km *Dunglow*—13km *Crolly*—17km *Gortahork*—16km *Dunfanaghy*—11km *Creeslough*—25km *Letterkenny*—N13. 37km **Derry**.

This distance will be considerably increased if the numerous alternative coastal circuits are included: the extent of each detour is given at their start. The excursion to Killybegs and Slieve League is recommended.

From Donegal (see above) we drive due W roughly parallel to *Donegal Bay*, with occasional views S towards the Sligo mountains and Ben Bulben, with distant Nephin Beg to the SW.

Beyond *Mountcharles*, a hillside quarrying village, we cross the base of the *Doorin peninsula*, with *Blue Stack* (672m) and *Binbane* to our right—A hill-road to the right (R262) climbs NW across country to (21km) *Glenties*, see below.

We traverse *Inver* and *Dunkineely*, the latter standing at the base of *St. Johns Point*, a narrow tongue of land, to the W of which lies *MacSwyne's Bay*, an inlet recalling the once powerful sept of that name who controlled the Barony of Banagh; their castle lies on the shore to the S. We bear NW over the Oily river, shortly passing a renovated *Round Tower* and (25km) reach a T-junction in the adjacent valley.

The left-hand turning leads in 3km to **Killybegs** (1,550 inhab.), a busy fishing-port, resounding to the keening of gulls, on one of the more attractive of the landlocked bays of Donegal. It is well-known for the manufacture of Donegal carpets. William Allingham, the poet, was a customs' officer here c 1849.

Hence we may return to the junction (see below), or continue W to make the circuit of part of the wild mountainous SW peninsula of Donegal: FROM KILLYBEGS TO MALIN MORE is 29km; and from thence to Ardara another 30km.

The R263 skirts *Fintragh Bay*, overlooked by *Crownarad* (493m), a shoulder of which we cross to *Kilcar*, charmingly situated at the confluence of two streams, and shortly beyond, enter *Carrick*, to the W of which towers *Slieve League*, its far side providing some of the most imposing cliff-scenery in Ireland. Carrick stands on the Glen river just above its mouth in the beautiful little fjord of *Teelin Bay*.

*Slieve League** (601m) is easily ascended by those with suitable footwear and a head for heights.

A lane to the right 1.5km S of Carrick, ascending to the right, later peters out, and is not recommended to motorists, but is best reserved for the descent by foot. The finest approach is by taking the next turning, at *Teelin*, which although narrow and humpy, takes us to the *Carrigan Head*, a bold promontory at the SE end of the cliffs, and then bears round, following a new track to a viewpoint on *Bunglass*

Point. Hence the whole curving seaward face of Slieve League is displayed, a precipice not only remarkable for its immense height—it falls practically sheer from the summit—but also for its colouring caused by the stains of metallic salts. In fair weather it may be visited by boat from Teelin.

At *Eagle's Nest* (534m) the cliffs are at their steepest, and between this point and the summit, providing splendid *•Views*, is the *One Man's Path*, a narrow edge 60cm wide between the steeply scarped landward side and the cliff—not to be attempted in blustery or misty weather—but which may be side-tracked by taking the 'Old Man's Path' a little below the crest on the landward side.

Regaining the road at Carrick, we turn left and cross moorland, after 3km leaving a rough road descending W to *Malin More*. After another 4km we climb down into the Glen valley and to **Glencolumbkille** (the glen of St. Columba; said to have been a favourite retreat of the saint and his disciples). On the hillside ascending N to Glen Head are the *House* (an oratory with its altar on the N side), *Well*, *Chair*, and *Bed* of St. Columba. *Glen Head* itself is a sheer precipice 227m high, with a signal tower above it.

Sturrall, the next promontory, is approached by a dangerous knife-edge ridge.—Continuing beyond the village, we pass (left) newly-built 'folk cottages' (which may be rented) and crossing a ridge reach *Malin More*, and at the S end of its bay, *Malin Beg*.—Beyond the latter is the little bay of *Trabane*, and to the W the island of *Rathlin O'Birne*, with a lighthouse. On the coast beyond *Sturrall* is the tiny harbour of *Port*.—1.5km along the direct Carrick road from Malin More, to the right, is the oval cashel (restored) of *Cloghanmore*, with two flag-roofed chambers, and on the other side of the road are two standing stones and a dolmen.

On regaining Glancolumbkille, we follow the Adara road, passing a well-preserved *Cross*, and climb due E. This road and that ascending the Glen valley from Carrick converge at *Meenanxeary*, whence we continue E up the desolate Crow valley towards *Crocknapeast* (502m) before bearing NE to the *Pass of Glengesh*. We descend towards *Ardara*, meeting the Killybegs road just S of the village.

Intrepid walkers may follow a rough track along the N coast of the peninsula from Glen Head over the cliffs of *Port Hill* (248m) and *Slievetooey* (443m) to the primitive hamlet of *Maghera*, with its waterfall, cliffs, caves and dunes, whence a coast road leads due E to Ardara.

From the T-junction N of Killybegs, the N56 climbs N up the Stragar valley to the 'Neck' of the *Ballagh Pass*, thence deceding to **Ardara** (650 inhab.)—pronounced with the last syllable accented—a centre of the Donegal homespun and knitting industry, standing at the head of *Loughros More Bay*.

Hence a DETOUR may be made to regain the road at (14.5km) *Maas*, by continuing due N to *Kilclooney*, with a huge dolmen (5 minutes' walk behind the church). Further to the W in LOUGH DOON are the remains of a huge oval fort known as *The Bawn*. Beyond the village we meet the road to *Maas* (right).—Turning left, we traverse *Narin* (or *Naran*) and adjacent *Portnoo*, two fishing villages facing the tidal islet of *Inishkeel*, with a ruined chapel. The views and walks in every direction are delightful. The road goes on, passing (right) *Dunmore Head*, and several small loughs with remains of island fortresses, to *Rosbeg* on *Dawros Bay*; from *Dawros Head*, beyond, there are fine views of the cliffs of Slievetooey (S) and Aran Island to the N.

The main road turns right along the Owentocker river from Ardara to (9.5km) **Glenties** (800 inhab.), another pleasantly sited angling resort near the confluence of the Stracashel and Owenea, where more knitting takes place, and with a modern church.

From Glenties the R250 drives NE to (16km) *Fintown*, beautifully situated at the far end of narrow LOUGH FINN (5km long), below *Aghla* (596m), connected by road to both *Ballybofey* (27km SE; see Rte 27) and *Letterkenny* (30km NE; see below), while from the N bank another mountain road leads NW to *Doochary* and *Dunglow*; see below.

The main road from Glenties turns NW to (7km) *Maas*, where we turn abruptly E and after 5km cross the Gweebarra estuary by a long bridge, with a fine view up the valley towards *Slieve Snaght* (683m) in the distance.

A minor road (R254) ascends the valley to (9km) *Doochary*, and is continued beyond past LOUGH BARRA (with retrospective views), and circling behind *Moylenany* (538m) meets the R251 by GARTAN LOUGH, 13km NW of Letterkenny. Near *Church Hill* is the *Glebe Gallery*; see below. Adjoining Gartan Lough to the N is LOUGH AKIBBON, where a ruined chapel above its W side is said to have been built on the spot where St. Columba was born in 521; it was later used as a burial-place for the O'Donnells. The ruined church at *Temple Douglas*, SW on the Letterkenny road, is where the saint is said to have been baptised.

Columba was a descendant of Niall of the Nine Hostages, and on his mother's side of the Kings of Leinster. Although the termination 'cille' (a church) to his name might confirm his devoutness, his character is better described by his other baptismal name, Crimthan (a wolf); but his relentless energy was quelled by his missionary visit to Scotland after the 'Battle of the Books' (cf. Cooladrummon).

The main road turns N across moorlands to (13km) **Dunglow**; 1,000 inhab.), an angling centre, the best sport being found in LOUGH MEELA, to the NW; *Maghery Bay*, 7km SW, has a fine sandy strand, and the strange rocky coast here is worth exploring.

DUNGLOW TO CROLLY BY THE COAST ROAD (23.5km). The R259 leads NW, skirting the island-studded bay, passing the old Rutland barracks and LOUGH MEELA, to (6.5km) *Burtonport*, a small fishing village with granite quarries, owing its name and origin to the 4th Marquess Conyingham (William Burton), who built the grain store.—About 3km NW is the lonely ruin of *Castle Port*. Close inshore is *Inishmacduirn* or *Rutland Island*, on which may be seen the sand-strewn relics of a futile attempt to establish a port here (1785) under the Lord-Lieutenancy of the Duke of Rutland. Napper Tandy made a landing here, for a few hours only, on 16 September 1798, together with a body of French soldiers, before being carried back aboard the 'Anacreon' in a state of inebriation.

Beyond it is the lofty **Aran Island** or **Aranmore**; in Irish *Árainn Mhór* (228m; 800 inhab.), with its lighthouse on its NW point, visible 25m (originally of 1798, but replaced in 1865). There is a regular ferry between Burtonport and *Leabgarrow* on the island, which, like the smaller islets of *Inishcoo* and *Eighter*, has fine sandy strands.—From Burtonport the coast road bears N across an area known as *The Rosses*, well-described by Lloyd Praeger as 'a land of innumerable lakelets, a windswept heathery region, with small peaty fields grudgingly yielding difficult crops of potatoes and oats and turnips, and roads meandering through granite hillocks'. The road passes the offshore island of *Cruit*, and beyond, *Inishfree Bay*, before turning inland through *Annagary* to regain the main road at *Crolly*.

The N56 from Dunglow leads NE, after 8km passing (right) LOUGH ANURE, dominated by *Crocknafarragh* (519m), and a large building started as a carpet-factory, which later became a toy-factory, before entering *Crolly*.

CROLLY TO GORTAHORK VIA THE COAST (27km). We turn NW for (left) *Bunbeg*, a little port, and further N, *Derrybeg*, beyond which, on the coastal slopes, are numerous houses and cottages, typical of the still 'Congested Districts'. We shortly round the hill known as *Bloody Foreland* (316m), the NW point of Donegal, so-called from its red hue when lit up by the setting sun.

11km due N lies *Tory Island* (317 hectares), a desolate place (on which a gunboat endeavouring to land rate-collectors was wrecked in 1884), inhabited by lobster-fishermen. It was once the stronghold of the Fomorians, a legendary race of gigantic pirates, whose chieftain was the one-eyed Balor of the Mighty Blows. St. Columba is said to have visited it in a corragh, and the *Round Tower*, tau cross, and other (re-arranged) antiquities there may be relics of a monastery he established.—Nearer the coast are the smaller islands of *Inishbofin*,

Inishdooey, and *Inishbeg*.—Rounding the head of *Ballyness Bay*, we leave (right)
the district known as *Gweedore* and enter that of *Cloghaneely*, regaining the
main route at *Gortahork*.

From Crolly the main road veers inland past the village of *Gweedore*,
an oasis in the wilds, which owes its existence to an hotel (closed) built
here by Lord George Hill (1801–79), who did much to improve the lot
of the poor inhabitants of this overpopulated district. Beyond it is a
power station on LOUGH NACUNG. To the left rises *Tievealehid*
(431m), while to the E we see the splendid conical quartzite peak of
Errigal Mountain (752m), the highest in Donegal.

The ASCENT OF ERRIGAL is usually made from Dunlewy (see below), and is
laborious but not difficult. The grass and heather slopes are succeeded by a
stretch of awkward loose stones, whence a steep incline leads to the first pinnacle
of the crest. This is connected with the main peak by the *One Man Path*, 27m long
and 60cm wide, the only dizzy part of the ascent. The N side towards LOUGH
ALTAN should be avoided, as it is covered by loose and dangerous scree. The
immense *View extends from Knocklayd, in Antrim, to Ben Bulben above Sligo,
and a fine panorama of coast.

Dunlewy is just off the R251 which forks right off the N56 just beyond
the power station.

DUNLEWY TO TERMON (29km) is an impressive but desolate road, to be
avoided in bad weather. To the SE of Dunlewy is the so-called *Poisoned Glen*, a
steep rift in the *Derryveagh Mountains*, and the water there was long unfit to
drink, owing to the poisonous spurge that grew on its banks. To the S rises *Slieve
Snaght* (683m), and to the NE, *Dooish* (633m). The road climbs NE, commanding
striking *Views; to the NW are *Aghla More* (582m) and the lower *Aghla Beg*;
between the former and Errigal lies savage LOUGH ALTAN. Further N rises the
escarpment of *Muckish* (670m). From *Calabber Bridge* the road bears round the
N spur of the Derryveagh range at *Kinggarrow*, and passes the N end of mountain-girt *Lough Beagh* (6.5m long), with a Deer Forest in the glen to the SW.
This is approached from a Visitor Centre by a private road on the S bank, passing
Glenveagh Castle (1870), beautifully sited on a rock promontory, with attractive
gardens and splendid rhododendrons.
    The area (9,667 hectares) has recently been designated the **Glenveagh
National Park**.
    Continuing E we bear left onto the R255 to regain the N56 just S of *Termon*; the
right-hand turning leads to LOUGH AKIBBON (4km S; see above), between
which and GARTAN LOUGH, at the *Glebe Gallery*, may be seen a collection of
paintings acquired by Derek Hill, some of them French Impressionists. This is
close to *Church Hill* on the R251, providing an alternative route to Letterkenny.

The main road from Gweedore circles N to *Gortahork*, where we bear
NE through adjacent *Falcarragh*, noted for the *Stone of Cloghaneely*
(which gives its name to the district) in the grounds of *Ballyconnell
House*.

It is said that the pirate Balor (see above) carried off to Tory Island a celebrated
cow belonging to MacKineely, the local chief, and hearing that the owner was
plotting retaliation, decapitated him on this stone, its red veining recalling the
bloody deed; another version is that MacKineely had seduced Balor's only
daughter. The resultant child, a blacksmith, in revenge for his father's death, ran
a red-hot iron through Balor's Cyclopean eye.

After 5km we pass in *Myrath* old churchyard (left) a monolithic cross
said to have been cut by St. Columba out of the rocks of *Muckish*
(670m; the 'Pig's Back'), a huge truncated cone to the SE, usually
ascended from Creeslough, see below.—16km (from Gortahork) lies
Dunfanaghy, overlooking *Sheep Haven* and dominated to the N by
Horn Head, a precipitous cliff 190m high, commanding splendid
views. By the shore to the W of the village is a colossal blow-hole
known as *McSwyne's* (or MacSweeney's) *Gun*, into which the tide

rushes with a deafening report in stormy weather. Hence cliff paths circle the cape, with its curious rock formations and uncommon seabirds.

Beyond Dunfanaghy the road turns SE, passing (left) *Portnablagh*, on a charming little bay opposite the *Rosguill peninsula*, while on promontories further S are the wooded demesne of the Capuchin Friary of *Ard Mhuire* (Ards), and at *Sheep Haven*, the tall but battered keep of *Doe Castle*, an ancient stronghold of the MacSweeneys, still surrounded by its bawn. It was the headquarters of Sir Cahir O'Doherty's ill-starred raid on Derry in 1608; although at first successful, he was forced to retreat and met his death within a year at Kilmacrenan.

9.5km *Creeslough*, with the *Church of St. Michael* (1971; by Liam McCormick and Partners).

CREESLOUGH TO LETTERKENNY VIA MILLFORD (44km). The R245 turns sharply NE.—A minor road shortly forks right for *Glen*, at the head of LOUGH GLEN.—Hence a track leads 5km S towards precipitous *Loughsalt Mountain* (470m), at the foot of which is a wild tarn of great depth (73m), reputed never to freeze. We may regain the main road N of Glen not far short of *Carrickart*, a tweed-weaving village, to the NW of which lies *Rosapenna*, on the narrow neck of the Rosguill peninsula.—Further N is *Downies*, with a fine strand and good views across Sheep Haven towards Muckish.—Hence the 'Atlantic Drive' circles the peninsula except for its NE promontory of *Melmore Head*. On the return, at the E foot of *Ganiamore*, we pass *Mevagh*, with a ruined church, inscribed stones, and other antiquities.

From Carrickart, the road skirts the W side of the 19km-long estuary of *Mulroy Bay*, almost landlocked, passing (left) near *Mulroy House*, the demesne of the earls of Leitrim, and *Cratlagh Woods*, where in 1878 the 3rd Earl was murdered for the callous eviction of any tenant who disobeyed him, and later cross a bridge over the Bunlin river, near which is a dolmen and a waterfall called *Goland Loop*, to enter **Millford** (or *Milford*; 900 inhab.), charmingly placed 2.5km N of LOUGH FERN.

Hence the DETOUR TO PORTSALON on the *Fanad peninsula* may be made by turning N onto the R746 skirting the E bank of *Mulroy Bay* below *Crockmore Hill* (further E, with a fine dolmen) via *Carrowkeel*. We then fork right almost parallel to the ridge of *Knockalla Mountain* (364m), called 'The Devil's Backbone'.— *Portsalon*, facing SE up LOUGH SWILLY (see below), finely situated opposite Dunree Head and the Urris Hills, has as its church bell the ship's bell of the bullion-laden 'Laurentic', sunk by a U-boat in 1917, the cargo of which was salved by divers in 1924. The far end of the peninsula may be circled, but it is not spectacular.—A road climbs SE round the N end of *Knockalla*, skirting the W bank of **Lough Swilly** (the Lake of the Shadows), in fact an estuary 48km long, with some impressive scenery at its seaward end. On 12 October 1798 the French frigate 'Hoche', with Wolfe Tone on board, was intercepted here by Sir John Warren's squadron, and its crew taken to Letterkenny. There Tone was identified, and transferred to Dublin Castle, where he committed suicide.—After some 11km we pass the ruined church of *Killygarvan* and the dolmen and cross-slab of *Dramhallagh* before reaching **Rathmullen** (600 inhab.). To the W rises *Croaghan Hill*, and further W is *Crockanaffrin* (347m), commanding a view of the fjord-like ramifications of Lough Swilly and Mulroy Bay.

Rathmullen was the scene of the 'Flight of the Earls' (1607), when the Earls of Tyrone and Tyrconnel, with about 100 minor nobility and followers, set sail for France, the terminating episode of the Elizabethan wars in Ireland. The ensuing confiscation of the earls' extensive estates led to the 'Plantation' of Ulster and all the events arising therefrom.

Rathmullen preserves the ruin of a Carmelite *Priory*, of which the tower and chancel were erected by the MacSweeneys in the 15C, while the W portions were rebuilt in 1618 by Bp Knox of Raphoe, to whom the lands of Turlough Og MacSweeney were awarded after the confiscations.—We reach the R245 11km SW at **Rathmelton** (pron. Ramelton; 950 inhab.), on a creek of LOUGH SWILLY, its harbour preserving some imposing old warehouses on the water's edge. It was the birthplace of the Rev. Francis Makemie (1658–1708), the real founder of the Presbyterian church in America; he emigrated in 1683. The curious E window of the church here may be as late as the 17C.—Some 5km SE lies *Fort Stewart*, a 17C ruin. The road leading hence to *Letterkenny* (12km SW of Rathmelton) passes the ruins of *Killydonnell Abbey*, a small Franciscan house founded in the 16C by an O'Donnell.

From Creeslough, the N56 leads SE, soon crossing the Owencarrow at *New Bridge*, with a fine view SW up Glenveagh (see above), and ascends to *Barnes Gap* between *Stragaddy* and *Crockmore*, with *Loughsalt Mountain* (470m; see above) further E, and descends into the Lurgy valley at *Termon*, and 3km beyond traverses **Kilmacrenan** in the Lenan valley. It preserves slight remains of a 15C Franciscan Friary and a later church tower, succeeding a church said to have been founded by St. Columba.— The *Rock of Doon* (3km W) was the site of the inauguration of the chief of the O'Donnells.

The road continues over rolling country to **LETTERKENNY** (6,450 inhab.), consisting mainly of one long street on the slope of a hill (*Leitir Ceanainn*, the hillside of the O'Cannons). The *Cathedral of St. Eunan*, decorated with a number of Celtic motives, and containing glass by Harry Clarke and Michael Healy, is in a 'free' Gothic style (1890–1901; by Hague and MacNamara).

At **Farsetmore**, NE of the town, took place a battle in May 1567 in which Shane O'Neill 'the Proud' was vanquished by Hugh O'Donnell. Many of his cavalry drowned while recrossing the estuary of the Swilly, where a sandbank is still named 'the Marcaghs' (or horsemen's) bed'.—At *Scarriffhollis*, below the hamlet of *New Mills*, 5km SW of Letterkenny, Sir Charles Coote's army destroyed the Bp of Clogher's forces in June 1650, the bishop-general being later captured; he was hanged at Enniskillen six months afterwards.

6.5km E of Letterkenny we fork left off the N14 to *Strabane* (see latter part of Rte 27; 19km beyond) onto the N13, running more or less parallel to the upper reaches of LOUGH SWILLY (see above) and traversing the villages of *Manorcunningham* and *Newton Cunningham*, 3km N of which stands the 16C tower-house of *Burt* (showing Scottish influence), with *Dooish Mountain* prominent to the right.—On reaching a T-junction one may either bear left round the high ground culminating in the *Grianan of Aileach* (see Rte 34B) to the frontier-post for entry to Derry from the N, or alternatively follow the right-hand fork (a slightly shorter road) to pass the border at *Killea*. For **Derry**, see Rte 34A.

29 Dublin to Donegal via Kells, Cavan, and Enniskillen

235km (146 miles). N3. 48km **Navan**—16km **Kells**— 19km *Viginia*—31km *Cavan*—17km *Belturbet*—R202. 29km *Swalinbar*—A32. 19km **Enniskillen**—14km *Irvinestown*—A35 and R232. 42km **Donegal**.

For the slightly longer alternative route from Dublin to Kells via Trim, see below.

Leave Dublin by skirting the N side of *Phoenix Park* (or by the Main Road through the centre of the park and *Castleknock*), cross the Royal Canal and traverse *Blanchardstown*. The castle from which Castleknock is named was built by Hugh Tyrrel, a Norman knight; its ruin dates from 1642, when it was taken with great slaughter by General Monk; its remains lie in the burial-ground of the Vincentian Fathers.—2.5km E stands *Dunsink Observatory* (Trinity College), founded in 1782, and designed by Graham Myers.

At 14.5km we reach the junction of the R156 (diverging left) for the DETOUR TO TRIM (also reached direct by the less interesting R154 from *Black Bull*, 5km further NE on the N3).

We first traverse *Dunboyne*, with a tall belfry, and the birthplace of Colonel Thomas Blood (1618–80), who nearly stole the Crown Jewels from the Tower of London in 1671.—After 22km we enter *Summerhill*, with a pleasant village green; in the demesne of the demolished Palladian mansion of the Langfords are remains of a castle destroyed in August 1647 when Colonel Michael Jones's victory over General Thomas Preston at *Dangan Hill* made Dublin safe for Cromwell. Elizabeth of Austria took Summerhill for the hunting season in 1879 and 1880.—Here we fork right onto the R158, shortly passing (left) the ruins, uninteresting in themselves, of *Dangan Castle*, the youthful home of the future Duke of Wellington, when it was the country house of his father, the Earl of Mornington. On the estate of Summerhill, near Dangan Castle, was born Ambrosio O'Higgins (?1720–1801, viceroy of Peru and Chile, and father of Bernardo O'Higgins (1778—1842) the liberator of Chile).—We cross the Knightsbrook river at **Laracor**, a quiet little village of which Jonathan Swift became incumbent in 1699.

Here are the paths where he used to stroll with 'Stella' (Esther Johnson) and Dr Raymond, the vicar of Trim; but the association is all that remains, for a modern church replaces that in which Swift used to preach to a congregation of a dozen. It retains the altar plate he used. The site is the only authentic feature of the house pointed out as 'Stella's', where she lived with her friend Mrs Dingley from 1701.

3km **TRIM** (originally *Ath Truim*, the ford of the elder-trees), the county town of Meath (2,150 inhab.), is charmingly situated on the Boyne, and preserves several interesting old buildings. The *Yellow Steeple*, the ruined 13C tower that rises above the roofs of the town, was part of the Augustine abbey of St. Mary, which is supposed to stand on the site of a convent founded by St. Patrick in 432 in conjunction with a bishopric of which his nephew, St. Loman, was the first holder. The *Sheep Gate*, near by, and the fragmentary *Water Gate*, to the W near the river, are the only two surviving in the old town wall. The facade of the old *Gaol* (c 1827) is by John Hargrave.

The *Castle, the largest Anglo-Norman fortress in Ireland, founded by Hugh de Lacy in 1173, was rebuilt by Roger de Pippard in 1220. The extensive ruins are dominated by a *Keep*, 21m high, which has a rectangular tower abutting each side. The outer wall, guarded by ten D-shaped towers, is surrounded by a moat into which the Boyne could be admitted at will. The barbican is well preserved.

Here Richard de Burgh, Earl of Ulster, held court in Edward II's time, and here Richard II confined his cousins Humphrey of Gloucester and Henry of Lancaster, afterwards Henry IV. It was the scene of several parliaments, and at one time housed a mint. Sir Charles Coote fell in its defence in 1642.

Talbot's Castle (modernised), near the Yellow Steeple, built in 1415 by Sir John Talbot, was bought by Esther Johnson ('Stella') in 1717 and sold by her the following year, at a profit, to Swift; the Dean likewise disposed of it, again at a profit, five months later; it was then converted into the diocesan school, where Arthur Wellesley (later the Duke of Wellington) received his early education, as did Sir William Rowan Hamilton, the astronomer. The Duke, who later (1790–95) represented Trim in Parliament, lived in Dublingate St, where he is commemorated by a pillar bearing his statue (repaired).

The tower of the *Cathedral* (since 1955, of the Protestant diocese of Meath), with a Sheila-na-gig, dates from 1449. To the N, outside the old walls, are the scanty remains of a *Dominican Friary*, founded by Geoffrey de Joinville, Lord of Meath, in the 13C.

To the W, on the N bank of the Boyne, at *Trimlestown* is a ruined 15C mansion garrisoned for ten years during the war against Cromwell.

At *Newtown Trim*, 1.5km E of Trim, on the direct Dublin road which here crosses the river by an old bridge, are the extensive remains of the *Cathedral of SS. Peter and Paul*, founded by Simon Rochfort in 1206 for Canons Regular. The church, on the N bank, is a good example of the transition from the Norman to the Early English style, with graceful lancet windows. At the other end of the bridge are the ruins of a *Castle*, with a large square keep, and a small chapel attached in the 13C to a priory of Crutched Friars. The neighbouring church contains fragments from the ruins and the tomb of Sir Lucas Dillon (died 1593) and his wife.

About 1.5km further on is the massive keep of *Scurlogstown Castle* (1080), with round towers at two of its corners.—*Bective* (see below) lies further NE to the right of the road to (14.5km) *Navan*.

The R154 continues NW from Trim to (12km) **Athboy** (*Ath Buidhe*, the yellow ford; 900 inhab.) to the W of the *Hill of Ward*, the site of the *Palace of Tlachtga*, formerly the scene of the festivities of Samhain, marking the end of summer.—Turning NE from Athboy we pass near the ruins of *Rathmore* church, with good 15C carving and the tombs of the Plunketts, whose keep stands near by, to regain the main road at (14.5km) *Kells*; see below.

For places of interest on the road between Kells and Mullingar, see the sub-route on p 371.

Keeping to the N3 beyond Black Bull, we reach (8km) *Dunshaughlin*, where the Protestant church preserves an ancient lintel with a primitive carving of Christ crucified between two tormentors.—At *Lagore* (*Loch Gabhair*), c 1.5km E, in the bed of a former lake, was a crannóg that was a residence of local kings c 650–950 and for a time the seat of the Ard Rí after the fall of Tara. It was destroyed by Olaf Guthfridson in 940, and excavated in 1934–36.

The minor road leading NW from Dunshaughlin approaches (4km) *Killeen Castle* (right) and, 2.5km beyond, *Dunsany Castle* (left), the ancient rival seats of the Fingall and Dunsany branches of the Plunkett family. Both were founded by Hugh de Lacy, and both were largely rebuilt in the 19C, the former by Francis Johnston in 1802 and later by James Shiel; the latter, preserving in the SW corner its Norman core, contains plasterwork by Michael Stapleton and a Gothick Library attributed also to Shiel; it was long the home of Lord Dunsany (1878–1957), the poet, and contains some works of art and family relics. The ruined church at *Killeen* (c 1465) preserves the tomb of its founder, Sir Christopher Plunkett; the old church at *Dunsany*, rebuilt by Nicholas Plunkett c 1450, contains a sculptured font and other Plunkett tombs.

The road goes on to (7.5km) **Bective Abbey*, on the left bank of the Boyne close to *Bective Bridge*, and one of the more picturesque of the ruined abbeys of Meath, founded in 1147 for Cistercians by Murchadha O'Melaghlin, King of Meath. It soon rose to importance, its abbot being a lord of Parliament, and here was buried Hugh de Lacy, procurator-general, accused of aspiring to the crown of Ireland and assassinated in 1186. The abbey was rebuilt on a smaller scale in the 15C and after the suppression it was adapted as a mansion (c 1600). The buildings surround a central cloister, and a strong battlemented tower rises at the SW angle. The dependencies, on the E side, have unusually thick walls incorporating chimney-flues.—To the NE stand the ruins of *Clady* church (13C), near a bridge, perhaps coeval.

Tara (see below) may be approached by turning NE from Bective along the S bank of the Boyne, and then right at the Ballinter crossroads. We pass (left) *Assey Castle*, and *Ballinter House* (18C; by Castle).

9.5km beyond *Dunshaughlin* on the N3, a left-hand turn shortly ascends the *Hill of Tara*, one of the more famous historic sites of Ireland (around which a thick mantle of romance has been woven). Little now remains apart from the hill on which there are a series of mounds, together with a church. In 1843 O'Connell chose this significant site for one of his 40-odd 'monster' meetings, attended by 100,000 or so, during his Repeal Campaign.

Teamhair na Riogh or *Tara of the Kings*, was originally the 'administrative capital' of the Kings of Meath (or North Leinster), and seat of the Ard Rí or High King. Every third year a 'feis' or assembly was held, each province having here their separate headquarters during such deliberations. It was apparently of importance as early as the Bronze Age, and remained so until the interdict of St. Ruadhan in 563, when King Diarmuid MacFergus was cursed for offering judicial violence to a kinsman, but was not finally abandoned until 1022. Under Cormac MacArt (227–66) the 'Teach Miodhchuarta' was erected for the triennial synods. It was his daughter Gráinne, betrothed to Fionn MacCumhail (Finn MacCoul), who eloped with Diarmuid O Duibhne.

On the summit of the hill, providing extensive views, is the *Ráth na Riogh*, the 'Kings' Rath' or royal enclosure, a slightly oval fortress (245m by 290m) with its earthern rampart and ditch. Within it are two mounds; on the E side, the *Forradh* or Royal Seat, and abutting it, in the centre of the enclosure; the *Teach Cormaic* (Cormac's House). On the latter, near an execrable statue of St. Patrick, is a pillar-stone marking the grave of insurgents killed at Tara in 1798, and fancifully named the *Lia Fáil*, as it is said to have formerly lain near the *Mound of the Hostages* (*Dumha na nGiall*; to the N of the enclosure), and was therefore the inauguration stone of the High Kings. The mound in fact covers a passage-grave of c 1800 BC.

To the S are traces of the *Rath Laoghaire* (132m across), or of Leary, King at the advent of St. Patrick in 432; and 1km beyond is the *Fort of Maeve*, another hillfort.

Passing the Mound of the Hostages, we traverse the *Rath of the Synods*, a trivallate earthwork (1–3C AD) unpardonably mutilated by misguided British Israelites at the turn of this century in quest of the Arc of the Covenant!—In the adjoining churchyard (where in the church a medieval window is preserved) is a pillar-stone known as *Adamnán's Cross*, with a weathered figure supposed by some to represent Cernunnos, the horned god of the pagan Celts.—Further N we see two parallel ridges, which mark the site of the great *Teach Miodhchuarta* (House of Mead-circling, of 'coasting'), assumed to be an assembly or banqueting hall, or even a ceremonial approach.—To the NW are three more circular earthworks, the nearest known as the *Rath Gráinne*; the others as the *Sloping Trenches* (*Claoin Fhearta*).

1.5km E of the main road, at *Skreen*, a well-sited hilltop village, is a ruined church of c 1341 with a later tower, and primitive cross; earthworks here are supposed to mark the site of a stronghold to which Cormac MacArt retired. To the N are the slight ruins of *Walterstown Castle*, 3km beyond which (NE) are remains of an ancient church and the fort of *Danestown*.

Continuing NW on the main road, we pass near the ruined 13C church of *Cannistown* (left) and descend to cross the river Boyne at *Kilcarn Bridge*.

Athlumney Castle, on the E bank, is a picturesque 16C manor, burned down, it is said, by Sir Lancelot Dowdall, a former owner, to avoid giving shelter to William of Orange; adjoining is a fine 17C house.—In the church of *Johnstown*, to the E, is the medieval font from the old church of Kilcarn.

After 2.5km we enter the busy but uninteresting town of **NAVAN** (4,100 inhab.) at the confluence of the Blackwater and the Boyne, but its inhabitants 'have turned their backs upon the stream, scarce a glimpse of which can be obtained from any of its narrow streets'. Known in Irish as *An Uaimh*, the town has a long history, but its fortifications erected by Hugh de Lacy have vanished and its abbey was destroyed in the Cromwellian wars. A wooden sculpture of the Crucified Christ by Edward Smyth (1792; his only recorded religious work) is preserved in the *Catholic church* (1836). W of the town is *Navan Mote*, an earthwork 16m high (not to be confused with *Navan Fort*, near Armagh). Some old mills remain by the riverbank. Lead and zinc deposits are being exploited in the vicinity, discovered in 1970.

Slane (see Rte 30) is 14km NW of Navan, beyond which the N51 continues E to (14km) *Drogheda* via (right of the road) *Newgrange*; see also Rte 30.

The Kells road ascends the W bank of the Blackwater, a lazy winding stream, the darkness of whose waters is attributed to a curse imposed on them by St. Patrick. After 2.5km we pass a turning (left) to (2.5km) *Ardbraccan House*, the later main block of which was begun in 1776, with wings by Castle erected after 1734. The church (1777) has a medieval belfry. The nearby limestone quarries provided stone for a number of Dublin's major buildings.—Beyond, to the right of the main road, is *Liscartan Castle*, a fortress held in 1633 by Sir William Talbot, with two square towers; adjacent is a pretty little church. *Rathaldron*, on the opposite bank, is another square fortress.—After a further 3km, and also on the far bank, is *Donaghpatrick*, the 'Church of St. Patrick', near a large rath with four tiers of ramparts. Beyond it, in a bend of the river, is *Teltown House*, taking its name from the *Hill of Tailte* on the N bank, on the summit of which is the *Rath Duhb*, or *Black Fort* (View), built by King Tuathal, and later a burial-ground.

Here took place the Aonach Tailteann, games in honour of the dead, held annually until 1168. An abortive attempt to revive these ancient antics was made in Dublin in 1924. Here also took place the 'Teltown Marriages', an informal agreement to cohabit for a year, after which, if the couple disagreed, they might stand back to back in the centre of the rath, and walking N and S out of the fort, were considered free to wed again, a practice which is said to have survived until the turn of the 19C.

KELLS (*Ceanannas Mór*; 2,600 inhab.), a small market-town, once a famous centre of learning, still retains a number of interesting remains of its illustrious past.

St. Columba, having received a grant of land from Diarmuid, son of Fergus Cerrbhol, founded a monastery here c 550. It flourished, producing in c 800 a magnificent decorated example of the Gospels, now to be seen in Trinity College Library, Dublin, and known as 'The Book of Kells'. A crosier made in the abbey is preserved in the British Museum. The monks of Iona, expelled by the Danes, took refuge here in 807, but between 920–1019 the abbey itself was four times plundered by the Danes. The town was burned in 1170, and again by Edward Bruce in 1315, and the monastery was dissolved in 1551. Roger Mortimer, 4th Earl of March, was killed in a skirmish here in 1398; Robert Barker (1739–1806), the reputed inventor of the 'panorama', was born here.

In the market-place is the *High Cross*, 2.5m high, with the top of its shaft and part of the wheel broken, and apparently used as a gallows in 1798, after which it lay prone for a century; the frieze of horse and foot soldiers on the original base is remarkable.—Hence we may ascend the street to the entrance of the churchyard. It is preferable to visit first (having obtained the key from a house on the right of the street here) the building known as *St. Columba's House* (c 807), a short distance further up the hill. This is a good example (but in need of restoration) of the primitive corbel-constructed steeply-pitched stone-roofed church (comp. Glendalough, Cashel, and Killaloe). The lower storey is barrel-vaulted; the original entrance to the upper storey has been walled up.

In the churchyard stands a *Round Tower*, c 30m high, and lacking its cap; it dates from before 1076. The entrance opening is round-headed; the windows above are square; the five (instead of the usual four) at the top are triangular-headed.—At its foot is the largest of the *Crosses of Kells*, over 3m high, and with a Latin inscription, unusual in Ireland; to the NW is the stump of another; beside the church is an interesting unfinished example. Adjoining is the detached belfry, rebuilt in 1578, and with a spire by Thomas Cooley added in 1783.

The *Catholic parish church* (1798) and the *Court-house* are both by Francis Johnston. Little remains of the other old buildings of Kells except part of a tower of Walter de Lacy's ramparts.

2.5km E, on the far bank of the Blackwater, is the demesne of *Headfort House* (now a school), preserving an Adam interior of c 1771.—3km to the N is *Dulane* church, with a fine old doorway.—See also the sub-route on p 371.

The Cavan road crosses the Blackwater at *Clavens Bridge*.

2.5km beyond at *Carnaross* we may turn left for the ruins of *St. Kieran's Chapel* and *Well*, on the S bank SE of the bridge; remains of four 'termon' or boundary crosses are still to be seen; another stands in a ford on the river.
    Legend relates that St. Columba, envious of St. Kieran's crosses, determined to steal one under cover of darkness; but St. Kieran awoke when he was half-way across the river, and in the ensuing struggle he was forced to leave it where it has remained ever since.

The N3 later skirts (left) LOUGH RAMOR before reaching (19km from Kells) the pleasantly-sited lakeside village of **Virginia** (650 inhab.), founded by James I at the colonisation of Ulster.

Swift wrote the greater part of 'Gullivers's Travels' in 1726 at the home of the Rev. Thomas Sheridan, whose grandson, Richard Brinsley Sheridan, also spent much of his youth at *Cuilcagh House*, 4km to the NE, S of the R178.—N of this road lies *Killinkere*, the ancestral home of the American general, Philip Sheridan (1831–88).—*Mullagh*, 9.5km SE of Virginia, was the birthplace of the poet and novelist Henry Brooke (1703–83), who retired here in 1774 and is buried in an unmarked grave nearby.
    11km SW on the R195 is **Oldcastle** (900 inhab.), 5km SE of which rises *Slieve-na-Calliagh* (*Hag's Hill*; 277m), the highest of the three summits of the *Loughcrew Hills*. About 30 chambered cairns have been excavated here, the most perfect of which, on the hill-top, is notable for its supporting wall of stones. To the N is a stone seat known as the Hag's Chair.—On the S side of the hill stood *Loughcrew*, the birthplace of the martyred archbishop of Armagh, Oliver Plunkett (1625–81). A later mansion on its site, built in 1823, was demolished in the 1960s after the third fire in 100 years.
    9.5km NW of Virginia is *Ballyjamesduff* (850 inhab.), which takes its name from General Sir James Duff (1752–1839), commander of the Limerick district in the troubles of 1798.—8km SW is LOUGH SHEELIN, on the SE bank of which rise the hill-top ruins of *Ross Castle*, an O'Reilly stronghold.

Beyond Virginia, the N3 ascends through hilly country, with a view NW of *Slieve Glah* (319m), and at 20km the road circles round to the W just short of *Stradone*.

STRADONE TO MONAGHAN (43.5km). The R165 (later R188), after traversing this village, bears right for (16km) **Cootehill** (1,550 inhab.), a pleasant little town taking its name from the Coote family, the former owners of **Bellamont Forest**, an imposing Palladian villa designed by Sir Edward Lovett Pearce in 1729–30 on DROMORE LOUGH, just to the N. It has a Doric portico and a central lantern, and coffered plasterwork ceilings.—To the right of the Monaghan road, overlooking the inner lough, is the demesne of *Dawson's Grove* (house demolished), with a *Monument* (1774; by Joseph Wilton) to Anne, Lady Dartrey (1733–69), in a domed 'island mausoleum' by Wyatt. It is protected by the Irish Georgian Society, but limbs have been broken from the statue by vandals.—Hence the R188 continues NE via *Rockcorry*, and traverses a 'drumlin' district to (16km) *Monaghan*; see p 321.

11km **Cavan** (3,250 inhab.), a county town, was the scene of the final defeat of the Duke of Berwick by the men of Enniskillen under General William Wolseley in 1690, who then burned the place. The castle of the O'Reillys has disappeared, and only the tower remains of the Franciscan church (originally Dominican) in which Owen O'Neill (died 1649) was buried. The pedimented *Court-house* is by John Bowden, designer of the *Parish church* of 1810. The building of the previous Gothick *Catholic Cathedral* (transported to *Ballyhaise*, 7km NE) was replaced in 1942 by an uninspired new church composed of an incongruous mixture of styles and of little aesthetic appeal.

3km NW is the *Farnham* demesne, with a house of 1700 enlarged in 1801 by Francis Johnston, beyond which is the circular 13–14C tower of *Clough Oughter*, built by the O'Reillys, possibly on the site of a crannóg, on an island in LOUGH OUGHTER, a labyrinthine lake, or rather a collection of islands and peninsulas, which, connected with UPPER LOUGH ERNE, is a feature of the landscape as far N as Enniskillen. The extraordinary contours are largely formed by the gradual decomposition of the limestone by the carbonic acid in the water.

Kilmore, 5km W of Cavan, the seat of a bishop since 1454 (now united with Elphin and Ardagh) has a Protestant *Cathedral* of 1858–60, incorporating a Romanesque doorway from the abbey of Trinity Island in Lough Oughter. In the graveyard is the tomb of Bp William Bedell (1571–1642), translator of the Bible into Irish, who had spent his last two years imprisoned in Clough Oughter (see above), scene also of the death of Owen Roe O'Neill in 1649.

Driving N from Cavan, we leave the road to *Ballyhaise* (5km NE) and (20.5km beyond) *Clones* on our right; see Rte 38B. For the road from Clones to *Enniskillen*, see p 322.

We diverge left on crossing the Annalee at (6.5km) *Butler's Bridge* for (10.5km) **Belturbet** (1,150 inhab.), a village on the Erne, which lazily threads its way through this apparently disintegrated region. Belturbet preserves the stump of a *Round Tower* and the remains of an old fort in its churchyard. It was described some 200 years ago by John Wesley as having 'Sabbath-breakers, drunkards, and common swearers in abundance'.

BELTURBET TO CARRICK-ON-SHANNON (62km). The R201 leads SW via (5.5km) *Milltown*, on a detached tarn, just S of which are the ruined church and 12C *Round Tower* (a stump 12m high) of *Drumlane*, probably an Augustinian Friary.—Some 6.5km W of Milltown is *Kildallon*, the home of the ancestors of Edgar Allan Poe, beneath the *Hill of Carn*, with its rath.—The road traverses (8km) *Killeshandra* (500 inhab.), frequented by anglers on Lough Oughter, and continues SW across country via *Mohill* to meet the N4 near *Drumsna*, 8km E of *Carrick*; see Rte 26A.

As the direct roads N from Butler's Bridge (see above) and from just W of Belturbet to Enniskillen may be closed, one should continue W on the R200 to (12km) *Ballyconnell*, with an early 17C church, to the SW of which Bronze Age skeletons have been excavated; there are a number of slight megalithic remains in the area. Although there is a minor border-crossing just N of Ballyconnell our route circles to the S of *Slieve Rushen* (405m, which marks the border), with BRACKLEY LOUGH on the left, to meet the R202 at (12km) *Derrynacreeve*. Here we turn right for *Swalinbar*, the frontier post (see Rte 26A), and thence to *Enniskillen*; see Rte 37.

For the direct road from Enniskillen to *Sligo*, see Rte 37.

The main road from Enniskillen to *Derry* is the A32 to (43km) *Omagh*, and thence the A5 to (53km) Derry via *Strabane*; see pp 322–3 and 303.

ENNISKILLEN TO BALLYSHANNON (48km; 21km S of Donegal). Crossing *West Bridge*, we pass (right) *Portora Royal School* and *Portora Castle*; see p 363. The A46 skirts the W bank of LOWER LOUGH ERNE, after 6.5km passing the former demesne of *Ely Lodge* (blown up in 1870), in which the stable block and dovecote remain of *Castle Hume*, Richard Castle's first architectural essay in Ireland (where he was invited by Sir Gustavus Hume), demolished by 1812 for the stone with which to erect Ely Lodge.—At *Monea*, 5km W on the far side of a ridge, is a ruined *Castle* of 1618 in the Scottish style; the church, beyond, preserves the E window (1449) of Devenish Abbey, transferred here in 1630.— Further N, we see from the loughside the offshore island of *Inishmacsaint* (*Inis muighe samh*, the isle of the plain of sorrel), with an early cross and ruined church, beyond which a track (right) leads to the ruins of *Tully Castle* (1610), built by the Humes. It was the scene of a massacre in 1641 when Roderick Maguire induced the garrison to surrender under promise of safe-conduct to Enniskillen, and then burned the place down.—Beyond this point we skirt the loughside, overlooked by the *Cliffs of Magho*, to *Belleek*; see below.

A recommended DETOUR may be made by forking left almost opposite Inishmacsaint, and after 2.5km bearing left again, shortly passing between two small lakes, beyond which a forest track ascends to the right through the *Blackslee* and *Lough Navar Forests*, to approach a belvedere some 300m above Lower Lough Erne, providing both a plunging and panoramic view. To the W beyond Donegal Bay is Slieve League; to the N rise the Blue Stack Mountains; and to the NE, Mullaghcarn, with the Sperrin Mountains beyond.

Regaining the main road, we turn right and keep right for **Belleek** (in Irish *Beal Leice*, the ford of the flagstones), a border village at the head of an artificial expansion of the Erne rapids, the height of Lough Erne being here regulated by a sluice. At Belleek is a pottery factory producing a fragile form of woven luster ware which has its admirers; the original porcelain, the delicate glaze of which was based on a French invention, was made in 1857–90 from clay and felspar dug at *Castlecaldwell*, some 6.5km E.

Crossing the border here we soon reach (8km) *Ballyshannon* (see Rte 27; and for the remainder of the route to *Donegal*, 21km N).—Travellers wishing to make the circuit of Lower Lough Erne turn E at Belleek onto the A47, described below, in reverse.

Our route N from Enniskillen skirts the E bank of **Lower Lough Erne** (29km long and 9km wide), its southern arm almost filled with a group of wooded islets. One of them, some 3km N of the town and reached by a ferry, is **Devenish** (*Daimh Inish*, the island of oxen), with a group of ruins associated with the name of St. Molaise of Devenish (6C). The principal building surviving is the particularly fine *Round Tower*, almost 25m high, notable for its masonry, its variously shaped windows, and its unique cornice of scroll-work with four sculptured heads beneath the conical cap. The *House of St. Molaise* and the *Teampull Mór* preserve only one round-headed door each; higher up is the *Tower* of the *Abbey Church* (1449) and part of the choir; to the S is a *Cross* of unknown date and unusual design.

The road shortly veers away from the lough to regain it, via *Irvinestown*, at (23km) *Kesh*. *Necarne Castle* (or *Castle Irvine*; c 1831, around its 17C predecessor) is 2km S of Irvinstown.

A more interesting and slightly shorter ALTERNATIVE road hugs the loughside via *Killadeas*, a little angling and yachting resort. In the churchyard, near the Irish yews, are three carved stones, the most important of which (?7–9C) has a crude figure of an abbot in profile on one side; on another is a face of the Boa Island type (see below).—We later skirt the demesne of *Castle Archdale* (left; see below), where a mansion of 1773 replaces a 'Plantation' castle (1615); it was a flying-boat base in 1939–45; its offshore islands are now a nature reserve.

Sculptures on White Island

A lane forking left skirts the shore of a bay in which lies *White Island (caretaker-boatman will ferry visitors from Castle Archdale). Here a small ruined church has a restored Romanesque S doorway and two windows of a similar style. The building protects seven curious figures of Christian inspiration (one a Sheila-na-gig; an eighth is a medieval mask), probably carved during the 7–9Cs, at one time built haphazard into the wall, and repaired since 1928.—The lane shortly passes the early 17C ruins of *Crevenish Castle* before entering **Kesh**, a loughside village where the traditional broad-beamed eel boats were constructed; some 7km NE stands *Drumskinny Stone Circle.*

The road now circles the N end of Lough Erne, where we follow the next right-hand fork, to (9km) *Pettigo*, see below.

The left-hand fork (A47) leads W to *Belleek* (see above) and (36km) *Ballyshannon*, first traversing the long narrow **Boa Island**. In the overgrown lakeside cemetery of *Caldragh* at its W end, signposted (left; but beyond that turning marked Lusty Beg Island), and 5 minutes' walk from the road, is concealed a squat Janus-formed statue known as the 'Lusty Man' beside a larger one. Both are earlier (possibly 5–6C) than those on White Island, and pagan. The road regains the mainland, passing on the next peninsula the ruins of *Castlecaldwell* (1610–19), visited by Arthur Young in 1776. At *Belleek* we cross the border.

Pettigo, the village frontier-post straddling the border, is the starting-point for the excursion to LOUGH DERG (9.5km long by 6km broad), 7km N among the mountains.

The lough is of no great interest in itself, but *Station Island*, towards the S bank, is said to be the scene of St. Patrick's vision of Purgatory. The island (on which penitential exercises are severe) sports a purgatorial neo-Byzantine basilica, octagonal in plan, and an hospice. The pilgrimage, which dates from c 1150, has persisted throughout the ages despite several attempts to suppress it due to concomitant excesses. On *Saint's Island*, to the NW, are remains of a monastery founded by St. Daveog, a disciple of St. Patrick, destroyed in 1632.

From Pettigo the R232 shortly bears NW away from Lough Erne, on the shore of which at this point are the ruins of the keep of *Termon Magrath*, a stronghold of that clan, bombarded by Ireton in the Civil War. We traverse the *Black Gap* and *The Pullans*, a region of little lakes and hills, before descending, with extensive views over Donegal Bay and the mountains beyond, to meet the N15, there turning right for **Donegal** itself; see Rte 27.

30   Dublin to Derry via Slane, Monaghan, and Omagh

233km (145 miles). N2. 47km *Slane* (for **Newgrange**)—21km *Ardee*—19km *Carrickmacross*—18km *Castleblaney*—24km **Monaghan**—21km *Aughnacloy*—A5. 19 miles **Omagh**—10 miles *Newtownstewart*—10 miles *Strabane*—13 miles **Derry**.

Leave Dublin by Church St (to the W of the *Four Courts*) and continue due N through the suburb of *Phibsborough*. Fork left after crossing the Royal Canal to *Finglas*, with an old cross and church founded by St. Patrick, beside which the Normans surprised and defeated Roderick O'Connor, the High King, in 1171.—8km NW, to the right of the main road, stands *Dunsoghly Castle* (15C), retaining its roof-timbers.— The long straight road leads to (21km) *Ashbourne*, the scene of a 5-hour battle during the Easter Rising in 1916 after 40 members of the Royal Irish Constabulary had been ambushed by insurgents led by Thomas Ashe, the local schoolmaster. The following year Ashe was arrested and died after being forcibly fed during a hunger strike in Mountjoy Prison.

6.5km beyond, the R152 forks right, passing (left) *Athcarne Castle* (1519), and *Annesbrook House*, with its huge Ionic portico, and Georgian-Gothic 'banqueting room' hastily added in 1821 to impress George IV when visiting Slane. As he preferred dining out of doors the effort was wasted.— 10.5km **Duleek**, where the first stone church (*Daimh Liag*, stone house) in Ireland is said to have been built by St. Patrick, and put in the charge of St. Cianan (Keenan). This was succeeded by a Priory founded in 1182, of which the ruined church remains (adjacent to a gutted church), with tombs of the Bellew family and a cross of the Kells type. In the village are an old *Bridge* and *Cross* (1601), erected by Dame Jennet Dowdall, and the castellated gateway of the demesne of the extinct earls of Thomond, *Duleek House* (c 1750), by Castle or his school.—*Drogheda* lies 7.5km further NE; see Rte 31.

6.5km beyond this turning is *Balrath*, with a 16C wayside-cross 'beautified' in 1727; the *White Cross*, a far more elaborate monument, another of those erected in the neighbourhood during the late 16C by Dame Jennet Dowdall, is 2.5km to the E.

Crossing the Boyne, we enter (11km) **Slane** (700 inhab.), a pleasant village with four matching Georgian houses facing each other diagonally in its centre, and the birthplace of the poet Francis Ledgwidge (1891–1917). It is overlooked by a hill to the NW (*View*) on which are the ruins of an *Abbey Church* and *College* of very ancient foundation, rebuilt in 1512. On the W side of the hill is a large *Rath*, 8m high. On the river bank near the parish church is the *Hermitage of St. Erc*, a Gothic ruin of various dates, dedicated to the first bishop of Slane, who mortified his flesh by standing all day up to his armpits in the Boyne. A five-storey *Flour-mill* (1766), described by Arthur Young as a 'handsome edifice, such as no mill I have seen in England can be compared with it' may also be seen on the Boyne here. It was probably designed by Hugh Darley.

A short distance W is **Slane Castle** (adm. only to the restaurant installed there), its demesne behind imposing gates (by Francis Johnson). It is a fine Gothick-Revival house incorporating an earlier castle built for William Burton Conyngham from 1785, largely by Wyatt and Johnston, with a round ballroom or library, the work of Thomas Hopper, with an ornate traceried ceiling. It was twice visited by George IV (whose portrait, by Lawrence, hangs there), who had a penchant for Lady Conyngham; the second time was in August 1821, after he became king.

The N51 leads E from Slane to (14km) *Drogheda*, passing near the necropolis of *Brugh* (pron. Broo) **na Bóinne**, as it was known in early chronicles and legends, with the three great tumuli of *Knowth*, *Newgrange*, and *Dowth* on a ridge above the river Boyne. These are perhaps the most impressive of Bronze Age passage-graves extant. There are 26 such graves in the Boyne valley, approx. 10 per cent of all those in Ireland.

They may be approached by turning right 3km E of Slane. The first mound, of **Knowth** (*Cnogba*), encircled by a kerb and 15 satellite tombs, preserves a rich collection of spiral, chevron, and zigzag carvings; a summit chamber, 4m in diameter, was discovered in 1942, and two passage-graves in 1967–68. The mound is closed to the public until excavations are completed.—To the SE rises the remarkable *Newgrange Tumulus*, for size and decoration hardly surpassed among European passage-graves. By the car-park is a small explanatory museum, where tickets are obtained and where one awaits the guide. The approach to the mound is across a field. The huge cairn of stones, 80m in diameter and 13.5m high, is covered with soil, from

The Threshold Stone, Newgrange

which trees and bushes have been cleared. It is surrounded by a circle of 12 of the estimated 38 pillar-stones originally there. Within them is a ditch, and the base of the cairn itself is encircled by a kerb of 97 large stones carrying a dry-stone wall. As at Dowth, some of the stones are incised with spiral and other motives, but their haphazard arrangement has suggested to Macalister that they were re-used stones from an earlier burial-field.

The main entrance, on the S side, was the object of considerable—some would say excessive—attention during the years 1962–76, when a wedge of quartz was discovered and replaced here. By the entrance is the famous *Threshold Stone*, carved with triple spirals, concentric circles, diamonds, and other motives.

Above, at either side of the entrance, the limestone facing has been encrusted quincuncially with sea-rolled pebbles. Its reconstruction following this controversial pattern was only commenced after numerous experiments by Professor O'Kelly with sections of the fallen material, and it has been claimed that only this design, or another very similar, could have made the pattern in which the fallen debris was found. It is of interest that the quartz had been originally quarried some 80km S, near Wicklow, and the sea-rolled pebbles had been gathered some 130km N in Co. Down.

A passage 1m wide, almost 19m long, and 1.5–2.5m high, faced with huge slabs, some also incised, leads to the tomb itself, a lofty domed chamber almost 6m high, roofed by corbelled (or beehive) vaulting (like the treasury of Atreus at Mycenae). It contains three recesses, partially patterned, and each with its hollowed stone trough or basin. Carbon-dating has confirmed (provisionally) that the tomb was constructed between 2800–2400 BC. In AD 861–62 it was rifled of anything portable by the Danes, who called it the cave of Acadh-Aldai. The guide will explain that only on 21 December each year will the first rays of sunlight enter and briefly illuminate the chamber.

To the W, on the far bank of the river, is *Rosnaree* (the wood of the kings), where Cormac of Tara was buried at his own request, all efforts to carry his body across to Brugh na Bóine being foiled by a sudden rising of the river. But here on 12 July 1690 the Williamites crossed to turn the Jacobites' left flank.

From Newgrange, the lane zig-zags NE to the great mound of **Dowth** (*Dubhadh*) encircled by a stone kerb and pierced by two passage-graves, one of which, difficult of access, is approached by a passage 8m long.

Dowth Castle is a ruin, as is the medieval church, probably built from stones from a vanished outer ring of the tumulus. To the E is *Dowth Hall* (c 1780; containing plaster possibly by Robert West). The eccentric 6th Viscount Netherville who built it is said to have 'attended' mass by sitting on top of the mound of Dowth and training his telescope on a distant chapel. John Boyle O'Reilly (1844–90; died at Boston, Mass.), the poet and Fenian, was born at Dowth.—The lane continues NE to cross the Mattock, 5km W of Drogheda, and the site of the Battle of the Boyne; see Rte 31.

SLANE TO NAVAN (14km). Running SW from Slane, after 3km the N51 passes (left) the formless ruins of *Castle Dexter*; on the far bank of the Boyne rises the wooded demesne of *Beau Parc House* (1755), and on the river itself, just below a bridge on the left, is *Stackallan Fall*.—At *Dunmoe* is a 16C castle on the river-bank, burnt in 1799, while opposite stands the ruined church of *Ardmulchan*.—To the right, before entering *Navan* (see p 313) we pass at *Donaghmore* (Domhnach Mór, the great church) a *Round Tower* (10C), 30m high, remarkable in having a carving of the Crucifixion above the door, and no belfry windows. Little remains of the adjoining church (?13C), said to occupy the site of the church of St. Cassanus, a disciple of St. Patrick.

From Slane we drive N. After 6km a right-hand turn leads 2.5km to *Mellifont Abbey, the first Cistercian house in Ireland, founded in 1142 by St. Malachi O'Morgair on the site of a 7C convent. Its ruins stand on the banks of the river Mattock, which here separates Louth from Meath. Of the church, consecrated in 1157, little more than the bases of columns and walls is left. The more interesting relics of the abbey dependencies are the massive *Gatehouse*, the *Chapter House* (miscalled St. Bernard's Chapel), with its groined roof, foliated capitals, and 14C tracery (restored), and the *Lavabo*, an octagonal building of which five sides still stand, each pierced by a round-headed doorway; it opens off the S cloister walk.

4km beyond this turning we traverse the village of *Collon*, overlooked to the E by the *Hill of Collon*, on the slope of which is *Oriel Temple*, once a demesne of Viscount Massereene and Ferrard, but since 1938 known as *New Mellifont*, and occupied by Cistercians. To the NW is *Mt Oriel* (244m).

After 6km a left-hand turn at *Anaglog Cross* leads to (1.5km) *Smarmore Castle* (14th and 19C), seat of the Taafe family.—At *Woodtown*, some 5.5km further W, are the clear remains of the Pale boundary, an earthen rampart and fosse above the river Dee.

Ardee (3,200 inhab.) takes its name (*Baile Átha Fhirdhia*, the ford of Ferdia) from the long combat in which Cuchulainn, the champion of Ulster, slew Ferdia, the Connacht warrior. It was once an important outpost of the Pale, and a borough until 1800. A motte called *Castleguard* or *Dawson's Mount* defends the ford, but the more recent *Castle*, restored in part, was founded c 1207 by the Anglo-Norman knight Roger de Pippard. Two monastic foundations (Carmelite and Augustinian, or Trinitarian) are assigned to him and his descendant Ralph (late 13C), and the remains of one of these are incorporated in the *Protestant Church*, which contains the head of a 14C (?) cross, and a Gothic font found in Mansfieldstown graveyard, near Castlebellingham. The *Catholic Church* (1829–60) is believed to occupy the site of the other. *Hatch's Castle* is a late-medieval fortified house in Market St.

For the road between Ardee and Dundalk, 21km NE, see the sub-route on p 371, in reverse.

The N2 veers NW from Ardee, and after 9km crosses the river Lagan into Co. Monaghan (Ulster) by the *Aclint Bridge*. An old fort here, and the *Lagan Ford* (replaced by a bridge 2.5km upstream) were the scene of negotiations for the truce of 1599 between Tyrone and Essex which led to the latter's downfall.

10km **Carrickmacross** (1,750 inhab.) was formerly reputed for its lace. Lace-making was introduced in 1820 and is still practiced by local nuns. A grant of land in the neighbourhood was made by Elizabeth I to the Earl of Essex, but little remains of his castle here, the site of which is occupied by the Convent of St. Louis. SW of the town is the wooded demesne and house of *Lough Fea*, designed by Thomas Rickman in 1827.

Shercock, 14km W, overlooks LOUGH SILLAN, in which some of the largest specimens of the horns of the extinct Irish elk have been discovered.—*Cootehill* (see p 314) lies some 21km further NW on the R189 to *Clones* (22km beyond; see below, and Rte 38B).

The N2 continues N, passing 1.5km W of the great motte of *Donaghmoyne*, once a Pippard stronghold, to (18km) **Castleblayney** (2,400 inhab.), a market-town taking its name from Sir Edward Blaney, governor of Monaghan under James I, who received a grant of land on condition of his erecting a fort between Monaghan and Newry. It stands on the shore of LOUGH MUCKNO (240 hectares), the largest and most beautiful of the many lakes in the district. *Hope* (or *Blaney*) *Castle*, adjoining the town, with a fine demesne, is now a convent.

CASTLEBLAYNEY TO ARMAGH (28km). The R181 leads 7km N to the frontier-post and, skirting (right) CLAY LAKE, veers NE through *Keady*, a market-town and once a linen-manufacturing centre, for *Armagh* (see Rte 38A), 12km beyond.

The main road continues NW through (12km) *Clontibret*. A little to the E was the scene of a battle in May 1595 in which Hugh O'Neill, second Earl of Tyrone, humiliated the forces of Sir Henry Bagenal, repeated three years later at the Yellow Ford. The place was also attacked by a mob of Loyalists, led by Peter Robinson, in August 1986.

The road then bears W to (8km) **MONAGHAN** (6,200 inhab.), the busy county town, with shoe factories. A crannóg in the grounds of a convent, to the SW, was the original headquarters of the MacMahons, lords of Oriel, but the town shows little trace of antiquity. It was incorporated by James I in 1614. Monaghan was the birthplace of the prominent 'Young Irelander' Sir Charles Gavan Duffy (1816–1903) and the historian J.B. Bury (1861–1927); John Wesley was arrested here in 1762.

The pedimented *Market-house* in the centre dates from 1791–92, and was designed by Samuel Hayes for the first Lord Rossmore; nothing remains of the Gothick pile of *Rossmore Park*. The *Courthouse* (1829) accommodates a *Museum*, containing the 13C bronze *Cross of Clogher*. On a hill to the E is the Gothic-Revival *Cathedral* of the R.C. diocese of Clogher, by J.J. McCarthy, built in 1861–92 but sheltering several discordant additions.

For the road to *Armagh* (27km NE) and *Clones* (19km SW) see Rte 38.

Tedavnet, 6.5km NW, takes its name from St. Damhnait, daughter of a 6C King of Oriel, who has been incorrectly identified with St. Dimpna of Geel in Flanders.—10.5km NE, at *Glaslough*, is the tomb of John Leslie (1571–1671), the 'fighting bishop' of Clogher; *Glaslough House*, also known as *Castle Leslie*, a mid 19C building by Lanyon and Lynn, with an earlier lodge by Nash, was the home of Sir Shane Leslie (1885–1970), author and eccentric.

MONAGHAN (OR CLONES) TO ENNISKILLEN (54km). The border is crossed by forking right onto the R187, 6.5km (4 miles) W of Monaghan, meeting the A34 10 miles beyond, and 3 miles N of *Newtownbutler*, only 5½ miles W of *Clones*, with its border-crossing. For the road (N54) between Monaghan and Clones, see Rte 38B.

Newtownbutler (600 inhab.) was the scene of the rout and massacre by the Protestants of Enniskillen on 31 July 1689 of a larger attacking Jacobite force.—UPPER LOUGH ERNE, a curious maze of straits and islands, now comes into view on the left.—On the island of *Galloon*, some 8km SW of Newtownbutler, are three *High Crosses*, two of them elaborately carved.—5.5km to the W is *Crom Castle*, seat of the Earls of Erne, a Tudor-Revival pile (1829), in the demesne of which, where stands a huge yew, is the older Plantation *Castle* (1611), burned down in 1764.—Turning NW, after 6.5km we leave on our left the ruins of the old Church of *Aghalurcher*, (?15C) its graveyard containing some curiously carved tombstones.—**Lisnaskea** (1,550 inhab.), where *Castle Balfour* (c 1618) refortified by General Ludlow in 1652, was burnt c 1800. The hill above the town commands a wide view over the labyrinthine lough. We continue NW more or less parallel with the course of the meandering Erne, connecting the upper and lower loughs, itself more of a lake than river, to meet the A4 3 miles from *Enniskillen*, which we enter after passing (right) the entrance to the demesne of *Castlecoole*; see Rte 37.

From Monaghan the N2 continues N, crossing the border just before (21km) *Aughnacloy*, its wide main street straddling a ridge, with views to the W towards *Slieve Beagh* (371m), to reach the Dungannon–Enniskillen road near *Ballygawley*; see Rte 37. The shell of *Garvey House* (1815, by Francis Johnston) is 2km W of Aughnacloy.—2 miles beyond, we traverse *Sess Kilgreen*, with a standing-stone inscribed with a rude cross, and remains of various cairns and passage-graves, etc. in the vicinity.

13 miles **OMAGH** (14,650 inhab.), the county town of Tyrone, long a garrison and market town, with a number of manufactures, is attractively situated at the confluence of the Drumagh and the Camowen, which unite to form the Strule. The castle played too important a part in the wars of the 16–17C to have survived and was finally demolished by Sir Phelim O'Neill in 1641, while almost exactly a century later the whole town was virtually destroyed by a ravaging accidental fire. Apart from its classical *Courthouse* (1820; by John Hargrave), the town contains little of interest; the *Cathedral* (R.C.; 1899), with two unequal steeples, is of no moment.

Hence an attractive ALTERNATIVE road (B48) climbs due N through the *Gortin Glen Forest Park* passing (right) *Slieveard* (422m) and *Mullaghcarn* (542m) to (10 miles) *Gortin*, a one-street village adjoining the demesne of *Beltrim Castle*, beyond which it continues via *Plumbridge* and crosses the W spurs of the Sperrin Mountains through the *Butterlope Pass* to *Dunnamanagh* to rejoin the main route 3 miles from *Derry*.

The A5 continues NW, after 3 miles passing (left) *Mountjoy*, where in a local farmhouse (restored 1968) was born Thomas Mellon (1813–1908), founder of the American banking empire. His family emigrated hence in 1818. An adjacent barn contains a collection of old farm implements. A growing *'Ulster-American' Folk Park* has been established since 1976 at nearby *Camphill* to demonstrate points of contact between the Old World and the New.

From the Information Office one may visit a forge and weaver's cottage (replicas) and a schoolhouse (re-erected) and likewise the cottage of John Joseph Hughes, 1st Archbishop of New York. He emigrated from Augher in 1817, and initiated the building of St. Patrick's Cathedral, New York, in 1858. In another section in the park a Pennsylvania farmstead, largely constructed of logs, has been erected.

We descend the Strule valley between two hills named *Bessy Bell* (left) and *Mary Gray* after the heroines of a Perthshire ballad by one of the Scottish lords of **Newtownstewart** (1,450 inhab.), which we soon enter. Delightfully situated on the Mourne, a stream formed by the confluence of the Strule with the Glenelly, the town is named after William Stewart, ancestor of the Lords Mountjoy, to whom the barony was granted by Charles I. James II spent a night here after the siege of Derry, ordering the castle of c 1618 to be dismantled and the bridge destroyed after his retreat.—To the SW is *Harry Avery's Castle*, a hilltop ruin ascribed to Aimhreidh O'Neill (died 1392).

It is said that this O'Neill had a sister with a pig's head. He offered a handsome dowry in compensation in order to marry her off, but any suitor who declined to carry out the bargain after seeing her would be hanged; 19 considered this the lesser evil.

3 miles SW is *Baronscourt, the seat of the Dukes of Abercorn, an early 18C house altered in 1791–92 by Sir John Soane, burnt out in 1796, and later transformed by William Vitruvius Morrison. The Palladian 'Agent's House' (1741) is also of interest.

From Newtownstewart we follow the road skirting the W bank of the Mourne via (7 miles) *Sion Mills*, with linen works, to *Strabane*, 3 miles beyond; see Rte 27, and for the road thence to **Derry**; see Rte 34A. *Letterkenny* lies 27km NW of Strabane.

31 Dublin to Dundalk, for Belfast

84km (52 miles). N1. 9.5km *Dublin Airport*—3.5km *Swords* (also by-passed)—(*Malahide* lies 3km to the E)—36km **Drogheda**—22km *Castlebellingham*—13km **Dundalk**. For the road beyond, see Rte 39 in reverse.

Driving N from O'Connell St we shortly bear right along Upper Dorset St, and cross the Royal Canal, and, soon after, the Tolka river.

To the left stands *Belvedere House*, late 17C with 18–19C additions. It has been a Jesuit seminary since 1841.—A short distance to the right, in *Drumcondra* churchyard, is the tomb of the architect James Gandon (1743–1823), buried beneath the same stone as his friend the antiquary Francis Grose (1731?–91); within the church is a monument by Sheemakers to Marmaduke Coghill (died 1739), builder of adjacent *Drumcondra House*, now part of All Hallows College.

On the outskirts of Dublin we pass (right) the church of *Santry*, with the only monumental brass outside the city, and the curious slate monument of Lord Santry (died 1673).— '*Woodlands*', 2.5km NE, is an interesting early 18C house designed by Sir Edward Lovett Pearce for the Rev. John Jackson, a friend of Swift.

We soon pass (left) the functional buildings of **Dublin Airport** (or *Collinstown*, 1937–43), by Desmond Fitzgerald; a small *Aviation Museum* may be visited.

SWORDS (11,150 inhab.), recently much expanded, was formerly a place of importance, with an abbey founded by St. Columba in 550 for St. Finan the Leper. It became so rich that it was called 'the Golden Prebend'; it was held by William of Wykeham in 1366. The ancient buildings of Swords include—a short distance W of the main street—a *Round Tower*, 22.5m high, of the earliest type, with a restored cap and a modern entrance at ground level; the 14C *Tower* of the abbey church; and the shell of the *Archbishop's Castle* (c 1200), many times burned by the Danes, within which the bodies of Brian Ború and his son rested on their way to Armagh on the night after the battle of Clontarf.

Malahide (see Rte 1G) is 3km E.—3km NW is *Rathbeale Hall* (c 1734), recently restored.

We cross the mouth of the Broad Meadow Water.

A right-hand turn leads 3km to *Donabate*, with a ruined castle, and in the C. of I. church, the exuberant stucco-work of the Cobbe gallery.—*Portrane*, 2.5km beyond, was once the home of Swift's 'Stella'.—Offshore is **Lambay Island**, a porphyry rock 127m high, preserving curious defence-works of 1551. It was the scene of the first Viking raid, in 795, and is now a bird sanctuary. The right-hand fork at Donabate regains the N1, passing (right) *Turvey House*, the 18C successor of a mansion built in 1565 with material from the ruins of the Austin priory of

Grace Dieu, and (left) *Newbridge House* (c 1737), probably designed by Castle for Charles Cobbe, later Abp of Dublin.

The right-hand fork at the next road junction leads to (3km) **Lusk** (5,800 inhab.), where the church preserves an ancient battlemented square tower supported on three sides by slender round towers with stepped battlements; within are 16–18C monuments; on the fourth side is a *Round Tower* of an early type, 24m high.—The road continues past the ruins of *Baldongan Castle* (13C) to the resort of *Skerries*, off which lie the rocks of that name, and the offshore *Rockabill lighthouse*.—Hence the main road may be regained at Balbriggan.

We traverse *Balrothery*, where the church has an old square tower with a *Round Tower* abutting (as at Lusk; see above), before reaching the coast at **Balbriggan** (5,600 inhab.), formerly reputed for its stockings, the manufacture of which was introduced in 1761. Here on 21–22 September 1920 the destruction of property and indiscriminate barbarity by a drunken rabble of 'Black and Tans' precipitated a chorus of disapproval from liberal circles in England.

8km inland is *Naul*, to the NW of which, on *Fourknocks Hill* (*Fornocht*, i.e. bleak place), are barrows excavated in 1950–52, yielding a quantity of Bronze Age artifacts, and a passage-grave of unusual regularity, decorated in the Newgrange style.

The N1 veers away from the coast, passing (left) *Gormanstown Castle* (1786; now a Franciscan house), which gives a title to the premier viscount of Ireland; the family vault adjoins the ruined church of *Stamullen*, further W. Evelyn Waugh, when considering buying the place in 1946, wrote of it as 'a fine, solid, grim, square, half-finished block with tower and turrets'.—At *Julianstown* we cross the river Nanny, on the bank of which (right) stands the castellated 17C mansion of *Ballygarth*, under restoration. The 'Tara Brooch' (see National Museum, Dublin) was found on the shore at *Bettystown* (3,000 inhab.), to the NE, in 1850.

DROGHEDA (pronounced Droyeda; 23,250 inhab.; in Irish *Droicheah Atha*, bridge of the Ford) is an ancient town, well situated some 5km from the mouth of the Boyne—crossed by a railway viaduct—with a good harbour, cement works, iron-foundries, breweries, etc.

It was a base of the Danish marauder Turgesius (Thorgestr), and later was a bridgehead of the Anglo-Normans of the Pale. In 1395 four Irish princes made their submission to Richard II in the Magdalen monastery here. Of the numerous Parliaments held at Drogheda the most notable was that of 1494, which passed *Poynings Law*, enacting that no future law passed by the Irish Parliament would be held valid unless ratified by the English Privy Council.

It was frequently the rendezvous of armies despatched to quell the rebels of Ulster, and it suffered two memorable sieges—in 1641, when Sir Phelim O'Neill was beaten off by Sir Henry Tichborne and Lord Moore until relieved by the Earl of Ormonde; and in 1649, when, after a stubborn defence by Sir Arthur Aston and 3,000 men, it fell to Cromwell on 10 September. In the massacre that followed its storming some 2,000 (Cromwell's own estimate) were put to the sword, and most of the rest transported to Barbados, a rancorous act among many which further stained his reputation throughout Ireland. In 1689 it was held for James II by Lord Iveagh, but surrendered the day after the Battle of the Boyne (see below). Drogheda was the birthplace of Eliza O'Neill (1791–1872), the actress, later Lady Beecher, but has produced few names of note.

A new bridge partially by-passes the town to the W.—S of the old bridge crossing to the town centre (Shop St) is *Mill Mount* (restored), the motte of the Anglo-Norman castle, near which are slight remains of town walls.—The *Tholsel*, by Francis Johnston, at the N end of Shop St, is now a bank. A short distance to the E are the twin towers of *St. **Lawrence's Gate** (13C), the only barbican remaining. In West St is *St.*

Peter's Church (R.C.), preserving relics of Oliver Plunkett (1628–81), Abp of Armagh, hanged at Tyburn during the 'Popish Plot' persecutions, and canonised in 1975.—Further W, near the site of the West Gate, are the ruins of St. Mary d'Urso, consisting of the central tower of the church and one arch spanning narrow Abbey Lane; these ruins are those of an Austin friary of the time of Edward I.

In Fair St, parallel to and N of West St, is the Courthouse, while further E, at the corner of William St and Magdelene St, stands St. Peter's (C. of I.), rebuilt in 1740–53, with a later tower and spire by Francis Johnston. It contains a 14C font (on a modern base), some good plasterwork of Italian workmanship, and monuments, among them that of Chief Justice Singleton, by John Hickey. In the churchyard are—on the wall—the macabre tombstone of Edward Golding and his wife (early 13C), and the graves of Oliver Goldsmith's uncle Isaac, and Bartholomew Vanhomrigh, father of Swift's 'Vanessa'.— Further N is the Magdalene Tower, (15C), all that remains of the Dominican abbey founded in 1224 by Abp Lucas de Netterville.

From Drogheda the N51 ascends the N bank of the Boyne, and in just over 1.5km reaches the remains of an obelisk near the mouth of the river Mattock that marked the site of the **Battle of the Boyne**, where on 1 July (old style) 1690, or 12 July by the modern calendar, James II's hopes of regaining the English throne were shattered.

On the S bank is Oldbridge, beneath the steep slopes of Donore Hill, on which James's army was drawn up. William of Orange (who was slightly wounded in a reconnaissance before the fight) detached part of his force to cross the ford of Rosnaree, to the SW, thus turning James's left flank, while the main body under General Schomberg rushed the ford opposite Grove Island. Schomberg, who showed great courage, was killed in an Irish calvalry charge, but in the meantime another force had crossed the Boyne further E, cutting off any retreat towards Drogheda, and James's army was forced to retire in confusion over the hill to Duleek.

William's forces amounted to c 36,000, mostly Dutch, Germans, Danes, and French Huguenots, while with James were about 25,000 Irishmen. James passed the night before the battle in the ruined church of Donore; King William's Glen, a little wooded ravine, marks the spot where he was wounded.

On the N bank also is the demesne of Townley Hall (1794, by Francis Johnston; his only Classical house), with a remarkable rotunda and staircase, now the agricultural research centre of Trinity College.

A minor road following the bank of the Boyne leads shortly to Dowth Hill and Newgrange; see pp 319–20; while 3km NW lies Mellifont Abbey, see p 321.

A short DETOUR may be made to the NE of Drogheda, descending the N bank of the estuary past (3km) Beaulieu House, a wide-eaved house in the Dutch style built in 1660–67 by Sir Henry Tichborne (died 1667) and his son, on the site of the medieval castle of the Plunketts, which had been O'Neill's headquarters during the siege of Drogheda. It was one of the first country homes in Ireland to be built without fortification. There is a macabre cadaver tomb-cover leaning against the church-tower.—Termonfeckin, 3km beyond, has a 10C cross of the Kells type dedicated to St. Fechin (died 665) and a 15C castle which until 1613 was a residence of the archbishops of Armagh. The home of Abp Oliver Plunkett was at Glass Pistol, 3km further NE near Clogher Head, commanding a distant view of the Mourne Mountains across Dundalk Bay, whence we may regain the N1 12.5km NW at Dunleer.

The N1 climbs N and at 7km veers NE.

The next left-hand turn off the left-hand fork at this junction leads very shortly to the ruins of *MONASTERBOICE (Mainistir Bhuithe), consisting of two churches, a round tower and three crosses, two amongst the finest of their kind, the relics of a community founded by St. Buithe or Boethius. The larger and older of the churches is almost 14m long; the nave, entered by a rude square-headed door, was connected to the fallen chancel by a round arch, which has likewise collapsed. The smaller church (13C) is nearer the tower. The Round

Muiredach's Cross, Monasterboice

Tower, 33.5m high, was probably built in the 9C; the entrance is 2m from the ground, and the small window above is the only one which is not square-headed. The burning of the tower in 1097 is the last recorded event in the history of the abbey. Of the three High Crosses, the *West Cross*, 6.5m high, is made up of three stones—the shaft, the wheel-cross, and the capstone, perhaps a replacement—on which there are c 50 sculptured panels. They are so weather-worn that only one-quarter of the subjects have been identified; these represent scriptural scenes (of which the Crucifixion occupies the centre of its W face) or grotesque beasts.—The monolithic *Muiredach's Cross*, nearest to the entrance, ascribed to Abbot Muiredach (died 923), is over 5m high and much less worn. New Testament scenes, including the Crucifixion, appear on the E side, and scenes from the Old Testament, and Christ in Judgment, on the W face; the summit represents a gabled building with a tiled roof. The *North Cross* retains its original base and head; the original shaft and an ancient sundial are preserved in its enclosure.

Regaining the main road, with occasional views ahead of Slieve Gullion and the Carlingford hills, we pass (left at 5km) *Athclare Castle*, a good specimen of a fortified manor-house, not far beyond which we traverse *Dunleer* (by-pass under construction), and (6.5km) **Castlebellingham** (850 inhab.) on the river Glynde, where the *Castle* (18C; now an hotel) replaces that of the Gernon family, burned in 1689 by the Jacobites as its then owner, Colonel Thomas Bellingham favoured and indeed acted as a guide to William of Orange; its demesne contains some fine old yews. In the churchyard lies Dr Thomas Guither, a 17C physician who is said to have introduced frogs into Ireland; James Napper Tandy (1740–1803), the erratic patriot, is also said to be interred here.

About 3km further on, to the W, is *Dromiskin*, where the stump of a *Round Tower* serves as a belfry, all that remains of a monastery whose abbot was St. Ronan (died 664); adjoining is the upper part of a sculptured cross.—2km W is fortified *Miltown Castle*.

10km **DUNDALK** (25,650 inhab.), the county town of Louth, in Irish *Dún Dealgan*, Dealga's fort, although a prosperous manufacturing town, with breweries, printing-presses, and engineering-works, etc., and with a safe harbour at the head of its bay, is of slight interest in itself, and can be a bottleneck for traffic.

The original dún was the motte of *Castletown*, a tumulus 2.5km W, and the possible birthplace of the legendary hero Cuchulainn, who also died near here in defending this key position on the road to the N (cf. *Clochafarmore*). The first name given to the present town was *Tráigh Baile* (Stradbally). Its subsequent history is one record of sieges. Edward Bruce, crowned King of Ireland in 1315, captured Dundalk the following year, but was also killed nearby in its defence in 1318. Later walled, it underwent six sieges between 1560 and 1650, and its remaining fortifications were dismantled in 1747. It suffered from fire during the 'troubles' of 1922–23.

In the town centre is *St. Patrick's Cathedral* (R.C.; c 1840), by Thomas J. Duff, in the style of King's College Chapel, Cambridge, in startling contrast with the Doric *Courthouse* (1813–18) to the N, by Edward Parke and John Bowden. To the E, off Castle Rd is the 15C *Tower* of a Franciscan friary (1240), the rest of which was destroyed in the 16C. In parallel Chapel Rd, nearer the centre, are the slight remains of a convent of Augustinian Crutched Friars. To the right of the main street leading N to the bridge is *St. Nicholas* (C. of I.), rebuilt in 1689 with the exception of its medieval tower, and altered early in the 19C by Francis Johnston. Adjoining the *Dún*, on which a folly was erected in 1780, is *Bellow's Castle* (1472–79), with a well-preserved keep with square angle turrets and crenellated parapets.

The interesting 13C fortress of *Castleroch* lies 6.5km NW of Dundalk.

For the sub-route from Dundalk to **Birr**, see p 371.

DUNDALK TO ARMAGH (52km). The R177 leads NW, reaching the border at 9km, being continued by the A29.—At 3½ miles beyond, the left-hand turn leads 3 miles to *Crossmaglen*, with a large market square, and adjacent to a British Army base, which has caused it to be a target of 'incidents'. N of the base is the well-preserved prehistoric grave of *Annaghmare*.—The main road shortly skirts (right) the *Dorsey*, an extensive entrenched oval enclosure (120 hectares), probably contemporary with the Black Pig's Dyke (cf.), before entering *Newtownhamilton*, whence we veer NW via *Keady* to (16 miles) *Armagh* (see Rte 38), also approached by a minor road (B31) forking right and driving direct through wooded country between *Deadman's Hill* (right) and *Carrigatuke*

(366m). For the road thence to *Belfast*, see Rte 38A; from Armagh to *Coleraine*, see Rte 36, both in reverse.

DUNDALK TO NEWRY VIA CARLINGFORD; the Cooley Peninsula (43.5km). Just N of Dundalk we turn right off the N1 onto the R173, skirting the N side of Dundalk Bay, at *Ballymascanlan* passing near the *Porleek Dolmen*, 3.5m high, adjoining a passage-grave.—After 17.5km the road turns N through *Grange*, with a quaint little church of 1762, passing to the W of *Greenore*, the terminus of a ferry from Holyhead between 1873 and 1926, and since 1960 revived as a freight port.

  Carlingford (650 inhab.), charmingly situated on its lough, commands good views of the Mourne Mountains rising beyond its far shore; it is said to have formerly possessed 32 'castles' in the days of the Pale, when every house on this border outpost was more-or-less fortified. The first old building seen as we enter is the *Abbey*, a Dominican house founded in 1305 by Richard de Burgh; the church preserves a square central tower and two W turrets. To the right further on is the *Parish Church*, also with a medieval tower; below it the *Mint*, a square tower with grotesque 15C Celtic-Revival carvings on its windows. Beyond this is the *Tholsel*, in part a rudely constructed town gate. In the main street is a square keep known as *Taaffe's Castle*, whence a short walk brings us to *King John's Castle*, built in 1210 by John de Courcy, a massive ruin occupying a horseshoe-shaped site overlooking the lough and enclosing a courtyard with a loopholed gallery.—*Slieve Foye* (587m), provides the highest of the Carlingford Mountains, provides a good view from its summit.—The road traverses *Omeath*, a small resort opposite *Warrenpoint*, to cross the border just S of the viewpoint of *Flagstaff* and adjacent *Fathom Wood* (bird sanctuary). It skirts the NEWRY CANAL and soon enters *Newry*; see Rte 39.

5km beyond Dundalk the main road to Newry passes (left) the hill of *Faughart*, an ancient fort 11.5m high, where Edward Bruce was killed in 1318 in a battle against Sir Edward Bermingham.

  We soon begin to ascend Ravensdale, the valley of the Flurry, gradually leaving behind the pastoral lowlands.

In the next valley to the W is the *Moyry Pass*, where Hugh O'Neill barricaded the road (further W) into Ulster for five years (1595–1600). The square tower was built by Lord Mountjoy in 1601.

We shortly reach the border-post, with *Slieve Gullion* (573m) rising abruptly to the left, and after 4 miles enter **Newry**; see Rte 39.

For the road hence to *Belfast*, 38 miles further NE, see Rte 39, in reverse; for the Mourne Mountains, see Rte 40.

32 Belfast

BELFAST (327,200 inhab., but according to the mid 1984 estimate, 303,500; it lists an additional 71,800 for the adjacent borough of *Newtownabbey*, a total of 375,300 for the conurbation), is the second city in Ireland and the industrial capital of Northern Ireland. It occupies an advantageous position at the mouth of the river Lagan and the head of Belfast Lough, to the W of which rises an amphitheatre of hills. It has extensive harbour installations and famous shipbuilding yards, while among its other important industries and manufactures are those of aircraft production, linen and synthetic fibre mills, ropeworks, etc. Its sudden growth during the last two centuries (in spite of a recent decline) explains why most of the architecture of the present city is a product of the industrial revolution and its aftermath, and little survives of the dignified late Georgian period, the lack of good building stone and the abundance of clay producing a largely red-

brick metropolis, although some of the larger edifices are of Portland
stone on a plinth of Mourne granite.

Tourist Offices. The *Northern Ireland Tourist Board Information Office* is at River
House, 48 High St, Belfast; there is also an office at Belfast International airport.
Local authorities have offices in 28 towns of N Ireland. The *Irish Tourist Office* is
at 53 Castle St. Both can arrange hotel bookings, etc.; see p 78.

AIRLINE OFFICES; *Aer Lingus*, 46 Castle St; *British Airways*, Fountain Centre,
College St; *British Caledonian*, 3 Rosemary St. *Belfast International airport*
(formerly *Aldergrove*) is 16 miles W of Belfast; the *Air Terminal* is at Great
Victoria St Bus Station. *Belfast Harbour Airport* is NE of the city.

SHIPPING OFFICES: *British Rail* (Sealink; Larne–Stranraer ferry), 24 Donegall
Pl.; *Belfast Car Ferries* (Belfast–Liverpool), Donegall Quay; *Townsend-Thoresen*
(Larne–Cairnryan), Larne Harbour.

RAILWAY STATIONS: *Belfast Central* (E Bridge St) for Dublin and the S; *York
Road* for the Larne line, and Londonderry.

BUS AND COACH STATIONS; *Gt Victoria St*, and *Oxford St*. The main coach
tour offices of *Ulsterbus* are also at Gt Victoria St.

AUTOMOBILE CLUBS: *AA*, Gt Victoria St; *RAC*, 79 Chichester St; *Ulster AC*, 3
Botanic Av.

Head Post Office: 25 Castle Pl.; with a Philatelic section.

Consulates: the US consulate is at Queens House, Queen St.

Other useful addresses: *Arts Council for N Ireland*, Bedford House, Bedford St,
for information with regard to Exhibitions, concerts, theatres, etc.; check also
with the Tourist Office, or in the press; *Central Public Library*, Royal Av.;
Linenhall Library, 17 Donegall Sq. N; *HMSO*, Chichester St; *Public Records
Office* (and *Ulster Historical Foundation*), 66 Balmoral Av.; *Ordnance Survey*,
Stranmillis Court; *The Archaeological Survey of N Ireland*, 66 Balmoral Av.;
Ulster Architectural Heritage Society (an admirable òrganisation founded in
1967), 181A Stranmillis Rd; *Presbyterian Historical Society*, Church House,
Fisherwick Pl.; *Ulster Archaeological Society*, Dept. of Archaeology, 17 Uni-
versity Sq.; *Ulster Arts Club*, 56 Elmwood Av.; *Ulster Folklife Society*, Ulster Folk
Museum, Cultra Manor, Holywood; see also pp 377–8.
    The *National Trust* is now at Rowallane House, Saintfield, Ballynahinch, Co.
Down. Their previous offices at Malone House, a 19C Belfast mansion, were
burnt out in November 1976 in an insensate terrorist attack. Its records and
photographic files were lost, and also the important Costume collection of the
Ulster Museum; a proportion of the furniture and paintings in its care was saved.

The *Port of Belfast* (see p 334) is, for reasons of security, closed to the casual
visitor, but visits may be arranged (preferably in small groups) on application to
the PRO at the *Harbour Office*, Corporation St.

The site of Belfast was in occupation during both the Stone and Bronze Ages,
while more than two dozen forts of the Iron Age (500 BC–AD 500) can be traced
on the hill slopes within a few miles of the city centre. John de Courcy, on
invading Ulster in 1177, erected a castle at the 'ford of the sand- bank' (*Beal-
feirste*). This, with the town which grew up around it, was destroyed by Edward
Bruce in 1315. The place then came into the possession of the O'Neills, Earls of
Tyrone, and when their lands were confiscated in 1603, Belfast was the spoil of
Sir Arthur Chichester, who colonised it with Devon men.
    In 1613 it was incorporated by Charter of James I, with the right of sending two
members to Parliament, and authorised to construct a wharf or quay. This
Charter was annulled by James II and a new one issued in 1688, but the original
was restored by George II. During the 17C progress was hampered by the
unsettled state of the country, and a protest by the citizens against the execution
of Charles I was met with a bitter response from Milton, levelled at the 'blockish
presbyters of Clandeboye' (the barony in which Belfast stood). Wesley, who
visited Belfast on several occasions, was equally critical, later commenting: 'I
never saw so large a congregation there before, nor one so remarkably stupid and
ill mannered'.
    The trade of Belfast, encouraged by Strafford (who purchased from Carrickfer-
gus, on the loughside to the NE, the monopoly of imported goods), was materially
benefited by the influx of French Huguenots after the revocation of the Edict of
Nantes (1685). They improved the methods of the already-established linen

Belfast Central

trade, which increased steadily during the 18th and 19Cs. In 1737 the 'Belfast News Letter' was first published. In 1784 a Corporation for 'Preserving' and Improving the Port and Harbour of Belfast' was set up, and at about the same time the architect Roger Mulholland planned a grid of streets as a framework for the future growth of the town. Cotton-spinning was introduced in 1777 and by 1810 engaged 2,000 people, while the revival of shipbuilding (initiated by William Ritchie in 1791) added a further impetus to growth. On 18 October 1791 took place the first open meeting of the Society of United Irishmen (three weeks prior to that in Dublin, founded by Napper Tandy), inaugurated primarily by Wolfe Tone and Samuel Neilson (1761–1803). The dredging of the Victoria Channel, from the port to the centre of Belfast Lough, was completed in 1849. In James Fraser's *Hand-Book for Travellers in Ireland*, published in the 1840s, he remarked of Belfast that 'Everywhere the superior arrangements, as compared with any other of our large towns, in cleaning, paving, and lighting, are evident, and there are none of those miserable suburbs we almost everywhere else meet with; so that, as a large manufacturing and seaport town, Belfast unites industry and elegance, with cleanliness and social order …'.

By 1800 its population (8,550 in 1757) had grown to c 20,000; in 1821, 37,000; in 1841, 70,000; in 1861, 121,000; in 1881, 208,000, rising to 400,000 by 1925. In 1888 Belfast, which had been incorporated as a borough in 1842 (and visited by Queen Victoria in 1849), was raised to the rank of a city, and its chief magistrate granted the title of Lord Mayor in 1892.

By the Government of Ireland Act, 1920, it became overnight the seat of government of Northern Ireland.

It was the scene of sectarian riots in 1935 (as it had been already in 1857, 1864, 1876, 1878, 1886, 1898, and 1912), apart from being a hotbed of trouble in 1920–22. (Charles Brett has pointed out that the dividing line recorded by the Commis-

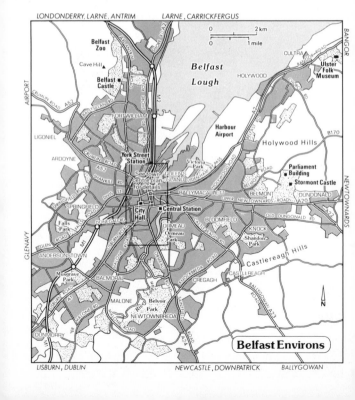

Belfast Environs

sion of Inquiry after the riots of 1886 follows almost exactly the barrier between the Falls and Shankill Road.) In spring 1941 it suffered a severe 'blitz' in which nearly 1,000 people were killed, during which the Dublin fire brigade was sent to their aid. (The aircraft factories of Short Bros. and Harland were sited adjacent.) In 1942 the first contingent of the United States Army to set foot in Europe landed here.

In 1964 took place what became known as the 'tricolour riots', in which the bellicose Rev. Ian Paisley became involved, and from 1968 the city again became a sectarian battlefield. In certain respects little has changed since Giraldus Cambrensis wrote of the Irish that they 'hurl stones against the enemy in battle with such quickness and dexterity that they do more execution than the slingers of any other nation'.

In recent years, as part of the Belfast Redevelopment Plan, large areas of the city have been cleared of their 19C slums, and strenuous efforts are being made—against considerable odds—to make the town look less tarnished.

Among natives of Belfast were: William Drennan (1754–1820), the poet, known for his apt phrase for Ireland, 'the emerald isle', and first president of the United Irishmen; Peter Turnerelli (1774–1839), sculptor; Sir Samuel Ferguson (1810–86), poet and antiquarian, born at 23 High St; William Thomson, later Lord Kelvin (1824–1907), the scientist; Lord Bryce (1838–1922), statesman and ambassador; Sir John Lavery (1856–1941), the artist; Sir Almroth Wright (1861–1947), the physician; Canon Hannay ('George A. Birmingham'; 1865–1950), and Forrest Reid (1875–1947), both novelists; Lord Craigavon (1871–1940), first Prime Minister of Northern Ireland, and his contemporary Joseph Devlin (1871–1934), the Nationalist leader; St. John Ervine (1883–1971), dramatist; Clive Staples Lewis (1898–1963), scholar; Louis MacNeice (1907–63) and William Robert Rodgers (1909–69), poets. Alexander Mitchell (1780–1868), born in Dublin, invented the screw-pile when in Belfast (1842), where he died; and John Boyd Dunlop (1840, in Ayrshire–1922) was a veterinary surgeon in Belfast from 1867, where in 1887 he invented the pneumatic rubber tyre. Anthony Trollope lived for 18 months in Belfast and adjacent Whiteabbey from 1853, where he completed 'The Warden'.

Note. Until the present 'troubles' are over it is unlikely that many visitors will wish to spend very long in the city, which has now less attractions than it might once have had. Vehicle access to a large central area is restricted, as shown on the plan, but directional signs pointing to some of the more interesting buildings have been placed there to assist the pedestrian visitor.

The main arteries of Belfast radiate from **Donegall** (sic) **Square**, the hub of the city, and still a centre of circulation. Here stands the **City Hall**, a ponderous Renaissance-style building of Portland stone by Sir Brumwell Thomas, completed in 1906, and improved by recent cleaning. It occupies the site of the old White Linen Hall of 1784. The central copper dome rises to a height of 53m, and the pile accommodates a number of sumptuous marble-decorated reception rooms, which may be seen on application.

The *Linenhall Library* (17 Donegall Sq. N) contains an important and rapidly growing collection of material, including ephemera, relative to the recent 'troubles', in addition to other collections. The W side of the square is taken up by the *Scottish Provident* building (1899–1902; by Young and Mackenzie).

At No. 1 Donegall Sq. N is the former warehouse of linen merchants, erected in 1869 by W.H. Lynn, and admirably restored by 1985 to house *Marks & Spencer*.

Parallel to the N front of the City Hall is Chichester St, leading E towards the river and the *Royal Courts of Justice* (1929–33; by J.G. West), another massive pile of Portland stone, with pavings, etc. of Irish granite. To the NE of the latter the Lagan is crossed by *Queen's Bridge*, opened in 1841 and widened in 1886, standing on the site of the Long Bridge of 1689 damaged by Schomberg's artillery in crossing it. Parallel to the N is *Queen Elizabeth Bridge* (1966). Another bridge spanning the Lagan slightly further N, is projected.

Beyond the S end of the Courts, East Bridge St leads past *Central Railway Station* to *Albert Bridge*, immediately to the SW of which is the *Maysfield Sports and Leisure Centre* (1977), with a riverbank marina.

Opposite the N front of City Hall is Donegall Place, extended by Royal Av. (on the right of which, in Castle Pl., is the new GPO) and York St. This last is prolonged through a somewhat derelict district of slum clearance to join the A2 or M2 motorway; this is also an approach via

Limestone Rd, forking left, to the old Antrim road (A6).—Smithfield Market, which went up in flames in 1974, is being replaced by a shopping centre.

Leading W off Donegall Pl. is Castle St, extended by *Divis St*, which is itself prolonged through a predominantly Catholic area by the *Falls Rd*, off which, in Derby St, is the externally impressive *Pro-Cathedral of St. Peter's*, completed in 1866 with spires added in 1886.—Royal Av. is crossed by North St, extended to the W by *Peter's Hill* and the *Shankill Rd* (a Protestant enclave), while roughly parallel to the latter, but further N, is the *Crumlin Rd*, leading to the Catholic district of *Ardoyne*: all names which have been in the news during recent decades as festering focuses of sectarian violence, but which themselves are of no intrinsic interest.

Off the E side of Donegall Pl. opens Castle Pl., with the new *Post Office*, prolonged by High St (with the *Tourist Office* at No. 48), beyond which (right) is *St. George's Church* (by John Bowden; 1816), with a classical portico from Ballyscullion (see Rte 33A).

At the E end of High St rises the *Albert Memorial* (1865, by W.J. Barre), leaning from the vertical due to subsidence.— Beyond, on the N side of Queen's Sq., stands the *Custom House* (1854–57, by Sir Charles Lanyon), with sculptures by S.F. Lynn, and containing a collection of paintings of maritime subjects. It overlooks Donegall Quay, the point of embarkation for the Liverpool Ferry, etc.

The **Port of Belfast** lies at the head of BELFAST LOUGH, c 19km from the open sea. In addition to being the largest port of Ireland, with an annual total movement of some ten million tonnes of shipping (including ferries), it is famous as one of the world's great shipbuilding centres, with the yards of *Harland and Wolff*.

There was a revival of shipbuilding in 1833 on the site of Queen's Island, which within a few years was virtually controlled by Edward James Harland, a Yorkshireman, who in 1858 recruited from Hamburg the marine draughtsman Gustav Wilhelm Wolff. Among numerous other liners constructed here was the 'Titanic' (1912).

The port contains four dry docks, including the huge 'Belfast Dry Dock', 335m long, which have seen the repair of some of the largest liners, and more recently, tankers, afloat; also c 13km of quays and some 500 hectares of water. Noticeable among a forest of some 40 cranes and gantries are the two cranes ('Samson' and 'Goliath'), one of which is 106m high and 140m long, straddling the 556m-long Harland and Wolff *Shipbuilding Dock*, where a tanker of 333,000dwt has recently been constructed.—Here also is a bulk liquid terminal of 200,000 tonnes capacity, and an oil refinery of 1.3 million tonnes capacity.

The *Sinclair Seaman's Church* in Corporation St, to the W of Donegall Quay, preserves some curious mementoes of maritime interest.

Facing Donegall St, which crosses Royal Av. diagonally some distance to the N, is **St. Anne's Cathedral** (C. of I.), a still-unfinished edifice in a hybrid Hiberno-Romanesque style, begun in 1899 from the designs of Sir Thomas Drew (died 1910), and continued by Sir Charles Nicholson (died 1949). It was built around the old parish church of St. Anne, demolished in 1903.

It is basilican in plan, with shallow transepts and an apsidal E end with ambulatory (completed 1959); the W front, with three portals, was dedicated as a war memorial in 1927. The *Nave*, 26m long, has a floor of maple and Irish marble, and at its W end is a maze. Here also is the tomb of Lord Carson (1854–1935), leader of the Unionists, with a supererogatory memorial on the S wall. At the SW corner is a richly decorated *Baptistery*, and opposite, the domed *Chapel of the Holy Spirit*. The capitals of the nave arcade, by Morris Harding, represent the occupations of mankind, above which are corbels commemorating leaders of the Church of Ireland.

Adjoining is the *Art and Design Centre* of the Belfast Campus of the

University of Ulster, an impersonal glass-fronted building typical of the 1960s.

Beyond the N end of Donegall St stands *Clifton House*, a Charitable Institute, designed by Cooley but probably built by Robert Joy, and opened in 1774.

Few ecclesiastical buildings in Belfast other than those mentioned below are of any moment. The *Cooke Memorial Church* in May St retains a classical portal; the interior of the old Presbyterian *Oval Church*, completed by Mulholland in 1783 and well restored after 'bomb' damage in 1972 and 1975, is of interest (in Rosemary St, just N of Castle Pl.); while in Alfred St, SE of Donegall Sq., is restored *St. Malachy's* (1844; by Thomas Jackson), with some impressive fan-vaulting. Hardly any others have escaped the 19C rage for the Gothic-Revival mould, and although some examples may be seen of the 'Scottish Tudor' and Hiberno-Romanesque styles, apart from those in more eclectic 'modern' forms, few merit any attention. Likewise, it must be admitted, the dour Victorian warehouses and factories of Belfast, apart from banks and other commercial buildings, although they may be of certain interest to the industrial archaeologist, have as little charm for the visitor as the low brick terraces which sheltered the shipyard, mill, and factory workers, and the modern tenements which have replaced some of them. But acquire the 1985 edition of Charles Brett's 'Buildings of Belfast 1700–1914' (for its introduction and foot-notes, particularly).

Wellington Pl. leads W from Donegall Sq. to College Sq ., with the *College of Technology* (1902–7) and the *Royal Academical Institution*, a day school (usually referred to as the 'Inst') at which Sheridan Knowles and James Thomson (Lord Kelvin's father) were masters. Erected in 1810–14, it was based on designs by Sir John Soane. Kelvin's birthplace (demolished) was in College Sq. E.—To the S, in Great Victoria Street, stands the *Opera House* (1894), designed by Frank Matcham (1854–1920), with a lavishly gilt interior, re-opened in 1980 after a thorough restoration. Also in this street stands the ornate *Crown Liquor Saloon* (1885, by Patrick Flanagan), an excellent example of Victorian architecture at its most exuberant, now the pro-perty of the NT and still used as a bar.

From the SW corner of Donegall Sq., Bedford St leads S past the *Ulster Hall* (1860: by W.J. Barre) to the junction of Gt Victoria St (itself extending S from College Sq.) and University Rd.

From this junction the Donegall Rd leads W to join the M1 motorway and the main road S to Newry, Dundalk, and Dublin, while the old Lisburn Rd bears SW.

Ascending gently almost due S along University Rd we pass on the left the original buildings of **Queen's University** (8,500 students), designed by Sir Charles Lanyon in a Tudor style.

Founded as Queen's College in 1845, and formerly associated with the other Queen's Colleges at Cork and Galway, it was later known as the Royal Univers-ity; the University of Belfast was incorporated separately in 1909.

To the E is the conspicuous *Assembly's College* (1853; also by Lanyon), a Presbyterian training school occupying a Tuscan Doric edifice, while opposite the University, in Elmwood Av., is the *Agricultural College*.

To the left just beyond Elmwood Av. is the entrance to the attractive **Botanic Gardens**, with a shapely glass-domed *Palm House* (1839; 1852; constructed by the Dublin iron-founder Richard Turner), rec-ently well-restored after years of neglect.

The Palm House in the Botanic Gardens

To the S are the new buildings of the *****ULSTER MUSEUM**, by
Francis Pym (1971), near the entrance of which is a re-erected Court
Cairn from Ballintaggart, Co. Armagh. The foundation stone of the
older building facing Stranmillis Rd, designed by J.C. Wynne, was laid
in 1924. The building also contains a library, lecture room, and café. It
is divided into five departments: Botany and Zoology; Geology; Antiquities; Local History, and Technology; and Art.

The recommended circuit is made by taking a lift to the TOP FLOOR,
thence descending on foot by a series of rubber-floored spiral
ramps.—**Art Collections**. Dates are given for those Irish artists not
included in the index. Not all the important works are on permanent
display, but a proportion of the following are likely to be seen: representative canvases by *John Lavery, Lucien Pissarro, Vanessa Bell,
Dubuffet,* and *Tapies,* and among notable individual works *Sickert,*
Suspense; *Stanley Spencer,* Portrait of Daphne Spencer, and Betrayal;
Hector McDonnell, Bewley's Restaurant II; *Anthony Green,* Second
Marriage; and *F.E. McWilliam,* Woman in Bomb Blast. Also notable
are *Henry Moore*'s sculptures entitled Oval with points, and Three-
piece reclining figure draped.

R6 Among over 1600 *****Watercolours and drawings**, a selection are
usually displayed of representative works by *Edward Lear, David Cox,
David Roberts, Samuel Palmer, Francis Wheatley, Cozens, Thomas
Shotter Boys, Paul Sandby, Rowlandson, Gerald Brockhurst, Varley,
J.F. Lewis, Percy Wyndham Lewis* (Seated Woman), *Philip Wilson
Steer, William Henry Hunt* (The Link Boy), *John 'Warwick' Smith,
Thomas Hearne,* and *Fuseli.*

Outstanding among the watercolourists are *Andrew Nicholl,* and
James Moore, of which the museum has an extensive collection,
George Petrie, William Miller (of Lurgan; died 1779), *Charles Ginner,*

John Percival Gülich, and *James George Oben* (O'Brien; fl. 1779–1819). A collection of paintings of over 180 Irish birds by *Richard Dunscombe Parker* (1805–81) is also of importance.

Other sections display *Colin Harrison*, Portrait of William Bogle; *Edward McGuire* (born 1932), Portrait of Seamus Heaney; *Louis Le Brocquy* (born 1916), Girl in White; *William Conor*, Jaunting Car; *Jack Butler Yeats*, On through the Silent Lane; *Sir William Orpen*, Self-portrait; *Nathaniel Hone the Younger*, Landscapes; *Joseph Peacock* (1783–1837), Festival at Glendalough; *James Glen Wilson* (1827–63), Emigrant Ship leaving Belfast; *W. Clarkson Stanfield*, Stack Rock, Antrim; *George Barret, senior*, The Waterfall at Powerscourt; *Nathaniel Grogan*, View of Kilkenny; *attrib. Philip Hussey*, The Bateson family; *Susanna Drury* (fl. 1733–70), two Views of the Giant's Causeway (1740); *Arthur Devis*, Portrait of Viscount Boyle; *Pompeo Battoni*, Portrait of the Earl of Hillsborough (1766). *Richard Wilson*, Landscape with Bandits; *Anon.* (English School, c 1600), Portrait of the 2nd Earl of Essex; *Turner*, The Dawn of Christianity; *Gainsborough*, Portrait of the 1st Marquess of Donegal. *Lawrence*, Harriet Anne, Countess of Belfast; *Reynolds*, Theodosia Magill, later Countess of Clanwilliam; *Margaret Clarke* (1881–1961), Portrait of Harry Clarke; *Hugh Douglas Hamilton*, Portraits of James Moore O'Donnell, and Colonel Hugh O'Donnell; *James Latham*, Captain Charles Janvre de la Bouchetière; *Lavery*, The bridge at Grès; *J.M. Wright the elder*, Gentleman in armour; and *Stubbs*, James Hamilton.

R2 Works of art displayed here include the Lennox Quilt (1712); Jewellery; *Irish Glass*, with examples of early Waterford ware, and the wheel engraved goblet of Abp Charles Cobbe (1743/5); *Irish Silver*

James Glen Wilson, Emigrant ship leaving Belfast (1852: detail)

tankards and porringers (among them the Dopping and Freke porringer of 1685), including the Great Seal Cup of 1593 (made for Adam Loftus, Abp of Armagh and first provost of Trinity College, Dublin), and a fine epergne of 1790.

The following sections of the museum display its *Natural History Collections* (including a skeleton of the extinct Irish Giant Deer; a Coelacanth dredged up off Madagascar in 1973; a Giant Japanese Spider-crab, etc.). In 1968 the *University Herbarium*, a collection of c 40,000 specimens of plants, largely formed by Charles Bailey (1838–1924), was donated to the museum. The *Geology of Ireland* is graphically displayed, as is the 'Giant's Causeway'.

An adjacent section is devoted to the raising of the *Girona Treasure* (cf. *Port-na-Spania*). The material salvaged from the galleass off Lacada Point (near the Giant's Causeway) by Robert Sténuit in 1968–69 was acquired by the Museum in 1972. It includes bronze cannon,

Thomas Robinson, Portrait of William Richie

breech blocks, and other artefacts, and also an invaluable hoard of jewellery, including a gold salamander set with rubies, gold chains, buttons, crosses, rings, cameos, and coins, etc.

In adjoining rooms are some of the treasures of the museum, among them a gilt bronze cross from Altikeeragh (Londonderry); silver mace of the borough of Cavan (by John Hamilton, Dublin, 1724); silver penannular brooch from near Ballymoney (late 9C), Irish made but Saxon inspired; amber necklace from Kurin Moss (Co. Londonderry, c 800 BC. The important finds from Nendrum may also be seen here.

In the *Archaeological Galleries* are a representative selection of Bronze Age gold ornaments; bronze cauldrons and other implements, including cordoned and collared urns (1750–1000 BC), and two types of cast bronze horns (c 800 BC); the Malone hoard of polished stone axes, etc. In this area also are general ethnological exhibits, and a section on local history.

On the approach to the GROUND FLOOR is the *Technological Gallery*, which we traverse before reaching the interesting collection of engines, many in working order, explaining Flax and Linen technology; also spinning-wheels, etc.

Visitors should not overlook the *Ulster Folk and Transport Museum*, at Cultra, some 7 miles NE; see Rte 41A.

Also in Stranmillis Rd is (right) the *Science Building* of the University (by John McGeagh), while from the far side of the Botanic Gardens the *Stranmillis Embankment* skirts the Lagan to Ormeau Bridge and Ormeau Rd (continued as the A24 to Downpatrick). Beyond the bridge, on the S bank of the river, is *Ormeau Park*.

33 Belfast to Derry

A. Via Antrim

73 miles. (116km). A6. 18 miles *Antrim*—17 miles *Castledawson* roundabout—19 miles *Dungiven*—18 miles **Derry**.

The M2 motorway, joined immediately N of the city centre (skirting the W bank of Belfast Lough) now extends some 23 miles NW from Belfast, providing a rapid exit from the city, rejoining the A6 between Antrim and Castledawson.

Leaving Belfast by Donegall St and Carlisle Circus, the road steadily climbs, with *Cave Hill* (368m) on our left, a popular excursion. It is the northernmost peak of a range of hills that overlooks the city to the W, the highest summit of which is *Divis* (478m), further S. The former, however, commands the best *View*, extending across Belfast Lough to Down and Strangford Lough, while on a clear day the Ayrshire coast and the Isle of Man may be discerned; to the W Lough Neagh is backed by the Sperrin and Carntogher ranges.

The easiest approach is from the Antrim Rd and Hazelwood Gdns, adjoining which is the *Belfast Zoo*. On the hillside stands *Belfast Castle* (1867–70, largely designed by W.H. Lynn in the 'Scottish baronial' style, with an incongruous stair added in 1894, and under restoration. On the summit are the earthworks known as *MacArt's Fort*, named after Brian MacArt O'Neill, killed by Lord Mountjoy in 1601; it is defended by a precipice on one side and a ditch on the other.

11 miles. **Templepatrick** (700 inhab.) is said to derive its name from

the Knights Templar. *Castle Upton* to the right, once the seat of the Upton family (Viscounts Templeton), was built in 1612 and remodelled in 1788–89 by Robert Adam, who also designed the Upton mausoleum in the churchyard; the mansion may be visited by prior arrangement. Further N, beyond the motorway, rises *Donegore Hill*, crowned by a prehistoric cairn; in *Donegore* churchyard is the grave of the poet and antiquary Sir Samuel Ferguson (1810–86).—At 6 miles (left) on the outskirts of Antrim we pass the slight remains of *Muckamore* priory (founded c 550 by St. Colman), and *Greenmount Agricultural College*.

ANTRIM (22,350 inhab.), a linen-spinning town on the Six Mile Water, is near the NE corner of Lough Neagh (see below), on which a steamer makes day cruises. Antrim was burnt in 1649 by General Monro. In 1798 it put up a stout defence and beat off the insurgents, lead by Henry Foy McCracken (soon after executed), although Lord John O'Neill, their commander, was killed. The *Protestant Church*, dating from 1596, has a spire of 1816 and some Renaissance glass. Near the *Court House* (1726) is the Tudor gateway to *Antrim Castle* (enlarged 1662, and rebuilt by John Bowden in 1813), a seat of Viscount Massereene and Ferrard. It was burned down in 1922 (accidentally), but retains its Dutch-style garden, with a T-shaped canal. Railway St leads to the *Round Tower*, the most perfect in Ulster (28m; with its conical cap restored), the only visible remains of the ancient monastery of Aentrebh; the door is almost 3m from the ground, and the rude masonry indicates an early date (c 900).

Belfast International Airport (formerly Aldergrove) is only 4 miles S of Antrim, but is more directly approached from the city (14 miles E) by the A52.

Immediately W of Antrim, the A6 skirts **Lough Neagh**, by far the largest lake in Ireland (and the British Isles); indeed it is more like an inland sea, being 18 miles long, 11 miles broad, and 65 miles round, with an area of almost 153 miles^2 (400km^2); it is bordered by every county of Northern Ireland except Fermanagh. Its banks are low—with a water level lower than in previous centuries—and in many places marshy, and it contains few islands, none of any size. Its insect population can be a nuisance. Ten rivers flow into it, and its outflow is the Lower Bann.

It contains char, pollan, and the gillaroo trout (*giolla ruadh*), and above all, eels, and is supposed to have petrifying properties. Hawkers used to walk the streets of Belfast with the cry 'Lough Neagh bones, put in sticks and taken out stones'. Of more interest is its marsh flora, ducks, and waterfowl generally, including among them the great crested grebe. Legend relates that the lough was created by the sudden overflow of a fountain which buried many cities, as quoted by Giraldus Cambrensis and alluded to in Moore's ballad 'Let Erin Remember'.

The road shortly passes (right) a large nylon-making plant, and (left) the lakeside demesne of *Shane's Castle*, preserving some ruins of the 16C stronghold of Shane O'Neill. Of John Nash's rebuilding of c 1812 only the greenhouse survived the fire of 1816. A second mansion erected in 1865 by Lanyon was burnt down in 1922.

The road veers away from the lough and traverses **Randalstown** (3,600 inhab.), a linen-bleaching and market-town known as Mainwater until its incorporation in 1683, with an oval *Presbyterian Church* of 1790, heightened in 1929, when oculi were inserted, and other early 19C churches; also of interest is the 18C former *Market-house*.

At *Toome Bridge* we regain Lough Neagh again at the outflow of the river Bann, with a large eel fishery, some 600 tonnes of which are caught each season.—The next right-hand fork leads towards the shores of LOUGH BEG, an expansion of the Bann, and the preserve of pike. On *Church Island* are 12–13C ruins adjoined by a spire erected by the Earl of Bristol in 1788.—Further N on the lake shore is a fragment of his former 'palace' at *Ballyscullion*, the portico of which now adorns the facade of St. George's Church, Belfast.

We turn left shortly through *Castledawson*, on the Moyola, and then right at a roundabout, after 5 miles reaching the A29 cross road (from Coleraine to Newry); to the right lies *Maghera*, see Rte 36. The scenery improves as we begin to climb the *Pass of Glenshane* through the *Sperrin Mountains* between *Carntogher* (462m; right) and *Mullaghmore* (555m; to the SW).

A minor but scenically finer road (B40) may be approached by turning left not far W of the Maghera junction, which regains the main road at *Killaloo*, 11 miles W of Dungiven.

We descend the Roe valley to **Dungiven** (2,200 inhab.), retaining the ruins of a fortified mansion of the Skinners' Company (1618), and of a *Priory*, approached by turning left on entering the town. The priory church, founded c 1100 by the O'Cahans and restored in 1397 by the Abp of Armagh, contains the elaborately carved *Tomb* of an O'Cahan knight (died 1385). In 1971 *Dungiven Castle* (1839) was the scene of an attempt to set up an independent Ulster parliament. John Mitchel (1815–75), the journalist and nationalist, was born near by, at *Camnish*.

At *Banagher*, to the SW, is a ruined church, the most interesting features of which are the W door, small and square-headed outside and large and semicircular within (as at Maghera), and the two loopholed S windows. In the churchyard is the tomb of St. Muiredach O'Heney, shaped like a mortuary house, with a figure in relief (?11C).—There is another similar but later tomb at *Bovevagh* church, 2 miles N of Dungiven.

The A6 continues W, with views S towards the Sperrin Mountains, the highest summit of which is *Sawel* (678m), after 9 miles passing (left) *Claudy*. Beyond Claudy we descend the charming wooded valley of the Faughan, which leads NW towards the banks of the Foyle, and **Derry**; see Rte 34A. It was near the bridge of *Burntollet*, c 7 miles from Derry, that in January 1969 a students' march was ambushed by Unionists, an action with far-reaching repercussions.

B. Via Coleraine

84½ miles (136km). A6. 18 miles *Antrim*—A26. 9½ miles *Ballymena*—19 miles *Ballymoney*—8 miles **Coleraine**—A37. 13 miles *Limavady* (the coastal road is 6 miles longer)—A2. 17 miles **Derry**.

For the road to **Antrim**, see Rte 34A, beyond which we bear right, and cross the motorway.—*Kells*, the seat of a once wealthy priory of a very ancient foundation, which has almost entirely disappeared, is passed to the E.

BALLYMENA (28,150 inhab.; P.O. 51 Wellington St), also by-passed, now the county town of Antrim, with a modern *County Hall*, owed its prosperity to the linen trade, but its reputation as the 'Aberdeen of Ireland' for its parsimony is no better deserved that that of Aberdeen itself. The old parish church (in Church St) retains a tower of 1721. In the S suburbs is the motte and bailey of *Harryville*.

1½ miles W of Ballymena lies the demesne of *Galgorm Castle* (17C), beyond which is the village of *Gracehill*, a Moravian settlement of 1746, with a typical central square.

The A42 leads NE of Ballymena, passing—in a loop of an extension of the M2 motorway by-passing the town—an ancient rath, to (3 miles) *Broughshane*, a village of no pretensions, but the home before he emigrated of Alexander Brown, founder of America's first bank, at Baltimore, and ancestral home of the hero of Ladysmith, F.M. Sir George White (1835–1912). The *Presbyterian Church* retains its wall of 1655 and a curious roof.—E of the village rises *Slemish* (437m), long assumed to be the mountain on which young St. Patrick ruminated while tending his master's swine.

The A43 leads NE from Ballymena towards the *Glens of Antrim* (see Rte 35), at first ascending a rather boggy upland, before approaching (left) *Parkmore Forest*, and descending Glenariff to reach the coast after 18 miles, just S of *Cushendall*.

The A26 bears almost due N, and is without interest except for the fine avenue of firs it traverses, off which after 11½ miles the A44 bears right for (15½ miles) *Ballycastle*; see Rte 35.

To the left of this road, 2 miles from the turning, is the fine motte of *Knockaholet*, built within a ring fort, beyond which (right) are the ruins of *Lissanoure Castle* on LOUGH GUILE, originally erected by Sir Philip Savage in the 14C, and rebuilt by Lord Macartney (1737–1806) in c 1787; it was dismantled in the mid 19C. Macartney, governor of the Cape of Good Hope in 1796–98, was the author of accounts of his earlier embassies to Russia and China, and of 'A Political Account of Ireland'; he was chief secretary for Ireland in 1769–72.—The road continues towards the coast via *Armoy*, with a *Round Tower* 10.5m high.

Ballymoney (5,700 inhab.), a thriving agricultural centre, preserves one street (Charlotte St) of late Georgian houses, a market-house of 1775, and an old parish church of 1637 superseded by St. Patrick's (1783).

James McKinley, grandfather of the American President William McKinley, was born 3½ miles N at *Conagher* in 1783; his birthplace is now an outhouse.—In *Drumabest Bog*, to the E of Ballymoney, four Bronze Age trumpets were found in 1840, and may be seen in the Ulster Museum, Belfast.

From Ballymoney we drive NW to **COLERAINE** (15,950 inhab.), in Irish *Cuil Rathain* (ferny corner), an irregularly built river-port at the head of the navigable reach of the Bann. Its prosperity dates from 1613 when the land was given by James I to the City Companies of London; but it claims a history going back to the 5C. Its whiskey distilleries and linen factories gave it an added prosperity, and its recent development has been given a further impulse by the founding in 1968 of the *University of Ulster* (part of which has been sited on its N outskirts since 1985) where functional buildings laid out in a spacious campus are too similar in style to new factories erected in the vicinity.

Its parish church, on an ancient foundation, was rebuilt in 1883, and no trace remains of the castle and priory except the rath at *Mountsandel*, in a wood 1 mile SE, which is supposed to mark the site of the fort of Fintan, King of Ulster, and of the later stronghold of De Courcy; it has also yielded flint implements of c 6650 BC, the earliest record of man in Ireland. In the town centre a stone bridge of 1844 spans the Bann, the 'fishy fruitful Bann' of Edmund Spenser, on which there is a commercial salmon fishery; upstream is the semicircular *Salmon Leap*. Coleraine was the birthplace of the artist and book illustrator Hugh Thomson (1860– 1920).

For the roads to Portstewart, Portrush, and the Giants' Causeway, see Rte 35; for roads S to Cookstown, Dungannon, and Armagh, Rte 36.

COLERAINE TO LIMAVADY VIA THE COAST (20 miles). The A2 drives NE, passing (right) the remains of *Downhill Castle* (badly damaged by fire in 1803 and again in 1851 but unroofed only in 1950; the demesne is open to the public). It was commenced c 1775 by Frederick Hervey, the urbane if eccentric 4th Earl of Bristol and Bp of Derry (1730–1803), an inveterate 'Grand Tourist', after whom innumerable 'Bristol' hotels in Europe are named. A statue, by Van Nost, of his brother, the 3rd Earl, was blow down by a gale from the summit of his Mausoleum (by Michael Shanahan), modelled on the Roman mausoleum at St. Rémy-de-Provence), and leans headless by the Bishop's Gate. A path leads past the castle to the ***Mussenden Temple** (1783–85), an elegant classical rotunda on the exposed cliff edge, erected by the earl as a compliment and memorial to his cousin Mrs Mussenden (NT). Less prejudiced than many, the Anglican bishop allowed a Catholic priest to celebrate mass here once a week, as there was no local Catholic parish church; and both the priest and his house were provided for in his will.—*Hezlett House* (1691), near by, is also open to the public.

The Mussenden Temple, Downhill

Beyond Downhill, the road skirts the cliffs before veering SW across the flat expanse of the *Magilligan Peninsula* (now defaced by an army camp and prison), with a 6-mile-long strand of firm sand, the haunt of conchologists. A *Martello tower* stands on the promontory at the narrow entrance of LOUGH FOYLE, which is connected by ferry with

Greencastle, backed by the hills of the *Inishowen Peninsula* (Co. Donegal); see Rte 34B.—The road swings S round the foot of *Binevenagh* (385m), its wooded escarpments furrowed by waterfalls, passing (right) at *Bellareena*, a 19C house, parts of which date back to 1690, and Folly Tower, to *Limavady*, see below.

The A37 drives SW from Coleraine, ascending past (right) *Sconce Hill*, crowned by the cyclopean fortress of *Dún Ceithern*, the legendary headquarters of the Red Branch Knights. On the E flank of Sconce Hill, near *Ballinrees*, was discovered (in 1854) the large hoard of Roman coins and silver dating from c AD 210, probably the loot of Irish pirates on English shores, now in the British Museum.—Descending between *Keady Mountain* (337m; left) and *Binevenagh* (see above), we pass (right) the demesne of *Drenagh*, with a house of c 1837, an early work of Sir Charles Lanyon.

Limavady (8,000 inhab.), a very ancient town taking its name, *Lim an mhadagh* (the dog's leap), from the site of a castle built by the O'Kanes or O'Cahans overhanging a deep glen 2 miles S up the valley of the river Roe, the original settlement. It was re-founded in the early 17C under the name of Newtown Limavady by Sir Thomas Phillips. The parish *Church* in Main St dates from 1750; the six-arched *Bridge* over the Roe was built in 1700.

James Monroe, 5th President of the United States, was descended from a family who took their name from nearby *Mount Roe*; William James Massey (1856–1925), Prime Minister of New Zealand in 1912–25, was born here, while Thackeray's 'Sweet Peg of Limavady' lived at an inn in Ballyclose St.

Between the town and the 'Dog's Leap' extends the demesne of *Roe Park*, in which a ridge, now called *The Mullagh*, is believed to represent *Drumceat*, the site of an ecclesiastical assembly in 574, attended by St. Columba, who sailed over from Iona for the occasion.

A road leads S along the attractive valley of the Roe, affording good views ahead of the Sperrin Mountains, to (9 miles) *Dungiven*; see Rte 33A.

The road to Derry—after passing (left) at *Ballykelly*, a fortified mansion of 1619 erected by the London Fishmongers' Company—keeps fairly close to the S shore of LOUGH FOYLE, with *Loughermore* (396m) rising to the S, and with the Inishowen hills ahead becoming more prominent.—At *Tamlaght*, 2 miles SE, are slight remains of a medieval church in a burial-ground on the site of a 6C monastery.—We turn SW, passing near *Culmore Fort*, on the estuary of the Foyle, built in 1824 within an old castle of the O'Docherty; there is a power station close by, beyond which, passing a number of industrial estates, we approach the transpontine suburb of *Waterside*, and cross the Foyle by the *Craigavon Bridge* (1933) into central *Derry*, see below. The new *Foyle Bridge* (1985) crosses the estuary to the N, providing a by-pass for those driving into Donegal and the Inishowen Peninsula; see Rte 34B.

34 Derry and the Inishowen Peninsula

A. Derry

LONDONDERRY (officially, although usually referred to as **Derry**; 62,700 inhab.; Post Office, 3 Custom House Quay) is the second city of Northern Ireland, an historic port, naval base, and garrison town. It retains its early 17C walls, which withstood a famous siege in 1688–89 (among others). They surround an oval hill rising steeply from the Foyle—here 275m wide—and crossed by a double-decker bridge, and since 1985 by the *Foyle Bridge*, further downstream, S of *Boom Hall*; see Rte 34B. The modern industrial town, noted for the manufacture of clothing, particularly shirts, etc., which has become more diversified during recent years, surrounds the old centre. It has suffered considerably during the last two decades from the discriminatory excesses of military and paramilitary forces and over-reactions to their continued occupation.

Waterside Railway Station (1873; by John Lanyon) is a short distance N of the E end of Craigavon Bridge. The *Bus Station* and *Tourist Office* are just NW of the Guildhall.

Derry, in Irish *Doire* (the oak-wood) had its origin in an abbey founded by St. Columba in 546, probably on the site of the present Protestant Cathedral. In 812 this was burned by the Danes in the first of many raids, and in 1164 Abbot Flahertagh O'Brolchain built the great church of Templemore where the church of St. Columba (R.C.) now stands. In 1311 the town was granted to Richard de Burgh, Earl of Ulster.
   In the autumn of 1566, in the rebellion of Shane O'Neill, Earl of Tyrone, the town resisted O'Neill's attack, although Edward Randolph, the English commander, was killed. Templemore was largely destroyed, and only the tower remained by the time Sir Henry Docwra had firmly established English dominance in 1570–1603. In May 1608 Sir Cahir O'Doherty laid waste the city, but was killed two months later, and his lands, together with those of Tyrone and Tyrconnel, were confiscated. Derry was handed over to the Corporation of London in 1613; its name was changed to Londonderry, and a large colony of Protestants planted. In 1649 Royalist forces under General Robert Stewart and Lord Montgomery of the Ards besieged the place for 20 weeks, but the defender, Sir Charles Coote, hired Owen Roe-O'Neill to relieve him.
   James II's army besieged it from 7 December 1688 to 12 August 1689, completely blockading it for 105 days by throwing a boom across the Foyle to bar the approach of provision ships. Fired by the apostolic fervour of the Rev. George Walker, the citizens stubbornly held out (in spite of attempts by Robert Lundy, the governor, to seek a compromise) until the boom was forced by the 'Mountjoy' on 28 July, and its relief concluded. Its gates remained open until 1940, when they were provisionally closed in the expectation of another siege.
   Its recent history has been less edifying. It was the scene in 1966 of what is now a classic example of gerrymandering in the arrangement, ostensibly for the purposes of local government, of its electoral wards. *Two* new constituencies were artificially created by extending the previous 'City' boundaries well beyond the Protestant suburb of *Waterside* to the E, into known areas of Unionist preponderance, while the anti-Unionists (largely Catholic) were crammed into the new South Ward (including *Bogside*). This produced a skilfully manipulated situation in which, although the anti-Unionists numbered 20,102 as opposed to 10,274, they were outvoted by 2 to 1 by the Unionists, who continued to control the town.
   On 5 October 1968 took place the first major confrontation between Civil Rights demonstrators and the police, repeated on 4 January 1969, the 'B Specials' justifying their reputation for intimidation and brutality, and reminding the older generation of the undisciplined activities of the 'Black and Tans' in Ireland in the early 1920s. On 12 August Bogside was in a state of siege, which has more-or-less continued ever since, and on 30 January 1972 British paratroopers killed 13 people, bringing home to the world at large the seriousness of the situation in

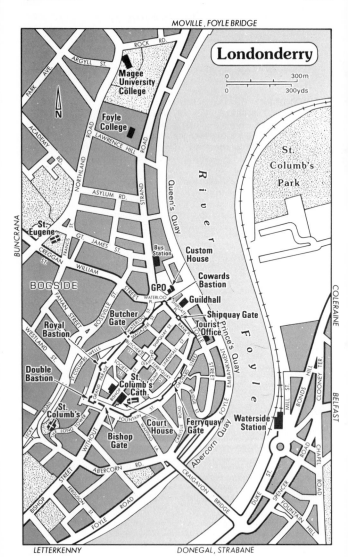

Northern Ireland. Whether there will be an end to hostilities before the tercente-
nary of Derry's much-vaunted siege is problematic.

Among Derrymen were the dramatist George Farquhar (1678–1707), and the
novelist Joyce Cary (1888–1957); Sir Robert Montgomery (1809–87), who suppressed the Indian Mutiny at Lahore, and was later Lt.-Governor of the Punjab,
was also born here.

The music of the 'Londonderry Air' is said to have been first noted down in
Limavady in 1851 by Jane Ross, on hearing an itinerant fiddler play the tune.

Having suffered through fire and sword throughout the ages, Derry
preserves comparatively few historic monuments, and not all of those
remaining are, in the present circumstances, easily approached. From
the W end of *Craigavon Bridge* (1933, and 365m long), replacing Carlisle Bridge, itself succeeding a timber bridge of 1791 by Lemuel Cox,
which here crosses the Foyle, Carlisle Rd ascends half-right to
Ferryquay Gate, that which was shut in the face of Lord Antrim's
troops in 1689 by the apprentice boys of Derry. Passing through this
we approach the **Diamond**, the central square of the old town and site
of earlier town halls. Hence, turning left up Bishop St, we soon reach
(left) the porticoed *Courthouse* (1813–17; by John Bowden). Beyond
stands *Bishop's Gate*, a triumphal arch erected in 1789, with sculptural
decorations by Edward Smyth of Dublin, but at present draped with
barbed wire.

Derry's *Walls (1617–19), the parapet of which has been laid out as
a promenade, are reasonably well conserved, but only a few of the
bastions have survived, among them (SW corner) the *Double Bastion*,
on which stands 'Roaring Meg', a brass cannon of 1642, which played
its part in the siege. *Walker's Monument*, erected in 1828 on Royal
Bastion, to the N, was recently destroyed. (Guided tours of the walls
take place in the summer, starting from the Tourist Office.)

A short walk downhill from Bishop's Gate (see above) via Long Tower St, will
bring one to the so-called *Long Tower Church* (*St. Columba's*; R.C.), with an
interior of interest, built on the site of Templemore (see history), the 'long tower'
of which, spared by Docwra, was destroyed in the siege. Here is preserved the
so-called *St. Colum's Stone*, a Bullaun removed in 1707 from its original site
beneath the Royal Bastion.

Turning down St. Columb's Court (adjacent to the Courthouse), in
which No. 1 is the home of the *Hon. the Irish Society* (1740), we reach
the **Protestant Cathedral** (St. Columb's), founded by the Corporation
of London. The nave dates from 1628–33, but the chancel was built
only in 1885–87, when the original plaster ceiling was replaced with
a wooden one. This 'Planters' Gothic' church has a spire, rebuilt in
1802–22, at its W end, and in the entrance vestibule, the bombshell
thrown into the city which contained General Richard Hamilton's proposed terms of capitulation, the historic and uncompromising answer
to which was 'No Surrender'. On the N wall is a quaint 17C monument
to John Elvin, Mayor, who died in 1676, aged 102. In the W gallery is
an organ-case of mahogany (1747). The *Chapter House* contains more
souvenirs of the siege and a walnut table belonging to the Earl of
Bristol, Bp. of Derry in 1768–1803 (cf.), whose palace faces the
courthouse.

Regaining the Diamond, where Butcher St leads to *Butcher Gate*,
overlooking the Catholic district of *Bogside* and *Creggan* beyond, we
descend Ship Quay St, which slopes steeply to *Ship Quay Gate*. To its
left is a terrace lined with old guns, and, beyond, the site of *Coward's
Bastion*, the safest sector during the siege.—Flanking Shipquay Pl. is
the *Guildhall* (1890; rebuilt in 1912 after a fire, and again in 1972 after
bomb damage), and with restored stained-glass and panelling. It

preserves the treasures of the Corporation, including the two-handed sword alleged to be that of Sir Cahir O'Doherty, who raided Derry in 1608.

From Waterloo Pl., just W of the Guildhall, William St leads towards the *Catholic Cathedral of St. Eugene*, a plain Gothic-Revival building (1853–73) by J.J. McCarthy, with a tall spire added in 1903.
    Two other buildings, N of the centre, are described below.

For routes from Derry to Sligo, and Omagh, see Rtes 27 and 30 respectively; for Enniskillen, Rte 29, and for Donegal via the coast, Rte 28; for Belfast direct, Rte 33A; via Coleraine, 33B: all these in reverse.

B. The Inishowen Peninsula

99km (61 miles). A2 and R238. 27km *Moville*—14.5km *Culdaff*—7km *Cardonagh*—30km *Buncrana*—14km *Bridge End*—4 miles **Derry**.

A circular tour of this peninsula, the northernmost part of Ireland, may be made with ease from Derry. The *Grianan of Aileach* (see below), the most impressive antiquity on the vicinity, lies 11km NW (by road), via *Bridge End*.

From Waterloo Pl. we drive N along Strand Rd, shortly passing (left) *Foyle College* (1814), the successor of the Free Grammar School (1617), where George Farquhar was educated. Among its pupils were Sir Henry Lawrence and his two brothers, and Sir Robert Montgomery, all distinguished for service in India, and J.B. Bury, the historian.—Further N is *Magee University College*, opened in 1865 by Mrs Magee of Dublin for the training of students for the Presbyterian ministry, and now part of the University of Ulster.
    Continuing N we shortly pass (right) *Boom Hall* (c 1770), marking the site where the boom was thrown across the Foyle during the siege of Derry, and beyond *Culmore* we cross the border into Co. Donegal.
    To the NW rises *Eskaheen* (419m), and, further N, *Crockglass* (398m), below which we skirt the broad waters of LOUGH FOYLE.—The direct road to (14.5km) *Cardonagh* (see below) ascends to the left at *Carowkeel*, 13km beyond which we enter the resort of *Moville* (1,250 inhab.), pronounced with the accent on the second syllable.— *Greencastle*, with a fort of 1812 and the ruined castle of Richard de Burgh (1305), lies some 4km beyond, opposite Magilligan Point, the narrowest part of the estuary. The road peters out at *Inishowen Head* (90m high), commanding a view of the coast to the E as far as 'the Giant's Causeway', and dominated by *Crocknasmug* (327m).

Just W of Moville a lane climbs inland to *Cooley*, with scanty remains of a church in a graveyard, beside which is an ancient cross preserving an impression claimed to be a footprint of St. Patrick on its slab; there are other archaeological sites in the neighbourhood.

The main road ascends *Bredagh Glen* between *Crockavishane* (left) and *Crockaulin* to traverse (9km) *Gleneely*, 3km beyond which a lane to the left leads to the ruined church and weather-beaten *Cross of Clonca* (or St. Bodan's Cross), preserving good ornamentation.— Further on (right) we pass a stone circle, probably Druidical, before entering *Culdaff*; *Culdaff House* (1779) has been rebuilt since burnt in the early 1920s.

A narrow road leads N to *Glengad Head*, where cliffs rising to over 150m command a view of the Scottish islands of Islay and Jura, and the Kintyre peninsula, and is continued to **Malin Head**, the most northerly point in Ireland, with a meteorological station. Although only 70m high, it has a fine sea view and is within easy reach of some splendid cliff and rock scenery. To the W is *Hell's Hole*, where the tide surges through a narrow rock-cleft and the prospect SW of the Clonmany hills opens out. The reef-girt island of *Inishtrahull*, had a population of about 50 until 1930 and now has three. Hence we regain the R238 S of the village of *Malin*, with a green, a ten-arched bridge, and a mansion of 1758 (to the N) overlooking the sandy expanse of *Trawbreagha Bay*.

7km SW of Culdaff, and 5km S of Malin, we enter **Cardonagh** (1,550 inhab.), the agricultural centre of the peninsula, preserving a 7C *Cross*, with an interlaced ribbon design and two stumpy guardstones, carved with naive figures (8C) opposite the church.—9km W is *Ballyliffin*, at the SW end of *Doagh Isle*, in fact a peninsula of dunes bounded to the W by the strand of *Pollan Bay*, at the N end of which is the ruined tower of *Carrickabraghy Castle*, an O'Doherty stronghold.—We continue S thence through *Clonmany*, with a view of *Raghtin More* (505m), with its glittering mica schists, to the W, beyond which rises *Dunaff Head* (189m) at the E point of the entrance to LOUGH SWILLY (cf.).

From Clonmany an interesting ALTERNATIVE route to Buncrana (30km) skirts the base of *Raghtin More* (see above) and veers S, climbing steeply (1:5.3 to 1:7) to the *Gap of Mamore* (262m; finest view in retrospect). *Mamore Hill*, the wild rocky peak N of the pass, is worth climbing for the view. The road, after descending, turns SW towards *Dunree Head*, where there is a fort of 1812 guarding Lough Swilly. The *Urris Hills* (420m), immediately above Dunree Head, are continued on the other side of Lough Swilly by the Knockalla Mountain. The road hence to *Buncrana* commands good views across the lough.

At Clonmany the main road turns S, ascending the valley past MINTIAGH'S LOUGH, a small tarn, passing near (left) *Slieve Snaght* (615m), the highest point on Inishowen. The road approaches Lough Swilly at **Buncrana** (3,150 inhab.), to the N of which, beside an old bridge over the Crana, is a square keep of the O'Dochertys, and near by, what was a fine 18C mansion, now decaying.

Skirting the loughside and circling *Mouldy Hill*, we traverse *Fahan*, where a monastery founded by St. Columba is represented only by the 8C *Cross-slab*, with its interlaced ribbon carving, known as that of St. Mura, a 7C abbot.—To the SW lies *Inch Island*, which, with most of the O'Docherty lands, was awarded to Sir Arthur Chichester after the Flight of the Earls.

Bearing inland, we may turn right along a minor road and then left to meet the N13. Opposite the junction is the interesting church of *St. Aengus*, a circular spired structure (1967) designed by Liam MacCormick and Una Madden, inspired perhaps by the ring-fort overlooking it to the S.—This is approached by crossing the main road and taking the first turning on the right, later climbing left.

The *Grianán of Ailech* is the principal antiquity in the neighbourhood of Derry, crowning a hill (244m), and commanding extensive panoramic views. Although over-restored and 'tidied up' unnecessarily in 1874–78, it is nonetheless one of the most remarkable concentric forts in Ireland. It was the residence of the O'Neills, Kings of Ulster, and was despoiled by Murtogh O'Brien, King of Munster, in 1101. Remains of three rough stone ramparts enclose the central cashel, a circular wall over 5m high and 4m thick at the base, and 73m round. In the thickness of the walls are defensive galleries.

Regaining the modern church, we turn right for *Bridge End*, and recross the border NW of Derry.—Alternatively, by turning left, we may

follow the N13 to (7km) *Newtown Cunningham* for *Letterkenny*; see
last part of Rte 28.

35 Belfast to Coleraine via the Antrim Coast

93 miles (149km). A2. 9½ miles **Carrickfergus**—15 miles *Larne*—26
miles *Cushendall*—16 miles *Ballycastle*—18 miles *Portrush* (via the
Giant's Causeway)—3 miles *Portstewart*—5½ miles **Coleraine**.

A direct road (A8) to (20 miles) *Larne* turns right off the M2 motorway 6½ miles
NW of Belfast, shortly by-passing (left) *Ballyclare* (6,150 inhab.) a busy market-
town and once a centre of the linen industry, and now with a synthetic fibre plant,
before traversing (6 miles) *Ballynure*, with the interesting remains of its old
church; from *Ballyeaston* (2 miles W), the grandfather of President Andrew
Johnson emigrated c 1750.—*Larne* lies 7 miles NE of Ballynure.

We follow the A2 N, skirting the W bank of BELFAST LOUGH, with *Cave
Hill* (see Rte 33A) rising to the left, and shortly skirt the 'new town'
known as *Newtownabbey* (56,150 inhab.), beyond which *Knockagh*,
with a conspicuous War Memorial, overlooks the road.
   CARRICKFERGUS (17,600 inhab.), once a flourishing port, and
now a yachting centre, with clothing factories and other small industries. The name 'the Rock of Fergus' recalls King Fergus MacErc, who
was shipwrecked off the coast c 320. It was here that the first regular
Irish presbytery was constituted in 1642. Both William Congreve and
Louis MacNeice spent part of their childhood here. The ancestors of
Andrew Jackson (1767–1845), President of the United States, were
natives of the town (but the thatched cottage 1 mile NE is not their
original home).
   The *'**Castle**, standing on a rocky spur above the harbour, is one of
the finest examples surviving in Ireland.

It was begun c 1180 by John de Courcy, who was defeated in 1204 by Hugh de
Lacy, Earl of Ulster. In 1210 it was besieged by King John. Edward Bruce, aided
by King Robert of Scotland, took it with difficulty in 1316, but it reverted to the

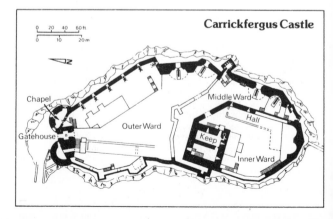

English on his death at Dundalk. In 1688–89 it was held for James II by Lord Iveagh, but Schomberg later captured it. Robert Monroe landed the first of several contingents of Scots in April 1642 to help the planters, and William of Orange disembarked here on 14 June 1690. In 1760 it was surprised and occupied briefly by a French expedition under Général Thurot, but his squadron was dispersed and he was killed in an engagement off the Isle of Man. John Paul Jones fought a successful engagement with HMS 'Drake' offshore in 1778. Garrisoned without a break until 1928, the castle now accommodates a museum.

The 13C *Gatehouse* admits to the outer ward; the storehouses on the left date from the 16C. From the inner ward we enter the imposing square *Keep* (before 1214), five storeys high (27.5m) with walls 2.5m thick.

The ground floor contains an ancient wooden canoe, and a steam fire engine of 1908; the next floor, with good views over the harbour, houses a collection of early prints and drawings, coins, clay pipes, armour, and cavalry uniforms (5th Royal Inniskilling Dragoon Guards, the Queen's Royal Irish Hussars, and the North Irish Horse). On the second floor is the vaulted *Great Chamber* (restored), from which a spiral staircase ascends to the 3rd floor (views).

Cross the main road and bear left to approach the church of St. Nicholas, contemporary with the castle, preserving late 12C pillars in its nave; the chancel, which is not in line with the nave, was completed in 1305–6. It suffered many vicissitudes, notably in the 14C, when the Scots and Irish ravaged the English possessions in Ulster, and in 1513, when the town was again set on fire by the Scots. Considerable restoration took place in 1614; the W tower dates from 1778. The N transept contains the *Monument of Sir Arthur Chichester, first Earl of Belfast (1563–1625), and his wife and infant son; below is a smaller effigy of Sir John Chichester (died 1597). Noteworthy in the nave (S side and W end) is the 16C stained glass, brought in 1800 from Dangan House, Co. Meath. The S porch (c 1614) is used as the baptistery.

A short distance to the N is the only other ancient building in Carrickfergus, the *North Gate* (restored), with remains of the *Town Walls*, together with *Dobbins Inn* (17C) in the High St, at the N end of which stands the blue-painted one-storeyed *Town Hall* (1797).

We shortly traverse the village of *Eden*, opposite the demesne of *Castle Dobbs* (1730; with later additions), built for Arthur Dobbs (1689–1765), Surveyor-General of Ireland, and Governor of North Carolina.

To the right lies the ruined church of *Kilroot*, the living of which was held by Swift for a year after his ordination in 1695, when he abandoned it as being uncongenial. His home, in which he wrote 'A Tale of a Tub', was burnt out in 1959 and demolished. It has been suggested that his later 'Polite Conversation' was a satire on local provincial society.

1½ miles N of Eden is the fortified Plantation farmhouse of *Dalway's Bawn (c 1609), the best surviving example in Ulster.

The road turns NW at **Whitehead** (3,550 inhab.), with a small harbour and the scanty remains of *Castle Chichester*, near which the road traversing 'Island' Magee bears off to the right. The Whitehead Excursion Station is also the headquarters of the Railway Preservation Society of Ireland. On summer weekends their steam train shuttles to Portrush from Belfast.

The narrow peninsula (7 miles long by 2 miles broad) called **Island Magee** separates LARNE LOUGH from the open sea. In the reign of Elizabeth I it was held by the Bissett family on the singular tenure of an annual tribute of goshawks, which breed on the cliffs. The finest of these cliffs, on the E coast, are known as *The Gobbins*. Portmuck (NE side) has a small quay, while *Brown's Bay* at the N end, with good sands, is also reached by ferry from Larne. The peninsula

achieved notoriety for the massacre of 1642, when numbers of the Catholic community are said to have been hurled off the cliffs, presumably in reprisal for the
massacre of Protestants in the previous year. It also had a reputation for witchcraft, and the last trial in Ireland for this crime took place in 1711, when a native of
the district was pilloried at Carrickfergus.

We skirt the shore of LARNE LOUGH past *Ballycarry* (left), the site of the
first Presbyterian church in Ireland, founded in 1613.—Beyond
Magheramorne, with Portland Cement quarries, we traverse the
village of *Glynn*, at the foot of the *Valley of Glenoe*, with its four
waterfalls.

LARNE (18,200 inhab.), a flourishing but dull industrial town, is the
terminus of passenger and freight services from Stranraer and
Cairnryan.

A new road now approaches the ferry terminus and harbour, and at
the end of a promontory (*The Curran*) is the stump of a tower, all that
remains of the Bisset stronghold of *Olderfleet Castle* (16C). It was here
that Edward Bruce landed in 1315. At the harbour entrance is a repro-
duction of a round tower.

Larne was the scene of the notorious 'gun running' of 25 April 1914, largely
organised by Carson for the Unionists, when 24,600 rifles and 3,000,000 rounds of
amunition acquired by Major Frederick Crawford from Hamburg entered Ulster.
Earlier in the century the stationmaster's wife, 'Amanda McKittrick Ros', wrote
here those literary curiosities 'Irene Iddesleigh' and 'Delina Delaney'.

The neighbourhood of Larne has yielded numerous mesolithic
artifacts.

Beyond the town begins the finest section of the road, built since the
1830s. It skirts the shore below steeply rising basalt or limestone cliffs,
passing through a tunnel known as *Black Cave*, and along *Drains Bay*,
by no means as unattractive as its name might imply, before rounding
the bold escarpment of *Ballygalley Head*. On the right an isolated rock
bears the remains of *Carncastle*, a haunt of the outlawed O'Halloran.

We traverse the village of *Ballygalley*, preserving a fortified manor
house (now a hotel) built by James Shaw in 1625, and *Glenarm*, an
ancient village with a small harbour, but covered with a shroud of
white dust from adjacent limestone quarries. It was the birthplace of
Eóin Mac Neill (1867–1945), co-founder of the Gaelic League in 1893.
In the glen stands *Glenarm Castle* (seat of the Earl of Antrim), a quasi-
feudal structure begun in 1606 and several times transformed since. In
the churchyard are the foundations of a 15C Franciscan monastery.

On the opposite side of the next bay is seen the resort of **Carnlough**
(1,400 inhab.), at the foot of Glencloy, traversed by a stream on which,
higher up, there are several little falls.—The coast now becomes once
more abrupt, the steep escarpment broken here and there by little
dells. Just before we round *Garron Point*, a road winds up to the left to
Garron Tower, a castellated mansion built by Lewis Vulliamy for
Frances, Marchioness of Londonderry, in 1848. *Knocknore*, to the SW,
commands a fine distant view of Mull of Kintyre, on the Scottish
coast.—Just off Garron Point is the isolated chalk stack of
Cloghastucan.

We now enter *Red Bay*, perhaps the most attractive part of the
coast, carved from the cliffs of Triassic sandstone on the NW or
Cushendall side, while to the S the hills gradually recede from the
road, their gullies marked by a succession of waterfalls.—*Waterfoot*
stands at the outflow of Glenariff, beyond which the road penetrates a
sandstone arch beneath the ridge of *Lurigethan*, and passes *Red Bay
Castle*, a ruined MacDonnell stronghold.

The **Glens of Antrim** is the name given to the series of valleys intersecting the range of hills between Larne and Ballycastle. There are nine: *Glenshesk, Glencorp, Glendun, Glenaan, Glenballyemon, Glenariff, Glencloy, Glentaise,* and *Glenarm.*

Among the more attractive is **Glenariff**, traversed by the road from Cushendall to Ballymena (18 miles SW). The finest part of the glen, notable for its waterfalls, is approached by a path crossing a bridge on the left. The road (A43) may be followed to (6½ miles) *Parkmore Station* (disused), whence the B14 leads back to Cushendall down Glenballyemon, beneath the slope of *Trostan* (550m), the highest point in Antrim.

Another short excursion may be made by turning left off the A2 1½ miles further N and ascending Glenaan to (5 miles) *Bryvore Water Bridge*, where, turning sharp right, we descend wild Glendun to *Cushendun* (see below).

Cushendall (800 inhab.) retains an ancient gaol-tower. The so-called *Ossian's Grave*, a two-chambered 'horned' cairn, lies 2 miles W, while the ruins of *Layde* church, with tombs of the MacDonnells, is on the direct road (right) to *Cushendun* (3½ miles N). The A2 circles inland and soon bears uphill to the left, and crossing the Glendun viaduct, zigzags up through woods.

Travellers with time are recommended to bear right to **Cushendun**, a well-sited little village on the outflow of the Glendun (*Cois abhann Duine*, the mouth of the brown river), near which are the scanty ruins of a castle (N) and some caves in the sandstone (S). Cushendun was the scene of the death of Shane O'Neill, murdered in 1567 by the MacDonnells after his defeat on the shores of Lough Swilly; his grave is marked by a cairn.—A narrow and winding minor road hugs the coast, here only 13 miles from the Mull of Kintyre, regaining the A2 at *Ballyvoy.*

The main road traverses a wide expanse of moorland, with Ballypatrick Forest to the left, crossing by a causeway the tarn of LOUGHAREEMA, which can suddenly run almost dry after heavy rain, and descends towards Ballycastle.—We pass (left) the ruins of *Bonamargy Abbey*, founded in 1500 by Rory MacQuillan, and burned in 1584 by the MacDonnells and the Scots. It was probably repaired and in use until 1642. Beside the church, refectory, and another stone-roofed room, the main interest is the MacDonnell vault, the burial-place of the earls of Antrim, beneath a chapel (c 1666), where lie Sorley Boy MacDonnell (1505–1590) and his son, the first earl (died 1636).—On the left rises conical *Knocklayd* (514m), crowned by a large cairn.

Ballycastle (3,300 inhab.), a well-situated resort at the junction of two valleys, with a view of Rathlin Island (see below), preserves a church of 1756, and a few early 19C houses, but its old stone harbour is now silted up. The cliffs to the E and W show the beginning of the dykes or intrusive masses of basalt which culminate in the Giant's Causeway further W. To the W is the small ruin of *Dunaneanie Castle*, the probable birthplace of Sorley Boy MacDonnell, and the scene of his death (see above).

In 1898 Guglielmo Marconi's first wireless installations for communication between a lighthouse and the mainland were set up at Rathlin and Ballycastle, assisted by George Kemp.

5 miles to the E is *Fair Head*, or **Benmore**, approached by a lane to the hamlet of *Cross*, a scarped headland rising to 194m above the sea, half this height consisting of a sheer cliff of basalt split into enormous columns, from the base of which a mass of debris slopes down to the water. A fine close view is obtained from the rough and somewhat dangerous *Grey Man's Path*, descending to the cliff-foot. Its summit commands an extensive view towards Rathlin, Islay with the Paps of Jura behind it, and the Mull of Kintyre, 13 miles NE.—Just behind the summit are three small loughs, one with a well-preserved crannóg. The cliffs of *Murlough Bay*, to the E, contain a coal seam worked from a remote period, the beach of which is now approached by a road.

Beneath the headland are the rocks known as *Carrig Uisneach*, the legendary landing-place of Deirdre and the sons of Uisneach on the voyage that ended fatally at Emania; while off the coast are the turbulent Waters of Moyle, where the Children of Lir, turned into swans by the jealous Boife, were forced to spend 300 years.

5 miles N of Ballycastle lies **Rathlin Island**, reached daily, weather permitting, by mailboat (and tourist boats in summer); at other times the intervening Race of *Sloch-na-Marra* (Valley of the Sea) can be unpleasant if not dangerous. Brecain, son of Niall of the Nine Hostages, was lost here with a fleet of 50 corraghs.

Rathlin is c 6 miles long, and has been described as being the shape of 'an Irish stocking, the toe of which pointeth to the main lande'. It is associated with St. Columba and St. Comhgall; and from its exposed position, was among the first places in Ireland to suffer from Danish incursions. Its main historical interest is that it contains *Bruce's Cave*, a cavern in the basalt near the NE corner of the island, which is said to have harboured the fugitive Robert Bruce in 1306, who was raised from the slough of despond by watching the perseverance of a pendant spider companion. It is difficult to approach except in calm weather. Near the landing-place is *Church Bay* is the *Manor House*, where the viscounts Gage formerly held patriarchal sway; to the E, *Bruce's Castle* stands on an isolated crag. Almost all the coast is cliff-bound, the highest, on the NW side, rising to over 120m, and the haunt of innumerable seabirds, particularly guillemots.

SE of Ballycastle is the valley of *Glenshesk*, where the MacDonnells were twice defeated: in 1565 at the hand of Shane O'Neill, and again in 1583, when fighting the MacQuillans. Above the road on the W side are the ruins of *Gobhan Saer's Castle*, in fact the remains of an old chapel said to have been founded by St. Patrick.—*Armoy*, on the A44, lies 7 miles SW of Ballycastle; see Rte 33B.

A short DETOUR from the A2, which drives W, may be made by following the B15 along the coast. The road ascends NW of the town, passing near a narrow headland on which are perched the ruins of *Kilbane Castle*, beyond which the cliffs become higher. On the right a path descends to the *Carrick-a-Rede* rope bridge (NT; in position from mid May to mid September) connecting a basalt stack to the mainland. The swinging bridge with its board floor looks more perilous than it is.—Traversing *Ballintoy*, off which lies *Sheep Island*, we regain the main road c 6 miles from Ballycastle.

Skirting *White Park Bay*, we pass (right) a turning leading to *Dunseverick Castle* (the fort of Sobhairce; a stronghold of the Mac-Quillans and O'Kanes). From this point a cliff path 4½ miles long has been constructed by the NT, bearing round Benbane Head to the *Giant's Causeway*, also approached—2 miles W—by the road.

The remarkable basaltic formation known as •**THE GIANT'S CAUSEWAY** was brought to a wider public notice by Dr William Hamilton (1755–97) in his 'Letters concerning the Northern Coast of Antrim' (1786), since when it has ranked among the natural wonders of the world. It had of course been visited previously, among others by Mrs Delany in 1758, and the Earl-Bishop of Derry built a footpath there for travellers interested in natural curiosities.

For the Causeway proper, see below. The cliff walk is first described, from E to W.

We first pass *Bengore Head* and then *Benbane Head* (112m), to the W of which is *Hamilton's Seat*, a favourite spot of the 'discoverer' of the Causeway (see above), and *Pleaskin Head* (122m). Between this point and *Chimney Point* (whose castellated appearance led vessels of the Spanish Armada to fire on it under the impression that they were attacking *Dunluce Castle*, further W) is *Port-na-Spania*, where the 'Girona', a galleass of the same Armada, ran ashore with the loss of 260 lives, including Don Alfonso de Leyva. The ship also happened to be carrying a large amount of treasure, much of it recovered in 1967–68 by a team of Belgian divers, and several of the more valuable items have since been displayed at the Ulster Museum, Belfast.—The path next passes the *Amphitheatre*, with columns broken up into terraces, before reaching the Causeway proper.

It has been estimated that there are c 37,000 basalt columns altogether, caused by a series of violent subterranean disturbances of volcanic origin some 60,000,000 years ago, which found a vent along a line from the Antrim coast to Skye, the effects of which may be traced through Rathlin, Islay, Staffa, (Fingal's Cave), and Mull. A great quantity of molten basalt was ejected to the surface, which when beginning to cool formed a number of nuclei equidistant from each other. These gradually absorbed the intervening mass into as many equal spheres, the intercolumnar pressures of which eventually caused them to assume a prismatic shape, hexagonal where the pressure has been regular, less often pentagonal, and on rare occasions with irregular numbers of sides, some even ten-sided. The cliffs of the causeway consists of two beds of columnar basalt separated by the bright red 'ochre bed', between 9m and 12m thick, formed by the weathering of the lava flow during a period of quiescence.

A panoramic view may be obtained from *Aird Snout*, a promontory E of the NT *Causeway Visitor Information Centre* (and restaurant; 1986), whence a bus shuttle-service is available to the base of the causeway for those who require transport. Boats may be hired to visit those caves not accessible at low tide. Visitors are warned that the surface of the basalt is often very slippery, and care should be taken when clambering about.

Susanna Drury, The Giants' Causeway (c 1739) Ulster Museum, Belfast

A road descends past the first headland, beyond which in the cliff to the right are seen some columns twisted into a horizontal position. On the next promontory are the *Little* and *Middle Causeway*, beyond which is the *Grand Causeway*, with several impressively regular formations. On the far side of the next bay is the so-called **Giant's Organ*, a perfect example of the columnar structure; the near by Shepherd's Path ascends to the cliff top, whence one may regain the car-park.

The principal caves are mostly to the W of the causeway proper. Among them are *Portcoon* (with a landward entrance NW of the hotel) and *Runkerry Cave* (over 200m long).

There are plans to restore part of the hydro-electric tramway, which once ran hence to Portrush, the first to be constructed on this principle (1883), and closed in 1949.

Leaving the Causeway, we turn inland to **Bushmills** (1,400 inhab.), noted for its whiskey-distilleries (which may be visited on weekdays), which had a licence to distil dated 1609, although whiskey was distilled for some centuries earlier. The town has also a Salmon research station. Hence the B17 leads directly SW to *Coleraine*.

The A2 shortly regains the coast before passing *Dunluce Castle, which, with its picturesque towers and gables, stands spectacularly on a projecting rock separated from the mainland by a deep chasm spanned by a bridge replacing a drawbridge. Probably built c 1300 by Richard de Burgh, Earl of Ulster, it was reconstructed c 1590 by James MacDonnell. It consists of a barbican, two main towers, and the remains of the great hall. The buildings on the mainland were erected after 1639, when part of the kitchen and eight servants subsided into a cave below during a storm.

Dunluce was taken by the MacDonnells (a sept of the McDonalds of the Isles) in the 16C, and Sorely Boy ('Yellow Charles') MacDonnell was a prominent figure in the struggle against the English and Shane O'Neill. Sir John Perrot entered the place after a nine-month siege in 1584, but Sorely Boy recaptured it and made peace with the English, although his son James assisted Cuellar and other Spaniards to escape to Scotland in 1588. Randal, James's brother, was made Viscount Dunluce and Earl of Antrim by James I. It fell into decay during the 17C wars.

To the W are the curious limestone formations known as the *White Rocks* (with numerous caves accessible by boat in calm weather), and offshore lie a line of reefs known as *The Skerries.* Beyond is the promontory of *Ramore Head*, on which stands the resort of **Portrush** (5,100 inhab.).

Coleraine lies 4½ miles SW, but the main road continues to the adjacent resort of **Portstewart** (5,300 inhab.), extending from the harbour on the E to *Black Castle*, a ruined O'Hara stronghold on the W, beyond which the cliffs die away into a sandy strand. Charles Lever worked as a dispensary doctor here, where he was visited by Thackeray in 1842.

The A2 turns S past (right) *Cromore House* (mid 18C; enlarged in 1834), now a post-graduate residence of the University of Ulster. For *Coleraine*, and for the road hence to **Derry**, see Rte 33B.

36 Coleraine to Newry, via Dungannon and Armagh

79 miles (127km). A29. 10½ miles *Garvagh*—10 miles *Maghera*—17½ miles *Cookstown*—10 miles *Dungannon*—13 miles **Armagh**—A28. 18 miles *Newry*.

This useful cross-country route through central Ulster leads S from Coleraine, and shortly bears left off the A37 to Derry.—*Garvagh* (1,200 inhab.), situated on a hill, was the seat of the Canning family and the birthplace of George Canning (died 1771), father of the more famous statesman.

6 miles SE is **Kilrea** (1,300 inhab.) an angling resort on the Bann. Some 5½ miles S of Kilrea, on the far bank, in a Georgian mansion at *Portglenone*, is a Cistercian monastery. Founded in 1951, it was the first in Northern Ireland since the Reformation; it contains columns and fireplaces from Ballyscullion (cf.).—*Maghera* lies 10 miles SW.

Foothills of the Sperrin range rise to the W, among them *Carntogher* (462m) and further SW, *Mallaghmore* (555m).

Maghera (1,950 inhab.) contains a ruined church with a square-headed doorway (?11C), with sloping side, enclosed by a square band of carving and surmounted by a curious Crucifixion.

Upperlands, 3 miles NE, was the birthplace of Charles Thomson (1729–1824), secretary of the first United States congress, known as the Continental Congress from its inception in 1774 until 1789. He designed, in 1782, the Great Seal of the United States, and was the final writer of (and first reader to the Congress of, in 1776), the Declaration of Independence.

We cross, to the S of the town, the A6 from Belfast to Derry (see Rte 33A), and shortly traverse *Tobermore*, with an old church rebuilt in 1816, and Presbyterian meeting-house of 1728.

Hence a wild mountain road (B47) leads SW via (4 miles) *Draperstown*, founded by the Drapers' Company of London, with ruins of an old church, beyond which it bears W over a S spur of the *Sperrin Mountains*, which is crossed between *Oughtmore* (right) and *Carnanelly*. The road then descends the Glenelly valley below the highest peak of the range, *Sawell* (678m; right), to cross the B48 at *Plumbridge* before meeting the A5 at *Newtownstewart*; see latter part of Rte 30.

The main road passes the village of *Desertmartin*, to the SW of which is *Slieve Gallion* (527m), where a track climbs to *Windy Gap* and the *Ballybriest* horned cairn.—2½ miles SE is the market town of **Magherafelt** (5,050 inhab.), granted to the Salters' Company at the settlement of James I. It has a curious 19C courthouse. *Moneymore* (1,250 inhab.), 5½ miles S, crossed by the main road, was the property of the Drapers' Company.—**Springhill** (NT), just to the SE of Moneymore, is a good example of a fortified manor house built by the Planters; it contains a collection of costumes.

The A29 bears SW, to the right of which, at *Lissan*, the militant cleric the Rev. George Walker was rector in 1669–74 (cf. Derry); the rectory was later redesigned by Nash.

Cookstown (7,650 inhab.), the dairying centre of the district, has a wide main street almost 1½ miles long, and is named after its founder

Springhill

Allan Cooke, who laid it out in 1609. The *Catholic Church* was erected by J.J. McCarthy in 1860.

SE of the town is *Killymoon Castle* (1803), a huge castellated edifice designed by Nash. Through its grounds flows the Ballinderry river, a good trout stream, which later enters Lough Neagh just S of the remains of *Salters Castle*, where the Salters' Company planned to build a town.

The B73 leads due E from Cookstown to (10½ miles) LOUGH NEAGH (see Rte 33A). On its insect-infested banks, slightly to the S, at *Arboe*, are the remains of an abbey said to have been the home and burial-place of St. Colman of Dromore (died 610). Beside the remains of the church is a *High Cross* (over 5.5m), with remarkable sculptures, but its upper part is damaged.

COOKSTOWN TO ENNISKILLEN VIA OMAGH (52 miles). Follow the A505 due W past (2½ miles; right) *Drum Manor*, with the remains of a small Scottish-baronial mansion surrounded by its Forest Park, in which a *Lepidoptera Reserve* has been established.—A short distance beyond, to the right, is the 18C **Wellbrook Beetling Mill** (NT), water-powered, restored, and in working order.

After another 1½ miles a lane (right) traverses the hamlet of *Dunnamore* to approach the extensive complex of seven stone circles (including three 'pairs'), nine alignments, and twelve cairns, at *Beaghmore, uncovered since 1945 by the removal of peat.

The main road continues W across country towards *Mullaghcarn* (542m) before bearing SW to *Omagh* (see p 323; 25 miles from Cookstown), beyond which we follow the A32 to (9½ miles) **Dromore**, a village where St. Patrick is said to have founded an abbey for the first woman who took the veil from his hands. On the site grew a Cistercian abbey burnt down in 1690; there are ruins of a church of 1694 nearby.—7 miles E is *Fintona*, an ancient O'Neill stronghold, where until 1957 a horse-tramway ran between the village and the station.—8½ miles *Irvinestown*, where we bear left, with the *Brougher Mountain* (316m), rising to the SE, to enter (9 miles) *Enniskillen*; see Rte 37.

---

2 miles S of Cookstown we pass near (left, on the road to *Stewartstown*, 3 miles beyond) the rath of *Tullaghoge*.

It was once the residence of the O'Hagans, Justiciars of Tyrone, who here inaugurated each O'Neill chief of Ulster. The last ceremony was held in 1595, but the inauguration stone was destroyed in 1602 by Lord Mountjoy. The family kept up its connection with the law, however, the first Lord O'Hagan (1812–85) having been twice Lord Chancellor of Ireland.

To the E of Stewartstown a lane leads past the remains of *Stuart Hall* (c 1760), the seat of Earl Castle Stewart, bombed in 1974 and subsequently demolished, and then S to *Mountjoy Castle*, overlooking LOUGH NEAGH, the ruins of a fortress of 1601–5, with good Tudor brickwork.—Hence we may approach Dungannon (8 miles SW) via **Coalisland** (3,300 inhab), the centre of the Tyrone coalfield, but which has never been profitably worked; some buildings of interest to the industrial archaeologist may be seen in the neighbourhood.

To the left of the A29 we pass the demesne of *Loughry* (now an agricultural college), the home of the Lindesays, where Swift was an occasional visitor.—Beyond *Dungannon* (see Rte 37) we bear SE past the present terminus of the M1 motorway, to *Moy*, on the Blackwater, with its tree-planted square. It owes its exotic air to its founder, James Caulfeild, Earl of Charlemont (1728–99), who built it on the plan of the Lombard town of Marengo. On the opposite bank of the river is *Charlemont*, where Mountjoy erected a fort in 1602 as a counter to the activities of Hugh O'Neill, which was held from 1642–50 by Phelim O'Neill, who killed the governor, Lord Charlemont, but was eventually driven out by Sir Charles Coote; it was largely burnt down in 1922.—*Armagh* lies· 7 miles S of Charlemont, but may also be approached by taking either of two short detours, while c 3 miles NE of Charlemont is **The Argory** (NT), a classical mansion of 1820, containing an unusual cabinet barrel-organ, and still lit by acetylene gas, said to be the only such surviving in the British Isles.

The B28 leads SE and then E to (4 miles) ***Ardress House** (NT) a late 17C mansion enlarged by the architect George Ensor for his own use in c 1775, and containing some very good plasterwork by Michael Stapleton; the halls has been well restored.—It was after a sectarian skirmish between a party of 'Defenders' and a gang of anti-Catholic 'Peep o'Day Boys' at the hamlet called *The Diamond* (2 miles SE), that the Orange Order was established, in September 1795.—2 miles S at *Loughgall*, surrounded by orchards, are two Planter's bawns; the poet W.R. Rodgers was Presbyterian minister here from 1934 to 1946; *Armagh* lies 5 miles SW.

The B106 leads SW from Moy to (4 miles) *Benburb*, with a ruined castle finely situated above the Blackwater, erected in 1615 by Sir Richard Wingfield, who also built the parish church. When Owen Roe O'Neill inflicted a crushing defeat here on General Monro and the Parliamentary army in June 1646, the beaten troops are said to have fled dryshod across the river on the bodies of the slain. The demesne, contains a mansion of 1887, a Servite *Priory* since 1949.—At *Blackwatertown*, 1½ miles E, stood the Earl of Sussex's *Portmore Fort* (1575), razed by O'Neill in 1595, and rebuilt in 1598, when at the *Battle of the Yellow Ford* on 14 August that year Sir Henry Bagenal's army, marching N to relieve the fort, were forced into a bog by O'Neill, and slaughtered.—*Armagh* lies 5 miles SE.

For **Armagh**, see Rte 38A. Hence the A28 leads directly SE to Newry via (6½ miles) *Markethill*, where *Gosford Castle*, the former seat of the Earl of Gosford, was visited by Swift in 1729; a later castellated pile was built from 1819–39; it has been used to store public records in recent years, but its Forest Park is open to the public.—For *Newry*, 11½ miles beyond, see Rte 39.

An interesting ALTERNATIVE route from ARMAGH TO NEWRY is that via *Tandragee*, 11½ miles due E on the A51, passing after 5 miles *Hamilton's Bawn*, where a bawn built in 1619 and destroyed in 1641 was the subject of a poem by Swift, and further E, MARLACOO LAKE, with its crannóg.—**Tandragee** (or *Tanderagee*; 2,200 inhab.), on the Cusher, a good trout stream in pleasant country, is dominated by its *Castle*, occupying the site of a fortress of the O'Hanlons, whose territory was confiscated under James I. It has been degraded to house a potato-crisp factory!

Redmond O'Hanlon, their outlawed descendant, was famous as the leader of the 'Tories', whose bands levied tribute on the Ulster colonists from their stronghold on Slieve Gullion during the years 1671–81 until their chief was treacherously murdered.

We now follow the depression, once a boggy wilderness, that marks the boundary between Armagh and Co. Down, after 2 miles bypassing (left) *Scarva*, the rendezvous of William III's armies in June 1690 before they marched to the Boyne, a gathering commemorated here annually by Orangemen, with concomitant contumely and much banging of their 'lambeg' drums, on 13 July.

In the demesne of *Scarvagh House* (c 1717; adm.) is a section of the so-called *Dane's Cast*, the prehistoric earthen rampart that marked the ancient boundary of the kingdoms of Ulidia (N Ulster) and Oriel (Armagh and Lough): it remains distinct as far as *Poyntz Pass*, and can be traced as far S as *Jonesborough*, beyond

Newry.—*Cairn Cochy*, a heap of stones 21m high, marks the site of a legendary battle in AD 332.—Redmond O'Hanlon (see above) is buried in the graveyard of *Ballynaback*, to the N of Scarva.

2 miles *Poyntz Pass* takes its name from Sir Toby Poyntz, who in June 1646 here defended the road into Down against Hugh O'Neill, Earl of Tyrone; 'Tyrone's Ditches' in the demesne of *Drumbanagher* (right) still mark the Irish entrenchments.—9 miles *Newry*, see Rte 39.

37 Belfast to Sligo via Dungannon and Enniskillen

129 miles (208km). M1. 40 miles (with exits for *Lurgan, Portadown*, etc.)—*Dungannon* lies 2 miles NW— A4. 13 miles *Ballygawley* crossroads—6½ miles *Clogher*—23½ miles **Enniskillen**—12 miles *Belcoo*—N16. 22.5km *Manorhamilton*—25.5km **Sligo**.

We drive SW from Belfast on the motorway, after 8 miles by-passing (right) *Lisburn*, and after another 15 miles (left) *Lurgan*—for both see Rte 38—skirting the SE corner of LOUGH NEAGH to the right; see Rte 33A.

To the right at exit 12 is the hamlet of *The Birches*, birthplace of Thomas Jackson, grandfather of General 'Stonewall' Jackson, who emigrated to America in 1765.—The SW bank of LOUGH NEAGH is 1 mile further N, off which lies *Coney Island* (3 hectares), one of the claimants to be the original of its American namesake. Nearer the shore to the W lie the ruins of an O'Connor stronghold, at the mouth of the Blackwater.

On reaching the end of the motorway we turn right for *Dungannon*; *Armagh* lies 11 miles SE.

Dungannon (8,300 inhab.), a textile-manufacturing town, was once the headquarters of the O'Neills, earls of Tyrone, but all trace of their castle has vanished; the *Towers* on Castle Hill were built in 1790. The *Royal School*, a foundation of James I, occupies a building erected by the energetic Abp Robinson of Armagh in 1789.

Among its pupils was General John Nicholson (1821–57), the hero of the siege of Delhi (born in Dublin of a Lisburn family), whose bronze statue once stood by the Kashmire Gate, Delhi.

Donaghmore, 2 miles NW, once the site of an abbey, preserves an imperfect sculptured *High Cross*—perhaps a combination of two—set up here in 1776, having been thrown down during the 17C troubles.—6 miles further N, near LOUGH BRACKEN, are the seven stone circles of *Moymore*, among other archaeological sites in the area.

On regaining the A4 (extending the M1 to the W) we shortly pass a right-hand turning to adjacent **Castlecaulfeild**, with the picturesque ruins of the Jacobean mansion (1612) of Sir Toby Caulfeild, ancestor of the earls of Charlemont: it was built on the site of a castle of the Donnellys and was burnt in 1641 by Patrick Donnelly. Wesley preached by its gate in 1767.—The *Church* (of the parish of Donaghmore) has a gabled porch of 1685; the S nave window and some figures on the N side of the tower were brought from the vanished church at Donaghmore (see above).

The bellicose Rev. George Walker (1616–90) was rector here from 1674 before going to the defence of Derry, and was buried here after his death at the Boyne. Charles Wolfe, the poet, served here as curate in 1818–21. His famous lines on the burial of Sir John Moore were first published in the 'Newry Telegraph' in 1817.

13 miles W of the Dungannon turning we cross the A5 just beyond *Ballygawley* (see p 322), near which, at *Dergenagh*, was the ancestral home of Ulysses S. Grant, President of the USA in 1869–77. We cross the Blackwater 5km beyond, at *Augher*, with the Plantation castle of *Spur Royal* (c 1615, on the site of an earlier fortress), restored and enlarged in 1832 by William Warren, the Sligo architect.—Some 3 miles N is the imperfect passage-grave of *Knockmany*, with remark able inscribed designs of the Early Bronze Age.

Clogher, now a mere village, claims to be the seat of the most ancient bishopric in Ireland (5C). The little *Cathedral* on the hill-top, rebuilt in the 18C, altered in 1818, and restored in 1956, is dedicated to St. Macartin (died 506), a disciple of St. Patrick.

After a period of amalgamation with Armagh (1850–86), the see was again made independent. The Clogh-oir ('Golden Stone') in the porch is most likely a relic of the 9C church; in the churchyard are two re-erected *High Crosses* (9–10C).

The first Protestant bishop was Myler Magrath, the pluralist, who became Abp of Cashel (cf.) in the same year (1570). John Stearne (1660–1745), the scholar, was bishop here from 1717, while Thomas Parnell (1679–1718), the poet and scholar, and friend of Swift and Pope, was archdeacon from 1706–16. Percy Jocelyn (1764–1843), bishop from 1820–22, was unfrocked for sodomy, and became a domestic servant. William Carleton (1794–1869), folklorist, and author of 'Traits and Stories of the Irish Peasantry' was born in the neighbouring hamlet of *Prolusk*.

We descend a wide valley with *Slieve Beagh* (371m) on our left, and after 7 miles traverse *Fivemiletown*, founded in the reign of James I, to the NW of which rise the *Brougher hills* (316m). We soon pass (right) red-sandstone *Colebrooke Park* (by William Farrell; 1825), once the home of 1st Viscount Brookeborough, Prime Minister of Northern Ireland 1943–63, near which is the charming 18C church of *Aghalurcher*, with a fine spire.—Beyond (6 miles) *Brookeborough*, with its tree-lined street, the road bears NW at *Maguiresbridge*, the name of which recalls the ancient rulers of the district, and soon after (7½ miles) traversing *Tamlaght* we reach (right) the main entrance to the demesne of *Castlecoole*.

*Castlecoole (NT; under restoration), approached by a long drive, is the fourth house on this site, an imposing mansion built in 1790–98 by James Wyatt (modifying the plans of Richard Johnston) for the Earl of Belmore, and containing notable plasterwork by Joseph Rose. From the *Hall*, containing portraits of George II and Queen Charlotte by Ramsay, one may visit on the ground floor the *Library*; the *Drawing-room* (note the Italian marble-topped table, and clock); the oval *Saloon*, with shaped doors by George Binns of Dublin, and two impressive cast-iron stoves; and the *Dining-room*, with furniture designed by Wyatt, including magnificent sideboards and wine-cooler. A *Bow-room* on the first floor displays Wyatt's drawings for the house; note the Chinese-patterned curtains. The lake in the grounds is the habitat of the oldest non-migratory flock of greylag geese in the British Isles. See plan on next page.

We shortly enter the outskirts of **ENNISKILLEN** (10,450 inhab.), the county town of Fermanagh, delightfully situated on the river Erne, between Upper and Lower Lough Erne. One may still quote a 'Hand-Book' of over a century ago, when it was remarked that 'although the houses of the town are by no means of a superior description, yet it has a clean orderly appearance'—admittedly not improved by its present barricades! Long known for its cattle market, and as an angling centre, it has also long remained staunchly Protestant, and has given its name (with a variant spelling) to two famous regiments, the Inniskilling Dragoons, and the Royal Inniskilling Fusiliers.

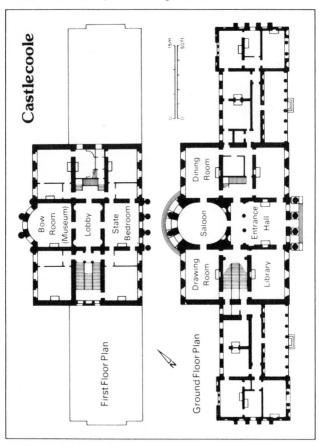

Castlecoole

Bow Room (Museum) — Lobby — State Bedroom

First Floor Plan

Dining Room — Saloon — Entrance Hall — Drawing Room — Library

Ground Floor Plan

Originally a stronghold of the Maguires, lords of Fermanagh, Enniskillen, at the confiscation of land after Tyrone's rebellion, was awarded to Sir William Cole (died 1653), ancestor of the earls of Enniskillen. He settled it with 20 English families, and defended the place in 1641, when the castle built on the site of Lisgoole Abbey (SW of the town, off the A509) was burned. In 1689 the men of Enniskillen beat of the troops of Tyrconnel, and pursued them as far as Cavan.

Boats may be hired at a jetty near West Bridge; a 'water bus' makes excursions down Lower Lough Erne.

The centre of Enniskillen is on an island; the High St (extending under various names, and from which traffic is diverted after 18.00) leads from *East Bridge* to *West Bridge*. The only building of interest in the street, apart from the (*William*) *Blake's of the Hollow* bar (1887), is the Protestant *Cathedral of St. Macartan* (1840), incorporating a tower of 1637 and font of 1666, while at the W end of the nave is the Pokrich Stone (1628), a memorial slab with a partly inverted inscription.—A turning to the left before we reach West Bridge leads down to the *Castle*, long used as barracks (and containing the *Fermanagh County*, and *Fusiliers' Museums*), but best seen from across the river; the attractive late-16C *Water-gate* and foundations of a 15C keep is all that remains.

Some distance to the W beyond the bridge stands the *Portora Royal School*, a building of 1777 housing a public school founded at Lisnaskea in 1608 by James I.

Oscar Wilde and Samuel Beckett were pupils. The poet William Dunkin (1709?–65) was master here from 1746 until his death. Dr Joseph Stock (1740–1813), headmaster in 1795, became Bishop of Killala (cf.) in 1798, where he was forthwith captured by Général Humbert, and later wrote an account of the French invasion. Just beyond, on the lough bank, are the ruins of *Portora Castle* (1615), built by Sir William Cole.

On *Fort Hill*, above East Bridge, a pleasant little park (views) surrounds a *Column* commemorating Sir Galbraith Lowry Cole (1772–1842), a Peninsular War General and later Governor of Cape Colony (in 1828–33).

For a description of roads on either bank of Lower Lough Erne, see the latter part of Rte 29.

Leaving Enniskillen, we cross West Bridge and follow the A4 to the W, skirting *Belmore Mountain* (400m) and (left) LOUGH MACNEAN LOWER, to the border village of **Belcoo**.

This may also be reached by two other minor roads: one circling N of Belmore via *Boho*, with a late 9C *High Cross* (imperfect); while a turning right off the A32 leads past **Florence Court** (see Rte 26), SW of which the summit of *Cuilcagh* (665m) marks the frontier. The limestone hills on both sides of the main road are riddled with caverns and underground streams.

From Belcoo, the B52 leads NW along the bank of LOUGH MACNEAN UPPER, to (13½ miles) *Garrison*, a small angling resort on LOUGH MELVIN, 5 miles S of *Belleek*; see p 296.

The main road crosses the border S of LOUGH MACNEAN UPPER, off which the R207 leads SW to Lough Allen (see Rte 26A), and ascends the Glenfarne valley between *Thur Mountain* (433m) and *Dough Mountain* (461m) to the right, and a range to the S, in which are numerous small tarns.—22.5km **Manorhamilton** (950 inhab.), superbly sited, takes its name from Sir Frederick Hamilton, to whom the manor was granted by Charles I; the ruined mansion (1641) is a good example of 17C building.

For the road hence to *Bundoran*, see Rte 27. Two alternative roads to Sligo are the R280, descending the Bonet valley to the SW to (c 13km) *Dromahair*, or the R286, ascending left off the main road 3km W of Manorhamilton, and descending towards the E shore of LOUGH GILL; for both, see Rte 26B.

The N16 continues W along the Glencar valley, dominated to the N by *Truskmore* (644m), the highest peak of the *Dartry Mountains*, and skirts *GLENCAR LOUGH, with its three waterfalls (right), either bank of which may be followed. At its far end we bear SW away from the conspicuous spur of *King's Mountain* and circle the steep escarpment of *Lugatober*, shortly entering *Sligo*; see Rte 26B.

38 Belfast to Athlone via Armagh and Monaghan

A. Belfast to Monaghan via Armagh

55 miles (88km). A1. 8 miles *Lisburn*—A3. 13 miles *Lurgan*—6 miles *Portadown*—11 miles **Armagh**—17 miles *Monaghan*.

Part B of this route provides a useful cross-country road for travellers approaching Galway and the SW of Ireland from Belfast; another, from Dundalk to Birr (for Limerick or Cashel) is described in the sub-route on p 371.

Leaving Belfast by the Dublin Rd (A1), we follow the Lagan valley, traversing residental suburbs, and passing the grounds of the *Royal Ulster Agricultural Society*, to (4 miles) *Dunmurry*, with a fine Presbyterian 'barn' church, above which rises *Collin Mountain*. To the E is *Dixon Park*, site of a Rose Show in July.

LISBURN (40,400 inhab.), an industrial town, has a triangular market-place, while the Castle grounds have been laid out as a public park. With its conspicuous spire (added in 1804), the **Cathedral** (1623, raised to its present rank in 1662) is the most interesting edifice, and a good example of 'Planters' Gothic', embodying Renaissance detail, but reconstructed in 1708, after the fire which ravaged the town the previous year.

Its most distinguished bishop (from 1661) was Jeremy Taylor (1613–67), who died here, but is buried at Dromore. In the churchyard are the graves of many of the Huguenots who introduced improvements in the manufacture of linen in 1699, under the supervision of Samuel Louis Crommelin (1652–1727).

In Castle St is a mansion (now a Technical College) built on the plan of Hertford House (London) by Sir Richard Wallace (1818–90), who was MP for Lisburn from 1873 to 1885, and founder of the Wallace Collection. The only Quaker school in Northern Ireland, founded 1774, is on Prospect Hill.

The B104 leads NW towards Lough Neagh, passing at *Brookmount* the birthplace of the composer and conductor Sir (Herbert) Hamilton Harty (1879–1941; buried at Hillsborough, to the S of Lisburn). Beyond Brookmount is *Ballinderry* church, built in 1665 by Jeremy Taylor, when living at Portmore Castle, now gone, and preserving its original furniture. Offshore in LOUGH NEAGH (see Rte 33A) is *Rams Island*, the largest of its few insignificant islands; with the stump of a *Round Tower*, 13m high.

We bear W from Lisburn on the A3, passing (left) the racecourse at *Maze*; to the S of the village are the notorious political prison of *Long Kesh*, and (after crossing the motorway) *Moira*, once famous for its gardens laid out in the early 18C by Sir Arthur Rawdon; it was the scene of the defeat of Congal, King of Ulster, by Dromhnall, the Ard Rí, in 637, the subject of a poem by Sir Samuel Ferguson.

LURGAN, which we now enter, once described as 'the cleanest, and most improved of our small inland towns', dates its prosperity from the introduction of the manufacture of linen-damask at adjacent *Waringstown* by Samuel Waring in 1691. After 1607 the district was taken from the O'Neills and given to Sir William Brownlow to 'colonise'; the demesne of the Brownlow's mansion, E of the town, is now a public park. *Waringstown House*, an early unfortified house, (built for William Waring; 1667) and the *Church* (1682; notable wood-work) adjoining, are good examples of Carolean architecture.

James Logan (1674–1751), one of the founders of Pennsylvania, emigrated from Lurgan in 1699; George W. Russell ('AE'; 1867–1935), poet, artist, and patriot, was born here, in William St.

The S shore of LOUGH NEAGH is less than 2 miles N.

Between Lurgan and Portadown rises the 'New Town' of **Craigavon** (52,500 inhab., including these former centres), built on a 'lineal' plan (or 'neo-ribbon' development), which was established in an attempt reduce the congestion of Belfast. It preserves the names—some have said provocatively—of James Craig, first Viscount Craigavon (1871–1940). The first Prime Minister of Northern Ireland (from 1921–40), he was, with Edward Carson, a fanatical opponent of Home Rule.

Portadown, on the S reach of the river Bann, is almost entirely a development of the 19C, with linen-weaving and handkerchief factories, and others manufacturing carpets and canning fruit from neighbouring orchards.

Sir Robert Hart (1835–1911), Inspector-General of Chinese Customs, was a native of Portadown. The embroidered saddle-cloth used by William III at the Boyne, now in the hands of the Orange Lodge, was formerly preserved in the *Carnegie Library* here; it had been in the possession of the Blacker family for over 250 years, but their elegant mansion of *Carrickblacker* (1692) has been demolished.

Tandragee lies 5 miles S; *Ardress House*, 7km W; for both, see Rte 36.

The road now traverses a fruit-growing district, passing (right) *Kilmore*, where the 'Round Tower' built into the massive square tower of the church is in fact a medieval staircase, and (left) the village of *Richhill*, with a Dutch-style 17C manor, to approach (11 miles) *Armagh*. The family of Francis Johnston, the architect, came from Richhill.

ARMAGH (12,700 inhab.), long the ecclesiastical capital of Ireland, and the seat of both Protestant and Catholic archbishops, is rich in historical association even if, because of its importance, it has suffered more from fire and slaughter than most towns of its size. Nevertheless a number of 18C buildings have survived, while the names of some of its principal streets—Scotch St and English St—recall the fact that it lay roughly on the border between the English and Scottish 'plantations' of Ulster, the former towards Tyrone, the latter towards Down.

The name *Ard Macha* (Macha's height) commemorates a legendary queen (4C BC), but there is little doubt that St. Patrick erected a church on a hill called *Druim-saileach* (ridge of sallow) within a short distance of the pagan sanctuary of Emania (see below). The plan of the rath surrounding the site of the church is still clear from the lay-out of the streets. It became a centre of monkish learning and attracted the attentions of acquisitive Danes in 841, and later of pillaging Anglo-Normans. Brian Ború and his son were brought here for burial after the Battle of Clontarf (1014).

In 1566 the town was laid waste by Shane O'Neill, who was forthwith excommunicated. St. Malachy (1096–1148) and Francis Johnston (1761–1829), the architect, were born here, as was the organist and composer Charles Wood (1866–1926). A native of the county was the Rev. Gilbert Tennent (1703–64), one of the founders of the 'Log College' at Neshaminy, from which grew Princeton University.

On the left of the approach from Belfast is the Mall (see below), above which on *College Hill* is the *Royal School*, founded by James I in 1608, and enlarged since, accommodated in a bulding of 1774, by Thomas

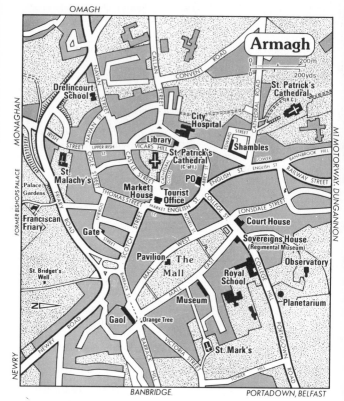

Cooley. Opposite is the **Armagh Astronomy Centre**. The *Observatory* here (possibly by Francis Johnston) has been in continuous use since established by Abp Richard Robinson in 1791; a *Planetarium* was opened in 1968, and since then a *Hall of Astronomy* (containing models of space-craft, etc.) and an Observatory for the use of the public, have been installed.

Facing the N end of the **Mall**, a long green partly lined by Georgian houses, is the *Courthouse* (restored), an attractive work by Francis Johnston (1805–9). On the E side of the Mall is the *County Museum, illustrating the life and history of the town and county of Armagh. The Ionic building was erected as a school in 1833, and opened in its present form in 1937.

Among paintings are two of Girls on a beach, and a Self-portrait, by 'AE' Russell; and a View of Armagh in 1810 by James Black. Other sections are devoted to folk craft; wood and metalwork; pottery and china; needlework; lace and linen manufacture; costumes, including uniforms of Armagh militia, yeomanry, and volunteers, and of the Royal Irish Fusiliers, etc.; local ornithology, wild life, geology; a collection of prehistoric artifacts found in the region, and general 'Armachiana'.

The *Regimental Museum* of the Fusiliers, whose headquarters are in Armagh, stands at the NE corner of the Mall.

From the S end of the Mall, overlooked by an imposing *Gaol*, Scotch St ascends to the centre. No. 36, a Georgian town house built for Leonard Dobbin, has been restored; its garden, in the course of excavation, may have been the site of St. Patrick's original church. From the *Market House* (1742; altered 1815), now a technical school, steep streets climb the cathedral hill, the ancient rath.

The **Protestant Cathedral** (usually locked; apply 3 Vicar's Hill, behind), with a battlemented central tower, owes its present appearance mainly to Richard Robinson (1709–94), archbishop from 1765, and later Lord Rokeby of Armagh, and to Lord John Beresford (1773–1862), archbishop from 1822. It is a plain well-proportioned building in the Perpendicular Gothic style, extensively restored in 1834–37 by Lewis Cottingham. Beneath is a crypt (?10C).

The interior contains some good 18–19C monuments, including that of Sir Thomas Molyneux (1661–1733) by Roubiliac; Abp Robinson, by Nollekens; and a recumbent statue of Dr Peter Drelincourt (1644–1722), dean of Armagh from 1691, by Rysbrack; also two fragments of an 11C Market Cross. The N Transept contains 17C memorials to the Caulfeild family, Earls of Charlemont, sculptured fragments from earlier cathedrals, and ancient idols. Hanging in the N nave arcade is a French standard captured at Ballinamuck by the Armagh militia in 1798.

To the SW, following the bank of the hill-fort of Ard Macha, is rebuilt *Castle St* (1730–40).

To the NW is the *Cathedral Library*, designed by Cooley, and endowed by Abp Robinson in 1771, with a Greek inscription above the entrance ('the healing of the mind'), and among the more important collections in Ireland.—Hence we may descend (right) past the *Infirmary* (1744; by George Ensor) and (left; at the bottom of the street) the *Shambles* (1827–29) to (right) Cathedral Rd.

The twin-spired *Catholic Cathedral*, dedicated to St. Patrick, was begun by Thomas Duff in 1838 and completed by J.J. McCarthy in 1873. It stands at the head of a long flight of steps, on the upper terrace of which are the statues of the two archbishops under whom the cathedral was started and finished; unfortunately the interior, meretriciously decorated, has hardly a redeeming feature.

SW of the Protestant Cathedral, in Navan St, are the buildings of *Drelincourt's School* (1740); while to the S, entered from Friary Rd, is the demesne of the (old) *Archbishops' Palace* (prior to 1767, to the design of Cooley), with a porticoed *Chapel* of 1781, and a classical interior. Near the gate are the ruins of a *Franciscan Friary*, founded in 1266, and destroyed 1565; and on an adjacent hill a huge *Obelisk*, raised by Abp Robinson.

An ancient coach road, leading due W from the cathedral hill, crosses the Callan by a charming old bridge, beyond which is *St. Patrick's Well*. 1½ miles further (right) rises **Navan Fort**, a huge elleptical mound (view) occupying the site of *Emania*, the legendary palace of the Kings of Ulster for over 600 years. It was said to have been founded by Queen Macha, and was the headquarters of the Red Branch Knights under Conor MacNessa. In c 450 it was overrun by tribes from Connacht and the city and palace irreparably destroyed.

ARMAGH TO AUGHER (24m.), FOR ENNISKILLEN. The A28 drives due W, shortly passing (right) *Navan Fort* (see above) and at 8 miles by-passing (left) **Tynan**, preserving four ancient crosses, probably dating from the 8C. Of these the most important is the *Village Cross* (4m high) and the *Terrace Cross*, with interlaced and spiral ornament, both removed from the *Eglish* churchyard c 1844; the latter, like the *Island Cross* and the *Well Cross* (with its wheel countersunk but not pierced) are in the demesne of *Tynan Abbey*; the last two were removed from Glenarb c 1844.

Turning N we enter **Caledon**, a 'model' village, formerly *Kennard*, taking its name from the earls of Caledon, whose extensive park, noted for its araucaria avenue, is adjacent. At the end of the 19C the park was inhabited by wapiti and black bears brought back by the 4th Earl of Caledon from America. It gained notoriety in 1968 for the discrimination shown against Catholic families in the allocation of council houses, which provoked later Civil Rights agitation. A monument to the 2nd Earl was senselessly blown up here in 1973. It was earlier the headquarters of Sir Phelim O'Neill in 1641, and the river was crossed here by General Monroe before the battle of Benburb (cf.). The *Castle*, built by Cooley in 1779, was enlarged in 1812 from designs by Nash, when the portico was added; it was the birthplace of F.M. Earl Alexander (1891–1969); the interior contains some good plasterwork; the gardens preserve the ruins of a 'Bone House' folly of 1747.—The road now bears NW to (7½ miles) *Aughnacloy*, the junction for the road between Monaghan and Derry (see Rte 30), and shortly turns left for (7½ miles) *Augher* (see Rte 37), passing (left) the bawn of *Favour Royal* (1611).

The A3 continues SW from Armagh, at 12½ miles reaching the border at *Tyholland*, 8km short of *Monaghan*; see p 321.

B. Monaghan to Athlone

120km (75 miles). N54. 19km *Clones*—L46 and L44. 25.5km *Cavan*—N55. 30.5km *Granard*—13km *Edgeworthstown*—41km **Athlone**.

From *Monaghan* (see p 321) we continue SW to **Clones** (2,350 inhab.), an agricultural centre retaining a few 18C houses. An ancient episcopal town (*Cluain Eois*, the meadow of Eos), its first bishop was St. Tigernach (died 548). It preserves of its abbey the remains of a *Round Tower* almost 23m high, of exceptionally rough masonry, a 10C sculptured *High Cross* (reconstructed, and placed in the central Diamond), and the nave of its church (c 1095). In the graveyard near the tower is a curious tomb shaped like a house-reliquary.—There is a Norman motte and bailey to the SW.

The old main road between Clones and Cavan is at present closed, and we therefore avoid the double border crossing by turning S onto the L46, passing (right) the demesne of *Hilton Park*, with a late Georgian mansion rebuilt after a fire in 1804, to *Scotshouse*. We later traverse *Ballyhaise*, retaining its market-hall built on arches, and the home in his youth of George Canning. *Ballyhaise House* (c 1733) was designed by Richard Castle; brick-built and with vaulted ceilings, it is now an agricultural college.

From *Cavan* (see p 314) we continue SW, leaving LOUGH GOWNA to the right, to **Granard** (1,300 inhab.), commanded by the huge *Motte* (disfigured by an image), of Hugh de Lacy's castle of 1191. The town also contains a large 19C *R.C. Church*, by John Burke.

4km SE, at *Abbeylara*, is a ruined church of 1214, with a Sheila-na-gig on its 15C tower, all that remains of its Cistercian abbey, pillaged by Edward Bruce in 1315.

The road traverses rather dull country to *Edgeworthstown* (see Rte 25A), 14km SE of *Longford*, which may also be approached direct from Granard.—19km *Ballymahon*, a large village pleasantly situated on the Inny, was Oliver Goldsmith's last home in Ireland, which he left for good in 1752. He was probably born (c 1730) at *Pallas* (4km E; house demolished), and baptised at *Forgney*, 4km SE; see p 291.

Castlecor House, 2.5km NE of Ballymahon, and now a convent, is a very curious building of c 1765, possibly based on Stupinigi, the hunting palace of the Duke of Savoy, near Turin. It contains an octagonal ballroom with a square central column incorporating four fireplaces.

Our road shortly enters Westmeath, the country of 'The Deserted Village', passing the 'Three Jolly Pigeons', which preserves the *name* only of the inn of 'She Stoops to Conquer'. The site of the village of *Lissoy* ('Sweet Auburn'), where Goldsmith's father was incumbent, and where the poet was brought up, was at the crossroads 2.5km further on.

At *Glassan* we strike the shore of LOUGH KILLINURE, a bay of LOUGH REE, on the bank of which, 5km NW, stands *Portlick Castle* (14–17C), and 7km beyond, enter **Athlone**; see Rte 19.

For the road hence to *Galway*, see Rte 19; for that to *Birr*, see Rte 20B, in reverse.

39 Belfast to Dundalk via Newry, for Dublin

50 miles (80km). M1. 10 miles, then A1 for 3 miles (left) *Hillsborough*—4½ miles *Dromore* (also by-passed)—6½ miles (right) *Banbridge*—13 miles A1 and then N1. 13 miles **Dundalk**.

For the road from Belfast skirting **Lisburn**, where we fork left, see Rte 38A.

From Dundalk, a cross-country sub-route describes the road hence via Kells, Mullingar, and Tullamore, to Birr for Limerick or Cashel; see below.

Hillsborough (1,200 inhab.) takes its name from Sir Arthur Hill (1601?–63), who built the well-preserved *Fort* in the park here in c 1650; William III is said to have passed the night here during his 1690 campaign. A Gothick tower-house was added in 1758. *Hillsborough Castle* (1797) formerly a seat of the Marquesses of Downshire, is now the official residence of visiting diplomats, etc. to Northern Ireland, and previously (1925–73) of the Governor. It was here, in November 1985, that Margaret Thatcher, PM of Great Britain, and Garret Fitzgerald, the Taoiseach of Ireland, signed a Treaty or Accord, in an attempt to end sectarian and political friction between the two countries.

The *Gates* (1745; possibly by the Thornberry brothers), brought here in 1936 from Richhill, are amongst the finest in the country. The *Church* was rebuilt in 1773 by the Earl of Hillsborough, afterwards 1st Marquess of Downshire; it contains remarkable Gothick woodwork, an organ of 1772 by John Snetzler, and a monument to Archdeacon Henry Leslie by Nollekens; Sir Hamilton Harty (cf. Brookmount) is buried in the churchyard. The *Market-house*, with its cupola, dates from 1790, by James McBlain. Harry George Ferguson (1884–1960), inventor of the tractor, was born at *Growell*, near Hillsborough.

Dromore (3,100 inhab.), on the Lagan, is the ancient ecclesiastical capital of Down, and believed to be the site of an abbey founded by St. Colman (c 510). In James I's reign the see was refounded and the cathedral rebuilt, but this was destroyed in 1641, and the present church erected in 1661 by Jeremy Taylor (bishop in 1661–67), who administered the see together with Down and Connor, which in 1842 were merged in one. Thomas Percy (of the 'Reliques'; bishop in 1782–1811) built the 'Percy Aisle' and rebuilt the tower; both he and Jeremy Taylor are buried here. Incorporated in the S wall of the chancel is St. Colman's 'pillow-stone', and in the tower porch are the 17C font and poor man's box. The *Bishop's Palace* is falling into ruin, as are Percy's essays in landscape gardening. The *Cross of Dromore* (8–9C; much restored in 1887) is preserved in the graveyard.

The parish stocks are in the Market Square, opposite the Town Hall.—Above the right bank of the river—well seen from the Hillsborough road—is a late 12C *Motte and bailey*, the finest example in Ulster.—2 miles W stands haunted *Gill Hall* (partially designed by Castle), long in a sad state of decay and recently burnt out.

Dromara, 6 miles SE, lies in the centre of the flax-growing district, and from it may be explored a range of hills to the S, culminating in *Slieve Croob* (534m), on which the Lagan rises; the view is surprisingly fine. *Craitlieve* is to the SW; S of its summit is the tripod-dolmen of *Legananny*.

Banbridge (9,650 inhab.), on the Upper Bann, is a prosperous industrial and market-town, with a steep but wide main street, the central part of which is at a lower level and passes under a cross-road.

A monument by W.J. Barre near the river commemorates Captain Francis Crozier (1796–1848), born here, and Franklin's second-in-command on his last ill-fated voyage.

Helen Waddell (1889–1965) the medievalist, is buried at *Magherally*, 2 miles NE.—6½ miles SE lies *Katesbridge*, to the E of which, at *Closkelt*, on the slope of *Deehommed*, with its cairn, a Bronze Age cemetery was unearthed in 1973.

At 3 miles we traverse *Loughbrickland*, a village dating from 1585–1600.

At *Emdale* (5 miles SE off the Rathfriland road on the left) are the remains of the cottage in which the Rev. Patrick Bronte (1777–1861), father of the more famous sisters, was born.

We pass (4½ miles; left) *Donaghmore*, in the graveyard of which is a fine 9–10C *High Cross*.

NEWRY (19,050 inhab.), an ancient frontier town, with a small port, appears to have ignored the condemnation of Swift's critical couplet: 'High church, low steeple, Dirty streets, and proud people'. It is connected with the sea at Carlingford Lough by the Newry Canal, commenced in 1729 and extending N to Lough Neagh.

Newry (*An Iubhar*, the yew-tree) is named from a yew planted by St. Patrick himself, according to the story. The town's strategic position at the gap in the mountains that separate the plains of Louth from those of Ulster has brought with it much fighting and hard usage. The castle was destroyed by Edward Bruce in 1315, and its successor by Shane O'Neill in 1566; and the town was set alight by Berwick in 1689.

Among distinguished natives are Lord Charles Russell of Killowen (1832–1900), the lawyer who vigorously advocated Home Rule, and leading counsel for Parnell (in 1888–9), and John Mitchel (1815–75), Irish patriot and author of 'The Jail Journal', who is buried in the old Meeting House Cemetery. Samuel Neilson (1761–1803), a founder of the Society of United Irishmen in 1791, was born at *Ballyroney*, 3 miles NE.

Little of old Newry has survived, although some 18C houses may be seen in Upper Water St and Trevor Hill. *St. Patrick*'s *Church* (that referred to by Swift), on the hill, is said to be the first church built for the Protestant faith in Ireland, but it was seriously damaged in 1689; it retains in the porch the arms of the founder, Sir Nicholas Bagenal (1510?–90?), marshal of Ireland. The *White Linen Hall* dates from 1783, while Francis Johnston may have designed the mansion of 1826 now accommodating the Bank of Ireland. The *R.C. Cathedral* (1825) is by Thomas Duff.

1½ miles NW is **Derrymore House** (NT: adm. by appointment), a late 18C thatched cottage ornée, in which the Act of Union is said to have been drafted in

1800. To the N is the 'model village' of **Bessbrook** (2,750 inhab.), founded by the Quaker linen manufacturer John Grubb Richardson (died 1753), with a fine granite-built mill; granite was also used for the neighbouring railway viaduct of 18 arches.

Some 2 miles E on the Hilltown road is *Crown Mound*, a motte and bailey 180m round.

5 miles SW rises *Slieve Gullion* (573m), with a passage-grave on its summit; at *Killevy*, on its E slope, is an old church, in fact two (?9C and 13C), with a huge lintel over the W door.

For the road circling the *Cooley Peninsula* to the SE, see latter part of Rte 31, in reverse.

The Dublin road drives due S to (3 miles) the frontier-post, shortly traversing a wooded valley below hills rising to 509m, and descends to *Dundalk*, for which, and for the road from the border to *Dublin*, see Rte 31 in reverse.

DUNDALK TO BIRR (168km). This useful cross road (N52) leads SW from Dundalk.

An interesting brief DETOUR may be made to *Louth* by following the R111 from Dundalk, bearing right off the direct road driving SW, after 8km passing (right) *Stephenstown House* (1750) before entering *Ardee* 13km beyond.—After 5.5km we pass (left) at *Clochafarmore* a standing-stone associated with the death of Cuchulainn, who tied himself to the stone and kept the army of Queen Maeve at bay single-handed until a raven alighting on his shoulder intimated to his enemies that he was dead, a scene commemorated by the statue in the Post Office in O'Connell St, Dublin.
  Louth, now a mere village, was once the chief place of the county. The religious house founded here by St. Patrick became one of the most famous in Ireland, producing (it is said) 100 bishops, but in the 9C it was pillaged by the Danes; the present ruins are those of a mitred abbey founded by Dermot O'Carroll, Lord of Oriel, in 1148. Adjacent is a derelict burial-ground. Near it is *St. Mochta's House* (restored), a small oratory of the saint (died 534), a companion of St. Patrick.—At *Inniskeen*, 7km N on the river Fane, is an imperfect *Round Tower*, 14m. high, the main relic of the monastery of St. Deagh (died 560), the successor of Mochta.— We traverse *Tallanstown*, on the river Glynde, 4km S of Louth, adjoining the demesne of *Louth Hall*, once the mansion of the Plunketts, Lords Louth, and 6.5km beyond, enter *Ardee*.

Continuing SW from *Ardee* (see Rte 30), after 17km we pass 5km S of *Nobber*, where Turlough O'Carolan (1670–1738), the last of the Irish bards, was born. After 13km we enter *Kells*; see Rte 29. At 12km we pass (right) the spectacular ruin of *Killna Castle* (1780), the seat of the Chapman family, an illegitimate scion of which was T.E. Lawrence ('of Arabia'); and 5km beyond (right) *Ballinlough Castle*, an early 18C castle to which a round-towered crenellated range was added c 1730, enlarged in 1780, and restored in 1939.—5km **Delvin**, a pleasant village on the Stoneyford river, with the remains of the 13C stronghold of the Nugent family; their ruined castle of *Clonyn* lies further to the W. Brinsley McNamara (1890–1963), the author of the controversial novel 'The Valley of the Squinting Windows', was born here.—21km *Mullingar* (see p 290), beyond which we pass near the E bank of LOUGH ENNELL and cross the N6 at (24km) *Kilbeggan*, passing *Durrow Abbey* on our right before entering (12km) *Tullamore* (see Rte 25A). The *Slieve Bloom* range rises to the S.—We bear SW again to (37km) *Birr*; see Rte 20B.

Hence the N52 continues SW to (39km) *Nenagh*, there turning right onto the N7 for *Limerick*, 40km beyond.—The N62 runs S from Birr via (19km) *Roscrea* to (19km) *Templemore*, (14km) *Thurles*, and *Cashel*, 19km beyond; see Rtes 7 and 4.

40   Belfast to Newry via Downpatrick: the Mourne Mountains

53 miles (85km). A7. 22 miles **Downpatrick**—A25. 6 miles *Clough*—
5½ miles *Castlewellan*—9½ miles *Rathfriland*—10 miles *Newry*.

For the ALTERNATIVE coastal route, attractive, but 13 miles longer,
continuing on the A2 from Clough via (6 miles) *Newcastle*—13½
miles *Kilkeel*—11½ miles *Warrenpoint*—7 miles. *Newry*; see p 376.

Clough may also be approached direct from Belfast on the A24 via (14 miles)
Ballynahinch (9 miles N of Clough); see below;—A third road (A22), skirting the
W bank of Strangford Lough, is described in Rte 41B.

Driving S from Belfast, we traverse the planned suburb of
Newtownbreda, with a parish church of 1747 by Castle. Part of the
demesne of *Belvoir Park* (home of the Duke of Wellington's mother)
has been converted into a housing estate since its 18C mansion was
demolished in 1961. At 6 miles we reach a road junction.

Castlereagh Hill, E of Newtownbreda, was the site of a residence of Con O'Neill
(died 1559), the last chieftain of his sept. 2 miles to the SW (via the B205) is the
Giant's Ring, a rampart enclosing a dolmen, and the site of several Bronze Age
burials; at *Drumbo*, to the S, is the stump of a *Round Tower* (10.5m high).

The right-hand fork (A24) leads due S to (9 miles) **Ballynahinch** (3,700 inhab.),
an agricultural town with chalybeate and sulphur springs, early 19C *Assembly
Rooms* with a Doric timber portico, a *Parish Church* of 1772, and a *Market-house*
of 1795; to the SW is the demesne of *Montalto*, with a mid 18C mansion.
  We pass, on leaving the town, the water-wheel of *Harris's Mill*.—To the SW
rises *Slieve Croob* (534m; cf) while the road S commands a fine view of the
Mourne Mountains.—After passing a small wood (left) a lane leads left to
Loughinisland, where, reached by a causeway, are three ruined churches, dating
from the 11C, mid-16C, and 17C.—For *Clough*; see below.

The left-hand fork—the A7—after 5 miles traverses the village of
Saintfield, the scene of a sharp engagement on 12 June 1798 between
the United Irishmen under Henry Monro and the Yeomanry under
Stapleton. Monro won a momentary success, but pressing on to Ballynahinch (see above) he was captured, and soon after hanged at Lisburn. Many of the United Irishmen lie in the graveyard of the Presbyterian church of 1777.—1 mile S are the gardens of *Rowallane* (notable
for its rhododendrons and azaleas).

On approaching Downpatrick, we pass (right), overlooking the river
Quoile, the ruins of **Inch Abbey**, founded in 1127 for Benedictines and
refounded for Cistercians by De Courcy in 1187; an earlier Celtic
house had been plundered by Sigtryg in 1002. The most striking feature of the ruins (late 12C) is the group of three pointed windows in the
chancel; S of the church are the remains of a quadrangle surrounded
by dependencies.

  DOWNPATRICK (8,250 inhab.), the ancient county town of Down,
overlooks the marshy vale of the Quoile, which flows into the S end of
Strangford Lough (to the NE). The trivallate *Dun*, 18m high, from
which the town is named, lies immediately to the N. Either this or the
cathedral hill, or the remains of ramparts to the SW of the cathedral,
may be the *Rath Celtchair*, named after one of the Red Branch Knights
whose residence it is believed to represent.

Downpatrick, the *Dunum* of Ptolemy, and the *Dun-da-lath-glas* (Fort of the two
broken fetters) of Irish chroniclers, was a place of importance before the arrival of
St. Patrick, who converted the local prince, Dichu, and founded a monastery on
land granted to him. After a period of Danish pillage, the church was rebuilt by

Bp Malachy O'Morgair in 1137. In 1176 John de Courcy took possession of the baronies of Lecale (in which Downpatrick is) and Ards, enlarged the church, and, it is claimed, brought the bones of both St. Brigid and St. Columba to lie beside those of St. Patrick. Having supported Arthur of Brittany against King John, De Courcy was treacherously seized while at prayer in the cathedral and his lands were awarded to Hugh de Lacy (1205). The cathedral was burned by Edward Bruce in 1315, and again in 1538 by Lord Leonard Grey, an act of sacrilege to which he largely owed his execution three years later. Thomas Russell (1767–1803), the United Irishman, was executed in Downpatrick.

An air of decrepitude pervades the town with its terraces of modest but neglected dwellings, although in English St., ascending steeply to the cathedral, the dignified Georgian houses are being restored; others may be seen in Saul St. and Irish St. The late 18C *Assize Court*, on the right, now house the local *Museum*, while a short distance down adjacent Mount Crescent is the *New Gaol* Gatehouse (1824–30). On the left, beyond the Courthouse stands a mellow red-brick building known as the *Southwell Charity*, erected and founded in 1733 by Edward Southwell as an almshouse and school, and possibly designed by Sir Edward Lovett Pearce.

We approach the E end of the pinnacled cathedral, in front of which stands a 10C *High Cross*, pieced together in 1897. The present **Cathedral** was built in 1790–1827, but preserves some portions of the older building, notably part of the E end, possibly the work of De Courcy, with its recessed doorway and trefoil niches. Within, arcades survive from the 13C and 15–16Cs, and the font (retrieved in 1931 from a farmyard after being lost for centuries) is believed to be Celtic work (11C). The walls are embellished with coats of arms of county families, and several of the early 19C box-pews have semicircular fronts. The rebuilt organ dates from the late 18C. In the wall beside the vestry door is an unusual diminutive figure of a cleric of c 1150, and in the porch is the *Cromwell Stone*, commemorating Edward, third Baron Cromwell (died 1607), governor of Lecale.

There is a good view of the Mourne Mountains from a terrace behind the cathedral. In 1900 a monolith engraved with the name 'Patric' was placed in the graveyard for no reason based on historical fact. No trace remains of the Round Tower which once stood to the S.

The *Tower* (1560) of the *Parish Church* (1735), in Church St, to the N of the town centre, behind the Post Office, may have been part of a castle erected by De Courcy. Thomas Russell (see History) lies in the graveyard.—To the SE in Stream St (an extension of Irish St) is the *Presbyterian Church* (1710), with an interior of interest.

1½ miles E of the town lie the *Wells of Struell*, beside which St. Patrick is said to have built a chapel; they are still resorted to. Adjacent is a stone-roofed bathhouse; another stands roofless.—1 mile N of them, on the direct road from Downpatrick to Strangford, are the insignificant remains of *Saul Abbey* (12C), where St. Patrick founded the monastery in which he died after 461, and near where, it is claimed, he landed on his first missionary journey, some time after 432.—Beyond, at *Raholp*, is a primitive church in ruins.

A rewarding DETOUR may be made to *Strangford*, 8 miles NE, on the A25. Shortly before entering the village we pass (left) the entrance to the extensive demesne of **•Castle Ward** (NT). This fine but eccentric mansion was built by an unknown architect for the first Lord Bangor and his wife, Lady Anne, between c 1762–68. He preferred the classicalx idiom (S front); she the then-fashionable neo-Gothick; there was no compromise, and the N front reflects the Strawberry Hill style.

Top: the South Front of Castle Ward. Below: the North Front

The couple later separated, understandably. Most of the original furnishings were dispersed before 1827, but the well-restored rooms have been refurnished with contemporary or early 19C pieces, family portraits, and early views of the building, etc. The *Laundry* should also be visited.—In the grounds are the previous *Castle* of 1610, a Palladian *Temple*, and to the N, overlooking STRANGFORD LOUGH, the ruined keep of *Audley's Castle* (c 1500), and a double 'horned' cairn near by.

Strangford, an attractive little fishing village, lies on the narrow strait between STRANGFORD LOUGH and the sea opposite *Portaferry* (see Rte 41A), with which it is connected by ferry. The *Castle* is a late 16C tower-house, one of many in the neighbourhood.

From Strangford, the CIRCUIT OF THE LECALE PENINSULA, the low-lying area to the SE and S of Downpatrick, may be made with ease, a distance of 22 miles to Clough.—*Kilclief*, to the S along the coast road (A2) preserves a tower-house of c 1430, 5½ miles beyond which, first passing the ruined medieval church at *Ardtole*, we enter **Ardglass** (1,300 inhab.), once the main port of Down and still reputed for its herrings. It was protected by seven 'castles' or fortifications, among them the *New Works* (probably fortified warehouses) erected by a trading company in the reign of Henry IV; and *Jordan's Castle* (containing a collection of bygones), where Simon Jordan held out for three years against Tyrone before Mountjoy came to relieve him in 1601.—On *St John's Point*, S of the next village of *Killough*, 'laid out' in the 18C, are the remains of a chapel (?7C). Hence the road follows the coast via *Minerstown*, on a long strand, to *Clough*.—c 1½ miles inland, beyond Minerstown, near *Lagamaddy*, is a fine double stone circle, important as a link between the 'henge' monuments and the grave mounds.

The A25 leads 6 miles SW from Downpatrick to the road junction of *Clough*, with scanty ruins of a 13C castle, whence we have a choice of two routes to Newry, the shorter inland road being described first.

FROM CLOUGH TO NEWRY, DIRECT (25 miles). The A25 continues SW to (5½ miles) **Castlewellan** (2,100 inhab.), a small market town with a wide main street and tree-shaded 'squares' laid out by the Earls of Annesley in 1750. Their demesne, to the NW of the town (where an earlier mansion was replaced by a Scottish-baronial style castle in 1856; now offices) is open to the public, and contains an *Arboretum* established in 1740. The estate is now owned by the Department of Agriculture, which has nurseries for re-afforestation here.

Passing (right) LOUGH ISLANDREAVY, we reach *Kilcoo*.

Hence the B8 forks left for (4½ miles) *Hilltown*, an angling resort on the Upper Bann, with the ruined church of *Clonduff* (the ancient burial-place of the Magennis clan, Lords of Iveagh) 1 mile E. Two roads cross the *Mourne Mountains*, which rise to the SE: the B27 climbs SE through the *Spelga Pass* to the source of the Bann, skirting a reservoir and turns S below (left) *Slieve Muck* (670m) before descending to *Kilkeel*, see below; the other (B25) leads S to Rostrevor.—*Newry* is 9 miles W of Hilltown.

The A25 continues W from Kilcoo to **Rathfriland** (2,250 inhab.), a well-placed 'Plantation' town, beyond which we veer SW to *Newry*; see Rte 39.

The COAST ROAD (38 miles). The A2 drives S from Clough to (2 miles) *Dundrum* (950 inhab.), a former port. Behind the village (reached by a lane opposite the Post Office and then first right) stands the *Castle*, begun by John de Courcy and dismantled by Cromwell, partly surrounded by a dry moat cut in the rock; it retains a fine cylindrical keep.

A right-hand fork just beyond the village leads shortly to *Maghera*, with an old church and stump of a *Round Tower* blown down by a gale in 1714, and 1 mile further, the village of *Bryansford*, to the S of which is *Tollymore Park*, long the seat of the Jocelyns, earls of Roden, with a number of pinnacled follies and the

Bryansford Gate (1786) remaining, and now a Forest Park noted for its conifers. The house itself was demolished in 1952. Park Field Museum, the first environmental centre in the British Isles, opened in 1965, was burnt to the ground in 1972, and many valuable specimens associated with the Mourne area were destroyed.—The road continues SW towards *Hilltown* (see above), with a fine view ahead of the **Mourne Mountains**. From E to W before us rise: *Slieve Donard* (850m), the highest in the range; *Slieve Commedagh*; *Slieve Bearnagh*, and *Slieve Meelmore*, with *Slieve Meelbeg* behind it.

The left-hand fork at Dundrum, passes (left) the *Murlough Nature Reserve* on the sand dunes (NT; 282 hectares), to reach the coast at the somewhat characterless resort of **Newcastle** (6,250 inhab.), but with a sandy beach, and dominated by *Slieve Donard* (850m), which may be climbed with ease. The 'New Castle', now almost vanished, was built on the site of an older fort by Felix Magennis in 1588 at the mouth of the Shimnagh, where the bridge now crosses it.

The ***Mourne Mountains**, in view throughout our route, although not an extensive range—c 15 miles in length by 8 miles in breadth—are the most beautiful in Northern Ireland.

The ascent of *Slieve Donard*, the highest peak, may be made by following a path up the N side of the Glen river, behind *Donard Lodge*. The view from the summit is superb in clear weather: Snaefell on the Isle of Man is clearly visible out to sea; the coast of Scotland can be seen to the NE; to the NW the mountains of Donegal are sometimes distinguished, while in the foreground lie the other peaks of the range.

The ***Coast Road**, which now climbs, affording several mountain views, after 2 miles crosses *Bloody Bridge*, where a stream descends between Slieve Donard and *Chimney Rock* and where a massacre of Presbyterians took place in 1641. We traverse the fishing-village and granite-quarrying centre of *Annalong*, to approach the fishing-port of **Kilkeel** (6,050 inhab.) near the NE outskirts of which is the dolmen of *Crabstree Stone*.

The Kilkeel river descends from the *Silent Valley Reservoir* and further NE, that of *Ben Croom*, providing water for Belfast and neighbouring towns.—Further W, the B27 ascends to the W of *Slieve Muck* (670m) before forking left to *Hilltown* (see above).

SW of Kilkeel, a road passes a large rath adjoining an unroofed 'giant's grave', an allée couverte 12m long, and after 4 miles enters *Greencastle*, where a huge Norman *Keep* (c 1260) guards the entrance to CARLINGFORD LOUGH. It was once a place of importance, having been the capital of the Kingdom of Mourne, and later one of the main English strongholds in the area. On the far bank of the lough stands *Greenore*. To its right is *Carlingford*, behind which rises *Slieve Foye* (587m); see the latter part of Rte 31.

The A2 leads W from Kilkeel, after 2 miles passing (right) *Mourne Park*, in which is a ruined court cairn; White Water, which flows through the demesne, is a good trout stream. On the right bank of the Causeway Water, which we next cross, stands the *Kilfeaghan* dolmen, with a 35-tonne capstone. The mountains, here a good deal lower, once more approach the coast, while Carlingford Mountain, on the opposite bank of the lough, is well seen.

Bearing N we reach **Rostrevor** (2,100 inhab.), to the E of which *Slievemartin* rises steeply, on a shoulder of which is *Cloghmore* (the great stone), a singular erratic 40-tonne block, fabled to have been hurled across the Carlingford Lough by Finn MacCoul. An obelisk commemorates the birth here of General Robert Ross of Bladensburg (1766–1814), who took Washington on 24 August 1814.

2 miles **Warrenpoint** (4,800 inhab.), a not-unattractive loughside resort, beyond which we follow the dual-carriageway ascending the bank of the Newry Canal, passing (right) *Narrow Water Castle*, a

square tower built soon after 1560 (restored), the bawn of which was altered in the 19C, and after 7 miles enter *Newry*, see Rte 39.

41 Strangford Lough and the Ards Peninsula

A. Belfast to Portaferry via Bangor and Donaghadee

43 miles (69km). A2. 5 miles *Holywood*—8 miles *Bangor*—7½ miles *Donaghadee*—22½ miles *Portaferry*.

Crossing *Queen Elizabeth II Bridge*, we bear NE on the Sydenham bypass along the E bank of BELFAST LOUGH, and after passing (right) *Palace Barracks* (on the site of a former residence of the bishops of Down), enter **Holywood** (9,450 inhab.).

It was originally called Ballyderry ('town of the wood'), and then had its name changed to Sanctus Boscus ('the Holy Wood') by the Normans. A church built here in the 7C by St. Laserain, was connected to Bangor Abbey. In the 16C a small Franciscan monastery was established, which with others in the district was burned by Sir Brian O'Neill in 1572 to prevent Queen Elizabeth's English troops from garrisoning them; its ruins lie at the end of High St.

Shortly after leaving the town we pass (right) the entrance to the demesne of *Cultra Manor*, now containing the combined *Ulster Folk and Transport Museum**, the latter part opened in 1976. It is one of the most interesting and important museums in Ireland, and deserves an extended visit.

Unlike some other fabricated 'folk parks', all the buildings in the open air have been brought from their original sites and re-erected in similar surroundings. They are furnished as they would have been at the turn of the century, admirably displaying agricultural and domestic equipment and other by-gones, and the unenviable conditions of a rural life now past.

Cultra Manor itself contains an extensive collection of objects and a reference library; the early photographs (c 1890–1920), taken by W.A. Green (1870–1959), the paintings of William Conor (1881–1968), and the prints of William Hincks (1783) are of great interest.

Among the buildings which may be visited are: two cottier's cabins; three types of farmhouse; a weaver's house; a more substantial two-storey house (a Rectory) of 1717; a Spade Mill from Coalisland (1840s); a Flax Scutching Mill, and Watchman's hut; a Forge (1830s); a Schoolhouse (1836), and Church (1790). The re-erection of other types of building is projected. Detailed desciptive leaflets are available.
 A road bridge spans the main road to the **Transport Galleries**.
 These are divided into various sections: *Archaic Transport* displaying examples of the shoulder creel (for carrying peat or potatoes); panniers; sledges or 'slipes'; slide-cars and wheel-cars; 'truttle' cars, and side-cars or 'jaunting' cars, etc. *Horse-drawn carriages* include dog-carts and pony-traps; the Waggonette Brake; the 'Phaeton'; the 'Victoria'; the 'Brougham'; a private Omnibus; a Stage Coach; and the Marquess of Abercorn's Dress Chariot (mid-19C).
 Next we see the *Bicycle Collection* of Thomas Edens Osborne (1885–1930), a lifelong friend of John Boyd Dunlop (1840–1922), the inventor of the pneumatic tyre, which so revolutionised transport; here are the Beeston Humber Ordinary of c 1885 (the 'Penny Farthing'), and its reverse; the earlier Dandy Horse (c 1810–

1865), the pedal Velocipede (c 1867); the 'Dublin' Tricycle (1876), and the Edlin Racing Safety (1889), the first to be fitted with pneumatic tyres (fixed by rubber solution directly to the wheel rims).

A third gallery displays a representative selection of veteran *motor-cars* from the MMC of 1903 to the Rolls-Royce Limousine of 1937, among them the Chamber's Car (Belfast, 1906), a two-seater Peugeot of 1913, the only surviving prototype of the Fergus Car (1915), a Humber (1924) and Lancia (1924), a Bentley of 1926, and Riley of 1936, etc.—Among *aircraft* are examples of the Short Bros and Harland vertical take-off plane, and the 'flying bedstead' (1953), and a full-scale model of a Ferguson monoplane of 1909.—A further section is devoted to the *shipbuilding* industry of Belfast, while among other individual exhibits are a Dublin-Kingstown railway carriage (1840); a horse tramcar from Fintona; a 'toast-rack' trailer car from the Giant's Causeway hydro-electric railway;¹ and a tinker's caravan.

On the lough shore near here is the North of Ireland Yacht Club, and at *Craigavad*, to the NE, the Royal Belfast Golf Club.

We shortly bear inland, passing (right) the demesne of *Clandeboye*, the seat of the Marquess of Dufferin and Ava. The chapel preserves an 8C cross-shaft from Bangor Abbey; 2 miles SE, at the far end of the estate, rises *Helen's Tower* (1858), erected in honour of Helen, Lady Dufferin (1807–67), grand-daughter of Sheridan, and composer of the ballad, 'The Irish Emigrant'.

BANGOR (46,600 inhab.) a flourishing resort.

It was the seat of a great missionary abbey (*Banchor*, the white choir) founded by St. Comhgall in c 555. Among his pupils were St. Columbanus and St. Gall, who went to evangelise the heathen Germanic tribes of central Europe. Its riches naturally attracted the Danes, who destroyed the monastery, but the abbey was rebuilt in c 1140. The Normans gave it to the Augustinians, but in 1542 it was dissolved. James I granted the lands to Sir James Hamilton (1559–1643), who in 1622 became Lord Clandeboye.

Main St descends to *Bangor Bay*, to the E of which is the strand of *Ballyholme Bay*. Near the inner quay is a small *Tower* built by Lord Clandeboye as a custom house in 1637, and now housing a tourist office. On a low hill above the town is *Bangor Castle* (1859), now the Town Hall, with a public park in its wooded grounds. It contains a small museum of relics from the abbey including a 14C Sanctus bell. Abbey St, at the foot of Castle Park, leads to the *Abbey Church* (rebuilt 1960), where a spire of 1693 surmounts the original central tower of the Augustinian church; several early 17C memorials are preserved, among them that of John Hamilton (died 1693) and his wife, by Scheemakers.

The COASTAL ROAD TO DONAGHADEE skirts *Ballyholme Bay* to *Groomsport*, where General Schomberg landed in 1689, but which is now spoilt by caravan sites. Beyond, three small islands come into view; the nearest and largest is *Copeland Island*, beyond which is *Lighthouse Island* (with no lighthouse), and *Mew Island*, with a lighthouse (1884), whose powerful beam guides shipping towards the entrance of Belfast Lough.

Donaghadee (3,850), a small resort, is the nearest Irish port to Great Britain. Until 1849 it was connected by a regular mail service with Portpatrick in Scotland, 21 miles NE, but this was abandoned in favour of the Stranraer–Larne route owing to the unsuitability of Portpatrick harbour. In 1818 Keats and Charles Brown, intending to visit the Giant's Causeway, came over in a packet, but having briefly seen Belfast, they re-embarked without further delay for Scotland. The *Lighthouse* at the end of the large *Harbour* was built by Sir John Rennie and David Logan. There are a few old houses surviving in the town, among them the *Manor House* in High St. A 'castle' of 1818 crowns the motte, from the summit of which the coast of Galloway may be seen in clear weather.

The **Ards Peninsula** may be conveniently visited from Donaghadee, but the roads are apt to get crowded at weekends. The barony of Ards occupies a tongue of land c 20 miles long and 4 miles broad which separates the Irish Sea from **Strangford Lough**. This arm of the sea is of much the same area as the peninsula, although owing to the narrow channel by which it is entered and the number of islands that encumber its shores, it has much more the appearance of a freshwater lough; most of the islands are in fact the summits of submerged drumlins, as in Clew Bay. The entire inner foreshore of the lough has been designated a wildlife and ornithological reserve.

The A2 skirts the E side of the peninsula between sandy beaches and caravan sites to (2½ miles) *Millisle*, to the W of which stands *Ballycopeland Windmill*, dating from the last decade of the 18C.—5½ miles *Ballywalter*, in the cemetery of which—to the NW—are the ruins of the 'White Church' of *Templefinn*, preserving three Norman grave-slabs.—We skirt *Ballywalter Park*, an Italianate palazzo (of c 1846, by Lanyon), built for Andrew Mulholland, to approach *Ballyhalbert*, where the road turns inland.—The small offshore islet known as *Burial Island* is pointed out as being the most easterly part of Ireland.—We shortly regain the coast at *Portavogie*, with its tiny harbour, and skirt *Cloghey Bay*, passing *Kirkistown Castle*, one of the better examples of a bawn erected by the 17C settlers.

The road beyond veers inland to approach **Portaferry** (2,150 inhab.), with a pleasant waterfront facing the narrow channel, 5 miles long and ½ mile broad, connecting Strangford Lough to the open sea, the swiftness of the current here giving the lough its Danish name of '*strangfjord*'. The new aquarium of the *Marine Biology Station* here may be visited.—2 miles to the E is *Quintin Castle*, an early 19C castellated edifice incorporating a 17C tower-house, and on the site of the stronghold of Sir Thomas Smith (c 1580).

The return trip may be made along the W side of the Ards Peninsula, skirting the lough to *Newtownards*, see below, or alternatively by taking the ferry across the estuary to *Strangford* (see Rte 40), 8 miles from *Downpatrick*, 22 miles from Belfast by the direct road. The minor road near the W bank of the lough is described in Rte 41B.

Driving N, we reach the lough side at *Ardkeen*—also approached by a minor road hugging the shore—where in c 1180 a *Castle* was founded by William le Savage, one of De Courcy's companions in the conquest of Ulster.—7½ miles *Kircubbin*, with a *Penal Law Chapel* of c 1780, restored, 4 miles beyond which is **Greyabbey**, a one-street village preserving in attractive grounds the ruins of a Cistercian Monastery founded in 1193 by Affreca, daughter of Godred, King of Man, and the wife of John de Courcy. Its chief features are the aisleless *Church, a good example of the Early English style, with a beautiful W doorway and fine lancets at the E end, and the refectory of which the S gable is likewise pierced by lancets. In the nave are two mutilated effigies of a late 13C lady and a 14C knight, rare survivals in the North.

The road next skirts the wooded grounds of **Mount Stewart** (NT). This seat of the Marquess of Londonderry and the birthplace of Viscount Castlereagh (1769–1822), who was nearly drowned in the lough in 1786, is known for its beautiful and luxuriant *Gardens*, designed by the wife of the 7th Marquess in 1921. The W end of the mansion, completed by William Vitruvius Morrison in 1828, dates from 1803. The octagonal *Temple of the Winds* (1780, by James

'Athenean' Stuart; restored) is a copy of the one in Athens. William FitzGerald was the stuccoman.

7 miles **NEWTOWNARDS** (20,550 inhab.), now a busy manufacturing centre, is an old town in spite of its name, dating from 1244, when a Dominican priory was founded here by Walter de Burgh, the *Church* of which still stands in ruins in Court Sq., off Castle St. Of the existing remains the nave is the only original part, the tower having been rebuilt under James I; in the SE corner is the Londonderry family vault. At the junction of High St and Castle St stands the octagonal *Old Cross*, reconstituted in 1666 with as many fragments of the original as had survived destruction in the rebellion of 1653. Overlooking the extensive market-place (Conway Sq.) is the dignified *Town Hall* (1765, by F. Stratford, a Bristol architect), revealing the Scottish traditon of stone-masonry.

About 1 mile E, on the S of the B172, are the 15C remains of the abbey church of *Moyvilla* (*Magh Bhile*), founded c 540 by St. Finian; several fine grave-slabs with foliated crosses of the 10–13C have been built into the N wall.

The A20 leads W past (left) Newtownards. We shortly approach the E suburbs of Belfast, passing near *Scrabo Hill*, on which rises a 41m-high tower (by W.J. Barre) erected as a memorial to the 3rd Marquess of Londonderry. To the right of the road is the dolmen known as *Kempe Stones*, passed before traversing industrial *Dundonald*, with a Rolls-Royce aero-engine factory, where the old village centre surrounds a Norman motte. For *Stormont* (right); see below.

B. Belfast to Downpatrick via Killyleagh

26 miles (42km). A20. 5m—A22. 4 miles *Comber*—11½ miles *Killyleagh*—5½ miles **Downpatrick.**

Crossing the Lagan by the *Queen Elizabeth II Bridge*, and driving due E, after 3½ miles we pass (left) the avenue leading up to the *Parliament Building* of Northern Ireland at *Stormont*, a severely plain classical building with a central portico (1928–32, by A. Thornley), on the right of which other government offices are housed in the Scottish-baronial *Stormont Castle*. At the approach to the former is a grotesque statue of Sir Edward Carson (1854–1935), the intransigent advocate of the continuance of Union; in the main hall is one of the first prime minister of the 'Six Counties' (1921–1940), Lord Craigavon.

Shortly beyond, we fork right onto the A22 for **Comber** (7,600 inhab.), a textile-manufacturing town, which may be by-passed, where the church of 1840 stands on the site of a Cistercian abbey. The main road drives directly SE to *Killyleagh* (see below), off which at the next fork a by-road turns left to skirt the island-studded W shore of STRANGFORD LOUGH (see Rte 41A), the foreshore of which is now a nature reserve. Keeping to the left at *Ringneill Bridge* we may visit *Mahee Island* by a causeway, beside which is the ruin known as *Captain Brown's Castle* (1570). On the island are the remains of the monastery of **Nendrum**, founded by St. Mochua (7C.), which were revealed and restored in 1922. The ruins, surrounded by the walls of a triple cashel, include part of a *Round Tower* (10C) and the church with its unusual sundial (?8C). The important finds from recent excavations may be seen in the Ulster Museum, Belfast. On the promontories and other islets are the ruins of several tower-houses erected in the 15–

16Cs and early 17C by the Ulster landowners.—From Ringneill Bridge, the road turns S via *Ardmillan* to rejoin the A22 5 miles N of *Killyleagh*.

Killyleagh (2,100 inhab.) was the birthplace of Sir Hans Sloane (1660–1753), the founder of the British Museum; while also, in the obscurity of this village, Edward Hinks (1792–1866), rector from 1826 until his death, gained the reputation of being one of Europe's foremost orientalists, having discovered the essential principles of Egyptian hieroglyphics and Persian cuneiform. The *Castle* has since 1610 been in the possession of the Hamilton family, sometimes earl of Clanbrassil and viscount Clandeboye. Reconstructed by Lanyon in 1850, it incorporates two round towers, one dating from the 13C, the other of 1666. Originally erected by De Courcy, it was later held by the O'Neills, and rebuilt by the Hamiltons after its destruction by General Monk in 1648. 'It pricks castellated ears above the smoke of its own village and provides a curiously exotic landmark, towering like some château of the Loire above the gentle tides of Strangford Lough', wrote Sir Harold Nicholson of his mother's home.

We turn SW through drumlin country to *Downpatrick*; see Rte 40.

INDEX

Topographical names are printed in Roman or **bold** type; the names of notable people in *italics*; while subjects are in CAPITALS. Loughs are indexed as a sub-group; no differentiation is made as to the position of the word 'lough', whether before or after the name. Dublin (and its inner suburbs) is also provided with a subordinate index. Irish place names (see p 13) are only included when they are in general use, although in fact there are Irish equivalents in almost all cases. When more than one place of the same name is listed, they are differentiated by the addition, in brackets, of the counties in which they lie, and the following abbreviations are used. If in the same county, the nearest town is placed within brackets.

Ant Antrim	Kild Kildare	Ros Roscommon
Arm Armagh	Kilk Kilkenny	Tip Tipperary
Car Carlow	Leit Leitrim	Tyr Tyrone
Don Donegal	Lim Limerick	Wat Waterford
Dub Dublin	Long Longford	Westm Westmeath
Fer Fermanagh	Mon Monaghan	Wex Wexford
Gal Galway	Off Offaly	Wick Wicklow

Atlas Section

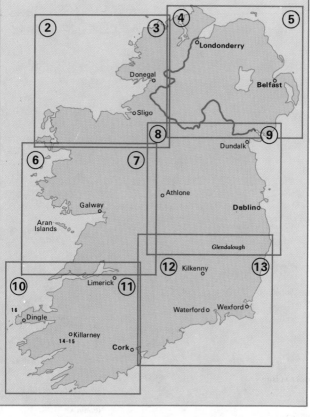

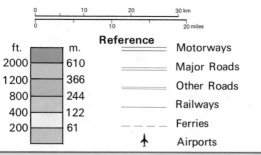

0   10   20   30 km
0   10   20 miles

ft.		m.
2000		610
1200		366
800		244
400		122
200		61

Reference

Motorways

Major Roads

Other Roads

Railways

Ferries

✈ Airports

② ③ ④ ⑤

ºLondonderry

ºDonegal

Belfast º

ºSligo

⑧ ⑨

Dundalk º

⑥ ⑦

ºAthlone

Dublin º

Galway º

Aran
Islands

Glendalough

⑫ Kilkenny ⑬
        º

⑩ Limerick º ⑪

16
ºDingle

Waterford º   Wexford º

ºKillarney
14–15
        Cork º

A T L A N T I C

O C E A N

Ross rk

Benwee
Head

Downpatrick
Hd.

Killala
Bay

*The
Mullet* Belmullet ○

Killala ○
Moyne Abbey +
Rosserk Abbey +

Bangor ○

Ballina ◉

Slieve Car ▲

Blacksod Bay

L. Conn

Nephin ▲

Croaghaun
▲ *Achill*
Keel *Island*

③

Tory I.

Tory Sound

Dunfanaghy

Creeslough

Muckish Mt. ▲

Errigal ▲ 56

L. Beagh

56

Aran I.

Derryveagh Mts.

Dungloe

Gweebarra Bay

56

Blue Stack Mts.

Glenties

Ardara

Blue Stack ▲

15

L. Eske

Glencolumbkille

Malin More

L. Derg

Slieve League ▲

Killybegs

56

Donegal

Pettigo

15

Donegal Bay

Ballyshannon

Boa Island

Bundoran

Inishmurray

L. Melvin

Lower Lough Erne

15

54

Benbulben ▲

Drumcliff

16

Manorhamilton

16

Sligo Bay

Sligo

L. Gill

59

Bromahair

Shannon

Cuilcagh

Collooney

O x   M t s.

L. Allen

17

4

L. Arrow

Slieve Anierin ▲

Tobercurry

Moy

L. Key

Charlestown

Boyle

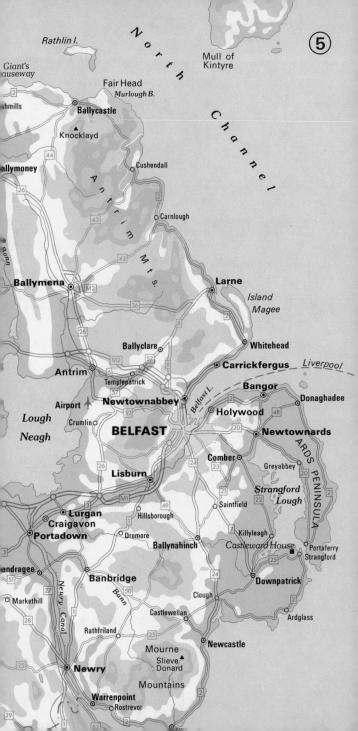

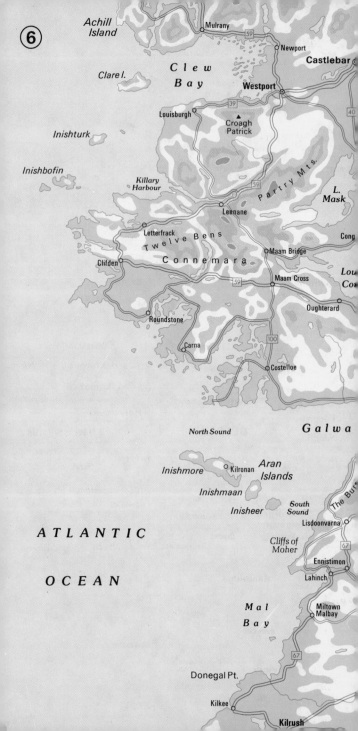

⑥

Achill Island

Mulrany

59

Newport

Castlebar

C l e w
B a y

Clare I.

Westport

39

40

Louisburgh

▲ Croagh
Patrick

Inishturk

Killary
Harbour

59

P a r t r y   M t s.

L.
Mask

Inishbofin

Leenane

Cong

Letterfrack

T w e l v e   B e n s

Maam Bridge

Clifden

C o n n e m a r a

Maam Cross

Lou
Cor

Oughterard

Roundstone

100

Carna

Costelloe

G a l w a

North Sound

Aran
Islands

Inishmore

Kilronan

Inishmaan

Inisheer

South
Sound

The Bur

Lisdoonvarna

67

ATLANTIC

Cliffs of
Moher

Ennistimon

Lahinch

OCEAN

M a l
B a y

Miltown
Malbay

67

Donegal Pt.

Kilkee

Kilrush

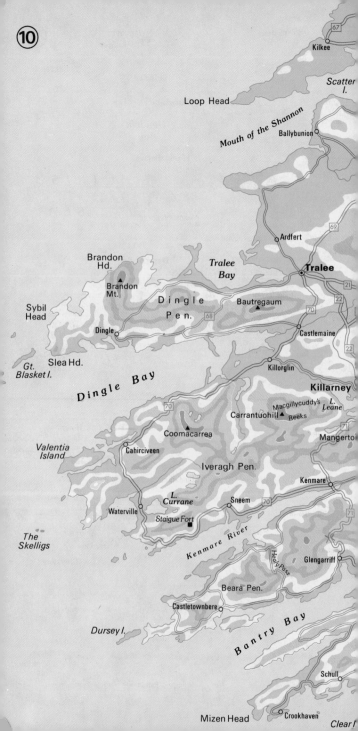

Kilkee

Scatter I.

Loop Head

Mouth of the Shannon

Ballybunion

Ardfert

Tralee

Brandon Hd.

Brandon Mt.

Tralee Bay

Sybil Head

D i n g l e   P e n.

Bautregaum

Dingle

Castlemaine

Gt. Blasket I.

Slea Hd.

Killorglin

Killarney

D i n g l e   B a y

Macgillycuddy's

L. Leane

Carrantuohill

Reeks

Valentia Island

Coomacarrea

Mangertol

Cahirciveen

Iveragh Pen.

Kenmare

L. Currane

Sneem

Waterville

Staigue Fort

The Skelligs

Kenmare River

Healy Pass

Glengarriff

Beara Pen.

Castletownbere

B a n t r y   B a y

Dursey I.

Schull

Mizen Head

Crookhaven

Clear I

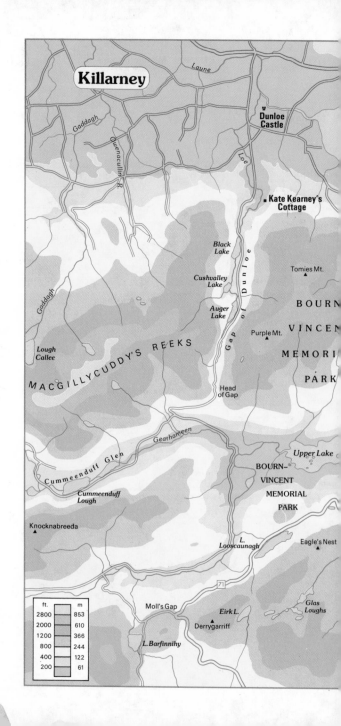

Killarney

Laune

Gaddagh

Gaddagh

Owenacullin R.

Dunloe
Castle

Loe

Kate Kearney's
Cottage

Black
Lake

Cushvalley
Lake

Auger
Lake

Gap of Dunloe

Tomies Mt.

BOURN

VINCEN

Purple Mt.

MEMORI

PARK

Lough
Callee

MACGILLYCUDDY'S REEKS

Head
of Gap

Gearhameen

Cummeenduff Glen

Cummeenduff
Lough

Upper Lake

BOURN–
VINCENT

MEMORIAL

PARK

Knocknabreeda

L.
Looscaunagh

Eagle's Nest

71

Moll's Gap

Eirk L.

Derrygarriff

Glas
Loughs

L. Barfinnihy

ft.	m
2800	853
2000	610
1200	366
800	244
400	122
200	61